ABOUT THE AUTHOR

Ghostly phenomena were a common occurrence in Brad Steiger's childhood home, and because these experiences were accepted by a mystically inclined mother and challenged by a skeptically inclined father, Steiger believes that he achieved a balanced attitude toward ghosts and hauntings that has served him well during his nearly 50 years as a psychical researcher. Since 1958, Steiger has been invited to dozens of private homes, office buildings, dormitories, hospitals, and sacred areas to investigate haunting manifestations. He has conducted investigations in 46 states, a number of Canadian provinces, and in foreign countries such as Egypt, Israel, Jordan, and Peru. He has witnessed spirit materializations, heard spectral voices, felt ghostly touches on his person, and once was even lifted into the air by hostile entity. In the early 1970s, the Steiger family moved into a haunted house that was home to several entities who tried every frightening method they could devise to drive them out.

His first book, *Ghost, Ghouls and Other Peculiar People*, a collection of his articles on ghosts and the paranormal, was published in 1965. Steiger has now authored or coauthored 150 books on the mysterious and unknown, including the classics *The Werewolf Book: The Encyclopedia of Shapeshifting Beings* and *Mysteries of Time and Space*. He continues to be drawn into haunted houses and hotels during his travels with his wife, Sherry, with whom he coauthors the "Miracle" series. Steiger appears frequently on radio and television, and he appears as a guest on the nationally syndicated *Jeff Rense Show* bimonthly to answer listeners' questions about ghosts in their own homes.

OTHER VISIBLE INK PRESS BOOKS BY BRAD STEIGER

Conspiracies and Secret Societies: The Complete Dossier
With Sherry Hansen Steiger
ISBN: 978-1-57859-174-9

Real Ghosts, Restless Spirits, and Haunted Places
ISBN: 978-1-57859-146-6

Real Miracles, Divine Intervention, and Feats of Incredible Survival
With Sherry Hansen Steiger
ISBN: 978-1-57859-214-2

Real Vampires, Night Stalkers, and Creatures from the Darkside
ISBN: 978-1-57859-255-5

Real Zombies, the Living Dead, and Creatures of the Apocalypse
ISBN: 978-1-57859-296-8

The Werewolf Book: The Encyclopedia of Shape-Shifting Beings
ISBN: 978-1-57859-078-0

ALSO FROM VISIBLE INK PRESS

Angels A to Z, 2nd edition
by Evelyn Dorothy Oliver and James R Lewis
ISBN: 978-1-57859-212-8

Armageddon Now: The End of the World A to Z
by Jim Willis and Barbara Willis
ISBN: 978-1-57859-168-8

The Astrology Book: The Encyclopedia of Heavenly Influences, 2nd edition
by James R Lewis
ISBN: 978-1-57859-144-2

The Dream Encyclopedia, 2nd edition
by James R Lewis and Evelyn Dorothy Oliver
ISBN: 978-1-57859-216-6

The Encyclopedia of Religious Phenomena
by J. Gordon Melton
ISBN: 978-1-57859-209-8

The Fortune-telling Book: The Encyclopedia of Divination and Soothsaying
by Raymond Buckland
ISBN: 978-1-57859-147-3

The Handy Religion Answer Book
by John Renard
ISBN: 978-1-57859-125-1

Hidden Realms, Lost Civilizations, and Beings from Other Worlds
by Jerome Clark
ISBN: 978-1-57859-175-6

The Religion Book: Places, Prophets, Saints, and Seers
by Jim Willis
ISBN: 978-1-57859-151-0

The Spirit Book: The Encyclopedia of Clairvoyance, Channeling, and Spirit Communication
by Raymond Buckland
ISBN: 978-1-57859-172-5

Unexplained! Strange Sightings, Incredible Occurrences, and Puzzling Physical Phenomena, 2nd edition
by Jerome Clark
ISBN: 978-1-57859-070-4

The Vampire Book: The Encyclopedia of the Undead, 3rd edition
by J. Gordon Melton
ISBN: 978-1-57859-281-4

The Witch Book: The Encyclopedia of Witchcraft, Wicca, and Neo-paganism
by Raymond Buckland
ISBN: 978-1-57859-114-5

Please visit us at visibleinkpress.com.

REAL GHOSTS,

RESTLESS
SPIRITS,

AND

HAUNTED PLACES

REAL GHOSTS,

RESTLESS SPIRITS,

AND

HAUNTED

PLACES

BRAD STEIGER

VISIBLE

INK
PRESS

Detroit

©REAL GHOSTS, RESTLESS SPIRITS, AND HAUNTED PLACES

Visible Ink Press™
43311 Joy Road #414
Canton, MI 48187-2075

Visible Ink Press is a trademark of Visible Ink Press LLC.

Most Visible Ink Press books are available at special quantity discounts when purchased in bulk by corporations, organizations, or groups. Customized printings, special imprints, messages, and excerpts can be produced to meet your needs. For more information, contact Special Markets Director, Visible Ink Press,at www.visibleink.com.

Art Director: Mary Krzewinski
Typesetting: The Graphix Group

ISBN 1-57859-146-5
CIP information is on file with the Library of Congress.

Printed in the United States of America
All rights reserved
10 9 8 7 6 5

Contents

Real Ghosts, Restless Spirits, and Haunted Places

The Real Reasons We All Love Ghost Stories

Whenever our family gathers for a holiday, eventually—usually late at night—talk turns to stories about the haunted house that we acquired in the summer of 1973. Although they are now in their 40s and late 30s, my four children have deep-seated memories of the occasionally nasty ghost that tried to drive us out of the old farmhouse.

We should have been forewarned about the haunting when a relative of the previous owner said that we had purchased the perfect home for a peculiar fellow like me, always chasing around the country looking for spooks. He laughed that I wouldn't have to leave the house to find a ghost.

The problem between our family and the ghost began after we had modernized the house with indoor plumbing, modern toilets, and a variety of electrical appliances in preparation for the winter months. When I was home alone one morning, I heard a series of mysterious thuds, thumps, and bumps sounding throughout the house. When I ran up to the attic to investigate, the thunderous sounds would move to the basement. This process was repeated a number of times until I grew tired of running up and down three flights of stairs and simply decided to ignore the manifestations.

Bryan, the oldest boy in our family, was treated to a similar performance a few nights later when knocking on the front door distracted him from his homework. Since he was home alone, he went to answer the door and was surprised to find no one there. Then a series of knocks summoned him to the back door. After playing a game of tag between the front and back doors, the disturbance finally sounded on both doors and all the downstairs windows at the same time. The absence of footprints in the freshly fallen snow proved that no human tricksters were playing a prank on him.

Steven, our youngest son, began to dread coming home after he left his after-school job because of the manifestations in his room, especially the rocking chair that would creak back and forth until nearly dawn. Kari, our eldest girl, heard her name being called in whispery voices that came from the attic. The children's mother often found herself locked out of the house when she stepped outside, and once she awakened to find herself being held down in bed by the ghost of an old man.

Julie, the youngest family member, became the victim of a bizarre facet of the haunting that would wait until she came home from school and was alone in the house before it began to torment her. The comingled sounds of voices and eerie music would grow louder and louder until she would be driven out of the house to seek refuge at a neighbor's home.

I had grown up in a house with paranormal manifestations and had seen my first ghosts when I was about four years old, but those entities in my old homestead were relatively quiet, and most certainly benign. My first articles on the paranormal appeared in 1957; my first book, *Ghosts, Ghouls and Other Peculiar People,* was published in 1965, so when we moved into the haunted house in 1973, I had experienced a wide variety of ghostly phenomena. Once I so angered a spirit that it smashed down a door and hoisted my fellow researchers and me in the air. By that time my family and I were experiencing regular encounters with unseen forces in our home, which was something quite different from ghost hunting in someone else's domicile. For months we underwent a supernatural barrage of phenomena, including mysterious lights appearing both inside and outside the house; footsteps moving up and down the stairs; and a noisy repertoire of assorted poundings, drummings, and tappings. Eventually, the phenomena seemed to grow more accustomed to our presence, or it wore itself out to a degree where coexistence with us became possible.

Interestingly, about four years ago Julie summarized that time as comprising some of the most horrible days of her life. More recently, she has been able to find positive aspects of the eerie ordeal. "Although it may have been totally terrifying at times, we did experience proof that there really is something within us that survives physical death," she said. Her frightening experience provided Julie with the rationale behind every ghost story that has ever been told: To experience a haunting, or to see a ghost, is to receive proof that life goes on beyond the grave. Accounts of haunting phenomena, no matter how terrifying they may be, provide evidence that existence continues for the spirit on more than one dimension, and that human beings are multidimensional entities that consist of mind, body, and soul.

My colleague Brian A. Schill of the American Society for Paranormal Research and Investigation (4661 Donovan Street, Orlando, Florida 32808; aspirusa@aol.com) has written a book entitled *The DNA of Ghosts* that explains the afterlife existence of the "ghost" within us in scientific terms. Schill points out that every living being has a bioelectric cycle that functions at 60 Hz. This cycle, he says, enables our hearts, brains, and central nervous system to function and communicate within the organism itself. Examining that medical truth within the context of the first law of thermodynamics (which states that energy can neither be created nor destroyed, only transformed), we are able to recognize that two-thirds of our life experience exists within our intangible mind and spirit (life force, soul, etc.), while the third part is made up of our physical body. If two-thirds of our total existence is in the form of intangible energy, what happens to this energy when we die?

With permission, I quote from Schill: "When a person dies the bioelectric energy is released from the body into the local environment where it may perform one of two actions. The unconscious energy may dissipate into the local environment and there will essentially be no manifestation thereafter or it may, through covalent bonding, remain in the local environment and attach itself to a certain place or object that the person was attached to in life, or any place that has an electron deficit (this is the theory behind 'repeat' hauntings). The energy may, upon rapid release from the physical body (such as in accidental death, tragic situations, or a rapid natural release, etc.) coagulate within the local environment over a short period of time, maybe only a couple of minutes or so, and amass to such a degree that the greater portion that was originally in the body has now become self-aware outside of the body." Psychological forces of conscious will may also trigger this type of reaction. When self-awareness occurs, there is generally a degree of confusion because of the new form that the person is in, one of pure energy rather than a physically manifested body.

Over many years, cases, and investigations, observers have documented that hauntings often have several striking similarities that cannot be ignored. The first of these similarities is that there are low-level electromagnetic field disruptions. These disruptions generally fall between 3 to 100 milligauss (Mg). The cause of these disruptions is the intangible biomagnetic field that makes up a ghost. This disruptive field would also explain why electronic devices malfunction on occasion.

The second similarity that has been documented is that the air temperature often drops between 10 and 40 degrees Fahrenheit. Temperature drops are thought to be due to the unintentional attraction and condensation of free electrons in an environment. The condensing of an energy field leaves a momentary void of heat in an area.

The third similarity is found in the infrared spectrum just below the level of visible light. This level of the electromagnetic spectrum seems to be where the greatest number of manifestations take place. Because infrared light borders on the lower portion of the spectrum of visible light (red, orange, yellow), this could possibly explain why glimpses of entities are seen with the peripheral portion of the eye instead of within the direct line of sight. Manifestations seen with peripheral vision also attract the attention of our unburdened subconscious rather than our conscious mind, which bears the fears of social restriction and repression when we experience something that is out of the ordinary. Because of ghosts' placement on the electromagnetic spectrum, this may explain why cameras are able to photograph them, recorders are able to pick up their voices, and so on.

If we wish to discuss the subject of ghosts thoroughly, we must also include near-death experiences, astral projections, poltergeists, appearances of human doubles, manifestations of religious figures, the mystery of spirit possession, the process of mediumship, the phenomena of glowing orbs, and the controversial matter of animal spirits. Each of these nonphysical phenomena comprises an intriguing facet of human experience that may one day help us define the farthermost reaches of the soul.

After researching the paranormal for more than 50 years, I spend little time these days theorizing about what ghosts may be. I accept the reality that within each of us there is a spiritual essence that is imperishable and eternal. I completely accept the existence of spirit phenomena, and I contend that it is extremely multifaceted. While I believe it may be difficult to separate ghostly manifestations into definitions of type and purpose that are truly distinct from one another, I submit that real ghosts and restless spirits often fit into the following categories:

1. *Spirit Residue:* If the strange noises you hear in your home are not due to a squirrel in the attic, clanging water pipes, or an overactive imagination, then they are probably caused by what I term "spirit residue." I have found that a large number of structural hauntings are caused by the residual presence of spirits. In these cases a powerful human emotion—fear, jealously, hate, pain—has somehow been impressed into the environment. It is my contention that the sounds and sights of the haunting may be perceived by the psyche of a sensitive individual as if they were images on a strip of motion picture film that keeps being fed through a projector again and again. The percipients of these kinds of hauntings cannot interact with the ghosts any more than one can interact with the images on a motion picture or television screen. Ghosts that have been seen by many witnesses over many years may literally begin to take on a kind of independent existence, much like psychic marionettes, responding to the fears and expectations of their human audience.

2. *Spirits of the Dead:* For many years I stubbornly and dogmatically held to the hypothesis that all ghosts are the products of psychic residue. I strictly separated evidence of the spirit's survival after death from accounts of ghosts.

However, as my on-site investigations increased in number, I encountered spirit manifestations that clearly seemed to be the result of identifiable intelligences that wished to communicate messages from the other side to loved ones or interested parties. Other haunting phenomena appeared to be caused by earthbound spirits of deceased humans that were unable to detach themselves from the people, places, and things of the physical world and had not progressed to the light of a higher dimension.

3. *Poltergeists:* In common parlance, any violent and disruptive haunting is said to be caused by poltergeists—raucous entities that toss objects about the room. In the view of many psychical researchers, such phenomena is born not in the psyche of a dead being but rather in a living being who is undergoing some kind of stress, psychic upheaval, or severe and dramatic psychological adjustment. Such an individual (most often an adolescent) expresses unconscious aggression toward others through dramatic manifestations of psychokinetic power (mind over matter), such as the overturning of furniture and the propelling of objects through the room. In some cases I have investigated, poltergeist phenomena have interacted with the haunting manifestations that already existed in the home, thereby producing intensely negative and disruptive energy.

4. *Spirit Parasites:* I used to be as dogmatically opposed to the concept of demonic possession as any modern investigator is supposed to be. Many years of research and encounters with entities that are unabashedly evil have convinced me that homes in which murders or other violent physical deeds have been committed may become repositories for nonphysical leeches of the soul that I prefer to call "spirit parasites." These beings are hideous and grotesque in appearance, often manifesting as reptilian-like entities. When humans make themselves physically and spiritually vulnerable through drug and alcohol abuse, promiscuous sex, and other excesses of the physical body, they may not be aware of spirit parasites in their presence that are capable of possessing and manipulating them.

5. *Spirit Masqueraders:* In my opinion some appearances of ghosts and spirits have nothing to do with psychic residue, psychokinetic explosions of a human psyche undergoing stress, or survival of the spirit after death. I believe these pseudohauntings to be the machinations of another order of beings that in the past we have called fairies, elves, or nature spirits. In contemporary times they may represent themselves as extraterrestrial visitors, but these entities have interacted with humans for centuries by abducting humans, making mysterious circles in crops, and deceiving humankind about the truth of who they really are. These beings are more nonphysical than they are physical. Indeed, they may be paraphysical interlopers from other dimensions. They are "in-between" beings, posing from time to time as ordinary humans, disguising

the fact that they are really phantoms, creatures that have materialized from some haunted dominion unknown to us. In some benign instances, they may be angels in disguise that have come to give comfort, aid, and inspiration. In some of the more frightening cases, they may be fallen angels that aim to deceive, lie, and enslave. Theoretical physicists now speak freely about parallel universes; perhaps from time to time these entities intrude into our world from a universe that may almost be a mirror image of our own. Or perhaps, as the ancient philosophers suggested long ago, the appearance of spirits is evidence that we are part of a larger community of intelligences, a complex hierarchy of powers and principalities, a universe of interrelated species, both physical and nonphysical.

And now I invite you to follow me as we explore the many dark and shadowed pathways that will lead us to encounter real ghosts, restless spirits, and haunted places.

ACKNOWLEDGMENTS

First, I must thank all those individual researchers and experiencers of ghost phenomena who submitted their personal accounts and photographs for inclusion in this book. If I should begin to name them, I would surely omit someone—so a big thank you to all who contributed to the authenticity of this book. Next I must thank my agent, Agnes Birnbaum, who continues to be a marvelous support to me and my work, and who arranged for me to enjoy once again the unique collaborative experience of working with the remarkably genial and always helpful Visible Ink staff—Marty Connors, Roger Janecke, and Christa Gainor. I also thank Neil Schlager and Vanessa Torrado-Caputo of Schlager Group for their editorial suggestions; Larry Baker for compiling the index; Mary Claire Krzewinski for page and cover design; and Marco Di Vita at the Graphix Group for typesetting. Finally, I owe a great debt to Sherry Hansen Steiger, my best friend, fellow researcher of the unexplained, and life partner, for her patience in enduring my long hours at the word processor and her courage in journeying with me to those haunted places where real ghosts and restless spirits await our investigation.

PHOTO AND ILLUSTRATION CREDITS

Photos and illustrations used in *Real Ghosts, Restless Spirits, and Haunted Places* were reprinted with permission from the following sources:

AP/Wide World Photos: 80, 118, 125, 133, 142, 205, 233, 260, 267, 282, 285, 287, 289, 294, 296, 297, 325, 327, 363, 385, 387, 388, 392, 416, 417, 430, 467, 480, 481, 494.

Rick Aiello: 16.

Loyd Auerbach: 489.

Gregory J. Avery (orbmasster@cox.net): 42, 44.

Merry Barrentine/Utah Paranormal Exploration & Research (www.uper.freewebspace.com): 438.

Clarisa Bernhardt: 238.

Cindy Blake/Michigan Ghost Watchers (www.ghostwatchers.org): 506, 507.

Barry Conrad: 543, 544.

Christina Crawford: 292.

Patrick Cross: 541.

Fortean Picture Library: 3, 57, 59, 64, 69, 72, 75, 83, 113, 151, 157, 164, 212, 215, 220, 226, 228, 231, 232, 235, 236, 239, 262, 263, 264, 265, 271, 272, 277, 304, 310, 313, 331, 337, 338, 340, 343, 345, 347, 349, 352, 358, 389, 394, 396, 397, 403, 404, 450, 451, 475, 485, 491, 501, 517.

Stacie Freeland: 86.

Terry Gambill/Ghosts and Haunts in Missouri (www.missourighosts.net): 13.

Rick Garner: 411.

Margaret Jackson: 371.

Dale Kaczmarek (www.ghostresarch.org) and Jim Graczyk (www.ghostguides.com): 318, 356.

Stella Lansing: 209.

"Mark": 511.

Neville Mitchell: 46.

Maureen Nelson/Washington State Ghost Society (www.washingtonghostsociety.org): 406.

Dr. Dave Oester and Dr. Sharon Gill/International Ghost Hunters (www.ghostweb.com): 523, 527.

Todd Roll/Wausau Paranormal Society (www.pat-wausau.org): 445.

Richard Senate: 19.

Dusty Smith/Daytona Beach Psychical Research Group (www.dbprginc.org): 307, 308, 309.

Sherry Hansen Steiger: 370, 373.

The Steiger Archives: 17, 33, 49, 77, 227, 290, 301, 418, 419.

The Steiger Archives/Benjamin Smith: 425.

Dave Van Slyke (www.ghosttoghost.com): 169, 470.

Ed and Lorraine Warren: 35.

1
Haunted Houses and Apartments

THE HAUNTING OF WILLINGTON MILL

During the last two months of 1834, the nursemaid employed by the Joseph Proctor family tried her best to ignore the eerie noises that she heard coming from the deserted room over the nursery. Each night when she was left alone to watch the children, she would hear the sounds—dull, heavy treading, like someone slowly pacing back and forth.

Finally she decided that she had had enough of the strange sounds that so disturbed her sleep. She was convinced that a ghost occupied the upstairs room. In a state of nervous agitation, she asked to be discharged from her service in the Proctor home.

Proctor saw no reason why he should attempt to talk the woman into staying with them. She was obviously a highly imaginative woman who had frightened herself by supposing that she was being visited by supernatural beings.

It wasn't long, however, before he—and his wife and the other servants—also heard the sound of heavy feet in the upstairs room. Although puzzled by the treading of invisible feet, the Proctors convinced themselves that there was undoubtedly a natural explanation for the strange sounds. In spite of their refusal to believe there was a supernatural element to the noises, the Proctors purposely omitted any mention of the disturbed room when they hired a new nursemaid on January 23, 1835.

On her first evening in the nursery, the girl came down to the sitting room to inquire who was in the room above her. The Proctors evaded her question, putting the whole matter down to the usual nightly noises of an old house.

[1]

The next day, Mrs. Proctor heard the steps of a man with heavy boots walking about in the upstairs room. Later that same day, during the family's dinner, the nursemaid came down the stairs and blinked incredulously at Mr. Proctor. She said that she had heard someone walking in the room above her for five minutes. She had come downstairs to assure herself that it wasn't the master of the house.

"But if it isn't you, sir," she inquired, "who is it?"

Proctor inspected the room that night. Trickery seemed out of the question. The door to the room had been nailed shut for some time; the room's only window had been boarded up many years before with wooden laths and plaster. Inside the room, the floor was covered with a thin, undisturbed layer of soot, which in itself was proof that not even a mouse had been walking about. Proctor descended even more mystified than when he had gone up to conduct his investigation.

On January 31, the Proctors heard a dozen loud thuds next to their bed as they were preparing to retire. During the next night, Joseph Proctor heard a metallic rapping on the baby's crib. There was a brief pacing overhead and then the sound of footsteps, which were never heard again in the upper room.

But what followed for the next several years included such a remarkable range of visual and auditory manifestations that the initial plodding footsteps were to seem like a baby's first steps in comparison. What is nearly as remarkable as the intense haunting of Willington Mill is the fact that the Proctors persisted in living in the house for over 11 years before finally surrendering to the paranormal disturbances that invaded their home.

Thomas Mann, the foreman of the mill that was separated from the Proctor's house by a road and a garden, told Proctor that he had heard a peculiar noise moving across the lawn in the darkness. At first, Mann thought it came from the wooden cistern that stood in the mill yard; he suspected that some pranksters were attempting to spill it. However, upon pursuing the noise with a lantern in hand, he found that the cistern had not been budged. Mann also told Proctor in the strictest confidence that even before this peculiar disturbance, he had on several occasions heard a sound as if someone were walking on the gravel path, but when he went to see who it was, he saw no one.

Shortly after Proctor's confidential conversation with Mann, both Mann and another neighbor observed the luminous image of a woman in a window of Proctor's house; both parties saw the ghost independently of each other. Mann gathered his entire family to witness the phantasm, which was fully visible for more than 10 minutes.

About a year after the phenomena at Willington Mill had started becoming increasingly frightening, Mrs. Proctor's sister, Jane Carr, arrived for a stay. One evening, a few minutes before midnight, she was awakened by a noise

A Haunted House.

very much like that of someone winding a large clock. After this bizarre noise, her bed began to shake, and she clearly heard a sound like that of a heavy sack falling on the floor above. Several strong knocks sounded about her bedstead, and the unmistakable sound of shuffling feet surrounded her bed.

In addition to the sounds of thudding feet, the ghost had soon acquired fists with which to pound on walls and added bed-lifting to its repertoire of supernatural phenomena. The invisible force manifested under the bed of the Proctor's eldest child and began to raise the mattress higher and higher, until the child finally cried out. Next, the *thing* hoisted the mattress of the bed on which Mrs. Proctor and a new nursemaid were sleeping. Mrs. Proctor described the sensation as feeling as if a large man were underneath the bed, pushing it up with his back. Later, the haunting developed an ability to whistle, talk, and materialize into a number of grotesque phantoms.

The Proctors' sons, Joseph and Henry, were awakened one night by a loud shriek that emanated from under their beds. Upon investigating, Joseph, Sr., heard an odd moan coming from somewhere in the room. One of the beds began to move, and the voice uttered what sounded like, "chuck-chuck." These sounds were followed by a noise similar to that of an infant sucking a bottle. The youngest child, Jane, was moved to another room, but her relocation did not spare her the torment of having her bed levitated.

The phenomena had begun to leave its domain on the upper floor, venturing to the lower floors during the night. The kitchen seemed to be a favorite target for its nightly forays, and on several mornings the cook would find the kitchen chairs heaped in a disorderly pile, the shutters thrown open, and utensils scattered about the room.

Mrs. Proctor's brother, Jonathan Carr, spent a night filled with so much commotion that he declared he would not stay in the house for any amount of money. Jane, Mrs. Proctor's sister, was much more strong-nerved than her brother; judging from the journal that Joseph Proctor kept, the young woman spent many evenings in the afflicted house. One night as she shared a room with Mary Young, the cook, the two women were terrified to hear the bolt in their door slide back, the handle turn, and the door open. As an invisible entity moved across the bed the women shared, the bed curtains began to rustle, and the bedcovers were suddenly lifted and thrown off the bed, revealing the two trembling figures. Both women saw a distinctly dark shadow against the curtains that hung from the bed frame.

Little Jane Proctor was sleeping with her aunt Jane one night when she saw a strange head peeping out at her from the bed curtains. The four-year-old girl later described the head as being that of an old woman, but she became much too frightened to continue her observation and tucked her own head under the covers.

Joseph, Jr., was disturbed nearly every night by some facet or other of the phenomena. He reported hearing the words "never mind" and "come and get" being repeated over and over, without any apparent meaningful application. As he attempted to sleep, he constantly heard footsteps shuffling around his bed, and he both heard and felt forceful thumps to his pillow and other bedclothes.

A medical doctor named Drury arrived and asked Proctor's permission to carry out an examination of the haunted upper room. Proctor consented and allowed the doctor and his companion, a young chemist, to make preparations to spend a night in the disturbed room.

At about 1 A.M., Proctor was awakened by a piercing scream of terror coming from the upper floor. Drury had come face to face with the ghost of the wizened old woman. The two curious would-be investigators spent the rest of the night drinking coffee in the kitchen. They left the house at dawn. Proctor noted in his journal that the doctor and the chemist had received a shock that they would not soon forget.

One of the most incredible materializations in Willington Mill was that of an entity resembling a monkey. One day eight-year-old Joseph, Jr., was seated atop a chest of drawers, pretending that he was making a speech to his sister, Jane, and his brothers Henry and Edmund, when his presentation was rudely interrupted. Suddenly, in full view of all the children, a monkeylike creature appeared and began to tug at Joseph's shoe strap.

By the time Joseph, Sr., came running in response to their excited cries, the children were scurrying about the floor, trying desperately to play with the mischievous monkey. Two-year-old Edmund, the youngest Proctor child, continued to look under chairs and tables until his bedtime, trying to locate the entity that he identified as a "funny-looking cat."

Years later, the memory of that incident was still vivid in Edmund Proctor's mind. In the December 1892 issue of the *Journal of the Society for Psychical Research*, he wrote: "Now it so happens that this monkey is the first incident in the lugubrious hauntings, or whatever they may be termed, of which I have any recollection. I suppose it was, or might easily be, the first monkey that I had ever seen, which may explain my memory being so impressed that I have not forgotten it.… My parents have told me that no monkey was known to be owned in the neighborhood, and that after diligent inquiry no organ-man or hurdy-gurdy boy, either with or without a monkey, had been seen anywhere about the place or neighborhood, either on that day or for a length of time.… I have an absolutely distinct recollection of that monkey, and of running to see where it went to as it hopped out of the room and into the adjoining [room]. We saw it go under the bed in that room, but it could not be traced or found anywhere afterwards. We hunted and ferreted about that room, and every corner of the house, but no monkey, or any trace of one, was more to be found." Aunt Jane Carr did not see the monkey, but she reported that she had heard what sounded like an animal jumping down off an easy chair.

The white face of what appeared to be an old woman was seen more and more often, but Joseph, Jr., soon added an old man to the list of materializations. One of the more astonishing visual materializations also occurred to the younger Joseph; the haunting force fashioned a double of the young boy. Imagine the boy's shock upon discovering his mirror-image peeking at him from the shadows beside his bed. He was about 10 years old when this facet of the phenomena manifested, so his powers of observation must be given some credence. Joseph, Jr., said that his spectral self-image, which was even dressed in a manner identical to his, walked back and forth between the window and the wardrobe before it gradually dematerialized.

Shortly after this dramatic episode, the Proctors decided that they had endured enough. Patient Quakers though they were, 11 years of living amidst incessant supernatural disturbances had been enough for them. They had also become fearful that the "plague-ridden dwelling" would inflict permanent injury to the minds of their children.

In 1866 Proctor obtained a residence at Camp Villa, North Shields, and after completing the arduous task of packing their belongings, he and his wife sent the servants and the children on ahead to their new residence. Mr. and Mrs. Proctor stayed behind, alone, to properly close up the house; their final night in Willington Mill was perhaps the most frightening of all.

The constant sound of heavy thuds prevented them from getting any rest at all. The house echoed with the sound of boxes being dragged down the stairs, but the house was empty, save for them. All of their boxes had been moved out earlier that day. Yet they continued to hear footsteps walking across the floors, dragging invisible furniture. The Proctors were, in effect, hearing a ghostly reenactment of all the noises made by the family and their servants as they were engaged in their various moving chores. The Proctors wondered with some panic if the ghosts were packing in order to move with them to the new house.

It was with indescribable relief that the Proctors arrived at the new residence to find it completely free of the former horror that had blemished 11 years of their lives. Their residency in the new home was blissfully untroubled by knockings, whistlings, footsteps, and phantasms.

After the Proctors moved from Willington Mill, the house was divided into two apartments. According to later testimonies of the new occupants, only the occasional haunting phenomena occurred. However, in approximately 1868, when two new families moved into the apartments, they were so greatly disturbed by ghostly manifestations that one family moved out and refused to return.

After a number of years had passed, the mill was closed and made into a warehouse, and the old Proctor house was divided into a number of small tenements. When Edmund Proctor visited the place around 1890, none of the tenants claimed to be troubled by ghosts. It appeared that whatever ethereal beings had plagued the house at Willington Mill had moved on.

THE DANCING GHOST OF ORENSBURG

On November 16, 1870, when he returned to his large country estate near Orensburg, in the Russian province of Uralsk, a wealthy landowner named Shchapoff found his household in an uproar over a dancing ghost.

According to Helena, his 20-year-old wife, their baby daughter had been fussy on the night of the 14th and had not been at all eager to go to sleep. Mrs. Shchapoff asked Maria, the cook, if she would see to the child.

Maria entertained the girl with her harmonica, while her mistress and the local miller's wife gossiped in the living room.

When Mrs. Shchapoff heard the sounds of the cook's feet tapping the floor in a brisk three-step dance, she remarked that when all else failed, Maria danced for the child, which always put the little one to sleep. The miller's wife was in the act of nodding her head in agreement when she suddenly opened her mouth in both surprise and terror, and screamed that there was someone looking in the window.

Mrs. Shchapoff turned and saw nothing to cause the woman so much alarm. The miller's wife was visibly shaken and disturbed and said that she thought that she had seen a horrid face looking in at them. Mrs. Shchapoff assured her that it was probably only a shadow of some sort. The awkward moment was interrupted as Maria entered the room and told her mistress that her child was now sound asleep. Mrs. Shchapoff thanked the cook and dismissed her for the evening.

A few minutes later, as the two women sat chatting, the miller's wife once again claimed that she saw something at the window. Mrs. Shchapoff rose from her chair to investigate, but she was halted in her journey to the window by the sound of an uproar in the attic above their heads. At first it seemed to be a flurry of wild rappings that had the two women staring at one another in wide-eyed confusion. Then the pace of the sounds slowed until they began to sound like the three-step Maria had been dancing for the child.

Mrs. Shchapoff was perplexed. What was that silly woman doing up in the attic? Did she never get her fill of dancing? The miller's wife questioned how the cook could have gotten up to the attic without their seeing her pass. Without speaking another word, the two women left the sitting room and walked quietly back to the cook's quarters. Opening the door just a crack, they were able to see Maria sound asleep in her bed.

Determined to see who had gone up to the loft unnoticed, Mrs. Shchapoff grabbed a lantern from a kitchen shelf, and the two women walked up the stairs to the attic. Although the sounds of the dancing continued, their lantern plainly revealed that there was no one in the loft. Then, as the women beat a hasty retreat down the stairs, the rapping seemed to race ahead of them, rattling the windows and pounding at the walls.

The miller's wife fled the manor to get her husband and the gardener, and Mrs. Shchapoff went to the nursery to check on the welfare of her daughter. By the time the miller's wife returned with her husband and the gardener, the rappings and dancing had attained such a volume that both Mrs. Shchapoff's mother and mother-in-law, as well as Maria, had been awakened by the racket. The two men searched the house and the grounds and found nothing that could explain the bizarre disturbance, which continued until dawn.

At 10:00 P.M. the next evening, the dancing ghost once again began its spirited interpretation of the three-step. The Shchapoff's servants patrolled the house and the grounds but could find no trace of the invisible dancer who continued to perform and to evade the searchers until dawn.

When Mr. Shchapoff returned that next afternoon from his business trip, he scoffed at his young wife's account and jokingly accused her of getting into his brandy while he had been away. Shchapoff was a no-nonsense landowner who had little patience with superstitious folktales and accounts of ghosts, dancing or otherwise. He grew very impatient when his mother and mother-in-law warned him that something supernatural had visited the house in his absence, substantiating Helena's story of a dancing ghost.

In a gruff and irritated manner, Shchapoff scolded the ladies for having sat around idly in the evenings, concocting a ghost story that had frightened the servants and distracted them from their work. He sent Maria to fetch the miller, a man he regarded as completely sensible and reliable, to set the matter straight.

The miller didn't disappoint him. While he admitted that there had been strange noises that had disturbed and confused the entire household, he stated that he had, that very day, removed a pigeon's nest from under a cornice of the house. It seemed likely to him that the bird had somehow been responsible for the weird noises that had so upset the women and the servants. Shchapoff knew that he could count on the miller to put an end to wild tales of a dancing ghost.

That evening after the rest of the household had retired to their rooms quite early, exhausted from their nocturnal ordeals of chasing the eerie tapping sounds, Shchapoff sat down in a chair in his study to read for a while before going to bed. At about 10 o'clock, he was distracted by scratching noises from above his head. Thinking at first that the pesky pigeon had come back to roost under the cornice, he became puzzled when he listened more closely to the sounds. He soon realized the sounds were not those of an animal; rather it sounded as though someone in the room above him was dancing a three-step.

Believing that Helena was having a bit of fun with him, Shchapoff put down his book and began climbing quietly up the stairs to his wife's room. He stood outside the door for a moment to be certain that he had accurately traced the sound of the dancing. Then, convinced that there was no doubt that the sounds were coming from Helena's room, he pushed open the door and stood ready to deliver a stern lecture to his young wife.

She lay in her bed, her eyelids closed, in deep sleep. The sounds of dancing had ceased the moment that he had opened the door. There was something strange going on here. Confused and more than a little baffled, Schchapoff started to close the door when a series of rappings sounded from above his wife's bed. He walked quietly to the wall, thinking he might catch a hidden prankster in the act of hammering on the bedstead. Just as he bent to listen more carefully to the noises, a rap sounded with such force next to his ear that it nearly deafened him.

His wife sat up in bed, screaming in shock and fear. She calmed when she saw her husband standing near her bedside. "What was that?" she demanded. "Did you hear it?"

Not wishing to alarm his wife, Shchapoff insisted that he had heard nothing. As if to call him a liar, two explosive knocks seemed to shake the house down to its very foundation. The angry landowner took his pistol from a drawer, slipped on his coat, and declared that he was putting a stop to the nonsense. He got his dogs, roused the servants, and told them that they were going to find out who was responsible for the outrage against his home.

However, Shchapoff found no prankster that night on whom he might vent his spleen. To those on the outside of the house, the rappings seemed to come from the inside. But those who remained indoors shouted that someone was trying to batter the house down from the outside. At last, Shchapoff had to admit defeat, and he dismissed his men for the night.

The next day, he enlisted the help of his neighbors as well as his own servants. The crew searched the entire house and examined every foot of the grounds. That night, at Shchapoff's request, his neighbors stayed to witness the disturbances. The uninvited invisible guest performed well. It danced above the heads of the searchers all night long—and, for a finale, it struck a door with such force that the heavy wooden planking was torn from the hinges.

By the next night, even the stubborn landowner had become a believer in the dancing ghost, and it was obvious that he dreaded the onset of a new round of the phenomena. He paced the floor nervously until ten o'clock, the time the manifestations usually began. But on this night, there was not a single scratching, rapping, or spritely danced three-step. Nor was there any sound from the loft on the next night. It appeared that the mysterious phenomena had quieted down in the Shchapoff country house. Or perhaps they might have if the Shchapoffs would have left well enough alone.

A month later, on December 20, the Shchapoffs were entertaining guests who openly expressed their skepticism of the phenomena their hosts described as having been active in the house. Angered that their guests would doubt his word, Shchapoff summoned Maria to the parlor and commanded her to perform a three-step, announcing in a loud voice that probably all the ghost needed was a little coaxing and it would come back.

At her master's insistence, Maria danced a brisk little three-step. The cook completed the dance, then looked around the room fearfully as a rapping began at the windows. The assembled guests listened incredulously as they heard an exact replication of Maria's dance coming from the attic overhead. The skeptical guests accused Shchapoff of having planted another servant up in the loft, but when a group of doubters went up into the attic to investigate, they found no one.

On New Year's Eve, 1871, Shchapoff again ordered Maria to dance a three-step in order to induce the dancing ghost to follow her with an act of its own. The country home was filled with guests who heard for themselves the ghostly echo of Maria's dance coming from the ceiling above their heads. The invisible performer became so animated and enthusiastic that for the first time it made some attempts at vocalization and sang some garbled snatches of Russian folk songs.

After such remarkable phenomena had been produced at two holiday parties, the stories about the mysterious goings-on at the Shchapoffs' country place spread across Russia. Soon, scientists and spiritualists sought an audience with the dancing ghost, using widely diverse methods of communicating with the strange force.

An investigator by the name of Dr. Shustoff explained the whole phenomena by invoking the magic name of electricity. He maintained that the soil conditions at the country place had produced the weird phenomena. He also theorized that somehow the electrical vibrations might be coming from Mrs. Shchapoff.

Dr. Shustoff's theory of prankish electrical currents was doomed when the phenomena began to give evidence of increasingly advancing intelligence that could respond to conversation and questions advanced by investigators. A psychic investigator named Alekseeff devised a series of knocks that he claimed allowed him to communicate with the entity haunting the country estate. According to information gathered by Alekseeff, Mr. Shchapoff had been cursed by the servant of a neighboring miller. For whatever reason, this angry servant so despised Shchapoff that he had maliciously set a devil on the wealthy landowner.

The provincial governor, General Vervekin, appointed a group of individuals to be the official investigators of the disturbances that plagued the Shchapoff estate. The team included Mr. Akutin, an engineer; the aforementioned Dr. Shustoff, an electrical theorist; and Mr. Savicheff, a magazine editor. This committee eventually decided that Mrs. Shchapoff had been producing the so-called supernatural effects by means of trickery, and Mr. Shchapoff received a sharply worded letter from the governor, warning him not to allow his wife to produce the phenomena again.

In spite of the governor's demands, the violence of the disturbances at the Shchapoff estate continued to increase. The ghost had acquired incendiary abilities, and Helena Shchapoff was the one who bore the brunt of the attacks. Balls of fire circled the house and bounced against the windows of her room, as if seeking to smash into the house and set it aflame. Dresses that hung unattended in closets burst into flame. Once, a mattress began burning underneath a guest as he readied himself for bed.

The ghastly climax of the haunting phenomena occurred when Mrs. Shchapoff appeared to become a veritable pillar of fire in front of the horrified eyes of the miller and another houseguest. A crackling noise had come from beneath the floor, followed by a long, high-pitched wailing. A bluish spark seemed to jump up at Mrs. Shchapoff, and her thin dress was instantly swathed in flames. She cried out in terror and collapsed into unconsciousness.

The houseguest leapt to his feet and valiantly beat the flames out with his bare hands. The most curious thing about the incident was that the courageous guest suffered severe burns while Mrs. Shchapoff received not a single blister, even though her dress was nearly completely consumed by the flames.

The Shchapoffs had had enough of their encounters with the dancing ghost. When the entity had contented itself with a nightly performance of the three-step, it had merely been a noisy nuisance. Now it had become a vicious terror, quite capable of dealing out fiery destruction. Mr. Shchapoff closed up his country place and made arrangements for a permanent move to the city of Iletski.

The phenomena ceased at once after the Shchapoffs had taken up residence in their town place. Although Helena Shchapoff recovered the health that had been rapidly waning under the onslaughts of the ghost, she died in childbirth eight years after their move.

The Orensburg haunting is an unusual case in many ways. Perhaps, as some have theorized, there actually was a curse levied on Mr. Shchapoff by a disgruntled servant of a neighboring miller. The projected hatred of such an individual may somehow have intensified what had begun as rather ordinary haunting phenomena (e.g., the face at the window, the imitation of the cook's dancing, the raps on the walls) and transformed them in a force of malicious evil.

EERIE FOOTSTEPS IN THE ATTIC

The town house that Karen and her husband bought in July 1992 was only 11 years old and in good condition. Shortly after they moved in, she began hearing someone walking in the upstairs hallway. At first she thought it was her son sneaking out of bed—which sometimes it was. But other times when she went to investigate, he was in bed, asleep. Karen never said anything about the footsteps to her husband, making the assumption that the sounds were the result of the house settling or her imagination.

The Personal Experience of Karen

"My husband is disabled, so he is home all day. Soon he began telling me that he kept hearing someone walking upstairs when nobody else was home but him. He said that he heard the sounds frequently, so I told him that I was also hearing things at night. Then our four-year-old son started telling us about the 'mice' that were in his room at night. I went into his room and lay down with him one night. I heard so many scratching noises on the floor and sounds like children running around the room that I scooped him up and got out of there. I put him in bed with us, and then we heard the walking sounds in the hallway.

"The next night, while my husband and I were in bed, we heard someone walking in our bedroom. The sounds started on my side of the bed, moved around the bed, then went out of the room, down the hallway and down the stairs.

"One night, my son came running out of his room into our bedroom, wide-eyed and out of breath, and said that there was a big dog in his room, and he wouldn't go back in there. He was awake until almost dawn before he fell asleep again.

"In the first month after we moved into the town house, we went through at least 100 light bulbs. We couldn't keep them burning. The ceiling fixtures and the bathroom, hallway, and kitchen lights blew out constantly—and within hours of each other.

"The previous owners had left several boxes and an old lead mirror in a plain wooden frame in the attic. I brought the mirror down from the attic and decided to hang it at the end of the hallway, opposite our son's bedroom door. There weren't any noises until after I hung it. And most of the noises were in that hallway or our bedrooms off of that hallway. My mother told me to get rid of the mirror, and the noises stopped after I carried it out and set it with the trash."

GHOSTLY RAPPINGS IN A MOBILE HOME

The following account came from a man we'll call Earl, who said that the events that occurred within the thin metal walls of his family's trailer home when he was a child had forever affected his life. Prior to his parents' divorce, Earl stated, the shower in the mobile home would turn itself on.

The Personal Experience of Earl

"My father always blamed it on my two brothers or me," he stated, "but we knew each other to be innocent. After the divorce, Father no longer wanted to sleep in the bedroom that he had shared with our mother, so he began sleeping on the couch. One night while he was sleeping, there came a loud rapping at our front door. Angrily he went to answer it, but there was nobody in sight."

About that same time, Earl wrote in his account of the haunting, the three boys and their father would awaken at nights dripping with sweat. "Father would discover the furnace had been turned up full blast. Since it wasn't winter, no one would have gone near the furnace."

Earl said that on many nights he would see the door to his older brother's room open by itself. "I would hear footsteps walk down the hall, enter the bathroom, flush the toilet, then walk into the room I shared with my younger brother," he said. "I would sit up in my bed, unable to sleep because I could feel a dark presence as the invisible spirit paced through our room. As a child, this experience intensified my fear of engulfing darkness."

One night as the four of them sat watching television in the living room, the hall light began to flicker on and off. "Father asked one of my brothers to turn it off," Earl said. "As soon as he would turn it off, it would turn itself back on. My brother turned it off once more before he came back into the living room. Just as he sat down, the light came on again and violently flickered off and on, as if in spite."

Investigator Terry Gambill took several pictures in a home that had been suffering from paranormal activity. While the majority of photographs he took turned out completely normal, he could not explain this particular frame, in which an entity is clearly visible.

The family didn't want to move, so Earl said that his father brought a minister into the trailer "to pray the spirit away" from their home. "A local preacher, Bible in hand, went into the middle bedroom where we all felt the spirit most often," Earl said. "While my brothers and I stayed in the kitchen to watch over a pot of pasta for the night's supper, we saw the dark shadow of a child form between the kitchen and the hallway. Father said that when the preacher walked into the bedroom with the Bible and began to pray, the entire room filled up with some kind of fog. The preacher thought the spirit left when the fog drifted out of the room."

Later that night, the family found out that it wasn't so easy to get the haunting spirit to leave. "There was such a pounding on the outside of the trailer that we ran outside to see whatever could be the source of the racket," Earl said. "Whatever it was, it could not be seen, and the pounding just kept hammering away, circling and circling the trailer until it finally quieted down."

After spending over a year with this restless spirit, the family gave up and finally moved out. "Later, we found out from a friend that the trailer burned down after we left," Earl said, concluding his account. "Almost 12 years later, we drove through the trailer park and discovered that our old lot was still vacant. The story had spread about the ghost that had haunted our home, and no one had ever wanted to set their trailer down on that spot."

GHOSTS IN RIVERHEAD, NEW YORK

Since the early 1970s, Lee Moorhead has been known as the "Psychic of the Hamptons" (see her website, <http://www.stargaze.com>, for more information about her work). In the following stories, Moorhead shares some of her experiences in the region of Riverhead, New York.

The Personal Experience of Lee Moorhead

"About 15 years ago, two ladies who owned the huge mansion on the north shore (known by locals as the Gold Coast) invited me to dinner on my birthday. I barely knew them, but they knew of me and were acquainted with my two friends who accompanied me. After cocktails and light chatter, we went into the dining room to have dinner, and my seat near the end of the table was facing the entryway.

"During the conversation, I happened to look toward the entry and saw an elderly lady dressed in a black coat and hat and carrying a large bag. I assumed it was either the housekeeper on her way out or possibly someone they had hired to cook the dinner, so I interrupted the conversation to tell one of my hostesses that the lady was waiting to see them. One of the women asked, 'What lady?'

"I said, 'The lady in the hall. She looks like she is ready to leave.' They told me that there was no one else in the house, and when I looked again, the lady was gone. They did tell me that they had learned that the house was haunted, but they had never known for certain.

"Later in the evening, they took me to the west wing. When I was taken into one of the rooms, I found it very cold, and I told them that a man had committed suicide in that room. Furthermore, I said that his spirit was still there, and the room would never warm up. I suggested they get holy water and sprinkle it in that room. They learned a few months later that a man had shot himself in the house, but the persons to whom they had spoken had no idea which room.

"Before I purchased a home in Riverhead, I rented a big old house in Aquebogue, on the north shore of Long Island, and gave my middle daughter what seemed like a very nice room upstairs. She would come downstairs crying every night that the lady in the white gown kept chasing her out of the room.

"I learned from the owner's grandsons that their grandmother, who was not totally sane, had lived in that room and never came downstairs. Her meals were brought up to her when she became old, and she ended up dying there in that house. I changed that room into the playroom and made a bedroom for my daughter out of the former playroom.

"I am very aware of spirit, and I know there is one who visits me in the most recent home I bought. Once in a while there is a knock on my bedroom door even though no one is here at home, and a few times the water turns on in the tub until I get up to walk in there, then it turns off. However, the water is there and the faucet is wet."

THE FACE ON THE TINTYPE

The Personal Experience of Richard Aiello

"The old barn on our property was built in June 1863, and it is still intact and as solid as a battleship. We had been installing some 4 x 4 posts in the barn to build stalls for our two Belgian mules. Now, the holes that we dug for these posts had to be deep, because the mules they would contain are big and powerful. At the depth of about three feet, I spotted something shiny in one of the holes. All three of us working in the barn saw the object fall out of the post-hole digger when it dumped the dirt. I picked it up and looked at it in amazement. It was an old tintype portrait of a bearded man.

"When I sent an image of the tintype plate to Eastman Kodak for analysis, they said that judging by the color of the picture and the clothing style of the subject, the portrait would be dated around 1845–1860. Amazingly, the tintype had been under the earth for 140-plus years and the frame had not rusted away, nor had the image disintegrated.

"But here is the kicker: When we first moved into this house, we often saw the image of a man looking in our large (4 x 8) window. We still saw it when we had the lights on bright and really lit up the room. The image was so detailed that sometimes I thought I was seeing my own reflection.

"The image on that old tintype is the same man that we would see looking in at us. And here is another eerie thing to contemplate: When we first unearthed the old tintype, its emulsion covering was clear. Now it has started to fog over and there is another image superimposed on the picture over the man's left shoulder. You can see the glint in its eye and the mustache, too. And it appears that other images are beginning to form."

The tintype found by Richard Aiello. Analysis showed that the portrait was taken c. 1845–1860.

OUR HAUNTED HOUSE IN NEW ENGLAND

Raymond Buckland is the author of 38 books on the mysterious and magical; his most recent is The Fortune-Telling Book: The Encyclopedia of Divination and Soothsaying.

The Personal Experience of Raymond Buckland

"In the early 1970s I left New York and relocated to New Hampshire, purchasing an old farmhouse near Lake Winnepesaukee. The house had been built around 1825 and was a two story with attached ell barn. From the beginning I knew the house was haunted. Most evenings my wife and I would hear footsteps in the upstairs bedrooms as someone paced the floors. Once, to our surprise, we heard the footsteps come down the main staircase.

"The stairs divided the house into two sections on both the lower and top floor. Downstairs, my study was off to one side, and the living room was on the other side; the front door of the house stood in the very middle, opposite the stairway. My wife and I were sitting in the living room when we heard the footsteps come down the stairs. We both turned expectantly to face the door, wondering who—or what—might make an appearance. Nothing! I got up and went to the door, looking out at the foot of the stairs. It was completely empty.

"Another time I was sitting in my study when I saw a ghost. A screened-in porch had been added to the front of the house at some time. The screen door was off at one end of the porch, closest to the driveway. While I was working in my study, I heard the screen door squeak open and then slam closed. I glanced up to catch a glimpse of a male figure walking across the

A photograph of the "Tulip Staircase Ghost" at the National Maritime Museum in Greenwich, England.

porch toward the front door. When the doorbell didn't ring, I got up and went to open the front door. There was no one outside. I would have heard the squeak of the screen door if anyone had gone back out, and the driveway was long enough that I would certainly have seen anyone hurrying away. But there was no one there. The porch was completely empty.

"On another occasion my wife's grandmother was staying with us for a few days. She slept in one of the front bedrooms, upstairs (the one from which we used to hear the footsteps). One morning she came down to breakfast and told us of an overnight visitor.

"'I woke up for no special reason about midnight,' she said. 'I saw a woman standing at the foot of the bed, looking at me. She was dressed all in blue, and after studying me for a while, she turned away and disappeared … just vanished into thin air!' There was always a nightlight burning in the bedroom, so she would have been able to see any such figure, and not just imagine it. We just accepted it as another of our family of ghosts.

"We always accepted the ghosts as friendly, and certainly never had any problems with them. We were sorry to leave them when we finally sold the house and moved away, some six years later."

From the Files of Ghost Hunter Richard Senate

Richard Leonard Senate has investigated well over 200 haunted houses, mostly in the western states. Senate holds a degree in history from California State University, Long Beach, and currently works as the historian for the city of Ventura, a position he has held since the mid-1970s.

During the summer of 1972, Senate encountered the ghostly image of a monk while working as part of an archeological dig at the old Spanish mission San Antonio de Padua (near King City, California). Because he had begun his research with little training in ghost hunting, Senate approached his first investigations into the appearance of the ghostly monk in the same manner he did an archaeological dig. In his opinion, such a model has proved successful over the years, because the systems used to unravel the mystery of an ancient culture can also be used to unravel the reasons why ghosts haunt a particular location.

Senate believes that the main focus of any psychic investigator should be to collect and save data on paranormal events, and then attempt to organize the information into a theory as to why a place is haunted (if it really is), and to name the identity of the ghost.

He openly admits that he doesn't know the exact nature of ghosts. "I still don't know what they are after all these years," he says, "but I know that something beyond our present knowledge is going on. Too many people have seen too many things over too many decades. They cannot all have been drunk or crazy. I have seen ghosts, and there is a great deal of truth to the old saying, 'seeing is believing.' I also know that no two haunted houses are alike."

Senate is the author of eight published books on the paranormal, including *The Ghost Stalker's Guide to Haunted California*, *The Ghosts of the Ojai Valley*, *The Haunted Southland*, and *Ghosts of the Haunted Coast*. In 1995 he became one of the first ghost hunters on the Internet with the website <http://www.ghost-stalker.com>.

"I believe the study of ghosts is currently in its infancy," Senate said. "We are at the same level as the study of electricity was in the time of Ben Franklin. I sometimes feel like I am out there in the storm with my kite and my key. Sure, I might get knocked on my butt, but I will find answers! Do I get scared sometimes? You would be a fool if you didn't. We are dealing with the unknown—adventures in a new country. Psychic research is the greatest exploration of them all!"

Paranormal investigator Richard Senate.

Richard Senate's Firsthand Account of a Very Haunted House

"The sun was setting when we drove up to the house. 'Strange,' I thought, 'it doesn't look haunted.' But then, the worst ones never do.

"Debbie Christenson Senate was with me on this investigation, and I watched her closely, knowing that her psychic gifts might pick up some impressions of the house even as we rolled to a stop in the wide driveway. She was silent, but a look of concentration was fixed on her face, and her eyes were glued to the window on the second floor. I felt certain that she would begin receiving some feelings regarding the place, because this house was perhaps the most active I had investigated in the last five years.

"I had received the call two weeks before. The family was terrorized by pounding footsteps in the night, moving shadows, and bizarre happenings, such as the curtains billowing out at odd times even with the windows closed.

"One night the poundings in the house and the boot-like footfalls grew so menacing that the wife believed that the house was being invaded and

Real Ghosts, Restless Spirits, and Haunted Places

called the police. The law enforcement officers arrived quickly to search the premises, but even with their dogs to sniff out any intruders, they found no one. The police then informed the residents that the house was haunted. The family had guessed as much, and after the police confirmed their suspicions, they began to collect information about the building's past.

They learned that a young man had taken his own life in the house a decade ago and that the present home had been built on the exact site where a large farmhouse had burned to the ground, taking six lives.

"The phenomena were persistent enough for me to organize an investigation. As always, Debbie was told as little as possible about the site. We do not wish prior information to taint her psychic impressions. She refused even to know the address or anything about the case until we were about to leave for the house in the Oxnard, California, area. We picked up two other researchers, who, in prior investigations, had managed to record strange, unaccountable voices on tape recorders. I hoped that they might find some useful EVP (electronic voice phenomena) in our walk though the house. I also brought a camera along to document the ghost hunt.

"As we drove up to the house, the family came out to greet us and ushered us into the large, tastefully furnished home. I had warned them not to say anything about the psychic events in the house until Debbie had a chance to look the place over. A sudden chill raced though her and she crossed into a hallway.

"'There is something here,' she said, looking down towards the door and bathroom off the hall. I could feel a coldness creeping over my legs. Was it just an overactive imagination or were the forces in the house reaching out to us?

"The others in the team were feeling it, too—that cold that comes from no place, yet everywhere. Debbie, now shaken, moved to the bathroom. 'This is where he is,' she said. 'There is a young man, a boy, and a woman.'

"Debbie didn't know that the hallway was the center of the disturbances in the house. The wife reported that she often felt as though she were being watched while she showered in that room. The feeling that we were being observed by an unseen presence continued up the stairs and even to the master bedroom, where a shadowy arm had materialized, only to vanish.

"After carefully searching the entire house, we retired to the living room to discuss our findings and the events that had taken place in the house. The owner informed us that almost every night the doors in the house would rattle violently, and they often heard the sound of children running alongside footsteps that sounded as if they were made by a large man wearing heavy work boots.

"Debbie felt that the haunting events were somehow linked to the house that had burned before the present home had been built. The rattling doors and footsteps were a reenactment of the last terrible moments when the house had caught fire, trapping the hapless residents inside. The fear and panic, Debbie believed, had left a psychic scar upon the location that had somehow been regenerated by the new family with young children.

"We all agreed that the house was indeed haunted and that there were prescribed things to do. One was to log the times when the events took place. It was determined that many of the events seemed to take place in the wee hours of the morning, and Debbie felt an explanation of the time factor was that it had been then that the house had caught fire long ago.

"For a short time, our visit to the house seemed to make things worse for the family, but the psychic events began to slow down and to occur less and less frequently, almost as if the spirits had become aware that it was their time to move on. When we listened to the tape recordings, a number of odd manifestations were discovered. There were gaps in the tape, odd clicks, and a voice, the voice of a woman, who said, in a whispered tone, 'I've got mine.'

"The meaning of these words remains unknown. The house is a mysterious place and events continue, but the worst appears to be over."

HAUNTINGS FROM THE FILES OF STEPHEN WAGNER

Stephen Wagner has been the editor of the website "About.com Guide to Paranormal Phenomena" since 1998 (<http://paranormal.about.com>). Wagner writes a feature article for the site each week, as well as editing the paranormal news and reviewing readers' true stories and photographs. "My view on ghosts and hauntings, specifically, is that there is overwhelming evidence that the phenomena are quite real," Wagner said. "What they are exactly and how and why they manifest in our reality is, of course, the mystery." Here are three interesting ghost stories culled from the many that Wagner has received from readers of his website.

A Little Peeking Ghost

When she was about 16, Marge and her two sisters shared a small apartment upstairs in their parents' home. Marge slept in the bedroom that was connected to the living room via a doorway with no door. Her sister Evelyne slept on the top of a bunk with their eight-year-old sister on the bottom. On this particular night, Marge lay in bed on her right side, facing the doorway, having a conversation with Evelyne, whom she could see in her bed.

The Personal Experience of Marge: "We were not talking scary stories or anything like that, just boys, school, and so forth. As we were speaking, I saw a cloud form past the foot of her bunk, gathering like a white mist. Evelyne's bunk had a footboard that came up about 18 inches, so it obstructed her view, but I could see the cloud take shape like a small person. It then put its hands on the top edge of the footboard and pulled itself up by its hands, peeking at my sister for a moment, then lowering itself, holding on, and peeking again at Evelyne from the side of the footboard. Then it was gone. I had stopped talking and just watched the thing for about a minute.

"Evelyne asked, 'Marge, did you just see something?' I answered that I had and asked what she had seen. She replied that she thought she had seen something small looking at her.

"I asked Evelyne if it had scared her. She answered no, because it had resembled a young person, maybe a child. I agreed and that was that. The apartment always seemed haunted, and there were many instances of odd happenings, but this one I remember clearly."

An Encounter with a Hugging Ghost

Darnell and her husband ran a small construction business and had been contracted to do a job in an older section of a nearby town. The house was built in the early part of the 1900s, and they were to gut totally the inside of the home and hang new drywall, put in new flooring and paint, and so forth.

The Personal Experience of Darnell: "One day I was in the kitchen, nailing down the plywood flooring. My children were with me and were busy playing in the yard by the back door and inside on the first floor—all of them nearby so I knew what they were up to. I was working at a steady pace, on my hands and knees working my way backward toward the stairs leading to the second floor off the back of the kitchen. I was tired and had stopped for a moment to catch my breath.

"I straightened up at the base of the stairs, still on my knees. I was suddenly hugged from behind by a small child. It was such a loving hug that I turned around to give whichever of my children had given me this wonderful feeling a hug in return. There was no one there.

"I immediately got a cold, eerie feeling and jumped to my feet. I called out to the kids. They were in my pickup truck parked a few feet from the back door, coloring in their coloring books.

"I packed up my things and left. I told my husband what had happened and the reason that I did not finish my work. He was astonished. He then told me that in the 1930s a small boy had been playing with his brother, who was emotionally disturbed, and had been accidentally pushed down the stairs and had died.

"When we returned the next day, the owner accused us of going upstairs in the bedrooms and unrolling rolls of wallpaper and pulling down the window shades and generally making a mess. While we worked in the days that followed, we could hear feet running back and forth upstairs. Tools were missing, and the owner kept accusing us of going upstairs where their personal belongings were and messing them up. We never went upstairs at all. We were told not to. We did not invade their personal space.

"We finally left the job unfinished because of these strange happenings. I could not seem to stay in the kitchen. I would get gooseflesh and feel strange sensations of happiness, loneliness, and love."

Ghostly Bells and Boots in a Lumberjacks' Bunkhouse

Dennis M. stated that his father was born in 1907 in Nova Scotia and had once worked in the woods as both a lumberjack and a cook. One night during the winter of 1935, just after the men had retired for the night, they were awakened by the sounds of a sleigh coming to the door.

The Personal Experience of Dennis M.: "They heard the bells on the horse, the sleigh runners squeaking on the snow, and the driver holler, 'Whoa!' Of course everyone got up and rushed to the door to meet the visitor. However, there was no visitor, no sleigh marks, no hoof prints from the horses, nothing.

"The event that finally chased everyone out of the bunkhouse was when the ghost drove the sleigh up to the door, got off the sleigh, opened the door and walked in. Dad said that you could hear the boots walking across the floor, clip-clop, clip-clop. It horrified everyone. Lumberjacks began throwing their boots and whatever else at the ghost. Dad said he finally got a lantern lit, and just like before, there was no evidence of anyone or anything being there."

JOIN ME IN THE CRAWL SPACE!

From the files of the "Ghost to Ghost" website (<http://www. ghosttoghost.com>)

The Personal Experience of Anonymous: "One day I was working with a friend in a brand new home in Ogden, Utah. We were doing the heating and air conditioning. My friend was checking the furnace and discovered it had a bad transformer, so he left to go get a new one.

"While he was gone I continued installing the ductwork. I got an eerie feeling and looked over my shoulder and saw an old woman standing at the base of the stairs. I figured she was the homeowner. I said 'hi' and asked her if she needed anything. She just shook her head 'no' and smiled. I went about my business.

"Then I felt the same eerie feeling. I looked over my shoulder and, there she was, about five feet from me. I got off my ladder and said, 'Can I help you?' She smiled and, once again, shook her head 'no.'

"Just then I heard my partner pulling around the house. I turned to see where the woman was and she was already by the base of the stairs, about 50 feet away. I said, 'Are you sure you don't need anything?' She just looked at me and motioned with her finger for me to come with her. Of course, I said, 'No way!'

"Then I heard my friend enter the home on the first floor. The old woman again motioned for me to follow her. She was backing toward a crawl space just under the stairs.

"I took my eyes off her for a second to try and figure out where my friend was and when I looked back, I saw the most horrifying old woman motioning to me with a bony, leathery finger. This time she said, 'Get over here!'

"I watched her disappear into the crawl space. That was it. I got out of there fast. Finally my friend joined me and I told him the story. He just laughed and told me to stay outside if it would make me feel better. And that's exactly what I did.

"I did some research on that area and learned that most of the land had been used as a Native American tribal burial ground. To this day I haven't returned to that site!"

How We Rid Our Home of Ghosts

The Personal Experience of Frank Joseph, author of Edgar Cayce's Atlantis and Lemuria *and* The Destruction of Atlantis: "In spring 2000 my wife Laura and I moved with our kitty Sally into a rented house overlooking the Wisconsin side of the Mississippi River. It was a small place, just the right size for the three of us, and out in the country, about two hours' drive from Minneapolis–St. Paul.

"Not even our landlord could determine the age of the original structure. A local man told us he saw it often as a boy, in the early 1950s, whenever he canoed past our neck of the river. In the mid-1990s the house was purchased by a retired couple from Arizona. They worked hard turning it into a sweet summer home, planting evergreen trees and a variety of flowers nearby. The exterior was remodeled in attractive redwood siding, while a new room with floor to ceiling glass panels provided a 180-degree view of the Mississippi.

"But winters in this part of the world can be brutal. Before the century was up, the pair returned to the milder climate of Arizona. Their dream vacation home was sold to a realtor, who put it up for rent. We moved in just seven months after our wedding, and could not believe our good fortune in finding such a wonderful little place.

"That first summer, I was walking with Sally in the backyard when a van pulled up into the driveway. An overweight man in his late sixties hauled his six-foot-plus frame out from the driver's side, while a cheerful little blond lady of approximately the same age emerged from the passenger's door. The big man did not look entirely pleased to see me, and pointedly asked what I was doing here.

"After I explained that I was a renter, he forced a gruff smile, while introducing himself and his wife as owners in the previous decade. His wife was obviously a genuinely nice lady and smiled to see that the perennials that she had planted so many years before were still in bloom.

"I had encountered her husband's type before. He inducted me into a private tour of the house he rebuilt, grandly boasting of this improvement or that addition, emphasizing the labor and expense that everything had demanded of him. I dutifully expressed appreciation at polite intervals. There was less sentimentality than ego in his presentation. He was obviously proud of having fixed up the old place, but I also sensed something akin to regret in his voice and choice of words. Perhaps Arizona wasn't all it was cracked up to be. When he learned the amount of money we were paying (an impertinent question, in any case), he expressed dismay, and promised to inform our land-lord that we were being charged far too little each month for the privilege of staying at 'his' house. I was glad when this oversized trouble-maker climbed back into his van and disappeared in the direction of the American Southwest before carrying out his threat. I hoped never to see him again.

"My hope came true. Two years thereafter I learned from someone in town who had known him during the brief period of his residence here that he had died recently in Arizona. In any case, I had by that time pretty well put him out of my thoughts.

"About the same time, however, a number of peculiar incidents at home began to convince Laura and me that we were being visited by a discar-nate entity. Nothing ever before suggested we were being haunted. But now we caught fleeting glimpses of a fast-moving shadow from time to time when we least expected to see such a thing. We did not mention these encounters to each other at first, dismissing them in our own minds as some kind of trivial optical illusion.

"It was only after the smells began that we spoke openly of the shadow. At first rarely, then more frequently, Laura and I might be at other ends of the house when we would be overtaken by a very pleasant scent. To me, it smelled like delicate perfume. Laura thought it was closer to a man's cologne.

"Sometimes we encountered the scent together, but in every instance it came and drifted away after only a few minutes. 'If we have to be haunted,' Laura said, 'it might as well be by a pleasant ghost.' Although the perfume or whatever was invariably associated with a feeling of [another] presence, neither of us were ever afraid.

"After about a month of such unpredictable visits, however, the quality of these redolent visitations began to deteriorate. I was working at my computer in the 'river room,' three rooms away from Laura, who was sitting up in bed, reading, when an unspeakably foul odor surrounded me. The stench was comparable to the most nauseating animal excrement one might encounter. It startled me, but I could not imagine its source. Then, almost as quickly as it manifested itself, the poisonous vapor was gone.

"Laura had been unaware of any foul stink in our home, but over the next few days and weeks, she, too, was sometimes overtaken by the repulsive smell of fecal matter, which seemed to come and go on a nonexistent breeze. Interestingly, the stench never pervaded the whole house, or even an entire room, but always confined itself to our immediate personal vicinity.

"Once, when Laura was outside tending the flowers growing under our front windows, she was suddenly enveloped in an invisible puff of strong cigar smoke. This incident confirmed our suspicions that we were being haunted by the recently deceased former owner, who had been a confirmed cigar smoker. Apparently, he was still annoyed that we were living in the house to which he had been so attached in life, and he wanted to stink us out.

"To fumigate our house of this unwanted bore, we tried several suggested de-haunting methods—all very nicey-nice appeals to his higher self to 'see the light,' while expressing understanding for his sense of loss, and so forth. Among other things, we tried smudging all the corners with burning sage and lighting candles for the departed. The evil smells continued unabated. In fact, things began to escalate.

"One night, while trying to fall asleep, I sensed a large, dark presence in the bedroom. It glided over to me and seemed to hover just over my head, and I was the recipient of a telepathic command: 'I want to know your thoughts!'

"At this point in our ghostly relationship, I was more annoyed than frightened, and I told our redolent houseguest, 'You can do whatever you want. I'm going to sleep.' With that, the disappointed shadow-man vanished. But only temporarily.

"Both Laura and I experienced horrific nightmares, real psycho-dramas that seemed to have nothing to do with our identity, as though they had been intruded somehow into our vulnerable subconscious minds. Still, we continued our feel-good New Age remedies, all without effect. Instead, we began to hear the sounds of terrific crashes, as though something huge had fallen over somewhere in the house, causing terrible damage. Once I thought the water heater exploded. Every time on investigation, however, nothing was found amiss.

"After the better part of a year, our patience had run out. One evening, while sitting down to dinner, the stench abruptly covered us like a putrescent cloud. We sprang to our feet, and as if with once voice we shouted in the direction of the stink: 'Get out of here! You're not welcome here! You don't live here—or anywhere—anymore! This is our house! We're here now, and you can't stay! No dead people allowed! Out, out, out! We don't care where you go, but you're not staying here! No freeloaders allowed! Get it straight: You're dead! You're dead! You're dead! Get out and never come back!'

"Since then, ours is the sweetest smelling little home you could ever know."

A Most Peculiar Barking Ghost

The Personal Experience of Patrick: "In 1990, shortly after Debbie, her three-year-old daughter, and I moved into this apartment, strange things began to happen. There seemed to be something else in the place with us. All these years later, I'm still asking myself what it was.

"Within the first week of moving in, I was awakened around 5:00 A.M. by what sounded for all the world like a small child, barking like a dog. I sat up in bed. Debbie woke a few seconds later and listened to the sounds with me. It came from the hallway, so we assumed that her then-three-year-old daughter had gotten up in the wee hours and was pretending to be a puppy—not all that unusual for a three-year-old.

"I got up to put her back to bed, but as I opened the bedroom door, the sound moved down the hallway and into the living room. I followed, and it kept moving and barking at a distance of what I'd estimate was about six feet in front of me. As I got to the living room, the barking moved on into the next room, the kitchen.

"I stood in the living room and rationalized for a moment. The lights from outside the building were spilling into the room, and it slowly occurred to me that if the baby had been playing, I would surely have seen her cross the room between the hall and the kitchen. I listened to the 'puppy' bark in the next room, and a chill went down my spine. I now had no idea what I was dealing with. The barking faded within the next moment, and I backed down the hall, ducking into the little girl's room and, of course, finding her sound asleep. I roused her and asked her if she'd been pretending to be a puppy? 'Nooo … ' came the expected, groggy response.

"I carried her back to our room and put her between us in the bed. I stayed awake until it was time to get up for work, making certain the 'puppy' didn't return. Of course, not certain what I'd do if it did. We never heard it again.

"A few months later, I was up in the middle of the night, using the bathroom. I was in total darkness. No windows in the room, no light, just darkness. Suddenly, from the area to my left, which would have been the bathtub, I heard very clearly—sharp and loud enough to make me jump—a voice shout, 'Belly Ache!'

"The voice was that of a child, but there was something rough, almost gruff, about it, as if the child in question was trying to 'do' a voice. Of course, I flipped on the light. Nothing. Not that I was totally surprised.

"Less dramatic incidents became frequent enough so that Deb and I began to half-joke about the apartment being haunted. Deb said that she had often seen the figure of a child moving up and down the hall past our bedroom door during the night. I remember her describing a little boy, enveloped in a soft, blue glow. She also admitted this could have been a series of waking dreams.

"The last incident that I'll relate happened shortly before we moved out. Again, it was late at night. Our kitchen faucet leaked and dripped fairly noisily on occasion. I lay in bed, listening to the drip. It had developed a steady rhythm, as drips will. Suddenly, the rhythm changed. The drip sound itself changed in pitch, and the thing literally played a tune. Now, I could write this off as my having fallen asleep and dreamed this, but at that point, after a few bars, Debbie groaned in disbelief next to me and asked, 'Was that *Funeral March of the Marionettes* [the theme music of the Alfred Hitchcock television series]?' 'Yeah,' I answered, nodding in the dark, 'that's what I heard.' We both sighed deeply and held each other close the rest of the night.

"While none of these incidents may fall under the classification of 'terrifying,' they were certainly disturbing. I was glad that we moved when we did. Whatever was in that apartment seemed to have a consciousness. It seemed aware of us."

LIVELY GHOSTS IN A WISCONSIN HOME

Brad Steiger's Investigation of a Haunted House: In 1970 I was among a number of researchers who accompanied the well-known psychic/sensitive and spirit medium Irene Hughes of Chicago to a very large home in Wisconsin that was afflicted by a wide range of haunting phenomena. From early reports, it seemed as though everything from dolls to dishes might become instantly transformed into ghostly guided missiles that would often pelt the occupants of the home but never seriously injure anyone.

When we arrived at the home on a Saturday in October, we were at once impressed by the size of the sprawling abode. According to some sketchy information that we had been given, the mansion had once belonged to an old lumber baron who had a rather dark reputation.

We had only been on the premises for a few minutes, and had just begun to interview the lady of the house when I excused myself to use the restroom. Interestingly enough, on the way to the restroom I ran into an obvious cold spot—a center of ghostly energy that is always many degrees cooler than the temperature in the rest of the house—but its significance soon diminished in comparison with a subsequent development.

While I was in the restroom, I could clearly hear the sound of what I believed to be the youngest girl of the family playing with her doll. She was singing a tuneless little song, the kind of melodic chant that appears to be universal with children—especially, it seems, with little girls—at play. From time to time, she would interrupt the humming of her sing-song to speak lovingly to her doll, and then she would call rather loudly for her mother. Then, when there was no response from her mother, she would return to her playing and singing.

As a father of two girls, who at that time were five and two, I fashioned a mental image of a little girl dressing her doll, combing its hair, creating her own world of imagination. I could clearly determine that the sound was coming from upstairs, almost directly above me.

When I rejoined the group, I excused myself for interrupting the conversation in progress, announced with some excitement that I had found a cold spot, then, with additional apologies for setting forth what may have been an already asked question, I inquired of the woman just how many children there were in the house at that time.

She replied that she had three children: a son in his late teens, who was often too frightened to come home and sometimes stayed with a friend; a teenage daughter in high school, who lived at home; and a six-year-old girl, the only child whom she had had by her second, and present, husband.

When I asked to meet any children who might be home on that Saturday afternoon, the woman said that she had sent her two daughters over to a friend's home. "I thought that you would rather work without the interruption or the presence of children," she said. Irene Hughes told her she had done the right thing, that our investigation would quite likely proceed much smoother without the presence of the children.

By now I was really puzzled. If our hostess had thoughtfully sent her children to a friend's home, who was the little girl playing upstairs? The woman blanched slightly and shifted uneasily in her chair after I had asked my question. "My little girl is at a friend's house," she said firmly.

"Then you'd better go upstairs and have a chat with her," I said. "She has apparently returned home. I clearly heard her in a room upstairs."

"Up-upstairs?" the woman echoed. Her hand clasped the arm of a friend whom she had asked to be present for support. "You heard a little girl upstairs?" I was by now becoming quite aware that the members of this family had a great deal of difficulty with their upstairs and that the woman sincerely believed her daughter to be at a friend's home. But my ears had heard too clearly the sounds of a little girl's sing-song voice. I could not be so easily convinced that I had heard anything out of the ordinary. Surely nothing supernatural. "A little girl I assume to be your daughter is upstairs," I said. "I heard her playing and singing."

"My little girl could … could not be upstairs," the woman answered softly. It was obvious that she was struggling to maintain control of her fear, trying not to permit her dread of the unknown to warp the sound of her voice. "She is afraid to go upstairs alone. She would never go upstairs. Upstairs is where … "

She seemed unable to complete her sentence and her trembling hands brought a coffee cup to her lips. "Upstairs is where most of the weird things happen in this house," her friend said, taking up the thread of the statement. "About the little girl. Did you hear it calling for its mother?"

I acknowledged that I had. From time to time, she would pause in her play and call for mother. The woman continued to explain. "They often wake up in the middle of the night or in the morning and hear that little girl calling for its mother. But whenever they check the kids, they find them all sound asleep."

Although the story was eerie and told convincingly, I still required a personal exploration of the upstairs, the attic, the basement, and the yard to persuade me that there was no actual, physical, real live little girl somewhere in that home. Once I had thoroughly searched the house, I conceded as gracefully as I could that our hostess was indeed telling the truth when she had told us that her little daughter was nowhere on the premises. If I truly heard what I believe that I heard in that Wisconsin home, then I either heard the sound of some lost and confused spirit-child, eternally singing and occasionally calling for its mother, or I heard some ethereal kind of phonograph record, eternally reproducing the sounds of a little girl who had once lived in that house.

However one might theorize about a haunting, the obvious truth of the matter was that the manifestations in that home constituted a persistent living nightmare for its occupants. The woman appeared almost to be suffering psychic battle fatigue from her constant confrontation with the paranormal incidents in her home, and she would not walk in any area of the house other than the kitchen and the living room without someone at her side.

We explored the basement, wherein she had so often heard heavy footsteps, thuddings, and scrapings. We visited each of the upstairs rooms and discovered two additional "cold spots." We ventured up to the attic where the family had so often heard the sound of heavy objects being dragged across the dusty floor. As we opened the door, we caught sight of a wispy something retreating to a darkened corner of the cluttered storage area. However, none of our investigating party could swear with certainty that what we had seen was a ghost or an ectoplasmic spirit, and not simply a floating bit of cobweb reflecting the sunlight.

Irene Hughes offered many psychic impressions as we walked from room to room. The woman of the house gave immediate feedback to the medium's comments, and in nearly all cases, she credited her with correct "hits."

As we walked through the house, we were treated to an occasional object that suddenly became airborne without any apparent physical cause for its levitation. These were small objects, mostly children's toys, such as an alphabet block, a plastic dish, and a little doll that had been made from a stocking. However, this particular haunting turned out to be even more complex than we had anticipated; there seemed to be factors working within the mother's own psyche that may have been psychically feeding the phenomena.

The teenaged daughter would often find her room in disarray when she returned home from school, and she noted that this bit of mischief would occur most often after a morning when she had taken careful pains to straighten up her room before leaving home. On the other hand, if she were to leave her room in a mess, she would find that some invisible helping hands had set the bedroom in order for her, right down to the last curler and comb in its proper place.

The phenomena seemed to be centered in the second floor and the attic, and the family reported that they often heard the sounds of something heavy being dragged across the floor. Although the house was quite large, the entire family circle, which was composed of father, mother, and three children, aged 19 to six, slept in two rooms downstairs. No one slept upstairs.

On occasion, the mother told us, the teenaged daughter would adamantly announce that she was not going to be driven from her room, and would often sleep alone upstairs for as long as two to three weeks. Then the sound of mumbled half words about her ears and the stroking of invisible fingers against her cheeks and hair would drive her back downstairs to join the rest of the family in the relative quiet of the two back bedrooms on the first floor.

The other center of the haunting appeared to be located in the basement. The phenomena in the eerie area under the house consisted primarily of knockings, thumpings, and the sound of footsteps running down the stairs and shuffling across the floor.

Certainly the most dramatic manifestation of the haunting was the materialization of four skeletons in one of the upstairs bedrooms. After appearing in startling blood red color, the skeletal figures would slowly manifest themselves into what appeared to be solid, three-dimensional representations of a man, two women, and a little girl. Each of the images appeared in period dress of what appeared to be fashions in vogue around the time of the 1890s.

Once the entities had fully materialized, a bizarre ethereal drama would unfold before any witness who might be present to observe the phenomenon. As the ghost of a lovely, long-haired blonde girl sat playing idly with her dolls, the man in the spectral reenactment strangled one of the women while the other stood by with a pleased expression of immense satisfaction. Over the years, various prior inhabitants of the house and other individuals who had witnessed the grim spirit portrayal had assumed that the haunting might very well have been set into motion by a tragic playing out of the eternal triangle. The ghastly reenactment seemed to be telling those shocked persons who had witnessed the grisly performance that at some time in the past the man of the house had strangled his wife to please his mistress.

Some cursory historical research and an examination of local folklore revealed a scandal regarding a lady of the house who had disappeared without a trace and a husband who had remarried after an extremely brief period of grieving. Local legend had it that the wife had been murdered by her husband and her body dumped in the nearby Mississippi River so that he might marry his mistress.

Although we were denied the dramatic reenactment during our visit to the home, the present occupants claimed to have witnessed the horrid pageant play in what had been their master bedroom immediately after they had moved into the mansion. Since that awful night, they had relocated their sleeping quarters downstairs, never to return again to the upstairs.

There was no immediate exorcism of spirit or entity that afternoon and evening of our first visit to the home, but after we conducted an in-depth counseling session with Mrs. Hughes and made a number of return visits to the place, the psychic storm that had swirled throughout the household was finally diminished. However, we did learn that the family eventually decided to leave the place to the very lively ghosts and move out. The last time I checked on the mansion in 1976, it remained unoccupied.

THE AMITYVILLE HORROR™, REVISITED

My friend and colleague Paul Barthlomew has been researching mysteries and anomalies for many years. He has investigated everything from ghosts to sightings of UFOs. Paul is also the coauthor of Monsters of the Northwoods, *which chronicles Bigfoot sightings, mainly in the New York and Vermont area.*

An Update on the House in Amityville, by Paul Bartholomew: "On December 27, 2002, George Lutz appeared on Art Bell's *Coast-to-Coast AM* talk radio show and revealed the real story behind what has come to be known as 'The Amityville Horror.' According to Lutz, 28 days after moving in, he, his wife Kathy, and their family fled their Amityville, Long Island, New York, Dutch Colonial home, leaving behind their belongings. It was the reported culmination of a supernatural siege that has since become entangled in Hollywood legends and lawsuits.

"The horror began on November 13, 1974, when Ronald Defeo slaughtered six members of his family. All of the bodies were found face down in their beds at 112 Ocean Avenue. On December 18, 1975, George and Kathy purchased the house—market value in 1974 of about $125,000—for a very reasonable $80,000.

"Father Ralph Pecorara was brought in to offer a house blessing. Lutz described him as an 'extraordinary man who spoke nine languages and held an Oxford law degree. He went from room to room and said prayers in each room, using holy water.... He was a bit uncomfortable in the upstairs back bedroom ... it was like he wanted to leave.'

"On an episode appropriately entitled *In Search Of ... The Amityville Horror* on Alan Landsburg's old *In Search Of ...* television program, the production crew arranged a silhouetted sequence with the priest, who spoke candidly in a rare interview: 'I was blessing the sewing room. It was cold in there.... It was a lovely day out and it was winter, yes, but it didn't account for that kind coldness. I was also sprinkling holy water and heard a rather deep voice behind me saying 'Get out.' It seemed so directed toward me that I was really quite startled. At one point, I felt a slap on the face. I felt somebody slap me and there was nobody there.'

"The priest claimed that blisters appeared on his hands after the blessing. He commented that he went to the doctor, but the physician couldn't explain the wounds. 'He thought it might be caused by anxiety and that's feasible, but I don't think I'm given over to psychosomatic responses. This blessing seemed to trigger or uncover the demonic nature of the home.'

"George Lutz recalled that during the last week they were living in the house they endured nightly occurrences of noises and foul odors. Kathy was

This photograph was taken inside a haunted house. In the top right corner of the image, a bright spirit can be seen reaching up toward the chandelier.

touched from behind by some unseen person. 'The lights would flicker, but they would not go out,' he said. He would often wake up to a strange musical sound, 'like musicians tuning up downstairs.'

"While many regard the Amityville case as a hoax, others argue over the real case versus the Hollywood version. In June 1979 American International Pictures conducted lie-detector tests on George and Kathy Lutz. They both passed.

"Also, back in 1977, Charles R. McQuiston, an acknowledged expert of the psychological stress evaluator, subjected a tape recorded interview with Kathleen Lutz to the machine and concluded she was being truthful. 'I'm convinced this woman is telling the truth—or what she believes to be the truth,' said McQuiston. 'There are no deceptive traces in her voice when she talks about turning into an old hag. She really lived those horrible things and she believes in what she is recounting.' [Kathleen Lutz, "The Amityville Horror: Our 28 Days of Horror in House Terrorized by Evil Spirits," *National Enquirer*, Dec. 13, 1977).

"Hollywood over-dramatized the case in many ways (*The Amityville Horror*, 1979). Among a number of embellishments, the walls really didn't ooze strange substances. The truth, according to Lutz, was that it was the keyholes from the old-style doors that emitted some strange substance. 'We had drips that got longer and longer,' he said. '[The mysterious drippings] were black ... almost like epoxy, and the longer we were in the house, the longer the drips came out of certain keyholes on the second and third floors.'

"Large numbers of flies did form against the sewing room window. 'Flies were always there ... they didn't go away,' said Lutz. The dog was scared to enter that room.

"The phenomena seemed to escalate until the night before they left. It was then that a fever pitch of paranormal events drove the Lutzses away. 'That night Kathy had levitated and moved away from me on the bed,' Lutz said. 'Kathy was asleep as she lifted off the bed and went towards the wall away from me. This is after she had turned into an old crone, a really ugly old woman, that literally took hours and hours for it to go away. Later she [transformed] again after we moved out of the house and moved in with her mom.'

"Many researchers investigated the home. Ed and Lorraine Warren, the well-known ghost researchers and demonologists, brought psychic-sensitive Mary Pascarella to the Amityville house. Recalling her visit to the Lutz home, Mary said that the couple 'were impeccably clean and the house was absolutely gorgeous.' Continuing with her recollection, the sensitive commented that what the Lutz family lost, 'they'll never be able to replace.... The reality is that there had to be something that drove them away.'

Paranormal investigators Ed and Lorraine Warren.

"Mary Pascarella said that when she was upstairs in the house, she had felt ill and tired and wanted to lie down and rest for a minute. She began to say her prayers, and as she was saying the 'Our Father,' she looked out of the bedroom door and there was 'a group of figures standing outside of the door saying the 'Our Father' backwards.... I took the holy water and threw it outside to the figures. I took the cross, and I raised the cross, and I said 'God is with me' and I threw it [at the figures] and like water on a fire, I heard this hissing sound.'

"Mary was deeply affected by her experience. While many critics have attacked the case, largely due to the discrepancies and dramatic license taken in the movie, she went on record on the September 15, 1979, Brian Dow radio show (WTIC, Hartford, Connecticut) to defend the case: 'You are dealing with something that is invisible and can't be seen ... and you are dealing in this case with something that is very malevolent.... I've never really dealt with anything on that level.'

"When appearing on the Art Bell show, Mary Pascarella added, 'There was a force or an energy in that house.... The house is deceptive. It will take an innocent person [and take hold of them].... The energy in that house remains. It may take a hundred years ... but it will implode again. That house is purely evil.'

"On a December 3, 1997, interview with Art Bell, Father Malachi Martin, who served as an advisor to two popes and was a best-selling author and expert on exorcism, said of the house in Amityville: 'I've been to it. The Amity horror was really a horror, it really was. It was real; it was generally gruesome and real, and it was very unpleasant.' When asked if the force was still in the home, Fr. Martin responded, 'I'd be inclined to think that it is there because it was never properly cleansed.'

"Roxanne Salch Kaplan and her husband, the late Stephen Kaplan, challenged the validity of the case and published a debunking work, *The Amityville Horror Conspiracy*. They noted changes in details from the hardcover version of the [events] to the paperback version. Kaplan took issue with Ed and Lorraine Warren in high-spirited debates on various talk shows and media outlets. The Warrens maintained that the case was an authentic manifestation of diabolical infestation. Their investigation produced paranormal photographs, including a still of a boy with glowing eyes near the staircase.

"Through lawyer battles and all out debates, the case has roared on for nearly 30 years, and it has taken its toll on the participants. The Lutzses are divorced, and George lives in Las Vegas. Kathleen Lutz is currently in poor health and often needs oxygen to aid her breathing. Jay Anson, who authored the best-selling book, *The Amityville Horror,* had a history of heart problems and died of a heart attack a couple of years after the book was published.

"George Lutz still speaks fondly of Kathy. 'Each of us were affected in a different way, and Kathy was damaged in a different way than I was,' said Lutz. 'I think that for her, in so many ways, it was much harder for her to recover over the years and be able to give it some distance.'

"Both Kathy and George feel sympathy for Ronald Defeo, who is serving a 25-year-to-life sentence at Greenhaven Correctional Facility in Dutchess County, New York. 'There has never been any doubt after living [in that house] that a sane person doesn't do this to his family. There's no doubt in our mind that he [Defeo] was influenced by that house and that he was controlled at least for a point. [The awareness of that] was so horrible that he couldn't live with it or realize it himself. Without extreme long-term psychiatric care, there's no hope of redemption of any kind in his life.'

"The famous house was bought by Barbara and Jim Cromartys in 1977, who lived in it for years without incident. In 1997 they sold it to a buyer for $310,000, about half its market value (Shelby Loosch, "Real-Life Houses of Horror," *National Globe*, Nov. 23, 1999).

"The Cromartys were adamant that there was nothing unusual about the home and that the only horror was that created by scores of annoying curiosity-seekers. 'The entire Thanksgiving (1977) weekend we were never alone. Thanksgiving Day we had 30 people here for dinner, and we had at least 300 people outside. I'm not exaggerating. Not all at once, but there would be a crowd of 40,' said Barbara Cromarty. 'Halloween, we hired a private security service. We had hundreds of people out there.' (Dennis Hevesi, "Haunted by a Horror Story," *Newsday's Magazine for Long Island*, Sept. 17, 1978).

"The Amityville Horror case has reached legendary status in the annals of paranormal history. It has infuriated, frightened, frustrated, and antagonized nearly everyone involved. And the controversy rages on."

INVESTIGATING GHOSTS AND HAUNTING PHENOMENA

Dale Kaczmarek, president of the Ghost Research Society in Oak Lawn, Illinois (<http://www.ghostresearch.org>), has been actively investigating haunting and paranormal phenomena since 1975. He has conducted on-site investigations of ghost lights, haunted houses, cemeteries, Native American burial grounds, murder sites, churches, and sacred sites. He appears regularly on numerous radio and television programs, and information about his research has been featured in more than 25 books. Kaczmarek is the editor of Ghost Trackers Newsletter *and the author of* Windy City Ghosts, Windy City Ghosts 2, A Field Guide to Spirit Photography, Glossary of Occult Terms, The Greater Chicagoland and Northwest Indiana Psychic Directory, *and many other books.*

Through the research, study, and investigation that he has completed, as well as through the continuing analysis of those investigations, Kaczmarek hopes to prove the existence of ghosts and life after death. "Whether I am investigating ghosts, hauntings, poltergeists, or any other form of the paranormal or supernatural, I always will follow the same guidelines and procedures to lead me to the end result or conclusion of an investigation," Kaczmarek said.

Listed below are the steps that Kaczmarek follows in investigating ghosts and haunting phenomena:

1) "When a case or person is called to my attention, the first step is to interview that person over the telephone and try to get all the relevant information concerning the case that can be obtained. We use a regular form that is filled out, and no questions are asked of the individual that might lead them to stretch the story out of proportion. Only general questions are asked at the conclusion of the telephone conversation or those questions that are meant to clarify certain information already given.

2) "Once that information is compiled, I personally sit down with professional psychics or clairvoyants with whom I frequently work to go over the information and telephone interview bit by bit to try to make some sort of determination of what might be going on prior to our arrival on the scene. This is how we are able to screen our cases, and such a procedure also gives the psychic that I have chosen the opportunity of asking questions of his/her own that I later pose to the client. We are careful not to form any concluding opinions at this point, but we do make additional notes of areas within the case that we will keep an eye on.

3) "The next step is to call the client and tell him/her what we feel may be going on and to set up a time when we might visit the house. I then tell the client to keep a diary of any strange or unusual events that may happen before our arrival date. It is important for the following data to be included in that diary: Date, time, which room, type of event, who was present or witness to the phenomena, the duration of the event, and a description of the event in the greatest detail. One of the things that we would be looking for in the above-mentioned diary are patterns that might begin to form. Over the years, we have discovered that most hauntings do have some kind of pattern or string of events.

4) "Prior to arriving at the location, I would pack the necessary equipment that I feel would be instrumental in solving the mystery of the event. This might include, but not be limited to, 35MM SLR cameras on tripods with cable releases that would be loaded with two different kinds of film. One would

have black and white infrared film pushed to 400 ASA, and the other would have a black and white high-speed print film to be used as a control film. Simultaneous pictures would be attempted and later compared for possible anomalies. Other equipment would include: portable voice-activated tape recorders, video cameras, cathode-ray magnetometers, spectrographs, microwave detection devices, negative ion detectors, infrared viewing devices, gauss meters, Geiger counters, as well as Instamatic SX-70 cameras.

5) "Upon our arrival at the location, we would first check with the diary our client has been keeping for further entries into the casebook. Then we would begin a slow walk around the location with the psychic or clairvoyant and with various forms of electronic equipment to see exactly what [could] be picked up. Pictures are taken randomly or at places the psychic designates as advantageous. Photographs are taken with both cameras, and the tape recorder is constantly going, recording the psychic's impressions and/or feelings.

6) "If any spirit or entity is contacted through the psychic, either telepathically or clairvoyantly, communication is attempted in an effort to determine why the spirit remains earthbound. The spirit is then convinced to move on through its own accord or with the help of the psychic. Since most spirits do not realize that they have passed over, that's usually all that is required to get the spirit to leave. We do not employ the use of Ouija boards, automatic writing, séances, or exorcisms since we feel that these are almost always unnecessary and are extremely dangerous if not done properly.

7) "After the film is returned from the laboratory, it is compared side by side with the infrared film. Many times strange images are seen, including strange shadows, anomalous lights, energy balls or streaks—and even faces, forms, and figures. If it is a natural image, then it should show up on both films. If, however, the image only appears on the infrared film, we can assume that it is supernatural event and invisible to the naked eye. Infrared film is sensitive to a narrow band between 700 to 1200 nanometers (one nanometer = one billionth of a meter).

8) "Besides the scientific and psychic investigations, additional research is done on the house and area in which it is built to determine the past history in general and such specifics as what originally was on the location, the former owners, and

any previous unusual or traumatic events or deaths. In this way an overall view can be put together, and a profile can be drawn up and documented. We do not normally charge for the investigation, however certain travel charges and cost of film and development are usually requested to help defray costs and to keep this valuable service going.

9) "Additional follow-up calls and/or visits are made if necessary to assure maximum efficiency and eventual resolution of the problem. While most events can be alleviated within a weekend, some hauntings have been known to go on for years. We absolutely guarantee the anonymity and confidentiality of all of our clients. The only people allowed to release such information are the client themselves."

2
Encounters with Glowing Entities and Ghost Lights

If such peculiar manifestations as orbs and ghost lights should be as intelligent as their actions often indicate, just what are they and what is their purpose? We have folklore that is at least 2,000 years old that equates these mysterious globes of light with spirits of the dead and with those beings we label nature spirits—the Devas, the elves, and the fairies.

The manipulation of glowing balls of light as a means of transportation may even be employed by angelic beings and spirit guides. Indeed, these benevolent beings may take form as globes of light before fully materializing in our dimension. In prior works, I have even conjectured that these orbs are themselves an intelligence that can manifest a physical appearance that is most compatible with the level of understanding of each individual witness.

And these glowing ghosts may be able to manifest even in space. Shortly after his epic solo orbit of Earth, Lieutenant Colonel John Glenn commented in *Life* magazine (March 9, 1962) that the strangest sight that he experienced during his initial flight into space came when he was crossing the Pacific toward the United States. He was checking the instrument panel, and when he looked back out the window he thought for a minute that he must have tumbled upside-down and was looking up at a new field of stars. He checked his instruments to be certain that he was right-side-up, then he looked again. "There, spread out as far as I could see, were literally thousands of tiny luminous objects that glowed in the black sky like fireflies," Glenn said. "I was riding slowly through them, and the sensation was like walking backwards through a pasture where someone had waved a wand and made all the fireflies stop right where they were and glow steadily. They were greenish yellow in color, and they appeared to be about six to 10 feet apart.... They were all around me, and those nearest the capsule would occasionally move across the window as if I had slightly interrupted their flow. On the next pass I turned the capsule around so that I was looking right into the flow, and though I could see far fewer of them in the light of the rising sun, they were still there. Watching them come toward me, I felt certain they were not caused by anything emanating from

[41]

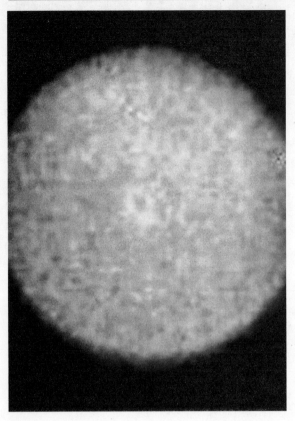

Close-up photograph of an orb seen by Gregory Avery.

the capsule…. As far as I know, the true identity of these particles is still a mystery."

The question remains: Are we dealing with separate phenomena in the differing fields of religious, scientific, and psychic thought? Or are we dealing with the same phenomena dressed in the specific nomenclature of these various disciplines? Will we ever be able to strip aside our preconditioned ways of looking at things to discover what these phenomena truly represent?

ARE ORBS INTERDIMENSIONAL VEHICLES FOR THE SOUL?

In his e-book *Colors of the Soul and Colors of the Web*, author George Michael states that when people come into contact with true orbs, they are viewing interdimensional vehicles, known to the Egyptians as "sun boats" and referred to in the Old Testament as "Merkabah." In schools of Jewish mysticism, including Kaballah, the Merkabah (Merkavah) is the Divine Throne Chariot described in the prophet Ezekial's mystical experience and is associated with the heavenly realms. In George Michael's view, the orb or Merkabah is how the soul gets around in the earthly dimension after its physical, material life has ended.

Real orbs, Michael says, can be sensed or heard. The sound they make is a super-high tone, chiefly heard inside the head, beyond normal hearing. Many individuals who have encountered true orbs have experienced the orb speaking telepathically to them.

According to Michael, orbs can assume many appearances, including globes, globules, balls of light, and hovering round balls, and they range in degrees of illumination from bright and glowing to faded and barely visible. There is great diversity among the erratic, fast-moving objects, Michael states, because there are many different types of orb phenomena. Some may even be separate life forms or nature spirits. The human spirit or ghost type, he says, is usually seen at about eye-level to about ceiling height and is often filmed in graveyards and haunted locations. The human spirit type may appear larger than some of the other types of orbs.

Another type of orb is used in conjunction with electromagnetic vehicles that shield the interdimensional beings inside, as well as serving as a means of propulsion. Although on occasion these orbs are seen at eye-level, they are primarily seen in the sky because of their higher dimensional level of existence.

Michael also believes that there is a type of orb that may be considered a spiritual aspect of extraterrestrial intelligence, much like the human spirit orbs are an aspect of us. Such orbs often have a more detailed and complex appearance, which may at times contain figures or faces. Although such orbs are rarely photographed, photos do exist.

PHOTOGRAPHING THE MYSTERIOUS ORBS

The Research and Photography of Gregory Avery

Glowing balls of light with various hues of color have come to be called "orbs," and they are seldom viewed by either photographers or subjects until they appear on the developed film. Orbs have appeared mysteriously on the photographs taken inside peoples' homes during festive occasions, such as birthday and engagement parties; in churches during solemn gatherings, such as funerals and memorial services; and at cemeteries, haunted houses, and sacred places. While some ghost researchers are quick to claim that these orbs are evidence of spirit entities, skeptics are just as quick to dismiss them as particles of dust, droplets of water, or natural electrical emissions rising from the ground.

Gregory Avery has taken photographs professionally since 1969, and since 1998 he has captured thousands of orb images. Avery says that while images of orbs may be taken by any camera, from the cheapest disposable flash camera to the highest-end megapixel digital camera, most of the images that he has captured were made with digital cameras. Digital technology allows images to be studied more closely and accurately by means of a computer.

"Flash seems to be required to image the orbs whether film or digital techniques are used," he said. "I know of one exception to this and that is a high-end multiple CCD (charged coupled device) digital video camera that recorded an orb flying through a researcher's backyard in daylight, and no flash, strobe, or additional lighting was applied."

In order to exclude the orb images as dust, moisture, raindrops, and so forth, Gregory recommends that the ghost researcher take several flash pictures back to back. If the orbs should be the result of such natural elements as those listed above, the first photo may reveal many apparently unexplained objects floating in the air, but there will be fewer in the second, and quite likely none in the third.

Orbs are very often seen in graveyards. While orbs are notoriously difficult to photograph, this picture by Gregory Avery is one of the clearest photographs taken of an orb in a graveyard.

"True orbs, for whatever reason, dart away during the flash," Gregory said. "The flash either over charges them, reveals them, or affects them in other ways that remain unclear, but they will move in different directions at high speeds, considering the speed of a flash."

Gregory states that the lens on his camera is always cleaned between images to guard against any elements of rain, fog, or other materials affecting the photograph in any way. He has conducted numerous tests to determine whether or not an orb is a genuine anomaly as opposed to a photographic, atmospheric, or optical artifact effect.

"Dust was thrown in the air," he explained. "Water was sprayed into the air. We acquired an artificial fog machine and photographed the plume. My fiancee Christine even blew bubbles into the air. All of these tests, and more, were conducted in order to produce those characteristics found in the true orbs' appearance, color, and geometry. We have been unable to duplicate the orb appearance or capture the astounding geometrical precision that genuine orbs have demonstrated."

SOME INTERESTING THOUGHTS ON ORBS

From Neville Mitchell, Australian Paranormal Researcher

"Firstly, you might remember me from a picture I sent you via my sister Valerie on the subject of Orbs. I would like to inform you that this phenomenon it seems is still occurring around us, and particularly around Valerie. Wherever Val goes, these orbs seem to follow.

"Valerie recently spent a weekend with us so we could explore the orb issue and subjects along this line. Val is a psychic, and she suddenly experienced a tingling sensation down her right arm. She immediately interpreted this as a sign that someone of a higher spiritual level has entered the conversation. We were then told that 'he' was standing between the two doors of my bedroom at that particular moment. I had my digital camera handy and immediately took a photo of that part of the room. Sure enough, right where he said he was, we could clearly see an orb between the doors. Its position proved to us that it could not be a reflection and was right where he said he would be.

"Other orbs joined the party, and I was able to get numerous pictures of them as they positioned themselves in front of nonreflective surfaces or solid objects such as the ceiling beams, lights and doors. We even have a green one. I later placed the camera on a tripod and took a series of pictures in an attempt to catch them moving without moving the camera. Four pictures in a row showed images in one, then the next picture was free of them, then they reappeared in the next but in different positions as if they were trying to demonstrate that they were truly intelligent life forms and could come and go at will. We were actually communicating with them, and they with us. Fascinating stuff.

"The next morning I woke early, and the previous night's orb encounters were still heavy on my mind. I wanted to come up with a better name to

Photograph taken by Neville Mitchell of the doorway in his bedroom where his sister Val told him an entity was standing.

describe these orbs as they were clearly more than just simple orbs to me—they were true life forms. With the aid of my trusty *Oxford Dictionary*, I eventually settled for 'Spherical Energy Life Forms' or SELF.

"Then it hit me. Isn't life a journey towards discovery of self? Is this the message I was to discover? Valerie emerged from her bedroom and told me to try and imagine two warring armies as just orbs with all their physical, three-dimensional baggage stripped away. I suddenly realized that when you attack another you are just attacking your-SELF. Life on planet Earth seemed to me to be one long process of learning how to shed unnecessary baggage on your pathway towards your higher SELF. The final baggage you shed is your actual physical form allowing you to pass on to the higher realms in your true form, your-self. Does this sound too bizarre? A further check of my dictionary revealed the word 'Sylph,' an elemental spirit of air. Maybe we already know the answers, but need a little help from our 'friends' to see what's right in front of us."

THE AUTHOR'S EXPERIENCE WITH A GHOST LIGHT ON A COUNTRY ROAD

Just before sunset one evening in the summer of 1953, I was finishing chores on our farm in Iowa when I heard screams coming from the country road at the end of our lane. There was still enough light for me to see three teenaged girls peddling their bikes as fast as they could manage on the loose gravel. Before I could get to my car and drive down to investigate whatever it might have been that had so frightened them, they were nearly out of sight.

Although we had a long lane, our rural community was small enough for me to be pretty certain who the girls were, so the next time I went to town, I located one of them and asked her what had caused them to scream as if their very lives were in danger. According to one of the girls, the three friends had decided to go on a twilight bike ride in the country. Just as they passed our lane, a large ball of glowing greenish white light rose up out of the ditch and began to bob about near them, as if checking out each one of them individually. They screamed and turned their bicycles around and headed back toward town, but the ball followed them for about a quarter of a mile before it turned around and left them.

I listened with polite interest to the spooky story. I was 17, a high school graduate for two months, so I could indulge the wild imaginations of three 15-year-olds. I was quite certain that the three girls had been frightened by a cluster of lightning bugs that had risen up out of the ditch.

However, a couple of nights later as I was driving home in my 1948 maroon Ford coupe, I was startled to see a greenish white glowing orb of light bobbing ahead of me, squarely in the middle of the road. The orb appeared to be about the size of a volleyball.

I didn't have time to slam on the brakes to avoid hitting the thing, and I had no idea if it would explode if I struck it, or smash in the front end of my car. To my everlasting surprise, the strange illuminated orb passed through the windshield of my Ford, remained a few moments directly in front of the steering wheel, right at my chest-level, then moved around me to pass through the rear window.

Although it had appeared to be a solid ball of some luminous substance, it had passed through the windshield and back window of the car without causing the slightest bit of damage. And whether it just thought it was fun to scare the bejabbers out of me, or if it was on some mysterious mission, the ball of light waited for me near the same clump of trees on the next two evenings. On those occasions, it merely raced beside the driver's side of the Ford, accompanied me to our lane, then sped on its way off into the distance.

Although I did not see the mysterious glowing orb again near our farm lane, I did have a similar encounter with such an object in 1985 while driving late at night in the desert country of Arizona. On this occasion, the ghost light shot in front of my car, then angled at great speed off the road and disappeared among the sage and cactus. Interestingly, in 2001, I learned via an e-mail from the wife of one of my high school buddy's sons that the greenish ball of light still manifested from time to time along the country roads of my home town.

BRAD STEIGER INVESTIGATES THE
GLOWING GHOST OF A MIDWESTERN MANSION

In July 1970 medium Irene Hughes and I brought a group of researchers to a university city in the Midwest, where we encountered a glowing spirit entity that so impressed itself on the psyches of certain members of our investigative group that for years afterward they reported awakening from nightmares, fearful that the ghost was forming again right in their bedrooms. Because the mansion that was home to the ghost has since been torn down and a new house built on the estate, I have changed the name of the previous owners and omitted the identity of the city in which the mansion was located.

My friend and associate Glenn had received a lead on this particular house from some police officers. Before the house had been vacated, two elderly sisters had lived there alone. According to a number of police officers, who had themselves witnessed the appearance of the ghost, nearly every night a glowing *something* would manifest in a lane that ran alongside the house. Then the manifestation would walk up to the house, enter it, and interact with the sisters.

On several occasions, the police had received calls from frightened neighbors who had seen the *thing*. These people thought the police should do something about the spook light, but the officers who responded to the call really didn't know how to handle what they assumed to be some kind of ghost. They would just sit in their squad cars outside the house and watch the two elderly women talking with the glowing light. After one of the sisters passed on and the other was taken to a nursing home, the ghost light continued to appear at the mansion.

On the first night we arrived in the city, our host suggested that we drive out to take a look at the ghostly site. It was midnight by then. Glenn was driving my station wagon, and he edged it cautiously into the lane of the estate. The headlights picked up the image of a wooden gate bearing a sign containing a strict warning that trespassers should keep out or risk being prosecuted. Glenn said that he had arranged for the caretaker to meet us at the estate the next day. He had also requested a police officer to accompany us just to be certain a passing squad car didn't pick us up as vandals.

Irene complained that it appeared as though we had entered a jungle. There was a heavy overgrowth of weeds and bushes. Thick, drooping branches of untrimmed trees virtually blanketed the narrow lane. Glenn said that from our present position we wouldn't be able to see more than the edge of what had once been one of the city's loveliest estates.

"What's that?"

I don't remember who first saw it, but no one had to point out that the dark and quiet scene was suddenly interrupted by a glowing intruder. There appeared to be a very large orb of light moving in front of us down the lane.

The moon was covered by clouds that night. Glenn turned off the headlights, and the strange orb glowed brightly in the total darkness. The nearest streetlight was completely cut off from the old estate by the thick wall of trees.

As we watched, the orb of light moved toward the old house. Everyone turned to look at Irene, who was seated in the middle of the backseat. In the dim glow of the dashboard lights, I noticed a rather strange expression on her face, and it had occurred to me that she had been extremely quiet during our excitement over sighting the ghostly figure.

"Shall we go right now and investigate the whatever it is?" someone wondered.

"No," Irene answered firmly, breaking her silence. "Not tonight. I have a very bad feeling that it would not be good for us to walk down that lane right now."

There was a certain tone to her voice that indicated that she meant exactly what she said. Her psychic impression told her that the time was not right to invade the darkened lane and approach the shimmering orb that seemed to be moving toward the deserted house.

"Let's leave … *now!*" Irene said suddenly. No one argued with her.

On the second night we approached the eerie mansion, it was nearly midnight once again. Earlier that day, in the company of the caretaker, we had walked around the house and allowed Irene to pick up psychic impressions about its past inhabitants. At first the caretaker had been very skeptical of what Irene was attempting to do. He had been quite reluctant to take time for such foolishness, and it had required a good

Medium Irene Hughes.

measure of Glenn's persuasive abilities to convince the caretaker that he should bother with us at all.

It was most interesting to watch the caretaker's obvious change of attitude as his exchange with Irene brought him deeper and deeper into a mysterious territory whose boundaries he had never before dreamed of transgressing. He knew that there was no way Irene could have gained such detailed and personal information about the house and its inhabitants, but somehow she seemed to have intimate knowledge of the family that had owned the mansion All Glenn knew about the house was that some police officers had seen strange lights moving around inside. Neither Glenn nor myself had researched the house in any manner whatsoever, and it is doubtful that even the most exhaustive search of public records would have turned up the personal minutiae that Irene had siphoned from the psychic atmosphere of the old house.

When I asked the caretaker afterward how he would assess Irene's percentage of accuracy, he grinned, and his answer came quickly and easily. "I'd have to give her a 90 percent," he admitted, "and it would probably be higher if there was some way to check out every name she gave. Just about everything she said fit in. I don't know how, but she really knew."

When we visited the estate on that second night, we had the caretaker and a policeman with us in the station wagon. We opened the gate and drove cautiously down the lane. When we were adjacent to the old house, Glenn stopped the car.

"Let us just sit quietly for a few moments, and permit me to gain some psychic impressions of the house by night," Irene requested. As our medium sat in meditation, I glanced absently out the windshield. Then I blinked my eyes rapidly. There was a glowing, mistlike substance forming directly in front of the station wagon's hood. The ghost was beginning take shape right before my eyes.

"What is *that?*" asked the police officer sitting beside me in the front seat.

This man was not the same open-minded police officer who had accompanied us that afternoon, nor had he been one of the officers who had previously witnessed the glowing entity in the lane. This fellow had joined us earlier that evening and had been openly skeptical, even mocking, toward our efforts of investigating haunting phenomena at the mansion.

Because he had declared himself a professional disbeliever in such things as ghosts, I could not resist having a bit of fun with him.

"What is what?" I asked blandly. "I don't see anything."

"There," he said in a harsh whisper. "Right there in front of the car! What in hell is that?"

I started to deny seeing anything one more time, but decided against further teasing the officer when I saw that he was nervously brushing the strap that held his service revolver in its holster. It was clear to me that this man was now dealing with something that his police manual had not prepared him for, and that he was having an extremely difficult time fitting the sight of the materializing entity into the worldview that he had only moments before held so sacrosanct.

At that moment, Glenn whispered over our shoulders in response to our overheard conversation. "I've been watching it for a couple of minutes now," Glenn said. "At first it was just a wispy tendril that seemed to come from that clump of bushes over there. Then it stopped directly in front of the car and began to take form."

By now everyone in our group observed the glowing, mistlike thing. We all sat in silence for a few moments watching as the orb grew larger and denser and began to assume a humanlike form. We decided to get out of the car for a closer inspection.

It was a very warm evening, but as I extended my hand into the midst of the glowing mist, I felt its very cold interior. Such a bold act may have been considered very rude by the entity, as the glowing image suddenly vanished. Before we could speculate on the ghost's rapid disappearance, Irene whispered loudly from the other side of the station wagon: "There are some people coming through the bushes by the house!"

I did not hear the sounds of footsteps and crackling brush myself, but others in the group swore that they could hear the approach of two or more people coming toward us. Then the footsteps stopped, and a member of our group directed everyone's attention to the appearance of glowing images between two trees. But before any of us could approach them, the lights went out as rapidly as extinguished candle flames.

"I swear the ghosts looked real to me, more than spirit," Irene said. Perhaps Irene's greater sensitivity enabled her to see images where we could only see the glowing mist and orbs. Irene suddenly put her hands to her ears and said that she heard the terrible sound of a woman screaming. "There! There in the bushes," she directed us. "Can you see her head?"

Glenn and I told her that we could see a glowing orb, but we were apparently not sensitive enough to tune into the vibrations on the estate and see distinctive features on the entities. "Well, there are plenty of vibrations around here to tune in to," Irene remarked. "This place is just drenched with psychic vibrations."

Other than Irene, none of us were able to observe the lights transform into clear images of men and women, and none of our group dared confront any of the glowing lights. It appeared as though the sound portion of the ethereal broadcast had been received well enough, as most of the members of our midnight expedition insisted that they had heard the sounds of footsteps and brush being parted, but other than on Irene's super-sensitive receiving set, the video portion of the program had been blurred. Every member of our party, including the police officer and the caretaker, had seen the ghostly glowing orbs, but only Irene Hughes had been able to adjust the fine-tune mechanism within her psyche clearly enough to pick up distinct images of the forms that had been preternaturally recorded on the grounds of the old estate.

There are a couple of eerie postscripts to this case. The first occurred approximately one calendar year after our visit to this home, when Glenn and I were conducting some follow-up research on the old mansion. We pulled into the lane about midnight in the company of three investigators, only one of whom had visited the place on a prior occasion. We took careful notice of a group of wires that stretched across the lane. Someone, undoubtedly the caretaker, had strung a number of white and red strips of cloth from the line. We switched off the headlights, got out of the vehicle, and prepared to await the ghost—which had been seen by Glenn and a university professor just a few nights before.

We did not have to wait long before a column of light about the height of an average human being appeared to the right of the automobile and made its traditional trek down the lane toward the old mansion. We viewed the glowing orb until it disappeared inside the house, then, satisfied that the phenomenon continued unabated, we turned to walk back to the car. As we were approaching the automobile, we were startled to see that a three-tine pitchfork had been shoved into the ground just a few feet in front of the vehicle.

We all knew that the pitchfork had not been there before we had switched off the headlights and began to walk down the lane. The pitchfork had been driven into the ground just in back of the white and red stripes of cloth on the wire that stretched across the driveway entrance. Since everyone had commented upon this colorful addition to the environment, we would certainly have noticed such an obtrusive element as a pitchfork added to the mix. If that shimmering column of light had truly planted that pitchfork before us, I had to admit that I was becoming concerned that we may have worn out our welcome at the haunted estate.

Three years later, on Halloween, Glenn learned that the old mansion was about to be torn down and replaced by a new home. We drove out to the estate for a farewell viewing, and on that particular occasion, even though it was Halloween, we saw nothing out of the ordinary. We decided that the glowing entity must have learned of the imminent destruction of the mansion and had at last moved on to a higher spiritual plateau.

Later that evening, we were invited to stop by a Halloween party in which a number of police officers were in attendance. Egged on by one of the officers who had experienced the haunting at the mansion on many different occasions, Glenn and I began to regale the partygoers with some spooky Halloween stories about our encounters with the glowing ghost.

The next day, before I left the city to return home, Glenn and one of the police officers stopped by the motel where I was staying to share the perfect capper to the haunting at the mansion. It seems that a couple of the police officers who had attended the Halloween party the night before had been highly skeptical of our accounts of the glowing ghost. Since they had to go on duty after the party, they decided to take the squad car out to the estate to see for themselves.

Amid howls of laughter, Glenn told me that the two officers had sat drinking coffee in the squad car, commenting derisively about our abilities as ghost researchers. Then, to their utter astonishment, the glowing entity materialized directly in front of their squad car. Begrudgingly admitting their terror, the two men confessed to their fellow officer that they had burned rubber getting out of the lane. From cynics to believers in ghosts in a matter of seconds.

OLD BRIT BAILEY'S LIGHT

Brit Bailey's dying request was that he be buried standing up. He proclaimed that he had spent his whole life stomping over the Texas prairies, and he didn't aim to stop when he died. They buried old Brit in 1833, but residents in the area of Bailey's Prairie, five miles west of Angleton, Texas, in Brazoria County, claim that the early settler has kept his vow to keep stomping around on the prairies.

The Thomas family moved into old Bailey's place shortly after he had been planted erect in the sod, and were the first to bear witness to the old-timer's ghost; it did not wait long to start prowling around. In her diary, Ann Rainey Thomas made a record of her sighting of old Brit's ghostly face looking through the window at her one night. Her servant girl, Melinda, reported that the ghost chased the hired hands away from the cows during evening milkings. All members of the household swore to have heard old Brit's shuffling footsteps moving around in the house after dark. Once when Mr. Thomas lay ill, he claimed that he clearly saw Brit Bailey in the room with him.

But it was not until the early 1850s that Bailey's glowing, ghostly image began to be seen away from his house, out on the open prairies. Colonel Mordello Munson and several of his guests saw a glowing ball of light drift inexplicably past his home at a very slow pace early one evening. Saddling their horses, the colonel and his male guests gave the strange globe of glowing light a hardy pursuit but were unable to capture it or clearly identify it. From that night on, "Brit Bailey's Light" has drifted across the Texas prairies that the old settler was so reluctant to relinquish.

THE GHOST LIGHT OF CHINATI MOUNTAIN

Since the days of the earliest pioneers and settlers, people in the area of Chinati Peak, located in the Chinati Range of southwestern Texas, have seen a glowing orb, about the size of a basketball, suspended in mid-air. The light that emanates from the unexplained object ranges in apparent intensity, from a mere twinkle to a blinding glare. The peculiar orb has been known to materialize, move about, split into twin spheres, and re-form in front of confused and astounded witnesses. According to area residents, the best spot for observing the ghost light is along Highway 90, between the towns of Marfa and Alpine.

Local legend attributes the source of the spook light to the spirit of the Apache chief Alsate, who was tricked into offending a tribal manitou after he had been betrayed by some Mexican soliders. According to legend, Alsate's eternal punishment is to wander the Big Bend region of Texas; it is the chief's glowing spirit that people see when they witness a manifestation of the spook light of Chinati Peak.

Some observers of the ghost light have attributed the source of the eerie illumination to the reflection of the moonlight on deposits of mica that are in the cliffs and crags of the mountain. However, this theory does not explain how the brightly glowing orb is visible on nights when the moon is hidden behind thick banks of cloud.

Some residents maintain that the ghostly light is seen under only two conditions: either just before or immediately following rain. Others argue that they have seen the light dozens of times when the land has been bone dry.

Rationalists explain the manifestation by stating that the mystery light has been caused by the reflection of automobile headlights coming down Paisano Pass; this hypothesis seems disproved by the light's ability to maintain a steady glow for several hours, without having to depend on the headlights of the occasional motor vehicle passing by. And then there is the troublesome fact that the earliest settlers and travelers in southwestern Texas mentioned seeing the ghost light. Covered wagons and stagecoaches were not known for having powerful headlights.

Whether the enigmatic light of Chinati Peak is caused by certain unique climatic conditions working on mineral deposits limited to that area, or whether observers really are seeing the glowing spirit of Chief Alsate, one indisputable fact remains: the spook light is there.

The Mystery Lights of Brown Mountain

Nestled far from the nearest city of Hickory, North Carolina, the Brown Mountain region has been the dwelling place of mysterious glowing lights for more than 200 years. From sunset until sunrise, globes of various colors, ranging in size from mere points to 25 feet in diameter, can often be seen rising above the tall trees and flickering on and off as they fall below the mountain pass.

Although the Brown Mountain lights were first documented in 1771 by Gerard Will de Brahm, a German engineer, they did not receive national attention until an account of the phenomena appeared in the works of the writer Charles Hoy Fort (1874–1932), who described how the lights chased early settlers along the various trails that lead to the sparsely placed cities.

Many legends have sprung up attempting to explain the origin of the lights; one states that they are caused by the spirits of Cherokee and Catawba braves who search the valley for the maiden lovers they left behind when they were slain in a big battle hundreds of years ago. Some area residents believe the battle still rages between spirits of the two tribes, for they claim that they have seen the lights fighting, butting into each other, and bouncing around, resembling extra-large basketballs in the process.

In 1913 the U.S. Geological Survey tried to explain the lights by attributing them to reflections caused by the headlights on locomotives or cars that run through the nearby Catawba valley. However, during the spring of 1916, when a flood prevented the use of all local bridges and the roads became too muddy for cars to travel, the Brown Mountain lights were seen in greater numbers than ever before. Besides, residents argued, the lights have haunted the region for hundreds of years, long before automobiles were invented.

Since the early 1900s, people have attempted to formulate scientific explanations for the Brown Mountain lights. Among the theories favored by those who would characterize the lights as naturally occurring phenomena are St. Elmo's fire (electrical discharges that sometimes occur during thunderstorms), fox-fire (phosphorescent illumination issuing from decaying matter), or simply moonlight shining on ground fog. While many individuals have tried to dismiss the idea that the lights are supernatural in nature, thousands of people have witnessed, photographed, and experienced bizarre encounters with the mystery orbs. In more recent years, certain researchers have attributed the eerie lights to entities from UFOs or Native American ghosts.

According to many who have seen the Brown Mountain lights, they are most often visible on partly cloudy nights when the moon is low. The prime viewing time is between 9:30 and 10:00 P.M. Although the sightings occur during all seasons, some who have empirically studied the lights state that the best time to see them is on a crisp autumn night after a rain.

Bob Downing, writing in the *Beacon Journal* (September 15, 2002), suggested the following viewing spots for those who wish to search out the Brown Mountain lights for themselves: "The Lost Cove Cliffs Overlook on the Blue Ridge Parkway … The Thunder Hill Overlook at Mile Post 290 … Wisemans View south of Linville Falls … an overlook on Jonas Ridge off state Route 181."

THE GHOST LIGHTS OF SILVER CLIFF

In the little town of Silver Cliff, found in the Wet Mountain Valley of Colorado, ghost lights have been seen in the local cemetery for more than a century. The lights can never be approached in order to gain a closer look. As soon as anyone comes too near, the lights disappear, only to pop up again in another section of the cemetery.

Local folklore has it that the lights were first seen by a group of miners passing by the cemetery in 1880. When the miners saw the flickering blue lights over the gravestones, they left the vicinity in a hurry. Since then, the lights have been observed by generations of residents of Custer County. The cemetery was the final resting place for many miners who lost their lives digging for precious ores in local caverns. According to legend, the flickering lights of the graveyard are the ever-glowing searchlights found atop the miners' caps; the lights guide the spirits of the long-passed miners, still searching for the silver they never found.

In 1880 Silver Cliff boasted a population of 5,087; by the early twenty-first century it had only a few hundred inhabitants and had almost become a ghost town. The story of the ghost lights of Silver Cliff first reached public attention in the spring of 1956, when an article on the mystery appeared in the *Wet Mountain Tribune*.

When some observers of the spook lights noted that the bluish colored illuminations could not be seen as clearly on the sandstone markers, many spectators became convinced that the lights were only a reflection of houselights in the valley. However, on August 20, 1967, the New York Times carried a story on the phenomena. In the article, county judge August Menzel gives the account of the night inhabitants of both Silver Cliff and nearby Westcliff turned off all of their lights, including street lights, "but the graveyard lights still danced."

Other rationalists have believed the Silver Cliff ghost lights to be caused by the reflections of stars. Yet the lights are just as clear on starless, moonless nights. Some have tried to prove that the lights are caused by phosphorescent ore, or glowing wood, but the darker the night, the brighter the lights. It has also been suggested that radioactive ores cause the flickering lights. Geiger counters have been employed to cover the entire area, but no radioactivity has been discovered.

THE SPOOKSVILLE GHOST LIGHT

One of the most famous ghost lights appears in the tristate area of Missouri, Arkansas, and Oklahoma. The ghostly light that has been seen in the area, sometimes referred to as the Spooksville Triangle, is even advertised as a tourist attraction.

The Spooksville ghost light resembles a bright lantern. Often the light dims before spectators, then bounces back over the mountains in a brilliant blaze of light. Hundreds of first-hand encounters with the mysterious ghost light are on record. These accounts demonstrate that actual experiences with the unknown are sometimes frightening and always interesting.

During World War II the U.S. Army Corps of Engineers scoured the entire area attempting to discover the cause of the light, using the latest scientific equipment. For weeks they tested caves, mineral deposits, and highway routes, exhausting every possible rational explanation for the origin of the mystery lights. They finally left, confounded.

Local resident Louise G. reported coming home in a school bus from a school carnival in Quapaw, Oklahoma, when a ghost light perched on the rear window of the bus, as if it were attempting to gain entrance. Everyone in the bus was thoroughly frightened, and several of the women were screaming. In *Ghost Lights*, a pamphlet written by Bob Loftin, Louise said that the light was so bright that it temporarily blinded the bus driver and he had to stop the bus. Just as the driver stopped, the light went away.

Chester M., a farmer near Quapaw, stated that when the weather would get intolerably hot, he liked to do his plowing in the evening. Chester recounted the

An orb or spook light seen between Joplin and Seneca, Missouri.

night that the ghost light "felt real neighborly" and hovered over the field where he was plowing. Chester was not bothered by the presence of the light until it suddenly darted at him. He said that he "absolutely froze stiff" on the tractor until the light sailed out of sight.

An Encounter with a Benevolent Ghost Light

In the June 1968 issue of *Fate* magazine, Arlene O. Meyers told the story of the encounter her mother, Laura Jeanette, had with a benevolent ghost light in the Willamette Valley of Oregon in the early 1900s.

Several times a year Laura and her husband loaded up the wagon, hitched up the horses, and made the two-and-a-half-mile trip into town, where they traded farm products for household goods. On this particular occasion their usual autumn trip had been delayed owing to the illness of Laura's husband, and it was already winter when they made the decision to go to town.

When they had finished their trading, they stopped off for supper with some relatives. During the course of the meal, Laura's husband became violently ill. The relatives insisted that he stay for the night, and Laura agreed that it would be best for her husband to remain unmoved until the cause of his illness could be established. But she could not think of remaining with him, as they had left their five children home alone, and they had no means of contacting the children to make them aware of their father's illness. Telling everyone she would send her two oldest boys the following morning to get their father, Laura began the trip home by herself.

When she got out onto the road, she discovered it was pitch-black. She began to fear she would not be able to see at all, and her thoughts strayed to the reports of a wild cougar that had been molesting cattle in the area. To forestall her fears, she began to pray.

A safe and peaceful feeling began to spread over her, and suddenly a light appeared in front of the horses, illuminating the road ahead. Laura breathed a sigh of relief. She had no need to fear the darkness around her, as her path was clearly lit. While she was unable to ascertain the source of the light, she felt it to be benevolent, and the light preceded her all the way home, illuminating every step of her way. When she arrived at the farm, she awakened one of her sons to help unhitch the horses.

The following morning the son came downstairs, and after hearing his mother's account of the light that helped her find her way home, he expected to find the stranger who had held the light. But there was no stranger present. Laura never wavered in her belief that it was an angel sent by God who had held the light.

A JACK-O'-LANTERN FOLLOWED HER HOME

The following encounter with a mysterious globe of light occurred in 1916, when Beverly K. was teaching at a rural school near Wellsburg, Iowa, and boarding with a farm family.

The Personal Experience of Beverly K.

"I was going with a young man in Wellsburg and very much in love," Beverly said, "but he had been acting differently toward me lately, and I was worried. It was in late May, near the end of the school year, and on this particular night I was restless and couldn't sleep. So even though the hour was very late, around eleven, I got up, dressed, crept silently down the stairs, walked out the door, and went for a stroll."

Orbs, fairy lights, spook lights, or will-o'-the-wisps have been seen for centuries. This illustration, from the 1845 edition of Thomas Milner's *Gallery of Nature*, depicts a will-o'-the-wisp.

Beverly recalled that it was a beautiful night, and a full moon was riding high in the sky. "It had been an unusually warm spring," she said, "and it was almost like summer. I felt quite exhilarated and not at all afraid. All the farmers in the neighborhood were fast asleep, so there was little chance of meeting anyone on the little-traveled dirt road."

Beverly was enjoying the solitude of her walk so much that she didn't notice how far she had gone. "It must have been two or three miles. As I realized that I must start back, the sky became overcast, covering the full moon and making the night darker and darker. My mood changed to an eerie sort of fear, and I kept walking faster and faster. Soon it was so dark that my fear almost became panic, for I could hardly see the road anymore."

At last she reached the crossroads near the farmhouse where she was staying. Suddenly she turned her head and looked over her shoulder. "There, just a few yards behind me, floating about three feet above the ground, was an orange-red ball or disc, following me at the same pace as I was walking. It glowed dully, but shed no light around it or on the ground. Almost as soon as I had seen it, it veered off to the side of the road, rose a bit, then sailed over the barbed-wire fence and disappeared in some shrubbery on the other side. It was with great relief that I got into the house and went back to bed."

Beverly didn't tell her landlady about the strange encounter for a day or two, because she did not want her to know about her midnight walk. "But finally my curiosity got the better of me and I did tell her about what I had seen," Beverly said. "My landlady merely nodded and said, 'We call them jack-o'-lanterns.' From her response it was obvious that lots of other folks had seen them, but I sensed that she didn't care to talk more about the subject so I dropped it.

"I'd heard of such things as the will-o'-the-wisp, but I always picture that as a rather formless white light, and this had been an orange-red globe. There were no swamps or marshes around, so it *couldn't* have been swamp gas. This strange ball of reddish light behaved as if it were intelligent, for it had been following me in a straight line. But as soon as it was discovered, it swerved aside and went into the bushes, as if in hiding. And hadn't there been something unnatural about the sudden darkness? This experience remains among my unsolved mysteries."

3
Poltergeists:
Unwelcome House Guests

Perhaps the most common conception of ghosts is that they are shadowy or invisible beings that throw dinner plates and pieces of furniture around rooms, occasionally materializing as fearsome entities, and sometimes levitating people for good measure. As we shall see throughout this book, there is actually a very wide range of phenomena that are popularly and collectively called ghosts. The ghosts that throw things and are generally responsible for rather dramatic household disturbances are known as "poltergeists," German for "noisy ghost."

Many contemporary researchers argue that such invisible housebreakers are really not messy and rude ghosts, but berserk bundles of uncontrolled psychokinetic energy, the direct action of mind on and over matter. Such investigators also attribute the violent disturbances that can manifest in a home or around certain individuals to the sexual changes and adjustments that accompany puberty, the early stages of a marital union, or feelings of inadequacy and frustration accentuated by some traumatic experience.

While there may be many instances in which the outbreak of poltergeist phenomena might be associated with the dramatic changes that adolescence brings to a child's psyche, many of the classic cases of noisy ghosts throwing objects and severely disrupting the normal flow of things occurred where no adolescent was present. If the extrasensory ability of psychokinesis, mind over matter, can somehow cause an individual to become an unaware participant in haunting phenomena, then we may have to expand our theory of the poltergeist to include those instances in which the human mind, under stress, fatigue, sleep deprivation, and so forth, may release uncontrolled spontaneous energy that has the power to activate and interact with dormant spirit forces.

[61]

THE THROWING GHOST OF SLAWENSIK CASTLE

On October 28, 1806, after Napoleon and the French army mauled Prussian armies at the battle of Jena, Prince Friedrich Hohenlohe-Ingelfingen (1746–1818) was declared a prisoner of war and taken to France. He was held captive, his future unclear, as Napoleon decided whether to use him as a political pawn, ransom him, or set him free. One of the most trusted members of Friedrich's council, August Hahn, had also been taken prisoner, but having won parole from the French, prepared to return to his homeland. The prince asked Hahn to oversee his castle at Slawensik, in Upper Silesia (today one of the most industrialized regions of Poland), until Napoleon saw fit to release him.

Although he was eager to return to his own home, Hahn's admiration for the prince demanded that he accept the responsibility. Hahn would have the company of his personal servant, Johannes, two of the prince's coachmen, and Frau Knittel, the caretaker who lived on the grounds with her son. However, in addition to the company of servants, Hahn wanted to insure the presence of intellectual fellowship as well. He entreated his boyhood friend Karl Kern, who had also been at the battle of Jena, to join him at the castle until they might return home. Kern consented to become a member of the group that would oversee their prince's empty home; the entourage arrived at Slawensik castle on November 19, 1806.

It was about nine o'clock on the third evening after their arrival when Hahn and Kern were pelted by a shower of limestone and other debris as they sat reading in the corner room they occupied on the first floor. In those times, lime was commonly used as an ingredient in plaster, mortar, and cement, so, believing the old castle ceiling was crumbling, Kern jumped to his feet, cursing the medieval structure for beginning to collapse around them. Hahn glanced warily toward the ceiling. There were no cracks in the ceiling. How could lime and debris fall on them from the ceiling if there was no hole from which they might drop?

The two friends stood up on chairs so that they might better inspect the ceiling. They were unable to detect one single sign of damage, but as they searched the area above them, lime once again began to rain down. Kern picked up a number of pieces from the fresh fall and commented that they felt very cold to the touch, as if they had come from an outside wall. Hahn continued to study the ceiling for some kind of opening through which the lime might have dropped. In the morning, he said, they would have to put the servants to work at repairs before the winter got any worse.

When the men awakened that next morning, they were greatly disturbed to find the room carpeted by the mysterious lime. Kern groused that the ceiling could have fallen in on them while they slept, but Hahn was quick to point out that there seemed to be no gaping cracks in the walls or ceiling that would have caused so much lime to fall.

On the fourth night of their stay in the castle, the bits of lime did more than fall from an apparently invisible crack. Large fragments began to fly about the room and pelt the two men. As they retreated to their bedrooms, hoping for safety, the sound of loud knockings began to reverberate down the ancient halls of the castle. Kern was convinced that Hahn was trying to frighten him and was somehow responsible for the occurrences. But while both of Hahn's hands were in full view of his nervous and angry companion, a loud series of knocks shook the room. Since the loud raps on the wall made sleep virtually impossible, Hahn began to record the unexplained phenomena in his journal. An attorney, Hahn was not a man who could be easily deceived or taken in by the work of a prankster.

When the manifestations began on the fifth night, Hahn and Kern were ready to investigate the rooms overhead. While Hahn remained below, Kern and the son of the castle's caretaker went to search the apartments above their rooms. All the rooms were empty. Later that night, Kern and Hahn were awakened by the sounds of what sounded like slippered feet moving across their room. They lit a candle and confirmed that they were the only individuals in the room. Before the end of the evening, the invisible slippers were joined by what sounded like a walking stick bouncing on one end.

By the next evening, the inhabitants of the castle had conducted an exhaustive search of all the possible "natural causes" for the disturbances. As the activity began to intensify, it became very apparent that there was a supernatural cause for the commotion. Candlesticks flew from one corner of a room to another. When the household sat down to dinner, knives, forks, plates, and foodstuffs became animated and airborne. Anything movable seemed to be possessed and have the ability to levitate about the room.

After three weeks of enduring sleepless nights, Hahn and Kern ordered the servants to move their things into the corner room overhead, where the sounds had initially seemed to originate. Hahn had not slept long when he was awakened by the sound of his friend whimpering. Hahn rolled out of bed and saw Kern staring into a mirror as though he were transfixed. He was extremely pale and trembling as if suffering from a high fever. After taking several moments to compose himself, Kern managed at last to say that while looking in the mirror, he had seen, clearly reflected, a feminine figure all swathed in white. At first he thought it was his imagination, but he could see his own reflection behind the ghostly woman.

When the phantasm's eyes had met his own, Kern perceived the face to be that of an old woman. Her features appeared quite tranquil and not at all disagreeable, but he could not help being filled with some sort of nameless

In 1887 the Fowler family suffered from poltergeist activity in their home, depicted here for the 1945 edition of Harry Price's *Poltergeist over England.*

dread. Hahn stepped to the mirror and demanded that the shape show itself to him. He stared into the mirror for 15 minutes before he finally abandoned his attempts to summon the ghost of the old woman. The following dawn, as soon as they heard the servants stirring, Hahn said that they might just as well have their things brought back down to the first floor.

After Hahn and Kern had spent a month at Slawensik castle, their weird tales of unearthly happenings began to spread abroad. Two Bavarian officers, Captain Cornet and Lieutenant Nagerle, both hard-nosed skeptics, decided to visit the castle and see what all the ghost business was about. Nagerle, the most vocal in his skepticism, offered to spend a night in the haunted corner room where Kern had seen the ghostly figure of the old woman

The men had not left the Bavarian officer alone for more than a few minutes when they heard the lieutenant cursing loudly. The usual noises of the disturbance were punctuated by the sounds of the officer's saber hacking away at table and chairs. When they opened the door to the room, they were

Real Ghosts, Restless Spirits, and Haunted Places

shocked to see Nagerle chopping at the air with his saber. It was difficult to believe that the officer, who moments before displayed such cynicism and bravery, had been reduced to a frightened man who ran about an empty room, slashing at an invisible enemy.

At the sight of his companions entering the bedroom, Nagerle seemed to shake off his fear and replace it with anger. As soon as the others had left him alone, he explained, the accursed thing had begun to pelt him with invisible objects. He had looked everywhere but could see nothing. His anger had gotten the best of him, and he had drawn his saber. Once again in control of his faculties, the lieutenant began to suggest that he might somehow have been tricked by Hahn and Kern. The two friends sat down with the officers and earnestly sought to convince them that they were not guilty of any connivance. Cornet also assured his fellow officer that he had not allowed Hahn and Kern out of his sight.

Then, while the four men sat talking around a table, candlesticks rose in midair and fell to the floor. A lead ball struck Hahn on the chest but did not harm him. The sound of footsteps began to pad about the room, and a drinking glass jumped off a stand and shattered against the floor. Although the Bavarian officers protested that such things were impossible, neither of them accused Hahn or Kern of being responsible for the manifestations.

The phenomena at Slawensik castle continued to increase in strength and ingenuity. Once, after Hahn had carefully prepared some water for shaving and had heated it to just the temperature that he desired, the warm water was sucked out of the basin and disappeared before he was able to moisten his razor.

Herr Doerfel, a local bookseller, had his hat hidden from him as he was preparing to leave the castle. After the household had looked for several minutes in vain, Doerfel's hat was seen floating teasingly in front of its owner. As the frustrated and frightened bookseller reached for his headpiece, it jerked out of his grasp. With Doerfel running in pursuit, the hat led its owner on a merry chase before it finally dropped at his feet.

Hahn, who was exhausted from months of sleep deprivation, firmly announced to the ghost one night that he did not want to have a single object thrown at him while he attempted to rest on his bed. It seemed for a little while as though the entity was going to cooperate with him. Hahn had just drifted off into a deep sleep when he was rudely awakened by a large quantity of water being dumped in his face.

Perhaps the strangest phenomena occurred while Hahn was absent, having left the castle to journey to the nearby city of Breslau. The months of disturbances had left Kern too nervous to endure a night alone in his bedroom, and so he persuaded Johannes, Hahn's personal servant, to spend the night with him. They had not been settled long before they saw a jug of beer rise slowly from a table and begin to pour its beverage into a tumbler. Then, before their unbelieving eyes, the glass was lifted and began to empty, just as if someone were drinking from it. As the glass was put back on the table, the men went to the spot where the invisible being had just drunk the entire tumbler of beer. There was not a drop of beer to be found on the floor. The men were terrified that the invisible thing could actually swallow liquid.

Nights later, as Hahn returned to the castle, he began to hear the sound of a dog following closely behind him. Thinking it was his greyhound, Flora, the attorney turned and called the dog by name. There was nothing to be seen. Hahn continued walking, still hearing what he believed to be a dog walking closely behind him. Even when he ascended the stairs leading to the front door of the castle, he could still hear the dog panting at his heels. Kern met him at the door, holding it open for a prolonged period of time after Hahn had passed through into the castle. Hahn promptly asked if he had seen a dog walking behind him up the stairs; Kern answered that of course he had. He had seen Flora behind him, and that had been the reason that he had taken hold of the door, to hold it open after Hahn had already passed into the castle.. He was afraid that Hahn seemed not to see her, and he was concerned that he might shut the door on her.

Hahn explained to Kern about the mysterious footfalls of the invisible dog that had been following him in the dark, and the two friends immediately began a search for the greyhound. If one of them had heard a dog, and the other had seen one, surely Flora must now be scampering about in the woods. They found Flora locked up in the stables. The coachmen assured them that the dog had not been set free at anytime during the day.

After this strange incident, the manifestations at Slawensik came to a halt. Hahn remained at the old castle for another six months until Prince Hohenlohe was released from imprisonment in France. Hahn concluded his journal on November 19, 1808—two years to the day that they had first arrived at Slawensik castle—with the words, "I have described these events exactly as I heard and saw them; from beginning to end I observed them with the most entire self-possession … yet the whole thing remains to me perfectly inexplicable."

Hahn did not seek to publish his bizarre journal until 20 years had passed. At that time, he submitted the manuscript to Dr. Andreas Justinus Kerner, the lyric poet, physician, chemist, and pioneer psychical researcher. When Kerner published the journal, it created an immediate sensation in Germany.

In 1830 Slawensik was destroyed by a fire caused by the direct strike of a lightning bolt. In the ruins, workmen discovered the skeleton of a man who had been walled up in a secret enclosure. His skull had been split and a sword lay by his side. To many, this discovery was a possible explanation for all of the disturbances that had plagued the castle.

THE STONE-THROWING DEVIL OF NEW HAMPSHIRE

In 1662 George Walton, an ambitious New Hampshire farmer who lusted over the acquisition of more land, eyed the few acres that bordered his farm with greed. The bit of land Walton craved was owned by an elderly widow who lived in a small cabin on the acreage. Walton knew that she had neither money nor influential friends, so he arranged to have her charged with witchcraft. Then, either through legal chicanery or bribing local officials, the greedy farmer obtained her land, which had been confiscated by the authorities after her arrest as a witch.

"You'll never quietly enjoy that ground," the widow cursed him.

Walton merely laughed at the old woman's malediction, but he did have the decency to drop his charges of witchcraft against the poor, now homeless, widow.

On a Sunday night shortly after Walton had moved his family into the widow's house, there came a fierce bombardment of stones against the roof and doors. Fearing an attack by warriors from a nearby Native American tribe, Walton shouted an alarm and reached for his musket. The occupants of the house cautiously looked out into moonlit fields and saw nothing. No one. Then, as they blinked their unbelieving eyes, the front gate was wrenched from its hinges by an invisible force and tossed high into the air.

Walton ventured out to investigate, his musket clenched firmly in his hands. A volley of stones was suddenly hurled at him, and he fled back into the cabin. As he slammed and barred the front door behind him, his family shuttered the windows. But shutters made no difference to the stones. In they came, through glass, through shutters, rolling down the chimney, smashing against the door. Objects in the room began to hurl themselves at George Walton. Candles were blown out. The bars on the doors began to bend under the solid blows of an invisible hammer. A cheese-press smashed itself against a wall.

Somehow, the Waltons managed to survive their first night of horror in the house. However, much to their dismay, the stone-throwing devil had not vanished with the coming of dawn and the cock's crowing. That day, haystacks in the fields were broken up and the hay tossed into the high branches of trees. As Walton attempted to go about his farmwork, stones pursued him.

Richard Chamberlayne, secretary to the governor of New Hampshire who later wrote a pamphlet on the "Diabolick Inventions of the Devil," lived with the Waltons for a period of time during the disturbances, which lasted for three months. Chamberlayne tried desperately to trace the source of the pelting stones and at first suggested that the activity might be the work of "naughty little boys." Chamberlayne had no sooner spoken these words of accusation than one of the boys, who had been helping the farm hands put up hay, was struck so hard on the back that he began to cry.

The Waltons' devil never developed a voice, but it was quite proficient at snorting and whistling. And although it kept up a steady barrage of stones, it was never too busy to smash pottery and slam furniture about the room.

Even if one feels that the greedy Walton deserved to have a "devil" set on him after he had displaced the poor widow and taken her land, one has to admire the perseverance of the man, who kept right at his farmwork in spite of the vicious personal attacks of the invisible stone thrower. Chamberlayne declared that Walton often received more than 40 "shrewd, hurtful blows" in a single day. Several rows of corn were uprooted as if by a sharp tool. Walton's farm hands had sickle blades broken by the stones, and tools were knocked out of their hands by the invisible demon. Chamberlayne himself once received a "smart blow on the leg."

After about three months, the bombardment of stones ceased. In 1662, as one might suppose, the entire disturbance was immediately accredited to the curse of a witch. To have thought otherwise would have been heresy—an ultimate lesson that 24 men and women learned when they were hanged, crushed, or died in prison as a result of the Salem witchcraft trials in 1692.

A TWO-WEEK BOMBARDMENT OF STONES FROM NOWHERE

Ivan T. Sanderson, world-famous zoologist, natural historian, and investigator of the unusual, once told me when I visited him at his estate in New Jersey that one should not use the term "throwing" when speaking of the poltergeistic manipulation of stones. "The stones are not thrown; they are dropped or lobbed or just drift around," Sanderson insisted.

Sanderson went on to declare that such cases are within the realm of physics rather than psychical research. Stone dropping, he said, is a purely physical phenomena and will, in time, be completely explained by physical principles. Newtonian, Einsteinian, or any others principles that concern our particular space-time continuum, however, may not explain this phenomena.

Sanderson told me that he "played catch" with flying rocks in Sumatra. "If somebody would measure their speed of fall on arrival," he maintained, "it might be demonstrated that they are obeying some law or, at least, following some pattern that is not entirely random. They might be obeying some other so-called 'law' of dynamics. If we could establish this, we would have at least two principles of dynamics in our space-time continuum."

The Oakland, California, police had been frankly skeptical when they received the frantic call from Mrs. Irene Fellows on August 17, 1943. Fel-

In 1973 a Brazilian family was plagued by a poltergeist that would slash their furniture.

lows had claimed that someone was pelting her stucco home on 89th Avenue with stones. She claimed that for two weeks, she and her granddaughters (Donna Lee, five, and Audrey, nine) had been bruised by stones that seemed to emanate from nowhere.

When two bemused patrolmen arrived to investigate the complaint, they were quick to notice that the walls and roof of the cottage were unmistakably pockmarked from the impact of falling rocks. Their amusement quickly turned to professional concern as they examined the indentations. Then, as they questioned the frightened woman, stones began to fly once again, hammering the roof with violent intensity.

"It has been like this since dawn," Fellows insisted. The police officers looked around outside, and even their trained, skeptical eyes could not ignore the many piles of worn rocks that littered the lawn.

An official investigation began on August 18. The police officers interviewed the neighbors—with special emphasis on the children—and exonerated all of them. Whatever was responsible for hurling the rocks reacted against the interference of the police by launching more malicious attacks on Fellows and her grandchildren. Several witnesses saw the inhabitants of the stucco cottage barraged by stones. Fellows was dealt a solid blow on the shoulder even as she talked with Sergeant Austin Page.

Sightseers began to arrive, and some of them boldly invaded the lawn to collect the "bewitched" stones as curios. Someone suggested that Fellows open a museum to display her "stones from the blue." One so-called psychical investigator stated that the family was being dive-bombed by seagulls that had obtained rocks from the beach.

Scientists from the nearby University of California investigated the house and acknowledged these brief facts: Whenever Fellows and her grandchildren left their home, stones from a cloudless sky struck one or more of them. Other stones fell on the cottage. No stones were visible until they hit their mark. The stones made no sound in flight. They came from all directions and fell with sufficient force to mark the house or bruise the bodies of three inhabitants.

At noon on September 1, Fellows, sleepless and exhausted, was talking with special officers Johnston and Nordendahl in her garden. The stones had been falling day and night for two weeks, and the elderly woman was on the brink of collapse. As the three of them were discussing the phenomenon, a huge stone suddenly crashed down at their feet. It was the last of the mysterious stones to strike the stucco cottage on 89th Avenue.

A Fiery Ghost Called Larry

The Stringers of London, England, had to call the ghost "Larry," because their four-year-old son kept asking about the column of vibrating light. The boy's father, Graham Stringer, explained to a reporter for United Press International that they didn't want to frighten him with a lot of ghost talk, so they preferred to treat the unexplained presence as a human being.

Larry would be benign most of the year, but beginning in 1958, the strange entity caused mysterious fires in the Stringers' home every Easter season. It was on Good Friday of 1958 that the Stringers first saw the ghost. It was a milky, fluorescent column of vibrating light about as tall as a man. Shortly after seeing the apparition, the Stringers smelled smoke coming from the baby's room. There they found that something had burned a hole through the center of a pile of the baby's clothes. It looked just as though a blowtorch had done it. Yet a pair of highly inflammable nylon stockings on the bottom of the pile was untouched.

In 1959 the Easter season once again brought Larry instead of the Easter Bunny. When Graham Stringer had a pair of shoes yanked out of his hands by an invisible force, he decided that it was time to call in the experts. A team of investigators from the College of Psychic Science was not able to achieve a conclusive analysis of the disturbances, but they identified the phenomenon as being poltergeistic in nature. Their series of psyche-probing questions established that Mrs. Stringer had experienced the visitation of a poltergeist during her adolescence. Mr. Stringer also recalled similar phenomena that had gone essentially unnoticed during their honeymoon.

Although the Stringers were prepared for Larry the fiery ghost when he returned in 1960, they were powerless to prevent the murky column of light from burning up another pile of clothes.

As the years progressed, their houseguest began to extend its annual stay. Clocks were still moving about on the mantelpiece, and objects were still floating around the apartment for several days after Easter Sunday. Stringer, a freelance photographer, also reported being enveloped in a gray, fluorescent cloud while working in his darkroom. "The room just lit up," he told reporters. "And there was Larry vibrating and glowing at my side."

In 1961 the Stringers attempted an exorcism with a Catholic priest administering the rites shortly before their annual visitor was due to arrive. It seemed to have worked, but their joy at the apparent ecclesiastical triumph over the ghost proved to be premature. Larry had simply taken a year's sabbatical.

During the spring of 1962, the Stringers' living room furniture burst into flames. Their son's bed was also consumed by flames that erupted spontaneously. On April 21, 1962, a spirit medium disclosed that Larry was in reality Mrs. Stringer's brother, Charles, who had died from burns 20 years earlier at the age of 18 months. Now that the spirit had made his identity known, the medium promised, he would leave the family in peace.

Whether Larry the ghost actually was Charles's spirit or whether the phenomenon was due to some long-repressed, subconsciously nurtured guilt on the part of Mrs. Stringer—who may, as a child, have considered herself in some way responsible for her brother's death—the Easter poltergeist did not return to the Stringer household.

A MESSY UNINVITED GUEST IN BALTIMORE

When a poltergeist is at its peak, the host may be beleaguered to the psychological breaking point. Psychoanalyst Dr. Nandor Fodor maintained that the poltergeist is an unquestionably sadistic force. Fodor theorized that the projection of aggression by means of unexplained biological agents, such as poltergeists, is one way in which an adolescent can release hostility against parents and other figures of authority and still maintain his conscious innocence.

In 1967 a lawyer's office in Germany was invaded by a poltergeist. This photograph reveals the poltergeist's favorite method of making its presence known: forcing chandeliers to swing aggressively.

Between January 14 and February 8, 1960, the Jones in Baltimore, Ohio, were the unhappy hosts of an uninvited guest that proved to be very messy. The poltergeist activity began when a row of Mrs. Jones's prized ceramic pitchers exploded one by one. Then, while the startled family watched in bewilderment, a flower pot lifted itself from a shelf and smashed through a nearby window pane. A sugar bowl floated up to the chandelier and scattered its contents in the candle holders. Pictures were tossed off the walls, and a brass incense burner became airborne and sailed six feet off a bookshelf.

Once when Mrs. Jones and her married daughter, Mrs. Pauls, were preparing a meal, a string of glasses danced off the shelf in the cabinet and shattered on the floor. After the women cleaned up the shards of glass, two dirty ashtrays flew into the kitchen and dumped their refuse on the floor. A table from the upstairs landing suddenly became animated and went bouncing down the steps, splintering into pieces at the bottom of the stairs.

The home-wrecking poltergeist did not ignore the basement in its domination of the Jones household. The caps of an entire case of soda bottles began to pop off in a series of explosions that sounded like a string of firecrackers on the Fourth of July. A well-stacked pile of fireplace wood erupted in violent bursts of energy that sent bits of bark and pulp flying across the floor.

No one received any real physical harm (and it is seldom that anyone ever does during a poltergeist attack) throughout the period of the psychic siege, but Mr. Jones was struck on the head by a falling can of sauerkraut as he stooped to pick up a can of corn that the invisible, rambunctious ghost had thrown. The can of sauerkraut barely bruised him, but Jones felt true anguish when he saw some of his most valued pieces of furniture rudely destroyed by the violent and unbidden guest.

None of the Jones household—Mr. and Mrs. Jones, their daughter, Mrs. Pauls, and their 17-year-old grandson, Ted—were injured in any appreciable way, but they all suffered terrible mental and emotional pain during that three-week period of siege under the attack of the poltergeist.

Many researchers have noted that, in addition to the sadistic attacks directed upon authoritarian figures (parents, older siblings, police officers, clergymen), the individual who serves as the poltergeist's energy center—the psychic "eye of the storm"—may receive wounds that appear to be the effects of stigmata. The individual may also experience painful swelling of the body, and vile and obscene writing may appear on walls or various personal objects. Whether such abuse is due to unconscious feelings of guilt is difficult to assess. It would seem that, in at least some cases, the agent of the poltergeist is subconsciously aware that he or she is responsible for the psychic storm that has been unleashed in the home.

Fodor was able to personally investigate the Jones case in Baltimore. He learned that the police department's crime laboratory could find no trace of any volatile substance having been placed in any of the moving or exploding objects. City engineers had gone to the home to test for earth tremors with a seismograph, but they had found nothing. A radio repairman had arrived with a theory that high-frequency radio waves had been responsible for the weird occurrences, but his sophisticated equipment could find nothing to substantiate his thesis. A local plumber had claimed the ghost was nothing but suction coming from the hot-air furnace, but none of his tinkering did anything to hinder the activities of the noisy demon in the Jones house.

Newspaper reporters, television crews, press photographers, and radio interviewers had stomped through every inch of the home and photographed the phenomena from every conceivable angle. Kooks, cranks, and cultists had plagued the Joneses, each with his own time-tested method of ridding a home of the unwanted force.

Fodor felt that he discovered the poltergeist with little effort at all. Seventeen-year-old Ted was a shy, brooding youth who had left school at the legal age because he said that his classes bored him. He liked to sit alone in his room and read. He confessed to the psychoanalyst that what he wanted most to do was to write short stories.

Fodor put the poltergeistic forces to rest by encouraging the teenager to do what he most desired: write fiction. A very simple exorcism, indeed, but it worked. When the youth realized that he had found a sympathetic audience for his opinions, and someone who would listen to a recitation of his ambitions and goals, the poltergeist activity ceased.

Fodor believed that the mechanics of poltergeist activity were accomplished by what he termed "psychic dissociation." The psychoanalyst theorized that the human body is capable of releasing energy in a manner similar to atomic bombardments. In the case of the Jones family, through psychic bombardments a projected energy force was apparently able to enter soda bottles and to burst them open from within.

Sacheverell Sitwell is another writer who expressed the opinion that poltergeists most often find their energy center in the psyche of an adolescent, who performs the ghostly effects, both consciously and unconsciously. "[The adolescent] is gifted for the time being with something approaching criminal cunning. The particular direction of this power is always towards the secret or concealed weaknesses of the spirit … the obscene or erotic recesses of the soul. The mysteries of puberty, that trance or dozing of the psyche before it awakes into adult life, is a favorite playground for the poltergeist."

Perhaps Fodor summarized the difference between ghosts and poltergeists when he told the press during his investigation of the Jones case that a ghost haunts a house and a poltergeist haunts a person. The psychoanalyst said that the poltergeist was very often not really a ghost "but a bundle of projected repressions."

POPPING BOTTLES ON LONG ISLAND

When 12-year-old James Herrmann, Jr., and 13-year-old Lucille Herrmann walked through their front door after school at 3:30 P.M. on February 3, 1958, they received a most bizarre "five-gun salute." The caps of bottles located in various rooms of the suburban Long Island home began to pop like champagne corks.

Scurrying from room to room, Mrs. Herrmann and her two children found that a bottle of bleach in the basement had blown its top. In the kitchen, they located an uncapped bottle of liquid starch. The bathroom yielded both an uncapped bottle of shampoo and a topless bottle of liquid medicine. Mrs. Herrmann also discovered that a bottle of holy water she kept in the master bedroom had been spilled.

Mrs. Herrmann called her husband, James, and reported the strange "poppings" that had occurred in their house. Mr. Herrmann was puzzled, but since no one had been hurt by the peculiar event, he decided that he would not come home any earlier than was his custom.

James Herrmann arrived home with a solution already fixed in his mind: some chemical reaction in the formulas of the various products had caused them to erupt. The fact that the bottles had all popped at once was undoubtedly due to some weird coincidence, and probably had resulted from excessive humidity or some such thing in the house. He was baffled, however, when he noted that each of the bottles had screw caps, which required several turns before they could be removed. If the bottles had had the crimped caps com-

In 1952 the Glynn family of Runcorn, Chesire, United Kingdom, suffered the exploits of a nasty poltergeist that would wreck entire rooms. The police even attempted to set traps around the home to prevent further abuse, but the attacks continued. In this photograph, John Glynn surveys his wrecked bedroom.

monly used on soda pop bottles at that time, his theory would have seemed much more valid. It seemed quite impossible that a chemical reaction could have blown off the screw caps without taking along the bottles' necks as well. He was relieved when his family gave every indication of having calmed down and no longer seemed to demand an explanation of the events from him.

There were no further disturbances in the Herrmann household until two days later. Then it was a repeat performance of the poltergeist's debut. The children walked in the front door from school and the fireworks began. A bottle of nail polish popped open, and so did a bottle of rubbing alcohol, a bottle of bleach, starch, detergent, and, once again, the holy water. All the caps were of the screw-on variety.

When the bottles began to pop on the next night as well, James Herrmann began to suspect that his science-fiction–loving son had somehow hatched a little plot whereby he might have some fun at the expense of his family. Herrmann conjectured that James, Jr., could have dropped some type of carbonate capsule into the bottles and loosened their lids in the morning before he left for school. He had probably succeeded in timing the explosions so he could be present to witness the startled expression on the face of his mother and sister.

Herrmann spent most of that weekend surreptitiously observing his son. He was determined to catch the boy in some action that would give him away as the agent behind the mysterious poppings. No one, therefore, could have been more surprised than Herrmann when, on Sunday morning, several bottle caps popped off and their containers began to jiggle on the shelves. He had kept an eye on the boy day and night. How could he have slipped anything into the bottles?

James, Jr., stood at the bathroom sink brushing his teeth and vigorously proclaimed his innocence. As Herrmann questioned his son, he was startled to see a medicine bottle move across the sink top and smash into the floor. Within seconds, it was joined by a bottle of shampoo.

James Herrmann called the police, begging the officer who answered to take him seriously. They were being bothered by bottles that popped their caps and flew about the room.

The officer accused Herrmann of drinking, but he agreed to send a policeman to investigate the disturbances. Herrmann had a good reputation in the community. It wasn't like him to annoy the police with wild stories.

Patrolman James Hughes had only been in the house a few minutes when several bottles in the bathroom fired a barrage at him. He rapidly concluded that the Herrmanns did, indeed, have very peculiar trouble. Detective Joseph Tozzi listened to Hughes's report with professional interest and concluded that if bottles were acting up at the Herrmanns, they were doing it with human help.

Detective Tozzi began his investigation on February 11. On that day, an atomizer in Lucille's room tipped over when no one was in her bedroom. Or, Detective Tozzi noted somewhat skeptically, no one claimed to have been in the bedroom. For the next few days, the disturbances were confined to the bottle of holy water in the parents' bedroom. On the evening of February 15, however, the manifestations became much more impressive. As the family sat watching television, a porcelain figurine was lifted from a coffee table and began to float through the air. After this demonstration of prowess on the part of their uninvited guest, the Herrmanns decided to call upon a priest to aid Tozzi in his investigations. Father William McLeod of the Church of Saint William the Abbott answered their plea for clerical help and administered a blessing to the home by sprinkling holy water liberally in six rooms.

But the priest was too late. "Popper," as the strange force in the Herrmann house had come to be called, had grown too strong to have its spark of psychic life extinguished by holy water. The Herrmanns soon discovered that

A still taken from the classic movie *Poltergeist*.

the invasion of privacy that began to occur when the news media gave their strange house a great deal of publicity was much worse than the Popper's antics. Letters in barely intelligible scrawls arrived, either condemning them for fraud or encouraging them to take heart and fight against the evil tricks of Satan.

Real Ghosts, Restless Spirits, and Haunted Places

On February 19 a porcelain figurine flew off a table and traveled more than 12 feet in the air before it smashed against a desk. On February 20 another figurine became airborne, a bottle of ink popped its cap and splashed its contents against a wall, and a sugar bowl took its leave from the dining table. Seventeen days after its arrival, Popper was steadily acquiring the strength to perform more dramatic and more spectacular demonstrations.

The Herrmanns, who had remained remarkably calm and patient throughout the phenomena, decided that they needed to get away from the house before their nerves gave out. While they spent the night of February 21 with relatives, Detective Tozzi stayed in the house that Popper had taken over with its infantile pranks. Although Tozzi's attitude toward paranormal manifestations had altered considerably from the first night that he had spent with the Herrmanns, it didn't bother him in the slightest to remain alone in the "haunted house." The night was quiet and without incident. There were no poppings, no moving of furniture, no flying figurines.

The truce at the Herrmann house ended on the night that the family returned. Once again the sugar bowl became so animated that it shot off the table and crashed to the floor. On February 24, Tozzi investigated a loud thud that had come from James, Jr.'s room. The officer was certain that no one had been in the room or near it, but upon entering the bedroom, he found that a heavy bureau had been tipped face down on the floor. The next night, the boy's phonograph began to orbit around the room while he was doing his homework. In the master bedroom, a statuette of the Virgin Mary flew more than 12 feet and struck the frame of a mirror across the room. A bookcase full of bulky encyclopedias was up-ended. A globe of the world shot down a hallway, narrowly missing Tozzi. A photographer saw his own flashbulbs rise from a table, float across the room, and bounce against a wall. For the first time, Popper began to knock on the wall, but no attempt at any sort of communication was attempted.

Tozzi was worried about the sudden flurry of violent activity on the part of Popper. Tozzi had previously arranged for the house to be checked by electricians and physicists in order to find a logical explanation for the events; even the Air Force had investigated to determine whether or not jet flight patterns might have somehow caused supersonic vibrations. He had taken the advice of occultists, self-styled preachers, anonymous letter writers. Any plan that had seemed remotely plausible, he had tried to apply to the Herrmann household. But nothing had worked. The manifestations seemed to be growing in strength and were becoming increasingly violent in their demonstrations.

Just as the detective was about to recommend that the family move to avoid personal harm, it seemed as though Popper had used up its last reserves of energy during the recent flurry of activity. The poltergeist said its farewell at ten o'clock on the evening of March 2. It sent a dish shattering in the dining room, a night table falling in James, Jr.'s bedroom, and a bookcase tumbling in the basement. With this parting gesture, Popper left the Herrmanns, never again to return.

REVISITING THE SALEM WITCH HYSTERIA AS POLTERGEIST ACTIVITY

Because of the accusations of a small circle of prepubescent girls, an entire community in the Massachusetts Bay Colony became crazed and allowed themselves to get caught up in the fear that many of their neighbors were secretly serving Satan.

A strong case might be made for the argument that the famous Salem witchcraft hysteria of 1692 is an example of poltergeist phenomena that got out of hand. The young girls, who claimed to have been bewitched by invisible spirits under the control of various elderly women in the village, complained of being pinched, having their hair pulled, and being stuck with pins. All these classic symptoms of a witch's wickedness we now recognize as familiar manifestations of poltergeist.

Pursuing this thesis just a bit further, we might observe that throughout the centuries witches have traditionally been ascribed certain powers, including the ability to command invisible agents, hurl stones at their victims, and torment people with night noises and destructive fires. All of these powers of the prototypical witch coincide with the attributes of poltergeist activity. Perhaps an accomplished witch in the classic sense, rather than the religious definition of the label, is simply one who has somehow retained that strange psychokinetic fragmentation of the psyche that sometimes occurs during pubertal change and has learned how to control it.

The madness at Salem began innocently enough in the home of the Reverend Samuel Parris, when his slave Tituba began telling stories of voodoo and restless spirits to his nine-year-old daughter Betty and her 11-year-old cousin Abigail Williams. Soon the exciting storytelling sessions in the Parris household were attracting older girls, such as 16-year-old Mary Walcott and 18-year-old Susanna Sheldon, who wanted Tituba to tell their fortunes and predict their future husbands, as well as tell them ghost stories. Although Parris and the other preachers fulminated from the pulpits about the dangers of seeking occult knowledge from spirits, the girls of Salem ignored such warnings in favor of a thrilling pastime that could help them through a long, cold winter.

Perhaps the psychic energies grew stronger when Ann Putnam, a fragile, highly strung 12-year-old, joined the circle in the company of the Putnams'

A "witch trials" memorial statue at the Salem Wax Museum of Witches and Seafarers in Salem, Massachusetts.

maid, 19-year-old Mercy Lewis. Ann had a quick wit, a high intelligence, and a lively imagination, and she soon became Tituba's most avid and apt pupil. Perhaps while a part of Ann's psyche was thrilled with the forbidden knowledge that Tituba was sharing with them, another more conservative religious aspect was racked with guilt for having flirted with devilish enchantment. Undoubtedly this conflict of conscience and the fear of discovery also affected the other girls.

Many contemporary psychical investigators who have been on the scene during the manifestation of a poltergeist have observed that the activity is more often associated with girls rather than boys. The reason for this may lie in the enormously complex physio-chemical changes that take place in the body of the girl entering puberty. Although the sex drive itself is usually stronger in the post-pubertal boy, the adolescent girl is confronted with much more dramatic physical alterations. The hips widen, the breasts form, and then there is the trauma of menarche, which can result in severe psychological shock to the girl who has not been adequately prepared for that initial flow of menstrual blood.

As the winter days passed in Salem, little Betty Parris became distracted from her chores, subject to sudden fits of weeping, and was often seen staring blankly at the wall. Shortly thereafter, Abigail got down on all fours and began barking like a dog or braying like a donkey. Mary Walcott and Susanna Sheldon fell into convulsions. Ann Putnam and Mercy Lewis also began to suffer seizures. Something evil had come to Salem.

When members of the Salem clergy began to ask the girls who it was that was tormenting them, Tituba was the first to be named by the "possessed" children. Nor did anyone doubt the naming of Sarah Good, an unpleasant woman who smoked a foul-smelling pipe and who had been suspected of spreading smallpox through witchcraft. But when Sarah Osburne was also named by the children, the village was shocked. Mrs. Osburne was a wealthy woman who lived in one of the most substantial homes in Salem. Nevertheless, warrants were issued for all three women.

From such a dramatic beginning, the list of names of the Devil's disciples who were tormenting the girls grew steadily longer. Two magistrates, John Hathorne and Jonathan Corwin, were sent out from the General Court of Massachusetts Colony to hear testimony that included tales of talking animals, dark shapes, red cats, and a Tall Man, who was undoubtedly the Devil himself.

When the pious, saintly 71-year-old Rebecca Nurse was arrested for witchcraft, the townsfolk of Salem began to realize that no one was safe from such accusations. Although the jury initially acquitted her, the judge ordered the jury to reconsider, and she was found guilty. She was hanged on Gallows Hill on July 19, 1692.

Massachusetts governor William Phips became outraged when his own wife was accused of being a witch. He ordered that there should be no further imprisonments for witchcraft in the state, and he forbade any more executions for the crime of witchcraft in Salem. Because of the governor's actions, the nearly 150 men and women who were still chained to prison walls were set free, and many who had been convicted of witchcraft were pardoned.

A RELENTLESS POUNDING ON THE WALLS

The Investigation of Sergeant Daniel G.

Police Sergeant Daniel G. related an encounter with a poltergeist that he and three fellow officers had in an apartment in a large Midwestern city.

The officers had no idea what to expect when they received the call around eleven o'clock on the night of October 12, 2000. All Sergeant G. and his partner Les H. had been told was that a lady had complained that someone was banging on her walls.

"We didn't know if we were going to have to quiet some noisy party animals in the next apartment or some cranky neighbor who might somehow be annoyed because he or she thought the woman was making too much noise in her apartment," Sergeant G. said.

When the two officers arrived at the address that had been dispatched to them, they quickly discovered that the complaint had been filed by a woman who lived on the third floor. That meant no one could be making noise above her, because she was on the top floor.

As the officers walked down the hallway toward her apartment, they could hear nothing that would qualify as raucous party sounds. Maybe they had lucked out, and the complaint of a disturbance had taken care of itself. But the minute the two officers stepped inside the apartment of Mrs. C and her 11-year-old daughter Sophie, they could hear terrible pounding sounds that seemed to be issuing from all around them.

As Sergeant G. stated in his report of the incident: "Mrs. C. appeared on the brink of nervous collapse, and her daughter was curled up on the couch. It was incredible. You stepped back out into the hall, and you couldn't hear a thing out of the ordinary. Yet the second you moved back into the apartment, you could hear what sounded like someone pounding the walls with a hammer. I told Les to check up on the roof while I tried to calm Mrs. C. and her daughter."

Mrs. C. told Sergeant G. that the disturbance began as they were finishing their evening meal, about six o'clock. They had been discussing some problem that Sophie had been having in school when the pounding began. The noise was not very loud at first; it sounded as if someone was knocking on the wall with his knuckles. They knew that they had raised their voices to some degree during their argument, and assumed that they might have disturbed the elderly man who lived in the apartment next to them, who was now complaining by knocking on their walls. Even though the argument between mother and daughter had ended and they were quiet in their apartment, the mysterious pounding got louder. Mrs. C. called her neighbor to see if he was indeed the one attempting to let them know that they had bothered him; the neighbor said that he had no idea what she was talking about. He had not been disturbed by their argument, and he certainly had not been pounding on their walls.

"I felt along the walls, but it was the strangest thing," Sergeant G. stated in his report. "The pounding didn't really seem to be coming from the walls at all. I couldn't really tell where the sounds were originating. Les came back down from checking the roof and said that he could find nothing up there that could possibly make such noises. I told him to call officers B. and L. to come and help us go through the apartment house. I thought right away that maybe someone had rigged some kind of electronic device in Mrs. C.'s apartment as some kind of cruel prank. Such proved not to be the case."

When officers B. and L. entered the apartment, the phenomena dramatically increased in scope and intensity. As all four police officers watched, the dinner plates, which had remained on the kitchen table from the family's interrupted dinner, were lifted into the air and smashed against the wall. As Officer B. rushed forward to examine the unexpected and unexplained mess, a kitchen chair scooted across the room, slamming into his knees and nearly tripping him.

"And all this time," Sergeant G. said, "the infernal pounding kept right on, not missing a beat. When the plates and the chair started to move, Sophie began to scream hysterically that she wanted to leave the apartment. At the same time, Officer L. covered his ears with his palms and said that he had to get out of the room. There was some kind of weird vibration in the place that was making his eardrums feel that they were about to explode."

This engraving of poltergeist activity in a French home appeared in Leo Taxil's book *Les Mystre de la Franc-maconnerie*, 1860.

Sergeant G. could clearly see that officer L. was in extreme distress. His face was ashen, and he appeared about to faint. "I ordered him to go down to the basement and check the heating to determine if there might be anything there to account for the strange disturbances," Sgt. G. said. "When Officer L. hesitated, I could tell that he was genuinely afraid to go alone, so I told Les to go with him. Officer L. is a big, tough guy, but he was scared of something in that apartment."

Officer B. called Sergeant G.'s attention to another kitchen chair slowly moving backward. As the confused witnesses watched, the chair did a complete flip, then gently returned to its upright position.

Unable to explain the source of the commotion and thus unable to provide a source of relief for the traumatized mother and daughter, Sergeant G. suggested they temporarily seek refuge elsewhere. "I asked Mrs. C. if she had someplace that she could go for the night. She said that she had a cousin who lived across town. I suggested that she call the cousin and request a night's sanctuary, pack a few things in a bag, and I would have Officer L. drive her and Sophie to wherever they needed to go. All this time, Sophie had been whimpering and crying, and, from time to time, emitting this hellish scream."

Once Mrs. C. and her daughter left the apartment, Officer H., Officer B., and Sergeant G. stayed at the locale, attempting to find the cause of the disruption. They remained in the apartment for another 50 minutes or so, but try as they did, they were unable to determine any rational cause for the pounding sounds. However, after the mother and daughter had left their apartment, one thing did become clear to the officers: the pounding was becoming less forceful and frequent.

"Approximately every ten minutes or so, the entire apartment would seem to tremble, as if we were experiencing an earthquake," he said. "And then the disturbances stopped altogether."

The officers checked everywhere in the apartment building for some kind of ordinary physical explanation for the things they observed and came up blank.

"From what I have read on the subject," Sergeant G. said, "a young person, especially a female, can serve as the center for these kinds of weird disturbances, and I wonder if Mrs. C. and her daughter had been experiencing an emotional conflict of greater duration than an argument about school over dinner that night." Officer Les H. interviewed a number of the neighbors who lived around Mrs. C. and her daughter, but none of them had been disturbed by any unusual sounds—certainly not the terrible pounding that was experienced by Sophie, her mother, and the officers they called upon to bring the disruptions occurring in their home under control.

Officer L. pointed out that there was a large cemetery across the street, and he admitted that he thought that he had seen and felt spirit presences in the apartment. Sergeant G. concluded, "Later, I learned that Mrs. C. and her daughter had moved out, because Sophie refused to return to the apartment. I think they also moved out of the city soon afterward."

A WEEKEND ENCOUNTER WITH A POLTERGEIST

The Personal Experience of Stacie Freeland

"I had heard about the movie *Poltergeist*, but I didn't expect to spend an evening with such a rambunctious entity. The event in question took place at a friend's family home in Vista, New York. There were six young, professional adults present for a weekend gathering, and all of us had driven up from New York City earlier that morning.

"It was a typical blustery, fall day, and the iridescent leaves that were falling when the wind tore them from their summer homes showered the ground with flashes of yellows, reds, and oranges, making perfect highlights to the all gray backdrop. The converted barn that we were making home for the weekend was situated on a lake and was completely surrounded by forest. There were plenty of activities to keep us all busy—firewood to be collected, beds to be made, food shopping, and other errands to run. After all the details had been attended to, we split up. Some of us went hiking in the woods, one read a book, and others went for a joy-ride in the convertible that was at our disposal. I'd opted for the hike in the woods with Maura, our hostess, the only other female present that weekend. By the end of the day, the weather had grown threatening, and the wind became aggressive and unpredictable. It was clear to all that it was time to go inside.

"We had left the windows and doors open to the fresh air all afternoon, and after closing the building up tight, we built a fire and removed the first course of the evening meal from the fridge to be heated on the stovetop. We were having homemade summer squash and red bell pepper soup. I'd been given the responsibility of choosing the music, and when Maura walked by me and asked that I keep an eye on the soup for a minute, I responded with a 'sure.'

"Maura had just shut the bathroom door when I heard a very strange sound coming from the kitchen. Before I could pick myself up and out of the cross-legged position into which I had folded myself, Maura, who had also heard the noise, came rushing out of the bathroom. Basically, we arrived on the scene together.

"Somehow, the soup had violently exploded, spewing a third of its contents into an area three feet in diameter in every direction. Feeling somewhat responsible, as I had remained in the living room rather than stationing myself in the kitchen, as Maura had been, I picked up the pan, thinking that a swift temperature change must have caused rapid-fire air bubbles to erupt. But when I felt the bottom of the saucepan, it wasn't even warm. 'That's really odd,' I said to Maura. We called the rest of the crew into the kitchen and inquired if anyone had tampered with the soup. Everyone claimed to be as confused as we were.

Stacie Freeland.

"We began the task of cleaning up the mess, and Maura became concerned that there might not be enough soup to go around. The clean up efforts took 20 minutes because we kept finding other places where the soup had splashed. The fan grate and light just above the stove was the hardest hit, and we used a lot of paper towels trying to wipe the infiltrated areas clean.

"Maura and I were still in the kitchen when Gordon, one of the houseguests, decided that he wanted a glass of wine. He had just opened the chosen bottle and was in the process of pouring from it when the wine glass he held in his hand flew in a perfect upward arch and then came straight down to the floor.

"I saw that the glass was taking very deliberate movements, and Gordon seemed to lack any control over the glass. It was as if an invisible hand had knocked it out of his grasp on purpose. We stood there, mouths slightly open, until Gordon asked, more as a joke than a serious question, 'Is there a ghost in the house?'

"'No, there are no ghosts,' Maura said emphatically.

"We all marveled at the fact that the wine glass had broken by the stem and not the delicate rim as would have been expected. 'Strange,' came Gordon's response.

"Maura was in the middle of handing out what was left of the homemade soup when, without warning, all of the lights in the house went out. We all became motionless as if our bodies had become pillars of salt. After a moment of silence, everyone started speaking at once.

"I heard someone blame Maura's husband Ed for this most recent situation. I quietly called out for Maura, and when she answered, I took a step closer to the sound of her voice. Then suddenly the lights came back on. Ed was visibly agitated, and he picked up the phone in order to call the electric company to inquire whether or not the pending storm was causing power outages. His face went ashen. 'What's wrong?' Maura demanded.

"'Well ... the phone is dead,' was his reply.

"All at once everyone began to offer possible causes. A few well chosen swear words were spoken, and again the entire house lost all power. Ed went to the window to see if the streetlights were off as well, because the power to the house was connected to the lines that fed the lights that lined the old country road. Those lights were on, which suggested a blown fuse in the house. The fuse box was in the basement, and no one offered to go down and check it out. It's funny how logic and rational thought disappear when there's an overload in the imagination. 'It's the storm,' someone said.

"By now Maura had lit some candles, and we at least had the glow of the tiny flames to guide our steps. We made our way to the dinner table in almost complete darkness and sat down just in time for the lights to return all foreign shadows to their proper places. 'That's no blown fuse!' Ed declared.

"This is going to be an interesting dinner, I thought to myself.

"A warm fire was behind us, and the conversation around the table soon became centered on the odd occurrences that had taken place in the house. Suddenly Gordon, who was seated opposite me, stopped with his spoon mid-way to his mouth. The manner in which his shoulders climbed up to his ears, and his head jerked ever so slightly to the right made me stop what I was doing and shift my full attention toward the direction from which his reaction had stemmed. I heard myself gasp.

"Within the indoor atrium—which had become sanctuary to a collection of antique weather vanes—a single weather vane, which hung from the ceiling by a chain, was swinging violently in a 180-degree angle! No other object was moving, not even a single fern frond swayed! Nothing! The pace with which the lone weather vane was swinging was even-tempered and exact. The violence with which it swung was very disturbing.

"Everyone was watching, unable to fully comprehend the event we were all witnessing. My husband Erik stood up from his chair and took a candle from the center of the table over to the atrium to search for a possible draft of some kind. None was found.

"All the while, the weather vane continued its mad antics, swinging closer and closer to the wall. There was an orb in the center of the weather vane made of some type of nonopaque glass, and if it were to hit the wall, it would shatter, which would leave us with a lot of explaining to do to Maura's father, who owned the place. I asked Erik, who was still standing, if he could stop the antique vane from swinging.

"Ed dramatically bellowed out, 'Don't touch it!' But Erik reached out and manually stopped the object from swinging. However, just as he did so, our friend Ed immediately started to have trouble breathing. Ed was hyperventilating and had to go outside into the cold night air to catch his breath.

"The wine was flowing in our blood streams now, and that seemed to help our ability to deal with the events of the evening. The dishwasher had been loaded and the table cleared. Nobody really seemed to want to talk about the incidents—perhaps because there was no way to agree upon an explanation. Soon, however, we couldn't help ourselves, and the discussion turned to what might be going on in the house. Ed was accused by one of the guests of having rigged the whole affair, but I more than doubted that was the case.

"The host decided that, if only to quiet the unrest we were all feeling, he wanted to play a game on the antique roulette wheel that stood in the hallway. On route to the hallway that housed the weathered roulette wheel, Ed stopped dead in his tracks. In the corner of the room that Ed was facing, there was a fine cloud of cold air visible to the naked eye. It was so cold we could see Ed's breath as he exhaled. Nowhere else in the house was it this cold. Everyone placed a body part in the cold spot to feel for themselves, and sure enough, the area was much colder than the thermometer outside, which read an even 40 degrees. 'This is really weird,' Ed said in a disbelieving tone.

"Ed then led everyone over to the roulette wheel. Everyone but me joined in the game of calling out a number to see if the wheel would stop on it. There were some failed attempts at matching the called number to that of the wheel, but when it was Ed's turn, he said something like, 'let's see if that old ghost wants to play with me!'

"He called out a number while challenging the specter to play, and I kid you not, during the next three turns, Ed called out the number and even before the wheel could come to a stop naturally, the wheel stopped abruptly on the exact number he'd called. Not once, not twice, but three times!

"I wasn't amused and directed my displeasure to the unseen player of the wheel. 'Get out of here,' I said to the invisible guest. 'We're bored with your silly antics. Go find some place else to camp out!'

"By now it was really late. Maura was the first to announce that she was off to bed and asked Ed to lock up the house. Ed chose me to go around the house and help him secure the locks on all the windows and doors. Together, we systematically locked up the entire house.

"The front door was the last on our rounds. This was an original door belonging to the barn from which the house had been converted. It was oversized, old, and very heavy. The door had a large black rusty bolt on it that acted as the knob, and it made a lot of noise when it was slid aside. I watched Ed as he used the weight of his body to aid him in shutting tight the wooden door. Once finished, he gave me a peck on the cheek and took himself up to bed.

"We four guests moved into the den area and sat about discussing the fashions and music of the the Jazz Age of the 1920s and 1930s. We had chosen to ignore the night's events, and we spent a pleasant half an hour talking about purely material things.

"Then I suddenly felt a cold blast of air. The chill was directly followed by a noise that amounted to an almost inaudible creaking sound. I looked at the three men who sat opposite me and shook my head. 'No, no way!' I said adamantly.

"I got up from the chair and in one step climbed up the three short stairs to peek around the corner to see if what I expected was true. The front door stood wide open—just hanging on its hinges, laying flat up against the wall. I couldn't believe it! The door hadn't made the hideously loud noise it generally made as the door scraped across the threshold, and that was what gave me the creeps! I asked Erik to please close and secure the door once again, and this prompted every one to call it a night.

"The other guests disappeared into their allotted bedrooms. Erik and I were to sleep in the den. For the first time that evening, I wondered if I could muster up enough energy to drive back to the city. Then I took stock of the hour and the amount that I'd had to drink. 'All right,' I said to the uninvited guest, 'if you are spending the night, then please go to bed now!'

"The lights in the den were on a rheostat. Directly following my tired, yet motherly, command to go to bed, the lights turned themselves up to full brightness. Erik and I were standing in the middle of the room, staring at each other, when the lights slowly came down to an almost-off position—then immediately climbed up again to the highest level of brightness. Finally, they turned and stayed off.

"That capped off the spooky events for that weekend. But the following weekend, just after midnight, I picked up the telephone receiver to be greeted by a very excited voice, repeating, 'It's happening again!' I thought it was a prank caller and almost hung up. When I realized it was Ed, I sat upright in bed and became alert.

"'What's happening again?' I asked him to clarify. Ed then proceeded to tell me that he and Maura had driven up to the house in Vista from Kennedy Airport after picking up some friends of theirs who had just arrived from Europe. They had told their friends the story from the weekend before and were met with disbelief and no small amount of chiding.

"Upon entering the country house, the two couples made their way to the atrium so that Ed could show the faithless just what he had been talking about. Ed turned on the light so that all could see, and much to the surprise of everyone, the weather vane was again swinging violently! Without interfering with the lightening-rod-gone-mad, Ed immediately phoned me. Why? Good question! I was five hours away in Pennsylvania. It was past midnight, and there was really nothing I could do over the phone, anyway! I told him to calm down and to tell the poltergeist to get the hell out of the house, NOW!

"There were no more phone calls and no further incidents. Ed's friends did walk away from the weekend with a bit more of an open mind, but Maura's father still doesn't believe our story."

4
Shadow Beings That Attacked

As we saw in chapter three, mischievous physical attention toward a particular member of a family can be a distinguishing characteristic of poltergeist cases. In this chapter, as we continue to identify diverse forms of ghosts, we examine cases in which the force of intelligence that directed the paranormal phenomena appears to have been motivated by malice more than mischief. Sometimes, for reasons that may never be adequately explained, ghosts violently attack individuals, inflicting physical torture and tormenting their victims on a daily basis. Victims have been known to suffer the attacks of malevolent ghosts for long periods of their lives.

THE GHOST OF OLD KATE BATTS, THE BELL WITCH

The disturbances experienced by the Bell family began in 1817. First, mysterious rappings were heard on the windows of the family's cabin, located near Clarksville, Tennessee. Then the entire family—parents John and Luce and their children Elizabeth, John, Drewry, Joel, and Richard—had their covers pulled roughly off their beds in the middle of the night. Twelve-year-old Elizabeth, known as "Betsy," also began to complain that a rat was gnawing on her bedpost while she attempted to sleep. Unable to find the suspected rat, the family members began to inspect the bedpost and were shocked to find that while they couldn't see a culprit, *something* was clearly gnawing on Betsy's bed; marks continued to appear on the wooden bed right before their eyes.

The family was also confounded by a noise that seemed to fill the entire home. Although Luce was not nursing any children at the time, the family heard what sounded like the sucking noise of a baby being nursed, and lips

[91]

smacking together. Several investigators of ghost phenomena have noted the peculiar sounds of psychic "nursing." Some researchers have noted that these haunting noises often signal the beginning of a particularly violent episode of disturbances. The phenomenon is a result of the manifestation of an entity in the form of an obscene infant, born from some dimension of reality that borders our own. Sacheverell Sitwell wrote that such a being might be "an embryonic phantasm" that comes into existence on "the borderlands, upon one frontier or the other, of human life…. It is in all things unholy, unhallowed, and not human."

When the Bell family arose the morning after their first night of unexplained disturbances, stones littered the floor of the front room, and furniture had been overturned. Without an apparent logical explanation for what had caused the vast array of disturbances, the children were wide-eyed and spoke of ghosts and goblins. John Bell lectured his family severely. They would keep the problem to themselves. He didn't want their family to become the subject for common gossip.

That night, Richard was awakened by something pulling his hair, raising his head right off the pillow. Joel began screaming at his brother's invisible attacker, and from her room, Elizabeth began howling that the gnawing rat had returned and was pulling her hair, too. Most of the family awakened the next day with sore scalps from having their hair yanked and tugged during the night, and John Bell reversed his decision. They needed help. That day he confided in James Johnson, the family's nearest neighbor and closest friend.

Johnson accompanied his friend to the Bell cabin that evening. The tale that Bell told was a strange one, but Johnson knew that John Bell was neither a drinker nor a liar. While he watched at Elizabeth's bedside that night, Johnson saw the young girl receive several blows on the cheeks from an invisible attacker. "Stop in the name of the Lord Jesus Christ!" Johnson adjured the phantom assailant. There was no activity from the ghost for several minutes, then little Betsy's hair received a yank that made her scream in pain. Again Johnson admonished the evil spirit, and it released the girl's hair. Johnson concluded that the invisible spirit understood the English language, and he also had the insight to perceive that for some reason, Betsy was the center of the haunting. The next day Johnson met with other neighbors, and they agreed to help the family as best they could.

A committee was selected to keep watch at the Bell house all night to try to keep the evil spirit from molesting Betsy. All this well-intentioned effort accomplished was to provoke an especially vicious onslaught of activity focused on the unfortunate girl. A number of neighbors volunteered to have their daughters sleep with Betsy, but the only thing this managed to bring about was the other girls being terrorized as well. Nor did it help to take Betsy out of the cabin and into the homes of neighbors, for the nasty, hair-pulling entity simply followed her to the other abodes.

By now the haunting had achieved wide notoriety, and the disturbances were thought to be the work of the ghost of old Kate Batts, an accused witch who, for some unknown reason, had returned to work evil upon the Bell family. Each night the house was filled with those who sat up trying to get the ghost to talk or to communicate with them by rapping on the walls or by making a smacking sound with its lips.

The entity soon became powerful enough to venture outside the cabin and away from Betsy, its center of energy. There seems little doubt that somehow the energy of the ghost was able to "feed" upon the psyches of the believers who gathered nearly every evening in the Bell home. Neighbors reported seeing lights like candles or lamps moving through the fields, and farmers began to suffer attacks of stones thrown by the Bell Witch.

Young boys in the area often played catch with the witch if she happened to throw something at them on their way home from school. Once an observer witnessed several boys suddenly get pelted with sticks that flew from a nearby thicket. The sticks did not strike the boys with much force, and, with a great deal of merriment, the boys gathered up the sticks and tossed them back into the thicket. Once again, the sticks came flying back out. This time the observer cut notches in several of the sticks before the boys returned fire. He testified that he was able to identify his markings when they were thrown back from the thicket.

While the witch loved to play with local boys from time to time, she was not at all playful with any scoffers who came to the Bell home attempting to expose the phenomena as trickery. Those who stayed the night had the covers jerked from their beds, and some were slapped soundly on the face. The blows were heard distinctly by the Bell family—it sounded like the open palm of a heavy hand striking flesh, one of them noted in a diary.

Spiritualists, clergymen, reporters, and curiosity seekers trooped to the Bell farm and tried to get the witch to declare herself and her intentions. Their efforts were finally rewarded when one day the ghost began to speak. At first the witch's voice was only an indistinct babble, then it evolved into a husky whisper that would only communicate at night, seeming to issue from the shadowy corners of the cabin. Soon after the ghost spoke in a full-toned voice, day or night.

To put a halt to the accusations of trickery or ventriloquism on the part of Betsy, John Jr. brought in a doctor, who placed his hand over Betsy's mouth and listened at her throat while the ghost's voice chatted noisily from a far corner of the room. The doctor stated firmly that young Betsy was not connected to the sounds in any way.

Twelve-year-old Betsy began to suffer from seizures and fainting spells, similar to those that spirit mediums undergo while in or entering a trance. Observers noted that the spells came on at regular hours, just before the witch would put in an appearance. After Betsy recovered, the ghost would begin to speak. Since it had gained the ability to speak, the ghost had been outspoken in its dislike of John Bell, Betsy's father. "I'll keep after him until the end of his days!" the ghost often swore to visitors in the Bell home. "Old Jack Bell's days are numbered."

Even before the witch had begun to manifest in the Bell home by causing the rapping on the windows and undertaking the hair pulling that so disturbed the family, John Bell had complained of a strange pain in his throat. He described it as feeling like "a stick stuck crosswise," punching each side of his jaws. As the visitation of the aggressive ghost continued, Bell was often plagued by a tongue that swelled against his mouth so that he could neither talk nor eat for 10 or 15 hours.

Some researchers have suggested that the onset of John Bell's physical afflictions and his daughter's psychic persecution was no coincidence. In his writings of the Bell Witch, Dr. Nandor Fodor made the observation that the swelling of Bell's tongue suggests that he may have been keeping a dreadful secret that sought physical release. Fodor also speculated that Betsy, approaching puberty, may have undergone a shocking sexual experience for which her father was responsible. "It was probably to save her reason," Fodor wrote, "that a fragment of her mind was split off and became the Bell Witch."

Fodor's theory presents the case of the Bell Witch as an occurrence of poltergeist phenomena, which may account for the remarkable range and power of the witch. However, the Bell Witch could also have been a negative entity that was attracted to the psychic energies that had been projected by sexual shock, pubertal change, and a father's guilt.

So what exactly was the entity known as the Bell Witch? Where did it come from? When a visitor questioned the witch concerning its identity, it once answered: "I am a spirit who was once very happy, but who has been disturbed and made unhappy. I will remain in this house and worry old Jack Bell until I kill him."

Later, the witch declared itself to be the spirit of a Native American warrior, and it sent the family on a wild "bone chase" to gather up all of its skeletal remains. "If my bones are all put back together, I'll be able to rest in peace," the entity lied to them. When the Bell family admitted that they had been unable to find any of the bones of the old warrior, the witch cackled and informed them that she was really the ghost of old Kate Batts. Kate Batts had been an eccentric recluse who had been branded with the title of witch by the citizens of Clarksville. When the word spread that it was the ghost of old Kate who was haunting the Bells, the entire mystery became much more believable to several doubting neighbors.

The Bell home became even more crowded when members of the witch's ghost family moved in with her. Four nasty entities named Blackdog, Mathematics, Cypocryphy, and Jerusalem, each speaking in a distinctive voice of its own, made every night a maddening, raucous party during their stay with their "mother." The sounds of riotous laughter rattled the shingles of the Bell home, and witnesses noted the strong scent of whiskey permeating every room in the house.

The Bell Witch was adept at producing odd objects from thin air. Once, at one of Mrs. Bell's Bible study groups, the ladies were showered with fresh fruits. Betsy's friends were treated to bananas at one of her birthday parties. "Those came from the West Indies," the witch told the delighted girls. "I picked them myself."

Although John Bell was the butt of malicious pranks and cruel blows, Luce Bell was looked after solicitously by the witch. Once when Mrs. Bell was ill, the witch was heard telling Mrs. Bell to hold out her hands. She did as she was asked, and a large quantity of hazelnuts dropped into her palms. "Eat them, poor Luce," the witch instructed her. "They will do you good." When Luce Bell weakly protested that she did not have the strength to crack the nuts, the witch volunteered to perform the act on her behalf. Family members and neighbors watched in wide-eyed awe as the nuts cracked open and the meat was sorted from the shells.

Besides the materialization of fruits and nuts, the witch was also adept at producing pins and needles. Luce Bell was provided with enough pins to supply the entire county, but sometimes the witch would impishly hide them in bedclothes or in chair cushions, with their points out to jab an unsuspecting victim.

Betsy's favorite brother, John Jr., was the only member of the family besides Luce to receive decent treatment from the witch. He could even talk back to the witch and get away with his sass. On the other hand, Joel and Richard were often whipped unmercifully by the ghost, and Drewry was so frightened of the witch that he never married, fearing that the entity might someday return and single out his own family for particular attention.

While other members of the family may have feared the witch, Elizabeth and her father received the brunt of the witch's ill nature. Besides the physical acts that injured Betsy's body, her life was also greatly affected by the witch. The cruelest example of the hold the witch had over Betsy's life was how it forced the termination of her engagement to Joshua Gardner (also spelled "Gardiner" in some sources). The entity protested so violently when the engagement was announced that it begged John Jr. to help it break them up. The witch warned Betsy that she would never know a day of happiness if she married Joshua. The witch screamed at Joshua whenever he entered the Bell home and embarrassed both young people by shouting obscenities about them in front of their friends. Richard Bell noted in his diary that the "vile devil" never ceased to torment Betsy. The witch insulted her modesty, stuck pins in her body, pinched and bruised her flesh, slapped her cheeks, disheveled and tangled her hair.

Frank Miles, a close friend of the Bell family, learned of the witch's objection to Betsy's engagement and vowed to stand up to the evil spirit on her behalf. According to the family members who witnessed the duel, Miles challenged the witch to take any form it desired, and he would take it on. He made motions in the air as if warming up for a wrestling or a boxing match. "Just let me get a hold of you, and we'll soon send you packing," Miles roared. "I'm not afraid of an invisible windbag."

Suddenly Miles's head jerked backwards as if a solid slap had stung his cheeks. He put up his forearms to block a series of facial blows, then dropped his guard when he received a vicious punch in the stomach. He slumped against a wall, desperately shaking his head to recover his senses. As an elderly woman in her eighties, Elizabeth still remembered how the dear man Miles had "fairly shook the house, stamping on the floor, swearing terribly" in his attempt to drive the spirit out of her life. "Begone!" the Bell family heard the witch's voice warn their courageous friend. "Or I'll knock your block off!" Reluctantly, Miles picked up his hat and coat. A man couldn't fight an enemy he wasn't able to see.

Although the valiant Miles had been pummeled into submission by the witch, others were still willing to stand up to the notorious witch. Word reached John Bell's old friend General Andrew Jackson, none other than "Old Hickory" himself, that a malignant spirit was interfering in the course of Betsy and Joshua's true love. At the urging of his wife, Jackson set out for the Bell farm in the company of several servants, and both professional "witch layers" (witch hunters) and "ghost layers" (ghost hunters). Along the way, the party picked up a number of other rugged individuals who swore that they could handle the Bell Witch.

As the Jackson party neared the Bell farm, Jackson's driver was startled when the wheels of the general's coach suddenly froze and would not budge. Jackson ordered the men to put their backs to the coach in an attempt to move it, but when the combined strength of men and horses could not make the wheels budge an inch, the general began to suspect that something other than natural forces were at work. Cackling laughter from a nearby bush alerted the ghost hunters to the presence of the Bell Witch. The entity welcomed the party to its domain, then uttered a command that unfroze the wheels of the coach. The general and his men had lost the element of surprise. The witch knew that they were coming.

That night, in spite of their previous boasts of an easy conquest, both the witch layers and the ghost layers fled in terror when the witch attacked them. According to accounts of the incident, General Jackson told John Bell that fighting the witch was tougher than having faced the British at the Battle of New Orleans. Although Jackson had planned to stay until the ghost had been faced down, he decided to leave with his men because his little army of ghost chasers had suffered enough.

With the decisive defeat of her champions, Betsy had no choice other than to give in to the witch's demands and break her engagement with Joshua Gardner. On the night Betsy returned the engagement ring, the witch's laughter could be heard ringing triumphantly from every room in the house.

With Betsy's marriage plans terminated, the ghost began again to concentrate its energy on the destruction of John Bell. Richard was walking with his father when John Bell collapsed into a spasmodically convulsing heap. Young Richard was terrified by the agonies that beset his father; he later wrote that his facial contortions were so hideous that they seemed to transform him into "a very demon to swallow me up." John Bell was brought home to his bed, where he lay for several days in a very weakened condition. Even during the man's illness, the cruel entity would not leave him in peace; rather, it continued to torment him by slapping his face and throwing his legs into the air.

On the morning of December 19, 1820, John Bell lapsed into a deep stupor. John Jr. went quickly to the medicine cabinet to obtain his father's normal prescription, but in its place he found "a smoky looking vial, which was about one-third full of dark-colored liquid." The witch cackled that it was no use to try to revive Old Jack. She had him at last. John Bell never woke again.

When John Jr. demanded to know where the vial had come from, the witch smugly answered that it had placed it in the medicine cabinet earlier that night. "I gave Old Jack a big dose of it while he was asleep. I fixed him!" the entity laughed. John Jr. sent for a doctor. When the physician arrived, he asked one of the boys to fetch a cat from the barn. While John Jr. held the cat, the doctor dipped a straw into the dark vial, and wiped it on the animal's tongue. The cat jumped into the air, whirled about the floor, and died "very quick."

The witch sang bawdy songs all during John Bell's funeral and annoyed the assembled mourners with the sounds of its crude celebration throughout the man's last rites. After the death of John Bell, the witch behaved much better toward Betsy. It never again inflicted pain upon her and even began to address her in terms of endearment. The psychic energy that had nurtured the ghost appeared to be waning. During the rest of the winter of 1820 and on into the spring of 1821, the manifestations decreased steadily. Then, one night after an evening meal, a large ball of smoke appeared to roll down from the chimney of the fireplace out into the room. As it exploded, a voice told the family, "I'm going now. I will be gone for seven years."

By 1828 Betsy had entered into a successful marriage; John Jr. had married and farmed land of his own. Only Mrs. Bell, Joel, and Richard remained on the farm. When the ghost returned to haunt the family that year, as promised, the disturbances it created consisted mostly of elementary pranks—rappings, scratchings, and pulling covers off of beds. The members of the Bell family living in the cabin agreed to ignore the unwanted guest. Their psychology worked, and the witch left them after two weeks of pestering them for attention. The entity sought out John Jr. and told him that it would return to one of his descendants in "one hundred years and seven."

Dr. Charles Bailey Bell should have been the recipient of the witch's unwelcome return visit, but Dr. Bell and his family survived the year 1935 without hearing the slightest unexplained scratch or rapping. Dr. Bell wrote the official record of the mysterious disturbances endured by his ancestors in *The Bell Witch: A Mysterious Spirit.*

Dr. Bell noted the precognitive powers of the witch in a series of "wonderful things" and prophecies that the entity revealed to his grandfather, John Bell, Jr. According to Dr. Bell, the witch predicted the Civil War, the emancipation of the slaves, the acceleration of the United States as a world power, the two world wars (the date for World War II was off by only four years), and the destruction of our civilization by "rapidly expanding heat, followed by a mighty explosion." The final prediction the witch provided was that the world as we know it would end; the witch provided no date for this to occur.

By the beginning of the twenty-first century, a private trust owned the land where the Bell family's abandoned cabin stands, and visitors were not welcome to explore the property. The only site associated with the Bell Witch that remains open to the public is the nearby Bell Witch Cave.

THE NASTY GHOSTS OF AMHERST

One night in September 1878, 18-year-old Esther Cox woke her 22-year-old sister Jane and asked if she felt something in bed with them. Although the two-story cottage they lived in on Princess Street in Amherst, Nova Scotia, Canada, was kept clean and neat, the possibility of a mouse invading their bed was not impossible. The two girls jumped out of bed with a scream and began to search their mattress. Jane spotted the straw of the mattress moving about and concluded that a rodent must be trying to make a nest.

The two sisters set to beating the mattress vigorously in an attempt to drive the tiny intruder out of their bed, but no mouse retreated from the straw of the mattress. The girls watched the mattress for a bit, detected no further movement, and concluded that the mouse must have escaped without their seeing it. Esther and Jane decided they had better get back to sleep before they awakened the rest of the household. The pair lived in the home of their sister Olive, who had married Daniel Teed. Daniel and Olive had two sons: Willie, five, and George, 13 months. Daniel's brother John Teed and William Cox, the brother of Olive, Jane, and Esther, also shared the Teed house. As they had not woken anyone as they searched for the mouse that disturbed their sleep, the girls decided to make no mention of the incident the next morning, as it would only result in laughter and teasing from John and William.

On the following night, Esther and Jane heard a loud scratching from under their bed. They lit a lamp to investigate, and a large cardboard box filled with patchwork suddenly flew out from under the bed. When Jane put it back in its place, it was once again thrust into the air. The girls were perplexed by the energetic "mouse" and began to call for help. Daniel Teed groggily slipped on a pair of trousers, entered the girls' bedroom, and kicked the box back under the bed, where it stayed. Grumpily, he cautioned them about repeating their little joke.

The girls were quite indignant at breakfast the next morning, when they were heartily teased by the whole family. The young women both felt that they were much too old to be considered empty-headed tricksters. That night the mood in the house quickly changed; as the disturbances became much more dramatic, those living in the Teed residence could no longer consider them a joke. When Esther woke up in the middle of that third evening, she gasped and cried out to Jane for help, as she feared for her life.

Jane lit a lamp, then nearly dropped it in horror as she took in the ghastly appearance of her sister. Esther's complexion had become a bright scarlet in color, and her eyes bulged from her skull. Her hair seemed to be standing on its end, and her flesh was extremely hot to the touch. Her entire body seemed to be swelling, as if someone were inflating her with a pump. Then the walls of their room began to rumble and shake, as if thunder had erupted within them.

Daniel and Olive appeared at the door to the girls' room. They had been awakened by the loud noises and wondered what on earth had been causing them. They were shocked at Esther's inflated appearance, then puzzled, when the girl's body suddenly seemed to begin deflating. Soon her flesh had returned to normal form and shape, and an exhausted Esther returned to her bed and slept peacefully. The family resolved not to say anything about the mysterious disturbances to anyone outside of the household.

Secrecy soon became an impossibility, however. The next night, the bedclothes flew off the girls and landed in a heap in a far corner of the room. Esther once again began to swell, and when John Teed came to investigate, a pillow shot from the bed and struck him full in the face. The young man could not be coaxed to re-enter the room, but the remainder of the household sat on the edge of the bed, using all their weight and strength to keep blankets over swollen Esther. While they fought with the bedclothes, a series of sharp explosions began to sound about the room. As the mysterious eruptions crashed and banged, Esther began to deflate just as she had done the night before.

Due to the inexplicable events of that evening, Daniel Teed resolved that he would have the family physician, Dr. Caritte, in attendance the following night. When the doctor arrived on the scene in preparation for the violent attacks, he examined Esther thoroughly. After having taken her pulse, he stated that the girl seemed to be suffering from some kind of nervous shock. The doctor's words seemed to be the signal the phenomena had been waiting for. Esther's pillow expanded as if it were a balloon suddenly filled with air. Although he had been frightened from the room on the night before, an emboldened John Teed re-entered the bizarre fray and grasped for the pillow. As if intimidated by his courage and his lunge toward it, the pillow deflated. But then, as if mocking its opponent, the pillow reinflated and wrenched itself from John Teed's closed fists.

The assembled members of the household and Dr. Caritte were drawn to the sounds of scratching on the ceiling above Esther's bed. Incredulously, they witnessed writing forming on the plaster. "*Esther Cox,*" wrote the invisible hand, "*you are mine to kill.*"

When Dr. Caritte returned the next evening, he admitted that what seemed to be afflicting Esther was a phenomenon beyond his medical knowledge. But as he knew she was experiencing the symptoms of nervous excitement, he had brought her a powerful sedative, the only thing that he could possibly prescribe. The effect of Dr. Caritte's bromide was completely different than what he had hoped for. As soon as the drug had eased Esther into a deep slumber, the noises began, louder than they had ever been. It sounded as though someone were up on the roof, attempting to pound his way into the house by means of a heavy sledgehammer. The doctor retreated shortly after midnight, and as he walked away down the street, he could still hear the powerful blows shaking the Teed home.

The disturbances continued in this manner for three weeks, with Dr. Caritte attending Esther three times a day, although his attempts to help her were in vain. Then, one night, the girl fell into a trance and spewed out the whole story of how she had escaped an attempted assault on her honor. Bob McNeal, a man who had worked with Daniel and John Teed and William Cox at the Amherst shoe factory, had arrived at the Teed home one evening and requested the pleasure of Esther's company on a buggy ride. He had only laughed when she had expressed her reluctance at going for a ride when the sky looked so black.

They had not ridden far when McNeal pulled into a wooded area outside of Amherst. He had wanted her to get down from the buggy and go with him into the woods. She had refused. Suddenly, McNeal leaped out of the buggy, jerked a pistol from a coat pocket, and leveled it at her breast. Either she came with him into the woods or he would kill her. Esther told him not to be a fool. Her honor could not be bought by the sight of a madman waving a pistol at her. McNeal cursed her with a foul stream of profanity. He cocked the hammer of the pistol, and for an awful moment, she wondered if he might not make good on his threat. Then the sound of wagon wheels began to creak toward them; another couple had sought the cover of the woods. McNeal thrust the pistol back into a pocket and climbed back into the driver's seat. Sullenly he stared at her, his eyes telling of terrible embarrassment and violent anger. He cracked the reins over the horses' backs and drove at a breakneck speed back toward the village. On the way home, it had begun to rain, but as if to punish her for not appeasing his lust, McNeal refused to put the hood of the buggy over them. He delivered her, soaking wet, to the Teed household at ten o'clock that night.

The family had known nothing of Esther's secret until that moment. When Esther regained consciousness, Jane told her what she had said, and Esther confessed that it was all true. Interestingly, McNeal had not been seen since the night that he had tried to seduce Esther. He had not reported for work at the shoe factory the morning after the attempted attack, and his landlady said that he had paid for his lodging and left. Evidently, shame for what he had tried to do to Esther and fear of the consequences had driven McNeal out of Amherst. He could not have known that Esther had not told her brother-in-law (who was his foreman at the shoe factory), or her sisters Olive and Jane. Esther had kept the memory of that terrible night tightly repressed and bottled up inside her.

"Could it be," Olive wondered, "that Bob McNeal was killed or took his own life and has come back to haunt Esther?" As if on cue, three loud knocks sounded on the walls of the room. Jane was slightly conversant with spiritualism and suggested that whatever it was that had been bothering their sister might be trying to establish contact with them. This comment, too, was met by the thudding of three raps.

Dr. Caritte quickly devised a simple code to communicate with the ghost. One rap was to represent "no," two raps would signify "no answer" or "doubtful," and three raps would stand for "yes." The ghost immediately used the code to answer elementary questions put forth by the household, but it ignored all attempts on the part of Dr. Caritte to establish a pattern of clues to determine the source of its existence.

By now the secret of the phenomena could no longer be confined to the walls of the Teed home. For one thing, neighbors and passersby had heard the strange sounds and had inquired what the cause was. Village clergymen began either to fulminate against Esther from their pulpits or to defend her. The Teeds' minister, Reverend R. A. Temple of the Wesleyan Methodist Church, had himself witnessed a pail of cold water suddenly begin to boil in Esther's presence.

Daniel Teed had just applied for police protection to keep the curious from turning his home into a public spectacle when Esther contracted diphtheria, and all manifestations ceased for a period of two weeks. Upon her recovery, she was sent to recuperate from her illness at the home of Mrs. Snowden, another married sister who lived in Sackville, New Brunswick, Canada. The phenomena did not follow Esther to Sackville during her stay.

When she returned to the Teed home in Amherst, everyone hoped that Esther was cured of whatever had ailed her. Daniel Teed had never been very sympathetic to Esther during the onslaught of the mysterious phenomena and had seemed more concerned about "what the neighbors would say" than he had been about her health. As an additional measure to help guard against a return of the unwelcome phenomena, and to allow Jane a new start, the Teeds gave Esther and Jane a new room.

On the first night of Esther's return to the Teed residence, lighted matches began to fall from the ceiling. All of the tiny flames were extinguished, but the incendiary activity had by no means ended. Rappings began to shake the walls, and by using the code that Dr. Caritte had developed to communicate with the strange presence, the family learned that the entity intended to set their house on fire. As if to signal that it meant business, a dress jumped from its place on a hanger and burst into flames as it slid under Esther's bed. For three days, the entire household kept vigil against the ghost's threat of destroying their home.

On the fourth day, just when they were beginning to think that the entity's threat might have been idle after all, Olive smelled smoke coming from the cellar. Grabbing one of the buckets of water that they kept at the ready, she and Esther found a pile of wood shavings blazing in a corner. The contents of the bucket seemed to have little effect on the flames. The sisters fled from the house, screaming for help, and ran into a passing stranger, who fortunately had enough presence of mind to beat the fire out with a doormat. Rappings were one thing, Daniel Teed decreed that night at dinner, but fires were something else. If their house had caught fire and the wind had been coming from a certain direction, half of the town of Amherst could have gone up in smoke. Teed said that he was sorry, but he just couldn't allow Esther to stay with them any longer. Olive may have looked askance at her husband, but there was little that she could say. He had, after all, been remarkably patient with his sister-in-law.

John W. White offered to employ Esther in his restaurant and provide lodging for her, but the well-intentioned gentleman soon regretted his decision to come to Esther's aid. The heavy door of his large kitchen stove refused to stay closed, even when braced by an axe handle. Metal objects clung to Esther's body as if she were a living magnet. Metal utensils that came into contact with her flesh became too hot for customers to hold. The furniture shifted about wherever she walked, and a 50-pound box once shot 15-feet into the air. White soon appealed to Daniel Teed to take Esther back because she was ruining his business.

Captain James Beck invited Esther to come to stay with him and his wife at St. John, New Brunswick, Canada. He had read of what had come to be known as the "Amherst Mystery" and wished to study the alleged agent of the phenomena at leisure and in his own home. However, Esther proved to be a big disappointment to Captain Beck and the groups of medical men and scientists who had gathered to examine her. For three weeks, the girl did nothing other than tell wild tales of three ghosts, "Peter Cox," "Maggie Fisher," and "Bob Nickle," who appeared regularly to threaten her with fires and stabbings.

Upon her return to Amherst, Esther spent another quiet sojourn at the farm of a Mr. and Mrs. Van Ambergh. As it seemed that the phenomena no longer plagued her, Esther was once again welcomed back into the home of Daniel Teed. Unfortunately, she had barely unpacked her things when the disturbances began with renewed vigor.

Teed felt that the situation with his sister-in-law was without resolve when a possible solution presented itself. A magician named Walter Hubbell offered not only to attempt to exorcise the ghost that afflicted Esther but also to pay rent if he might stay in the house and observe the disturbances firsthand. The day that Hubbell moved into the Teeds' home was marked by a particularly violent onset of phenomena. His umbrella was jerked out of his hand and tossed into the air. A large butcher knife appeared and menacingly headed in his direction. Whenever he entered a room, all the chairs therein would fall over or dance about noisily. "The ghosts don't like you," Esther said finally, by way of understatement.

Hubbell was undaunted, even pleased, that the manifestations had become so robust since his arrival. Throughout his six-week stay, Hubbell witnessed a *potpourri* of haunting phenomena, including ghosts whistling and drumming "Yankee Doodle"; furniture moving about and shaking on its own; the blasting of what sounded very much like a trumpet, although no one in the home owned such an instrument; and the subsequent materialization of a very tangible German silver trumpet no one had ever seen before.

Hubbell's stay in the Teed home was not without its dangers. Several knives and a large glass paperweight were thrown at him by the invisible intruders, the latter narrowly missing his head. He also sustained a variety of bruises from his encounters with the furniture, which would move about on its own. Esther, too, seemed to suffer more personal attacks after the observer had arrived in the house. Once, 30 pins materialized before her eyes and drove themselves into different parts of her body. On another occasion, after Esther had returned to the house from church, an old bone that had been lying in the yard flew toward her head, cutting it open.

Hubbell had not been completely honest with the Teeds when he told them that be wished only to observe the disturbances caused by the ghosts. As an accomplished stage magician, the man had found himself completely awed by the girl's ability to produce genuine spirit phenomena. He envisioned Esther on tour, with him acting as her manager. He had also begun to take copious notes for a book that he intended to write on the Amherst mystery. It didn't take Hubbell more than a few hours to convince Daniel Teed that he should be permitted to make all the arrangements necessary to put his sister-in-law on the stage. Olive and Jane objected to their sister being on public display, but Teed squelched all arguments by pointing out that their home had been wrecked. Esther had caused all the destruction they witnessed around them by setting her ghosts loose on them, Teed complained. It seemed only right and proper that she should pay them back in some way for all the grief that she had caused the family.

In an attempt to prove that his scheme would benefit the Teed family, Hubbell rented a large auditorium and sold tickets to a curious crowd who had come to see Esther produce "wonders and miracles" on stage, but Esther's debut was a disaster. Not a single supernormal act took place, and the restless audience was soon chanting for the return of their money.

Daniel Teed had endured his last humiliation. He ordered both Esther and Hubbell from his home. The magician shrugged his shoulders and left for St. John, New Brunswick, to begin writing his book on the Amherst mystery. Esther was taken in by the Van Amberghs, who had not suffered during her last visit and who had grown fond of the girl.

Shortly before the publication of the book on the Amherst mystery, Hubbell tried to contact Esther by mail. He was shocked to receive a letter from Jane, informing him that her unfortunate sister was serving a jail sentence for arson. She had been charged with burning the barn of a farmer named Arthur Davison, for whom she had been working as a servant girl. This alleged barn burning was the last record of the nasty deeds of Esther's fiery spirits.

Hubbell's book, published during the latter part of 1879, was an instantaneous success, and by 1916 the ghost story had gone into ten editions. The magician had accomplished what be had set out to do: make a great deal of money on someone else's real magic.

Esther went on to marry Mr. Adams of Springdale, Nova Scotia, Canada. Her second husband was Mr. Shanahan of Brocton, Massachusetts. From time to time, Esther endured some supernatural manifestations, but nothing of significance. Esther Cox Shanahan died in 1912.

ATTACKED BY AN INVISIBLE MONSTER WITH FANGS

The teenaged girl writhed on the floor of the Manila, Philippines, jail cell and moaned as if she were in terrible pain. Suddenly, she sat upright, her eyes wide, her arms flailing at an invisible foe. "Here he comes again!" she screamed. "The monster has come again to bite me!" The police officer who had been posted to observe 18-year-old Clarita Villanueva shook his head sadly at the distraught young woman's hysterical screams. He did not believe her wild tale of some bug-eyed monster with a black cape that flew around trying to chew her up.

When the police had found Clarita, she had been walking about on the streets of Manila, sobbing for someone to protect her from a monster. Her strange behavior had attracted a small crowd of observers from a nearby tavern, who had stood by cheering her on as she struggled with her invisible attacker. She had been taken into custody under the suspicion of being either a drug addict or an alcoholic. It was a warm, sultry night in May 1951, just the kind of night that the police knew would bring out all of the city's undesirables. This girl was obviously one of them, the officer at the scene thought to himself.

When police medical officer Dr. Mariana Lara gave the teenager a cursory examination, he diagnosed her as having suffered an epileptic episode and advised that she be closely watched so she could not injure herself. He left the police station quite sure in his diagnosis.

"Don't worry," the police officer guarding Clarita's cell reassured her as she crouched in terror behind the bunk in her cell. "No monster can get you in there. He couldn't get through the bars."

"But he is coming!" Clarita shrieked. "And he is drifting right through the bars!"

Then, before the officer's startled eyes, livid teeth marks began to appear on Clarita's upper arms and shoulders. He quickly opened the cell door, knelt beside the girl and helped her to her feet. The girl screamed again, and more bleeding wounds and welts appeared on her arm. It was as if an invisible monster had wrapped its entire mouth around her slim arm and had sunk its teeth deep into her flesh. The officer helped Clarita into the hall, and together they fled the cell to seek out his captain. The captain quickly assessed that the situation was far beyond anything his expertise as a law enforcement officer had prepared him for. Within a short time, the chief of police, the city's mayor, and the medical examiner had all gathered around Clarita, attempting to decide what could be done to help the girl.

Mayor Arsenio Lacson and the chief of police had already completed their examination of Clarita by the time Dr. Lara returned to the jail, muttering his disapproval at being dragged out of bed in the middle of the night to observe a young woman whom he had already diagnosed as suffering from epileptic seizures, and obviously inflicting wounds upon herself.

Self-inflicted? The two men frowned at the medical examiner. How could she bite herself on the back of her neck? Gently, Mayor Lacson questioned Clarita while the doctor examined her. What was attacking her? The girl sobbed that she certainly did not know its name. It resembled a man with a long, flowing black cape. It was very ugly and came at her with its fangs bared and ready to sink into her flesh. The medical examiner traced a forefinger over the indentations in the girl's skin. They certainly appeared to be the prints of teeth. And, he had to admit, the girl did not appear to be drunk or under the influence of any drugs.

The police chief noted the date, May 10, 1951, on the calendar. A religious man, he had briefly entertained the notion that this might be the onset of a manifestation of stigmata, a replication of the wounds that Christ suffered during the crucifixion, but there were no special holy days in the Philippines during the month of May.

Clarita spent the rest of the night on a bench in the front office of the police station, closely attended by an officer who bad been assigned the task of keeping watch for a monster he had not seen with his own eyes. The next morning, the girl was brought to court to face the charges of vagrancy that had been levied against her. There, before the incredulous eyes of the entire court, Clarita endured another attack by her invisible monster.

Reporters rushed to stand beside her for a closer look. Dr. Lara took the girl in his arms as she swooned from the excruciating pain of the unseen jaws that had attached themselves to her flesh. "This girl is definitely not having an epileptic fit," Dr. Lara told the reporters. "These teeth prints are real, and they are most certainly not self-inflicted." There was no need to attest to the reality of the teeth marks to the reporters. They were serving as startled witnesses to the cruel indentations that were appearing on the girl's arms, shoulders, palms, and neck. Dr. Lara told a police officer to send at once for the mayor and the archbishop. "This is outside my realm of physiology and medicine," he said. "Perhaps a clergyman will be of more value in this case than a doctor."

By the time Mayor Lacson arrived, the unfortunate girl had become a veritable mass of deeply embedded teeth prints and swollen and bruised flesh.

"You poor girl," the mayor commiserated, taking one of Clarita's hands into his own. Then, while he held her hand, deep teeth marks appeared on opposite sides of her index finger, as if a hungry fiend were trying to chew the digit off. Dr. Lara called for an ambulance, and both he and Mayor Lacson rode with her to the hospital. The driver thought that Clarita was a victim of some horrible beating until the teeth began to attack her in the automobile. He drove the ambulance through Manila traffic, one eye on the road and the other on the tortured girl in the back. Throughout the 15-minute ride to the hospital, Clarita shouted that there were two creatures attacking her, each of them with large, baglike eyes and awful teeth. As the doctor and mayor watched in horror, teeth marks appeared on both sides of the girl's throat and on the hands that Mayor Lacson held in a vain attempt to comfort her.

The unexplained attacks ceased when Clarita entered the hospital. When she was released six weeks later, she had recovered her health almost completely. Clarita never again suffered from the terrible invisible jaws that had torn at her flesh, but her body would forever bear the scars of those vicious attacks by her invisible assailant. "What happened to Clarita Villanueva is a complete mystery, something that simply defies rational explanation," Dr. Lara commented. "I don't mind saying that I was scared out of my wits."

DEVIL VOICES AND VICIOUS DARK, SWIRLING ENTITIES

The Personal Experience of Randy

"**I**n this one house we lived in for a while, we were troubled by entities that seemed set upon us by a curse of black magic. From time to time, we would see a hooded figure moving about the house. Once, my daughter Cindy saw the figure with its cowl down around its shoulders; it appeared to be the image of an older man with thinning white hair on the sides, and bald at the top. On another occasion Cindy saw the hooded figure with some kind of cat-like creature that stood about three feet tall, with pointed ears and a long tail. The hooded figure stopped and looked at her, then moved on and disappeared.

"One night in her room, Cindy heard a whole bunch of voices whispering, but she couldn't understand them. They were all jumbled together. Another time when she was in the kitchen, someone said her name right in her ear, although no one was in the room with her. Recently, she heard a voice that she described as a demon voice: throaty, hoarse, and very mean. It said to her, 'Cindy, show yourself to me!' She could pinpoint the exact location the voice had come from. It unnerved her so much that she fled her room and wouldn't sleep until the sun came up. So far, that's the last encounter that she's had.

"I've only seen the hooded figure that bothered Cindy once. The creature that bothered me was a black, floating, swirling mass, about four feet high and three feet wide, and [could] change shape. I only saw it about four times, but I would wake up sometimes and feel it sitting on my chest, choking me. I actually felt it when I grabbed it and threw it off of me. When I got out of bed to confront it, it disappeared into a wall.

"One night about two in the morning, something hit the wall with such force that it knocked all the pictures off the dresser and cracked the dresser mirror. It looked like there had been an earthquake in that one particular spot. Even the pictures hanging on the wall were knocked on the floor.

"Sometimes I would feel the thing behind me, watching me. It always attacked at the most vulnerable times. But I always confronted it. I wasn't afraid of it. But we decided to move after a month or so to keep all of our furniture from being smashed to pieces by the thing."

AN ENTITY SAVED HIS BABY SISTER BUT TORMENTS FRIENDS

The Personal Experience of Will

"My father's side of the family have a good-sized farm in North Carolina with a large house. Around 1986, when my sister was learning to walk, she managed to crawl up a long set of steps that lead to the third story of the house when no one was looking. When my Mom and Grandma couldn't find my sister, they rushed about the house looking for her, and found her just as she was going to attempt to walk down the stairs. As Mom and Grandma stood, unable to help, at the bottom of the steps, my sister began tilting as if she was going to fall. However, *something* grabbed the collar of her shirt, and she was pulled backwards to safety. No apparition was seen, but the collar of her shirt clearly was pulled back by something invisible.

"We often hear strange noises in the home, and we have occasionally seen eerie shadows. However, the most disturbing events occurred around 1994 when my friend Matt went to the farm with us to celebrate my twelfth birthday. Matt was 13 or 14, and because of the spooky stories that we had told him, he was visibly scared once he saw the old farm house.

"We drew pictures of airplanes in the living room the first night he stayed there, and before we went to bed upstairs, we placed them in a neat pile. We also turned off the light in the living room. After we had been in our upstairs bedroom for a while, Matt said he needed to use the bathroom. I walked downstairs with him to make sure 'nothing got him.' We walked into the living room, and to our shock we found our drawings strewn about, and the light on.

"Matt was even more shaken, and insisted that he wanted to sleep in the same bed with me, in case something should attack him. The next morning, he said that he had heard something come up the steps in the middle of the night. He heard it go through the room in which my older sister was sleeping, then enter the center room of the third story where my parents were sleeping, and then enter our room.

"Matt said that the ghost walked up to the foot of the bed, then pressed down hard on him, making it impossible for him to yell. He said that although he managed to nudge me, I sleepily responded by mumbling, thinking that my younger sister was bothering me. Matt was relieved that nothing further happened to him the rest of the trip, or on following visits to the farm.

"However, one of my other friends once came with us to the farm, and became so frightened upon entering an upstairs room that he shook visibly for hours on end and was unable to sleep. He wouldn't even let us turn out the lights until 1:00 A.M. As before, though, everything was normal on the second night of the visit."

5
Spirit Parasites That Possessed

After a careful consideration of nasty entities that attack people, such as those presented in chapter four, perhaps we are now ready to face the grim possibility that there are some spirit beings that have become agents of evil and wish to possess the bodies of the living.

Many men and women who were granted the blessing of seeing the ghostly image of their loved ones pass to the "other side," or who received messages of comfort from recently deceased individuals, have often told us that those souls were met by angelic beings or more advanced spirits who assisted them in evolving to higher planes of awareness. As these souls progressed, all of their ties to their prior physical existence faded into irrelevance. Sensual memories of their previous material life were forgotten.

But, on occasion, it seems that something goes wrong on a soul's evolution into the light. If individuals have spent their entire lives on Earth in pursuit of sensual pleasures, their psychic, soul personalities may experience the same hedonistic drives after death. They may undergo traumatic shocks when they slowly realize that they no longer have physical bodies, and may attempt to return to all of their old, pleasurable places. If there were additional negative factors in an individual's life, such as a bitter dispute left unsettled, an old score left unpaid, or an argument left unresolved, then these restless spirits might hunger to return to the physical world in order to obtain revenge.

Hedonistic or vengeful discarnate spirits refuse to allow the natural order of spiritual progression and their evolution to higher levels of awareness to ease their desires, pain, and anger. They wish only to return to the world of the living. These disembodied entities will seek out vulnerable humans to whom they can attach themselves.

Humans are most susceptible to invasion by spirit entities at the following times: when they are fatigued and exhausted; when they have undergone a period of severe emotional stress, turmoil, or anger; and when they are under the influ-

[111]

ence of drugs, alcohol, or any other mind-altering substances. Young people, with their unfettered imaginations and undisciplined lives, are also very susceptible to possession, especially if they are excited, even titillated, by the lure of exploring the unknown through devices such as the Ouija board. Venturing into the dark areas of the occult or attempting communication with spirits become especially dangerous when attempted by those who have not taken the time to study the arcane. Explorations into the world of shadows require discipline and experience with the precautions that must be exercised before venturing into realms that can be very dangerous. If undisciplined, untutored people should be under the influence of drugs or alcohol when they are trying to make contact with the spirit world, the result may be temporary or extensive possession by a spirit entity who enthusiastically takes advantage of the psychic doorway that has been unknowingly opened by the unprepared.

In addition to spirits of the dead that take over the minds and bodies of people who are emotionally or physically weak, there also appear to be discarnate entities that have never been human but who strongly desire to occupy the body of a man or a woman. Nonhuman entities want to feel the emotions and sensual expressions that are unique to the human experience. These beings very often identify themselves as agents of evil. Traditionally, they have been called demons. I choose to label them as spirit parasites, nonphysical beings from other dimensions of reality that have the ability to seize the controlling mechanism of a host body, undermine the victim's will, and direct the enslaved human to perform harmful acts against himself and others.

DR. WILSON VAN DUSEN ON THE HIERARCHY OF SPIRITS

Psychologist Wilson Van Dusen, Ph.D., has developed theories regarding reality and mysticism through empiric research. His books include *The Presence of Other Worlds* (1994), *Testimony to the Invisible: Essays on Swedenborg* (1995), and *Beauty, Wonder, and the Mystical World* (1999). For anyone interested in examining ghosts, spirits, and other paranormal phenomena from as broad a perspective as possible, Van Dusen's research is rich, powerful, and thought-provoking.

Van Dusen is a scholar of the life and works of Emanuel Swedenborg (1688–1772), an eighteenth-century intellectual colossus and Renaissance man. Swedenborg wrote 150 books in 17 sciences; was an expert in numerous crafts; was an accomplished musician and politician and a prolific inventor; and was fluent in nine languages. Those who recognize his name today usually think of Swedenborg as a Swedish mystic who claimed that he had daily communication with angels, demons, and other inhabitants of the unseen world and whose experiences with remarkable psychic phenomena were well documented.

The untrained novice should avoid use of items like the ouija board, which will often attract lesser entities.

Through the course of his study and research, Van Dusen found what he believed to be evidence supporting one of Swedenborg's most unusual doctrines: that the lives of human beings are dependent on a relationship with the hierarchy of spirits. In his position as a clinical psychologist in a state mental hospital, Van Dusen set out to describe his patients' hallucinations as faithfully as possible. Although he noticed similarities between the descriptions given by his mental patients and Swedenborg's discussions of the relationships of humans to spirits, it was not until three years after Van Dusen had completed collecting data from his patients that he discovered the striking similarities between what his patients had shared with him in the twentieth century and what Swedenborg described in his accounts centuries earlier. In his opinion, Swedenborg's descriptions of experiences with what we today call the "paranormal" seemed to mirror his own patients' experiences and help explain otherwise puzzling aspects of hallucinations.

After dealing with hundreds of individuals who suffered from hallucinations, schizophrenia, alcoholism, brain damage, and senility, Van Dusen discovered that he was able to communicate with the hallucinations his patients endured. He began to look for patients who were able to distinguish between their own thoughts and the products of their hallucinations. The doctor told the patients that he wished to gain as accurate a description of their experiences as possible. He promised no special reward and offered no hope for recovery. Some patients, he learned, were embarrassed by what they heard or saw. In other instances, the hallucinations were reluctant to interact with Van Dusen, as they were frightened of the psychologist. Once he had reassured the patient and the hallucination, Van Dusen attempted to establish a relationship with both his patients and their hallucinations, which remained invisible to him.

Van Dusen's methodology was to interview his patients or their hallucinations directly. He instructed the patient to give a word-for-word account of what the voices answered or what was seen. In this way, the psychologist could hold long dialogues with a patient's hallucinations, recording both questions and answers. Van Dusen's only purpose was to come to as accurate a description as possible of the patient's experiences, treating the hallucinations as reality because that was what they were to the patient.

On numerous occasions, Van Dusen found that he was engaged in conversation with hallucinations and that the dialogue was far above the patient's level of comprehension. He found this to be especially true when he contacted the higher orders of "hallucinations," which he discovered to contain and exist in a symbolical depth beyond the patient's normal understanding. The psychologist also learned that in most cases the hallucinations had come upon the patients very suddenly. A consistent finding was that the patients believed that they had somehow established contact with another world, dimension, or order of beings.

Van Dusen soon learned that all of his patients objected to the term "hallucination." Each had coined his own term, such as the "Other Order," the "Eavesdroppers," and so forth. The voices the patients heard were completely audible and human languages and on occasion would assume the qualities of someone known to the patient in an attempt to deceive them. Such pranks and the shouting of vile and obscene messages and threats were the work of the "lower order" of entities.

Members of the lower order suggested lewd acts and encouraged the patient to indulge in them—then they would scold the patient for having even considered such thoughts. These beings sought to find a weak point of conscience and work on it interminably. According to Van Dusen, "They invade every nook and cranny of privacy, work on every weakness and credibility, claim awesome powers, lie, make promises, and then undermine the patients' will. They never have a personal identity, though they accept most names or identities given them." Van Dusen found the lower order consistently antireligious, and some actively obstructed the patient's religious practices. Occasionally they would refer to themselves as demons and speak of hell.

The higher order of hallucinations stood in direct contrast to such demonic manifestations, but Van Dusen found that they made up only a fifth or less of the patient's experiences. The higher order respects the patient's freedom and does not work against his will. While the lower order prattles on endlessly, the higher order seldom speaks. Van Dusen also discovered that the higher order is much more likely to be symbolic, religious, supportive, genuinely instructive, and communicate directly with the inner feelings of the patient. In general the higher order is richer than the patient's normal experience. The psychologist likened the higher order to Carl Jung's theory of archetypes, whereas he compared the lower order to Freud's concept of the id. "In contrast to the lower order, the higher order thinks in something like universal ideas, in ways that are richer and more complex than the patient's own mode of thought," Van Dusen said. The communications from the higher order can be very powerful emotionally and carry an almost inexpressible ring of truth. "The higher order tends to enlarge a patient's values, something like a very wise and considerate instructor," he commented.

After intensive study, Van Dusen concluded that there were a number of points of similarity between Swedenborg's description of a spiritual hierarchy and his own findings. Van Dusen's patients acted independently of each other and yet gave similar accounts. "They also agree on every particular I could find with Swedenborg's account," he said. "My own findings were established years before I really examined Swedenborg's position in this matter." In Van Dusen's opinion, it seemed remarkable that, "over two centuries of time, men of very different cultures, working under entirely different circumstances, on quite different people could come to such similar findings.... Because of this I am inclined to speculate that we are looking at a process which transcends cultures and remains stable over time."

Van Dusen also wondered whether the hallucinations of his patients, described by the vast majority of his colleagues and psychological literature as being "detached pieces of the unconscious," and the phenomenon of spiritual possession "might not simply be two ways of describing the same process. Are they really spirits or pieces of one's own unconscious?"

Van Dusen reflected that it may be necessary to change how we approach an understanding of reality, because, "as Swedenborg has indicated, our lives may be the little free space at the confluence of giant higher and lower spiritual hierarchies." Humans contend that we have free will, but in actuality, we could be "freely poised between good and evil" and under the influence of cosmic forces most of us don't even believe exist. The decisions made by human beings, believing that they are exercising their free will, may actually be, "resultant of other forces."

Most people find the thought that they might be at the mercy of unseen forces very discomforting, and they will argue, quite forcefully, that they have free will to choose their own destiny. Others who have come face to face with the unknown are less certain and are willing to ponder the possibility that entities from some other dimension of reality may seek to influence, disrupt, or control our lives.

POSSESSED BY SPIRITS FOR 26 YEARS

Shortly before the two priests were to begin the exorcism in the convent, Father Theophilus Riesinger, the exorcist, complimented Father Joseph Steiger for having the bravery to allow him to perform the rites in his parish. "The devil does not deal softly with those who attempt to interfere in his work," Father Riesinger said solemnly.

The two men had been friends for many years, and since the woman afflicted by demonic possession lived near Father Steiger's parish, Father Riesinger had prevailed on him to allow the convent in his Earling, Iowa, parish to be used as the place in which to conduct the exorcism. According to Father Riesinger, Anna, the woman who lay quietly in a room awaiting the holy rites, had been the victim of violent and loathsome demonic attentions since she was 14 years old. On several occasions, she had tried to commit suicide in order to rid herself of the terrible voices that screamed in her ears. Now the poor creature was 40 years old. Marriage hadn't helped her; dozens of doctors hadn't helped her; someone *had* to help her.

Yet Father Steiger had to admit to his friend that it seemed strange that, in 1928, two priests were about to begin the ancient rites of exorcism in an attempt to cast out a devil in, of all places, Earling, Iowa. Although he believed the case to be genuine and he had deep faith that Father Riesinger would in some manner be able to give the poor woman some peace, he still couldn't help thinking that the whole process seemed so medieval.

But what else could be done? Here was a woman who could not receive the sacraments because of taunting voices in her head that mocked her; a once-pious young girl who could not even go to confession without attempting to strangle the confessor; a woman who never got past the eighth grade but could give a literal translation of Latin prayers and correct her priest when he mispronounced a word. The bishop had been studying this case since 1902, 26 years prior, so no one could accuse him of having made a hasty decision when he declared Anna's affliction to be, unmistakably, one of diabolic possession.

That was why Father Riesinger had been sent to Iowa to conduct a rite almost forgotten by clergy and laity alike; a rite that could not be conducted without the full approval of church superiors. Father Riesinger was a cleric who had long since been convinced that the world was very different from what most people believed, and that the modern age had not succeeded in altering the basic truths and balances that were presented in the scriptural texts. In his view of reality, the struggle of Good versus Evil was still very much a part of contemporary existence. With God's good help, he believed they could rid the woman of the demons that possessed her.

On September 1 the exorcism began. Father Steiger stepped aside to allow Father Riesinger to enter the room at the end of the hall, where the possessed woman lay afflicted. The exorcist swept past him in the austere hooded robe he wore as a member of the Order of Friars Minor Capuchin. His long white beard and the oversized crucifix that rested in the cincture of his robe, like a broadsword ready for diabolic fray, made him seem otherworldly. Although he was nearly 60 years old, Father Riesinger was still a strong, muscular man, with a body that had been kept in good physical condition by a regimen of disciplined monastic living.

A special mass had been said that morning, and the mother superior stood by the possessed woman's bed with a number of sisters. To begin the rites, Father Riesinger made the sign of the cross, and all present joined in the opening prayer of exorcism, the Litany of All Saints. The woman began to tremble, then a dreadful growl filled the room. Father Steiger was amazed to note that in spite of the rising chorus of animal howls that were ostensibly coming from the woman, neither her tongue nor her lips moved. The exorcist raised his voice in an invocation, but he had only uttered a few words when an incredible phenomenon occurred. Before the nuns who surrounded Anna could intervene, the trembling woman on the bed was suddenly carried through the air to the doorway of the high-ceilinged room. As if she had been filled with helium, the bedeviled woman remained fixed in midair. The nuns screamed in horror and amazement. "Bring her down!" Father Riesinger's voice sounded loud and steady. "Help me," he pleaded with Father Steiger. "We must not let hysteria take control here, or we are beaten before we begin." Father Steiger and Father Riesinger calmed the nuns and then, with effort, brought the tormented woman down from the ceiling.

"She's lapsed into a coma," Father Riesinger told the others. "That may mean the devils have taken full possession and are about to speak." The exorcist intoned his litany. The unconscious woman's body jerked about, and a violent moaning and yelping sounded from her closed lips as Father Riesinger recited certain holy names. Undeterred, the priest continued the rites of exorcism.

Cardinal Jorge Medina Estevez of Chile holds the book *De Exorcismis et Supplicationibus Quibusdam* (Of all kinds of Exorcisms and Supplications), comprising the Vatican's new guidelines on exorcism. The new guidelines, presented in 1999, are the first updates to rules that have been in place since 1614.

By late afternoon, Father Steiger had to excuse himself to disperse the crowd that had gathered outside. People had been able to hear the terrible howling coming from the convent and had come to determine its cause. To quell rumors that a nun was being murdered, Father Steiger was forced to tell the people that a rite of exorcism was in progress. Before he left the astonished crowd, he beseeched the faithful to remember the tormented woman in their prayers. When he returned to the room, he found the sisters in a state of profound anxiety. Anna's body had become bloated beyond recognition. Father Steiger felt his stomach jolt as he looked at the grotesquely distorted woman writhing on the bed. Could they be certain that they were not killing her?

In a soft but firm voice, the exorcist told them that Satan would use every device within his power to make them quit the rites and leave the poor woman in his embrace. He advised the nuns to take turns getting outside and walking around a bit to get some fresh air. He also recommended that the mother superior draw up a schedule for the nuns to work in shifts, so that there was always a fresh group of people ready to care for Anna. "That's right, old man," came a voice from within the possessed woman, "those screaming brides of Jesus are going to need all of their strength!" At last the howling and growling had evolved into a voice. Father Steiger stared in wonderment as the mocking entity spoke from the woman's tormented body without utilizing either her lips or tongue.

Father Riesinger moved in on his adversary without a moment's hesitation. He demanded to know how many devils inhabited the body of the woman. The gutteral voice declared that there were many of them, far too many for the exorcist to handle. The gauntlet had been tossed. Now the battle would begin in earnest. As if to strike an immediate blow at Father Steiger's sensitive stomach, the woman began to vomit foul excrement. Some of the obnoxious matter resembled vomited macaroni, other chewed and sliced tobacco leaves.

Real Ghosts, Restless Spirits, and Haunted Places

Nausea would seize the woman as many as 20 times a day, and some of the substances seen in her vile outpourings were things that could not have been ingested by a human body. The retching continued at a prodigious rate, in spite of the fact that the woman was conscious each day for only a little while in the morning and took only very light nourishment before the rites of exorcism were renewed. Father Steiger worried that Anna would waste away from dehydration, but the exorcist advised him that Satan would not go so far as to kill her.

Father Riesinger determined that the woman had been possessed by two types of demons, those from the realm of fallen angels who had never lived on Earth as humans, and those that had once been humans living on Earth. He had also singled out their leader, Beelzebub, who told Father Riesinger that although the priest fought a hard battle, he would not win the woman away from the demons that had possessed her. Anna had been theirs since she had been 14 years old. According to the demon, her own father had cursed his daughter, asking the forces of evil to take her as their own. The devil Lucifer had been happy to oblige the curse and had commanded the demons to enter her.

Beelzebub conversed with the exorcist in German, Latin, and English. The demon's command of each language was so perfect that he took great delight in correcting Father Riesinger whenever he mispronounced a word. But the priest was not interested in playing word games. He wanted to learn why a girl's own father would bring down the hordes of hell upon her. "Ask him yourself!" Beelzebub snapped one day, when the exorcist had been at him without pause since early morning.

"You mean," Father Riesinger asked incredulously, "that he is one of the devils within her now?" Beelzebub laughed and said that the spirit of Anna's father, Jacob, had been within her since the moment he dared to curse his daughter into damnation. When the exorcist commanded the spirit of Jacob to come forth, a different demon made its presence known. A deep bass voice thundered through the room with such vehemence that Father Steiger excused himself from the room. The new speaker claimed to be Judas Iscariot, the betrayer of Jesus. The spirit of Judas told Father Riesinger that it was his demonic mission to make Anna commit suicide—preferably hang herself, as he had done.

At this point the possessed woman's face contorted grotesquely, and a terrible stench filled the room. Anna's thin and emaciated body inflated like a balloon, and the stench became so overwhelming that the sisters were forced to flee the room for fresh air. Only the exorcist stood his ground. The entity that spoke from Anna's body claimed to be the Prince of Darkness himself. Father Riesinger challenged Satan by stating that he was fighting a losing battle, for the exorcist had the love of Christ on his side. "Such things are beyond your understanding," Satan responded. "But this whole issue began before time itself, and in accordance with a set of strict laws."

Father Riesinger advanced on Satan with a large wooden cross that a sister had left in the room for him. Satan laughed and told the exorcist to put aside a silly toy made of papier-mâché. Father Riesinger looked down at the cross and saw that what had once been a firm, wooden cross was now simply papier-mâché. The exorcist was momentarily flustered and was then bombarded by two hours of uninterrupted mocking laughter from the demons inside of Anna.

When Father Steiger rejoined his fellow priest, he received a verbal assault from the demon. "So there's the sniveling pup who brought this whole thing about, is it?" Satan snarled at the parish priest. "I'll attend to you, Joseph Steiger. I'll set the entire parish against you. Such hatred will build up against you that your parishioners will demand your removal!"

That night at dinner, while the nuns watched over the entranced woman, Father Steiger spoke earnestly to the exorcist. He was becoming concerned about what people in the parish thought about the whole affair. The exorcism had continued for days with the endless screaming, cursing, and growling. Father Steiger had even overheard some parishioners saying that those who are able to conjure up Satan must be in his power themselves. With a deep, weary sigh, Father Riesinger told his fellow priest that he had begun to fall right into Satan's plan. It was part of the demon's strategy to sow seeds of doubt in his soul. What a victory it would be for Satan if he could turn two old friends against one another. Father Steiger left the dinner table for a place where he could be alone in quiet prayer and meditation. When he rejoined Father Riesinger in Anna's room, he felt confident and grateful that he had not fallen into Satan's snare.

Seemingly surprised to see Father Steiger rejoining the spiritual combat, the demon's voice became low and filled with menace. He informed Father Steiger that he'd had better priests murdered on their own altars! He'd had priests butchered alive. He'd had them skinned, baked, boiled, and burned. He even had Jesus hung on a cross and Peter crucified upside down. After a series of rambling threats, the demon vowed that he would personally attack Father Steiger on the following Friday.

When that day arrived, Father Steiger received an emergency call from one of his parishioners who lived far out in the country. Father Steiger got into his car and began to drive to the home of the individual who had asked for his help. Although he knew that the demons that had taken control of Anna had threatened to strike against him on that day, the priest did not hesitate for a second. As he approached a bridge, a black cloud descended on his car, obscuring his vision. The priest lost control of the vehicle and crashed. The car was totaled, but Father Steiger escaped from the wreck in a state of nervous excitement, his life intact.

When he returned to Anna's room, the demonic entity that had threatened Father Steiger's life laughed at his appearance and asked how the priest liked the car crash "for openers." Then the demon promised the priest a lot more fun. Later that night, the "fun" came to Father Steiger's room. Eerie, rat-like noises scampered across his floor until dawn. Doors opened and slammed shut. His bed was suddenly jolted several times, which kept him on edge all night long.

After two weeks of harassment against the priests and nuns involved in the exorcism, Satan took leave of Anna's body and left the battle to his demonic underlings. A few nights later, during the Litany, another voice spoke from Anna; it was Jacob, her father. To show contempt for the exorcist, a torrent of filth and vomit gushed forth from Anna's mouth. Father Riesinger was forced to change his robes four times that next day. After one terrible vomiting session, the voice of Mina, Jacob's mistress, came forward to admit that she, too, dwelled within Anna's tormented body. Mina laughed that Jacob may have cursed his daughter, but she had murdered four of her children.

Father Riesinger had been in the throes of exorcism rites for 20 days, a period that was without precedence in the Roman Catholic Church. Although he was growing physically weak, he refused to slow his pace. He sensed that the demons were also losing strength; they had begun to plead for control of Anna's body and soul. The exorcist resolved to continue his rites around the clock, from dawn to dawn without ceasing. Either he would drop from exhaustion or the devils would quit the body of the possessed woman.

For 72 hours without rest, Father Riesinger pressed the exorcism on. The entities began to cry and to plead for mercy. They agreed to quit Anna's body, but they begged to be directed into another mortal dwelling of flesh and blood. The exorcist was not about to enter into such a hellish bargain. With prayers for strength and guidance, he stepped up the pace of the rites. At 9:00 P.M. on September 23, 1928, Father Riesinger had sustained the rites of exorcism for 23 days, and the devils had finally endured enough. Anna's body stiffened like a plank and stood upright, with only her heels touching the bed. The sisters gasped. Was she about to spring for the ceiling again?

Father Riesinger motioned for them to remain calm, and he drew his large crucifix from his robe. He warned the devils that he would bide no deception. He did not want a single one of them going back on their word and remaining within the woman. As they left, he commanded each of them to call out its name. Terrible moans filled the room, and then the demons began to call out their names as they left Anna's body. "Beelzebub! Judas! Jacob! Mina!" the voices cried. The entities departed, and as if from a great distance, the priests and nuns could hear the echoes of tormented wails chanting over and over again: "Hell! Beelzebub! Hell! Judas! Hell! Jacob! Hell! Mina! Hell … hell … hell."

On the bed, the woman lay freed from her bondage. The ordeal had been extremely hard on her, and her features were gaunt and haggard. Anna tried to form her lips into a smile. "God bless you, Father," she said in a hoarse whisper. Suddenly a vile odor filled the room, and a nun screamed that the demons had returned. Father Riesinger calmly told them to open the windows and air out the convent, explaining that it was just the demons' parting shot. "Be assured," he told them. "It is ended."

Anna went home to a new life, free for the first time since that terrible day when, as a 14-year-old girl, she had been cursed by a "loathsomely unchaste" father.

The Roman Catholic Church decreed the case to be an authentic instance of diabolic possession. The exorcism that took place in Earling, Iowa, remains the only case in which an account of the rites surrounding an exorcism have been released by the church body. On July 23, 1935, the Most Reverend Joseph F. Busch, Bishop of St. Cloud, Minnesota, placed the church's *imprimatur* on a clerically approved summary of the case, which had been prepared by the Reverend Celestine Kapsner, O.S.B., of St. John's Abbey, Collegeville, Minnesota. Father Kapsner's account was based on an earlier record of the case by the Reverend Carl Bogl.

It is recorded that by 1935 Father Riesinger had performed 19 successful exorcisms.

ENCOUNTERING SHADOW BEINGS AND SPIRIT POSSESSION DURING WINTER BREAK

The Personal Experience of Michael

"I have spent the last 13 years trying my best to forget the events that took place that week in 1989, but [the week] sticks in my memory like it happened yesterday.

"It was winter break at college, and I was bracing for a week alone on campus, as my school was in Tennessee and my home was in New Hampshire; I was unable to make such a long trip home. My friend Jim invited me to I join him and his family that week in Ann Arbor, Michigan, and I accepted.

"On the trip to Michigan, Jim told me that his younger brother Mark was doing a favor for someone who was out of town. He was house-sitting for them while they were gone, seeing that their dog was fed and hanging around the place once in a while so it looked lived in. We arrived at Jim's house in Ann Arbor on a cold and rainy night. I met his family, including his brothers Mark and Chucky, who was the youngest of the family at about 13.

"Jim, Chucky, and I rode along with Mark when he went to check on the place where he was house-sitting, and on the way over, he told us about some strange things that had happened to him while he was there. Mark said that late one night, around 2:00 A.M., when he was sitting alone upstairs in the master bedroom watching television, he heard voices downstairs. At first he was afraid that someone had broken in without his realizing it. All the lights downstairs were out, and when Mark turned the volume down on the television set, the voices became louder. He went out into the hall and looked out over the thin metal railing by the stairs. He heard loud whispers at the bottom of the stairs, but he couldn't make out what they were saying. Then he saw a large, dark shadow of a woman coming up the stairs, and as it approached the whispers became louder, and seemed to be emanating from the shadowy figure. Mark even heard footsteps as the entity came up the stairs.

"Mark said that he had been really scared. He ran back into the master bedroom, sat in a chair, and changed the station on the television to a Christian channel. Mark grabbed a Bible and held on for dear life. He sat there with the volume up and his Bible in hands, but he could still hear the dark figure moving up the stairs and toward the room he was in. The footsteps and the voices kept growing louder. Then the shadow of a woman appeared in the doorway to the room he was in. It disappeared as quickly as it had manifested. Mark felt a cold wind pass by him, and the curtains billowed as a shadowy figure went out the window that he had opened earlier to get some fresh air.

"By the time we turned up the road to the house, Mark had finished his story. We prayed, and tried to prepare for anything. The house was large, dark brown or black, and the yard had a metal fence that separated the property from a cemetery. It may have appeared to be a normal house by day, but at night it looked like something right out of a horror movie. We pulled into the driveway, and up to the house.

"When we got out of the car, Mark pointed to the second storey of the house, and pointed out the window of the master bedroom where he occasionally watched television. As I looked up to the window, I saw a bluish, flickering light, and I asked Mark if he were absolutely certain that he had turned off the television the last time he had used it. He replied that he was sure. When we reached the door to the house, we found the dog scratching wildly against it. We opened the door, and the dog shot out into the yard as fast as a bullet out of a gun, and as he ran he kept looking back at the house, as if he wanted to get far away from it.

"The first impression I got when we entered the house was that the atmosphere was so tense, it could be cut with a knife. This was the first time I actually sensed the presence of a spirit. Mark began to perform his duties as house-sitter; he just had to check phone messages, make a call or two, take the mail inside, and so forth. I was convinced that, in spite of what he had said, Mark had left the television on in the master bedroom, so Jim and I were about to go upstairs and turn it off, but suddenly we had a spooky feeling, like we were being closely watched. I looked around and Chucky was gone. Expecting him to have gone outside, I went out to check on him. As I had expected, he had gone outside, and was staring up at the master bedroom. I was shocked to see that it was totally dark in that room, even though I knew light had filled it only moments before. At that point we knew something weird was going on, but we were not freaking out. We told Mark to complete his business so that we could get out of there as soon as possible.

"As we were waiting for Mark, we began to hear footsteps coming from the upstairs hallway. Then we began to hear the same kind of whispers that Mark had talked about, as if many voices were speaking at once, in an unintelligible murmur. They were coming from upstairs, and getting louder with every footstep. I stood at the bottom of the stairs, and heard the footsteps and voices moving down the stairs, toward us. I called Jim over, and he heard and sensed the same thing. The voices and footsteps were getting closer to us.

"By that time, Mark had finished with his chores, and we were getting ready to lock up. Jim went out dragged the dog back into the house against the animal's will; it was obvious that house was the last place it wanted to be. Chucky had wandered outside again, and I once again found him staring up at the window of the master bedroom. He stood there, staring, as if in a daze, but he broke out of it when the flickering, bluish lights suddenly returned. I told Chucky to stay were he was, and I went back inside.

"Just as we were ready to leave, a shadowy figure came out of a dark room that was at the end of the downstairs hallway, and began moving toward us. I was a Pentecostal Christian at that point in my life, as were Jim and Mark, and we believed that we were in the presence of devils. We began to rebuke the creature in the name of Jesus, as we had been taught to do in such situations. The spirit, entity, or whatever it was, did not go away, but it stopped moving toward us. Once again we began to hear voices and footsteps coming toward us from the stairs, and so we ran out of the house, locked the door, grabbed Chucky—who was still staring up at the window of the master bedroom—got in the car, and drove away.

"We assumed that would be the end of it, since we didn't have to go back to that house, but we were wrong. The night before Jim and I were to go back to school, I could not sleep. I had the feeling that someone was watching me very closely, just as I had when I had entered the house where Mark was house-sitting. This unnerved me as there was no reason that should have happened in Jim's house. I took a blanket [and] went downstairs, to just hang out and read. Chucky came downstairs and said that he wanted to talk, so we did,

A man in Malajpur, India, takes his wife, who he believes to be possessed by evil spirits, to the temple of Furu Deoji Maharaj. The village holds an annual exorcism rite at the temple to exorcise those under the spells of ghosts, devils, and evil spirits.

and then we decided to have a prayer. Jim and I were both studying to be preachers, so we believed in faith, and spiritual warfare. Chucky told me that he wanted to receive what Pentecostals call the baptism in the holy ghost, during which people speak in other tongues. We knelt by the couch to pray on our knees, and Chucky sounded like he was speaking in tongues, but then something happened.

"Chucky had been kneeling, with his head bowed for prayer, when suddenly his entire body flew back, and on to the floor. His eyes rolled into the back of his head. At first I misinterpreted this as another Pentecostal experience called being 'slain in the spirit,' when God lays you out like a light, and communes with you. It didn't take long for me to figure out that this was not the work of God. Chucky began writhing on the floor, speaking in weird tongues that I had never heard before, and his eyes looked totally glazed over. I knew he was possessed. At that time, because of my Pentecostal faith, I believed Chucky was possessed by *the* devil or a devil, but now I believe it was the evil entity or spirit from the house Mark had been house-sitting for, and that it had followed us back to Jim's house. That was why I couldn't sleep. I had been aware of its presence on some level of consciousness.

"I was just about to get Jim and Mark when Chucky stopped writhing and sat straight up, as stiff as a board, and spoke in a deep voice completely different from his own. He spoke in an unearthly voice, deeper than anything I had ever heard. He pointed at me and said in a dark, evil tone, 'YOU!' To this day I don't know what that was all about. In my youth and pious pride, I thought the devil was aware of who I was because I was such a good Christian. I ran upstairs and got Jim, Mark, and their parents. We got our Bibles, and for the next hour and a half we tried to rebuke the evil spirit that had entered Chucky. Chucky sat up and bellowed 'YOU!' again, once to me and once to Jim. The more we rebuked, prayed, and quoted Bible verses, the harder Chucky writhed and the deep, dark evil voice within him shouted many foul things at us.

"All these years later, I can't believe that there was any way this young kid with a high-pitched voice could have faked that deep voice. We were grasping at straws, but we were unwilling to give up on Chucky. The next time Chucky started writhing and spewing his dark tongues, we all rebuked the devil in the name of Jesus, and placed our King James Bibles on his chest at the same time. Chucky shook violently, but this brought him back; whatever possessed him had fled. His normal voice returned.

"Even now, I get chills thinking about that night. Chucky described what it was like when the evil spirit possessed him. He said that gruesome creatures were holding him in a place where everything was white. He had no idea what was going on outside his body. As I said, back then I believed in devils. I do not now, but I do believe there was something evil in that house. I am reluctant to tell this story, for I have found that most people just don't want to know the truth about what's out there."

THE EVIL THAT CAME ALONG WITH A SECOND-HAND SOFA

The Personal Experience of the Emminger Family

In late August 1996, 34-year-old Patricia Emminger told me that she moved from Anaheim to Fremont, California, with her husband, Gary, and their two children, five-year-old Wendy and four-year-old Mark. Because they could not afford a large moving van and were moving into a much smaller house, they had been forced to sell many of their larger possessions, including much of their furniture. When they moved into their new house, Patricia was pleased to discover that the previous tenants had left a large sofa. She ran a dust cloth over the sofa and was happy with how handsome it looked; she couldn't imagine why anyone would leave behind such an attractive piece of furniture behind.

One night, shortly after they had moved into the house, Patricia sat alone, watching a favorite old movie that she had put in the VCR to help her wind down before bedtime. The rest of the family was asleep. The movie was nearly over when she noticed a dark shadow to her left. However, when she focused her eyes directly on the spot, she could see nothing. Patricia decided that her eyes were undoubtedly becoming tired. It was, after all, nearly one o'clock.

A few moments later, when she had resumed watching the movie, she saw the shadow again. This time it crossed directly in front of her, moving toward the couch. But once again, when she focused directly on the thing, she saw nothing but the shadows of the dark room. Patricia shrugged, distracted from the movie. "Are you a ghost?" she asked, speaking toward the area in front of the couch where she had last seen the shadow. "I don't happen to believe in ghosts, but if you really are one, you appear harmless enough. Stick around if you want to." Patricia turned off the television and went upstairs to bed. By morning she had forgotten the entire episode with the mysterious shadow.

The next day was a particularly difficult one for Patricia at her office. After the dinner dishes were stacked in the washer, it felt good to curl up on the big couch with a good book. Gary watched television for a while, then confessed that he was quite tired. He gave her a good-night kiss and headed up to bed. Patricia settled back into her book, figuring she was good for a few more chapters before she became too groggy to continue reading. Several moments later, a peculiar sound caused her to raise her eyes from her book, and she was surprised to see the shadow again. As on the previous evening, it crossed in front of her, but then it settled on the other end of the sofa. "Okay," Patricia said, stifling a yawn. "If you want the sofa tonight, be my guest. I am simply too tired to care. I'm going to bed."

The next afternoon when the Emmingers returned home after work, they found that they had received a message from Gary's older sister, Carrie, reminding them that, as planned, she would be arriving the next day for a visit. At 46, Carrie was 10 years older than her brother. Carrie's husband had been killed in a small plane accident six years before. They had never been able to have children, and her niece and nephew were like surrogate children to Carrie.

Carrie arrived early the next morning, just before Patricia and Gary left for work. The children jumped up and down with enthusiasm for their favorite aunt. They were especially delighted with Carrie's visit because that meant they could stay home with her rather than attending nursery school.

That afternoon when Patricia returned home from work, she found that Carrie had prepared a delicious roast with all the trimmings. Later the older woman helped her change Wendy and Mark into their pajamas as well as read them a bedtime story. Yes, it would be wonderful to have Aunt Carrie around for a few days. In fact, she could come visit as often as she liked. Once the kids were settled, the adults made some coffee and settled down in the living room for the delightful business of catching up on each others' lives. During the course of conversation, Carrie commented on the attractive new sofa. "New to us," Gary said. "The previous owners left it here."

Talk of the couch reminded Patricia of the shadow that she had seen the past two evenings. Risking their laughter, she told them that on the nights when she had stayed up late, she had been aware of something kind of wispy floating around her. Carrie laughed, affecting an expression of mock horror. Was she to sleep in a haunted house? Gary arched an eyebrow quizzically, wondering if this was some kind of rehearsal for Halloween, which was only a few weeks away.

Suddenly Patricia felt a strange chill shudder through her body. It was as if her disclosure to her sister-in-law and husband had seriously offended the unseen guest in the room. All at once she felt surrounded by ugly, malignant hatred. She experienced a fear of the unknown. Gary wanted to know if there was something wrong, but Patricia decided that she had said enough. Patricia successfully rerouted the conversation to other subjects, but her mind was occupied with the strange shift in the house's atmosphere. Then she became aware of *something* moving up the stairs toward the children's bedroom. She stiffened with fear as she realized that whatever it was, she had offended it, and it had decided to get even with her by going for her children.

Patricia was about to jump up and cry out in dread, when they all heard Mark screaming from upstairs. She was several steps ahead of Gary and Carrie as they all raced upstairs for the children's bedroom. "A ghost," Mark sobbed as Patricia held him in her arms. "An ugly ghost was in our room!"

"You know there's no such thing as ghosts, Markie," Carrie told him. "And even if there were, you know that they would be afraid of your Aunt

Carrie!" Wendy sat up, blinking her eyes at the sudden light in the bedroom, confused by her brother's screams. "No such thing as ghosts," she echoed, pulling a pillow over her head. Mark continued to cry softly, cuddling against Patricia's breast as she sought to soothe him. "It held out its hand and kept bending its finger at me, like it wanted me to follow it somewhere," he said between tearful gasps.

After they had the kids settled down, the three adults went back downstairs to the kitchen. Gary poured himself a fresh cup of coffee and asked Patricia if she had tried out her ghost routine on the kids earlier in the evening. Patricia stared her husband straight in the eye, and assured him that she would never do such a thing. But at the same time, she wanted so very much to tell Gary about the awful, ineffable *something* that she had sensed heading toward the children's room with malicious intent. She wanted to tell him, but she knew he wouldn't believe her. It was difficult for Patricia to turn out the lights that night. She walked through the house, trying to catch sight of the elusive shadow being. It was nowhere to be seen. But everywhere she walked, she felt surrounded by cold hatred.

The next morning at breakfast, everything seemed as it should be. Five-year-old Wendy was her bubbly self, full of cheer and giggles. Only Mark seemed to be aware of a subtle change in the home's atmosphere. Just before noon the next day, Patricia received a telephone call from Carrie. She hated to bother Patricia at work, Carrie said apologetically, but Mark claimed to have seen the ghost again. He said that it was waiting for him in his room.

Patricia left work early that afternoon, and when Gary came home that evening, the family went for pizza and a movie afterward. It was her plan to distract both the children and the adults from thoughts of ghosts. Lights went out early in the Emminger home that evening. Sadly, they did not remain that way for very long. The family had been asleep for only a few hours when Mark's terrified screams once again filled the house. As Patricia entered the room, she was shocked by the chill in the air. Although she could see nothing, she was certain that the evil, shadowy force had been after Mark again.

It took two hours for the three adults to calm the children, for that night Wendy thought she, too, had seen the ghost. When the children were once again asleep, Patricia decided that she must tell Gary about the shadow being that she had seen.

Her husband listened patiently to her account of the *something* that moved between the couch and the television set, and the sense of evil that she felt in the house. Although she could see that Gary clearly did not believe her, she went on describing the cold, unseen thing that she had witnessed moving up the stairs to the children's room. Gary offered his opinion, which was that there might be some physical or psychological reason why Mark was having ghost dreams, and he made Patricia promise that she would take him to a pediatrician as soon as possible.

Patricia was able to get an appointment for Mark for the next afternoon. The doctor seemed unperturbed by the whole affair. He said that many children of Mark's age experienced nightmares. He advised parents to stress that the monsters are not real and not to encourage their child's fantasies. He gave Patricia a prescription for a mild sleeping aid, just in case it became necessary to help the boy sleep more soundly. The sleeping aid proved to be woefully ineffective against the nocturnal visits of the ghost, for once again Mark awakened everyone with his screams of terror.

For three nights, their son had been victimized in the darkness. As Patricia cradled her son in her arms, she sensed a mocking presence all around her. "If you feel frightened now," the unseen entity seemed to tell her, "be aware that this is nothing like the fear that you will soon suffer."

The next day when Patricia returned home from work, Wendy rushed excitedly to her arms and gave her an enthusiastic kiss as a greeting. When Patricia inquired why Mark did not seem to want a hello kiss, he jerked his face away from hers with a scowl of disgust. "I can't stand you," he snarled. "I don't want to be near you. I won't kiss you again ever." Patricia was shocked and hurt. She glanced at Carrie and saw the look of astonishment on her face. This was definitely not their loving little Mark speaking.

That night during dinner, Mark continued to refuse to permit his mother to touch him. His sister could cuddle him; Aunt Carrie could kiss and hug him; Daddy could wrestle and play with him; but Mommy was not allowed to get near her little boy.

On her way home from work that next evening, Patricia stopped at a toy store and bought presents for Wendy and Mark. When she arrived home, Wendy met her at the front door with her usual kiss, but Mark only glowered at her. Wendy responded to her surprise gift with little cries of pleasure and appreciation. Mark refused even to open the brightly colored wrapping paper, and his lips curled back in a contemptuous sneer. "You can't buy my kisses with presents!" he said, spitting out the hateful words. Patricia was determined to remain calm. She could see the emotional turmoil that boiled within little Mark. Suddenly he broke into a run and hurled himself into her arms. "Mommy, I do love you," he cried. "Sometimes ... I don't understand ... what...."

Patricia sat on the floor and pulled her son onto her lap, kissing his forehead, hugging his tiny frame. Then, all at once, Mark's face changed again. His lips twisted into an evil sneer. With a violent shudder of his body, as if he were repulsed by his mother's very touch, he slid out of her lap. "Why can't you just leave me alone!" he shouted as he ran from the room. "I don't love you anymore!" Patricia sat on the floor in despair. Wendy stood near, uncertain what to do. She wanted to comfort her mother but felt that she should remain silent. Patricia put her hands to her face and began to sob disconsolately.

Later that evening when the children were sleeping, Patricia, Gary, and Carrie sat at the kitchen table to discuss the awful change in Mark's behavior. It soon became apparent that Gary had already made up his mind that their son should see a psychiatrist. "He keeps insisting that he sees an ugly ghost, day in and day out," Gary argued his decision. "Now he's undergone a complete personality change and refuses to allow his mother to touch him. I think we owe it to Mark to put away our prejudices regarding mental illness and take him to a psychiatrist."

Patricia pleaded for her husband to listen to what she considered the true cause for their son's aberrant behavior. "There is something evil and awful in this house, and slowly but surely it's entering Mark's mind and causing him to act as he does. Don't you see that this thing is trying to possess our son?" Gary replied coldly that neither he nor Carrie saw any shadowy thing moving around the house.

Although Carrie had been sitting quietly, reluctant to enter a family discussion of such perplexing depth, she now volunteered yet another possibility. Perhaps Mark resented not having his mother at home. They all knew that he hated nursery school. "Maybe by saying he doesn't like you," Carrie theorized, "Mark is really saying that he doesn't like it when you *leave* him."

Patricia was impressed by Carrie's insights. Maybe she had hit upon the real reason for Mark's sudden change of personality. Perhaps the "shadow" that she had seen when she was trying to relax after a hard day at work was really a shadow of guilt moving across her psyche, an attempt to get her to stay home and be a good mother. But could they afford for her to quit her job? Could they make it without a second paycheck? Gary answered they could certainly afford it until Mark got better and felt all right again about her working. "Maybe the move and all was just too much for the little guy," he said.

Patricia was determined to do anything to help her son. She gave notice at the dental office that next afternoon, and she expressed the hope that the job might still be waiting for her after things got straightened out at home. That night, after everyone else had retired for the evening, she sat up late in the living room, mulling over the bizarre situation. Mark seemed to be sleeping peacefully. Could the week of terror really have resulted from her son's feeling of desertion when she left for work?

Suddenly she felt the room's temperature drop. Warning alarms went off in her brain, and she feared raising her eyes to look around the room. As the deathlike chill permeated the room, an atmosphere of hatred seemed to solidify. She knew that something monstrous and evil was in the room with her.

There, in front of her, was the shadow that she had first seen a week ago. Both the hands and face of the dark form now appeared lighter, and Patricia was able to make out features on its face. The thing was grossly emaciated, and yellowish green skin stretched tautly across its high cheekbones. Long hair flowed to its shoulders. Its thin, outstretched arms supported bony hands and fingers that looked like claws. Dark, soulless eyes stared hollowly at her, and the ghastly image curled its lips into a vile sneer. Patricia's body began to tremble as she realized that this was the same sneer that she had seen on Mark's face that day when he refused to accept the toy she had brought him. At last she was certain she knew what the being intended to do with Mark. It intended to steal his soul and inhabit his body.

Slowly the loathsome form dematerialized before her eyes. The chill lifted from the room. With a sudden jolt of fear, Patricia ran to the children's room. She sat on Mark's bed and gathered his sleeping form into her arms. Somehow she must find a way to thwart the evil creature's plan to possess her son's body. A sound from the hallway startled her. Unconsciously, with a mother's basic reflex, she tightened her arms around her son. "My God, I saw it!" Carrie exclaimed. "My God, Patricia! I was in the kitchen, warming some milk to help me sleep. I saw that thing take shape. What was it?" Tears of relief flooded Patricia's eyes. Carrie had seen the thing! Now she had an ally in her war against the hideous shadow creature. "It ... it wants Mark, doesn't it?" Carrie asked in a voice barely a whisper. The two women awakened Gary and handed him a steaming cup of strong black coffee. "You will listen to us," Carrie told him.

More than an hour and several cups of coffee later, Gary could still do little more than shake his head and rub the stubble on his chin. "It's all so primitive and superstitious," he said at last. "An evil spirit trying to possess our son. How could that be?" For several silent minutes, Gary looked into the eyes of his wife, then those of his sister. "I've got to believe the word of the two women in the world that I love and trust the most," he said. "If you both say that you've seen the thing, then I believe you."

Patricia explained that she had come to believe that the spirit was able to draw energy from their thoughts and strong emotions. They must try not to show any signs of fear.

Dinner the next evening was very quiet. Throughout the meal, Gary sat lost in thought, scarcely eating his food, glancing cautiously from time to time at his scowling son. Carrie also seemed nervous, and even Wendy noticed that her aunt's hands shook as she passed the bowl of mashed potatoes. Since Mark's behavior had changed, the bedtime ritual at the Emminger home had been altered. Patricia had confined her attention to Wendy, and Gary had assumed the responsibility of putting Mark to bed. Mark had never

A man performs a dance to drive away evil spirits at a Buddhist temple during a festival in Taipei.

rejected affection from his father, yet that night he suddenly snapped at Gary and refused to allow either of his parents to touch him. "You've been listening to her lies," the boy snarled, indicating his mother. "Now you're as bad as she is. I don't like you anymore either!"

A stricken look crossed Gary's features, and Carrie hurriedly entered the room. "Aunt Carrie will help Markie with his jammies, okay?" But he had nothing but scorn for his beloved Aunt Carrie as well. "Why don't you go home?" Mark asked, his voice full of venom. "No one wants you here. You're old and fat and ugly."

After the three adults left the children's bedroom, determined to remain calm, the windows in the living room began to make a fearsome noise. Although there was no wind outside, the glass panes shook violently. Then the drawn curtains began to flail wildly, knocking a vase to the floor and noisily tipping over several framed family photographs on a small table. A number of books flew off a shelf. Gary got to his feet, his eyes wide with unnamed fear. "This is too much," he said. "I can't believe these things are happening to me in my own home!"

Patricia begged him to ignore the manifestations, but as soon as she spoke, she heard a voice inside her head that echoed with malice: "*You can't ignore me. I am stronger than any of you!*" Patricia realized that the thing was communicating with her telepathically. Inside her mind, she defied the intruder: "*We are stronger than you. We are strong together! Now get out of this house. You are not wanted here!*" The only reply was menacing, low-pitched laughter; from the look on Gary's face, he, too, had heard the ghastly sound.

"That's it," he said. "I'm out of here. I'm taking Wendy, and I'm getting out of this hell hole." Patricia pleaded with her husband, stating that they had to stay strong, but Gary admitted that he couldn't handle what was happening in his home. Things like this were not supposed to be able to happen. He had been taught his whole life not to believe in the supernatural.

"I can't take it," he said, his eyes wide with fear. "I'll be no use to you anyway." Carrie agreed with her brother. "Let him take Wendy and go! His fear will only feed the thing." Patricia made one last attempt to regain her husband's support in the fight against the ugly shadow being, but then two of the picture frames that had been pushed over by the animated drapes exploded loudly, sending glass fragments across the room. "I'm sorry," was all Gary could say before he ran upstairs to the children's bedroom to get their daughter.

After Gary had left with Wendy, the window panes began to vibrate with such violence that it seemed as if they would shatter at any moment. The draperies continued to flap noisily, as though they were flags on a pole, resisting a strong wind. Carrie reached for the Bible on the coffee table, clutched it in her trembling hands, and began to pray for deliverance from evil.

Within a few minutes the wind from nowhere died down, and the draperies once more settled quietly against the windows. "Keep praying," Patricia said to Carrie. "I'm taking the Bible with me, and I'm going into the kids' bedroom. I think the thing knows that tonight is its last chance to possess him. I feel that it is about to go after Mark with all of its strength."

Patricia gathered her sleeping boy into her arms and tried to prepare herself for whatever was to come. Within moments she felt the chilling approach of the detestable being, and its ghastly form began to materialize before her. An eerie sepulchral haze surrounded the entity as it moved inexorably toward her. Its bony arms were outstretched, and an almost irresistible force seemed to flow from its yellow-green claws. Patricia could not empty her mind of the thought that if those vicious hands should ever touch her, her very essence would be ripped from her.

The being stepped closer, and for one terrible moment Patricia felt herself faltering. Her mind began to swirl, and she knew that she was losing strength to the entity's demoniacal power. From far away she could hear its soulless laughter. The sound of that pitiless cackle was all that Patricia needed to rally her inner resources. "I will not let you take my son!" she shouted at the thing.

Somewhere deep inside of herself, Patricia tapped a source of primeval energy. Centuries of culture and sophistication melted away, and she was simply an enraged mother protecting her young. She held the Bible in front of her as if it were a shield and advanced toward the evil creature. "I am stronger than you, you reject from Hell," Patricia snarled at the entity. "My love for my son is stronger than your will to possess him."

As Patricia continued moving forward, she was rewarded by the sight of the creature beginning to move backward. Feeling a tremendous surge of power and thrusting the Bible toward the entity, she spoke with authority: "God's word is stronger than you are. God's love is stronger than you are. You are beaten! Leave my son; leave my house! The power of love has defeated your power of evil!"

The entity continued to retreat, growing smaller and fainter as it moved backward. Patricia continued to hold the Bible in front of her, only dimly aware that they were moving down the stairs toward the living room. Then it suddenly occurred to her that the entity was headed toward the sofa. "So that's it!" she exclaimed. "Now I know where you came from, you miserable scum!"

Patricia could see Carrie was still seated on the sofa, and she could hear her prayers entreating God, the Holy Spirit, and all the saints to banish evil from the house. "Carrie, get off the sofa … right away!" Patricia shouted. "The thing is headed for the sofa. That's where it came from!" As if moving awkwardly in a dream, Carrie did as she was told.

Patricia continued her advance on the being, watching it become increasingly dimmer as it neared the sofa. Its vaguely luminescent quality had vanished, and Patricia was staring at the formless shadow that she had first seen seven days before. It hovered above the sofa for only a few seconds before it seemed to evaporate into the cushions.

Both women were startled by the sound of the front door closing. Gary was returning with Wendy cradled in his arms. "I couldn't stay away," he managed an apology for his former cowardice in the face of supernatural evil. "I thought you might need my help." Patricia kept her eye on the sofa. "Yes, honey, we need your help all right. Take this damned sofa from our home right now!"

With only the pale light of a crescent moon to guide them, Patricia and Gary made a desperate trip far beyond the outskirts of the city. When they found a desolate spot where it seemed completely safe and far away from any trees or foliage, they dumped the sofa, doused it with lighter fluid, and set it on fire. When the sofa had been completely consumed by the flames and they had stamped out the last glowing sparks, Patricia sighed that it was over at last.

Later that night, when she checked in on her sleeping children, Mark rolled over on his back, sleepily kissed her, and whispered, "Good night, Mommy. I love you so much." When Patricia rejoined Gary and Carrie in the kitchen, there were tears glistening in her eyes. "Thank God," she sighed in a meaningful prayer of thanks. "We won!"

POSSESSED BY A SPIRIT PARASITE

If someone you know has demonstrated a dramatic alteration in their behavior, and you are certain that he or she does not abuse drugs and has no previous history of mental problems, that person may have been invaded by a spirit parasite. Consult with a physician, a psychologist, or a psychiatrist and consider possession by a spirit parasite as one of many possible diagnoses. Those who suffer from invasion by an uninvited entity may begin to exhibit the following changes of personality or behavior:

1. They may begin to hear voices directing them to perform acts they would have never even considered earlier.

2. They may frequently see the image of the spirit parasite as it existed in its physical life as a human. In the case of a nonhuman entity acting as spirit parasite, the being will appear in its demonic countenance.

3. The spirit-possessed often feel themselves lose consciousness, although they are physically able to continue interacting with other people, and people around them believe they are conscious. They often have no memory of their black-outs later.

4. On occasions, sometimes even in the midst of conversations, their conscious mind may be blocked, and a trancelike state will come over them.

5. They may begin walking differently, speaking in a different tone and manner, and behaving in strange, irrational ways.

6. They may begin doing things that they have never done before. Friends and family will remark that they are behaving like a totally different person.

7. In the very worst cases, the parasite being will consume its victim's life. The evil spell may reach its climax with the possessed individual committing murder, suicide, or some violent antisocial act.

Remember that spirit parasites cannot achieve power over anyone unless they are somehow invited into someone's private space or attracted to an individual by his or her negative thoughts and actions. A person will become especially vulnerable to spirit invasion if they abuse alcohol or drugs or exploit someone mentally, physically, or emotionally.

Evil or negativity is an imbalanced, chaotic, destructive energy, the opposite of growth and productivity. When an individual is negative, depressed, and discordant, he or she opens the psyche to invasion by a parasite from the lower frequencies of the spirit world.

One should be wary of an indiscriminate exploration of the occult or of "ghost hunting" in haunted houses or places. Without proper discipline, study, and discernment, the ill-prepared are liable to interact only with those entities who will seek to deceive and entrap them.

Experienced psychical researchers understand that the physical world is closer to the realm of the lower, more negative, spiritual frequencies of the spirit world than it is to the dimension of higher beings. Because we exist in a material world, our psyches will always contain more aspects that are similar to those of the lower vibratory realm than the higher spiritual planes.

If you should have an encounter with a negative being from the more chaotic regions of the spirit world, you will quite likely experience a prickling sensation that will seem to crawl over your entire body. You will instantly be filled with an awareness that you have entered into a very dangerous liaison. If you continue the contact, you will experience a mounting sense of terror or a distinct sensation of unease, depending upon the strength of the discordant vibrations emanating from the spirit parasite. If you should find yourself in such an encounter, utter prayers of love and harmony and ask angelic or higher spiritual guides to surround and protect you.

Those who have accumulated many years of experience researching and exploring the unseen world have come to understand that the spirit world is populated by all manner of discordant entities, as well as more benevolent and benign beings. Experienced ghost researchers have become aware that troubled spirits will continue their contentious ways beyond physical death, and they will often attempt to influence the minds, and therefore the lives, of those who will receive them. Those psychical investigators who have spent many years perfecting their knowledge of the unseen world have also become aware that many of the inhabitants of other dimensions of reality have never been human. While some of these discarnate entities envy human flesh and human experiences, other such beings hold the human species in the greatest contempt and seek devious ways to humiliate and destroy their victims. The best way to avoid a negative encounter with a spirit parasite is to always seek to elevate one's thoughts, works, and deeds to the highest levels.

6

Spirits Seen at
Deathbeds and Funerals

We cannot state when, or if, the earliest members of our species (*Homo sapiens*, c. 30,000 B.C.E.) conducted burial rituals of a nature that would qualify them as believers in an afterlife, but we do know that they buried their dead with care and consideration and included food, weapons, and various personal belongings with the body. Even earlier Neanderthal species (c. 100,000 B.C.E.) placed decorative shells and bones, food, and stone implements in graves with the deceased, which they often covered with a red pigment. Because of the placement of such funerary objects in the graves, it seems we can deduce that even these prehistoric people believed that death was not the end, and that there was some part of the deceased that still required nourishment, clothing, and protection in order to journey safely in another kind of existence beyond the grave. There seems little question that the graphic paintings found in the European caves of the Paleolithic age (c. 50,000 B.C.E.) clearly indicate that early humans sought to placate the spirits of the animals they killed for food, dispel the restless spirits of the humans they had slain in disputes, and to bring peace to the spirits of their deceased tribal kin. Therefore, it seems quite likely that for 50,000 years, human beings have believed that one of the most common places to witness the spirits of the deceased is around deathbeds and at funerals.

THE RESEARCH OF CARLA WILLS-BRANDON

C arla Wills-Brandon, Ph.D., has spent more than two decades investigating the mystical experiences of the dying and those who were at their bedside. According to Wills-Brandon, who has collected nearly 2,000 modern-day deathbed vision accounts: "Deathbed visions come in all shapes and sizes. As physical death draws near, some people receive visitations from deceased relatives while others encounter angels or other religious figures."

Many of the accounts collected by Wills-Brandon mention a wisp of "something" leaving the physical body at the moment of passing. "Those who are about to leave will often talk about seeing beautiful landscapes on the other side and then state with conviction that this is where they will be after they pass," she said.

A licensed marriage and family therapist who shared a private practice for 20 years with her husband of 25 years, Michael Brandon, Ph.D., Wills-Brandon is the author of *One Last Hug Before I Go: The Mystery and Meaning of Deathbed Visions* and *A Glimpse of Heaven: Spiritually Transformative Mystical Experiences of Everyday People*. Her extensive research has convinced her that deathbed visions bring comfort not only to the dying but also to those who love them. "In most cases, once one has had such a vision, death is no longer something to fear," she said. "This phenomenon is nothing new. It has been described over and over again, across all cultures and religions, for as long as time can remember."

As Wills-Brandon reminds us, deathbed visions of the soul leaving the body have been experienced by humans in all cultures and religions; in fact, the existence of the soul is one of the few things upon which the major religions agree. In Judaism, Christianity, Hinduism, Buddhism, and Islam, the soul or spirit is the very essence of the individual, more important to his or her identity than the physical body, which is only a temporary possession that will turn to dust:

1. "The body is the sheath of the soul." (The Talmud [Judaism])

2. "Then the Lord God formed man out of the dust of the ground, and breathed into his nostrils the breath of life; and man became a living being." (Old Testament, Genesis, 2:7 [Judaism/Christianity])

3. "And He originated the creation of man out of clay, then He fashioned his progeny of an extraction of mean water, then He shaped him, and breathed His spirit in him." (The Qur'an, 32: 8–9 [Islam])

4. In Hinduism, the soul is a fragment of the Divine Self, the Atman. "Now my breath and spirit goes to the Immortal, and this body ends in ashes; OM, O Mind! Remember the deeds. Remember the actions." (Isha Upanishad 17)

5. The great Hindu work, the Bhagavad Gita, contains the oft-quoted lines that tell us the spirit within is unborn, eternal, immutable, indestructible, immemorial, and unchanging. "As a man abandons his worn-out clothes and acquires new ones, so when the body is worn out a new one is acquired by the Self,

who lives within.... The Self cannot be pierced or burned, made wet or dry. It is everlasting and infinite, standing on the motionless foundation of eternity. The Self is unmanifested, beyond all thought, beyond all change." (Bhagavad Gita, 2: 19–25)

6. Buddhism perceives the spirit as the end-product of a life of conditions and causes. "Behold this beautiful body, a mass of sores, a heaped up lump, diseased ... in which nothing lasts, nothing persists. Thoroughly worn out is this body.... Truly, life ends in death.... Of bones is this house made, plastered with flesh and blood. Herein are stored decay, death, conceit, and hypocrisy. Even ornamental chariots wear out. So too the body reaches old age." (Dhammapada 147–51)

7. The teachings of Seicho-no-le, a new religion becoming popular in Japan, state that the nature of human beings is primarily a spiritual life, "which weaves its threads of mind to build a cocoon of flesh, encloses its own soul in the cocoon, and for the first time, the spirit becomes flesh. But understand this clearly: The cocoon is not the silkworm; in the same way, the physical body is not man but merely man's cocoon. Just as the silkworm will break out of its cocoon and fly free, so, too, will man break out of his body-cocoon and ascend to the spiritual world when his time is come." (Nectarean Shower of Holy Doctrines)

ANGELS OR SPIRITS?

One can engage in a ceaseless and tiresome debate about whether people are really seeing angels at the deathbeds of their loved ones or if spirits pose as heavenly messengers to soothe the fears of the dying and their family members. It can also be argued that angels assume the image of beloved deceased family members in order to help the dying make the transition between life and death.

According to the monotheistic traditions of Judaism, Christianity, and Islam, humans do not become angels when they die. The scriptures of these faiths state that angels were created as an order of spiritual beings prior to the creation of humans and thus remain as entities separate from human beings. Angels serve as God's messengers, intermediaries between humankind and the divine, and as guardians and guides for men and women while they live on Earth.

To the dismay of traditional theologians in the United States, Canada, Great Britain, and Europe, the spirituality of contemporary generations is becoming increasingly centered on angel phenomena. Books on angels became popular in the mid-1990s, which encouraged the proliferation of

Angels are one of the most common forms that individuals see during out-of-body projections, near death experiences, after death has occurred, and during times of emotional turmoil.

numerous stores specializing in angel merchandise—everything from statues of the heavenly creatures to a variety of scents designed to attract them to one's home can be purchased. Since the terrorist attacks on September 11, 2001, belief in angelic beings has become more widespread. Members of organized religious bodies blame the recent popular interest in angelic beings on the fact that large numbers of young adults and teenagers have grown up with no organized religious instruction. These individuals consider the faiths of their parents as tarnished and marginalized structures that are no longer able to offer any practical rules for life and its myriad mysteries.

Michael Valpy, a religion and ethics reporter for the Toronto *Globe and Mail* (December 24, 2002), interviewed Thomas Beaudoin, a theology professor at Jesuit Boston College and the author of *Virtual Faith: The Irreverent Spiritual Quest of Generation X*, who verified that the angel phenomenon was extant wherever he encountered young Christians, Jews, or Muslims. Beaudoin commented that young people speak of angels in personal terms, which reflects their need for mentors and role models in an age when heroes and heroines are in short supply. In addition, Beaudoin said that a belief in angels demonstrates a conviction that human existence is too profound to be terminated by the act of physical death as well as a desire to be connected with those who have passed away.

Other theologians, such as David Reed of the University of Toronto's Anglican Wycliffe College, have stated that angels are extremely believable and accessible as spirit guides. Leonard Primiano, a teacher of religion and folklore at Pennsylvania's Cabrini College, said that young North Americans are interested in everything that is supernatural—UFOs, ghosts, and angels. As the majority of young people believe that angels are the spirits of people who have passed on, they are regarded as proof of life after death. To have a faith in angels is to have faith that the human soul lives on after the grave.

The popularity of a growing number of "channelers," who claim to contact angels, illustrates the manner in which the concepts of angels and spirits of the dead have blended in contemporary times. Just as mediums claim to be able to contact the spirits of the deceased and obtain guidance and wisdom for the living, there are angel mediums, or channelers, who claim the ability to establish communication with angels and relay information that will help their clients solve their material, human problems.

In December 1999 Emma Heathcote, a researcher and Ph.D. candidate at Birmingham University in the United Kingdom, appeared on a popular television program on the British television station BBC to appeal for reports from individuals who had encounters with angels. In November 2000 she stated that she had heard from 800 individuals—Christians, Jews, Muslims, agnostics, and atheists—who claimed to have experienced interaction with angels. The respondents stated that the angels had appeared to convey a message, to provide comfort, and in some instances intervened to prevent serious accidents.

In January 2001 the Allensbach Institute, a surveyor of public opinion in Germany, released poll findings that indicated that 30 percent of the German population believed in angels, and one-fifth of that group claimed to have seen an angelic being.

On December 20, 2001, Scripps Howard News Service and Ohio University released a report stating their research indicated that belief in angels cuts across almost all ranges of education, income, and lifestyle. Women and young people were slightly more likely to believe in angels, but a majority of demographic groups in the United States had faith in these supernatural beings. According to their survey, 77 percent of adults answered "yes" to the question, "Do you believe angels, that is some kind of heavenly beings who visit Earth, in fact exist?"

The fact that angels and spirit beings from some heavenly realm are synonymous in the minds of the great majority of individuals only mildly affects the research of those who pursue the matter of ghosts and the great mystery of life after death. Whether these entities are separate beings who work together to bring peace and comfort to the dying and their families, or facets of the same benevolent force that manifest in a manner most acceptable to the dying and those at their bedside, for thousands of years individuals have proclaimed that these angels do exist.

A Survey of Doctors and Nurses on Deathbed Visitations

Reports of deathbed experiences have long intrigued medical doctors and nurses. The work of researchers such as Dr. Elisabeth Kubler-Ross, Dr. Raymond Moody, Dr. Kenneth Ring, Dr. P. M. H. Atwater, and Dr. Carla Wills-Brandon have allowed us to gain greater understanding of this most personal phenomena.

Interestingly, a systematic investigation of deathbed reports was not attempted until the early 1960s, when a pilot study by Dr. Karlis Osis sought to analyze and establish patterns in the experiences of dying persons (*Deathbed Observations by Physicians and Nurses*, Parapsychology Foundation, Inc., 1961).

Osis gathered 640 doctors and nurses to participate in the survey-based investigation; their selection was based on their specialized training, ability to make accurate medical assessments, and proximity to dying patients. Each respondent to Osis's questionnaire had observed an average of 50–60 deathbed patients, totaling more than 35,000 cases. The initial survey was followed up with telephone calls, additional questionnaires, and personal correspondence.

A total of 385 of the participants reported 1,318 cases in which deathbed patients reported seeing apparitions of previously deceased loved ones or ghosts of individuals who were known to them. Scenes of wondrous beauty or visions of heaven were reported by 248 participants in 884 instances.

The physicians and nurses stated that the experiences left nearly all of the patients in a state of peace or exaltation. In about half of the cases, the spirits of loved ones or religious figures seemed to manifest in order to guide the dying patient through the transition from death to the afterlife. Those who had visions of the other side seemed serene and elevated in mood. One distinct observation from Osis's study was that few patients appeared to die in a state of fear.

Interestingly enough, patients with a higher degree of formal education seemed to experience deathbed phenomena more often than individuals with less formal education, which contradicts the allegation that uneducated, superstitious individuals have such experiences. Those with strong religious beliefs most often identified a saintly figure or saw heaven, but holy and angelic figures were often reported by patients with no religious affiliation.

Another interesting finding of the study was that deathbed visions are reported more often in cases where the dying patients are fully conscious and appear to be in complete control of their senses. Sedation, high fever, and barbiturates seem to decrease, rather than increase, the ability to experience deathbed phenomena. Brain damage and brain disease were found to have no impact on the kind of deathbed experiences that were relevant to Osis's survey.

The study also discovered cases in which those who had gathered around the deathbed collectively witnessed apparitions. There were numerous instances of a telepathic or clairvoyant interaction between patients and the physicians and nurses that attended them; a good number of participants reported that they had undergone a change in personal outlook or philosophy after having witnessed the experience of a dying person.

THE DEATHBED RESEARCH OF REVEREND W. BENNETT PALMER

During the course of his extensive research into deathbed visions, Reverend W. Bennett Palmer commented that bedside witnesses typically see a mist or cloud-like vapor emerging from the mouth or head of the individual who is dying. Shortly after, the vaporous substance takes on a human form, which is generally a duplicate of the living person. However, in most cases any physical deformities or injuries the individual may have had are partially or wholly absent. Angels or spirits of deceased loved ones are often seen accompanying the newly freed spirit form to higher dimensions of light.

In numerous reports, the moment of physical death is not witnessed, but the deceased is seen leaving the Earth plane for the higher world, most often accompanied by angelic beings. While spirits or angels are often seen ascending upward with the newly deceased, this seems to simply be a mode of disappearing, rather than an indication that other dimensions or planes of existence are in any particular spatial area.

"A fact often noted in connection with deathbed visions is that they are quite different from a patient's delirium and are coherent, rational, and, on reflection, apparently real," Palmer said. "It has also been observed that visions of the dying are different from visions of those who only think themselves to be dying, such as those undergoing a near-death experience. However, visions of the dying are similar to those who claim to have been out of the body during altered states of consciousness.

"Revelations concerning the nature of the future life which are received in deathbed visions seem to be regarded with favor by all churches, and no stigma attaches itself to the deathbed visionary experience," Palmer continued. "Persons having deathbed visions often claim to have seen the dead—or what is so regarded—and to have had them reveal knowledge of events which could not be known in any normal way. Frequently, the person having a deathbed vision claims to see a person in spirit who is not known to be dead. Later, investigation proves that the person was deceased at the time of the visitation.

"Another aspect of deathbed visions," Palmer concluded, "involves visions of angels and other Holy Figures seen by other persons in the presence of the dying."

Transcending the Final Boundary

In his years of research, Palmer has noted that people who are about to transcend their physical existence often mention a final boundary. After the person who is dying has passed that line of demarcation, they cannot return to their physical body. In fact, they are often prevented from crossing back over the line and returning to their physical life.

The environment and the scenery described in deathbed visions is said to be a scene much like what we experience on Earth, only it becomes more beautiful as the spirit progresses. Eventually, the environment becomes ineffable, incapable of description in human terms or in earthly comprehension.

In instances where one has achieved a glimpse into heaven, or higher planes of existence, the forms of deceased relatives and friends and esteemed or saintly figures are often seen. Angels are frequently seen in the company of deceased loved ones. The angels may come to sing heavenly music, to summon the soul from the dying body, or to accompany the newly released spirit to the other world. Most of the individuals who have witnessed spiritual or angelic presences at deathbeds are able to describe the beings in great detail, including their eyes, hair, apparel, as well as other attributes and accouterments.

DEATHBED VISIONS AS TOLD TO REVEREND W. BENNETT PALMER

Cloud-like Vapors and Luminous Clouds

Bill W. told Palmer that he saw the spirit of his brother as it disengaged from the dying body. The cloud-like vapor took on human shape, clapped its hands in joy, and passed upward through the ceiling in the company of an angel.

Jerry C. of Denver, Colorado, stated that when his 10-year-old son died, he saw the child's spirit leave the body as a luminous cloud and rise upward toward the ceiling.

They Joined the Angels Two Days Apart

Mr. and Mrs. S., two members of Palmer's congregation in New Port Richey, Florida, were very ill and had been placed in separate rooms of their home to insure periods of peace and uninterrupted sleep for both of them. One afternoon, as Mr. S. rested in his bed, he saw the form of his wife pass through the wall of his room, wave her hand in farewell, and rise upward in the company of an angel.

A few minutes later a nurse came into his room and informed him that Mrs. S. had passed away. "I know," he said, holding back his tears. "She had enough of this desperate struggle to maintain life. She came to say goodbye, and to ask me to join her with the angels." Mr. S. died two days later.

An Oval Light Met by a Lovely Angel

When Mrs. Ernestine Tamayo entered her husband's sickroom in order to bring him the newspaper, she saw a large, oval light emerging from his head. The illuminated oval floated toward the window, hovered a moment, and was met by a lovely angelic figure. Within seconds, both the oval of light and the angel had vanished.

"I knew that Miles was dead even before I reached my husband's bedside," she told Palmer. "I had seen his angel guide come to take him home."

OTHER DEATHBED ACCOUNTS

The Spirit of a Beautiful Woman Came for Mary

Dr. E. Hanner, a retired general practitioner from Michigan, said that he would never forget the time back in 1939 when he visited a sick child who was slowly dying from the ravages of typhoid fever.

"This girl that I was tending was the youngest child of the Reddings, a family of hardworking German Catholics," Hanner said. "I was a staunch Baptist, and in those days, in some of the more remote rural regions of the state, there were certain prejudices that were strongly maintained between Catholic and Protestant. But when one of the children in any of the Catholic families was sick, it didn't matter to them if I worshipped crows or trees. I was the only doctor in town, and they wanted me there looking after their kids."

Late one afternoon in August, just after Hanner had finished examining the seven-year-old girl, he heard a rustling sound off to his right side. "I assumed that I was hearing the sound of the mother's dress, so without turning around, I expressed my sad regret that I didn't think there was anything more that I could do for little Mary. Her condition had not improved, and it seemed to be quickly worsening. I suggested that they call their priest for last rites. My pills and powders could not help her any longer."

When there was no response, Hanner turned to see a beautiful young woman he guessed was in her late teens standing just a few inches from him. "She had dark brown shoulder-length, and she was dressed completely in white," he recalled. "I knew that she was not any member of the family, for the oldest of the Redding children was only 13. She seemed not to pay any attention to me, and she brushed by me to approach the girl in her bed."

Hanner was astonished when the lovely young woman bent over the child, then lifted the spirit form of the little girl into her arms. "I was so stunned by the action that I thought my knees would buckle. I was witnessing a sight that few mortals are privileged to see," he continued. "Little Mary's spirit was identical to her physical body, except it was translucent, and it no longer bore the ravages of the terrible illness that she had suffered for over a month." What Hanner beheld next was even more startling. The beautiful lady in white passed right through the wall with the child's spirit in her arms.

He sat quietly in a chair for several minutes, attempting to recover his mental balance. When he felt that his wits had returned and he could examine the girl, he verified what he already knew. Little Mary had died at the very moment when the beautiful woman in white had lifted her soul from her body.

A few minutes later, Hanner walked down the stairs of the farmhouse to give the weeping parents the sad announcement that their youngest child had died. Hoping to somehow alleviate their grief, but stumbling for the proper words, he offered his sincere conviction that he had seen an angel take Mary's soul to Heaven.

"I stayed with the family, offering what little comfort I could," Hanner said. "A while later, as we sat in the parlor drinking coffee and discussing funeral plans, I saw a picture of a beautiful young woman amidst a number of other photographs on a shelf near the upright piano. I involuntarily gasped, and said that before me was a photograph of the angel who had lifted Mary's soul from his body. Mrs. Redding told me that the portrait was of her sister Rose Ann.

"Mrs. Redding told that me that the portrait was Rose Ann's high school graduation picture and that it had been taken shortly before she was killed in an automobile accident," Hanner said. "Rose Ann had just turned 18, and she had died in 1930, nine years earlier."

Hanner said that when he swore that the lovely young woman who had ascended with Mary's spirit in her hands looked exactly like Rose Ann, the Redding family seemed to receive great comfort from his words. "They knew me as a man who was a bit hard-nosed and not given to exaggeration, or flights of imagination," he said, concluding his account. "And what I saw that afternoon in that Michigan farmhouse provided me with all the proof that anyone could ever need that there is life after death."

Grandfather Accompanied Catherine to the Other Side

Lisa Shellenberg of New Hampshire wrote that she saw the spirit of her grandfather James Hedrick in the sickroom of her 30-year-old daughter Catherine, just 10 hours before Catherine's death. It was her grandfather's spirit, she testified, who later called Catherine's soul body out of her physical form.

Shellenberg stated that she lost consciousness at the time of her daughter's death, and she was taken out of her body, together with Catherine's spirit, by her grandfather. For several hours she was with her daughter in the spirit world. Here, Shellenberg said, she saw many angels and spirit beings. Finally, Grandfather Hedrick told her that she must return to her body. She bade Catherine farewell, and she was soon in her flesh form once again.

"I had always had a special connection with Grandpa James," Shellenberg said. "It really didn't surprise me that our connection would extend after death and that he would grant me that last journey with Catherine as she passed away."

The Kiss of a Stranger Foreshadowed Death

Beth Domke of Omaha, Nebraska, said that her 15-year-old daughter Stacy was caring for the infant child of a neighbor in a nearby park when a strange man approached them and stopped before the bench on which they were sitting.

Stacy had at first become very nervous, fearing that the man might have malevolent intentions toward the baby. Her mother had cautioned her so often about child molesters and abductors. But she later told her mother that there was such a feeling of peace and love that issued from the man that she relaxed and smiled up at him. Not only did he seem kind and friendly, but there was something about him that seemed so familiar to her.

She was startled, however, when, without saying a word, the man suddenly leaned forward, kissed the baby on the forehead, and walked briskly away. Stacy said that he walked so fast that it seemed as though he had just disappeared.

Confused and experiencing vague feelings of guilt, Stacy stopped by their apartment before she returned the baby to its mother and told her own mother about the incident. "Stacy said the man appeared to be in his fifties or so, tall, silver-haired, very distinguished in his appearance," Beth Domke said in her account of the incident. "Stacy kept saying over and over that the stranger had seemed so nice, so loving." Domke assured her daughter that she had not done anything wrong. No harm had been done, but she should be more cautious regarding strangers in the future.

That night, according to the baby's parents, a knock was heard at their front door. When they answered, they found no one there. In a few minutes, the sound was heard again. On an impulse, the mother went into the room where her baby was sleeping. To her great sorrow, she found that the child was dead. Later, an autopsy revealed that she had died from sudden infant death syndrome.

When the Domkes visited the bereaved family the next day to express their sorrow over the family's loss, Stacy nearly became hysterical. Assuming that her sensitive daughter was reacting strongly to the death of the baby, Beth got Stacy out of there as quickly as she could. "On the way home," Beth wrote, "Stacy told me that she had freaked out because she had seen a ghostly image of the man who had kissed the baby in the park standing directly behind the grieving mother, resting a hand on her shoulder, as if it were trying to comfort her."

At first she thought that he was the Angel of Death, but then she saw a photograph of a man and woman on the mantle piece. "That was when Stacy realized why the man had seemed so familiar to her. She remembered the first time that she baby-sat for the family, and the mother had showed Stacy a photograph of her parents. She said that her mother was still alive, but that her father, whom she had loved so very much, had died several years ago. Stacy insisted that the man in the park was the spirit of the woman's father."

In her account of her daughter's remarkable experience, Domke stated that she believed the spirit of the woman's father had come to escort the soul of his infant granddaughter to the afterlife. Domke reasoned that the family had heard the spirit knock at the front door as it came for the soul of the child, and it knocked again as it left.

An Angel Came to Get Mommy

Richard Riggs's wife and nine-year-old daughter were killed in an automobile accident that left his six-year-old daughter Robin severely injured. Riggs entered little Robin's hospital room and steeled himself for the awful task of informing her about the death of her mother and sister.

But before he could break the sad news to Robin, she told him that she already knew about the deaths. "While I was lying hurt on the ground," she stated, "I saw an angel come to get Mommy. The angel started to go back up into the sky, but it stopped, came back for Becky, and took both of them into Heaven."

An Angel Tapped at the Window

Pastor Raymond Tigge had known for several months that his child, Samuel, would not recover from his lengthy illness. One warm July night, the entire family decided to sleep in the coolest room of their home. Tigge said that he and his wife were both awakened by a soft tapping at the window near their bed. They then saw an angel come through the window, walk over to the sleeping boy, kiss him, and leave.

A few days later, in an effort to divert the boy's mind from his illness, a friend asked Samuel what he wanted for Christmas. The boy shook his head soberly and replied that he would be in Heaven. He wouldn't need any toys there. Within a week, Samuel Tigge died.

His Friend's Soul Left During the Funeral

Dr. D. P. Kayser said that while attending the funeral of Dr. A. N Costello, a colleague whom he had known for more than 30 years, he watched his friend's soul leaving the body. "There was no question in my mind that Angelo was truly, clinically dead before the funeral," Kayser stated, "but I had once heard it said that 'real death' is not accomplished until the soul actually leaves the body."

This engraving by William Blake depicts the author's vision of death.

Kayser knew that his friend's life had been one of kindness and service. "Angelo had always been a sincere, practicing Catholic, but even so, I was quite startled when I saw the spirits of a group of white-robed children materialize. Assembled near the coffin were more white-robed spirits, some of whom I recognized as deceased friends, relatives, and patients of Dr. Costello's."

As the funeral service progressed, Kayser was somehow able to observe the process of death: "I saw a vapor or mist gradually rise from the body in the casket. When the transition had been completed, the mist gradually took on the image of Dr. Costello. Almost at that very moment, a very beautiful angel, robed in the purest white, approached the newly liberated spirit. In its hands, the angel bore a lovely wreath, the center of which supported a large white flower. With this floral diadem, the angel crowned the spirit body of Dr. Angelo Costello.

"When the spirit form was completely separated from the physical body, the image of my friend, the angels, and the attending spirits appeared to float away together."

A Dream of His Sister's Death

Charles Downey had a dream that told him his sister Jean was dying. Since he had experienced similar dreams before the deaths of other members of his family, he was inclined to pay heed to the nocturnal revelation. "Either it's a dark Irish curse or a blessing," Downey said. "I had experienced a similar dream before the death of our mother, our cousin Paul, and a close school friend. Because of such a sorrowful track record, I knew that I had better pay attention to this sad dream about Jean."

When a telephone call from his brother-in-law David confirmed Jean's approaching death, Charles and his wife Marcy left immediately to be at her bedside. Jean's eyes did not open, but somehow she knew who was present in her room and even where they were standing. As Charles bent to kiss her cheek, Jean spoke in a voice barely audible: "Don't worry, Charlie, they've come for me. Mom, Dad, Paul, Uncle Sean, they're all here, waiting for me, just outside the window. And there's a lovely angel with them. She'll escort us to our heavenly home."

David was standing by the window when Jean asked him to step aside so the angel and the others might enter to take her home. Confused, David moved back from the window, and all those present in the room were startled when a whiff of wind suddenly stirred the curtains at the same time that Jean took a final breath.

Charles Downey wrote that his sister's face bore a lovely and restful smile as her soul departed with members of her family and her angel guide.

An Angel Appeared with Her Parents to Take Her Home

The Personal Experience of Steve Preteroti: "I saw three separate clouds float through the doorway into the room where Rochelle lay dying. The clouds enveloped the bed. As I gazed through the mist, I saw what at first appeared to be the form of a woman take shape. It was transparent and had a golden sheen. It was a figure so glorious in appearance that no words can describe it. The beautiful entity was dressed in a long, Grecian robe, and there was a brilliant tiara on her head. It had to have been an angel.

"The majestic figure remained motionless, with its hands lifted over my wife, seemingly engaged in prayer. Then I noticed two other figures kneeling by Rochelle's bedside. I recognized them at once as the forms of her deceased parents. They had come in the company of an angel to guide my beloved Rochelle to heaven. My wife's spirit duplicate appeared over her physical body, hovering above it horizontally. It seemed to be connected to Rochelle's body by a cord.

"The whole experience lasted for five hours. As soon as my dear wife had taken her last breath, the glorious angel, the spirits of Rochelle's beloved parents, and the spirit form of my wife vanished."

The Manifestation of an Angelic Comforter

Reverend Maurice Elliott and Irene H. Elliott state that they were present at the bedside of a dying woman when an angel-comforter appeared by her and said, "I have come to take you home." According to the minister and his wife, other angels and the dying woman's deceased friends and relatives also joined the angel-comforter. Shortly after, a white, hazy mist rose above the woman, hovered there for a few moments, and eventually congealed to take on perfect human form.

After the soul-body had been released from its physical shell, the woman's spirit left in the company of the angels and those dear ones who had already become residents of a higher dimension.

An Angel Severed the Cord

Don P. said that directly above his dying brother Nick, he saw a shadowy form floating in a horizontal position. The form evolved into an exact image of Nick's physical body. "Then I saw an angel materialize and sever a cord which appeared to have connected Nick's spirit form with his physical body," Don stated. "Once the cord had been separated, Nick's spirit form and the angel disappeared together."

7

Ghosts That Returned to Bid Farewell

A downed aircraft in France, a hotel room in Calcutta, a favorite niece in England, a family friend in yet another locale—as we shall see from the following account, time and space mean nothing to ghosts who come to bid farewell. There are two features in the case of Captain Eldred Bowyer-Bowyer that are common in the phenomena of the recently departed saying goodbye. The first is that the ghost appears very lifelike; in fact it looks so much like the human being it represents that it is almost always mistaken for the actual living person. The second is that such ghosts materialize when people least expect them. They suddenly pop up, completely unannounced by prior feelings of distress or anxiety about the person whom they represent. The visions usually manifest while the percipients are engaged in their normal duties or while they are preparing for sleep.

The Reverend Arthur Bellamy told the highly respected psychical researcher Frederic W. H. Myers about the lady he saw one night sitting on his wife's side of the bed while she was sound asleep. He stared at the strange woman for several minutes, especially noting the elegant styling of her hair. Then she vanished.

When Mrs. Bellamy awakened, her husband described the mysterious visitor. He was startled to learn that the description fit that of a schoolgirl friend of his wife's. The two friends had once made a pact that whichever of them died first would appear to the other after death. The astonished Reverend Bellamy asked if she remembered her friend having any distinguishing physical characteristics, so that they might be certain it had been the same individual. "Her hair," his wife replied without hesitation. "We girls used to tease her at school for devoting so much time to the arrangement of her hair." Later, the clergyman saw a photograph of his wife's friend and identified her as the ghost that had appeared at his wife's bedside.

It would appear, judging by the cases we will encounter in this chapter, that at the moment of physical death, the soul—the essential self in all persons—is emancipated from the confines of the body and is able to soar free of time and space. In some instances the soul is able to make one last, fleeting moment of contact with a loved one. These projections at the moment of death indicate that *something* non-physical exists within the human body and is capable of surviving physical death.

THE PILOT KEPT HIS PROMISE

The Case of Captain Eldred Bowyer-Bowyer

On March 19, 1917, Captain Eldred Bowyer-Bowyer was shot down in his plane over France; on that same day he was to be named the godfather of his half-sister's baby. Mrs. Spearman, who was staying in a hotel in Calcutta, India, was fussing with her baby when she suddenly turned around and saw her half-brother standing behind her. Delighted that he had been transferred to India just in time to attend the baptismal service, Spearman turned to set the baby down. When she turned back around to embrace her brother, and faced the spot where her brother had stood only moments before, she found that he had vanished.

At first Spearman thought that he had to be playing a trick on her. She called for him and searched everywhere, but he was nowhere to be found. Puzzled, she made her way to the church. It was not until two weeks later that she read in a newspaper that her half-brother had been shot down on the very day that he had appeared in her hotel room.

On the day of his death, Bowyer-Bowyer was also seen by his young niece in England. At about 9:15 A.M., the girl ran excitedly up to her mother and informed her that "Uncle Alley Boy" was downstairs! Her mother smiled and reminded the girl that her uncle was in France, but the excited girl insisted that she had seen "Uncle Alley Boy" downstairs.

A third impression of Captain Bowyer-Bowyer was received by a Mrs. Watson, an elderly friend of the airman's mother. On March 19, she wrote Mrs. Bowyer-Bowyer—to whom she had not written for 18 months—that she had great feelings of anxiety about Eldred.

THE PHONE WAS OUT OF ORDER, SO HER SPIRIT CAME TO SAY GOODBYE

In the summer of 1913, Stella (Libby) Rife moved away, leaving behind Bernice Moore, her best friend and "double cousin." Bernice's father was Stella's maternal uncle, and her mother was Stella's paternal aunt. The two girls had been fast companions and confidantes until the Rifes moved from Lansing, Michigan, to Jackson, Michigan.

Three years later, on the evening of December 19, 1916, Stella and a girlfriend were home alone, getting ready for an evening out with some other young women. Stella was leaving her room and descending the brightly lit stairway when she suddenly froze. "Standing in the bright illumination stood my cousin Bernice," she recalled ("My Proof of Survival," *Fate* magazine, February 1968). "She looked terrified. I saw her clearly, yet I knew she could not be there."

Stella ran hurriedly down the stairs, brushing past the apparition and out the front door. She did not stop until she was a block away from the house. Her girlfriend caught up with her, and Stella tried her best to explain what had so startled her.

When they met their friends later that evening, one of the young women, who worked as an operator for the telephone company, appeared to be troubled. Even before they had greeted one another, she asked Stella if they were aware that their phone was out of order. Someone in Lansing, Michigan, had been trying to call the Rife family, the operator said, but as their phone line was down, she said that she would deliver the message personally, since she would be seeing Stella soon.

On November 16, 1968, Robert A. Ferguson addressed a spiritualist convention in Los Angeles, California. Several Polaroid photographs were taken during his speech; this one allegedly shows Ferguson's brother, Walter (who died in action in 1944, during World War II), standing next to him.

The message was that Bernice Moore had died that evening. When the telephone could not be used to communicate the message, the spirit of her cousin traversed time and space and manifested before Stella to say farewell.

A WHITE FORM, GLIDING AWAY, STRUCK THE DOCTOR

Mrs. Margaret Sargent, a certified nurse, was caring for a young woman in Augusta, Georgia, when, at about 11 P.M., the patient took a dramatic turn for the worse. The physician did not wish to awaken the patient's mother, for fear of adding to her emotional stress. Sargent later recalled that they knew the patient had previously expressed that she wanted to have her mother present at all times, "but since she had become unconscious, we did not think it necessary to satisfy that desire" (Sylvan Muldoon and Hereward Carrington, *The Phenomena of Astral Projection*).

The doctor and nurse recognized that the girl was going to pass on, and they stood solemnly by her bedside, anticipating the moment of the young woman's death. Sargent was sitting at the foot of the bed when she glanced up and saw "a white form advancing, a robed form." She was unable to see the robed figure's face because it was turned away from her, but she was clearly able to observe its form, as the figure remained for a moment by the inert physical body of the young female patient. "Then [it] passed swiftly past the doctor and glided toward me, but always turning its face in the opposite direction," she said.

Just before the apparition passed through the wall to the room in which the patient's mother lay sleeping, it paused to strike the doctor a smart blow on the shoulder. Startled, the physician turned around, saw nothing, and remarked perplexedly to his nurse that something had struck him on the shoulder. Sargent managed to overcome her awe and tell him that the woman who had just passed by him was the one responsible for the blow. "What woman?" the doctor asked. "There is no woman in this room but that poor dying young lady on the bed. But someone struck me. What does this mean?"

Before either of them could speculate further, the patient began to mumble in a feeble voice. To their complete astonishment, the woman had regained her senses. She remained conscious for another 24 hours before she died with her head resting on her mother's arm.

CONTACTS BETWEEN THE LIVING AND THE NEWLY DEAD

A Personal Recollection and Commentary by Franklin R. Ruehl, PhD

"**A**re the dead able to make contact with the living after having passed over? Or does communication between individuals terminate upon death? My mother, Florence Ruehl, had a dramatic experience some years ago that indicates communication can take place even after the physical body dies. Back in 1955 we were living in a second-floor apartment in Glendale, California. On the evening of Tuesday, April 5, my father, a bookkeeper, was at the office preparing tax forms, while I was in my room doing homework. My mother was in the living room, dancing to music playing on the phonograph.

"Suddenly, at approximately 8:10 P.M., a small human form materialized in the room, just a few feet away from her. It was a dwarf-sized man, about three feet tall, dressed in colorful cowboy attire, complete with a 10-gallon hat and leather boots. The entity simply stared at her, with a smirk on its face, but said nothing. Then, after a minute, it slowly faded away into nothingness.

"Mother was shaken and called out to me. Describing the incident, she asserted that the man she saw was, without a doubt, her father, and she was certain he had just visited her from beyond the grave—despite the fact that, as far as she knew, he was in good health at the age of 64 and living in Pittsburgh.

"Now, it should be stressed that in life he had been of ordinary stature, about five-feet, eight-inches tall. And, to her knowledge, he had never expressed any interest whatsoever in the Wild West, being a lifelong easterner. Moreover, he was always very loquacious, unlike the taciturn entity that appeared to her. But, in spite of all of these contradictions, she had absolutely no doubt that it was his spirit that had appeared to her. While the entity had smirked at her, she did not feel that it had been menacing. On the other hand, she did not feel it had been friendly, either. The two of them had been more or less estranged for several years and rarely communicated.

"Her apprehensions were confirmed the very next morning when a telegram arrived about 10 A.M., informing her of her dad's demise from a heart attack the previous evening, shortly after 11 P.M. EST, which had been the exact hour he had materialized before her. My mother Florence often thinks about her brief encounter with the paranormal and has stated: 'I recall that night as vividly now as when it first transpired. There is absolutely no doubt in my mind that the spirit of my father appeared before me!' As to the being's small stature and cowboy outfit, she hypothesizes, "Perhaps he longed to be a child once more, and conceivably, he harbored a secret wish to play at being a cowboy, even if only for a brief instant in time."

His Father's Last Message

Such transitory contacts between the living and the newly dead are well chronicled in parapsychological literature. As an intriguing example, there is the case of prolific horror/sci-fi director Reginald Le Borg, who helmed such films as *Voodoo Island, The Mummy's Curse, The Black Sleep,* and *Diary of A Madman*, starring such luminaries as Boris Karloff, Bela Lugosi, Vincent Price, Basil Rathbone, John Carradine, George Zucco, and Lon Chaney, Jr.

While living in Los Angeles in 1938, Le Borg was awakened by an unsettling dream one warm night at 2:15 A.M. In the dream, his father had shouted, "Stay here! Don't say no!" The men had a long-standing quarrel, rooted in Le Borg's decision to travel to the United States and pursue a career in Hollywood. Le Borg immediately felt a presentiment of death concerning his father, which was verified later that morning, when a telegram arrived informing him that his dad had indeed passed away. He later learned that the precise time of death corresponded to the moment he had awakened, and that his last utterances as he lay dying were, "Stay here! Don't say no!'"

Such cases offer powerful testimony to the theory that the human spirit persists after death and often attempts to make final contact with a loved one in some way. When loved ones are estranged, it is especially common for contact to occur after death, whether it takes the form of a dream, vision, or momentary materialization.

"Don't Touch Me. I Must Return."

In August 1954, when Larry Exline finally got a two-week vacation with pay, his wife Juliette was overjoyed. Larry had been working so hard, and this vacation would give him an opportunity to go fishing in Nevada with a friend.

On August 29, Juliette awakened in a cold sweat. She was certain that she heard Larry's voice calling her. The voice was faint, as if it were coming from a great distance, but she was certain that this was Larry's voice. He sounded like he was suffering and in pain. Juliette slid out of bed, turned on a night light, and stepped into the hallway. At its far end she saw her husband, clutching at the wall in an attempt to stand up. His clothes were drenched with blood. She screamed as she rushed toward him. "Don't touch me," he warned her with a sob. "I must return." She begged him to explain where had to go, and why, and told him to wait, that she would call a doctor.

At that instant, the telephone rang. It was a sheriff from Ely, Nevada, calling to inform Juliette that her husband had been killed instantly in an automobile accident. "Oh, no," she said. "My husband's here!"

She hurried back into the hall, "But Larry wasn't there. He indeed had 'gone back'" (Juliette L. Exline, "My Proof of Survival," *Fate* magazine, July 1969).

A Mother's Kiss from Beyond the Grave

Ken Lehmann left the bedside of his mother feeling sad and depressed. His mother's battle with cancer had been long and painful and had left him emotionally exhausted. Ken's father had passed away four years earlier, and his mother had been in ill health since that time. "Please go home and get some rest, Kenny," his mother had told him. "You must not stay here another night worrying over me. Go home and see to Audrey and the children." Ken said that he would go home and look in on his wife and kids, but then he would return to the hospital to be at her side.

When he arrived at home, he saw that the kids were already tucked in their beds, so he sat and talked with Audrey and told her that he was certain that his mother would soon pass on. "I really didn't want to leave her alone," he said softly, trying to hold back the tears. Audrey urged him to get a little rest before he returned to his vigil at the hospital. She told him that she had a sales presentation to finish before she went to bed, so she would be up if the phone rang. Ken checked his watch and decided that he would nap for a bit before he returned to his mother's bedside.

"I couldn't have slept more than 30 minutes when I felt what I knew to be the touch of my mother's lips on my cheek," Ken said. "It was a kiss of such sweetness and love that it could only have come from my mother. I opened my eyes and sat up. I had left a small lamp on in the room, and there, in the dim light, I could distinguish a kind of mist that had assumed human shape. Although I could not make out any distinct features, I knew that it was Mom. I felt the strongest emanations of pure love flowing to me from that vaporous form. Then it floated out of sight through the ceiling."

When Ken called the hospital a few moments later, he was not surprised to learn that his mother had just died. "The kind nurse spoke a few words to console me," Ken said. "But I had just received the greatest sort of consolation from my mother, who had come to show me that there is life beyond physical death. And no one will ever be able to convince me that it was not my mother who gave me that wonderful goodbye kiss!"

"I'm All Right Now"

When Colette Bransen awakened on that chilly November morning in 1983, she arose with an acute feeling that something was very wrong. As she prepared breakfast, she carefully examined her 13-year-old daughter Melissa and her seven-year-old son Tim. Since they seemed well and happy, Colette knew that something had to be wrong with her husband, Jeff, who was institutionalized in a veterans' hospital nearly 200 miles away.

Jeff, a Vietnam veteran, suffered from a progressive disease that he had contracted while in the service. He had dealt courageously with his illness, but in the spring of 1981, the stresses of rearing a family, adjusting to society, and battling a steadily debilitating disease had caused him to suffer a nervous breakdown. Tragically, Jeff had succumbed to a more complex mental illness soon after he had recovered from his breakdown.

Colette went to work that November morning feeling extremely distracted and ill-at-ease. "I was lucky my boss didn't fire me," she said. "I was continually drifting off into thoughts of great concern for Jeff." That evening when she returned home, she was no longer able to contain herself. She knew that it was always difficult to talk to one of her husband's doctors in the hospital, but she also knew that she must try to do so in order to set her mind at ease.

She managed to get through to a doctor who informed her that Jeff's condition remained unchanged. Furthermore, the doctor grumbled, his condition was not likely to change for several months, perhaps years. She would just have to content herself with the knowledge that he was being well cared for and that the medical staff was doing the best they could under the circumstances.

The doctor's brusque assurances did nothing to calm Colette's concern. In fact, the words designed to pacify her had achieved the opposite effect. She was all the more convinced that something was wrong with her husband. "After the kids were in bed, I retreated to my own private altar that I had constructed in a corner of my bedroom," she said. "I read from the Psalms, the New Testament, then lighted some candles and incense and began to pray. After a period of intense meditation, I soaked in a warm tub and went to bed."

Colette was awakened from a deep sleep by the sound of her husband calling her by his pet nickname for her, "Hey, Bright Eyes, wake up!" The sound of Jeff's voice raised her spirits. "Perhaps I was in that in-between space between sleep and consciousness, for I felt there was nothing strange about Jeff's standing firm and solid at my bedside," Colette said. "As I reached out to touch him, I asked with an inner knowing, 'You're all right now, aren't you, Jeff?'"

Colette's fingertips touched the firm flesh of Jeff's hand, and he closed his own fingers tightly around them. "Yes, Bright Eyes," he replied. "Everything is all right now. Always remember that I loved you so very much. Kiss the kids goodbye." And then he disappeared. Colette's hand only clutched a memory. She turned on the light and took careful note of the time on her clock radio. It was 2:08 A.M.

"I had no doubt that the visit I had just experienced was the result of my husband's death," Colette said. "I knew that Jeff had come to say goodbye."

She had just finished making the children's breakfast when the official call came from the veterans' hospital at 7:30 A.M. A sympathetic doctor expressed his condolences, then informed her that Jeff had died at about two o'clock that morning. Melanoma metastasis of the brain had snuffed out his life. "He died at 2:08, to be precise," Colette said aloud, not really knowing why it felt so important to correct the doctor.

There was a moment of awkward silence, and then the doctor was asking if someone from the hospital had called her earlier with the news of her husband's death. "None of your staff disobeyed your orders not to call me until 7:30," Colette said. "I'll be ready to drive to the hospital in an hour or so. I'll explain it to you when I see you." It was on that long 200-mile journey to the veterans' hospital that Colette once again heard Jeff's voice.

"He told me that he was now free, free of pain, free of confusion," she said. "And he told me that we would always be together on some level of awareness. I know that ever since his death, his spirit has always looked after our children's welfare from his dimension of being, and I have felt his loving presence in my own life on many occasions."

"I Will Never Leave Your Side"

Gretchen, 28, of Spokane, Washington, had always been very close to her maternal grandmother, Deborah K., who had been living in a nursing home in Rochester, New York. Grandma Deborah was in essence her mother, for Gretchen's mother died when she was four years old and Deborah had reared Gretchen as her own daughter.

"My mother and I had been living with Grandma when Mom became terribly ill with cancer," Gretchen said. "My father had been killed in Vietnam, and Mom and I had gone to live with Grandma in 1970. If it were not for the photo album I had with pictures of Mom in it, I would actually have very little memory of her. I remember that she was sick a lot. And I dimly recall her telling me that she would not be coming home from the hospital, that she was going away to be with Daddy, but that Grandma would take good care of me."

Gretchen had been filled with regret over the fact that her uncle, Ted, had placed Deborah a nursing home. She knew that Deborah was 77 years old and had been quite ill, but Gretchen was sad that when she had her first child, her grandmother would be so far away. Gretchen told her husband Larry how much she wanted her grandmother to be with her when the baby came, but she knew that even if they could afford to fly her to Spokane, she wouldn't be able to make the trip by herself.

On the night of October 17, 1992, two days before her baby was due, Gretchen experienced a very difficult night. She was highly nervous and extremely uncomfortable. When she did slip into brief periods of fitful sleep, she would dream of terrible things happening to the baby during the delivery. She looked at the alarm clock for what seemed the thousandth time that night, saw that it was 2:15 A.M., sat up in her bed, and began to weep.

"That was when I saw Grandma standing by the side of the bed," Gretchen said. "I know I was not dreaming, because I had been so anxious and restless, and I had just sat up in bed, wide awake and irritable." Gretchen remembered clearly that her grandmother just stood beside her quietly for a few moments before she spoke soothingly to her: "Everything is going to be all right, honey. You just stop your crying and fussing now. Be brave and be Grandma's big girl. I'm going to be with you every minute of the delivery. I will never leave your side. Everything will be fine. Now, blow Grandma a big kiss, and remember that I will always love you!" Gretchen found herself blowing a kiss toward Grandma's smiling face, and then the image of her beloved grandmother disappeared.

Gretchen cried out Grandma's name and awakened Larry, who sat up rubbing his eyes, wondering if she was having labor pains. "I told him about

This picture was taken immediately after two-year-old Greg said "Nanna's here."

my vision of Grandma, and how good it had made me feel," Gretchen said. "I always knew that Grandma and I could communicate telepathically, so, in one sense, her image appearing to me in a vision did not really surprise me that much. Anyway, I knew that I would be able to get some sleep."

At 5:47 A.M. Gretchen was awakened by labor pains. Larry knew that this was no false alarm. At 1:27 P.M., Deborah Esther was born. She was named after Gretchen's grandmother and Larry's mother. As truthful and dependable as always, Gretchen's grandmother had accurately predicted a safe delivery. And Gretchen did feel the loving presence of her grandmother supporting her throughout the entire painful process of giving birth.

That evening, after Gretchen had rested, Larry sadly presented her with a telegram from the nursing home in Rochester. With tears blurring her vision, Gretchen read that Grandma Deborah had died in her sleep. Larry pointed out the time that Deborah had passed away. "Honey, according to the people in the nursing home, your grandmother died this morning at about 5:15. Allowing for the difference in time zones, that would be about 2:15 our time, just when you said that you had a vision of your grandmother telling you that everything was going to be all right."

"Grandma was with me in spirit to watch over the birth of little Deborah Esther, and to see that she safely made her entrance into the world," Gretchen said, concluding her account. "Maybe it is like that song says, when one of us dies there will be another child born to take our place and to carry on."

"Remember Me with Kindness"

In 1972, while he was stationed in Germany, Stanley met a beautiful girl named Karla with whom he enjoyed a wonderful relationship. They were both in their early twenties, and they discussed marriage many times. Even though he had decided upon a career in the navy, there were times when he considered leaving it all for a life with Karla in Germany. Once, Stanley went so far as to buy an engagement ring, but he never showed it to Karla. Somehow, the time just didn't seem right to make such a commitment.

When it came time for Stanley to return to the United States, the two lovers were faced with a moment of truth. They spent their last weekend together in a lovely old hotel, and as they were finishing what they knew might be their last meal together, they once again spoke of marriage. As they were slowly sipping cool glasses of wine from the Rhine region, Karla said that she couldn't see herself marrying anyone but Stanley. Stanley admitted that he felt the same way about her. "Perhaps, then, we should see how we feel after you return to the States," Karla suggested. "Let us correspond. Let us see how we deal with the absence of one another. Let us test our love, and see if we should be married." They touched wineglasses and toasted Karla's proposal.

After Stanley's return to the United States, the two lovers began a passionate correspondence. Six months later, however, Stanley began to realize that he was concentrating more intensely on his navy career. The navy allowed him opportunities for advancement, and that meant putting his spare energy into preparing for exams, not writing love letters.

Stanley conceded that he began slacking off on the commitment to maintain an active correspondence. The frequency of his letters to Karla began to slow down. While he had once written a letter a day, it soon became one a week, and finally one a month. Karla's letters continued at a steady pace for a few months, then she began to match his schedule of once or twice a month.

About that time, Stanley met Darcy, a navy brat whose her father had devoted his entire career to the navy. Darcy really understood his love and commitment for the sea. Shortly after his engagement to Darcy, Stanley wrote to Karla and told her the news about his approaching marriage to another woman. "I never received an answer to my letter," Stanley said. "I felt bad. I wondered how I would have felt if Karla had been the one to have sent me such a letter. But I couldn't help feeling that I had done the best thing for both of us."

After his marriage, Stanley reported to duty aboard a destroyer based at the Virginia Beach, Virginia, shipyards. Darcy remained at home in Massachusetts while Stanley's ship was deployed to the Middle East and then passed into dry dock. It was Stanley's intention to move Darcy to Virginia Beach as soon as soon as he could.

Late on the evening of June 15, 1975, Stanley, a payment disbursement officer, was in his office preparing for payday only a few days away. He sat at his desk, typing up the pay roster until about 12:20 A.M. He had just leaned back in his chair to doze for a few minutes when he was awakened by a soft tapping at his office door. Assuming it was the security watch, he rather grumpily opened the door.

To Stanley's complete and total amazement, the image of Karla stood in the doorway, dressed in a diaphanous white nightgown. "Karla looked just the way that she had the day that we said goodbye in Germany," Stanley said. "And it hurt me to see that she had been crying." Stanley was speechless. At last he managed to ask her how she knew where to find him, and how she had been able to get aboard the destroyer without security stopping her.

She ignored Stanley's questions but spoke directly of other matters. "Stan, I am here to tell you that I understand about Darcy—and I forgive you." Stanley began to speak, but Karla held up her hand to silence him so that she might continue. "I knew that you were right in doing what you did," she said in a soft voice. "So I accepted another's proposal of marriage not long after I received your letter." Karla blinked back the tears that had gathered in her eyes and asked Stanley to promise to always remember her with kindness. Stanley nodded, choked with emotion. "With great kindness, Karla," he managed to whisper. "And with love."

Karla smiled, turned to leave, then looked over her shoulder and added, "And please be happy in your life with Darcy." Karla stepped away from the doorway and walked quietly and quickly down the passageway until she was out of sight. Stanley cannot estimate how long he sat quietly in reverie after Karla left him. He does remember being roused by the security watch that checked in on him. "Did you happen to see a pretty blonde woman in the passageway a few minutes ago?" he asked the security watch. "Yeah, right," the man laughed. "I thought you were supposed to working in here, not dreaming. Are you all right?"

Stanley mumbled something that somehow satisfied the watchman, then went back to work on the pay roster. But he was unable to remove the incident from his mind; whatever had occurred in those incredible few moments had completely disoriented him. He tried desperately to sell himself on the concept that he had dozed off and had a vivid dream, perhaps partially inspired by the guilt that he still felt toward his breakup with Karla. Stanley was unable to accept this rationalization. He knew that he had been awake when he had seen Karla.

Stanley set aside his paperwork and wrote a letter to Karla, detailing his remarkable experience. "I wanted to know if she might be ill, or if she might have been thinking intently of me at the time that her image had appeared in my office aboard the destroyer," he said.

A few weeks later, Stanley received a reply from Karla's mother, who informed him that Karla had died instantly in a head-on automobile crash in the early morning of June 16. The time of Karla's death was equivalent to about 12:20 A.M. on June 15 in Virginia Beach.

"Mrs. G. told me that she had been looking for my address to inform me of her daughter's death just as my letter arrived," Stanley said. "Only days before Karla's fatal accident, she had spoken of me and said how sorry she was that she had not answered my letter about my marriage to Darcy. Mrs. G. also verified that Karla was engaged to be married at the time of her death. The bond of love that we had once shared somehow enabled her to bid me a tender and forgiving farewell."

THREE STORIES OF A LAST FAREWELL FROM GHOST TO GHOST

These three moving accounts are provided through the courtesy of the Ghost to Ghost website (<http://www.ghosttoghost.com/stories.htm>).

One Last Time: From Gina in England

"**W**hen my mother was younger she knew an old man who [lived] up the road from her. When she walked to school each day, he made sure that he would walk her most of the way there. He would never leave her to walk alone, never.

"One day at around 9 A.M., which was the time she would set off for school, he came and walked with her as he normally did every school day. Once they had reached the end of the street he told her he had to cut off and go to the shop to buy some food. This was not what he would normally do, but my mother just thought it was not a big thing. She tried to turn around to wave and say goodbye, but she said she just couldn't turn around. It was as if something was stopping her from doing this.

"When my mother got home from school, she told her mother what had happened that morning. Her mother told her the old man had died at around [the same time he had been] walking with her. Also, a neighbor [had been] worried about my mother because, as she was walking to school that day, she [had seen] my mother talking to herself. What the neighbor [hadn't realized] was that my mother was actually talking to the old man who was walking with her to school—one last time."

A Visit from Grandpa: From Soraya, Age 15

"All my life I [had] dreamed of meeting my grandfather who lived in Iran. I am sorry to say that I never got to meet him [while] he was alive. Three days after the new millennium arrived, he passed away from a stroke. When my mother told me, I cried in my room for a long time. After I finished my tears, we went to my cousin's house to talk [and comfort each other].

"My Uncle told us that Grandpa [had] told him and his other siblings … that when he died he didn't want it to make people sad. When we got home I cried in my bed. I cried until, after awhile, I felt someone standing at the edge of my bed. I looked up. Nothing was there, but I felt someone's presence. I believed it was my grandpa trying to stop me from feeling sad. He leaned over and rubbed my cheek in a circular motion, and I could feel his hands were very warm. I stopped crying, and had a huge smile on my face because I finally got to meet my grandpa.

"A couple days later I heard my dad crying downstairs as I did my homework. I [had] never heard my dad cry before, but I knew it was because he was sad about his father. That night I told him about what happened, and he asked 'When he touched your cheek, did he move his hand in a circular motion?' And I said, 'Yes!'

The crystal goblets Betty gave to her best friend as a wedding gift.

"He told me that his father did this to comfort all his children. I was happy to tell my dad about this because he wasn't as sad after he knew his dad was still there. Now I know that it really was my grandpa that night. Sometimes I wish he would come back, but I know I will see him again someday."

The Crystal Goblet: From Dave in Ohio

"My mother grew up in a small town outside of Erie, Pennsylvania, called Wesleyville. Her best friend Betty lived directly across the street. They walked to school together, played, went to movies—all the things that best friends do—until my grandfather announced to my mother that they were moving to Ohio. My mother, who was 16 at the time, was dismayed, to say the least. What would she do without her best friend?

"The moving day came and the best friends promised to stay in touch. And they did—through the remainder of the Great Depression and through World War II. After the war, each served as maid of honor in the other's wedding. When it was my mother's turn to be married, Betty gave her a beautiful crystal goblet as a wedding gift.

"Things went well throughout the 1950s. Betty and my mother each had two sons. Betty's family came to Ohio to visit with us frequently, and we went to Erie to visit with them. And then, in 1958, Betty came down with a terminal illness. Her condition deteriorated rapidly and we knew the end was not far away. One night [as my mother was lying awake thinking of her best friend, she heard] the sound of breaking glass from the dining room. She instinctively looked at the clock and it was 3:00 A.M. She got up, turned on the lights and went to investigate. She looked all over and didn't see anything unusual—until she looked into the cabinet where she displayed her crystal. There, lying on its side and broken, was the goblet Betty had given her [13] years earlier. Nothing else in the cabinet was disturbed in any way.

"My mother went back to bed, trying to figure out what could possibly have caused the goblet to fall over inside a display cabinet. No one had disturbed it. My dad was sound asleep in their bedroom and my brother and I were asleep upstairs.

"The next morning, at about 7:30, Betty's husband Don called to tell us that Betty had passed away during the night. 'What time?' my mother asked. '3:00 A.M.,' replied Don.

"This story is true, exactly as I described it. Did Betty cause the goblet to fall over as a sign to my mother? A sign that, although gone from this plane of existence, she lived on in another realm?

"My mother and I [have] discussed this event many times over the years, trying to come up with an alternative explanation. We know the goblet didn't fall over due to an earthquake. We have tremors occasionally in Ohio, but they are exceedingly rare. Had there been even a mild earthquake that night it would have been in the newspapers and we would have remembered it. Besides, the base of the goblet was wide enough that a moderate shaking of the ground would not be sufficient to knock it over.

"Had it fallen over in the daytime, my brother and I would [have been] natural suspects. But it was 3:00 A.M., and we were sound asleep in our upstairs bedrooms. My mother, a light sleeper, would have heard us coming down the stairs.

"And why did that one goblet fall over while everything else in the cabinet was undisturbed?

"My mother and I, both rational people, are convinced Betty herself knocked it over at the time of her passing. We believe it was her way of saying 'farewell.'"

FROM THE FILES OF PROFESSOR IAN CURRIE

Professor Ian Currie, a former lecturer in anthropology and sociology at Guelph University in Ontario, Canada, and author of the book You Cannot Die, *shared the following cases.*

Early one morning a United States serviceman stationed in Germany showed up quite unexpectedly at his family home in a Detroit suburb. His mother, who was in the middle of preparing breakfast, was both startled and overjoyed and set another plate for her son.

"Sorry, Mom," he said, declining the meal with a gentle smile. "I can't stay for breakfast. I just wanted to say goodbye." The young soldier waved farewell and walked out the door. His heartbroken mother ran after him, shouting for him to return and stay longer, but he had completely disappeared. A few hours later, an officer appeared at their door to inform the family that their beloved son had been killed in a training accident 6,000 miles away in Germany. He had died half an hour before his mysterious visit.

In another case from Professor Currie's files, two friends became business partners and opened a Boston clothing store, but one later skipped town with all of their money. In spite of the partner's treachery, the business went on to prosper. Half a dozen or so years later, the owner of the clothing store was stunned when his old friend and former partner walked in the door. The prodigal partner waved aside all amenities and immediately got to the point of his visit. He said that he had come back to apologize for what he had done. The old friends embraced, and the partner that had been left with the store forgave his old partner for stealing from him. The long-lost friend's face brightened at once. "Thank you," he said, then quickly left the store. It was several days before the businessman learned that his ex-partner had died three hours *before* he walked into the store to ask forgiveness.

"SORRY FOR ALL THE TROUBLE I'VE CAUSED YOU"

The Personal Experience of Brad Steiger

Some years ago I appeared on a radio show in St. Catharines, Ontario, Canada, and a young woman called in to relate the experience that proved to her that some part of us survives physical death.

One night she was awakened by the form of her brother standing at the foot of the bed. "I'm sorry, sis, for all the trouble that I may have caused you. I love you," he told her. The sound of someone speaking stirred the woman's husband from his sleep as well, but by the time he had truly awoken, the image of his brother-in-law had disappeared, and only the couple was left in their bedroom.

The woman insisted that she had seen her brother standing in their bedroom, and she described in detail what he had been wearing. She had particularly noticed that he had been wearing a plaid shirt that she had never before seen him wear. No sooner had she completed her description of the apparition when the telephone rang, and the woman was given the tragic news that her brother had been killed in an automobile accident. Later, when the couple visited the morgue to identify the body, both of them were startled to see the corpse attired in a plaid shirt just like the one that she had described.

WAITING TO SAY GOODBYE

In some instances, rather than manifesting at the moment of physical death, spirits of the deceased wait for a more appropriate time to say a final farewell. Some witnesses report receiving a last goodbye days, weeks, or months after their friend or family member died. Spirits may even deliver an ethereal reminder of their presence years after they have passed away.

They Said Farewell Through Music on the Radio:
The Personal Experience of Patrick

"My mother died from brain cancer in 1981. A few weeks after her funeral, I had the radio on as I was going through things in my parents' room. The radio was tuned to the country music station that my mother had enjoyed during her life, and music filled the room. Suddenly, without an introduction from the deejay, a song called 'Softly as I Leave You' by Elvis Presley began to play. I was familiar with the song but had never, ever, heard it before on the air. The song is about a man who is dying in the hospital and awakens one day feeling himself slipping away. He sees his wife sleeping in a chair next to his bed, and rather than wake her, he writes a note in which he says that he will leave her softly, long before she will miss him, long before her arms can beg him to stay for another hour or another day.

"I felt emotions well-up inside me, and I was almost in tears as I sat and listened to the song. My mother had died before we had the chance to say goodbye. Due to her illness, she had been staying at my sister's home, and on the morning of her death, I'd left her and gone to my own home to sleep. She had died 'long before I missed her,' as the song said. I got a very powerful impression that my mother was somehow using the medium of the radio to say goodbye. Elvis had been her absolute favorite performer in life; no reason he wouldn't still be in death.

"In 1986 my father passed. Before going to my father's viewing, I went out to warm up the engine of the car, and when I turned on the radio, Roy Orbison's song 'For the Good Times' immediately came across the speakers.

The lines about not being so sad that things are over, that life goes on and that we should be glad that we had some time to spend together, made me cry, and I turned the radio off. After my mother died, my father and I had lived together. We'd never been close, but in the five years after Mom's passing, we'd grown to appreciate each other. And, yes, I was very, very glad that Dad and I'd had some 'time to spend together.' Those words of the song couldn't have summed up my feelings any better if I'd written it.

"A year later something else very significant happened to me. A close friend of mine was diagnosed with a life-threatening illness. He'd made me promise not to tell anyone else in our circle, and only one other mutual acquaintance knew the situation. After he'd told me, I'd gone to pick up another friend, and we were en route somewhere when the friend asked me what was wrong. I replied that there was nothing wrong, but he persisted in pointing out that I was acting like something was bothering me. I reached over and turned on the radio. The chorus of Billy Joel's 'Only the Good Die Young' blared through the car. I turned off the radio. Coincidence? I really don't think so."

Joe Came to Say a Last Goodbye: The Personal Experience of Rick Aiello

"I first met Joe eight years ago when I was introduced to him by the woman from whom we bought our home. We were about to close on our new house in the picturesque Finger Lakes region of New York, and wanted to take another look at the property. Anita, the seller, thought it would be appropriate for my wife and I to meet the man who would be our closest neighbor. We went up the road and found Joe working on his tractor. Anita introduced him to us as, 'The hardest working man in the county.'

"Joe was a family man who, regardless of the fact that he always had two jobs, was always there for someone in need. As a displaced city dweller, I felt unprepared for the obligations of maintaining my new rural property. I suddenly had three acres of lawn and many more acres of brush and weeds to keep in check. Because Joe did landscaping as his second job, he had all the equipment to get the job done. He made it clear that he would help out with the mowing and bush hogging.

"Joe had a great love of animals. No matter how tired he was or how late he was for dinner, he would always take the time to come to the aid of an animal. He'd pick up a kitten that had been dumped on one of our rural roads by someone who thought the animal 'would be better off in the country.' When he rumbled up our long driveway, we never knew what Joe would have in the cab of his truck until he stopped and opened the door of his cab.

"In the summer Joe would take a week off his regular jobs and rent a bulldozer. He would move earth and build ponds and have an all around good time. Joe built two ponds for me in the eight years I knew him. Every time I see my geese paddling around, I thank Joe.

"Joe would also take care of my snowplowing, showing up at four in the morning, the time he usually started his day. It was always a reassuring sound, hearing Joe rumble through the snow, plowing a clear path up to my house. When he would make his first pass up to the house, I would bolt out of bed and run downstairs to greet him. While the big diesel dump truck idled, I would jump into my boots and run outside to join him in the warm cab of his truck. We'd talk about the deer he had just seen or the fox that had been chasing his chickens. We would chat as he was finishing my driveway, then he would be gone for the rest of the day.

"In November 2001 Joe had a sudden and unexpected heart attack at the age of 44. We were all devastated. Joe had been such a big part of so many lives. After his death, there were many stories exchanged of all the selfless deeds he had done for so many people. Joe was a good and caring man, and he would never be so inconsiderate as to leave without saying goodbye. As in life, he did not let me down in death.

"One month after his death, my wife and I were awakened by the sound of a diesel truck. Upon hearing that big noisy truck I instantly woke up, as I had for the past eight years. I bolted out of bed, took a few steps, and only then did I realize that I could not possibly have heard Joe's truck. I had to have been dreaming!

"But there I was, standing up, wide awake, listening to this truck idling up next to the house. I rushed downstairs, fully expecting to see Joe's big truck sitting there, with him waving for me to join him in the cab. I reached the bottom step and looked out the patio door, still hearing the truck. The moment my eyes met an empty driveway, the sound stopped.

"I instantly felt depressed, confused, and cheated. But when I went back upstairs and discussed the event with my wife, she confirmed that she, too, had heard the truck. I realized that Joe had come to say goodbye in a way that I would understand, for I had never missed [an opportunity] to run downstairs and greet him when I heard his truck. I didn't feel cheated anymore. I felt blessed and honored that he remembered me. It seems like only yesterday when my good friend pulled up to say his last goodbye."

A Cautionary Note

There are shadow beings and spirit parasites that inhabit unseen areas at the edge of our material world who take delight in assuming control over humans, or even in entering and taking possession of a physical body. The following two accounts indi-

cate that caution must be taken even when one is led to believe that they are interacting with a departed family member or a dear friend. As I have emphasized repeatedly throughout this text, there are entities in the spiritual dimension that will masquerade as something or someone they are not. They do this for the sole purpose of deceiving us and wreaking havoc in our lives.

"Shouldn't Daddy Be Resting in Peace?" The Personal Experience of Cindy

"I 've been having periodic paranormal experiences since my father's passing back in August 1998. For the first three years after his death, the episodes were especially frequent. What would you say if I told you I had actually had physical contact with my late father? I know it's my father, because I've seen him at very close range.

"He makes physical contact with me when I'm sleeping. When he enters my body, it feels like a blob of electrical energy has taken me over. It paralyzes me from my mouth to my toes, but not my brain! When I force myself to say, 'Daddy,' he immediately leaves my body. Then I remain quiet and still. It's one hell of an experience.

"When he enters my bedroom on other visits, I can feel the energy; it's as if someone is in my room. I work the midnight shift at my job, and I've had experiences there as well. They all involve my 'old man.' Sometimes, it is a little scary because he will just suddenly make an entrance. It still takes a little getting used to.

"I must clarify that these experiences happen while I'm fully awake. They have only happened one or two times after I was already asleep. I'm under the impression that he is checking up on me, to see if everything is okay. He has used other methods to contact me, to let me know he is with me. I've told my brother about what has happened, and he, too, has had a few experiences, but nothing—and I mean nothing—compared with my experiences. My brother is still not certain whether he should accept the contact. He has doubts. I seem to be the stronger one—or the most receptive.

"Shouldn't my father be resting in peace by now? Or can he find a way to come back and forth from his dimension to ours? I'm into sci-fi, paranormal activity, and so forth, and very open minded to the possibility of such phenomena. To have such events actually happen to me makes me a true believer. I haven't told my mother about these visits from Dad because of her Christian beliefs. I also don't want to scare her."

Author's comment: I didn't wish to scare Cindy, but I advised her that her love of her father and her open-mindedness to the paranormal may have made her susceptible to the deceit of an astral masquerader who was taking pleasure in entering her body from time to time under the guise of being the spirit of her deceased father. Maintain-

ing contact with the spiritual essence of a departed loved one is something quite differ-ent from permitting a nonmaterial spirit to possess one's material body. In this author's opinion, one should always resist the advances of any spirit being who attempts to occupy one's body—whether its alleged identity is known or unknown. Nor should a person ever allow a spirit entity to engage in acts of physical intimacy.

Discerning the Spirits:
The Personal Experience of Jack, a Member of Alcoholics Anonymous

"At AA meetings, I became friends with a lady I will call Mary, who was 10 years older than I, and who had been sober 29 years. She had once been a speaker in AA, traveling around the country, speaking at meetings and AA conventions. She had curtailed many of her activities after she had fallen ill with hepatitis C. Before Mary died from the disease, we had become very close friends.

"The night of Mary's death, I was awakened by the sense of a presence in the room. I felt it draw near and envelope me. It felt like electricity, but without the pain. It was like nothing I had ever felt before or since. It sur-rounded me like a hug, and I felt a kiss on my cheek. Then it was gone. I sat up in my bed and said out loud, 'Good-bye, Mary.' I knew it had been her and that she had not left without saying goodbye.

"The next night I felt another presence in my room, but this was not Mary. It felt darker. It made itself known by pressing down on the side of my bed as I tried to sleep. I would turn to see who was there and see nothing. A couple of nights later, I heard something rattle in the bathroom. It sounded like someone was shaking a jar of vitamins that I kept there. When I got up to investigate, the jar was right where I had left it. At first I thought that the sounds might have been caused by mice, so I set out traps. But there were no mice to catch.

"A few days passed, and then one night I was nearly overcome by the smell of rotting flesh. I got out of bed and checked the pantry, refrigerator, and trash. But the smell had not come from either of those places. Angrily I shout-ed out, telling whoever or whatever it was that it was not welcome.

"The next night I was listening to *The Jeff Rense Show*. Brad Steiger was the guest. I decided to call, and after telling him the story, he suggested that I perform a cleansing ritual and prayer. I did this and it worked! The apartment became silent."

The Cleansing Ritual

Visualize yourself surrounded by violet light and ask that your spirit protector or guardian angel connect you to the highest vibration of your concept of God, the

Great Mystery, or the Source of All That Is. Visualize and feel the violet light moving over you in a wave of warmth. See and feel it touching every part of your body and spirit, and those of any others who are present. Then say aloud to your spirit protector/guardian:

"Assist me in calling upon the highest of energies from the Great Mystery, the Source of All That Is. Summon the law of harmony, for I (and those with me) have found myself (ourselves) in a dark place of shadows that resist the light. Permit the violet light of transformation and cleansing to move around and through this dwelling place. Allow this cleansing energy to purify and elevate all negative energies, all improper memories, all entities of evil purpose, all spirits who delight in wrongdoing, all lower vibrations that encourage impure desires. Allow the transforming energy to replace all darkness with light. Remove all chaotic energies and replace them with the purest of energies, the power of love, and the glory of all good and benevolent spirits. Bless us with the light, so that I (we) may go forth on this new day (night) of cleansing, rejuvenated with perfect physical and mental health, perfect joy, perfect illumination, and perfect wisdom. Amen and so let it be!"

8

Ghosts That Warned of Approaching Danger or Death

SAVED FROM A NAZI TORPEDO BY HIS MOTHER'S GHOST

The Personal Experience of Victor L.

"**D**uring World War II, I had the misfortune of being on a freighter that was temporarily stranded in the middle of the Atlantic Ocean. Our engine broke down about seven days out of port, and even though we were part of a convoy headed for Italy, the demands for materials made by the war forced the rest of the ships to leave us behind while they went on ahead.

"From 1942 to 1943 the waters of the Atlantic were thick with Nazi submarines, and they all had commanders eager to sink ships that might be helping the Allied forces. We were all tense and nervous, expecting to see two or three of those terrible metal 'fish' streaking toward our helpless vessel at any minute.

"By the third day of bobbing in the water like a sitting duck during hunting season, the crew had become really jumpy and tense. We had a few guns on deck, but we all knew that they would be of little use against submarines unless they surfaced. And it was hardly likely that a commander would waste the time and effort to surface in order to engage us in an old-fashioned sea battle, when launching a couple of torpedoes at our ship from the safety of Neptune's domain would do the trick.

"In late afternoon of the third day, I was on my bunk, trying to get some rest before my next watch. I was completely alone in the quarters. I was awakened by the sensation of a warm hand nudging my shoulder. I grunted and tried to shrug off the annoyance that was interfering with my sleep, but something seemed very familiar about the nudging. I opened my eyes and saw the

Real Ghosts, Restless Spirits, and Haunted Places

image of my mother standing next to my bunk. She was still pushing at my shoulder, and when my eyes widened in astonishment at her presence, she smiled at me. 'Vic, honey,' she told me in her usual softly pleasant voice, 'you had better get up now. It is time to get up.' Before I could respond in any manner whatsoever, the form of my mother disappeared.

"My mother had been dead for eight years. For a minute or so I thought that maybe I had been dreaming; perhaps reliving a day in my childhood when my mother had woken me up so that I could get ready to go to school. But the more I thought about the apparition, the more I began to feel so damn uneasy that I wanted to get dressed and get out of the bunk room as quickly as I could.

"Since I did not wish to be alone after that strange experience, and I still had a couple of hours before I was due to report to my watch, I decided to go down to the engine room and talk with the engineers who were working on the repairs. I had no more than nodded hello at one of the firemen, who was a good buddy of mine, when a tremendous explosion shook the entire freighter and knocked us all off kilter. I went down on one knee, and a couple of the men fell flat on their backsides.

"No one had to tell us that we had been hit by one of the German [navy's] torpedoes. Within a matter of minutes, all of the crew members had crowded into lifeboats and were rowing away from the sinking ship. Fortunately there were no casualties. But as I looked back at the slowly sinking freighter, I clearly saw that there would have been a fatality if the ghost of my mother had not awakened me when she did. From my position in the lifeboat I could see that a massive hole had been blasted in the starboard side of the ship; I had been sleeping directly above the spot of impact only moments before the torpedo had struck. My mother had somehow managed to go on recess from heaven so that she would be able to wake me up just in time."

THE VOICE OF HER DECEASED HUSBAND CALLED HER NAME

In March 1992, 71-year-old Kristin F. wrote me a detailed letter describing how she had been sleeping soundly in her comfortable two-bedroom cabin in northern Minnesota when she distinctly heard the voice of her late husband, David, calling her name.

The Personal Experience of Kristin F.

"I sat up in bed and fumbled for the light, glancing wildly about the dark room. I knew with every fiber of my being that I had not been mistaken about the source of the voice. I would forever recognize the sound of my beloved David's voice, even though he had been taken from me by a heart attack five years before.

"I finally managed to locate the light switch, and I got out of bed, slid my feet into warm slippers and pulled on my robe. It was a chilly night in late November, and I knew the floorboards would be cold. '*Kristin,*' the voice spoke again, seemingly just over my right shoulder. 'Look sharp, girl,' I heard David say. 'Something is burning! You are in danger, my beloved. Look sharp, now!'

"I spun around, hoping to catch at least a fleeting glimpse of my husband's spirit. I saw nothing. But the voice was so distinctly David's. Years ago, after we had been amused by a British movie in which a military man had always prefaced his commands with a snappy 'look sharp,' we had used the phrase teasingly whenever we wanted the other to get right at a domestic chore.

"The cabin's furnace was electric, and I had adjusted the thermostat before retiring. I knew that I had not left on any electrical appliance, such as a toaster or an iron. David had been almost phobic about the idea of our house burning. His maternal aunt's house had caught fire when he was just a boy. The lovely old house had burned to the ground, but even worse, David's favorite cousin, Kathy, had been horribly burned and left badly scarred.

"Once, three or four years after we were married in 1943, David had awakened in the night and found some trash smoldering in the kitchen wastebasket. He was mortified when he discovered that he had carelessly dumped an ashtray with a live butt into the trash, and he was horrified when he considered that he could have been responsible for setting our house on fire. He had become even more fearful of fire, and he quit smoking, cold turkey, that very night.

"As I made my way into the living room to investigate further, I pondered these things, and began to consider quite strongly that my mind might have played back a kind of mental tape of David's voice. I heard a noise in the backyard and looked out a window to see a graceful family of deer moving down toward the lake. An owl hooted mournfully from somewhere deep in the forest. All was peaceful and as it should be.

"I had just about convinced myself that I had only awakened from a strangely vivid dream, when, as if in answer to my mental debate and its rational conclusion, I heard David's voice once again. This time the message was brief and forceful: 'The cabin is on fire!'

"Becoming even more confused, and perhaps a little frightened, I walked from room to room in the ranch-style cabin. Nothing! I could find no sign of any threatening flames. Earlier that evening when I had taken my nightcap of warm cocoa, I had built a nice, crackling wood fire in the fireplace. The fire had burned out hours earlier. There were only a few glowing embers still visible behind the fire screen.

"'*Fire!*' David's voice was insistent, demanding. I began to cry in frustration. 'Where?' I asked. 'Please tell me where!' I leaned back against the wall next to the brick chimney in a state of seeming near collapse, and then, suddenly, I felt that the wall was hot. When I turned to place my open palm against the wall, I was horrified to find that it was extremely hot to the touch. Through a tiny crack between the fireplace mantel and the wall, I could see raging flames. The house was on fire!

"I forced myself to remain as calm as possible, and headed for the telephone in the kitchen to dial 911. Although the village was small, it had an excellent volunteer fire department. I knew that they would get to me as quickly as possible. After I cradled the receiver, it seemed as though I had, at last, become truly wide awake. I could quite clearly hear the terrible, crackling sound of the fire spreading toward the roof. Tendrils of dark smoke were moving across the living room like the greedy fingers of fire seeking objects for consumption. I decided it would be safer to await the fire department in the yard, and even as I was pulling on a heavy coat to wear over my robe, I heard the eerie wail of a siren shrilling a summons to the volunteer firemen. 'Thank you, David,' I said to the stars. 'Thank you, my darling, for saving my life.'

"The prompt action of the local firefighters prevented the complete destruction of our cabin, but the estimated cost of the repairs played a major factor in my decision to move into an apartment in a larger nearby city. I miss the solitude of our cabin by the lake, but I strongly sense that David's spirit feels better now that I am closer to our friends and family, and am not so lonely."

THE SPIRIT OF THEIR MOM WAVED THEM BACK FROM DANGER

The Personal Experience of Susan

"We lost our mother when I was just a young girl of 12, and we were living in Yreka, California. The other kids and I were terribly despondent over the loss of Mom, and Dad was taking her death just as hard as we were. There were four of us kids. I was second oldest. Debra was 14, Paula was eight, and Douglas was six. We all cried ourselves to sleep every night for weeks after Mom's funeral in March 1973. We could hear Dad crying in his room, too. We all just missed Mom so much.

"Daddy stuck it out in Yreka until school was dismissed for the summer. Then he decided that it would be best for the entire family if we moved to another town and made a fresh start. There were just too many memories of Mom in Yreka, he told us. It would be easier for all of us to get on with our lives if we weren't thinking about Mom all of the time.

"Dad decided that we should try a whole new and different lifestyle while we were at it. Through one of his cousins, he had heard about this old farmhouse outside a small town in Oregon, and he thought that we should check it out. On June 16, when we stepped out of our station wagon, we kids took one look at the ramshackle house and started to pray that Dad wouldn't like it out in the country.

"The house was big enough. It had six bedrooms, a large country kitchen, and a neat living room with window boxes. The problem was, it was really run-down, and needed a lot of fixing up. Debra and I knew that Mom's illness had cost Dad a lot of money. And then, of course, there had been the funeral expenses. While the low asking price of the big old house might appeal to Dad's busted budget, we hoped that he would realize how much money we would have to spend to fix the place up to make it really livable. Paula and little Doug were excited about the large barn, the various outbuildings, and animal sheds. They immediately began to dream about having horses to ride.

"While Dad discussed terms with the landlord, the four of us kids set off on a tour of inspection of the sprawling house. We had already decided who got what room, and even climbed the dusty steps to the attic, where we found some potential treasure chests of old clothes and hats that some family had left behind. They would be just great for playing dress up. Finally, only the basement remained for us to explore. Paula protested that she didn't like basements because they were dark and smelly and spooky. Little Douglas was certain that monsters were living under the stairs, and his large blue eyes grew even wider at the thought of braving the dark unknown. I teased them for being little sissies, and I promised that we would find some neat things that someone had left down there. However, Paula was adamant that she and Dougie would stay upstairs while Debra and I explored the underworld.

"'If we're going to live here,' big sister Debra told them, 'you can't be afraid to go down in the cellar.' Paula could not suppress an involuntary shudder. 'Oh, I hope we don't have to live in this creepy old place.'

"'That's for Dad to decide,' Debra reminded her. 'Come on, now, I'll take Dougie's hand, and Paula, you take Susan's hand, and we will all run down the basement stairs together. You can't be afraid if we are all together.'

Reluctantly Paula and Douglas did as they were told, and we were about halfway down the stairs when we all came to a sudden stop. There at the bottom of the stairs was *Mom!*

"All of us saw a clear image of our deceased mother. Later, when we discussed what we had seen, each one of us described her in the same way. She had on this really pretty sundress with big flowers on it that all of us had loved so much. Her long blond hair was braided, like she often fixed it in warm weather. But most of all, we saw her beautiful smile. She was smiling up at us so lovingly. I will never forget the image that I saw of Mom that day in that old basement.

"We all probably would have run into the arms of our lovely, smiling mother if she had not begun to make motions that we should go back up the stairs, and not continue our descent into the basement. When Paula moved down a couple more steps toward Mom, she frowned and made a motion that Paula should stop. I know that we were all crying and calling out to her, saying that we wanted to hug and kiss her, but she kept waving her arms and motioning us to go back. Just when we were about to ignore Mom's gestures and run down the steps toward her, the image of our mother disappeared.

"We ran upstairs to get Dad, and tell him that we had seen Mom at the bottom of the basement stairs. Since we were all crying and talking at the same time, he could hardly ignore us or argue that we were all seeing things.

"When the landlord, an elderly man in his eighties, finally understood that we were talking excitedly about something in the cellar, he became very agitated. 'No, no, you mustn't let those kids go down in the basement!' he said, extra loud because of his partial deafness. 'There's an old cistern down there right at the bottom of the stairs. The boards have rotted away, and I'll have to fix it before anyone goes down there.'

"Dad was shocked that the landlord hadn't mentioned such a potential spot of danger immediately, but it was easy to see that the elderly gentleman had trouble keeping his mind on more than one thing at a time. And he had quite obviously forgotten long ago how young children want to explore old houses when given the opportunity.

"When Dad went to investigate, he found things exactly as the old man had described them. The cistern, an uncovered well about eight feet deep with about three feet of water at the bottom, was right in the shadows at the bottom of the basement stairs. The way that we had been running down those stairs, we all could have fallen into the well and been severely injured, perhaps even killed. At that very moment Dad decided against renting the old farmhouse, and he never once doubted us when we told him that our beautiful mother had returned with her loving smile to save our lives.

"'Because she was the one who gave you life in the first place,' Dad said, 'it surely does stand to reason that she would do her best to protect your lives even from beyond the grave.' Dad got tears in his eyes and added, 'Now you kids know for certain that love never dies.'"

THE GHOST OF A NEIGHBOR SAVED THEM FROM A DEADLY FIRE

In September 1994 the ghost of their dead neighbor saved Maybelle Johnson and her family from a possible death by fire or smoke inhalation.

The Personal Experience of Maybelle Johnson

"At the time of the fire I lived with my husband, Lamar, and our three kids in a four-storey apartment building in a suburb of Charlotte, North Carolina. That winter our neighbor, Jeanette, a sickly young woman in her early twenties, began suffering with advanced stages of leukemia. Jeanette had been such a cheerful, hardworking lady that it was hard on all of her friends to see her becoming so ill and in so much pain.

"When Jeanette's steady boyfriend stopped coming around to see her, I tried to make more time in my busy schedule, so that I could spend it with her. It was hard to get away from my duties, what with three little kids and a job, but Jeanette had always been there to help me with babysitting and other things whenever she could, so I wanted to offer some kind of support in her hour of need. I usually had to wait until Lamar was home from work because I didn't want any of our babies saying anything hurtful to Jeanette. You know, like asking her why she looked so awful and stuff like that. Jeanette died in April. She was courageous and cheerful to the very end. I so admired her spirit, and all of us in the apartment building considered it a real tragedy that such a good person had to die so young.

"One night, about a month after Jeanette's passing, I was in bed with my husband, just starting to drift off to sleep. I had been feeling kind of restless with worry about bills and stuff. As I was finally falling asleep, I rolled over on my side, and there, solid as life, standing right by my side of the bed, was Jeanette.

"I wasn't scared of her being a ghost and all, but I admit that I was startled to see her there. I blinked my eyes and shook my head. When the image of Jeanette remained at my bedside, I giggled and said out loud, 'I always thought that if I ever saw a ghost, I would be scared silly. But I'm not at all afraid of you, Jeanette.' Jeanette's spirit-form smiled at me, but her features immediately became very serious in appearance. 'Girl,' she said, 'if you don't get up and get your family out of here, you're gonna be a ghost just like me!' With that warning pronounced, Jeanette's image vanished, but she certainly had my complete attention. I wasn't ready to be a ghost yet. I had three little kids to get raised.

"I elbowed my husband to wake him, and told him that I had just seen Jeanette's ghost, and she said that we had to get out of the house. Lamar rubbed his eyes and grumbled at me. 'It's two o'clock. What are you doing waking me up at this hour? You know I've got to be at work by six. I need my sleep.' I told Lamar again that Jeanette's ghost had come to me and told me to get us up and out of there fast, but he just grumbled that it had only been a dream, and that I should let him get back to sleep.

"After a few more minutes of arguing about the reality of Jeanette's ghost and the urgency of her warning, I finally convinced Lamar to get out of bed to at least look around our apartment. Lamar had no sooner shoved his feet into his slippers at the side of the bed when he said that he smelled smoke. Suddenly wide awake, Lamar ran to the door of our apartment and opened it to find the hallway beginning to fill with thin clouds of smoke. 'Oh, my God,' he shouted back to me, 'the place must be on fire! You get the kids up and dial 911, and I'll wake the others in the building!'

"Within minutes we had vacated our apartment and spread the alarm that saved the lives of the other tenants in the building. Because of the early detection of the fire, the firemen were able to keep damage to a minimum. It was later revealed that the new occupant in Jeanette's old apartment, a heavy cigarette smoker, had accidentally dropped a lit cigarette in the cushions of an easy chair before he had gone out to shop at an all-night supermarket. In the days that followed, I was not at all shy about letting everyone know that they all owed their continued existence on the planet to Jeanette's ghost."

Her Husband's Spirit Watches over Them

In 1992, after one of our seminars in San Diego, Margaret G. told my wife Sherry and I this inspirational account of her deceased husband's continued interest in his family.

The Experience of Margaret G. Retold by Brad Steiger

"I was half asleep one night, reading the newspaper in my reclining chair in the front room, when I thought I heard Cissy, my three-year-old daughter, whimpering in her bedroom," Margaret said.

"About the same time I heard the trash can in back of the house go clattering into the alley. Cautiously I peeped out a window in the kitchen and caught a glimpse of a man standing in the shadows beside the garage."

Margaret did her best to quiet the trembling fear that seized her. Taking a deep breath to center herself, she walked purposefully back into the front room and called the police.

"I sat in my easy chair, using all of my willpower to retain control, praying earnestly that a police car would pull up in the alley before I could count 10. Then I heard my little girl whimpering once again. Suddenly a new terror seized me and sent my heart pounding: What if there was already an intruder *inside* the house?" Margaret opened the door to Cissy's bedroom and was unable to suppress her cry of horror when she saw a man leaning over her daughter's bed. Her brain struggled with a hundred different fears. She was alone. The police were nowhere in sight. Did the intruder mean to hurt her child?

But then, to her complete amazement, she heard the man singing softly to Cissy. Within another moment she was able to focus her senses sharply enough to recognize the tune as a song from the sixties that had been a favorite of her husband's. "Who … who are you?" Margaret asked the man. He had drawn the hood of a sweatshirt over his face so she could not distinguish any of his features in the dim light of the child's bedroom. "Who are you?" she repeated, trying to control all inflections of fear in her voice.

As the man raised his head and turned, Margaret was startled to see the face of her husband, William. In the next instant the image vanished. "I was about to collapse, but that's when the police officer knocked on the front door," Margaret said. "He was just checking to see if everything was all right, and he told me that they had just picked up a man in the alley behind our house because they immediately recognized him as a known burglar. According to the officer, the man had a rap sheet of prior offenses as long as his arm."

Margaret thanked the officer for his quick work in apprehending a criminal who had quite obviously targeted her house that evening. "Glad to be of service, ma'am," the police officer said, "but you are extremely lucky that your husband was at home with you tonight."

"My husband?" Margaret echoed hollowly.

"Yes," the officer went on. "You see, most burglars just like to slip in and out of a house without even being seen, but this man is different. He's got a real sadistic streak. If he should happen to see a woman home alone, he doesn't mind breaking in and hurting her while he loots the place. And if there should happen to be a youngster around, he doesn't hesitate at all to beat up the kid, too."

Margaret had to ask for confirmation of what she had seen in Cissy's bedroom just before the officer had knocked on the door: "Are you saying that the burglar saw my husband in the house?" The police officer nodded. "Yeah, the burglar said that he kept peeping in your windows, but he always saw this big man standing right beside your chair. A couple of times he went around to try to enter through the child's bedroom, but then he saw your husband in there, bending over your daughter's bed, singing to her. He said your husband had on a hooded sweatshirt like he had been working out or running or something. So it's a good thing he had come home and was in the house." The officer frowned quizzically, glanced around the front room. "Where is your husband now? Did he go to bed or something?"

"Officer," Margaret answered, "my husband William died nearly two years ago. He and a couple of his buddies were out jogging on the beach when he decided to add some hurdles to the run by running and jumping over the tops of some large rocks that were still exposed by high tide. He slipped and fell when a large wave suddenly crashed into the rocks. He was pulled out to sea immediately. The heavy, hooded sweatshirt that he was wearing quickly absorbed water, and probably was a factor in his drowning. His body washed up on shore the next morning."

The officer became very quiet, excused himself, said goodnight, and left. "I don't know if he believed me or not," Margaret said. "I really didn't care. I knew that William's great love for us had drawn him back to protect us on the night when we were threatened by a man who would have stolen our valuables and harmed us physically. And I will never forget the glimpse that I received of him in Cissy's room or the beautiful sound of his singing over his daughter's sleeping form. In addition to saving us from pain and theft, William gave us the greatest gift imaginable: proof that there is life and love beyond the grave."

A GHOST SAVED HER FROM ATTACK BY A RAPIST

The Personal Experience of Dorothy

"My experience with a benevolent ghost took place just a few months after I married David in 1970. We didn't have much money in those days, and we lived in a pretty rough section of Kansas City. We moved into the third house in a string of five, run-down, identical houses that had all been built sometime around the turn of the century. We kept telling ourselves that one day we would have it better.

"I usually got home from my job as a waitress two hours before David came home from the factory where he worked. David said it was humiliating that I had to do such menial work. In his family, the man of the family had always supported his wife. He only accepted the idea of me working because he knew it would help us achieve a better life more quickly, but he insisted that, because of the rough neighborhood we lived in, that if I had to work, then I had to be home before dark. To make matters even worse, young women in our neighborhood had been targeted by a rapist who had slashed and raped at least half a dozen women, murdering one.

"Three nights a week David went right to night school after work, so I had to keep his dinner warm until after ten o'clock. It was tough on both of us, but we hoped that those business courses that David was taking would eventually prove to be our ticket to better times.

"It was on a chilly October night that the incident occurred. David was still at school, and I was keeping his dinner warm in the kitchen. I was relaxing in the living room, my bare feet were up on a footstool, and I was reading a new book. I didn't expect David for at least another hour, and it felt so good after being on my feet all day to just to sit and take it easy for a while. At about 10 minutes to nine, though, I thought it was time to check David's meal to be certain it didn't dry out.

"When I reached the door between the living room and the kitchen, I was suddenly stopped dead in my tracks by some invisible force that prevented me from passing through the doorway. Some unseen, solid barrier that I actu-ally felt pressing against my chest and arms was holding me back. Stunned, doubting my own senses, I lunged toward the doorway with all of my strength. I was thrown back with such force that I lost my balance and dropped to one knee. I have always been a tall woman, standing just over five feet, ten inches; I was 22, very athletic, solidly built, and weighed about 140 pounds when this occurred. I had grown up on a Missouri farm doing a man's work, and I was completely shaken by the experience of being knocked to my knees by some-thing I couldn't see.

"I slumped against the side of the sofa and studied the open doorway. I don't really remember how long I sat there trying to figure out what it was that had prevented me from entering the kitchen. I thought for a few minutes that maybe I had been working too hard, with too little sleep, and was having some kind of breakdown. The doorway was clear. I saw absolutely nothing that could have blocked my path to the kitchen, so I got back up and rushed the doorway once again.

"This time I saw a flash of brilliant blue light as I struck the impenetra-ble invisible barrier, and I felt a fairly powerful electric type of shock that knocked me back on my posterior. I shook my head to clear it of the fear and confusion I was feeling. When I looked up once again at the open doorway, I saw a blue light shimmering there. For just a few seconds the light took the shape of a tall, powerfully built man, and then it faded away. I was completely awestruck. There was a ghost in our house that wouldn't let me enter the kitchen. A shiver went up and down my spine and centered in my solar plexus. David and I had no idea the place was haunted.

"Slowly I got to my feet and approached the doorway. This time I gin-gerly poked a finger through the doorway and saw the blue light manifest again. As incredible as it may seem, I saw my fingertip rest lightly against the dimly defined, upraised palm of a big man that was made entirely of shimmer-ing blue light. When I tried to pass through the doorway, the spirit's palm moved from my fingertip to my chest, and once again I felt it push me back into the living room.

"When the telephone in the living room began to ring, I was so startled that I felt as though I'd jumped to the ceiling. It probably rang three or four times before I had the presence of mind to answer it. It was my next-door neighbor, Pearl. In a hoarse whisper, she told me to be quiet, and just listen carefully to what she was about to say. 'You know that these five houses in a row are all built just exactly alike,' she said, 'so I know just where your tele-phone is. You just sit there and talk to me and don't move away from the sofa.'

"My head was swimming. First a ghost made of blue light blocked my path to the kitchen and now my next-door neighbor was telling me not to move from the telephone. Pearl kept her voice low, but her words were beginning to gain powerful meaning. 'Now, don't you be afraid, but I can see a man standing right outside your kitchen door. He's got a big butcher knife in his hand, and it is plain to see that he has been waiting for you to come back into the kitchen.' I could not suppress a gasp of horror. I felt a cold sweat break out over my entire body.

"'Now don't you go screaming, or being afraid,' Pearl said sternly. 'He can't see you there on your sofa when you talk on the telephone, so you just stay there!' 'But he has a *knife?*' I whispered into the receiver. 'Do you think … that he … ?'

"'I think he might be the rapist-slasher, all right,' Pearl said matter-of-factly, 'so you just sit tight. I called the police the second I spotted him walking up our back alley, so they should be here any minute now.' Just then, in answer to my unspoken prayer, I heard the sound of police sirens. 'Praise the Lord,' Pearl said, 'I can hear the police cars coming right now! You just sit tight, honey, until they come into your house.' I remained frozen in place, and then, almost simultaneously, there was a knock on our front door, and the sound of scuffling and shouts outside the kitchen.

"Poor David came home just as the police were handcuffing and leading away the man who had been waiting outside our kitchen to attack me. The way David came bursting into the house trembling, shaking, and with tears in his eyes told me, far more than words could ever say, that he really loved me.

"A police officer told us that the rapist was a small, slight man, who had apparently been attracted to me by my size, and had thought that I would make a great conquest. But the little monster was also a coward, intimidated by my height. Apparently that was why he had waited in the kitchen to attack me by surprise, rather than approaching me in the living room where I had been reading.

"When I told David about my incredible experience with the ghost that would not permit me to enter the kitchen, we both knew that my life had been saved because of its actions. David said that it had to have been my guardian angel protecting me, and I had to agree."

9
Inspirational Messages from the Other Side

A STRANGE SPIRIT MANIFESTED AT HER SICKBED

In November 1839, when Mary Jobson was 12 years old, she began to suffer from a strange illness that afflicted her frail body for nearly 11 weeks. The mysterious rappings that came from the area around Mary's bed only added to the concern her parents felt as they attended their sick daughter. At first, they had thought that their child had been pounding on her bedstead while she was delirious with fever, but they had been in her room and had heard the knocking while her hands remained beside her in bed. The rappings proved to be an elementary beginning to the phenomena that would soon manifest in the Jobson home.

The knockings evolved into violent explosions and loud rumblings that were so loud that the tenant who lived below Mary's room often yelled that he feared the ceiling was about to crash down on him. Footsteps stomped loudly about Mary's bed, closet doors opened of their own accord, water seemed to fall from the ceiling, and an invisible organ began to play sweet and ethereal music. Finally, a strange, whispering voice that seemed to come from nowhere began to predict events that would occur to the Jobson family, which later proved to be accurate.

The Jobsons' family doctor retained his skepticism about the phenomena, as did John Jobson, but the spirit manifestations, especially the "heavenly" voice, began to attract wide attention. The voice declared that it issued from a benevolent spirit and was able to administer good advice to those who came to hear it. The voice told the distraught parents that their child had been temporarily "possessed" by a good spirit. The Jobsons were told that

[191]

though Mary appeared to suffer, she did not. She did not know where her body was. Her spirit had left its physical body, and the good spirit had entered it. Mary's skeptical father demanded some form of physical proof from the voice, and a large quantity of water was dumped at his feet. Jobson called for more water, and a deluge was forthcoming. He called out for proof again and again, until he had commanded the water to be dumped at his feet 20 times and the bedroom was drenched.

Mary's teacher, Elizabeth Gauntlett, was summoned by the voice while she was doing housework in her own home. "Elizabeth Gauntlett, one of your scholars, a certain Miss Mary Jobson, is ill," the voice said. "Go and see her; it will be good for you." Gauntlett asked the voice for the address of her pupil and went to visit the girl as the voice instructed. The teacher received "many marvelous signs" while she was at the bedside of the young girl.

Mary's bedroom became a sort of shrine as her body became a "speaking-trumpet" for the voices of departed friends, loved ones, and the revelations of the good spirit. "Look up, and you shall see the sun and moon on the ceiling," the voice once said. Before the bewildered eyes of a roomful of witnesses, the planets appeared above them as celestial orbs of yellow and orange. John Jobson immediately set about whitewashing the figures, but he soon learned that the voice had intended its artwork to be permanent. He put his brushes away when he discovered, after several coats of whitewash, that the figures still remained visible.

The celestial music that attended the manifestation of this spirit was most intriguing. Not only did the sound of a melodious organ continually fill the room with the sound of hymns, but on several occasions lovely voices of an invisible choir sang as accompaniment.

In spite of the voice's assurances that Mary was not really suffering, her young body continued to exhibit the characteristics of an extremely long convalescence. Finally the voice announced that on June 22, Mary would be the recipient of a miracle. Their doctor advised the Jobsons that the miracle could come none too soon. Mary was physically ill, and if the strange, undetermined disease continued its peculiar course, death would be imminent.

When the appointed day arrived, Mary's strength seemed to be rapidly diminishing. Her fever had risen, and the doctor was not optimistic about the young girl's chances of seeing another day. At five o'clock, the voice instructed Mrs. Jobson to lay out some clothes for Mary. Too dazed by grief and worry to refuse, the woman did as she had been told. After this was done, the voice ordered everyone from the bedroom with the exception of Mary's two-year-old brother. The Jobsons and the doctor spent an anxious 15 minutes outside the door of Mary's room before they heard the voice cry: "Come in!"

When they entered the room, Mary sat smiling in a chair, completely dressed, bouncing her baby brother on her knee. From that moment on, she seldom suffered from any illness and never received another visitation from the "good spirit." She matured into a very well educated and highly respected young woman. In spite of the "undetermined disease of the brain" she suffered from for seven months, Mary Jobson apparently suffered no psychic scars from the possession by a most unusual ghost.

SHE VISITED THE OTHER SIDE BEFORE HER DEATH

The American Society for Psychical Research's 1918 *Journal* contains the remarkable account of a 10-year-old girl named Daisy Dryden. In October 1864, during the last three days of her life, Daisy had numerous out-of-body experiences and visited the "other side." While outside of her physical body, Daisy, the daughter of Reverend David Anderson Dryden, a Methodist minister, encountered the spirit of her little brother Allie, who had died seven months earlier. She conversed with him, as well as with many other spirit beings. Before Daisy's death, her mother made a detailed record of the visions and heavenly scenes her daughter witnessed.

Although the doctors had assured the Dryden family that their daughter would soon recover from her bout with typhoid fever, Daisy told them that Allie had informed her that she would soon be joining him in the spirit world. Then, seemingly aware of both the material and the nonmaterial worlds, Daisy wondered aloud if she would still be able to visit the loved ones that she would leave behind on the Earth plane. "I'll ask Allie if it will be possible," she said to those friends and family members gathered around her bed. After a brief pause she relayed her brother's answer: "He says that it is quite possible and that I shall return sometimes, but you will be unaware of my presence. Nevertheless, I shall be able to talk to you."

Two days before she died, Daisy's Sunday school teacher came to see her, and before she left, the well-intentioned lady said to the child, "My dear little Daisy, you are about to pass over the dark river." When she had gone, Daisy asked her father what her teacher had meant by the dark river. Reverend Dryden did his best to explain how the river was meant as a metaphor representing the dividing curtain between life and death. "What nonsense!" his daughter exclaimed with a burst of derisive laughter. "There is no river here at all. There is no dividing curtain. There is not even a line between this world and the next." Stretching out her little hand, she continued her description of the world that follows death on this plane. "What is here is there. I know it is so, because I can see you all here, and I can see the others over there at the same time."

When Daisy's mother asked her to explain what she meant by her reference to "over there," the child said, "It is impossible for me to explain to you—it is so different from our world that I can't make you understand what I mean." Her mother moved to her bedside and held Daisy's hand. "Dear Mama, I wish you could see Allie," Daisy said, smiling as she spoke. "He is quite close to you." Instinctively, Mrs. Dryden turned around, but Daisy continued: "He told me that you would not be able to see him, because your spiritual eyes are shut. I can see him, because my spirit is now tied to my body by a very fine thread of life."

The next day, when her Sunday school teacher returned, Daisy informed the woman that her two children were present. The teacher's children had gone to the other side many years before, but if they had lived, they would have been young adults by that time. All of the people present that day were quite certain that Daisy had never heard anyone speak of the woman's children, so she would have known nothing about them before seeing them in the spirit world. When Daisy's teacher asked her to describe the children, she could not relate to the girl's descriptions of them as mature individuals. "You are describing grown-ups," the teacher protested. "They were just little children when they passed on." Allie explained through Daisy that children do not stay children when they cross to the other side. "They grow up, just as they do in this life."

The Sunday school teacher shook her head in wonder. "But my little daughter Mary fell, and was so injured that she could not stand up straight."

Daisy smiled and assured her that her daughter was all right now: "She is straight and beautiful; and your son is looking so noble and happy."

In the report of Daisy's final days, her mother wrote that another family friend came to pay her respects and was informed that her daughter, who had died some years before, was also now an adult on the other side. The family friend did not recognize Daisy's description of her daughter until she said, "She used to have a mole on the left side of her neck, but she does not have it now." With this added bit of information, the woman was convinced.

Mrs. Dryden asked her daughter how she was able to converse with Allie. "I don't hear you speak, nor do you move your lips." Daisy smiled and replied, "We speak with our thoughts." Mrs. Dryden wished to know in what form Allie appeared to her. "He is not dressed as we are," Daisy explained. "His body is clothed in something dazzlingly white. It is wonderfully bright. Oh, Mama, you should see how fine, light, and splendid his robe is—and how very white!" Reverend Dryden cited the psalmist of the Old Testament who declared, "He is clothed with light." "Oh, yes, father," Daisy agreed. "That is very true."

Daisy loved to hear her sister Loulou sing some of her favorite hymns. In one particular stanza, when Loulou was singing about the wings of angels,

Daisy began to giggle. "Oh, Loulou, it is so funny. We were always told that angels had wings. But it is not so. It is a mistake. Angels do not have any wings at all." Loulou found such an assertion difficult to accept. "But they must have wings, dear Daisy. Or else how could they fly down from Heaven?" Daisy explained further, "They don't fly. They just come. Do you know, the very moment that I think of our brother Allie, he is here at once."

Mrs. Dryden, who had been listening to the conversation between her daughters, wanted to know how it was that Daisy managed to see the angels.

Daisy was quick to admit that she did not always see them. "But when I do, the walls seem to vanish and I can see ever so far away—and I see crowds and crowds of spirits. Those spirits who come close to me are those whom I knew in my life, but others I have never seen before."

On the day of her death, Daisy asked her mother for a hand mirror. Dryden hesitated, fearing that her child would be horrified by her haggard features. But after calmly considering her reflection in the looking glass for several minutes, Daisy said, "My poor body is used up, like one of Mama's old dresses that she hangs up in the wardrobe and never wears again. But I possess a spiritual body, which shall replace my old one. I have already got it on me, and it is with my spiritual eyes that I see the spirit world—even though my earthly body is still attached to the spiritual one. You will place my body in the grave, because I shall have no further use for it, but I shall be clothed in another body much more beautiful than this one—one just like Allie's! Mama, darling, don't cry, for if I have to go away, it is for my benefit. God knows what is best."

The child asked that her mother open the window, and Mrs. Dryden complied with her request. "I want to have a last look at the beautiful world," Daisy said, "for after the sunrise tomorrow, I shall be no more." Daisy requested that her father raise her up a little. "Goodbye, goodbye, my pretty world. I still love you, but, nevertheless, I don't wish to remain here any longer."

Mrs. Dryden's journal recorded that at a quarter to eleven that night, Daisy called out to her father, "Papa, lift me up. Allie has come to look for me." When the child had been placed as she wished, she asked that someone sing a hymn. "Go and get Loulou," one of the adults in attendance at Daisy's bedside said. "She's the singer in the family."

"No," Daisy said in a soft voice. "Please don't disturb her. She's asleep." Then, just as the hands of the clock pointed at eleven, Daisy lifted up her hands and said, "I am coming, Allie!" It was at that moment, Mrs. Dryden stated, that her daughter stopped breathing.

Daisy Dryden's heavenly visions made quite an impression upon psychical researchers of the day. Professor James H. Hyslop of Columbia University, author of *Science and a Future Life* (1905) and *Borderlands of Psychical Research* (1906), conducted a full investigation of the case and reported that he could confirm every detail. Bozzano quoted the case in his *Phenomenes Psychiques* (c. 1923) as did George Lindsay Johnson in his *Does Man Survive?* (1936) .

In his summation of the Daisy Dryden case, Johnson affirms that in his opinion, "This case affords one of the most convincing proofs of the continuation of life after death and of the survival of all our faculties that it is possible to obtain.... [Daisy's] artless patter is of infinitely more value—and far nearer the actual truth—than all the learned philosophy and disquisitions of scientists and divines. As Jesus exclaimed, 'I thank thee, Father, Lord of the wise and the learned, Thou hast revealed them to the childlike.'"

SPIRIT MESSAGES TO LOVED ONES LEFT BEHIND

In 1968 we began distributing the Steiger Questionnaire of Psychic and Mystical Experiences. *Respondents sent us the following messages they received from loved ones who had crossed over to the other side.*

Heaven Is the Summation of Perfect Harmony and Love

1. "From what the spirit of my husband Sam has told me," Bridget C. said, "Heaven seems to be the summation of perfect harmony and love. He says that it is a person's inner life that makes for righteousness and happiness."

2. Ann H. said that her mother's spirit informed her that the entities in heaven were always busy with pleasant activities. "It seems as though the spirits in the next world are always learning and continually engaged in meaningful pursuits and recreations."

3. Marion Palmer said: "In heaven, love is the great guiding star. Love fills the spirit entities with the highest joy. The spirit of my sister Jackie has told me that the souls of all those in heaven are filled with [unimaginable] happiness. She said that the divine energy of living, being, and becoming permeate their essences with an intensity [of] which we on Earth can have no conception."

Hell and Belief Constructs

Hell appears to be the negation of all virtues and pleasures. Rather than a specific place, it seems to be more of a condition, or state of being, that embodies the summation of all misdirected energies, such as greed, lust, malice, hate, and jealousy.

At the moment of physical death, spirits newly freed from the confines of flesh are profoundly influenced by the belief constructs they maintained while on Earth. A Roman Catholic, therefore, will often perceive a saint or the Virgin Mary waiting to welcome him to the next world. A practicing Jew may have Moses or Abraham greet him. An angel or Jesus may be waiting to open the gates of heaven for a Protestant. After the spirit has adjusted to existence in the afterlife, however, religious concepts evolve into matters of little or no importance.

Paradise

According to numerous reports, a person does not go directly to heaven after he or she dies. The newly deceased finds him- or herself in what is commonly referred to as "paradise."

"Georgia said that it is a kind of gathering place for all newly arrived spirits," Douglas J. said, referring to the communication that he had received from his wife in the next world. "She said that the place has nothing to do with whether or not you lived a good life or a bad life. Everyone goes there, regardless. It is something like a kind of resting place before the spirit moves on."

Douglas stated that he had looked up the word paradise in a dictionary and discovered that it is a Persian word for a park or garden. "From what I can ascertain," he continued, "it is after the spirit entity has been deceased for a while that it begins to grow weary of the familiar scenes of life on Earth. I am certain that it all depends upon the individual entity and the personal circumstances of his or her passing, but it seems that the spirits must be willing to set aside their material interests before they are ready to progress more completely into the light of higher awareness."

The Wonder of the Afterlife

Peggy Ann L. said that she sometimes felt that the spirit of her husband Patrick found it impossible to convey the beauty and the brilliance of the next world in mere mortal words. "I am not certain if Patrick is simply unable to describe the wonder of the afterlife, or if my finite mind is simply unable to grasp it all. Patrick told me that at first everything in the next world was so marvelously different from existence on Earth that he found it impossible to grasp. Now, I fear that Patrick has given up the task of allowing me to perceive the glory of the afterlife. He said that I will just have to wait and see it all for myself."

Remaining Unaware of the Transition of Physical Death

Throughout history, spirits have stated that in the afterlife, days, months, or even years might pass before an entity might realize that it had passed over.

After having passed on in September 1987, the spirit entity of Camille A. told her sister Louise that many spirits remain oblivious to the death of their bodies because they may be in a kind of dreamlike state immediately after death. According to Camille, "This kind of spirit dreaming is different from Earth dreaming in that the dreamer will never again awaken to physical realities. When the spirit does awaken, it will do so in a world of new realities that are unknown to it. It will only be some time later that such materialistic entities will emerge from their stupor and gradually become convinced that they are no longer living in the physical world."

Meeting Friends and Relatives

As a general rule, it seems that regardless of the kind of life a person might have led, the moment people die a spirit entity (usually a friend or relative) comes to meet the newly deceased and becomes a kind of guide. The guide's mission is to greet, comfort, and show the new spirit around. Without such guides, the recently deceased would feel desperately lonely and confused the moment they wake up to their new life.

"My wife Ramona told me that she was met by her grandparents and by her best friend Carmen, who had been killed in a car accident," said Joaquin S. "I had been so sad, so frightened, until the spirit form of my wife told me that she was not alone on the other side. It brought me great peace, just knowing that she had someone with her."

Spirit Duplicates

Many of those who have received messages from spirits have been repeatedly assured that objects in the Earth plane have their spiritual counterparts on the other side. "We have our spirit duplicates of everything that you can see around you," Edward B. heard the spirit voice of his wife Donna tell him. "We have trees, flowers, animals, mountains, rivers, and seas."

The inquisitive Edward insisted on receiving a more complete description of the environment of the next world. "We have clouds and rainy days, storms and lightning," the spirit entity continued. "We have the 1,001 forms that make mother nature so beautiful. We have houses and books and clothes. Everything on Earth has its mental duplicate or counterpart in the spirit world."

On the Other Side, the Living Are the "Spooks"

In an interesting twist, Kathy B. said that the spirit of her sister Barbara communicated that those of us who dwell on the physical plane are deemed "spooks" by the entities in the next world. "Life is intensely pleasurable here,"

Barbara said from the other side. "Although you think of us over here as ghosts, to us it is the other way around. We look upon you as spooks and shadowy beings, because you are transparent to our mental vision. From our perspective, it is we who are the real thing. We appear to one another as perfectly solid."

There Is No Pain in the Next World

The spirit of Frank M. appeared to his wife Teresa and told her that since spirits have no physical bodies, they have no nerves and therefore cannot feel pain. "Life cannot help being more virtuous here," he said. "Spirit entities do not harm or kill one another, because our bodies cannot be harmed or murdered. There is not the slightest temptation to steal, because there would be nothing to steal that we cannot form mentally with our own minds. It is pointless to tell lies, for the obvious reason that we can read one another's thoughts. We do not eat and drink, therefore drunkenness and gluttony cannot exist.

"Although we keep a concept of sexual identity, we do not marry. And because we have no physical bodies there can be no such things as adultery, lust, or jealousy. The concept of [possessing another being] has completely disappeared. We are no longer attracted to the promise of the physical delights of the body, but to the prowess of one's mental strength and the beauty of one's soul."

Beyond the Fourth Dimension

Sherrana P. had been deceased for nearly three years before her spirit entity appeared to her husband Ronald. "Darling, if you can grasp the concept that thoughts are things," the spirit told him, "you will be in a marvelous position to understand many of the essential mysteries of the universe, including life after death. Because of my more rapid ethereal vibration, I can appear before you in your more physically dense world. Likewise, I can easily walk through your doors and walls, because they are objects of the third dimension. I now exist beyond the fourth dimension."

Warnings About Spirit Entities in the Lower Vibrations

"If you should encounter spirit entities who appear interested in matters of the flesh, and who are selfish and exploitative," warned the spirit entity of Jack K., "you have met beings from the lower and less spiritual planes of existence. On planes of higher spiritual vibration, love is the chief emotion."

Kris C.'s spirit essence told her mother that like-minded souls are attracted to one another. "Here, the happiness of the soul depends upon its own resources. We do not work to earn money for the pleasures of existence. We are free to utilize our individual talents as we prefer. Because our thoughts and our characters are completely open and naked for all to see, there is no attempt at pretense. Spirits of similar vibrational frequencies just naturally move toward one another.

"Those souls who, for whatever reason, are slow to adjust to the next world may stay on the lower planes for years. Some exist for quite some time in a kind of mental darkness. That is quite sad, for the heavenly life is one of growth in wisdom, insight, and love."

The Realms of Spiritual Expression

The spiritual essence of Floyd A. materialized before his wife Lillian to explain three distinct realms, or dimensions of spiritual expression. "In the afterlife," he said, "there is the etheric, the mental, and the spiritual. Your plane, my dear one, is the world of matter, wherein you have a physical body that is controlled by your mind. On the other side, however, we manifest a mentally formed etheric body that is controlled by our spirituality. The key to all of this is to interpret the physical in terms of the mental, and to control the whole by means of the spiritual."

Al M. had been confined to a wheelchair for 11 years before he passed on in September 1988. "Time and space do not have the same meaning over here," his spirit told his wife Terry. "I can travel from one spot on the Earth to another, simply by thinking it to be so. I'm not confined to that darn wheelchair any longer, darling, and I'm traveling all over the place now."

Spirits Communicate by Telepathy

According to Goldie C., her father's spirit form told her that telepathy was the normal means of communication among spirits, as well as between spirit beings and humans. "Telepathy dispenses with the clumsiness of language and renders sound superfluous," the spirit said. "It is this mechanism that permits spirit entities to communicate with the living in whatever country they may exist. It is also such a mechanism that allows spirits from ancient times to be able to be understood by men and women in the twentieth century."

Medical Diagnosis from the Next World

The spirit of Philip A. appeared to his wife Sonya and told her to go at once to her physician to have a lump in her left breast examined. "Phil could see inside my body," Sonya said. "He explained that their sense of color on the other side is vastly superior to ours, and their range of sight extends far beyond our small share of the spectrum. Their sight moves beyond even what we know as the ultra-violet range. Phil said that everything that was around me in my environment appeared totally different to him, and different from the way that he had remembered it.

"Phil surprised me when he said that there was no sunlight in the next world, but that everything was intensely bright, regardless. I guess that was why my physical body was more or less transparent to his spiritual eyes. His sight could penetrate between the molecules of my body, just like X-rays do."

Watching over Loved Ones on Earth

Marie R.'s three children were all under five years of age when her husband Larry was killed in 1952 during the Korean conflict. Even today, more than 50 years later, Marie still feels the guiding and protecting influence and spiritual presence of her husband, and she feels that she knows why this is so.

"I have come to understand that when the spirits in the next world develop spiritually, they pass to a higher spiritual sphere," Marie said. "Most spirits who graduate to that higher plane eventually lose all their interest in the mundane, the material, the earthly. The higher the spirits evolve, the less often they will be concerned with Earth plane considerations. In fact, the highly progressed entities will rarely come to anyone on Earth *unless* there should be such a strong bond of affection between the spirit and those left behind that the entity will frequently return to monitor their loved ones until the time that the loved ones join them in the next world. I know that Larry's spirit remains concerned about us and that he awaits our joining him on the other side."

The Next World Is One of Thought Forms

Tiffany J. said that the spirit essence of her husband Norman has told her the principal difference between life on Earth and the other side is the fact that we living humans exist in a material world wherein everything is governed by physical laws.

"In the next world," Tiffany stated, "the spirit beings live on a mental plane, and thought replaces physical action and crude matter. Thoughts are things, and the limitations of time and space do not exist for them.

"Another main difference," she added, "is that over there, love is the principal energy that controls every thought, every deed, every vibration."

Ghosts Are Merely Humans Freed of Their Physical Limitations

In his quest to solve the enigma of life after death, scientist George Lindsay Johnson thoughtfully observed what he believed to be an axiomatic truth: "The Universe is a vast exhibition of intense activity, movement, and intelligence—a becoming through perpetual evolution. This consists of two systems—the natural or physical, and the psychic or spiritual world—and each of them is governed by its own laws, which are entirely different in their action. These two world-systems are perpetually acting and reacting on each other; the physical world being subservient to the spiritual world, and controlled by it. Furthermore, the inhabitants of the spirit world are merely human beings freed from the limitations imposed upon them by their physical bodies."

10
Ghosts That Gave
Proof of Their Existence

THE SCRATCH ON HIS SISTER'S CHEEK

In 1876 Mr. F. G., a traveling salesman, was sitting in a hotel room in St. Joseph, Missouri. It was high noon, and F. G. was smoking a cigar as he wrote out orders. Suddenly conscious of someone sitting on his left with one arm resting on the table, the salesman was startled to look up into the face of his dead sister, a young lady of 18 who had died of cholera in 1867.

"So sure was I that it was she," he wrote later in an account to the American Society for Psychical Research (*Proceedings*, S.P.R., vol. VI, no. 17), that I sprang forward in delight, calling her by name." As he did so, the image of his sister vanished. F. G. sat back in his seat, stunned by the experience. The cigar was still in his mouth, a pen in his hand, and the ink was still moist on his order form. He was satisfied that he had not dreamt the vision of his sister; he was wide awake.

"I was near enough to touch her, had it been a physical possibility, and noted her features, expression, and details of dress.... She appeared as if alive. Her eyes looked kindly and perfectly naturally into mine. Her skin was so lifelike that I could see the glow or moisture on its surface, and, on the whole, there was no change in her appearance." F. G. was so impressed by the experience that he took the next train home to tell his parents about the remarkable visitation. His mother nearly fainted when he told them of "a bright red line, or scratch on the right-hand side" of his sister's face.

With tears streaming down her cheeks, F. G.'s mother told him that he had indeed seen his sister, for only she was aware of the scratch that she had

[203]

accidentally made on her daughter's face after her death. She had carefully tried to obliterate all traces of the slight scratch with the aid of powder, and "she had never mentioned [it] to a human being from that day." F. G. noted later that he found it impossible to believe that it was solely a coincidence that his sister visited him when he did. "A few weeks later my mother died, happy in her belief she would rejoin her favorite daughter in a better world."

In discussing this case, the noted psychical researcher Frederick W. H. Myers, author of the classic work *Human Personality and Its Survival of Bodily Death* (coauthored with Edmund Gurney and Frank Podmore, publishing posthumously in 1903), wrote that in his opinion, the spirit of the daughter had perceived the approaching death of her mother and had appeared to the brother to force him into the role of message bearer. Also, by prompting F. G. to unexpectedly return home at that time, the spirit enabled him to have a final visit with his mother.

Myers is further intrigued by the fact that the spirit figure appeared not as a corpse but as a girl full of health and happiness, with the symbolic red mark worn simply as a test of identity. Myers discounted the theory that the spirit figure could have been a projection from the mother's mind. Myers, who founded the British Society for Psychical Research in 1882, along with Henry Sidgwick and Edmund Gurney, concluded the following regarding the famous "scratch on the cheek" case: "As to the spirit's own knowledge of the fate of the body after death, other reported cases show that this specific form of *post-mortem* perception is not unusual. However explained, this case is one of the best attested, and in itself one of the most remarkable, that we possess ... it certainly seems probable that recognition was intelligently [intended]."

RAYMOND'S LAST PHOTOGRAPH

The noted British physicist Oliver Lodge was knighted in 1902, while he was serving as the president of the British Society for Psychical Research. In 1913 Lodge was elected president of the British Association for the Advancement of Science. In the eyes of his more conservative scientific colleagues, his brilliant work with electricity and the early forms of radio more than compensated for his fascination with the spirit world. In August 1915 Lodge received what he considered absolute proof of survival after death when Leonora Piper, the famous spirit medium from Boston, relayed what he believed to be convincing messages from the spirits of two close friends and associates, Fredric W. H. Myers, who died in 1901, and Edmund Gurney, who died in 1888.

While Lodge and his wife, Lady Lodge, both believed that life continued after physical death, it did not prevent them from grieving after the death of their son, Raymond, when he was killed in service on September 14, 1915.

In the 1999 movie *The Sixth Sense,* actor Haley Joel Osment (left) plays a young boy who is able to see ghosts. The young boy realizes that the ghosts come to him for help in resolving issues from their lives. Shown at right is Bruce Willis.

Although they both grieved for their son, they used the understanding they had of the next world to attempt to communicate with their son in the next plane of existence. On September 25 Lady Lodge sat with the medium Gladys Osborne Leonard to contact her son. The medium described a photograph that had been taken of Raymond with a group of fellow officers. The Lodges had numerous portraits of their son in uniform that had been taken in the early months of World War I, but they did not possess a single photograph like the one the medium described. Intrigued by Leonard's insistence that such a photograph existed, Lady Lodge could only shake her head in puzzlement, for she knew of no such photograph. "He is insistent that I should tell you of this," Leonard told Lady Lodge. "He stands with his fellow medical officers, his walking stick under his arm."

After Lady Lodge shared the information with her husband, Sir Oliver was impressed with the emphasis that the medium had set upon Raymond's desire that she should tell them about the photograph. According to Lodge's report on the case (*Proceedings*, S.P.R. vol. XXIX), on November 29, a letter was received from a Mrs. Cheves, who was a stranger to them but who was the mother of a friend of Raymond's. Cheves informed the Lodges that she had a photograph of a group of medical officers, in which Raymond and her son were present. Would the Lodges, inquired Cheves, like a copy of the photograph?

Although the Lodges responded immediately, the photograph did not arrive until the afternoon of December 7. In the meantime, Lady Lodge had gone through Raymond's diary, which had been returned to the Lodges with Raymond's belongings, and had found an entry dated August 24, which told of such a photo having been taken. "The exposure was only made 21 days before his death," Lodge wrote in his report, "and some days may have elapsed before he saw a print, if he ever saw one. He certainly never mentioned it in his letters. We were therefore in complete ignorance of it."

While the Lodges were awaiting the photograph from Cheves, they visited another medium whose guide contacted the spirit of Raymond and gave them additional details concerning the group picture. "Raymond is doubtful about the stick," the spirit said through the medium, "but he says there is a considerable number of men in the photograph; that the front row is sitting, and that there is a back row, or some of the people grouped and set up at the back; also that there are a dozen or more people in the photograph, and that some of them he hardly knew." Raymond also named two friends who were prominently featured in the photograph and said that he was sitting down with officers behind him, one of whom annoyed him by leaning on his shoulder.

When the photograph was delivered to the Lodge home on the afternoon of December 7, the Lodges immediately noted that the picture offered a poor likeness of Raymond but excellent evidence that their son had communicated to them from beyond the grave. The walking stick was there, though not under Raymond's arm, as Leonard had said. The fellow officers whom Raymond had named through the second medium were in the photograph, and the general arrangement of the men was as the mediums had described it.

"But by far the most striking piece of evidence is the fact that someone sitting behind Raymond is leaning or resting a hand on his shoulder," Lodge said. "The photograph fortunately shows the actual occurrence, and almost indicates that Raymond was rather annoyed with it; for his face is a little screwed up, and his head has been slightly bent to one side out of the way of the man's arm. It is the only case in the photograph where one man is leaning or resting his hand on the shoulder of another."

After receiving the photograph, the Lodges contacted Cheves to learn where they might obtain prints of other photographs that had been taken at the same time. Upon examination of all accessible prints, the Lodges found that the basic group pose had been repeated with only slight variations for three different photographs. The Lodges felt the existence of the photographs offered proof of life after death; the degree of proof was greatly enhanced by the fact that one medium had made a reference to the existence of Raymond's last photograph, and another medium, unknown to the first, had supplied the details of the photograph.

In his book *My Philosophy* (1933), Lodge wrote, "I am absolutely convinced not only of survival, but of demonstrated survival, demonstrated by occasional interaction with matter in such a way as to produce physical results."

JAMES CHAFFIN'S OTHER WILL

On September 7, 1921, James Chaffin, a farmer from Davie County, North Carolina, died as the result of a fall. Although Chaffin was survived by his widow and four sons, the will that had been duly attested by two witnesses on November 16, 1905, left all of his property to the third son, Marshall.

One night in June 1925, James Pinkney Chaffin, the farmer's second son, saw the spirit figure of his father standing at his bedside. The specter told him of the existence of another will. According to James, his father appeared before him that night as he often had in life, wearing a familiar black overcoat. "You will find the will in my overcoat pocket," the spirit said, as it took hold of the coat and pulled back the lapels to expose the pocket it referred to.

The next morning James arose convinced that he had truly seen and heard the spirit of his father, and that the spirit had visited him for the purpose of correcting some error. After his death, the black overcoat had been passed on to his eldest son, John, so James traveled to visit his brother in order to examine the pocket of the overcoat. The two brothers found that the lining of the inside pocket had been sewn together, and when they cut the stitches, they found a roll of paper that bore the message: "Read the 27th chapter of Genesis in my daddies Old Bible."

James was convinced that the spirit had spoken truthfully, and he took witnesses to the home of his mother where, after some search, they located the dilapidated old Bible in the top drawer of a dresser in an upstairs room. One of the witnesses found the will in a pocket that had been formed by folding two of the Bible's pages together. Their father had made the new will on January 16, 1919, 14 years after the first will. In this testament, the farmer stated that he desired his property to be divided equally among his four sons with the admonition that they provide for their mother as long as she lived. Although the second will had not been attested, it would be considered valid under North Carolina law if it could be proven that it had been written entirely in James Chaffin's own handwriting.

Marshall Chaffin, the sole beneficiary under the conditions of the original will, had passed away within a year of his father. Marshall's widow and son prepared to contest the validity of the second will, and the residents of the county anticipated a long and bitter court battle between members of the Chaffin family. The scandal mongers were immensely disappointed when 10 witnesses arrived in the courtroom prepared to give evidence that the second will was in James Chaffin's handwriting. After seeing the will, Marshall Chaffin's wife and son immediately withdrew their opposition. It seemed evident that they, too, believed the will had been written in the hand of the testator.

James later told an investigator from the Society for Psychical Research's *Journal* that his father had appeared to him before the trial and told him that the lawsuit would be resolved in such a manner. James said, "Many of my friends do not believe it is possible for the living to hold communication with the dead, but I am convinced that my father actually appeared to me on these several occasions, and I shall believe it to the day of my death."

Investigators from the Society for Psychical Research were unable to establish any kind of case that James had a subconscious knowledge of the will in the old Bible, or of the message in the coat pocket. Fraud had to be ruled out because of the ease in which 10 reliable witnesses, all well acquainted with Chaffin's handwriting, could be summoned to testify to the authenticity of the will's handwriting. Charges that the will was fake seem negated by the immediate withdrawal of the contest by Marshall's widow and son once they were allowed to examine the document. Evidently they, too, recognized the handwriting of the elder Chaffin.

The *Journal*'s summation of the strange case of Chaffin's will stated the difficulty in attempting to explain the case on normal lines. "If a supernormal explanation [is to] be accepted, it is to be noted that the present case is of a comparatively infrequent type, in which more than one of the percipient's senses is affected by the phantasm. Mr. J. P. Chaffin both 'saw' his father and 'heard' him speak. The auditory impression was not strictly accurate: what was in the overcoat pocket was not the second will, but a clue to its whereabouts, but the practical result was the same."

GRANDAD CAME TO SAY GOODBYE

On the night of June 11, 1923, a sleeping Gladys Watson was awakened by the sound of someone calling her name. As she sat up in bed, she was able to discern the form of her beloved grandfather leaning toward her. "Don't be frightened, it's only me. I have just died," he told her. Mrs. Watson started to cry and reached across the bed to awaken her husband. "This is how they will bury me," her Grandad Parker said, indicating his suit and black bow tie. "Just wanted to tell you I've been waiting to go ever since mother was taken."

The Watson's house was next door to Lilly Laboratories in Indianapolis; their bedroom was dimly illuminated by lights from the laboratory that allowed Gladys to see her grandfather clearly. Before Gladys was able to awaken her husband, her grandfather had disappeared.

After waking her husband, he insisted that Gladys had suffered a nightmare. "Your grandfather is alive and well back in Wilmington," he told her. Mrs. Watson was firm in her conviction that she had seen her grandfather, and that it had not been a dream. He had come to bid her farewell. At 4:05 A.M. the Watsons called Wilmington, Delaware, where Gladys's family lived. Gladys's mother, Mrs. Parker, was surprised to receive the call. She had been up most of the night with her father-in-law and had decided to wait until morning before calling the Watsons to let them know that Grandad Parker had passed.

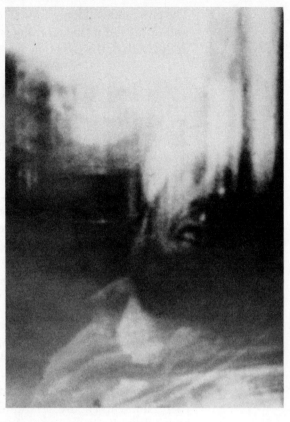

Materialization of a spirit entity.

Gladys was awakened by the apparition of her grandfather at approximately 3:30 A.M., and the Watsons had called Wilmington at about 4:05 A.M. central time. Gladys's grandfather had died at 4:00 A.M. eastern time—half an hour before Gladys saw him.

Gladys wrote an account of her experience for the American Society for Psychical Research's *Journal* (vol. LXV, no. 3). In her account she mentioned that both she and her husband were children of Methodist ministers "schooled against superstition from the time of their birth." When Gladys was asked by an A.S.P.R. investigator whether the experience of hearing her grandfather speak could be compared to hearing someone in the flesh, or to hearing with one's "inner ear," she answered that it had been as if her grandfather had been there in the flesh, speaking in a soft yet determined voice.

Gladys's father, Reverend Walter E. Parker, Sr., corroborated his daughter's story in a letter to the A.S.P.R. in which he wrote: "Gladys had always been my father's favorite grandchild, and we had promised to let her know if and when he became seriously ill. (He made his home with us.) He took sick the day before. We called the doctor and thought he was going to be all right.

The end came suddenly around four o'clock in the morning. We were going to wait until later in the morning to get in touch with Gladys. I believe sincerely in the truth of this experience as my daughter writes it."

A DEBT REMAINED TO BE PAID

In his book *The Dead Have Never Died*, Edward C. Randall wrote of 20 years' worth of experiments he conducted with the medium Emily S. French. French was deaf and extremely frail, and Randall felt that her loss of hearing provided an excellent condition for testing the authenticity of her powers as a medium. Randall stated that because of her deafness, French would often fail to hear the spirit voices that would sound about her. French would continue speaking, without regard for the entities she might be interrupting. No mediumistic trick could enable one to speak in three or four different voices at the same time, each voice discussing some topic completely unrelated to the others. Randall admits that such conditions often made for confusion, but in his estimation, greatly increased the validity of the more than 700 sittings he held with French.

On May 26, 1896, the Brown Building in Buffalo, New York, collapsed while undergoing repairs. The city was filled with rumors about the number of people who had lost their lives in the tragedy. At a sitting with French that evening, four voices identified themselves as victims of the accident and gave their names and addresses. Randall writes that these were verified when the bodies were discovered some days later.

At another sitting, Randall, a lawyer, said that the voice of his father was heard. The senior Randall told his son that one small item in the settlement of his estate had been overlooked. Randall spoke a bit harshly to the voice, chiding the spirit that during his life his father had always been preoccupied with amassing money. "The estate has already been divided," Randall told the spirit voice. "Why bother me with this now?" The spirit of Randall's father replied that he had worked too hard for his money to allow an asset to remain undiscovered.

The voice proceeded to tell of a small sum of money lent to an individual in Erie, Pennsylvania. Before the note's maturity, the deceased had filed it with the protonotary in Erie. Although there would be no record of the loan in his books, the voice told Randall, he could find the judgment of the note on record in the protonotary's office. "I want you to correct it," the voice concluded.

Randall was surprised when he was able to locate a transcript of the transaction his father's spirit had mentioned, and with such evidence, he obtained payment for the note, with interest. Randall questioned all of his father's former employees to determine if anyone other than the makers of the note and the protonotary in Erie had had knowledge of the debt. He could find no one who had known of the loan. It would certainly have been impossible for French to have known about the undisclosed dealings of a man she had never met. "My father's voice was clearly recognizable on that occasion, as it has been on hundreds of others," Randall wrote. "I cite this instance for the benefit of those who measure everything from an evidential standpoint."

The Spirit Remembered a Forgotten Kindness

Arthur Findlay, a stockbroker and accountant from Glasgow, Scotland, began to investigate psychic phenomena in 1918. Although Findlay began his studies as a skeptic, he soon found himself becoming increasingly convinced that John C. Sloan—whom he had originally intended to expose as a fraud—had authentic powers as a medium.

After more than 50 sittings with Sloan, Findlay became convinced not only of the medium's integrity but of human survival after death. In his book *On the Edge of the Etheric*, Findlay relates the following case as one he considers completely free of any suggestion of fraud, telepathy, or clairvoyant interaction.

In 1919 Findlay took his brother John to a séance with Sloan, where a voice calling itself "Eric Saunders" manifested, claiming to have been an acquaintance of John's. John denied ever having known a man of that name, but the voice persisted that they had known each other in the army. "Where might that have been?" John asked. "Among other places, I served at Aldershot, Bisley, France." As John recited a number of locations that had figured prominently in various British campaigns, he deliberately omitted naming Lowestoft, where he had actually spent most of his army life training machine-gunners. "I knew you at none of those places you have listed," Saunders said. "We knew each other near Lowestoft." John managed to repress his surprise and excitement and countered with the question: "Why did you say *near* Lowestoft?"

"Because we were not actually in Lowestoft, but in the village of Kessingland, which is located near the larger city," the voice replied. John conceded this statement was correct. Then, piqued by his inability to remember the man and still suspicious of some kind of fraud, he continued his questioning. "Who was our company commander?"

The voice replied that the commander's name had been MacNamara and scored another hit. Then, to test the voice further, John said, "You must have been one of my Lewis gunners."

"No," the voice answered, evading the trap, "you instructed us in the use of the Hotchkiss, not the Lewis." Saunders's disembodied voice continued to answer all the questions correctly. The spirit said that he had been killed in

Ken Webster of Dodleston, Chester, United Kingdom, lived in a home that had often suffered from paranormal activity. In May 1985 he started to receive messages on his computer, and then written by hand on his floors, from one "Tomas Harden" living in the sixteenth century, who said Katherine Parr was his queen. This photograph shows messages left on the floor of Webster's house.

France when he had crossed the channel in the big draft of August 1917. John asked the voice what it meant by the "big draft."

"Don't you remember?" the spirit of the machine-gunner wondered a bit incredulously. "There was an extra large draft of men to France that month, and even the colonel came out on the parade ground to make a speech to us." John commented that this was correct. It was, in fact, the only occasion that he could remember in which the colonel had personally said goodbye to the men. Now that the identity of Eric Saunders seemed to have been established, John asked the next logical question. Why had the machine-gunner returned to speak to him? "Because," the voice said with some emotion, "I have never forgotten that good turn that you did for me."

"Eric Saunders" seemed to fade away before further explanation could be delivered identifying the good deed that had been done. After the séance, John told his brother that he could vaguely remember securing leave for one of his gunners under rather unusual circumstances, but he could not honestly remember if Saunders had been that trooper's name.

Six months after the séance, John was able to meet with the man who had been his corporal. The corporal could not remember an Eric Saunders, but he had brought a notebook with him in which he had entered the names of all the men who had served under him. In the 1917 records for the company, they found the name of Eric Saunders with the notation "August, 1917." A red line had been drawn through the name and the words that followed it. John's former corporal explained that he had always drawn a line through the men's names when they were shipped overseas into combat.

John was left to marvel at the proof of survival that had been given to him by a machine-gunner who had remembered a long-forgotten act of kindness.

A Mysterious Visit from the Spirit of a Priest

The Personal Experience of Anita Stapleton

"Is life after death only a matter of religious beliefs? Is it just wishful thinking? Comfort for the bereaved? Or has it ever been proved? These questions pass, at one time or another, through the minds of most people. There have been many stories about visions and apparitions, verbal and written messages from 'beyond.' Are they genuine, or were they caused by imagination, hallucination, self-hypnosis, mental telepathy, or any other form of brainpower? As a person with an inquisitive mind, I have reflected upon these questions many times, until one day I received an answer most unexpectedly.

"That day in 1989 had been a normal one for me in my home in Labrador, Queensland, Australia. I had gone about my daily chores, watched television in the evening, and finally went to bed, while my husband was still watching the late movie on TV.

"The bedroom was not dark, because the bright light of a full moon [entered] through the window. I had just lain down, ready to go to sleep, when I suddenly noticed that I was not on my own. Right in front of the wardrobe and looking directly at me was a middle-aged man, dressed like a Catholic priest. I rubbed my eyes and pinched my arms to make sure I was fully awake. Yes, I most certainly was. Was I having hallucinations?

"The priest was still standing there, looking at me. He was [a rather] frail man with hollow cheeks. His face showed traces of a hard life and illness. If he had any hair at all, it was covered by his hat. He looked so real, not like a ghost. I was not a bit scared, because he radiated vibrations of utter peace and tranquility. There was nothing to be afraid of, so I decided to talk to him, keeping my voice as low as possible. 'Hello, Father,' I said. 'God bless you.'

"'And God bless you, my child,' came the priest's prompt reply. He was well-spoken, his voice soft. His English accent was not hard to distinguish. After giving me a few personal messages and stressing the point that there is survival after death, he told me who he was. [His name] was Frederick William Faber, and he had lived in England from 1814 to 1863. When I remarked that at the time of his passing he was only 49 years old, he confirmed this and added that he had died of a kidney disease. After quietly talking about religious matters for a few more minutes, he bade me farewell and disappeared.

"My mind was boggled. As late as it was, it was impossible to think of sleep. I wrote down my unearthly visitor's name and other details. Then I told my husband what had happened. Naturally, his first reaction was disbelief, and [he asserted] that I had been asleep and dreaming. Of course, I knew I had been fully awake. The whole thing, however, seemed so incredible that doubts came into my mind. The name Faber seemed a bit unusual for an Englishman. Being of German descent, I know quite a few Germans by that name. I recalled a girl, Hildegard Faber, who had gone to school with me. Was this some trickery by my subconscious mind? The incident troubled me for days. How could I ever find out the truth?

"Then my husband reminded me of Somerset House in London, where a record of every person born and deceased in Britain is kept. However, he did not know how far back these records went. Father Faber, if indeed he had existed, had been dead for over 100 years. Should I write to Somerset House? I hesitated. I did not want to make a fool of myself in case the whole thing was just a hallucination. A few days later, however, I took the plunge and wrote to Somerset House, requesting a search. I was sent a form to fill in, giving details of the required person, and I was asked to include a small search fee. This I did immediately. I waited for a reply from Somerset House. This suspense-drama

In April 2000 a family in northern Wales had strange figures appear on the walls of their home. Crosses, circles, Welsh words, and figures of monks were all visible.

would soon reach its climax. Either I would be told that there was no record of this person or ... I did not dare finish this thought.

"Two weeks later an airmail letter from London arrived. The sender was Somerset House. My hands were shaky. I trembled like a leaf. I was barely able to open the letter. Then I almost fainted. The letter contained a certified copy of a death certificate. It stated that Fredrick Will Faber's death had occurred on September 26, 1863, and that he had been 49 at the time of his death. [He] had been a doctor of divinity, in Brompton, County of Middlesex. The cause of [his] death was stated as kidney disease. In other words, the official document in my hands confirmed what the apparition had told me.

"If this is not a genuine case of a visit from beyond the grave, what is it? An authority like Somerset House would not send a fictitious document halfway around the world to back up someone's fantasy or hallucination. To the best of my knowledge, Father Faber had not been a well-known personality, so books would not have been written about him [that] I might have read and forgotten about. Nobody alive today is old enough to remember him.

Real Ghosts, Restless Spirits, and Haunted Places

"While it is true that I have been in England, I did not visit any cemeteries there, which rules out the possibility that I may have seen his name on a tombstone. I am absolutely positive that I had never before heard of Father Faber. As much as I rack my brain, I cannot find a logical explanation, but I now know for sure that there is life after death. To me it has been proven beyond the shadow of a doubt."

Author's note: Various Roman Catholic references stated that Father Frederick William Faber was a man of great charm and an eloquent preacher. Father Faber was a well-known writer of hymns, such as "The Shadow of the Rock," The Eternal Father," and "Sweet Savior, Bless Us Ere We Go." While Father Faber might be known to certain theologians, we are likely to concede Anita Stapleton's contention that he would not be well known to a layperson. The mystery is why Father Faber's spirit should appear to a housewife in Australia and offer her proof of survival after death. As Anita writes, she considers the visitation a great blessing.

THE RED-HEADED MAN IN THE CLOSET

The Personal Experience of Tom: From the Ghost to Ghost Website

"In the mid-80s we bought a 200-year-old farmhouse. Some records came with the house, so we had an idea of some of the changes and remodeling [that had been] done over time. The oak pantry door had once been the main entrance to the house. This door latched with a three-inch iron thumblatch, but we often found it open when we came in from being outside or when we got up in the mornings. I would blame my wife for not shutting the pantry door, and she would blame me. Finally it got so annoying that we put a chair against it to keep it closed. That worked for a couple of weeks.

"One night, preparing for company, I was mopping the floor in an unused room that had another old main doorway. This door was never used and was bolted from the inside. Yet I found muddy bootprints coming from the door and crossing the room.

"In the kitchen a bit later I told my wife about the bootprints. She joked that they must have been made by the guy who kept coming in the pantry door, and we had locked him out. Looking toward the pantry she said, 'It's OK, if you prefer this door, go ahead and use it.'

"Immediately the latch clicked and the door swung open, pushing the chair aside. Needless to say cold chills ran through both of us. We never worried about the pantry being open again and never saw anything else.

"But apparently our three-year-old son did. Sometime after the incident when the door swung open at my wife's invitation, our son came downstairs and told us that he'd been talking about farming with the red-headed man in his closet. Many kids have an imaginary friend, so we gave it little thought. However, he continued to talk about the red-headed man who told him about farming [and] wagon-making and warned him to be careful around the river. When we asked about the farmer, our son described him as short, with a red beard, and stooped over with a limp.

"A couple of years later, while doing research to register the home with the National Register of Historic Places, I discovered that the man who had lived in the home before the turn of the century was short, bearded, red-haired, and built buckboards for a living. He had also walked with a limp due to an accident.

"Immediately after his death, his son did the remodeling involving the pantry door, and turned what had been a sleeping room facing south into the upstairs closet. As for the warning to our son about the river, I learned that the red-headed farmer had had two children drown in the river about a mile away from the house."

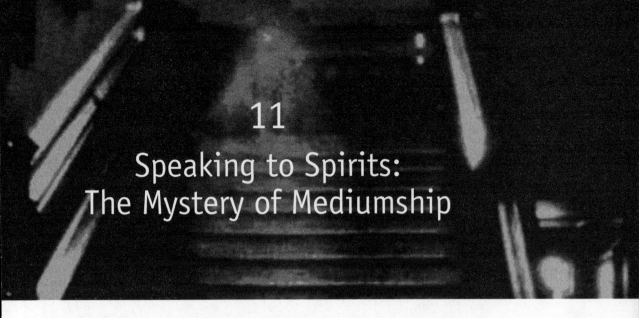

11
Speaking to Spirits:
The Mystery of Mediumship

MEDIUMS, SHAMANS, AND SPIRIT CONTACT

The idea that we survive physical death, that some part of our being is immortal, profoundly affects the lives of those who harbor such a belief. While Christianity, Islam, Judaism, and many other religions promise their followers some form of a life after death, throughout all of human history many thousands of men and women have felt that they have received proof of life existing beyond the grave, based on the evidence of survival that manifests through spirit mediums.

I first began investigating and researching spirit mediums in 1957 and subsequently had "sittings" with dozens of men and women throughout the United States and Canada who believed that they had become qualified in some special way to form a link between the living and the dead, and to relay messages of comfort, support, and personal information from the next world. While some mediums gain impressions from the spirits in a fully conscious state, others enter a trance, which is often accompanied by manifestations that appear to defy known physical laws, such as objects moving without having been touched, the levitation of the mediums' body, and the materialization of spirit forms. Perhaps the essential attribute that qualifies one to be a medium is an extreme or abnormal sensitivity that allows spirits to more easily access an individual's psyche. For this reason, mediums are often referred to as "sensitives."

After nearly 50 years of research into various aspects of spirit communication and related phenomena, I have reached the opinion that those with mediumistic abilities are individuals whose psyches preserve certain of the ancient qualities and requirements of shamanism. A shaman is one who serves

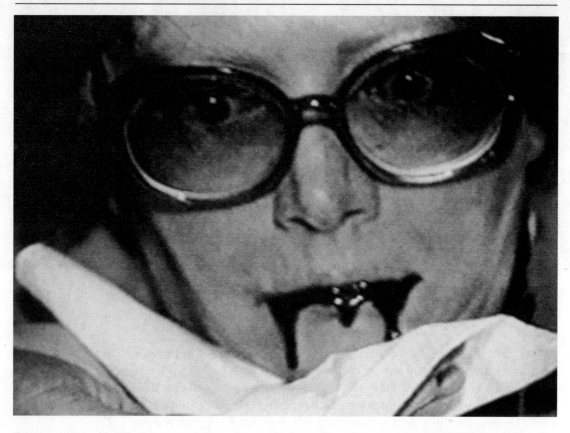

During a séance, blood begins to exude from the mouth of a medium. Seventeenth-century alchemist and freemason Prince Raimundo de Sangro de Sansevero was reported to be manifesting through this medium.

his people by acting as an intermediary to the spirit world. Originally, the term "shaman" was applied to the spirit doctors and exorcists among the Tungus group of Siberia, but in recent years the title has also been applied to the medicine men and women of the various North American tribes who also serve as mediums, healers, and visionaries for their people. Many tribal traditionalists still revere the wisdom that is shared by the men and women who maintain the shamanic traditions, traveling to the other side in the company of their spirit helper.

Anthropologist Ivar Lissner, who spent a great deal of time among the Tungus of Siberia, as well as native peoples in North America, defines a shaman as one "who knows how to deal with spirits and influence them.... The essential characteristic of the shaman is his excitement, his ecstasy and trancelike condition.... [The elements that constitute this ecstasy are] a form of self-severance from mundane existence, a state of heightened sensibility, and spiritual awareness. The shaman loses outward consciousness and becomes inspired or enraptured. While in this state of enthusiasm, he sees dreamlike apparitions, hears voices, and receives visions of truth. More than that, his soul sometimes leaves his body to go wandering."

During séances, spirit mediums are very often in a trance state and claim to be under the direction of a spirit control or spirit guide that serves as an intermediary between themselves and the spirits of deceased men and women. Once contact has been made with particular spirits in the other world, the guide speaks through the medium and relays messages to the sitters, those men and women who have assembled in the séance room for the opportunity of hearing messages from their departed loved ones.

In the shamanic tradition, the spirit guide or spirit helper is usually received by those who choose to participate in a vision quest. Before initiates embark upon this ordeal, tribal elders and shamans tutor them for many weeks on what to expect and what is expected of them. In many shamanic traditions, the spirit helper serves as an ambassador from the world of spirits to the world of humans, and often manifests in animal form to serve as a kind of chaperone during visits to other dimensions of reality.

For the more contemporary spirit mediums, who often prefer to call themselves "channels," the guide may represent itself as a being who once lived as a human on Earth or as a light being, an extraterrestrial, or even an angel. Regardless of the semantics involved, in my opinion, today's mediums and channels follow the basic procedures of ancient shamanic traditions.

MEDIUMS AND THEIR SPIRIT GUIDES

In western society, the concept of a spirit guide goes back to antiquity. The great philosopher Socrates furnishes us with the most notable example of an individual in ancient times who freely referred to his guiding voice as a "daemon" (not to be confused with "demon," a fallen angel or a negative, possessing entity). "Daemon" is better translated as guardian angel or muse. The philosopher believed that his guardian spirit kept vigil over him, warning him of approaching danger.

Spirit mediums believe that while they are in a trance, they fall under the control of a particular spirit that has become their special guide. Their guide speaks through them and works all manners of mysterious phenomena on their behalf. Although this spirit was once a living person, it has, since its time in the spirit world, become greatly elevated in spiritual awareness.

Some psychical researchers have theorized that the spirit guide may actually be a little-known power of the mind that enables the medium's subjective level of consciousness to dramatize another personality, complete with a full range of personal characteristics. Other researchers maintain that the only difference between those individuals who proclaim themselves to be psychic and those who call themselves spirit mediums is that psychics attribute their talents to some manifestation of extrasensory perception—such as clairvoyance, precognition, or telepathy—while mediums attribute their powers to an interaction with unseen spirit intelligences. While many mediums may admit that the subjective mind is not entirely eliminated when they are in a trance, they insist that their subconscious mind is taken over and controlled by a spirit entity of great compassion and wisdom.

In his autobiography, written in collaboration with Marguerite Harmon Bro, the highly respected medium Arthur Augustus Ford (1897–1971), an ordained minister of the Disciples of Christ Church, explained the working relationship that he enjoyed with his spirit guide, Fletcher. According to Ford, Fletcher had been a boyhood friend who had been killed in action during World War I. When Ford wished to enter a trance, he would lie down on a couch or lean back in a comfortable chair, breathing slowly and rhythmically until he felt his energy draw in at the solar plexus. Then he focused his attention on Fletcher's face, as he had come to know it, until gradually he felt as if his guide's face had pressed into his own. At the instant the faces merged, he experienced a "a sense of shock," as if he were fainting or "passing out." At that point, Ford lost consciousness, and when he awakened at the completion of a séance, it was as if he'd had a "good nap."

Olof Jonsson, one of the greatest mediums of the twentieth century, once told me that while he accessed the universal mind through meditation, he was aware of spirit beings on other planes of existence. Jonsson was the psychic-sensitive who participated in astronaut Edgar Mitchell's Apollo 14 ESP experiment between Earth and the Moon in February 1971. He said that humans might interpret these intelligences in any way that would be most compatible with our own psyches. "One person might perceive such an entity as an Indian," he said, "another as an old wise man, yet someone else as a holy figure. But all these seemingly separate beings are bodiless forms of benign intelligence. These intelligences cloak themselves as Tibetans or cosmic teachers because the human brain will more readily accept an entity that looks like a human being, rather than a shapeless, shimmering intelligence."

Jonsson said that he believed that spirit beings have the ability to absorb our actions and thoughts so that they may know how to better direct us toward cosmic harmony. "These beings avoid language and work with us on an unconscious level," he said. "Telepathy affords us proof that language means nothing to the unconscious. We do not think in words, but in ideas and feelings. What language does God speak? The feelings and the harmony communicated between the unconscious levels of self comprise the one 'language' that all people understand."

Bertie Catchings, a remarkable psychic-sensitive and spirit medium from Texas, once remarked that when a person dies, the soul becomes more alive than it was in the flesh. She was able to relay messages from the deceased to their loved ones because, in her view, "The spirit wishes to communicate with loved ones and let them know that they are alive and that they are well off in another dimension." Catchings said that many spirits feel surprised and elated when they truly find out what has happened to them. "They usually have so many friends and family members on the other side that they enjoy quite a reunion, quite a wonderful occasion." Regarding her spirit guides, Catchings said that sometimes she would be awakened in the middle of the night by a pleasant voice speaking to her. "I am told things that are going to happen or things that I must do," she explained. "I am used to these things. They don't bother me."

In a controlled experiment, Deon Frey, an exceptionally powerful medium, sent her spirit guide, Dr. Richard Speidel, from Chicago to London, England, to move a large mirror that hung above the heads of the witnesses. Frey received her first visit from a spirit on the night her father died. "I was 15," she told me. "Eternal life was proved to me that night. The spirit of my father, who had never been a churchgoer or a believer in the afterlife, appeared at my bedside and said, 'If I live after death, then everyone lives.'"

According to Frey, Dr. Richard Speidel first appeared to her in 1942. He was of sober appearance, dressed formally in a black coat and bow tie. "I have been sent to be your guide and your teacher," he told her.

I conducted many séances with Frey acting as the medium, and she believed, as I do, that those who apply themselves to serious study, discipline, and discernment have the ability to develop mediumistic or shamanistic abilities. "The creative God force works through us at all times," she said. "The more we use it, the more we are able to grow within ourselves. You must learn to experience the light, let it flow through you, giving it force so that others may feel a portion of it through you. Become a channel for the light, and you will leave a portion of it with whomever you meet."

Popular Chicago psychic-sensitive Irene F. Hughes, the medium in investigations presented in chapters one and two, explained how she can tell when her spirit guide wishes to bring forth a message from a discarnate entity on the other side. "I am quiet, completely relaxed, deep in meditation," she said. "I may be alone at home or among friends in a prayer circle. A tingling sensation, similar to a chill, begins on my right ankle, then on my left. Slowly the tingling spreads to cover my entire body. It is as though a soft silken skin has been pulled over me, glove-tight—even over my face, changing its features—yet comfortable and protective. At this point I am on the way to that golden flow of consciousness that we earthlings term the spirit plane. I am in semi-trance. Were I in full trance, I could not recall a single detail."

As she immerses herself in the spirit plane, Hughes says that her body becomes as "icy cold as death itself," yet a delightful warmth engulfs her inner self. Soon, her spirit teacher Kaygee appears, smiles, bows to her as a trusted friend, indicating approval of her incursion into the spirit world. By a slight waving of his hand, he ushers in those of the spirit plane who wish to speak through her. "I am bound to my spirit teacher by ties that are ethereal, yet mighty as a coaxial cable," she said. "Every thought that flashes through his consciousness becomes crystal clear also in my consciousness."

MEDIUMS, CHANNELS, AND ESP

As mentioned above, certain psychical researchers maintain that the principal difference between a psychic-sensitive and a trance medium is that psychics attribute their abilities to a manifestation of extrasensory ability, such as clairvoyance, precognition, or telepathy. Spirit mediums credit their abilities to interaction with spirits. Some researchers have observed that the intelligence exhibited by the alleged spirits seems always on a level with that of the individual through whom they manifest. These psychic investigators may admit that on occasion the information relayed often rises above the medium's known objective knowledge, but they point out that the limits of the subjective mind are not yet ultimately defined.

Skeptics point out that the spirits can often be controlled by the power of suggestion and can be made to respond to questions that have no basis in reality. These critical investigators state that they have been able to establish communication with an imaginary person as readily as a real one. Some mediums have found themselves the object of ridicule or exposure when they have relayed a "spirit message" from a fictitious individual whose identity was supplied by a skeptical researcher or when they have given profound ghostly advice from a person who is actually still alive.

In the 1970s, after the publication of Jane Roberts's books *The Seth Material* and *Seth Speaks*, "channeling" became a more popular name for mediumship. Roberts made spirit contact with an entity named Seth while in a trance state. Her husband, Robert Butts, recorded the thoughts, ideas, and concepts communicated by the ethereal being. The material dictated by Seth was of very high quality, extremely provocative, and well-suited to a generation of maturing flower children and baby boomers. It wasn't long before Seth discussion groups around the nation were reciting concepts such as "we each create our own reality," "our point of power lies in the present," and "we are all gods couched in our own creaturehood." Nor was it long before large numbers of "channelers" emerged throughout the land. For a time it seemed as though every strip mall boasted the office of a professional spirit communicator.

Often, these individuals were "instant mediums," suggestible men and women who had attended a new age workshop, or read *Seth Speaks*, and then became convinced that a spirit guide was speaking freely through them. Most of these gullible and self-styled channelers soon returned to their day jobs. On the other hand, there were more talented and convincing individuals who attained large audiences of devoted followers and achieved international celebrity status. In the mid-1980s it was standing-room-only when Jach Pursel channeled "Lazaris," Kevin Ryerson hosted "McPherson," and J. Z. Knight strutted across the stage and issued teachings for "Ramtha," a 35,000-year-old warrior from the lost continent of Lemuria.

Whether it was in the minds of their audiences or in the minds of the channelers, the concept of a medium apparently seemed to conjure up images of the traditional, darkened séance parlors of an earlier time that seemed distasteful and outdated in an age of technology. In the twenty-first century, spirit communicators very often relay messages from guides and master teachers in the full light of a platform setting or a television studio. Whatever title is preferred by those who claim to relay messages from the spirits, the process of communication remains the same: spirit entities occupy the physical body of the channelers or the mediums and speak through them. Individuals such as Sylvia Browne, James Van Praagh, and John Edward have moved into the national spotlight with their own syndicated television programs and a seemingly endless number of media appearances, and the interest in after-death communication has never been stronger.

Beginning in the latter decades of the nineteenth century, spirit mediums began to contend with an increasingly materialistic and mechanistic science that did a great deal to obliterate the idea of a soul and the duality of mind and body. The concept of an eternal soul was steadily eroded by an emphasis on brain cells, conditioned responses, and memory patterns that could exist only while the body remained alive.

Sometime in the 1940s, Dr. J. B. Rhine summarized the research that had been conducted on spirit mediums and concluded that results were mixed. However, in March 2001 scientists involved in a unique study of spirit mediums at the University of Arizona announced that their findings were so extraordinary that they raised fundamental questions about the survival of human consciousness after death. Professor Gary Schwartz, who led the team of researchers, concluded that there were highly skilled spirit mediums who were able to deal directly with the dead, rather than merely with the minds of the sitters. In the opinion of the scientists, all the data that they gathered was "consistently in accord with survival of consciousness after death." Based on all their data to date, Professor Schwartz said, "The most parsimonious explanation is that the mediums are in direct communication with the deceased."

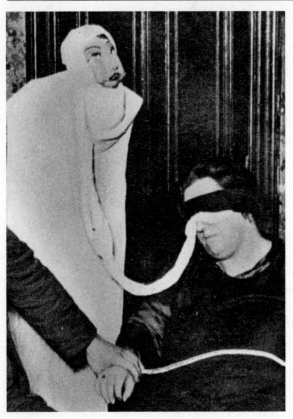

During a séance held in the 1930s, medium Helen Duncan helps an ectoplasmic spirit materialize.

MATERIALIZATION: THE ULTIMATE MEDIUMISTIC MANIFESTATION

Perhaps the ultimate in séance phenomena is the materialization of a spirit form that is in some way recognizable to one or more individuals present. In spiritualist churches and camps, such a phenomenon is often accomplished through the utilization of a cabinet from which the materialized spirit emerges and communicates with those gathered around the medium. Spirit cabinets may be elaborate wooden structures, or they may simply be blankets strung across wires in order to give the medium some privacy while in trance.

In his book *This Is Spiritualism*, Maurice Barbanell (1902–1981), the founder and editor of *Psychic News,* wrote, "The miracle of materialization is that in a few minutes there is reproduced in the séance room the birth which normally takes nine months in the mother's womb." Numerous psychical researchers have claimed to have seen a nearly invisible cord that links the materialized spirit figure to the medium, making the obvious comparison to an umbilical cord. The name that spiritualists give to the substance that the spirit image is comprised of is "ectoplasm," and they contend that it is drawn from the medium's body. French researcher Dr. Charles Richet christened ectoplasm in the 1920s, but Baron A. von Schrenck Notzing, a German investigator of the paranormal, gained a medium's permission to "amputate" some of the material and to analyze it. He found it to be a colorless, odorless, slightly alkaline fluid with traces of skin discs, minute particles of flesh, sputum, and granulates of the mucous membrane. Barbanell claimed that his spirit guide "Silver Birch" explained that ectoplasm is ideoplastic in its nature, and as such it may be molded into a representation of the human body by the psychic "womb" of the medium. Spirit beings compound ectoplasm until it assumes a human form that "breathes, walks, and talks, and is apparently complete even to fingernails."

I have witnessed what I would consider to be authentic ectoplasm issuing from a spirit medium on only about half a dozen occasions. There remain very few contemporary mediums who even attempt to produce ectoplasmic materializations during a séance. Today, the vast majority of séances conducted by professional mediums fit into three categories:

1) "Direct-voice" communication, during which the spirit guide speaks directly to those present through a medium in a deep state of trance.

2) "Twilight" communication, in which the medium is in a lightly altered state of consciousness and relays messages from his/her guide in a conversational exchange with those present.

3) A "reading," in which the medium is in a fully conscious state and presents a series of images and messages that are "shown" or "told" by spirits who have some personal connection to the sitters.

A MESSAGE TO MOTHER FROM BEYOND THE GRAVE

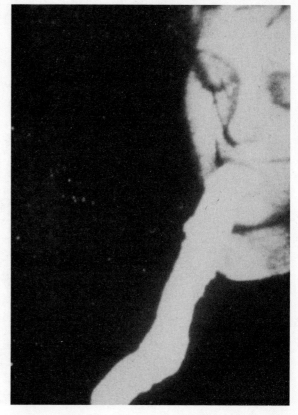

This medium reportedly materialized ectoplasm, or spirit essence, which is spewing from her mouth.

On February 10, 1933, Maurice Barbanell sat in a darkened room with medium Estelle Roberts (1899–1970) as the spirit voice of a young girl began to speak hesitatingly through Roberts. "Come along," said Barbanell, who was also an accomplished medium, to encourage the disembodied voice. "Come and talk to me."

"I am Bessy Manning and I want you to send a message to my mother," the voice told him. "Mother has been reading some of your articles about direct-voice séances in *Psychic News*. Please tell her you spoke to me." Barbanell assured the spirit voice that he would send a message the next morning. Pleased with his response, Bessy continued: "Tell Mother I still have my long braids. I am 22 and have blue eyes. I died with tuberculosis last Easter. I have brought along my brother Tommy who was killed by a motorcar accident nine years ago. Could you bring Mother here?"

Barbanell was sympathetic to the request that was put to him during that direct-voice sitting with Roberts, but he needed more essential information to fulfill the spirit's request. "I must know where your mother lives," he told her. The reply came without hesitation: "14 Canterbury Street, Blackburn."

Scene from a séance.

The next day Barbanell sent a telegram to Bessy Manning's mother telling her that Red Cloud, Estelle Roberts's spirit guide, had brought her daughter to a séance the night before. The address that the spirit had given to Barbanell proved to be correct. Within a few days, Barbanell had received a letter that told of the Mannings' "glorious happines" at the contact they had made with Bessy. Mrs. Manning substantiated the information the spirit had given Barbanell during the direct-voice séance. Bessy had passed on the preceding Easter, and her brother had been killed in an automobile accident nine years before.

"I regard Bessy Manning's return as flawless evidence for the after-life," Barbanell stated in his books *The Trumpet Shall Sound* (1933) and *This is Spiritualism* (1959). "No theories of telepathy or the subconscious mind can explain it away. No suggestion of collusion or any other kind of fraud can be entertained. Mrs. Manning had never met Estelle Roberts, or corresponded with her or any member of her family. Neither had she written to me or anyone who attended these direct-voice séances. Yet her daughter's full name and address had been given, accompanied by a complete message which was accurate in every detail."

Barbanell later arranged for Mrs. Manning to travel to London so that she might speak to the voice of Bessy and judge for herself whether or not her daughter had survived the grave. "I heard my own daughter speak to me, in the same old loving way, and with the same peculiarities of speech," Mrs. Manning wrote to Barbanell. "She spoke of incidents that I know for a positive fact no other person could know. I, her mother, am the best judge, and I swear before Almighty God it was Bessy.... I have no fear of so-called death. I am looking forward to the glorious meeting with my loved ones."

ARTHUR FORD'S TELEVISED SÉANCE WITH BISHOP JAMES PIKE

In February 1966, at the age of 22, the son of Episcopal Bishop James A. Pike committed suicide. On several occasions shortly after his son's death, Pike found pins paired together like clock hands, indicating the time of James Jr.'s suicide.

On September 3, 1967, through the mediumship of the Reverend Arthur Ford, an ordained minister of the Disciples of Christ Church, Pike heard spirit messages that he believed to be from his deceased son. The séance, which took place in Toronto, Ontario, Canada, was unique in that it did not take place in a darkened room, hidden away from the public. Rather, it was taped and broadcast on a Canadian television network. Allen Spraggett, the man who arranged the televised séance, was at the time the religion editor for the *Toronto Star*, and a former pastor of the United Church of Canada.

On September 17 the program was televised and precipitated a great furor in the field of psychical research. Pike was a controversial figure who was frequently spotlighted in the news for his dispute with the church over interpretation of certain traditional doctrines, and he stood his ground on the matter of communication with the dead. He later told media representatives that he firmly believed that he had spoken directly with his son during the séance, without the intermediary aid of Ford's customary spirit control, Fletcher. However, when we later discussed the séance, Spraggett told me that Fletcher had initially brought forth Pike's son as well as other communicating personalities, and Fletcher had continued to serve as a control throughout the séance.

Just prior to the beginning of the séance, Ford went into a trance. He placed a dark handkerchief over his eyes, commenting that it was easier to go "to sleep" when one is not surrounded by light, and the bright lights of the television studio would make the acquisition of a trance state that much more difficult. "So many people associate spirit contact with dark rooms," Ford said, "so I'll leave you [Bishop Pike and other observers] in the light. Any [genuine phenomenon] that takes place in the dark can usually take place in the light."

Once Ford had attained a state of trance, Fletcher soon made an appearance. Fletcher said that he had two people eager to speak with Ford, and others who were waiting. The first communicating entity revealed himself to be James A. Pike, Jr., a young man who had been mentally disturbed before his death. He spoke of how happy he was to be able to talk to his father.

Next Fletcher introduced George Zobrisky, a lawyer who had taught history at the Virginia Theological Seminary. Zobrisky said that he had "more or less shaped" Pike's system of thought, a point that Pike readily conceded. Then the spirit of Louis Pitt sent greetings to Pike, who recognized Pitt as having been the acting chaplain at Columbia University before Pike had become chairman of the department of religion.

Next, Fletcher described an older gentleman whose lectures Pike had often attended. The man had a Scottish name, and in life had owned two cats that had formerly belonged to James Jr. "And there is something about Corpus Christi." Pike said that there was a college at Cambridge by that name. Spraggett asked Fletcher if he could not provide a name. The spirit control stated that the name sounded something like "McKenny, McKennon, Donald McKennon." Pike confirmed that Donald McKinnon had been the principal influence on his development while he had been at Cambridge.

The last spirit that came forward told Fletcher that he had called himself an "ecclesiastical panhandler" in life. Pike seemed to recognize the appellation at once, but Spraggett asked Fletcher for a name. "Oh," said the spirit control, "like Black or something. Carl. Black. Block."

"Carl Block," Bishop Pike clarified, "the fourth bishop of California, my predecessor. I admired and respected you, and yet I hoped you weren't feeling too badly about some changes." Speaking through Fletcher, Block told his successor that he had done a magnificent job, and that he had magnificent work yet to do.

Pike later told the Associated Press that he did not see how Ford could have done any research before the séance that would have revealed so many intimate details about his life, or roles that certain individuals had played in shaping his thinking. Pike felt that the details had been quite cumulative. They were not just bits and pieces or an assortment of facts. "They added together," he said. "They made a pattern. Also, the persons who communicated had one thing in common—they were in varying ways connected with the development of my thought. They knew me at particularly significant times in my life, turning-points."

Spraggett told the Associated Press that while he accepted the possibility that true spirit contact had been achieved by Ford, he believed that the

At a séance held on December 25, 1919, Polish medium Franek Kluski reportedly materialized a spirit (center).

séance could also be explained in other ways; extrasensory perception or psychic communication may have also taken place between Ford and Pike.

Martin Ebon, formerly an administrative secretary for the Parapsychology Foundation located in New York, responded to a request for comment by saying that Pike represented "the kind of searching individual and researcher who has found subjective proof in an area where many scientists ... hold that objective proof cannot be found with current investigative methods." Ebon speculated that while the séance may not offer conclusive proof of life after death, it demonstrated a "high and specialized form of E.S.P." He concluded that, "The medium could have picked Pike's memory."

Parapsychologists, ever mindful of scientific method, were careful to qualify their remarks regarding the séance by stating that not having been present, they could not evaluate what had taken place, and that one really could not determine very much from a single séance. Dr. Karlis Osis, director of research for the American Society of Psychical Research, said that there have been some facts discovered through parapsychological research that suggest

Real Ghosts, Restless Spirits, and Haunted Places

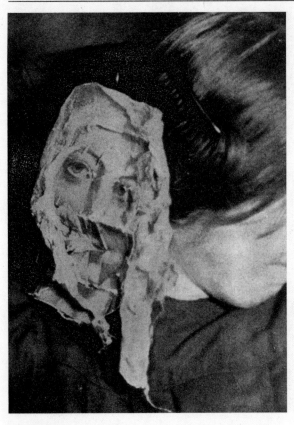

An ectoplasmic face materializes on the neck of famous medium Eva C.

the possibility of existence after physical death. Dr. J. B. Rhine of the Foundation for Research on the Nature of Man, stated that it has been established that the human mind has a nonphysical capacity, but stressed that he could offer no conclusion in regard to the validity of the communication that Pike had received.

Even before the séance in which he communicated with his son, Pike had expressed belief in the possibility of contacting the dead. Shortly before the séance, he answered a question on the subject, stating that he firmly believed in life after death. He also held that on occasion there could be communication between those on this place of existence and the next.

In 1967 Pike and his wife, Diane Kennedy Pike, wrote the book *The Other Side: An Account of My Experiences with Psychic Phenomena*. In 1968 he stepped away from his position in the church to form the Center for Religious Transition. Pike died on an expedition that he and Diane took to the Judean desert in 1969. In 1970 Diane published *The Search*, which chronicled the last days of her husband's great spiritual quest.

In 1972, while I was speaking with Diane regarding spiritual matters, she said that she thought it was important to make a distinction between messages that came through from the spirit world and a higher dimension of awareness. "If higher beings choose to relate something to humans," she said, "I think they do so in a very selective fashion. I am sure that there is always some distortion that goes on when [messages] are brought in from other states of consciousness into expression on this plane. Many times people seem to get into mental things that are really out of their own idea realm. They think they are communicating with higher intelligences, but really they are not. Of course, the trick becomes, how do you know the difference?"

Diane said that her personal feeling was that Jesus's test of spiritual manifestations ("By their works, you shall know them") is really the safest one. In her opinion, those who have received a revelation from the higher realm will manifest high characteristics or qualities in their life and understanding. There will emerge in them a deeper sense of peace as a result of their communication, and a deeper sense of wholeness. "I think a person who is on his own mental trip will manifest what we call ego qualities, which is a kind of deceptiveness, self-assertiveness, pride and so forth, which are not really characteristics of highly developed spiritual people," she said.

Diane added that any spirit communication or alleged revelation from a higher realm that is fear-oriented "is obviously not of the higher spiritual realm." In her opinion, a "so-called revelation that indicates that you should fear something coming to you from somewhere else, or that incites fear in other people when you tell them about it" should be immediately disregarded by the percipient.

In 1981 Diane assumed the name "Marianne Paulus" and wrote a series of books carefully designed to present "Ancient Wisdom" teachings in a manner that was more approachable to contemporary men

Harry Houdini.

and women. She currently resides in Scottsdale, Arizona, where she has established the Teleos Institute with her colleague, Arleen Lorrance.

ARTHUR FORD AND THE HOUDINI CODE

Arthur Ford's abilities as a spirit medium often led to controversy. In 1929 he received a message that he believed to have originated from the spirit of the late master magician Harry Houdini (1874–1926); Ford conveyed the message to Houdini's widow, Beatrice (Bess). A storm of fierce arguments, both pro and con, immediately erupted in the media. It was a well-known fact that before his death, Houdini had left a coded message with his wife that he would attempt to send her proof of life after death from beyond the grave. Some feature writers championed the authenticity of Ford's message from Houdini, while others quoted his widow as saying that the message was not correct.

However, according to Ford's supporters, on February 9, 1929, Bess wrote the medium and stated, "Regardless of any statement made to the contrary: I wish to declare that the message, in its entirety, and in the agreed upon sequence, given to me by Arthur Ford, is the correct message prearranged between Mr. Houdini and myself."

Eventually it came to be widely known that the various words in the Houdini code spelled out the secret message, "Rosabelle, believe." Ford's detractors argued that there was nothing paranormal involved in the medium providing the secret message to Houdini's widow. They stated that Ford had carefully studied an interview Bess had given in 1928, in which she had inadvertently revealed the code to several reporters. She had explained that the message her late husband would give from the next world was based on their old vaudeville mind-reading routine that used a secret spelling code.

THE MATERIALIZATION OF ROSALIE

On December 8, 1937, Harry Price had just concluded a radio broadcast regarding psychic phenomena when a listener contacted him with an interesting revelation. Price was informed that the listener regularly participated in a family séance that was held every Wednesday evening, at which the family materialized the spirit of a child. Price was invited to attend on the condition that he would never reveal the location of the séance circle or the identity of the members. In addition, he had to promise not to touch the spirit without the permission of those in the circle. If he would agree to those terms, the family would permit the researcher to attend one of the séances and to exercise any controls or conduct any examination that he wished. Price readily agreed to the family's stipulations and made arrangements to attend a séance on December 15.

When he arrived at the home, Price was given some background information on the spirit child, Rosalie; she was the daughter of one of the sitters, whom Price referred to as "Mrs. Z." in his notes. The girl had died of diphtheria in 1920. One night in 1925, Mrs. Z. had sensed the etheric presence of her daughter and heard the child's voice calling to her. Before dawn, Rosalie had materialized and had become sufficiently solid for her mother to clasp her hand.

When members of her family and certain close friends learned of Rosalie's remarkable return, they offered to donate their time for one night each week for the purpose of establishing a systematic schedule that would encourage the spirit to visit her mother on a regular basis. The séances had proved to be most successful, and by the time they invited Price to join them, the circle had been meeting weekly for 12 years.

Price subjected the room to a thorough examination before the sitting. He removed all ornaments, the clock, and any small items of furniture so that the room might be as bare as possible. He locked the door and slipped the key into his own pocket. The door and windows were sealed with adhesive tape. The fireplace was covered with sheets of paper. Every drawer was emptied; every cushion examined; and every inch of the floorboards was sounded. With apologies to his hostess, Price sprinkled liberal coatings of powdered starch around all the movable objects that remained in the room, and in front of the door and fireplace. When Price had completed these extensive preparations, he indicated that the séance could begin.

Price's notes reveal that it was just a few minutes after 10:00 P.M. when Mrs. Z. told the others that she sensed the presence of Rosalie. The mother began to weep softly, and she cautioned the other members of the circle not to speak. The room was by no means dark. A small lamp gave enough light for Price to clearly distinguish the shape of a small girl materializing beside him.

"May I touch Rosalie?" Price asked when it seemed that the materialization had been completed. The researcher was given permission to put out his hand to touch the spirit child. He found her flesh to be somewhat cooler than that of a living

The spirit of Katie King materialized during séances held by Florence Cook. This photograph of "Katie" was taken in 1873.

human. His fingers moved up to test the soft, silken quality of Rosalie's hair. Then, with the mother's permission, Price lifted the spirit girl to his knee, just as he might any living child. To his astonishment, he was able to hear a heart beating when he placed his ear to Rosalie's chest. The rate of her pulse was 90 beats a minute. Price turned her face toward the lamp and noted that Rosalie's classical features would have "graced any nursery in the land."

With Mrs. Z.'s indulgence, Price queried the girl about conditions in the spirit world. Interestingly, Rosalie responded to none of these questions, but when the investigator asked her if she loved her mother, the spirit child responded rapidly in the affirmative. Mrs. Z. could no longer contain herself, and she went to Price's chair and took the spirit child from his lap. Price later noted that all the women in the circle were weeping, and that he also was deeply affected by the emotional scene. After Rosalie had been with the circle for a total of about five minutes, she slowly began to fade back into her ethereal state. Within a few moments, the spirit child had completely disappeared.

On February 12, 1897, a spirit entity named Y-Ay-Ali appeared to medium Mme. D'Esperance.

Price called for the lights to be switched back on and conducted an immediate inspection of his seals and coatings of powder. He found all of the tape intact, and discovered no tracks of any kind in the powdered starch that he had dusted about the room. When Price made public certain details of the remarkable return of Rosalie, many other investigators were greatly intrigued by his account and wished to learn more about the incredible materialization of a spirit child. Price remained true to his word and never disclosed the names of the individuals in the circle that summoned Rosalie back from the grave each Wednesday night.

Already a controversial figure in psychical research, Price damaged his reputation by refusing to reveal the actual names of the alleged spirit circle and by denying other researchers the opportunity to violate the sanctity of Mrs. Z.'s home so they might conduct experiments of their own to corroborate his account.

Through an interesting chain of circumstances, in the early 1970s I was granted the privilege of receiving a great many of Price's original notes and manuscripts, including his account of the famous Rosalie materialization. To personally examine Price's own account of the experience, one of the most controversial in psychical research, was to be touched by the investigator's excitement of discovery and to be moved by the deeply felt emotion of Mrs. Z. and her circle. The sincerity expressed in the manuscripts does offer the testimony that the strength of a mother's love may be able to summon the spirit of a deceased child to revisit Earth for a limited period of time. While no additional disclosures were revealed in Price's notes—such as the actual identity of Mrs. Z. or the individual members of the spirit circle—and there was no supplementary data that would offer absolute proof to stun the skeptic into silence, it remains for each of us to decide the truth of the account for ourselves.

CLARISA BERNHARDT: SEERESS, INTUITIVE, MEDIUM

I first met Clarisa Bernhardt, a Swedish-American/Cherokee psychic-sensitive, in her native Oklahoma in 1973. Over the years, Bernhardt has gained an international reputation as the "Earthquake Lady" for her accuracy in predicting seismic rumbles. She has served as a medium for entities who wish to communicate from the other side, and become known as one of the most accurate psychic-sensitives in the world. She has also become a dear friend to my wife Sherry and me.

While Bernhardt accepts the designation of "spirit medium," she does not have a single spirit guide on whom she relies. Rather, she feels receptive to guidance from angels and other higher intelligences from what she terms our great "cosmic family." Bernhardt prefers the term "interdimensional commu-

Medium Clarisa Bernhardt.

nication" to describe her contact with spirit beings. She has certainly met a good number of ghosts during her work as a psychic-sensitive. "Some of my ghostly encounters were startling," she said. "Some were scary, and some were very helpful to [me] or to others." In explaining how her psychic mechanism works, Bernhardt states that requires neither a spirit control nor a trance state to pick up details from those who have passed to the next world.

Clarisa Shares a Ghostly Encounter

"On one occasion when I was visiting in North Texas, I was requested to come to the home of Wilma S. [The] loss of her mother had been hard for her and all her family, for everyone was extremely fond of 'Granny.' When I arrived at the home with an [acquaintance of mine from] the local newspaper, I was told by the family that they had felt the late woman's presence in the home very strongly for the past week. When I walked into the hallway, I could see an energy field [that] was frantically moving about. It suddenly moved quickly towards me, and [I tried to move out of its path just as quickly].

"It stopped, and then moved back to a door near the end of the hall, flitting back and forth. I felt an overwhelming vibration of anxiety in the atmosphere of the home, so I asked everyone to please be quiet so that I could concentrate on what was happening. [Then, alone, I] went ... back into the hall area and walked toward the door where the energy seemed to concentrate its activity. Then I froze, for I saw this image of a woman, and she was throwing herself at this door. I could hear a crash as she would hit it. And then I was overcome with information that there was great danger for her family. After the spirit in the hallway had demonstrated such an incredible explosion of energy, it was suddenly gone.

"I went back to the front area of the home and asked what was behind that door at the end of the hallway. Wilma said, 'Oh, there's a stairway that goes down to the basement and into the cellar.' I inquired when they had last gone down there, and Wilma responded that it had been about a year, for there

During an 1873 séance, several photographs were taken as medium John Beattie attempted to contact the spirit realm. This photograph reveals that something was in the room with Beattie during the séance.

were lots of things that were stored there. I advised them of the message her mother had given me about the danger that was in the cellar and that it should be checked immediately. Wilma said that she would have it looked into.

Real Ghosts, Restless Spirits, and Haunted Places

"When we walked out of the house, I was given a quick tour of the grounds of the house. As we approached the garage [that] supported an apartment on the second floor, I once again heard the spirit of Wilma's mother. [She told] me that she had buried some money in the area. She also said something about some old silver spurs that were worn on cowboy boots. I mentioned both of these comments to the S. family.... We said goodbye, and I left, hoping that the S. family would follow my advice.

"A couple of months later when I was in Sedona, Arizona, for the winter, I received a phone call from Doug, a nephew of Wilma's, who told me that I should know that his aunt had followed through on my spirit message from his grandmother. When Wilma opened the basement door, it had immediately become obvious that there was a gas leak. By making such a discovery ... a tragedy was avoided. Doug also advised me that a pair of silver cowboy spurs had been found buried near the fence when some post work was being done. They also uncovered several canning jars filled with $50 bills—a very specific and helpful communication for Wilma and her family."

12
Ghosts That Came Back to Life

OUT-OF-BODY PROJECTIONS

Throughout all of human existence, men and women have testified to the existence of another kind of ghost, one that is an extension of the living rather than the dead. While in the ecstasy of meditation or the illumination of the semiconscious state of physical pain and suffering, people through the ages have testified to having left their physical body to briefly travel through other dimensions of reality in their spirit bodies before they returned to the material plane. Thousands of people have claimed to have seen the spiritlike image of a friend or a relative appear before them while the living counterpart of the apparition was known to be residing thousands of miles away. Numerous individuals have claimed to have had an out-of-body experience during sleep, and have maintained that they witnessed activities during their strange "dreams" that were later verified. Some even argue that they have received or conveyed messages of great personal importance during astral flight.

Based on my research and personal experiences, I have found that out-of-body projections seem to fit into one of seven general categories:

1) The projection of the soul while the subject is asleep.

2) Projection while the subject undergoes surgery, childbirth, tooth extraction, etc.

3) Projection during an accident, when a subject receives a terrible physical jolt and his/her spirit seems literally thrown from the physical body.

4) Projection during intense physical pain.

5) Projection during a high fever or severe illness.

6) Projection during pseudo-death (the near-death experience), wherein the subject "dies" for several minutes and may appear to a living percipient with whom they have an emotional link, or may travel to other dimensions of existence before being subsequently revived and restored to life.

7) The conscious out-of-body projection in which the subject deliberately seeks to free his/her spirit from the material body.

In December 2001 an article in the British medical journal *Lancet* reported on a study that examined 344 patients from 10 hospitals in the Netherlands who had been successfully resuscitated after suffering cardiac arrest. Researchers spoke to these survivors within the week after they had suffered clinical death and been restored to life, and found that 18 percent of the patients recalled some portion of what happened to them when they were clinically dead. Another 8–12 percent remembered having near-death experiences, such as seeing lights at the end of tunnels or being able to speak to deceased friends or relatives.

In the past three decades a great deal of attention has been paid to the near-death experience (NDE), both by medical doctors and individuals claiming to have experienced the phenomenon. Among the stellar researchers drawn to study NDEs have been Dr. Elisabeth Kubler-Ross, Dr. Raymond Moody, Dr. Kenneth Ring, Dr. Karlis Osis, Robert Crookall, and Dr. P. M. H. Atwater. Dozens of books have been published that generally describe the phenomenon as occurring when someone appears to have died and is then returned to life, complete with a story of having been drawn down a tunnel toward a light in the company of angels or relatives. Somewhere in their out-of-body travels to the world beyond death, these disembodied souls are told that their time is not yet completed on Earth. They must return to life, often with instructions to complete a particular mission.

The well-known psychical researcher Harry Price put forth the view that the whole point of our life on Earth might very well be to provide us with a stockpile of memories out of which we might construct a meaningful image-world at the time of our death. Such a world would be a psychological world and not a physical one, even though it seems to be quite physical to those who would experience it. Price conjectured that the other world would be the manifestation of the memories and desires of its inhabitants, including their repressed or unconscious memories and desires. It might be every bit as detailed, vivid, and complex as this present perceptible world that we experience now. We may note that it might well contain a vivid and persistent image of one's own body.

According to Price's concept of survival, the surviving personality is actually an immaterial entity: "But if one habitually *thinks* of oneself as embodied (as one well might, at least for a considerable time), an image of one's own body might be, as it were, the persistent center of one's image world, much as the perceived physical body is the persistent center of one's perceptible world in this present life."

Although this is a book about real ghosts, I include a chapter about these "ghosts" that came back to life because of the testimony they provide, which demonstrates not only the existence of a soul and life after death, but that ghosts are real. And, as the reader shall see, the serious study of the near-death experience is nothing new.

GHOSTS OF THE LIVING

Soaring Above His Body

Richard Evans of St. Louis, Missouri, was crossing a busy intersection when a car roared around the corner and was on top of him before he could jump back to the curb. He wrote that in an eternal moment before impact, his true "soul body" seemed to jump out of his physical self. The *real* Evans seemed to soar high above the street, and he could see the automobile about to hit his physical body. "I had a stunned deer-in-the-headlights look on my face," Evans wrote, "but there was a lady watching from the curb who seemed about ready to go into hysterics. I knew the car was going to hit me, but it seemed as though my real consciousness was not terribly concerned."

Richard Evans then saw his body go sailing through the air like someone had drop-kicked a football. He did not feel any pain in his physical body, and he seemed to have a strange feeling of indifference to the man he saw flying through the air. He had no sense of consciousness connected with the body that had just been struck by the speeding automobile. He was the dispassionate observer.

A crowd began to gather around Evans's crumpled body. Evans, still floating somewhere above the street, wanted to leave the scene, to soar free in space, but something held him to the pitiful scene below him. A wail of sirens directed his attention to a rapidly approaching police car, then to an ambulance following closely behind. A doctor leapt out of the vehicle and knelt beside the body. Evans saw the doctor fill a syringe from a small bottle, then shoot the liquid into his arm.

The substance that was injected into his body from the syringe was like a magnet and pulled Evans back into his body. He described the sensation as feeling like he was "one of those balls on a rubber string that had been thrown as far as the string would stretch and was now being pulled back." The next thing Evans knew, he was back in his physical body, blinking his eyes. Everything was blurred. And, most of all, he was conscious of the terrible pain. He devoutly wished he were back soaring above the street, away from the agony of his injuries.

Visited by Her Injured Mother

It was 2:00 A.M. on July 17, 1957, when Patricia Mann opened her eyes and glimpsed a shadowy form that resembled her mother. "Come, I need your help," the apparition said to her. Her mother lived 10 miles away from her, but Patricia was convinced that the ghostly form was truly her mother. She picked up the telephone and dialed her mother's number. She could only get a busy signal. A call to the telephone company produced the information that the line was out of order.

Somehow Patricia Mann knew that she could not wait until morning to find out if her mother needed her help. She dressed hurriedly and drove to her mother's house. When she arrived, she found all the lights on, and she could hear the television set blaring at full blast. She pounded on the door and called her mother's name, but received no response. Finally she found an unlocked window and crawled through. She found her mother lying in a pool of blood, clutching the telephone receiver in her hand. Patricia called an ambulance.

After her mother's forehead had been stitched up in the hospital's emergency room, she told Patricia what had happened. Patricia later summarized the strange experience: "[Mother] had fallen, and from the gushing blood she knew she had sustained a deep cut. She was trying to phone me when she blacked out, but she remembered calling my name. She also knew that it had been about 2:00 A.M. when she fell" (Patricia Mann, "True Mystic Experiences," *Fate*, February 1967).

Her Spirit Gave Her Body a Rest

One night Sara Norris arose sleepily from her bed and reluctantly left the hollow of warmth next to her husband. It was 3:00 A.M. and time to feed the baby. As she wrote in her response to the *Steiger Questionnaire of Mystical and Paranormal Phenomena*, she walked into the kitchen and turned up the gas flame beneath the old pan in which she warmed the baby's bottle. While she waited for the water to heat, Sara looked out over their moonlit farmyard and listened to the night noises.

She had felt exhausted when she had gone to bed that evening. She had carried the heavy load of her pregnancy through an exceptionally hot summer. The delivery had been long and difficult, but Sara had left her hospital bed to come back to the farm and help with the harvest. She had not been able to get caught up on her sleep. There were the late meals that had to be made for all of the extra help that had been brought in for the harvest, and they could not afford to hire someone to assist her with the housework. Then, while her husband slept, she had to get up during the night to see to the baby. She would have given nearly anything to be able to sleep one night through. Just one night of sleep without interruption.

The bottle was ready. She tested it on her arm, walked into the baby's room, and slid the nipple between the baby's lips almost before he was able to cry. Sara did not want to awaken her husband or the two other children who slept in the next room. Nor did she wish a piercing scream to shatter the bliss-ful dreamlike state she moved in.

It was as she returned to bed that Sara was startled to see her own sleep-ing form lying next to her husband. The form was unmistakably her own body: hair in disarray, mouth slightly open, one forearm resting across her brow. But how could she be in two places at once? There was a tingle of fear … a strange tugging sensation … then Sara jerked awake with a jolt. A dream. It had all been a bizarre dream.

But the baby was in bed, content with his bottle, working the rubber nipple in his tiny mouth. It would seem that Sara's soul, her nonphysical true self, separated itself from her sleeping body so that the bone-tired shell of her physical self could rest undisturbed. Her spirit saw to the baby. Not only had she freed the spiritual essence from within her physical body, Sara was able to see her own ghost.

A Doctor Becomes a Spirit and Returns to His Body

When Dr. Wiltse of Skiddy, Kansas, believed that he was dying, he called to his family and friends to bid them farewell. His attending physician, Dr. Raynes, later testified (*St. Louis Medical and Surgical Journal*, 1889; reprint-ed in *Proceedings*, vol. VII, Society for Psychical Research, 1892) that for the duration of four hours, Wiltse lay without pulse or perceptible heartbeat. Raynes did state, however, that he may have witnessed very slight gasps occa-sionally emitted by his patient.

During this lengthy period of clinical death, Wiltse found himself in what he later termed a state of "conscious existence" that bore no relationship to his physical body. He began to rock back and forth, trying to break the ten-uous bond of tissues and fibers within his physical form. He began to feel and hear "the snappings of innumerable small cords," as his spirit began to retreat from his feet and collect in his head like "a rubber cord shortens." Shortly after that, the doctor felt that his true self had gathered in the area of his head, and he began to emerge through his skull. In his report he stated that he distinctly remembered resembling "something like a jellyfish as regards to color and form." [*Author's note: Many men and women who project from the Earth plane in their near-death experiences often discard concepts of body image and report perceiving themselves as a "shiny cloud," a "bright balloon," an "egg yolk," or "something like a jellyfish."*]

As his true self emerged from his skull, Wiltse experienced the floating sensation so common to near-death projections. He felt himself bobbing gently up and down until his exertions landed him squarely on the floor. At that point, he gradually arose and expanded himself to the full stature of his regular physical body. "I seemed to be translucent, of a bluish cast, and perfectly naked," he said. The doctor cast a glance at his woeful physical body on the sickbed and decided that he had no further use for it. Without further ado, he headed for the front door.

As he reached the door, Wiltse observed that he was suddenly fully clothed. At the same time, he noted that two of his friends were standing by the door and that they were completely unaware of his presence. With a great deal of surprise and amusement, Wiltse discovered that he could pass directly through his friends; he did so and continued on out through the door. He never saw the street more distinctly than he saw it then, he stated. Glancing around, he noticed that he was still attached to his body in the house by means of a small cord, like a spider's web. Then the doctor found himself soaring high above the neighborhood, enjoying the aerial view that his unique situation afforded him. However, just as he was relaxing into his newly achieved emancipation from the confines of bodily flesh, Wiltse found himself on a road with steep rocks blocking his path. He attempted to climb around them, but as he was doing so, a black cloud surrounded him and he found himself back in his bedroom, once again confined to an ill body.

Witse's experience raises many mundane questions: for instance, why is it that those who undergo near-death experiences usually see themselves clothed, rather than naked, as Wiltse first saw his body? I believe that since near-death experiences involve the essential stuff of human personality, the projected mind may—if it wishes to do so—"create" its clothing by exercising the same kind of mental machinery that is utilized in dreams. Wiltse's case provides us with a very good look at some of the mechanics of the near-death experience. When he first projects his true self from the skull, he perceives himself as "something like a jellyfish as regards color and form." Then, because his mind had been conditioned on the temporal plane to think in terms of physical body concepts, the "jellyfish" expands into the full stature of a naked human male. When Wiltse confronts his sober-faced friends at the door, he suddenly finds himself clothed. Even though he is certain that they cannot see him in his spiritual body, a lifetime on the Earth plane living in a conservative culture had conditioned him not to go about in the nude. It may well be this same psycho-spiritual mechanism that explains why we never perceive naked ghosts.

It is worth noting that Wiltse's near-death experience terminated when he was confronted by steep rocks that blocked his journey. Generally speaking, there seem to be two types of environments in near-death experiences:

1) The environment of this planet Earth, in which the projected personality observes the actions of people in faraway places and sees actual occurrences at great distances that can later be substantiated.

2) The environment of other planes of existence or dimensions of reality, in which the projected personality may encounter entities that he perceives as angels, masters, guides, saints, or the spirits of loved ones who have previously passed away. The geography of these spiritual planes seems to be quite similar to that of Earth, and the individual's religious views often determine whether the plane is interpreted as heaven, paradise, or a place of eternal bliss.

The "rocks" that halted Wiltse's advance may indeed have been rocks on another plane of existence, or they may have been formed by his own mental machinery as a symbol that he was not meant to venture farther but was instead supposed to return to his physical body.

Aloft in the Spirit Body

Dr. Robert Crookall, author of such classic works as *The Study and Practice of Astral Projection*, has reported on a case of near-death experience that was first published in the *Moscow Journal* in 1916. The subject of the NDE was a Russian who had rejected the idea that the spirit survives in any kind of afterlife.

The subject remembered feeling dizzy during a stay in a hospital. He called for a doctor, then became aware of a "certain state of division" within himself. He was conscious of his physical self, yet at the same time, he had a feeling of indifference toward his material body. It seemed as if he was actually two beings—one, the main part of him, was concealed somewhere deep within; the other, his physical body, was external and less significant. He felt the "main part" of himself being drawn *somewhere* with irresistible force. He felt like something he had been allowed to use for a brief period of time was being recalled and pulled back to its source. At the same time, he was filled with the conviction that his essential self would not disappear.

The entire medical staff seemed to be crowded about his bed. The "main part" of him moved forward, and he saw his physical husk lying there on the bed. He tried to grasp the hand of his material body, but his spirit hand went through it. Struck by the strangeness of the situation, he wanted someone to help him understand what was happening. He called to the doctor, but the air did not seem to transmit the sound waves of his voice. He tried everything he could think of to make his presence known, but none of the medical staff seemed aware of his "real" self. Had he died? He found this inconceivable, for death meant the cessation of being, and he had not lost consciousness for even one moment. He was as aware of himself as ever. He could see, hear, move, touch, think. Even when the doctor declared that it was all over for him, the perplexed Russian refused to accept the idea of his death. A nurse turned to a religious icon and asked for a blessing on the man's soul. The words had scarcely been uttered when two angels appeared at his side. They picked him up by his arms, carried him right through the wall into the street, and began to ascend quickly.

Although it was evening and dark, he saw everything clearly. He was able to perceive a much greater expanse than he would have had with his ordinary vision. On the ascent, they were suddenly surrounded by "a throng of hideous beings, evil spirits" that tried to snatch him away from the angels. The man, who had proclaimed himself an atheist during his life, found himself praying for deliverance, and to his astonishment there suddenly appeared a "white mist which concealed the ugly spirits." The ascent upward was halted when an intense light appeared before them and a voice thundered: "Not ready!" At once, the angels began to descend with him.

At first, he did not understand the meaning of the thunderous words from the light, but soon the outlines of a city became visible. He saw the hospital, and then he was being carried into a room completely unknown to him. In this room there stood a row of tables, and on one of them, covered partially with a sheet, he saw his dead body. His guardian angel pointed to his body and told him to enter it. At first the Russian felt as though something was pressing against him; the sensation was unpleasantly cold. An awareness of ever-increasing tightness continued, and just before he lost consciousness, he felt very sad, as though he had lost something.

When he became aware of his surroundings the head physician sat at his bedside, astounded by the medical miracle that he had witnessed. The subject had no doubt that his soul had temporarily left his body and then returned to it.

Report to the Royal Medical Society, 1937

When the Royal Medical Society of Edinburgh met on February 26, 1937, Sir Auckland Geddes, a medical doctor and professor of anatomy, read a most unusual paper before the august body of medical professionals. A colleague who wished to remain anonymous had experienced what we today would call a near-death experience, which he wanted to bring to the attention of his fellow professionals. When the anonymous physician had been near death, he realized that his "being" had separated from his physical body. Upon recovery, he immediately began to dictate his amazing experience to his secretary.

According to his account, one evening shortly after midnight, the doctor was stricken with gastroenteritis so severe that by ten o'clock the following morning he was too ill to even ring for assistance. However, though the doctor's body was in terrible agony, his mental faculties remained quite clear, and he began to review his financial affairs, firmly convinced that his death was imminent. It was at that point that he realized that he appeared to have two levels of consciousness, one of which was separate from the other. Later, while dictating the experience to his secretary, he labeled these two states of consciousness "A" and "B." His ego—the true spiritual self—was the "A" state of consciousness. The "B" consciousness remained with the physical body.

The physician observed that as his physical health continued to deteriorate, the "B" personality began to fade, while the "A" personality began to embody his complete self. As the process continued, the "A" personality vacated the physical body entirely, and he was able to observe his body lying inert in the bed. As his awareness increased, he realized that he could also see his entire house and garden. Testing his new range of existence, he discovered that he could instantly travel to any earthly place that occurred to him.

He became aware of the presence of a guide or mentor who explained to him that he was in another time dimension of space, a fourth dimension in which *now* was equivalent to *here*. This fourth dimension corresponded in its makeup to everything that existed in three-dimensional space. Moreover, everything in the third dimension also existed in the fourth. The doctor's guide pointed out that in the fourth dimension, he appeared as a blue-colored cloud. In his report to the medical society, the physician apologized for the lack of words to describe his extraordinary experience. No words adequately put forth his actual feelings and sensations. He stated that his spirit mentor had impressed on him that "all our brains are just end-organs projecting as it were from the three-dimensional universe into the psychic stream ... and flowing with it into the fourth and the fifth dimensions."

Many more mysteries were revealed to the physician when one of his servants entered his bedroom and discovered his employer's dying body. He watched his servant rush to the telephone and place a hasty call to one of the physician's colleagues, at the same time, he saw that physician take leave of his patients because of the emergency. When his colleague arrived, the doctor's "A" consciousness could hear the man think, "He is nearly gone!" He was able to hear the man speaking to him, but he was unable to respond. He was no longer in the "B" consciousness that resided in his physical body.

The visiting doctor pulled a syringe out of his medical bag. The "A" consciousness of the physician saw this act and became very angry, as it did not wish to return to the "B" consciousness. As the injection flowed into the doctor's body, however, the "A" consciousness once again began to take notice of his heartbeat and gradually allowed itself to be pulled back into the physical body. Finally, the doctor became fully aware of his complete self once again and realized he was lying on his bed. He felt intensely annoyed, because he had just begun to understand where he was and what he was seeing. He was angry at having been pulled back into his body. "And once back, all the clarity of the vision of everything disappeared, and I was again possessed of a glimmer of consciousness which was suffused with pain."

In his concluding remarks, Geddes told the members of the society that their colleague's experience had helped him define "the idea of a psychic continuum in which we all exist."

The Day I Became a Ghost, by Brad Steiger

On my parents' wedding anniversary, August 23, 1947, when I was a boy of 11, I had a near-death experience as a result of a terrible accident on our family farm in Iowa. My body lay crushed and bleeding, sprawled where the mangling, metallic blades of the farm machinery had dropped it. Almost at once my essential self left my body and distanced itself from the tragic scene.

Although I could clearly perceive the events taking place below me, I felt only dimly associated with the dying farmboy who lay bleeding in the hay stubble. I felt the concern and panic of my seven-year-old sister who was running for help, but I had no connection to the emotions she felt. I had become an orange-colored spheroid, intent only on soaring toward an incredibly beautiful and brilliant light above me. I felt blissfully euphoric, and I began to revel in the glory of a marvelous sense of oneness with the power and intelligence of All-That-Is.

Then I discovered that bilocation was a facet of my spirit body. I could be in two places at once. I could exist physically in my father's arms as he carried my terribly injured body from the field; and at the same time, I could be above us, watching the whole scene as if I were a detached observer. When I became concerned about my mother's reaction to my dreadful accident, I made an even more incredible discovery: the "real me" could be *anywhere* that I wished to be. My spirit, my soul, was free of the physical limitations that we humans incorporate into our definitions of time and space. I only had to think of my mother, and there I was beside her.

I put the newly found freedom to other tests. I thought of my friends—one at a time—and I was instantly beside each of them as they worked with their fathers on their own farms. I was a ghost, a spirit. I was able to pass through walls, soar through the clouds, and be wherever I wished. It was wonderful. From time to time I would feel a fleeting pinch of regret over having left my family and my friends, but whenever the sorrow of earthly separation impinged on my newly extended consciousness, I was shown something that I can only describe as a series of brilliant geometric designs. It was as if these colorful patterns were somehow a part of the great tapestry of life; my ability to perceive these figures illustrated the order and the rightness of existence. To view this cosmic panorama was to peek into God's notebook and see that there truly is an underlying meaning to existence on Earth. Suddenly it became obvious that there is, indeed, a divine plan; life on Earth is not simply the result of some cosmic accident. Yes, I was dying, but that was not really the end of me. Nor was it the end of the world. Life on Earth would be able to continue without me.

Viewing these geometric designs completely removed my fear of death and allowed my spirit essence to move closer to the light. At the same time, the light appeared to be intelligent and to manifest a kind of benevolent presence that brought me immense peace and tranquility. As I drifted closer to the brilliant light, I had a sudden sense of longing for my simple and pastoral life on the farm with my parents and sister. At that instant, a geometric mobile manifested before me, and it seemed that in a flash I was shown the great secret of all existence. How I wish that I could have retained that knowledge, but I was left with "the peace that passes all understanding."

I was in and out of my body during the desperate 140-mile run to a hospital in Des Moines. Whenever the real me would enter the body of the dying 11-year-old boy, it seemed to reject the choice and return to the dimension of spirit where there was no pain. Rather inconveniently, I returned to my physical body just as the surgeons were preparing to operate. I returned with such force that I sat up, shouted, and pushed an intern off balance. It took the calming and caring tones of love from a Roman Catholic nun to pacify me until the anesthesia could take effect.

I began to sense a kind of intelligence or personality within the light itself, and I asked it if I might leave the operating room. I was just bobbing around above my body, and I really didn't want to watch the surgery. The accident had given me numerous skull fractures and had essentially scalped me. In answer to my prayer, I remember being taken to what appeared to be a kind of ideal little village, complete with a bandstand, ice cream vendors, and friendly people walking about.

During the two weeks of my hospital stay, the nuns seemed to have sensed that I had been "somewhere" and had seen "something." They asked me again and again about my experience as a spirit being, traveling between the two worlds. A mystery had been pierced, they told me. I would never again have to ask the troubling question about whether we humans survive the experience of physical death. I would be able to testify that there truly was an existence that transcended the material realm. Because of what could well have been a fatal accident, I was given the ability to understand that we do survive physical death in our spiritual essence, our souls. I knew with an unshakable certainty that we are spiritual beings. Regardless of the technology that may surround us, the physical environment that may complement or discourage us, political or cultural boundaries, we are spirits inhabiting a physical body—the things of the spirit world are the most lasting.

I have never felt chosen or special because of my near-death experience and the cosmic geometric designs I was given the opportunity to see. But I believe I was blessed with the chance to *know* what so many others accept on the basis of faith. Having received proof of existence in the afterlife, I became convinced that I am to here to testify that the human spirit is eternal, and that benevolent spiritual beings of light exist to help us and to guide us in our spiritual evolution.

For many years after my near-death episode, I assumed that my viewing of the geometric designs had to be classified as an ineffable experience, impossible to translate into physical expression. Whenever I attempted to articulate the cosmic panorama and describe the geometric patterns for others, my mind would literally blank-out due to the lack of an appropriate vocabulary. From time to time, I would meet other individuals who'd had a near-death experience and had seen geometric visions similar to mine, and they would agree that these awesome messages from All-That-Is are beyond words.

In 1988 my wife, Sherry, began conducting healing seminars utilizing computer derived images of fractal geometry, and in these sessions I finally saw images that were close approximations of what I had been shown during my NDE. I was struck with a powerful shock of recognition when she projected these brilliant images during her seminar. Interestingly, the effect on the audience was profound, and many individuals claimed healing experiences after viewing the images.

LEARNING TO CONTROL AND PROJECT THE GHOST WITHIN

The cases presented thus far in the chapter have dealt with the inadvertent projection of the "astral" self, but a great many people have exercised this function of the transcendent self to the extent that they can project their "ghosts" at will. The pioneer psychical research Frederic W. H. Myers wrote that cases of astral projection present "the most extraordinary achievement of the human will. What can lie further outside any known capacity than the power to cause a semblance of oneself to appear at a distance? What can be a more central action—more manifestly the outcome of whatsoever is deepest and most unitary in man's whole being? Of all vital phenomena, I say, this is the most significant; this self-projection is the one definite act which it seems as though a man might perform equally well before and after bodily death."

Sylvan J. Muldoon was one of the earliest practitioners to claim that the process of instigating an out-of-body experience can be learned, developed, and mastered by a serious student. In his two books, *The Projection of the Astral Body* (1929) and *The Case for Astral Projection* (1936), Muldoon offers a detailed record of many experiments he has personally conducted and provides a systematic method of inducing the conditions necessary for astral projection. According to Muldoon, it is possible to leave the body at will and retain full consciousness in the "astral self." Muldoon is also cognizant of the "silver cord" mentioned by many individuals who have had a near-death experience as the link that connects the spirit and physical bodies. This cord, says Muldoon, is extremely elastic and permits a journey of considerable distance. Muldoon claims that while he was out of his body, he was able to move objects and gain information that he could not have acquired via any of the normal sensory channels.

Muldoon is generous in providing the reader with copious descriptions of the mechanics involved in astral projection so that the truly interested student can follow the procedures and experiment on his or her own. The fundamental law of projection, according to, Muldoon, is expressed in these words: "When the subconscious will becomes possessed of the idea to move the body, and the physical body is incapacitated, the subconscious will moves the astral body out of the physical body."

The Projections of S. H. Beard

In his groundbreaking book *Phantasms of the Living* (1886), Edmund Gurney wrote of the remarkable experiments conducted by S. H. Beard. Beard began his experiments with astral projection on a Sunday evening in November 1881, after he had read philosophical material about the great power that the human will is capable of exercising. Beard exerted the whole force of his being on the thought that he would make his spirit-form manifest before his fiancée, Miss L. S. Verity, on the second floor of her home at 22 Hogarth Road, Kensington, London, England; his experiment was a success.

Three days later, when Beard called upon Verity, she excitedly told him that both she and her 11-year-old sister had nearly been frightened out of their wits by an apparition that had looked just like him. When Verity's sister confirmed the appearance of such a phantom, Beard, who had not revealed the part he had played in the mysterious visitation or broached the topic with his fiancée, felt quite pleased with his experiment.

Verity later told Gurney that she had seen Beard in her room at about one o'clock. She stated that she was perfectly awake and "much terrified." She had awakened her sister with her screaming, and the 11-year-old girl also saw the apparition. Neither Verity nor her sister had ever experienced hallucinations of any sort on any prior occasion. Beard had not yet disclosed his actions to his fiancée because he was by no means finished with his research.

For his second experiment, he willed his presence before Verity's married sister, whom he had met only briefly once before. Beard walked up to the bed on which the woman lay, took her long hair into his hand, and then lifted her hand.

When Gurney learned of Beard's second successful projection, he wrote him a note urging Beard to let him know when he planned to conduct his next experiment. Beard complied, and in a letter dated March 22, 1884, he simply told Gurney, "This is it." This message was explained in his next letter, which was received on April 3. A statement from Verity was enclosed: "On Saturday night, March 22nd … at about midnight, I had a distinct impression that Mr. S. H. B. was present in my room, and I distinctly saw him whilst I was wide awake. He came towards me and stroked my hair.… The appearance in my room was most vivid and quite unmistakable." Verity testified that she had voluntarily given Beard the information without any prompting on his part. Beard concluded his experiments after this episode, for Verity's nerves "had been much shaken, and she had been obliged to send for a doctor in the morning."

A Famous Writer Turns Himself into a Ghost

The American novelist Theodore Dreiser often told the story of the night that he entertained the English writer John Cowper Powys. On that particular night, the Englishman had to leave rather early, and both men expressed regret that their evening had been so short. Seeing that Dreiser's disappointment was genuine, Powys told him, "I'll appear before you, right here, later this evening. You'll see me."

"Will you turn yourself into a ghost?" Dreiser asked, chuckling at the Englishman's peculiar sense of humor.

"I'm not certain yet," Powys told him. "I may return as a spirit or in some other astral form."

Several hours later, as Dreiser sat reading in his easy chair, he glanced up and was startled to see Powys standing before him, looking exactly as he had earlier that evening. When the writer moved toward the apparition and spoke to it, Powys's astral projection disappeared.

SEEING YOUR OWN GHOST

Another phenomenon that must be closely related to the projection of the astral self is that of the appearance of one's own double. This phenomenon is called "autoscopic hallucination" and appears to serve no particular purpose, such as providing a warn-

ing or disclosing valuable information. In fact the only service it appears to provide is to allow an individual the opportunity to see his/her own body image without having to use a mirror. The April 1966 issue of Fate contained an article entitled "Have You Seen Your Double?" in which Dr. Edward Podolsky wrote of a number of cases where people had reported seeing their own ghosts. According to Podolsky, there are two main theories that discuss possible causes of autoscopy. One is due to "the result of some irritating process in the brain, particularly of the parietotemporal-occipital area (the visual area)." The other, a psychological theory, sees autoscopy as a projection of memory pictures "that may be projected outside the body as very real images" when conditions of stress or other unusual psychological situations arise.

The Experience of Harold C. from Chicago

In March 1958 Harold C. returned home after a hard day at the office with a splitting migraine. As he sat down to dinner, he saw, sitting opposite him, an exact replica of himself. This astonishing double repeated every movement he made during the entire course of the meal. Since that time, Mr. C. has seen his double on a number of occasions, each time after he has suffered from a migraine.

The Experience of Samuel V.

Samuel V. of Kansas City, Missouri, was startled to see an exact double of himself mirror his every movement as he went about his gardening chores. The double was visible for about two hours.

The Frightening Case of Jeanie P.

The case of Jeanie P. is the most frightening of those recounted by Podolsky. As she was applying her makeup, she saw an exact duplicate of herself that was touching up *her* features. Jeanie reached out to touch the double, and the image reached out to touch her. Jeanie actually felt her face being touched by her mysterious double.

THE VARDOGR

Neither of Podolsky's theories regarding autoscopic hallucinations explains the Scandinavian phenomenon known as the *Vardogr*. Wiers Jensen, editor of the *Norwegian Journal of Psychical Research*, wrote a series of articles on the Vardogr as early as 1917. The individual that possesses a Vardogr unconsciously employs it as a type of spiritual forerunner to announce his or her physical arrival.

"The Vardogr reports are all alike," wrote Jensen. "With little variation, the same type of happening occurs: The … Vardogr *announces* his arrival. His steps are heard on the staircase. He is heard to unlock the outside door, kick off his overshoes, put his walking stick in place, etc. The listening percipients—if they are not so accustomed to the prelude of the Vardogr that they remain sitting quietly—open the door and find the entry empty. The Vardogr has, as usual, played a trick on them. [A few] minutes later, the whole performance is repeated—but now the reality and the man arrive."

Based on the research he conducted *c.* 1917, Jensen theorized that only Scandinavians and the Scots experienced the phenomenon of the Vardogr. I have learned that this bizarre spiritual forerunner is not limited to these ethnic groups, but being of Norwegian and Danish descent, I can attest to the reality of the Vardogr, a unique manifestation of a living ghost.

The first really dramatic encounter with a Vardogr that I can recall occurred one Saturday night when I was about 16. I had arrived home before my parents, and I went upstairs to my room to lie down on my bed and thumb through a new magazine I had purchased that evening. I had not been there long when I clearly heard noises downstairs. As I have stated elsewhere in this book, my childhood home was a center for a lot of ghostly phenomena, such as doors opening and closing, the footsteps of unseen guests, and the occasional manifestation of spectral beings. But the sounds I heard that night were not the "spooky" sounds; what I heard downstairs sounded like my parents and sister entering the house. First there was the opening of the front screen door, then the squeaking of the inside door. Next, the sound of feet walking up the three steps to the inner hallway, followed by the subsequent sounds of footsteps moving about various rooms as they prepared for bed. "Goodnight!" I called downstairs after a few minutes. Both my parents and sister had bedrooms on the first floor, so they would not be coming upstairs to retire.

There was no answer. I flipped through a few more pages of the magazine, thinking that my parents and sister had not heard me as they prepared for bed. "Goodnight down there!" I shouted after a few moments, a bit louder that time. Again no answer. By that time it had become very silent downstairs. Too silent for those footsteps to have belonged to my family. My mind was instantly flooded with a variety of startling images. Maybe intruders had thought my house was deserted and had decided to enter the house. Had my shouts alerted them to the presence of a lone occupant? What would their next move be?

Just as the icy fingers of fear had begun to trace a slow, deliberate path up the length of my spine, I once again heard the familiar sounds of my parents and sister arriving home. The noises were precisely as they had been before, only this time when I shouted my goodnight, the voices of my parents and sister quickly responded.

The next time I experienced my parents' Vardogr was no less eerie, and neither were any of its subsequent arrivals. Each time it tricked me as thoroughly as it had before. My sister fell victim to its spooky pranks as often as I did. One night my parents arrived home to find her in a state of near panic. She had been sitting in a chair with her back to the door. She had heard the door open and close and the sound of footsteps enter the house and approach to the spot directly behind her chair. As she was engrossed in the book she was reading, she had not bothered to turn around at the sound of the opening door. After a few moments had passed, she began to wonder why her mother and father preferred to stand behind her chair in complete silence. Imagine her horror when she turned around and saw no one was there.

Weirs Jensen notes that as a general rule, the Vardogr announces itself only by imitating the sounds made by inanimate objects, such as "the sound of the key in the lock, the placing of overshoes in their proper spots, the stamping of shoes on the floor. The jingle of horsebells and the cracking of whips may also be heard."

It is interesting that in his early research, Jensen singled out Scandinavians and Scots as the primary progenitors of the Vardogr. Some years ago, I shared an office suite with two friends who were both of Scottish descent. The combination must have produced a powerful Vardogr, for on many occasions, Glenn or Dave would enter my office to confer with me, only to find that I had not yet arrived. They would later swear that they heard me arrive, move my chair into position in front of my trusty 1923 Underwood typewriter, and begin tapping out words on the keys. When I would arrive at my office, I would often find my two puzzled friends standing in my office, wondering what joke I would try playing that morning. They soon learned about the reality of the Vardogr. Their spiritual forerunners fooled me from time to time as well.

Since my wife, Sherry, is also of Scandinavian descent, our two Vardogrs have played tricks on us on innumerable occasions. In some instances, the pranksters have almost precipitated arguments when one of us wants to know why the other came home and then left again, only to return a few minutes later. Then, laughingly, we realize a Vardogr has tricked us again. Our particular combination of personalities has strengthened our Vardogrs to such a level that they have been able to duplicate our voices, which can prove really perplexing and somewhat disturbing.

Not long ago, I received a letter from Mr. K. L. H. regarding his son's Vardogr: "I came across one of the archived shows on the *Jeff Rense Program* where you mentioned a phenomenon called the Vardogr. This immediately gave me cause to ponder some recent events in our home. I have a small office-studio in our basement where I have my computer, my musical instruments, and some recording equipment. My son's room is immediately above this office. He is 13.

"Every weekday he arrives home from school at about 3:30. When I hear him come home, I always go upstairs to ask about his day, but sometimes I find that he is not actually home yet, in spite of hearing the sounds you would normally expect to hear from a teenager coming home. Before hearing the program, I just brushed it off as normal house noises, or the cat, or whatever; but after I heard the show, I decided to try an experiment.

"The first day, I made sure the cat was not in my son's room, and I closed his door. I was certain that all TVs, radios, and so forth were turned off. Then I went back downstairs and listened.

"Sure enough, at about 2:30, I started hearing sounds from upstairs, just like he was arriving home from school. I heard footsteps, doors opening, and so forth. I was so sure that these were actual sounds that I figured the experiment was a bust on the first try. But after going upstairs, I discovered to my surprise that no one was home!

"The second day was an almost exact duplicate of the first. The next day I decided to place a tape recorder in his room, and I was able to actually record the sounds!"

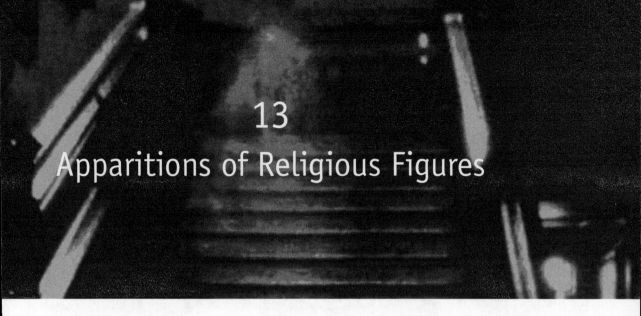

13
Apparitions of Religious Figures

POPE JOHN XXIII APPEARS TO SISTER CAPITANI

In early 1967 Dublin's *Irish Independent* carried the account of a dying nun's miraculous healing, which was brought upon by a visit she had from the spirit of Pope John XXIII. Sister Caterina Capitani, a nun of the Sisters of Charity of St. Vincent de Paul, suffered from severe gastric hemorrhages, a condition thought to be incurable. However, because the unfortunate sister endured continual hemorrhages, physicians decided to attempt an operation in Naples, Italy. Two surgeries were performed but they were unsuccessful, and when an incision on her abdomen opened, Sister Capitani's condition steadily worsened to the point where she collapsed.

Desperate to attempt any new therapy, her doctors sent the nun south, hoping that the change of air and locale might help her, but she was soon returned to a hospital in Naples when it was decided that she was dying. Sister Capitani later recalled that she had been all alone in her hospital room when her miraculous healing took place. She had been lying on her side when she suddenly felt someone place a hand on her abdomen. Summoning all her strength, she turned around to see who was in the room with her, and she saw Pope John standing beside her bed. Although he did not manifest in his papal robes, Sister Capitani said that she had recognized him easily.

In a quiet yet authoritative voice, the ethereal image of Pope John, who had died four years earlier on June 3, 1963, spoke words of great comfort: "Sister, you have called to me so many times, as have so many of the Sisters of Charity of St. Vincent de Paul, that you have torn out of my heart this miracle. But now do not fear. You are healed!" The spirit of Pope John then told Sister

[259]

Pope John XXIII lying in state inside St. Peter's Basilica on June 6, 1963.

Capitani to call in her doctors and fellow sisters so that tests could be run. He assured her once again that no trace of her illness would remain. Just before he vanished, he told Sister Capitani to go to Rome and pray at his tomb.

The moment the spirit of the deceased pope disappeared, Sister Capitani rose from her bed and was elated to realize she felt no pain. When she summoned the sisters and doctors into her room, they were amazed to find that the scar on her abdomen, which had been open and bleeding, was now completely healed. There was, in fact, no longer any scar or any other physical sign indicating that there had been a gaping wound on her abdomen just moments before. Sister Capitani was not expected to survive the day, yet that evening she was up and eating her supper with her community. According to the *Irish Independent*, the miracle healing of Sister Capitani by the ghost of Pope John XXIII occurred in May 1966. "Ever since," the account reads, "[she] has lived a healthy life. This is a phenomenon that cannot be explained in a human way."

Psychic News, the well-known British spiritualist weekly, agreed that the miraculous healing of Sister Capitani was a splendid event that could not be "explained in a human way," but it could not resist musing that when such an intervention by spiritual entities occurred among conventional Christians, the act is often deemed a miracle. However, whenever similar phenomena occurs among members of spiritualist groups, orthodox clergy are likely to denounce the "miracle" as the work of the devil.

The observation made by *Psychic News* seems a fair one. While the healing of Sister Capitani may well be attributed to a nonphysical being, was it truly the spirit manifestation of Pope John XXIII, or could it have been some other benevolent being who chose a form acceptable to the nun to better perform the act? And is the reported healing by an intervening ghost or spirit entity any less valid than a miraculous act performed by a religious figure or saint?

It has been repeatedly emphasized in this book that there is no intention to undermine or criticize any reader's personal religious faith. The author freely acknowledges that miracles do occur and that appearances of religious figures are commonly reported expressions of an individual's mystical experiences. This chapter does not seek to challenge any belief system that regards certain manifestations of religious figures as authentic. The transient materialization of benevolent spiritual beings is a universal phenomenon reported by members of all religious faiths. However, the entities who represent themselves as a particular figure may not always reveal their true identities. Indeed, they may reveal themselves in an image that may be more easily recognized by the percipient as an agent of help and healing. It will be for each individual reader to decide if the accounts that follow were truly manifestations of the holy figures that witnesses believed them to be, or if they were guardians and benefactors from the spirit world who materialized to offer guidance and healing.

APPEARANCES OF JESUS

While evangelical Christians proclaim that they have a friend in Jesus, it seems strange that virtually no apparitions of Christ have manifested to large groups in the same way that the Blessed Mother has appeared before audiences of thousands of devout and penitent believers.

In his response to the *Steiger Questionnaire of Mystical and Paranormal Experiences*, an Episcopalian priest wrote that he was awakened one night by the image of Jesus, who placed a kind of "burning coal" on his lips: "I began to speak. My wife woke up and she heard me speaking in what she later said was the strangest, most beautiful language that she had ever heard." The next day, during a meeting with his bishop, he eloquently expressed his congregation's needs and won his superior's support for greater financial aid. "I know that without the appearance of Jesus and his help, I would have been intimidated, tongue tied, and argued ineffectually with the bishop for my cause," the priest said.

E. Debat-Ponsan's rendition of Christ appearing to soldiers on a battlefield.

Perhaps the Christian tenet that Jesus is a *personal* savior enables Christian mystics and repentant sinners alike to claim a spiritual interaction with a powerful being they believe to be Jesus Christ.

An Apparition of Jesus Cured His Addiction

A young salesman wrote to testify how he had been mired in the despair of drug and alcohol addiction. His addiction had reduced him to a shaking skeleton who barely weighed a hundred pounds. What transforming influence and power had redeemed him from his miserable existence?

One day he walked into a dirty motel room with a bottle and his usual bad attitude and realized that someone had left a Gideon Bible open on the bed. As he bent down to move it aside, the book flipped open and certain words in the text seemed to be glowing a bright red: *Lo, I am with you always, even to the end of the world.* The salesman mumbled sarcastic words to the effect that Jesus certainly had never been with him. Then there was a brilliant flash of light and he realized that an image of a bearded man in a robe stood there before him. "He reached out to touch me, and it was like electricity going through me," the salesman said. "I felt pure, loving energy moving through every cell of my body. I know that it was Jesus who appeared in my room that night. He was gone in the next blink of an eye, but he took all my addictions, all my pain, and all my weaknesses with him. I have not taken any drugs or alcohol since that day 11 years ago."

APPEARANCES OF MOTHER MARY

The most common appearance of a religious figure in the western world is that of the Madonna, Mother Mary, who has appeared to people of many religions and cultures. For some reason, the devotion that many Roman Catholics have for the Virgin they believe to be the mother of Jesus Christ is often confused as ownership of the Blessed Mother. This is far from the truth, although it cannot be denied that the most best-known apparitions of the Madonna have been to Roman Catholics in countries where membership in that denomination is particularly high.

At the old castle in Hohenbaden, Germany, a vision of Virgin Mary was seen. The Virgin promised to stop the plague that had been raging in the surrounding area.

Those who interpret the beautiful image of Mary in a more universal way believe that these manifestations may be that of the Magna Mater, the Great Mother, a personification of Gaia, the planetary feminine intelligence, come to warn her many human children to take better care of their environment and the creatures that inhabit it. Others theorize that the apparitions of the Madonna may be that of benevolent nature spirits who choose to appear as a beautiful young woman in order to appear less threatening to the visionaries. Indeed, the majority of individuals respond better to the gentle scoldings of a loving mother than the angry growls of a stern father.

It should be acknowledged that most claims of reported miracles and appearances of religious figures are not sanctioned or authenticated by the clergy of any organized religion. Although visitations by Mother Mary are reg-

Nineteenth-century print of the Virgin Mary appearing to Melanie Mathieu and Maximin Giraud at La Salette, France, on September 19, 1846.

ularly reported around the world, the Roman Catholic hierarchy officially recognizes only seven appearances of Mary:

1. Guadalupe, Mexico: In 1531 an Indian named Juan Diego saw Mother Mary four times and was given a serape as evidence of her heavenly visitation. Currently, there is a petition to have Juan Diego canonized and made a saint, but a vocal minority of priests and church historians oppose the movement on the grounds that there is no convincing proof that Juan Diego ever existed. Some historians argue that he was probably fabricated by Spanish conquerors as a device to convert native tribes to Catholicism.

2. Paris, France: The Holy Mother appeared to a nun in 1830 and asked her to fashion a medal to commemorate the Immaculate Conception.

3. La Salette, France: A weeping, sorrowful Mary manifested to two peasant children on September 19, 1846, and instructed them to do penance for their sins.

4. Lourdes, France: Identifying herself as the Immaculate Conception, Mary appeared 18 times to 14-year-old Bernadette Soubirous between February 11 and July 16, 1858. During one of her visits, Mary promised that a spring would appear at the site of her visitation, and the waters of the miraculous spring are today world-famous for their healing powers.

5. Fatima, Portugal: Mother Mary appeared to three children near the town of Fatima and instructed them to say their rosary frequently. During her six visits between May 13 and October 13, 1917, Mary issued a number of prophecies, one of which is still said to be held secret by the Vatican. (See longer account about Fatima below.)

6. Beauraing, Belgium: Between November 29, 1932, and January 3, 1933, five children at a convent school experienced three remarkable encounters with Mother Mary in the school garden.

7. Banneaux, Belgium: Mother Mary appeared to an 11-year-old girl eight times between January 15 and March 2, 1933, in the garden of her parents' humble cottage.

There are a number of other visions of Mary that have been highly publicized; some have received full approval from the church, while others have not:

1. Garabandal, Spain: A series of 2,000 ecstatic visions of Mother Mary began for four children after they attended a Sunday Mass in 1961. The visitations continued until 1965 and produced numerous prophecies and astonishing miracles. (See longer account below.)

2. Zeitoun, Egypt: As many as a million witnesses may have glimpsed the figure of the glowing Madonna standing, kneeling, and praying beside a cross on the roof of St. Mary's Coptic Church. Miraculous cures manifested among the pilgrims from 1968 to 1971. (See longer account below.)

Since 1981 the Virgin Mary has appeared and spoken to children in Medjugorje, Bosnia-Herzegovina.

3. Medjugorje, Yugoslavia: In 1981 six children near the village saw Mother Mary holding the infant Jesus. The holy figure appeared almost daily for five months, leaving behind a continuing legacy of miraculous healings.

4. Bayside, New York: From 1970 until her death on August 3, 1995, the "Bayside Seeress," Veronica Lueken, issued pronouncements from Mother Mary against the spiritual abuses of contemporary society.

The Dancing Sun at Fatima

When two bursts of lightning flashed across the cloudless sky on May 13, 1917, the three children who were outside the village of Fatima, tending to the flocks of Antonio dos Santos, immediately stopped what they were doing and looked quizzically at one another. Lightning did not come in a clear sky. Ten-year-old Lucia dos Santos and her cousins, seven-year-old Francisco and nine-year-old Jacinta Marto, focused their attention on the leaves of an old oak tree that was situated on a plateau named the *Cova da Iria*. To their astonishment, in the tree they saw a strange globe of light emanating a kind of iridescent radiance.

The children became frozen with fright when they saw an aura develop in the center of the globe of light. Then the image of a lovely young woman who appeared to be about 18 years old manifested within the illuminated ball. As they stared, wide-eyed in awe, she told them not to be afraid. The children wanted to know who the woman was. "If you return to this very spot on the 13th of every month until October, I will tell you then who I am," she said to Lucia, who quickly repeated her words for the other two. (From the very beginning, Lucia was the only one who could actually hear the words of the beautiful woman.) "For now," the lady said, "you must keep my appearance a secret. You must tell no one that you have seen me. And you must say your rosary every day!" Then the ghost, spirit, or whatever it was vanished almost as suddenly as it had appeared.

Lucia, Jacinta, and Francisco did say their rosary every day, but the children were unable to remain silent about the wondrous vision that had manifested before them while they were tending to the sheep. All three of the children received the same reaction from their families. They were scolded for lying. Within a few days, the parish priest stopped by their homes and made known his intense displeasure with children for having made up silly ghost stories, but he ended up believing them.

The story of the mysterious lady had spread throughout the surrounding villages, and on June 13 nearly 60 of their neighbors accompanied the three children to the high plateau where the spirit had said she would appear again. Try as they might, the assembled townsfolk saw nothing, but Lucia claimed to see a flash of lightning. The townsfolk watched and listened as Lucia asked the unseen visitor a number of questions. Francisco and Jacinta testified that they, too, could hear the lady. Although the visitation did not last long, the message from the beautiful lady was both sorrowful and startling. Francisco and Jacinta would soon be completing their earthly mission and return to heaven, but Lucia would remain to spread her message.

Although the village of Fatima was populated by only a few hundred inhabitants, word of the miraculous manifestations quickly spread throughout Portugal. By the time July 13 arrived, 5,000 thousand pilgrims joined the three children at the foot of the oak tree. During her third visit, the lady identified herself as the Immaculate Heart of Mother Mary. Lucia repeated the words

Every year thousands of worshipers gather at the Fatima Sanctuary in Portugal.

Mary shared with her so that all the pilgrims could hear the messages. Lucia announced that World War I would soon end but that there was a proviso to Mary's message. Humanity had to cease offending God, or another, more terrible war would begin.

After word of Mary's third visitation had been widely circulated, Lucia, Jacinta, and Francisco were arrested and placed in jail. At that time the civil authorities sought to control and minimize the influence of the Roman Catholic Church. Although Portugal had always been known as the "Land of Mary," its traditional monarchy had been replaced by a revolutionary republican government. The new regime had already sought to abolish the Catholic sacraments, and it boasted that in two generations the Roman Catholic Church and all its practices would be eliminated from Portugal. The government believed that the three peasant children from the hills of Fatima were going to instigate a religious revolution. The only hope the state had was to expose the children as liars or intimidate them into making full retractions about their supposed visions. But the three little visionaries remained steadfast. Even the prospect of being tossed into boiling oil did not deter them from testifying to the validity of their experiences.

On August 13, the day of Mary's next visit, 15,000 thousand pilgrims gathered at Cova da Iria. When they learned that the three children had been placed in jail, they were outraged. The authorities soon discovered that they had stirred up more unrest among the population than they had estimated. A staggering number of people believed in the visions that the children reported. Before thousands could march on the jail, a decision was quickly made to release Lucia, Jacinta, and Francisco. A few days after their release, the children kept their fourth appointment with the lady. Although they went to the site on a day when she was not scheduled to manifest before them, she did appear.

On September 13, the day of the fifth visitation, the children were nearly crushed by the vast crowd that went to the site hoping to see the appearance of Mary. Among the pilgrims in the great assemblage were those begging for healing and for the forgiveness of sins. The blind, crippled, maimed, deaf, and terribly ill had all come to Fatima to pray for a personal miracle. As they stood before the oak tree, the three children began to say the rosary, and shortly after they saw the flash of light that prefaced the beautiful lady's arrival, and then she manifested before them. She told Lucia that she would heal some of those who had come expecting miraculous cures, but in October she would perform a miracle so that all would believe. She also promised that during her next visitation, a number of other holy figures would accompany her.

It is well known that the Roman Catholic Church has a number of committees and ecclesiastical authorities that examine all matters pertaining to miracles and visitations from holy figures. The Reverend Doctor Manuel Nunes

Formigao was assigned to investigate what was happening near the tiny village of Fatima, and he was immediately struck by similarities between the visitations at Fatima and those that had occurred at La Salette, France, in 1846. At that time two shepherd children had seen Mother Mary in a vision and had been told to warn others that great calamities would come to France if its citizens did not cease offending God. Lucia admitted that she had heard of the visitations at La Salette, but she said that the story had never crossed her mind until the priest reminded her of it. Although Reverend Formigao was impressed with the children's sincerity, he remained uncertain how much of their story was simply fantasy. He told his superiors that he had to wait until October 13, the day of the next appearance, and attend the visitation himself, which would allow him to appraise the events and make an objective judgment.

By early morning on October 13, 1917, all roads to Fatima were clogged with people who had come from all over Portugal and the rest of Europe to see Mother Mary's promised miracle. They came hobbling on crutches, carrying children who were too ill to walk, and hoisting others on stretchers. Some had walked all night, rich and poor alike, all hoping for a cure, revelation, or absolution. An estimated 70,000 people managed to gather on the Cova da Iria by noon. To add to the discomfort, confusion, and impatience of the vast crowd, it began to rain.

At noon, Lucia stood beside her cousins Francisco and Jacinta at the oak tree and commanded the vast crowd to close their umbrellas. After several minutes of standing unprotected in the downpour, the crowd began to get restless. It was a chilly day in October, and everyone was soaked. Suddenly Lucia cried out that everyone should kneel down. Thousands strained to see and hear the vision that the 10-year-old girl was able to see, but even the most devout among them were unable to behold Mother Mary. Lucia told the crowd that the lady wanted a chapel to be built in honor of the Lady of the Rosary. Lucia asked the lady about the healing of sick persons and the conversion of sinners, and the lady replied that some of those who had gathered on the plateau that day would be healed, but all must amend their lives and ask forgiveness for their sins. The rain stopped abruptly, and the clouds parted, allowing the sun to appear in a patch of bright blue sky. Lucia, Jacinta, and Francisco watched as the lady ascended into the sky, and then, alongside the sun, they beheld St. Joseph with the child Jesus, and Mary robed in white with a blue mantle.

While no one else assembled that day saw the holy figures described by Lucia, they were able to see something as astonishing. According to thousands of observers, the sun began to spin, extending fiery fingers across the blue sky. As the sun danced and spun, Earth itself appeared to change colors. At first the terrain seemed cast in a red shadow that evolved into shades of orange, yellow, green, blue, indigo, and violet. According to witnesses, this eerie phenomenon was repeated three times. Then to the complete horror of the assembled pilgrims, the sun began to plunge toward Earth. As if with one voice, thousands of men and women screamed at the terrible sight. Thousands fell to their knees in terror, pleading with God to have mercy. Others silently stared upward, too frightened even to pray. Most of the 70,000 people who gathered outside Fatima that day believed that it was the end of the world. The dramatic demonstration of supernatural power continued for 10 minutes. Finally, as if in answer to the crowd's collective prayer for mercy, the sun ceased its devastating plunge to Earth and began to climb back to its position in the heavens.

Avelino de Almeida, editor of the newspaper *0, Seculo*, had joined the crowd that day as a skeptical journalist who was very much opposed to the beliefs of the Roman Catholic Church. But on October 13, 1917, he admitted that his cynical view of religion and his doubts concerning miracles had been severely shaken. Writing for *0, Seculo*, he stated: "Certainly beyond all cosmic laws were the sudden tremblings and movements of the sun, dancing as it were … before the astonished multitude who gazed in awe. It remains for the competent to pronounce on the dance macabre of the sun, which today at Fatima has made hosannas burst from the breasts of the faithful and naturally has impressed … even freethinkers and other persons not at all interested in religious matters. To this unbeliever, it was a spectacle unique and incredible…. I can still see the immense crowd turn toward the sun, which reveals itself free of the clouds, and I hear the nearest spectators crying, 'Miracle, miracle!'"

After the dancing sun was seen at Fatima, Lucia, Francisco, and Jacinta became instant celebrities, darlings of the secular press. Wherever the children went, crowds gathered to ask them weighty questions about the meaning of life and the world beyond death. Reporters were never far from their sides, and every word that the children uttered was dutifully recorded and published. Photographers followed the children everywhere, hoping for a golden photo opportunity.

Although Mary had told Jacinta and Francisco that they would soon die, they remained untroubled. In fact, they told anyone who asked about the brief duration of their earthly mission that they were looking forward to returning home to heaven. However, Jacinta had always been a very sensitive, somewhat intense child, and she was greatly disturbed by the "worship" of the pilgrims that followed them. She became increasingly withdrawn and began to experience prophetic visions of her own. Most of her visions were quite violent and ghastly in nature, and she revealed that she had been shown terrible bombings in France and Holland. London and Frankfurt, she said, would be in ruins as the result of bombs that would rain death from the skies. All these awful things, she foretold, would take place 25 years later (that would be in 1942, when the destruction wrought by World War II would be devastating Europe and Great Britain).

This photograph was taken in Karascond Church, Hungary, in 1989. The vision of the Virgin Mary and Jesus was not seen by the photographer through his lens as the picture was taken, but it was seen by Karoly Ligeti, an art restoration specialist who was working on the scaffolding above.

In early 1919 Francisco became ill with influenza. On the morning of April 3, the 11-year-old boy received his first communion. On April 4, at ten o'clock in the morning, he died. Jacinta fell victim to influenza a few months

Karoly Ligeti holds a photograph of the vision he saw in Karascond Church, Hungary.

after her brother's passing. Several doctors recommended that Jacinta undergo a complicated chest surgery, and arrangements were made to take her to a hospital in Lisbon. Before she was transported to the city, the nine-year-old girl told Lucia that the Holy Mother had told her she would die alone in Lisbon.

There are many stories concerning the Holy Mother's appearances to Jacinta as she lay struggling for life in the hospital so far from her village. Jacinta repeated a good number of Mary's prophetic visions, and she uttered personal predictions for those around her that left many astounded. In one instance, one of her doctors asked Jacinta to pray for him before she went to heaven. Jacinta sighed and tearfully informed the physician that he and his daughter would enter the heavenly gates before she did. The startled doctor left Jacinta's room shaking his head in disbelief, but it was not long before he and his daughter were killed in a tragic accident. On the afternoon of February 20, 1920, her attending nurse found Jacinta dead, a beatific smile upon her lips as if she were welcoming the spirits that had come to take her home.

Shortly after the deaths of Jacinta and Francisco, Lucia entered a convent school and took the name of Sister Maria das Dores, "Sister Mary of Sorrows." The young girl proved that she had taken Mary's words regarding her life seriously and spent her life perpetuating the message, mystery, and wonder of Fatima.

The astonishing collapse of the Soviet Union in 1991 came as less of a surprise to those who had faith in the predictions made to the three children outside the Portuguese village in 1917. Millions of men and women throughout the world believe that the dissolution of the communist superpower was the work of the Holy Mother and was intended as the fulfillment of a promise that she had made to Jacinta, Francisco, and Lucia 74 years earlier. The children were given three prophecies, the first of which forecasted the end of World War I (which was still raging at the time of the visitations) but promised that an even greater war would rage if humankind failed to repent for its sins. The second prediction foretold the advent of the Russian Revolution and the subsequent rise of communism, which would spread atheism throughout the world. However, Mother Mary promised that if the pope, in concert with the bishops of the world, consecrated Russia in her holy name, the nation would eventually be converted. In 1984 Pope John Paul II consecrated Russia to the Virgin Mary at St. Peter's in Rome. Seven years later, the Soviet empire crumbled.

Lucia kept Mary's third prophecy a secret, but she was said to have entrusted its contents to Pope John XXIII in 1960. The prediction remains the source of much controversy and speculation. It was said to have been made public at the request of Pope John Paul II on June 26, 2000; the prophecy revealed that a "bishop dressed in white" would be shot during a period when the church would suffer from widespread persecution. Pope John Paul interpreted the prediction to have been realized when he was wounded in an assassination attempt in 1981. After the secret third prophecy had been made public, Pope John Paul proclaimed its message an invitation for all believers to pray for peace in the world. In January 2002 Sister Lucia, who at that time still lived in a Carmelite convent in Coimbra, Portugal, denied rumors that she had received new revelations from Mother Mary.

An Angel and a Beautiful Lady Appear at Garabandal

On June 18, 1961, four young girls were playing on the outskirts of the small village of San Sebastian de Garabandal, Spain, when they heard what they believed to be a loud clap of thunder. The sudden sound heralded the appearance of a bright figure that they immediately recognized as an angel. The magnificent being identified himself as the Archangel Michael. Conchita Gonzalez, Maria Dolores Mazon, Jacinta Gonzalez, and Maria Cruz Gonzalez had gone to the area to play, not to have a mystical experience. Maria Cruz was only 11; the other three girls were 12. They were all from very poor families, and in spite of the common factor of the Gonzalez surname, none of the girls were related. Michael appeared to them many times throughout the month of June. Finally he promised them that they would be able to meet the Blessed Mother on July 2.

Located in northern Spain in the rugged area of the Picos de Europa Mountains, Garabandal had, at that time, a population of about 300 people. There was no doctor in the village, nor was there a resident priest. But there were dozens of devout and curious townsfolk who vowed that they would accompany the four girls to the spot where Archangel Michael had predicted Mother Mary would appear.

At six o'clock in the evening on July 2, the girls walked to the area where they had first seen the Archangel Michael. According to the young revelators, shortly after they arrived at the spot, the Holy Mother appeared in the company of two angels, one of whom was Archangel Michael. The girls went into ecstatic states, and witnesses later declared that their faces reflected the same type of light that they claimed to see issuing from the Blessed Mother. The girls described Mary as having been dressed in a white robe with a blue mantle and a crown of golden stars. They said that her hands were slender. Her hair, deep nut brown, was parted in the middle. Her mouth was very pretty, and she had a fine nose. To their eyes, she appeared to be a young woman of about 18, rather tall. The girls excitedly agreed that there was no voice in the world like hers. Mother Mary had manifested, the girls said, as Our Lady of Carmel.

During 1961 and 1962 Mother Mary appeared to the girls several times a week. Whenever the visitations occurred, villagers and pilgrims alike saw the girls enter into ecstatic or trance states that would last from a few minutes to many hours. Numerous eyewitnesses said that the faces of the girls held an extraordinary sweetness when they were enraptured by the Blessed Mother. It was as if they were transformed by an inner light, and their beautiful faces were reflecting a holy glow from a divine spark within. Many witnesses observed that the girls seemed transported to a dimension of reality where time did not matter. They never gave the slightest sign of fatigue or discomfort, in spite of the fact that they were often kneeling on rocks with their heads violently thrown backward. On cold days the children came barefoot in the snow and listened to the messages of Mother Mary for hours.

There were thoughtless, insensitive skeptics who would hit, burn, and stick the girls with needles during their periods of ecstasy. None of these cruel stimuli elicited the slightest physical response from the four girls. On one occasion an inconsiderate photographer flashed powerful beams of light in their eyes while they were in a trance. Under normal circumstances a light that strong would have burned their retinas or perhaps caused blindness, but their eyes remained wide open and joyful, and none of the girls even blinked.

On May 2, 1962, an angel told Conchita that on July 18, God would perform a miracle and allow a sacred host to be seen on her tongue before she received a wafer during communion. When Conchita went to receive communion on the appointed day, she dropped to her knees, opened her mouth, and put out her tongue to receive the host. As excited pilgrims drew near with lanterns and flashlights, photographer Don Alejandro Daminas, who was standing only three feet away, was able to get clear pictures of a host materializing on her tongue. Those who witnessed the miracle stressed that Conchita's arms were at her side the entire time. She never raised her hands to her mouth to place a communion wafer on her tongue.

Over a period of 19 months, the Blessed Mother and Archangel Michael appeared to Conchita and the other three girls on some 2,000 occasions. Witnesses observed the girls levitating during their ecstasy, rising as if they were going to kiss or embrace the holy figures. Sometimes they were seen being slowly lowered to the ground, their backs ramrod stiff and straight. Once, a large crowd saw the girls walking in mid-air.

A young Jesuit priest named Luis Andreu begged the girls and the Blessed Mother to be granted the ability to behold the wondrous sights that the blessed girls were permitted to see. Father Andreu's request was acknowledged, and he was given permission to participate in a holy visitation. Although thousands assembled that day to watch the simple farm girls converse with unseen holy personages while they were in ecstatic states, Father Andreu was the only one among them who was able to see the angels and the Holy Mother. The healthy, robust young priest left Garabandal fervently proclaiming his great, ineffable joy. Thirty-six hours after his remarkable interaction with the supernatural, Andreu was in the midst of telling a friend that he had just experienced the happiest day of his life when he suddenly died. Doctors at the clinic where the young priest's body was examined stated that they could find no discernable causes for the man's sudden demise. His fellow priests stated that Luis had simply died of joy.

Conchita Gonzalez received her final visitation from Mother Mary on November 13, 1965. Conchita said that she was shown a preview of the awful chastisement that would be humankind's fate if the warnings of Mary were ignored, and she urged everyone to repent quickly.

Mysterious Lights Atop St. Mary's in Zeitoun, Egypt

On April 2, 1968, two mechanics working in a garage across the street from St. Mary's Church in Zeitoun, Egypt (a suburb of Cairo), were startled to see what looked like a nun dressed in white standing on top of the church's large dome. The two men decided not to waste a single moment in fearful speculation. One of them ran into the church to get a priest; the other telephoned for a police emergency squad. When the priest ran from his church and looked up at the dome, he was the first to recognize the remarkable event that had occurred: Mother Mary had manifested.

The white image of the Blessed Mother glowed as the priest and the mechanics stared in amazement for several minutes. As an excited crowd of witnesses began to amass, the vision disappeared.

While it is true that the majority of Egypt's inhabitants are Muslim, the country is also home to a fairly large population of Coptic Catholics. As news of the Holy Mother's appearance spread through Zeitoun, Cairo, and all of Egypt, thousands began to gather around the majestic church to see the Queen of Heaven for themselves. On April 3, when the mysterious image reappeared on the dome of the church, a large crowd was there to greet her with awed shouts of jubilation and whispered prayers of supplication. As if responding to the devout and enthusiastic reception, she returned to the church on April 9. Amazingly, the glowing manifestation of Mary appeared atop the dome of St. Mary's Church sporadically during a period of three years. Millions witnessed the visitations, and numerous photographs of the spiritual phenomenon exist.

The apparitions were most often heralded by mysterious lights, which were said to flash somewhat like sheet lighting. These unusual displays of illumination would continue for about 15 minutes before the image of Mary would appear in a brilliant burst of light. According to witnesses, the peculiar flashes would sometimes manifest directly above the church, while at other times they would appear in strange clouds that occasionally formed over St. Mary's. Even on days when there was hardly a cloud to be seen in the sky, unexplained cloud formations were often reported over the church's dome. The clouds would often descend from the dome and settle over the multitudes of pilgrims that would encircle the church. Many witnesses claimed that the clouds were scented like incense. Later, Bishop Gregorius declared that it had been determined that the clouds *were* formed of incense, although one million censers could not have produced clouds of that size.

Another aspect of the phenomenon was the mysterious appearance of glowing, birdlike creatures that often materialized before and after the apparition of Mother Mary. According to numerous journalists who traveled from all over the world to record the miraculous phenomena of Zeitoun, the entities resembled glowing white doves. Other observers argued that the airborne beings were larger than doves, more the size of pigeons. However, one account stated that the mysteriously illuminated figures could not have been ordinary birds because they flew too rapidly and never moved their wings. The spotless figures emitted white light, and they appeared to glide into and around the image of Mother Mary. The mysterious birds materialized, appeared, and disappeared without making any sound.

In his book *Our Lady Returns to Egypt*, Reverend J. Palmer, an American priest who traveled to Cairo to witness the miracle for himself, documents the various forms of the Blessed Mother that manifested atop St. Mary's dome: "At first she appeared above the dome in traditional form, wearing the veil and long robes associated with other appearances, such as at Lourdes and Fatima.... Mary [did] not stand motionless, but [was] seen bowing and greeting the people in silence. She [bent] from the waist, [moved] her arms in ... blessing and sometimes [held] out an olive branch to the people." Palmer stated that Mary appeared "between the trees in the courtyard in front of the church ... under each of the four small domes, through the windows of the larger dome, and ... walked on the flat church roof so as to be seen by those standing on all sides of the church."

In 1968 crowds of people would gather outside the Coptic Orthodox Church of St. Mary in Zeitoun, Egypt, to witness the visions of the Virgin Mary, which were often visible for hours at a time.

The visions of the Blessed Mother continued to manifest at the church from 1968 through 1971. The duration of her visits varied greatly, from a few minutes to several hours. One evening in June 1968, she was seen from 9:00 P.M. to 4:30 A.M. Strangely enough, Mary chose to remain silent from her majestic and commanding pulpit atop the church outside of Cairo. Although thousands of people claimed miraculous cures as they looked upward at the glowing figure of the Holy Mother, no one announced any special messages from Mary. There were no warnings of impending Earth changes, admonitions to repent or to cease sinning, and no predictions, secret or otherwise.

TWENTY-FOUR SIMILARITIES IN APPEARANCES OF GHOSTS AND HOLY FIGURES

Reverend B. W. Palmer, a retired Methodist clergyman from Haines City, Florida, spent many years collecting accounts of contemporary visions of religious figures from around the world. His exhaustive research on the subject, which he kindly shared with me, indicated that there are at least 24 ways that religious figures commonly utilize to manifest before groups of people. The reader can easily determine that the list might also apply to the materialization of ghosts and spirit entities:

1. The skies suddenly open up, and the religious figure appears to descend to Earth.

2. In the presence of a human witness, the religious figure appears to descend in a shaft of light.

3. The holy being appears or disappears through a solid object, such as a door or a wall.

4. Witnesses may hear footsteps outside their house. When they hear a knock at the door, they open it and behold a religious figure.

5. A figure may appear as though it is a picture on the wall.

6. Witnesses may awaken because they feel a spiritual presence in the room or they may feel someone's touch. When they open their eyes, they see a religious figure bending over them.

7. An angel may first appear to witnesses and lead them to the materialization of a holy figure, such as Mother Mary, Jesus, or Moses.

8. A witness may see the face of a religious figure appear above a person who is desperately in need of help.

9. Witnesses may hear a voice that tells them to go to a certain place and to do a certain thing. When they comply, they encounter the Holy Mother, Jesus, or other figures.

10. The images of religious or holy figures may appear in the sky, greatly magnified.

11. Witnesses may be awakened by what they initially think is the very bright reflection of the moon. Shortly after, they see the image of the religious personage.

12. The Virgin Mary has often manifested within clouds, and then her image pulls away from the clouds and glides toward witnesses. She has also been seen retreating back into clouds as she disappears or makes her departure.

13. A cloud or a heavy mist may materialize in a witness's room. Out of that mist, an image of the religious figure will appear.

14. During the Fatima miracle, the Holy Mother appeared to the three children in exactly the same way. As often as they were interrogated, all three consistently gave the same description of what they had seen. However, in many cases, religious figures appear to several witnesses at the same time, but the figure is seen in different ways by the individual percipients. To one witness at the scene, the figure may appear as a ball of light; to another, a flash of lightning; to yet another, a disembodied voice.

15. On some occasions, the being may appear in a room occupied by many people and yet is seen by only one or two witnesses.

16. The image of a holy figure may appear in the dreams of witnesses. Many times such a manifestation will bring about healing.

17. After a figure has manifested, it may vanish suddenly or fade away slowly, moving into a cloud, door, the floor, or ceiling. The figure may also walk away from the witnesses, fading from view as it moves farther and farther away.

18. As with the visions of Mother Mary at Fatima, very few witnesses are usually able to see, hear, or receive messages from the figure, even though there may be thousands of people at the scene of the manifestation.

19. The religious figure often manifests in a strange light that illuminates both it and the witnesses.

20. In a number of visions, the witnesses said that they did not see the holy figure, but they were aware of its presence due to a supernatural light or voice that came to them.

21. Numerous men and women have claimed that during an out-of-body or near-death experience, a holy figure appeared to guide them.

22. In out-of-body or near-death experiences, people have also claimed that a holy figure appeared with deceased friends or relatives.

23. During out-of-body or near-death experiences, individuals have seen the lower-levels of the spirit worlds, where good spirits, holy figures, and angels attempt to assist low-level entities by giving solace and comfort.

24. After near-death experiences, men and women have returned to consciousness stating they journeyed to heaven, where they saw a holy figure together with deceased friends or relatives and attending hosts of angels.

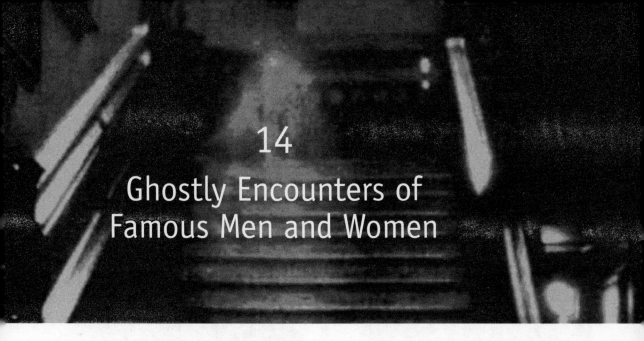

14

Ghostly Encounters of Famous Men and Women

THE LITTLE RED GHOST OF FRANCE

France has a ghost whose history is so well-established that it is mentioned in scores of books, official records, and even Napoleon's diaries. According to legend, the ghost known as "the little red man," appeared to some of the nation's most notable personalities for more than 260 years, garnering a reputation as a harbinger of tragedy. The ghost seemed to center its activity in Paris, at the Louvre and Tuileries palaces.

Catherine de Medici is said to have been the first person to have confronted the apparition. In was in 1564, during the construction of the Tuileries, that de Medici came face to face with a gnome-like creature dressed completely in scarlet. It soon became apparent to haughty Catherine that her unannounced companion was not a man of flesh and blood, and she interpreted the strange visit as an omen of bad luck. As Catherine had already begun to foment trouble between Roman Catholics and Protestants in France, and she induced the king to order the terrible St. Bartholomew's Day massacre of the Huguenots, scarlet was an appropriate color for the ghost to have worn.

The little red man appeared to Henry IV just before the monarch was assassinated by an insane schoolteacher in 1610. In 1792 startled chambermaids discovered the scarlet-clad gnome in the bed of Louis XVI when the threatened king was making a futile attempt to escape the machinations of the French revolutionaries. A few months later, guards claimed to have seen the little red ghost in the prison where Louis and Marie Antoinette awaited their turn with the guillotine.

[281]

Napoleon Bonaparte, by Paul Delaroche.

The red-hued entity first appeared to Napoleon in 1798, during the military leader's Egyptian campaign. The spirit is said to have materialized before Napoleon and to have made a bargain with the ambitious officer. According to the terms of the contract, Napoleon was to enjoy victory and triumph on the battlefields of Europe for a decade. The strange visitor said that he had advised the rulers of France in the past and declared that he had appeared to Napoleon in order to counsel him as well. The ghostly advisor told the military genius that he had been at his side since he had been a schoolboy. "I know you better than you know yourself," the spirit chided him. The entity told Napoleon that his orders to the French fleet had not been obeyed. While the Egyptian campaign had begun on a note of triumph with the Pyramids, the ghost told him that the enterprise would fail; Napoleon would return to France and find her closed in by England, Russia, Turkey, and an allied Europe.

As the scarlet ghost predicted, the Egyptian campaign failed. In 1809, after the Battle of Wagram, Napoleon made his headquarters at Schonbrunn, and his mysterious advisor once again appeared to him. Napoleon had conducted 10 years of successful campaigning, and he asked his supernatural advisor for five more years of guaranteed triumph. The ghost granted his request with the admonition that the greedy conqueror should not launch a campaign that would take him on Russian soil. Napoleon ignored the warning and met with a disaster that proved to be more significant than the physical defeat he suffered at Waterloo.

The red ghost made his third and final appearance before Napoleon on the morning of January 1, 1814, shortly before the emperor was forced to abdicate. The gnome first appeared to Counsellor of State Molé and demanded that he be allowed to see the emperor on matters of urgent importance. Molé had been given strict orders that the emperor was not to be disturbed, but when he told Napoleon that a red man wanted to speak with him, the emperor asked for the mysterious stranger to be granted immediate entrance.

It is said that Napoleon beseeched the ghost for time to complete the execution of certain proposals, but the prophetic messenger gave him only three months to achieve general peace or it would all be over for him. Rather than attempting to bring peace to Europe, Napoleon desperately tried to launch a new eastern campaign. Such a move left Paris to fall into the hands of the allies; and on April 1, three months after the red man's final visit to the emperor, Talleyrand and the senate called for Napoleon's abdication.

The ghost's last reported appearance occurred in 1824, when Louis XVIII lay dying in Tuileries Palace. The mysterious, gnome-like apparition has, however, earned itself a strange but secure position in French history.

KING CHARLES XII OF SWEDEN MEETS THE LITTLE GRAY MAN

Interestingly, King Charles XII of Sweden sought the counsel of a little gray man with a ruddy complexion, who gave Charles a ring that vanished on the day of the ruler's death. As he cut a mighty swath across Europe, Russia, and Turkey, the young King Charles became known as the "Alexander of the North." As his bravery and feats in battle became legendary, Charles resisted his mysterious counselor's entreaties to make peace. In 1718, as the Swedes were besieging Fredrikshald, one of Charles's officers noticed that the ring the king had worn throughout his reign was no longer on his finger. Moments later, Charles fell dead from a head wound.

A PROPHETIC SPIRIT APPEARED TO GEORGE WASHINGTON

In 1880, 81 years after George Washington's death, the *National Tribune* ran a story that had often been told by Anthony Sherman, a man who had been a close friend to Washington. The story related Washington's encounters with a prophetic visitor from the spirit world. According to Sherman, in the winter of 1777 a despairing General George Washington was studying maps and making military plans in his cabin at Valley Forge when he saw a rising, curling vapor filling the room. An astonished Washington watched a dark-haired, long-robed entity materialize before him. At first the general thought it was the ghost of a Native American taking form, but then he heard three loud blasts from a trumpet and a deep, commanding voice say, "Son of the Republic, look and learn."

The vapor that surrounded the ghost glowed with surging life as it formed an image of the globe. The entity dipped water onto the forms of Europe, Asia, and Africa, and Washington was horrified when thick black clouds began to arise from each continent. The odious clouds merged into one dark mass that began to move toward North America. Within the black cloud, Washington saw hordes of armed men land and begin to devastate cities that had sprung up only moments before. Washington's ears rang with the roars of the cannons, the shouts and cries of millions who had become locked in mortal combat. Above the sounds of strife, the mysterious voice once again admonished him to "look and learn." Then the shadowy figure sprinkled water upon North America, and the invading armies were swept away.

Washington told his friend Sherman that when the invading armies were swept away, he was once again able to see villages, towns, and cities springing up. In a loud voice the spirit cried out, "While the stars remain, and the heavens send down dew upon the earth, so long shall the Union last." As the vivid scene faded, Washington once again became aware of the mysterious figure in the shadows of his rude cabin at Valley Forge. "Son of the Republic," the figure said, "what you have seen is thus interpreted. Three great perils will come upon the Republic. The most fearful for her is the third. But the whole world united shall not prevail against her. Let every child of the Republic learn to live for his God, his land, and his Union." With those words, Washington told Sherman, the spirit being vanished. Revitalized in body, mind, and spirit, Washington rose from his chair convinced that he had seen a vision that had presented him the birth, progress, and destiny of the union. He was filled with a renewed conviction that the revolution would not fail. As miserable and depressing as the conditions were during that terrible winter in Valley Forge, the ragged, freezing, starving soldiers would not be defeated, and the goals of freedom and independence would be won.

THE GHOST OF WASHINGTON HALTED ROBERT E. LEE

It was September 1862, and the inexperienced Union troops had been shattered in battle after battle by the sharp-shooting, determined Confederate forces. President Lincoln had called on General George B. McClellan to take charge of the chaos and whip the Union troops into shape.

A 1795 oil painting of President George Washington by Rembrandt Peale.

McClellan slumped wearily over the desk in his tent. Before him lay campaign maps, battle reports, and a large scale map on which all known Confederate positions had been marked. His eyelids drooped, and he fell asleep on his desk.

His slumber did not last long. A booming voice suddenly filled his campaign tent. "General McClellan, do you sleep at your post? Rouse yourself, or before you can prevent it, the foe will be in Washington!" Wondering if some bold messenger had arrived with news of an impending confederate attack, McClellan snapped to attention. When he opened his eyes, he beheld a luminous apparition of George Washington. General McClellan later told the Portland, Maine *Evening Courier* that the spirit of Washington wasted no time in delivering his message: "If God had not willed it otherwise, before tomorrow's sun had set, the Confederate flag would have waved above the Capitol and your own grave! Note what you see. Your time to act is short!"

After Washington's ghost made a gesture, a living map detailing the most current Confederate troop positions appeared in front of McClellan. He grabbed a quill from his desk and began to jot down all that he could see. He was very much aware that if the Confederate armies took Washington, D.C., they would break the spirit of the entire union. The living tableau changed, allowing McClellan to see maneuvers the Confederates planned in the future. He furiously marked the positions that the map revealed to him on his own campaign maps. "You have been warned in time, General McClellan," the spirit of Washington said softly. With those words, the image of George Washington began to fade and McClellan once again found himself alone in his tent.

At first he thought the experience had merely been a vivid dream, but then he saw the markings and the symbols of Confederate maneuvers he'd made on his campaign maps. He would give the orders to move out at once.

Because of the knowledge that McClellan gained during his unusual paranormal experience, the Union troops were able to halt the Confederate invasion of Washington at Antietam and pursue General Robert E. Lee by anticipating several of his subsequent campaigns. McClellan later wrote of the ghostly manifestation in these words, "Our beloved, glorious Washington shall rest … until … he may once more become a Messenger of Succor and Peace from the Great Ruler, who has all nations in his keeping."

LINCOLN, THE PRESIDENT WHO CONSULTED "SPOOKS"

During his lifetime, Abraham Lincoln—one of the most revered presidents in the history of the United States—was constantly chided for his consultations with the spirit world. Shortly after he was elected president, the Cleveland *Plain Dealer* lashed out at him for "consulting spooks." The president-elect's candid reply was, "The only falsehood in the statement is that the half of it has not been told. The article does not begin to tell the wonderful things I have witnessed."

Lincoln openly admitted having consulted the mediums and spiritualists of his day. Reared in an atmosphere where people sought advice from the spirit world, Lincoln was never a skeptic. Historians and biographers have made little fuss about recording that he inherited a strong spiritual heritage from his mother and her family. His consultations varied from those received from backwoods "granny women" when he was in his youth, to sittings with the most famous mediums of the day during his tenure as president.

In times of great crisis, the president's wife, Mary Todd Lincoln, would arrange séances to calm her husband. Some of the gatherings took place in the White House itself. One of Lincoln's favorite mediums, Nettie Colburn, and other spiritualist channels would relay information from the spirit world that the thoughtful president would consider with all the intensity of his serious nature. Other participants in these séances were Colonel S. P. Kase, Major

President Abraham Lincoln sitting with his son Tad on February 9, 1864.

Vanvorhees, and Daniel E. Somes. Lincoln admitted that the messages he received from the spirit world enabled him to come through crisis after crisis. His influence extended to other figures of the time—even hard-nosed Union general and future president Ulysses S. Grant later turned to spiritualism.

Lincoln's Ghost Still Walks White House Halls

While Lincoln consulted the spirits in life, after his assassination in 1865 his ghost has been seen by many witnesses. President Calvin Coolidge's wife claimed to have seen Lincoln's ghost in the Oval Office; his hands were clasped behind his back as he looked out a window toward the Potomac River.

Perhaps because Franklin Roosevelt's years in the White House were full of strife due to World War II and his spirit was often troubled, Lincoln's ghost appears to have been most active during Roosevelt's 13-year occupancy of the White House. A clerk in the White House claimed to have seen Lincoln's ghost sitting on the edge of a bed and pulling off his boots. In a famous incident, Queen Wilhelmina of the Netherlands, a guest at the White House, was awakened late at night by a knock on her bedroom door. When she opened the door, she saw Lincoln looking at her from the hallway.

First Lady Eleanor Roosevelt used the Lincoln bedroom as a study. Although the first lady never claimed to have seen his spirit, she stated her belief that Lincoln watched over her as she worked in the room.

One would expect Lincoln's spirit to be courteous and always knock before entering a room. Presidents Theodore Roosevelt, Herbert Hoover, and Harry Truman all claimed to have heard what they believed was Abe Lincoln's spirit walking through the hallways of the White House and stopping to knock at their doors.

Ronald Reagan was certain that when his dog Rex began to bark, the canine had sensed the ghosts of Lincoln, Dolly Madison, Andrew Jackson, and Abigail Adams, whose spirits have all been sighted in various rooms of the White House. It is said that Regan's daughter Maureen, who slept in the Lincoln bedroom during visits, saw Lincoln's ghost on several occasions.

Valentino's Spirit Remained in Falcon Lair

Shortly after Rudolph Valentino's untimely death in August 1926, stories began to circulate that the great Latin lover's ghost haunted his favorite places. Falcon Lair, the dream home he had built on Bella Drive for his bride Natacha Rambova, became the most commonly reported site for ectoplasmic manifestations of the departed Valentino.

Fans whose worship of the great lover approached idolatry began to haunt the grounds in hopes of catching a glimpse of Valentino's ghost. The more important and persistent of the faithful somehow managed to wrangle invitations to spend a night in the glamorous mansion. A chosen few were fortunate enough to stay in Valentino's own bedroom.

Like children awaiting a visit from Santa Claus, the excited and expectant fans would lie in his room, ready to receive and transcribe any messages Rudy might choose to deliver from beyond the grave. All of Valentino's faithful knew that he firmly believed in the afterlife and that he had often spoken of his spirit guide, Meselope. If his ghost did not manifest during a visitor's stay in Falcon Lair, they concluded that the fault lay either with themselves or with adverse spiritual conditions in the atmosphere.

One story about the appearance of Valentino's ghost involved a caretaker who ran down the canyon in the middle of the night, screaming at the top of his lungs that he had seen Rudy. Another popular legend told of the stableman who left the grounds without collecting his belongings after he had seen his master's ghost petting his favorite horse. The myth makers made a great deal over the fact that the New York jeweler who had won the bid for Falcon Lair later backed out of the transaction. Those who supposedly knew the details claimed that the restless spirit of Rudolph

Actor Rudolph Valentino.

Valentino had not wished to be usurped by the physical presence of one who dealt with materialistic items such as jewelry. In another story, a woman from Seattle visited the caretakers of Falcon Lair and later claimed that when she had been alone in the mansion she heard muffled footsteps and saw doors open and close. She had been completely alone in the house except for Rudy and Brownie, Valentino's two favorite watchdogs who were trained to bark or snap at everyone except their master. Strangely, the dogs didn't bark, they only whimpered at what may have been their master's ghostly footsteps.

FIERY GHOSTS IN THE HOME OF JOAN CRAWFORD

Over a period of 20 years in her extensive film career, Joan Crawford transformed herself from the embodiment of the devil-may-care flapper, a symbol of America's "flaming youth," in *Our Dancing Daughters* (1928) to the heroine of America's favorite melodramas in films such as *Rain* (1932) and her Academy Award–winning performance in *Mildred Pierce* (1945). Many con-

Publicity shot of Joan Crawford.

sidered Joan Crawford the quintessential glamorous Hollywood movie star, as well as a leading lady whose strength and charisma were a match for any of the top-billed actors of her day, including Douglas Fairbanks, Jr., Franchot Tone, and Phillip Terry. These men were, perhaps without coincidence, also three of her four husbands. The fourth was Alfred Steele, chairman of the board of Pepsi-Cola Company.

In 1978 Christina Crawford, Joan's adopted daughter, released her book *Mommie Dearest* and shocked moviegoers around the world with her heart-wrenching revelation that growing up with one of Hollywood's most famous leading ladies was not full of sweetness and light like fan magazines had portrayed. *Mommie Dearest* was on the *New York Times* best-seller list for 42 weeks and was made into a 1981 film starring Faye Dunaway.

In 1989 my wife and I heard rumors of haunting manifestations in Joan Crawford's former home on Bristol Avenue, and Christina Crawford seemed genuinely surprised that we were aware of the manifestations. When we interviewed her for *Hollywood and the Supernatural* (1990), Christina said, "Not many people know that the house I grew up in may be haunted. It's not in print anywhere." When asked if she remembered unexplained phenomena occurring in the home when she lived there as a child, Christina admitted that she had vivid memories of some strange things. "When you are severely abused as a child, you tend to block out some things," she said. "But I'm positive that there were manifestations occurring when I was little.... I saw them! There were places in the house that were always so cold that nobody ever wanted to go in them. As a child, *I saw things in the house!* There was, of course, no context or framework in which to put what I saw and felt. I had nobody to speak to about the occurrences."

Christina recalled that any time she would become extremely frightened and would get out of her bed to try and find somebody to comfort her, she was always treated as though she were being a "bad child" who didn't want to go to sleep. "I used to have terrible nightmares and that kind of thing," Christina recalled, "but a lot of it had to do with the fact that I saw *things* in the night; so the solution to that finally was just to leave the lights on everywhere. One of the things I saw seemed like an apparition of a child ... or children."

Christina told us that she had not been back to the house since she had left for college at the age of 17, back in 1956. When we interviewed her in 1989, she had just learned that the new owners of the house had called in the Reverend Rosalyn Bruyere of the Healing Light Center to work with the house. Reverend Bruyere told her that she had discovered many spirits in the house and that there had been signs of ritual abuse in one of the rooms. Christina told us that other people had heard children's cries coming from within the walls. "Every single owner has had trouble," she said. "The *first* one was Crawford herself. She built the majority of the house. It was a small cottage when she bought it. Every single family that has lived in that house has had horrible things happen ... illnesses, alcoholism, addictions, relationship problems, and now, evi-

Christina Crawford.

dently with the current owner, the walls are breaking out in flames! I've heard that in particular it's the wall that was behind Crawford's bed."

Christina said that it would not have surprised her in the least if the "haunting" spirit in the house was Joan Crawford. "She was capable of real evil," she told us. "My brother and I were absolutely terrified of her. In fact, there is a passage in *Mommie Dearest* that describes 'the look' on her face when she tried to kill me when I was 13. My brother and I talked about it extensively. It was not of an ordinary human being!"

Christina said that Joan Crawford sold the place to Donald O'Connor, who sold it to the Anthony Newleys. They sold it, she thought, to the new owners, who were friends of the Reverend Rosalyn Bruyere, and they asked her to heal the house.

When we were able to contact Reverend Bruyere, she confirmed that the former Crawford house was afflicted with spontaneous fires, primarily in the wall behind where Joan Crawford's bed used to be. Reverend Bruyere expressed her opinion that the house had been supernaturally poisoned in some way, even before Crawford had moved into the place, but that the evil in the house had added to Joan's neuroses. The noted healer, who in this case served as an exorcist to clear the home, said that she found the haunting existing in levels. "It was a place of conspicuous negativity. I called it an 'astral central,' a gathering of spirits that were attracted to the negative vibrations. I picked up on gangland figures, corrupt politicians. There is an area in the house where a child [not Christina] had been tortured and molested. Terrible things went on in that house."

Reverend Bruyere felt that ghosts were trying to burn the house down. "Once the Beverly Hills Fire Department spent four days there attempting to solve the mystery of the spontaneous fires that would break out on the walls. I feel the spirits were trying to burn the house down to protect some horrible secret. There is something hidden there. I am certain that there are bodies buried in that basement. The house had become an astral dumping ground, but it seems clean now."

In 1992 the family that occupied Joan Crawford's former home graciously allowed my wife and I to film a segment for a Halloween television special in areas of the house that had seemed to be the most haunted. To their immense relief, spontaneous fires were no longer breaking out on the walls. The appearance of apparitions throughout the house and grounds had not ceased. They reported seeing ghostly images in a number of locations, especially the pool house, where they believed they had seen an image of Joan Crawford and an unidentified man playing billiards. They also reported hearing the clicking sounds of the billiard balls coming from the house when they knew no one was there. Another interesting manifestation sometimes seen in the large front room was what appeared to the ghost of a Native American shepherd.

Our hosts also allowed us to film in their basement wine cellar, where Reverend Bruyere had psychically detected the presence of buried bodies and a "terrible secret." Sherry and I immediately sensed that the atmosphere was very powerful, but the basement provided us with nothing other than eerie shots for our program. The only spirits we saw were in the bottles racked along the walls.

THE LITTLE BOY GHOST IN RICHARD HARRIS'S LONDON HOME

Irish actor Richard Harris (1930–2002), who starred in films such as *This Sporting Life* (1963), *Camelot* (1967), *A Man Called Horse* (1970), and *Cromwell* (1970), lived in a haunted English mansion for a time. The actor described the place as glorious. The home had a dining room with stained-glass windows decorated with signs of the Zodiac, a library with carved biblical figures, and a frieze of strange wild plants designed to appear as though one were in the sea looking at the sky with stars in the background. Harris said that he discovered the home when he was 24 years old. One morning, he woke up in the garden of the London house. He had no idea how he had gotten there, but he knew that he had to own that beautiful house.

Fourteen years later, Harris learned that the owners were interested in selling the house to a developer. The actor would not disclose exactly how he managed to close the deal in his favor. He simply said that it was a mystical thing that was meant to be. Harris said that right before he moved into the house, he had a burglar friend check out the mansion. He wanted to see just how burglar-proof the house was, and he thought that no one could offer a better evaluation of a house's security than one who made his living invading them.

The man managed an easy entrance, then just as he was preparing to leave, he heard the sound of a child crying. Since he knew the house was empty, the burglar was puzzled and stood still for a few moments, attempting to determine the direction the sound was coming from. When he heard the cry again, the man knew that he had made no mistake. A distressed child was

Actor Richard Harris, 1965.

sobbing somewhere within the dark old mansion. The burglar reasoned that a child must have somehow managed to enter the house during the day and had become lost in one of its many rooms.

The burglar tracked the sound to an upstairs room. The child cried quite vigorously as he reached the room. The man pushed open the door to the room and found himself in a room completely devoid of any other living human. Moonlight passing through a large window bathed the room in sufficient light to permit an immediate evaluation. As an eerie silence fell upon the old mansion, the burglar realized he was quite alone. The man reported back to his friend Harris and provided him with the necessary details on how to make the old mansion a bit more burglar-proof. Then he added, "But that's a strange house you've got there, mate."

Harris said the ghost that roamed the house was that of an eight-year-old boy. He knew the ghost's age because old records revealed that an eight-year-old boy had been buried in the house's tower. The restless spirit became an intriguing part of the actor's life. He even had the ghost perform for friends. But Harris also confessed to having had some terrific rows with the spectral lad. The ghost would often awaken him at two in the morning, banging closet doors and running up the tower stairs. Harris explained to the ghost that it had better be good, because an actor needed his sleep. If the ghost wouldn't quiet down, Harris threatened to have it exorcised. Finally, Harris built the ghost a nursery, complete with toys, at the top of the stairs. After he made that concession, the ghost behaved a bit better.

The Beatles Contacted Their Deceased Manager

Brian Epstein, former manager of the Beatles, died in London on August 27, 1967, following an overdose of sleeping pills. In the wake of this tragedy, the Beatles—George Harrison, Paul McCartney, Ringo Starr, and John Lennon—found themselves adrift in a sea of intense soul searching and developed a strong interest in the hereafter. McCartney remarked that since the earliest days of the Beatles, Epstein had been their guiding light. He had showed them everything and taught them all they knew. Epstein had always known the best thing to do for the Beatles. Without him, they would not have enjoyed the level of success they had.

The Beatles' search for the meanings of life and death led them down many paths. They tried the way of transcendental meditation but became disillusioned with their teacher and began to look elsewhere for knowledge. In 1968 Harrison felt that he received Epstein's first message from the other side. Harrison told the others that the message had not come in words, but in a compelling feeling that had come to him while he had been relaxing in his home. The band had always believed that Epstein's spirit would be with them. They had never been able to accept the fact that death would mean that they would never be able to speak to him again. All four felt certain that if Epstein had found the bliss he had been seeking, he would try to let them know. In order to encourage Epstein's messages from the other side, a séance was arranged.

The first attempt to communicate with Epstein was an amateurish affair, with the four musicians sitting quietly for 90 minutes with their hands spread on a round table. When the session broke up, the Beatles expressed their determination to have another go at it with a professional medium.

After a careful selection process, the Beatles found an elderly gentleman who came highly recommended, a medium of the finest reputation. During their initial séance with the medium, the Beatles heard a voice coming out of the darkness that they definitely thought was Epstein's. The spirit voice told them that he was happy in the afterlife and that he was pleased that they had sought to communicate with him. Epstein gave other brief messages then faded back into silence.

Encouraged by their success, the Beatles arranged for two more séances. They later said that Epstein came through again, but that he did not add a great deal to the messages from their first sitting. The Beatles were convinced that they had spoken with their departed friend. Each identified the particular inflections and voice patterns of Epstein's voice. They had great respect for the abilities of the medium who brought their friend back to them, but they refused to divulge his name. Whether the spirit of Epstein predicted the break-up of the Beatles was not known, but the four young musicians stated that they had never felt more together as a group than they did during those evenings around the séance table.

THE SPIRIT MESSAGE THAT ENCOURAGED BARBRA STREISAND TO FILM *YENTL*

Barbra Streisand, the famous singer, actor, and director, told Claudia Dreifus (*The New York Times*, November 11, 1997) of the indecision she felt about

Barbra Streisand, 1993.

directing the 1983 film *Yentl*. As she was internally debating the matter, she went to visit her father's grave for the first time. She admitted that she had not done so earlier because she was angry "that he died on me." Later that same day, she invited a medium, "a nice Jewish woman who had a spiritual guide," to her older brother's home.

During the séance, the table began to move and Streisand later confessed that she became so frightened that she ran into the bathroom. After she had regrouped her courage and rejoined the séance, she observed the leg of the table raise and lower itself to the floor and spell out "M-A-N-N-Y," which was her father Emanuel's nickname. Then she received the messages, "S-O-R-R-Y" and "S-I-N-G-P-R-O-U-D." Streisand said that the messages she received from the medium's guide were a definite signal to her that she should direct the movie. She has said that of all the films she has made, she is most proud of *Yentl*, because it was dedicated to her father.

HE FACED GHOSTS IN FRONT OF THE CAMERA AND LIVELY SPIRITS IN HIS HOME

In his later films, British actor Donald Pleasance (1919—1995) epitomized the very essence of the eerie. Pleasance carved out a niche for himself in horror films with the release of the cult classic *Halloween* (1978) and its four subsequent sequels, and he also appeared in numerous other movies that featured hauntings and apparitions.

In the early 1970s Pleasance and his wife, Meira, bought a seventeenth-century home in Strand-on-the-Green, England. The large home had been divided into two separate houses, and as both were up for sale, they decided to buy both. And that was when the fun began.

Shortly after moving in, the Pleasance family began hearing strange thumping sounds. Although they checked throughout the house, they could not find the source of the mysterious noises. Pleasance admitted that at first he was frightened to death. But the family gradually came to realize that the sounds were distinctly like those of children running, and they had an insight. They knocked down the walls that separated the home into two houses, and allowed the ghosts of children once again to run through the house, as they had probably done many years before when they were alive and it had all been one big house.

Once the Pleasance family had determined the origin of the thumps and bumps, they had no problem with the concept of sharing their home with the ghosts. The sounds, Pleasance observed, were sounds of joy. They could feel that the children seemed happy to once again have a free run of the place after all those centuries.

SHARON STONE SAID THE ONTARIO SET WAS HAUNTED

Actress Sharon Stone, 1998.

When Sharon Stone was filming the movie *Cold Creek Manor* (also called *The Devil's Throat*) in the North Dumfries, Ontario, mansion used in the motion picture, she said that the entire crew experienced "incredibly spooky stuff." Stone thrilled reporters at a Milan, Italy, fashion show by telling them about the frightened crew members who reported seeing the ghost of a little girl who wandered around the 150-year mansion where doors would open and close of their own volition.

Joan Chaplin, one of the owners of the mansion, told Jeff Pappone of the *Ottawa Citizen* (January 14, 2003) that the members of the movie crew were not the first people to report seeing a ghost in the home. A visitor had once told her that he had seen a woman sewing at a sewing table in a bathroom. Research indicated that a former owner, Margaret Keefer, had used the room on the west side of the house as her sewing room; it had since been converted into a bathroom. Chaplin said that she had not seen any ghosts in the mansion. The atmosphere of the home gave her a "really nice feeling."

Cambridge archivist Jim Quantrell said that the ghost of the little girl that was seen by the film crew might have been one of the daughters of Matthew Wilks, who purchased the mansion in 1858. The girl died at about the age of 15, but no one had previously reported seeing her ghost wandering throughout the house.

JULIANNA MARGULIES CONTACTED SPIRITS AS A CHILD

In the motion picture *Ghost Ship* (2002), Julianna Margulies, a former star of the television series *ER*, portrays a member of a salvage crew that discovers a lost ship and decides to tow it back to port. When they board the vessel, they discover that it is full of fiendish phantoms that they must vanquish if they are to survive.

Margulies confessed to reporter Rachel Blackburn that when she was a little girl, her family lived in an old barn that was built in 1348 and had been converted into a house. She and her sisters sensed something in the old place, but they weren't afraid. When she was about 13, she and her sisters made their own Ouija board to try to communicate with any spirits that might be near them. Apparently contact was made, for Margulies recalled that they all asked "Are you here?" and then what they were doing felt "freaky and wrong," leaving Juliana in tears. Although she no longer works the Ouija board, she said that she definitely believes in ghosts.

THE GHOST OF SUPERMAN

Mystery still surrounds the death of television's "Man of Steel," George Reeves (1914–1959), who starred in the television series *Superman* (1950–1957). Numerous witnesses claimed to have seen his restless spirit in the home on Benedict Canyon Drive where his body was found. Although Reeves's death on June 16, 1959, was ruled a suicide, friends, relatives, and thousands of fans still insist that it was murder. Singer Don McLean wrote the song "Superman's Ghost" in tribute to the anguish experienced by those who still mourn the actor.

People have reported seeing Reeves's ghost wearing a bathrobe, quite likely the one he was wearing the night of his death. One couple, ignorant of the history of the home on Benedict Canyon Drive, moved out after confronting his spirit. Others claim to have seen his ghost dressed in his full Superman costume, cape blowing in some nonexistent breeze.

THE NIGHT MARILYN MONROE RETURNED

During the summer of 1946, Bob Slatzer met Norma Jean Baker in the lobby of Twentieth Century–Fox Studios. He was a correspondent for an eastern newspaper, and she was a young model trying to get work by making the rounds. They struck up a conversation and made a date for later that evening. Thus began a long relationship that led to their brief marriage in 1952. Even after Norma Jean had been transformed into the Hollywood love goddess known as Marilyn Monroe, they remained close friends until her death in 1962. Since her passing, many strange things have manifested in Bob's life that have convinced him that her spirit is still with him. In 1973 he participated in an experiment that actually caused Marilyn Monroe's spirit form to materialize.

Slatzer had known Anton La Vey, the author of *The Satanic Bible*, for about two years when he learned that La Vey was fascinated with Marilyn Monroe. One night La Vey contacted him and told him an astrological "dark moon" would occur on Saturday, August 4, just as it had 11 years earlier when Marilyn had died. La Vey needed someone who knew Marilyn very well to help him manifest her spirit. Bob agreed to participate in La Vey's plan, and later that night they went to Marilyn's former home on Helena Drive. La Vey had received permission from the then-current owner to be at the house. Although she closed the gate that led up to the home, she allowed them to sit in the cul-de-sac that led to the property. They positioned their car against the gates, looking out, and there was no one else around.

Slatzer sat in the front passenger's seat, next to Anton. Mrs. La Vey was in the backseat. La Vey had a tape recorder with songs from Marilyn's pictures, and about 11:45 P.M., he turned it on at a low volume. He also had a small penlight he used to read something he had written. Slatzer remembered that it was sort of like La Vey was speaking in tongues or chanting. "About 12:15 A.M., the night was still," Slatzer told us when we interviewed him about the extraordinary encounter for *Hollywood and the Supernatural*. "Not one single blade of grass was moving. The leaves on the eucalyptus tree by the comer of the house were still. All of a sudden, a terrific wind came up. The tree looked as if it were in a hurricane for three or four minutes—yet nothing else on either side of the road was moving. Then from out of nowhere—I didn't even turn my head or blink, and I have 20-20 vision—this woman appeared! It was as if somebody suddenly set her there. She had on white slacks with a little black-and-white, splash-pattern top, little white loafers, and I could see a shock of blond hair. She started walking toward the car. I had goose bumps all over!"

After recovering from his shock, Slatzer began to think like a journalist. He wondered if the whole thing was a setup by La Vey, a kind of publicity stunt, but he didn't think that La Vey would do anything like that. He seemed too intense and serious about his work. As the figure of the woman began walking slowly toward the car, Slatzer asked La Vey, who was sweating profusely, if he wanted to turn a light on. La Vey indicated that they should remain silent. "The figure came slowly toward us and stopped about 30 feet in front of the car," Slatzer said. "Anton had dimmed the music a little and finished his chant when she was about halfway to us. All of a sudden, she veered off to our left. There used to be a big tree there, and she just stood there, almost as if she were made of cardboard, with kind of a wooden look, but the figure was highly recognizable as Marilyn Monroe!"

Slatzer told us that at that moment he truly became a believer in the paranormal, in life after death. "Marilyn was so real!" he recalled. "Mrs. La Vey had practically turned white and looked almost petrified! Anton … well, his breath was taken away, I can tell you that!" The image of Marilyn Monroe hesitated for a minute, her hands clasped. It appeared that she was looking past their car rather than directly at them. Slatzer thought it seemed as if she was looking past the gates, as if she wanted to enter the gates and go in but didn't want to pass the car. Then she turned to her left and slowly started to walk down the middle of the boulevard.

When the ghost of Marilyn Monroe was about three-fourths of the way down the street, Slatzer decided to get out and walk after her. As he approached her, the ghostly image turned, walked to the middle of the street, and *vanished* into thin air! "I saw this happen with my own eyes," Slatzer said. He had walked hurriedly through a small drainage ditch about two and a half feet wide in his attempt to catch up with Marilyn's ghost. He noticed his wet shoes had left an imprint on the road. The apparition of Marilyn had been taking short, small, measured footsteps, and had also walked through the ditch, but it left no footprints.

Slatzer told us that he had repeated the story to only two people: psychic-sensitive Clarisa Bernhardt and Norman Mailer, who had written a book about Marilyn Monroe. "When I got through telling it to him, he said, 'I do not disbelieve it. I do believe these things—and that is quite a strange experience.'"

CLARISA BERNHARDT AND THE CROSSOVER CLUB

"The astral plane hangs heavy over Hollywood," our good friend and psychic-sensitive Clarisa Bernhardt observed. "There are too many people there who were unprepared to make their transition to a higher dimension. Part of my work with the spiritual Crossover Club is to encourage these confused entities to move on, to leave the Earth plane, and to walk into the light."

In 1982, two years after the death of Mae West, Bernhardt was asked to serve as the medium at a séance held in the lounge of Hollywood's Ravenwood Apartments on Rossmore Avenue, where Mae had lived for nearly 50 years. "Immediately I could feel a sense of joy coming from Mae's spiritual vibration," Bernhardt said. "She was extremely psychic herself when she was alive, and she doesn't like the term 'séance.' She prefers 'interdimensional communication.' I think the most important thing that came out of the meeting was Mae telling us about the Crossover Club, a group of spirits who help new entities adjust to life in that new dimension. She told us that she would soon be qualified to assist and to greet some of those who will be coming to the other side."

The information about the Crossover Club was of great benefit to a medium like Bernhardt, but the participants in the séance were more interested in receiving specific references about Mae West's life to convince them that they were, in fact, communicating with the late actress's spirit. Several of West's closest friends were there, and Bernhardt was able to channel information that convinced them that her spirit essence was truly present.

"I received a communication about a problem with Mae's leg," Bernhardt said. "She had broken an ankle back in the 1940s, but no one else had known about it. Her spirit also referred to some inspirational writings of hers that she now felt might be helpful to others. She said that she had written 10–15 sheets of onion-skin paper and placed them in a thin brown cover. A friend

Actress and "sensitive" Mae West.

of hers confirmed that such papers did exist." When Bernhardt told the sitters in the spirit circle that West expressed concern about a ring that had been lost, a friend of the actress immediately recognized the incident to which the spirit referred to. He stated that only West and he knew about the lost ring.

Since that session in 1982, Bernhardt has assisted many spirits as they attempted to adjust to the other side. "It is so important that we all keep our spiritual house in order," she said.

Bernhardt has told me of an experience that she had shared with Dotty Knight, the widow of the late actor Ted Knight, well known for his portrayal of the egocentric Ted Baxter on *The Mary Tyler Moore Show* (1970–1977).

"I first met Ted Knight when he was appearing in a stage presentation of *You Know I Can't Hear You when the Water's Running*, produced by Rita Streamer at her Santa Monica Theatre Playhouse in West Hollywood," Bernhardt said. "My late husband Russ was doing some public relations for Ted on that project through his Russ Bernhardt Enterprises. Russ and Ted had been friends a long time, and Russ did special publicity assignments for Ted. As a result I got to know and become friends with Ted and his wife Dotty. They were both aware of my strong intuitive ability, which seemed always to produce accurate and unexpected information for them. My talent was particularly interesting to Ted.

"I recall that once I dreamed that Ted was possibly going on a boat ride, and the message was clear that he should not go. I called him and relayed the message. He listened and was very quiet. And then he said to me in a manner very much like his television personality 'Ted Baxter' that he didn't even know a close friend with a boat. I felt a bit uncomfortable, but that was the information that spirit had given me, so we said goodbye.

"[Less than an hour later] my phone rang. It was Ted, and he [told] me that a close friend had just called and invited him to go for a ride on a new boat he had just bought. Ted said he thought it was incredible that I had told him about that unexpected invitation in advance, and I was delighted that my dream information for him was correct. Ted said that he declined the invitation, and although he later learned that nothing occurred when the others went in the boat, the message that I received had been specifically for him, and he told me he truly felt that if he had gone perhaps he would have fallen overboard or something.

"Ted passed away in 1986, and Dotty and I have remained good friends. After Ted's passing, it was no real surprise to me that he began to appear to me in dream-visions. Sometimes he gave simple messages. Other times he expresses his concern for Dotty or other members of his family.

"The message that truly got Dotty's attention [was] when I gave her a telephone call after not having spoken to her for some time and told her that I had just received a rather strange message from Ted. Dotty was immediately interested to hear his message. So I told her that Ted had said to tell her that it was okay to sell the house, but [not to] sell the silverware. And that was the message. Dotty responded with an outburst of joyous laughter, and she confirmed to me that she was in the process of selling the house and a lot of things associated with the past, but she said to me, 'Clarisa, I won't sell the silverware.'

"Just recently, when Dotty and I were visiting by telephone, as we sometimes do, she asked, 'Do you recall when you told me about the message from Ted that I was not to sell the silverware? Well, I made a point not to sell it, because silverware was very important to Ted. He collected it. I just wanted to be certain to tell you that I truly believe you really did hear from him.'"

15
Animal Ghosts—
Domesticated and Wild

Do Pets Go to Heaven?

My wife and I write a column called "Frequently Asked Questions" for the Internet magazine *Beliefnet* (<www.beliefnet.com>). In June 2001 we gave our answers to the questions, "Do pets go to Heaven?" and "Can pets be reunited with their owners in the afterlife?" To briefly summarize, we stated that 45 years of research have convinced us that just as there is life after death for humans, animals also have some form of existence on the other side. Just as our beloved pets are our loving companions in the material world, we believe that our spiritual essences remain connected somehow beyond the grave.

We quoted Janice Gray Kolb, author of *Compassion for All Creatures*, who expressed her conviction that the breath of God "breathed into man was the same breath breathed into the animals, birds, and other creatures. Genesis 1:21–22 (New American Catholic Bible) says, 'God saw how good it was and God blessed them.'" In her opinion, God's blessing of the animals is further proof that all creatures have a soul. "Blessed," she explains, "means 'to make holy,' 'sanctify,' 'to invoke divine favor upon.' God blessed his creation of man and woman and thereby granted them a soul. Why else would God have blessed the animals if it were not to bestow a soul upon them?"

Tulsa, Oklahoma, attorney M. Jean Holmes is convinced that any distinction between humans and animals that may allegedly be found in scripture is the result of a translator's "philosophical construction." In her book *Do Dogs Go to Heaven?*, Holmes argues that an examination of the original Hebrew texts for concepts such as the "soul" and "spirit" reveals that the authors of various books of the Bible believed that animals have souls and spirits, just as humans do.

[303]

In 1926 Lady Hehir and her Irish wolfhound Tara were photographed by a friend. The developed photograph showed the head of a small dog right above the rear of the wolfhound. Lady Hehir immediately recognized the small dog to be her cairn terrier Kathal, which had died six weeks before this photograph was taken. The two dogs had been inseperable friends, and the spot where this photograph had been taken was a favorite of theirs.

Real Ghosts, Restless Spirits, and Haunted Places

Most pet owners will agree that their pets will be numbered among their best friends in heaven, as they are on Earth. In conjunction with our column in *Beliefnet,* the editors decided to run a poll of their readers to gain a clearer picture of how many pet owners believed that they would be reunited with their pets in the afterlife. An astonishing 85 percent said that they did believe that their pet had a soul and that they would see them again one day on the other side. However, when ABC News picked up the item for a telecast, they expanded the base of the poll beyond the readers of our column to include the general public, and then only 43 percent of pet owners surveyed answered "yes" to animal companionship in the beyond.

We still maintain that those pet owners who have taken a good look into the eyes of their beloved animal friend will not deny that the same breath that God breathed into humans was also breathed into animals, birds, and other creatures.

SNOOPY CAME BACK TO SHOW THAT HIS SPIRIT WAS OKAY

The Personal Experience of Patrick

"[In 1971, when I was 10,] I had a dog I absolutely loved that was killed (as many dogs were before leash-laws were commonplace) when he was struck by a car. It was the first time I'd ever experienced the loss of something I'd loved so dearly and I was devastated. I grieved for what seemed to be weeks.

"The dog's name was Snoopy, he was a little black and white mongrel, marked very distinctly, with a black mask over his eyes and a black spot on his back. He didn't look like any dog I'd ever seen before or since. Snoopy was killed in October of 1971. Late one afternoon in the summer of [1972], every kid in the neighborhood was involved in a giant game of hide-and-seek and I was 'it.' Most of the game was taking place in our field, which consisted of about two acres of wild wheat, roughly waist-high to a 10-year-old. I counted to whatever number I was supposed to before I ran off into the field to find my hidden friends. It was near dusk, and we were trying to get as much playtime in as we could before our parents started calling us in.

"I headed into the wheat … and nearly tripped over *my dog, Snoopy.* Snoopy was less than five feet in front of me. It was Snoopy. There was no mistaking the markings, and he still had his winter coat. He looked at me and wagged his tail. He was happy. A few seconds later, he turned and trotted away. The wheat didn't move as the ghost of the dog traveled deeper into the field. I followed but quickly lost sight of him. A moment later, I came upon a concrete block that was against the fence. It was what we had used for the headstone when we'd buried the dog. The letters that my mother had written on the block with a permanent marker on the block had almost faded away: *Snoopy, October 28, 1971.*

"I stood and stared at the stone for a moment, realizing what had just happened. Snoopy had wanted to see me again, and he had wanted me to see him again … and we did … and he was okay … and he was happy. A 10-year-old boy who'd lost his best friend slept a little better that summer's night knowing that his friend was still around and that he just might be with him again someday."

BROWNIE, THE GHOST DOG OF DAYTONA BEACH

A Personal Investigation by Dusty Smith, Founder of the Daytona Beach Psychical Research Group (<http://www.dbprginc.org>)

"**A**t one time the most popular resident of the Daytona Beach downtown business area did not come in the form of a human. The most popular ambassador Daytona Beach has ever had was a dog that came to be called 'Brownie.'

"[Somehow] this weary, yet wise, canine traveler made his way to Daytona Beach. Like many before him, and many more after him, Brownie explored the sidewalks and storefronts of Beach Street for several days before staking a claim. Brownie's first, and best, friend was Ed Budgen, Sr., the owner of the Daytona Cab Company, located on the corner of Orange Avenue and Beach Street. When Brownie met Ed, he offered Brownie part of his lunch. Being the smart and resourceful dog the he was, Brownie gladly accepted the free meal. Brownie quickly learned how to capitalize on this gracious human trait. Many of the downtown workers and restaurant owners would feed him scraps on a regular basis.

"Brownie took up residency at the Daytona Cab Company. Brownie's new friend Ed even made him a doghouse from a cardboard box. Eventually Brownie's home became a bit more upscale. It was quite an elaborate home, complete with Brownie's name on it and a collection box. Many people donated to the 'Brownie care fund.' This fund would provide food, veterinary care, and money for Brownie's annual license.

"One local resident remembers that Brownie became a Daytona resident in 1940. At that time downtown shopping was popular. Brownie quickly became know as 'the town dog.' It was customary to greet Brownie on a shopping spree. His reply would always be a wag of his tail.

"Brownie became a trusted companion to many of the local cab drivers. He took it upon himself to accompany the police on their nightly rounds. Brownie would assist the officers by sniffing at shadows in dark alleys, and he would stand beside officers while they checked on local businesses.

"Brownie's fame grew, but his ego didn't. Even after being written up in national magazines and newspapers as 'Daytona Beach's dog.' As they walked and shopped along Beach Street, many visiting tourists would seek Brownie out in order to have their picture taken with the country's most popular dog. Ed's wife Doris remembers Brownie getting Christmas cards and presents from all over the country. Doris would respond on Brownie's behalf and include a photo of the famous dog.

"Brownie passed of old age in October of 1954. Many fine folks from across the country felt the loss and sent letters and cards of condolence. Brownie's bank account had enough money in it to purchase a headstone and construct a plywood casket. City officials provided a resting place in Riverfront Park, which is directly across from the place that Brownie had spent the best years of his life. There were 75 people in attendance, including four pallbearers, at Brownie's funeral. As Mayor Jack Tamm stated in Brownie's eulogy, 'Brownie was indeed, a good dog.' Many shed a tear.

One of the few remaining photographs of Brownie.

"Now that I have told you about Brownie's life in this world, let me tell you how I met Brownie in the next world. On one of our little outings, I decided it might be worthwhile to go and visit Brownie's resting place. We arrived at Riverfront Park at about 11:00 P.M. I took off in one direction, and my fellow researchers, Kyle and Tracy, went in the opposite. Normally we would stick together, but we had no idea exactly where Brownie was buried. Riverfront Park is quite large with many fishponds, small footpaths and bridges, and beautiful gardens. I walked to the south [and] they went north. My radar must have been in tune that night because I walked straight to Brownie's grave.

"When I turned around to see where Kyle and Tracy had gotten to, they were completely out of sight. I decided to have a little chat with Brownie and take a few pictures. I introduced myself and explained to him how I had read about how famous and humble he had been. I noticed the shrub to the north of his headstone was supposed to be in the shape of a dog, but was a bit lack-

Grave of Brownie the dog.

ing. Boxwoods can be hard to train sometimes, especially when they are so close to a saltwater source. Anyhow, I noticed how wonderful Brownie's headstone was; the mayor's quote that Brownie had been 'a good dog' was inscribed at the bottom.

"As I stood there thinking about what a wonderful impact Brownie had on this town and the folks who were lucky enough to encounter him, I suddenly felt sad. I wondered how many people still remembered this fine animal. Obviously the grass was mowed on a regular basis, but how many even knew of this location? Did someone still come and talk to Brownie? Did anyone ever bring him flowers or maybe lay a dog biscuit down for him? Did Brownie still recall what it felt like to be petted?

"My belief is that we take these feelings and thoughts onto the other side with us. How sad would it be if no one remembered to remember us? I realize that in 100 years there [will] be no one around to remember who and how we really were. But couldn't someone make the afterlife a little special for this obviously special dog? Yep, you're right, it would be me! I decided at that moment to take Brownie on as my very own spirit pet. I would visit him as often as I could. Talk to him, offer him biscuits, or as they are known in my house, 'cookies.'

"I noticed a park bench just west of Brownie's place of rest. It seemed to be so inviting. Sitting on a park bench, dog at your side, listening to the wind, and watching the traffic go by. I told Brownie that if he cared to join me, I would be more than happy to sit with him for awhile. After several minutes, I felt warmth at my left leg. Could it have been Brownie? Or just a warm breeze coming in off the inter-coastal waterway? Just then I noticed Kyle and Tracy headed my way. The warmth was gone. I spoke to Brownie again, 'Thank you for taking time to sit with me. I needed to feel a loyal friend tonight. I do hope you will reveal yourself in a picture. You *are* a good dog,' I said.

"I snapped a picture of where I had been sitting with what I felt was my new friend, Brownie, the spirit dog. I looked at the LCD screen on the digital camera and noticed a bright orb in front of the palm tree. When we returned home and viewed the digital photos, I was delighted. Not only had we gotten some decent orb activity, Brownie had made his presence known. I looked at the picture for less than two seconds before realizing it had a face in it. Not an ordinary face though, Brownie's face! It seems to me that this famous ambassador is still doing his job: sitting next to visitors or weary travelers in a cool shady corner of the park; keeping an eye on the passing traffic; walking alongside pets that still reside in this world; maybe even romping through the park to visit with other worldly residents. Whatever the case, Brownie is still doing his job."

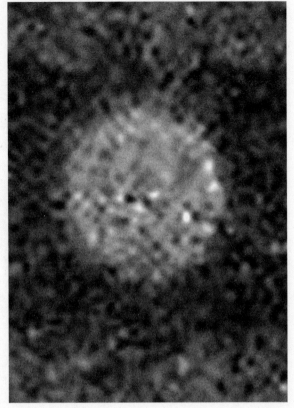

A close-up of Brownie's orb.

HIS CATS WERE GHOST DETECTORS

The Personal Experience of Eric Wilson

"In the late 1990s our family moved into an old two-story house that still had asphalt shingles, real wood flooring, and a genuine dining room complete with a swinging door into the kitchen. We chose the place because of its proximity to my work and its old style interior beauty. I took a small room with French doors as my office. All of our bedrooms were upstairs, so I didn't have to worry about waking anyone up during my late-night activities.

"Shortly after we moved in, I began noticing some noises in the living room when I worked late in the evenings. I chalked it up to one of the cats, who had a tendency to get wild. But as the weeks passed, I kept hearing noises outside of the room and became curious. They seemed to happen around 1:00 A.M. on a regular basis, so I started timing my activities to make sure I was in the living room at that time. At 12:55 A.M., I would go out and relax in the dark living room, hoping to solve the mystery of the sounds. At first nothing happened. Every time I would go out there, no noises. If I stayed in my office, I'd hear them. I had almost decided that my theory of the cats being responsible was correct. Then one night they were all in the office when the noises started.

"Late one Friday night, while I sat in our dark living room, I made careful note of the location of our cats. At 1:00 A.M., I heard someone coming down the stairs. The cats also heard the movement and went to the stairs

In 1974 Alfred Hollidge took a photograph of his cat, Monet. When the picture was developed, he noticed a second cat in the photograph, which Monet seemed to be looking at. The appearance of the second cat has not been explained.

expectantly. Step by step I heard someone come down the stairs, but no one was there. Then, as the footsteps reached the bottom step, the cats ran toward the unseen entity as if their favorite friend had just entered the room. As the sounds of someone walking moved across the living room, they followed. I heard the doorknob rattle as if someone was checking the lock. I think that was the point that the invisible being decided that it was okay to be around our family.

"After the initial display, we had things going on all the time. It was almost as if two families lived in the house. Doors would open; floorboards would creak. One night I woke up to find that every light upstairs had been turned on. I was panicked, thinking that we had a break-in. But there were no physical intruders. My little girl was sick at the time, and I think the spirits were insisting that I check on her. The ghosts even tried helping with the cats. Our cats are spoiled and prefer to drink running water out of the faucet in the bathroom. We'd often turn the water on and let them get a drink. Several weeks after the upstairs lighting incident, I was in my office and heard the water come on in the bathroom sink at full force. After the first time, it wasn't uncommon to hear the water turn on in the downstairs bathroom. It was pretty amazing though, to realize something could actually turn the handle on the cold water from fully off to fully on. We had many paranormal occurrences at that house, and we loved living there."

"I'M A GHOST IN THE FORM OF A WEASEL"

While it would seem that the great majority of accounts of animal spirits tell of benign and loving entities that return to their owners for a final visit, or to provide a reassurance that life goes on beyond physical death, there are tales that speak of more hostile and frightening animal beings.

It was in the fall of 1931 that a mysterious entity manifested in the home of James T. Irving and his family on the Isle of Man. His daughter, Voirrey, saw it first, just seconds before Irving caught a glimpse of it himself. It was as large as a full-grown rat, with a flat snout and a small yellow face. Voirrey suggested that perhaps it had been the creature responsible for the scratching noises they had heard in the parlor on the previous night.

The strange animal was not satisfied with simple pranks and disturbances for very long. It began to mimic the calls and cries of the family's barnyard animals. Irving then made the remarkable discovery that the creature was extraordinarily intelligent. Members of the family only had to call out the name of an animal and the mysterious creature would respond with the correct imitation. The night noises began to increase, and the family was beginning to find them less than pleasant. Their strange visitor would blow, spit, and growl from the dark corners of the bedrooms, keeping the family awake all hours of the night. Once, in an effort to lull herself to sleep, Voirrey began to chant nursery rhymes aloud. She was startled to hear the weird animal begin to repeat the rhymes after she had finished. In an excited voice, she called to her parents to come and share her discovery. The creature had developed the ability to talk! The Irvings stood at the door of their daughter's bedroom and exchanged incredulous stares. The animal's voice, although a full two octaves higher than any human's, was clear and distinct as it sing-songed nursery rhymes.

The mysterious animal quickly put itself on intimate terms with the Irvings, addressing them by their first names, "Jim" and "Maggie." It carried on long conversations with them and announced that it had chosen to make its home with them. The Irvings were not very enthusiastic about having the strange animal become a permanent resident. The family got so little sleep that they were almost to the point of selling the farm and leaving. However, they realized that it would not be easy to sell a farm that was not only quite isolated but also haunted. And their talking rodent was no longer a secret. On January 10, 1932, the Manchester *Daily Dispatch* and the London *Daily Sketch* both ran articles on the mysterious "talking weasel."

"Have I ever heard a weasel speak?" wondered a reporter for the *Daily Dispatch*. "I do not know, but I do know that I heard, today, a voice I never imagined could issue from a human throat." The journalist found the Irving family "sane, honest, and responsible folk not likely to indulge in difficult long-drawn-out practical jokes to make them the talk of the world." As the number of newspapermen wanting information about the ghost increased, James Irving insisted that there were no ghosts on his farm. He explained that it was only a strange animal that had taken up residence on his property.

Since the peculiar animal's arrival, the "talking weasel" had caused ghostly poltergeist phenomena to occur. Strange scratchings and unexplainable sounds were followed by furniture and small objects moving about on their own. But this ghost did something that that no other entity of its ilk has ever done before or since: during the course of its stay with the Irvings, it left the family more than 50 rabbits on the kitchen floor. Each of the rabbits had been strangled. If a true weasel had done the stalking, it surely would have used its teeth on the throat of its prey. As the phenomena increased and the entity became stronger, it claimed to be a mongoose born near Delhi, India, and it often used Indian words and sang Indian folk songs. The creature's claim that it was a mongoose was reinforced by the fact that a farmer in the local village of Doarlish Cashen had once brought a number of the animals from India to kill off the rabbits that had become a threat to his field crops. No one ever received more than a glimpse of the animal that had moved in with the Irvings, but those who did see the strange thing described it in terms that might well have applied to a small mongoose.

James Irving began calling his uninvited guest "Jef." This name met with the approval of the self-proclaimed mongoose, who told Irving that when he was in India, he lived with a tall man who wore a green turban on his head. Jef also informed Irving that he was born on June 7, 1852, which made him 79 years old.

Jef's activities were by no means confined to the Irving cottage. He wandered far afield to stalk rabbits for the family meal, and he took delight in hiding in village garages and in bringing back gossip to share with the Irvings. The weird entity also had a cruel streak that it most often unleashed on the villagers. Once, it harassed a group of men repairing a road by carrying off their lunches. Several of the workmen swore that they had seen their lunch bags being toted off by some invisible force. Another time, Jef was blamed for striking a garage mechanic with a large iron bolt. Irving later said that Jef had boasted of the deed.

Arthur Springer, a retired inspector for Scotland Yard, took this photograph in 1916. The dog was not present in the frame when the photograph was taken.

The famous psychical researcher Harry Price sent an associate to the Isle of Man to investigate the news stories that he had begun to collect on the Irving family and their unexplained guest. It was a rare stranger who made a favorable impression on Jef, and Price's investigator, a Captain Macdonald, was no exception to the rule. From the safety of his hiding place, Jef screamed that the man was a doubter and demanded that James Irving send him away. When Macdonald tried to coax Jef out of his crack in the wall to pose for a picture, the entity displayed its ill humor by squirting water on the investigator. Later, it hurled a needle at the man, which missed him and struck a tea pot. Irving tried to console the researcher by revealing that Jef often threw things at the family. When the mongoose was seen sitting on a wall in the farmyard, Macdonald pleaded with Voirrey to take his camera and see if she could approach Jef and get a picture of him. The girl began walking toward him, speaking to the entity in a low, pleasant voice. She lifted the camera to take Jef's photo, but he was gone before she could click the shutter. Captain Macdonald received little more than the entity's curses for his troubles, but at least he had heard the mysterious mongoose speak and got a glimpse of it. When Price went out to the island to investigate the disturbances for himself, the temperamental Jef was silent during the entire duration of his stay.

The entity demanded to be served food by the Irvings and was especially fond of bananas and pastries. Although it often seemed genuinely concerned about the family's welfare, the mongoose did not relish any open expression of affection. Once Mrs. Irving put her hand into Jef's hiding place and began to stroke the animal's fur. She instantly withdrew her hand with a sharp cry of pain. Jef had bitten her and had drawn blood. The fact that Mrs. Irving had actually touched the manifestation encouraged Harry Price to suggest that the family attempt to obtain a bit of Jef's fur for laboratory analysis. As if it had read their thoughts, the mongoose awakened the family late one night and promised the Irvings that it was going to present them with a special gift. Jef directed them to a particular bowl on a shelf in the kitchen. The Irvings turned on the lights and hurried quickly downstairs to seek out the appointed bowl. There, in its center, was a tuft of fur. The next morning, James Irving mailed the fur off to Price, who, in turn, relayed it to the London Zoo. Unfortunately, it turned out that the cunning Jef had simply played a prank. The fur was that of a dog, not a mongoose.

Determined to obtain some shred of tangible evidence of the creature's physical existence, Price sent the Irvings four plasticine blocks on which Jef could stamp the impressions of his feet. James Irving set the blocks in Jef's hole in the wall and coaxed his strange house guest to imprint its feet in the doughy material. The next morning, the family awakened to Jef's cursing that making impressions in the plasticine was "hard as hell," but he had done it, and he bade them to go and look. That time it seemed as though the entity had really cooperated with the family's wish to secure a permanent memento of its visitation. Excitedly, James Irving shipped the casts off to Price and anxiously went back to his farm to await the results of analysis and identification.

Mr. R. I. Peacock of the British Natural History Museum's zoological department concluded that one print might have been made by a dog, but the others were of no mammal known to him, unless they belonged to an American raccoon. In Peacock's opinion, he doubted if the casts represented foot tracks at all. He stated that the tracks had most certainly not been made by a mongoose. R. S. Lambert, an associate of Price's, suggested that Jef was voice and nothing more, but witnesses claimed to have seen something scampering about that was decidedly a physical being. Throughout the duration of the phenomena, James Irving wrote in a journal. In the journal he stated: "The mongoose said to my wife, 'I know what I am, but I shan't tell you. I might let you see me, but not to get to know me. I'm a freak.... If you saw me [as I truly exist] you'd be petrified, mummified.... I'm a ghost, in the form of a weasel.'"

Jef continued to live with the Irvings for four years, alternately chatting with them or cursing them. Then, the mysterious talking mongoose simply seemed to fade into nothingness, becoming but another of the Isle of Man's many legends. In 1947 a farmer actually shot a mongoose near the village of Cashen's Cap. There was a great deal of conjecture on the part of the villagers whether or not this animal might have been a descendant of one of the mongooses turned loose in 1914, but the farmer was certain that the creature had not spoken to him before he pulled the trigger.

GHOST DOGS FROM BACHELOR BOULEY'S HELLHOLE

Russell Madsen said that not far from where he grew up in Missouri there was a long lane that led to an old haunted, burned-out farm known as Bachelor Bouley's Hellhole. There are a number of local legends about Bachelor Bouley. Some say he lived with a pack of hounds he used for hunting; others say he was a bootlegger and that his still blew up his house. There's the legend that Bouley practiced black magic, and one night when his satanic majesty came to collect Bouley's soul, the devil's flaming footprints caught Bouley's house on fire. Still others insist that one night some angry prohibitionists in a frenzy of self-righteousness judged Bouley an old reprobate who sold moonshine to minors, and burned the house to the ground with him and all his howling hounds inside.

Madsen said that there are two consistent elements in the legends about Bouley:

1. He was a cranky old recluse whose only companions were a dozen or more hunting dogs that lived, ate, and slept with him in his ramshackle farm house.

2. The angry spirits of the hounds that were burned alive with their master still protected the place.

According to Madsen, over the years it had become a rite of passage for teenage boys to drive out to Bachelor Bouley's Hellhole and tempt the ghost hounds to chase them. Over the years dozens of people have sworn that something hellish resides on the property, and there have been all kinds of testimonials about ripped clothes, clawed fenders, and scratched faces that were attributed to Bouley's hellhounds.

"When I was 16, my buddies and I heard that a bunch of senior football players had driven out to Bachelor Bouley's and gotten the devil scared out of them," Madsen said. "They said they heard the hounds baying, howling, and jumping around their car. The toughest guy among them got out of the car and swore that something ripped the sleeve of his letter jacket. The others pulled him back in and they burned rubber getting out of there."

Madsen and his friends Don, Todd, and Joe decided to test their manhood against Bouley's hellhounds. Don drove the group out to Bouley's house, because he had managed to get his father's new station wagon by telling him that the gang was going to a drive-in movie. When they pulled up next to the charred ruins of the house, Don shut off the headlights because he said that he wanted to be able to see if the ghost dogs' eyes really glowed in the dark. According to Madsen, they heard noises that sounded very much like a pack of very large dogs surrounding their car. "Within moments we could hear and feel some very solid *things* bumping up against the sides, hood, and rear of the station wagon," he recalled. "Joe wanted to get the hell out of there. Todd just sat there shivering. I pleaded with Don not to get out and investigate as he claimed he was going to do before we left town."

And then the howling started. A high-pitched, mournful howling that Madsen said he would remember for the rest of his life. "Todd clamped his hands over his ears and began to cry," he said. "Joe, sitting in the front seat beside Don, punched him in the shoulder and shouted at him to burn rubber and get us the hell out of there. Don seemed paralyzed, as if he had somehow been placed under a spell by the terrible frequency of the ghost dogs' ear-piercing howls. At last, he managed to shake himself free of the fear or the fascination that had held him immobile, and he tore out of the place as if we were truly escaping from the outer rim of hell."

The following day was a Saturday, and when Madsen went over to Don's house to talk over the incredible events of the night before, he saw that the new station wagon was covered with dozens of scratches that looked like they had been made by the paws of very large dogs. Don's father was angry and demanding to know what kind of drive-in movie would produce effects like that.

Russell Madsen concluded his story by stating that none of his friends ever went back to Bachelor Bouley's Hellhole. "But I hear that teenage boys still have to drive out to Bouley's," he said. "Like I said, it's like some kind of rite of passage for boys in that region."

THE GHOST DOG THAT SMOTHERED A CHILD

One of the most frightening accounts in the annals of the paranormal is this report of a ghostly dog—or an evil entity manifesting in the form of a dog—that suffocated a child.

In May 1955 the Pell family moved into their new home on Coxwell Road in Birmingham, England. During their first weekend in the house, they were awakened by the sound of a slamming door. Frank Pell was puzzled because he knew that he had carefully locked all the doors before retiring that evening, so he got out of bed to investigate. As he stood in the kitchen, he heard a scraping sound like the noise of a scrambling animal. After that the house was silent, and Pell returned to bed.

As time passed, the Pells received nightly visits from an array of strange sounds. The greatest concentration of noises occurred around midnight, and no matter how the doors had been secured, they would bang to-and-fro as if they had a will of their own. Eerie whispers and incomprehensible phrases echoed in the air around the family. Both Frank Pell and his wife lay awake at night, listening and wondering, knowing that what was happening in their home could not have a natural explanation. Their dream house had begun transforming itself into a nightmare.

Once while she was cleaning the bedroom, Mrs. Pell felt a cold draft and what she described as "icy, intangible fingers" running over her body. Even though the sense of evil had clearly presented itself to the Pells, both were sure that fear of it would only give it greater power over them. They reasoned that only those who feared supernatural forces could be harmed by them.

Then one hot June morning, the family awakened to find that their baby had suffocated during the night. The child had been in the best of health and no mark of violence appeared on its body. Shortly after the child's burial, one of their sons startled them by asking if the baby had gone with the little white dog. The Pells knew that no dog had ever entered their house, so they asked their son when he had last seen the white dog. "On the night the baby left us," the boy replied. "The dog was sitting on the baby's face." Mrs. Pell became hysterical, and Frank could not calm her. The thought that a supernatural force had suffocated her baby to death horrified her. Although they summoned a priest to exorcise the negative spirits from the house, the bumping and banging continued with even greater regularity.

Although the photographer did not notice anything unusual when this picture was taken, when it was developed strange figures resembling a woman and a dog were noticed in the doorway. This family had just moved into this house, which they later found out had been inhabited by an old woman and her bulldog.

By early July the feeling of evil in their home had become very strong, and Frank Pell feared for his wife. One day he rushed to the stairs where a frightening scene awaited him. His wife stood on the upstairs landing, transfixed with terror. Her limbs had stiffened and her hands clutched frantically at her side. The veins along her neck had swollen. Her eyes bulged with terror, and her mouth gaped open in a silent scream. When Pell ran up the stairs to help her, he ran directly into an invisible force that would not let him pass. It seemed to shroud him like net. At last he broke through the wall of evil with a powerful lunge. At that instant, his wife's screams filled the house.

Without bothering to pack, the Pells took their children and left the house. Later, friends collected their belongings. They, too, heard the strange whispers and the weird thumpings, and once they finished packing, no inducement could bring them back into the house.

16

Restored Scenes of the Past

Can a scene from the past return and assume temporary physical reality once again? The conventional idea of time existing as some sort of stream, flowing along in one dimension, is obviously inadequate. In this view, the past does not exist; it is gone forever. Neither does the future exist, because it has not yet happened. The only thing that one can rely upon is the nebulous present. But if the past completely ceased to exist, we would have no memory of it. Yet each of us has a large and varied memory bank. The past, therefore, must exist in some sense. Perhaps the past does not exist as physical or material reality, but in some sphere or dimension of its own. It may be, as some researchers have theorized, that our subconscious minds—our transcendental selves—do not differentiate between past, present, and future. To the subconscious mind, all spheres or dimensions of time may exist as part of the "eternal now."

A materialized ghost may seem as solid as any human. Modern science no longer regards solids as "solid"; rather, they are understood to be congealed wave patterns. Psychical researcher James Crenshaw notes that the whole imposing array of subatomic particles—electrons, protons, positrons, neutrinos, mesons—achieve particle-like characteristics in a manner similar to the way that wave patterns in tones and overtones produce characteristic sounds. Crenshaw theorizes that ghosts may be made up of transitory, emergent matter that appears and disappears. This matter "can sometimes be seen and felt before disappearing.... [It] behaves like ordinary matter but still has no permanent existence in the framework of our conception of space and time. In fact, after its transitory manifestations, it seems to be absorbed back into another dimension or dimensions."

[319]

GHOSTS OF THE PAST

Psychoanalyst Dr. Nandor Fodor theorized that genuinely haunted houses were those that had soaked up emotional unpleasantness from former occupants. Years or even centuries later, the emotional energy may become reactivated when later occupants of the house undergo a similar emotional disturbance. Therefore, a haunting—composed of mysterious knocks and rappings, opening and slamming doors, cold drafts, appearance of ghostly figures, etc.—is produced by the merging of the two energies, one from the past, the other from the present.

According to Fodor's theory, a reservoir of absorbed emotions that lies dormant in a house can only be activated when emotional instability is present. Thus, homes that have a history of happy occupants are in little danger of becoming haunted.

There is another kind of paranormal phenomenon in which an entire section of land seems to be haunted. In most cases of this particular type of haunting, a tragic scene from the past is recreated in precise detail, as if some cosmic photographer had committed the vast panorama to ethereal film. Battles are waged, trains are wrecked, ships are sunk, the screams of earthquake victims echo through the night—exactly as they took place months, years, or centuries before.

Thomas Edison theorized that energy, like matter, is indestructible. He became intrigued by the idea of developing a radio that would be sensitive enough to pick up the sounds of times past—sounds that were only audible to the psychically sensitive. Edison hypothesized that the vibrations of every word ever uttered still echoed in the ether. If this theory should ever be established, it would explain phenomena such as the restoration of scenes from the past. Just as the emotions of certain individuals permeate a certain room and cause a ghost to be seen by those possessing similar telepathic affinity, so it might be that emotionally charged scenes of the past become imprinted upon the psychic ether of an entire landscape.

An alternate theory maintains that souls or energy emotionally held to an area may telepathically invade the mind of a sensitive person and enable him/her to see the scene as "they" once saw it.

It cannot be denied that some locales have definitely built up their own atmospheres over the years and that such auras often give sensitive people feelings of uneasiness, fear, and discomfort. Whether this may be caused by energy, psychic residue, or an impression of the actual event in the psychic ether is a question that remains unsolved at the present stage of parapsychological research.

A Ghostly Reenactment of a Village Fair

On a rainy evening in October 1916, Edith Olivier was driving from Devizes to Swindon in Wiltshire, England. The evening was so dreary that Olivier earnestly wished to find a nice, warm inn in which to spend the night. After she left the main road, she found herself driving down a strange avenue lined by huge gray megaliths. She concluded that she had to be approaching Avebury. Although Olivier had never been to Avebury before, she was familiar with pictures of the area and knew that the place had originally been a circular megalithic temple that was reached by long stone avenues.

When she reached the end of the avenue, she got out of her automobile so that she might better view the megaliths. As she stood on a large bank of earth, she saw a number of cottages among the megaliths, and was surprised to see that, in spite of the rain, there seemed to be a village fair in progress. The laughing villagers were walking merrily about with flares and torches, trying their skill at various booths, and applauding lustily for the talented performers at various shows. Olivier became greatly amused at the carefree manner in which the villagers enjoyed themselves, completely oblivious to the rain. Men, women, and children walked about without any protective outer garments and not a single umbrella could be seen. Olivier would have joined the happy villagers at their fair if she had not been growing increasingly uncomfortable in the rain, which was becoming steadily heavier. She decided that she was not made of hardy stock like the villagers, and got back into her automobile to resume her trip.

Olivier did not visit Avebury for another nine years. At that time, she was perplexed to read in a guidebook that, although a village fair had once been an annual occurrence in Avebury, the custom had been abolished in 1850! When she protested that she had personally witnessed a village fair in Avebury in 1916, Olivier was offered a sound and convincing rebuttal from a local guide. Even more astounding, perhaps, was the information she acquired concerning the megaliths. The particular avenue she had driven down on the rainy night of her first visit had disappeared before 1800.

Witnessing an Ancient Rite of Animal Sacrifice

When the Beckers of Ebenezer, New York, built their new home, they knew that the lot they had purchased had originally been part of the Seneca Indian reservation. On the night of February 22, 1966, Carolyn Becker took her dog for a walk along the Cazenovia Creek. Suddenly from out of nowhere, she heard the howl of a strange dog. Her dog heard it, too, for his hackles rose as he froze in his tracks and pricked up his ears.

Then on the bank of the creek, a tall pole decorated with cloth strips of vivid colors appeared. Carolyn said that she watched in astonishment as a buckskin-clad Native American man wearing a headdress was strangling a beautiful white dog. As she stood observing the strange scene, the man began to wrap the limp body of the dog in brightly colored strips of cloth. Then he wound strands of wampum around the dog's broken neck. She saw campfires that were dimly glowing, heard throbbing drums in the distance, and the smell of tobacco smoke invaded her senses. The scene soon faded, and the woman and her dog were left standing and shivering in the snow.

After doing some research on the customs of the Seneca, Becker realized that she had witnessed the Seneca's New Year jubilee ceremony, in which a pure white dog was sacrificed for the tribe's sins. Becker searched through the old records of the reservation and learned that the ceremony had last been held on those grounds in 1841. She could only deduce from this information that time had somehow turned backward to allow her to witness this ceremony.

A Ghostly Street Fight

Francis J. Sibolski said that over a 20-year period, he has witnessed a phantom street fight take place outside of his home 13 times. His wife has also witnessed the fight on several occasions. Sibolski claims that from his front window, he has seen a 1937 Plymouth taxicab pull up and disgorge two angry men in their twenties. The punching and mauling lasts about three minutes, then the smaller of the two men jumps into the waiting taxicab and speeds off. The larger man rummages for a cigarette, shakes the last one out of the pack, crumples the package and throws it on to the sidewalk, and begins to walk toward the corner. Before the taxi reaches the corner or before the big man has taken more than a few steps, the tableau fades away. However, the cigarette package has existed for several minutes, sometimes even hours, *after* the tableau has vanished

Sibolski said he researched the incident to the extent that he was able to identify the two men [now both deceased, though one was still alive when Sibolski began witnessing the restored scene from the past]. He obtained testimonials from those who remember the original altercation. Sibolski once approached the phantom scene and attempted to become a part of the past. When he came within six or seven feet of the fighters, his nostrils and throat suddenly became congested with a taste and smell that recalled colds he suffered as a child. While he was capable of moving, he had no desire to. He retreated to his porch steps feeling very odd and watched the act complete itself.

Driving Down a Street Out of Time

Restored scenes of the past are not all as dramatic as observing an ancient rite of animal sacrifice or witnessing a phantom street fight. All Alan did was take the same route home that he had traveled for years. Without deviating from his habitual route, Alan suddenly found himself driving down a street completely unrecognizable to him. Everything seemed quiet—too quiet for his liking—and when he tried to pick up a station on his car radio, all he got was static. The only other car in sight was extremely old and parked in front of a little diner named "Henry's." When Alan reached the intersection, he remembers experiencing a "funny feeling like going through cool water." After that, everything was all right. Alan knew where he was, and he came out just where he should have been all along.

Alan claims to have driven that route a couple of thousand times without ever having seen a diner named Henry's. Even if he had taken a wrong turn, his knowledge of the town would have enabled him to recognize the street. He asked friends if anyone knew of such a diner, but no one had ever heard of a Henry's. Finally, in city records he found that a diner with that name had once existed in 1914, on a street that had been destroyed by fire in 1923 and rebuilt in 1926.

Sharing a Campground with Ghosts

In August 1941 Leonard Hall and a number of friends on an extended fishing trip decided to camp out along the Upper Current River in the Ozarks. Just before sunrise, Hall was awakened by the sound of many voices speaking in a strange language. He opened his eyes, and to his amazement he saw that another party of campers had moved into the area while he and his friends had been sleeping.

Several figures were silhouetted against a roaring fire about 100 yards from his tent. Hall was further astounded when he saw that the entire clearing along the riverbank was ringed by campfires. The majority of the figures were recognizable as Native American men dressed only in breechcloths. They spoke a language unknown to him, but Hall could hear other people speaking what sounded like Spanish. When he realized that he was hearing Spanish voices, he rubbed his eyes and pinched himself to make sure he was awake, for there, sitting around a campfire in the Ozarks, were men sporting the armor of Spanish *conquistadores*. Hall feared that he was experiencing either an extremely vivid dream or some dreadful mental aberration. He did not awaken his companions to confirm what he was witnessing. Instead, he returned to his sleeping bag and managed to doze off again, somewhat fitfully.

The following morning, with the incomprehensible scenes of the night fresh in his mind, Hall made a careful check of the riverbank but failed to unearth any evidence that he and his friends had shared the site with other campers. Hall's curiosity was aroused, however, and he decided to do a bit of private research. He did not release his findings until several years later. In the interim he learned that bands of *conquistadores* under the leaderships of Hernando de Soto and Francisco Vasquez de Coronado had actually been in the area of the Upper Current River in August 1541. In his story, eventually written up in the St. Louis *Post-Dispatch*, Hall wondered if having camped on the same stretch of ground the adventurers had chosen exactly 400 years earlier had allowed him to view what happened in another time.

He Was Trying to Get to His Wedding on Time

In his book *Orbits of the Unknown*, John Macklin related the experience of Father Litvinov. Just before midnight one evening in 1933, Father Litinov opened the door to his church in order to admit a young man who had a look of horror on his face and was wearing ornate knee breeches. Once the priest managed to calm his visitor's hysteria, he heard a most incredible story.

The young man said his name was Dmitri Girshkov, and he claimed that he was to have been married that day. On his way to the church, he had stopped by the cemetery to visit the grave of a boyhood friend. As he stood there paying his respects, he was startled to see an image of his friend, who had been dead for over a year. As he turned away from the cemetery to make his way back to the village, he became terrified when he realized that nearly everything in his small Siberian town was different. Before Father Litinov could say a word, Dmitri ran from the church, shouting in anguish that he had to find his family, friends, and bride. Father Litvinov noticed a strange light and a gray mist around the young man, and in the blink of an eye, he had vanished.

Greatly intrigued by the provocative experience, the priest went through old parish records. He discovered that in the past two centuries, a schoolmaster and two other priests experienced encounters with the boy who stepped out of the past (or who stepped into the future, depending upon one's point of view). In his parish records he also found the name of Dmitri Girshkov, the young man who had stopped by a friend's grave on his wedding day in 1746 and then mysteriously disappeared.

The Strange Adventure of Petit Trianon

When Eleanor Jourdain and Anne Moberly took the train from Paris to Versailles on August 10, 1901, they did not expect to meet Marie Antoinette. They also did not expect to encounter people speaking in an archaic French dialect, or dressed in costumes that dated from the late eighteenth century. These and other mysterious circumstances transformed a tourist's visit to the palace grounds.

Like all tourists, the two academics, Moberly and Jourdain, principal and vice principal of St. Hugh's College, Oxford, began their promenade with

The Château de Versailles.

a visit to the long rooms and galleries of the palace. It was a pleasant afternoon. The late summer had been hot, but on this day a protective curtain of gray cloud had been drawn across the Sun, and a cool breeze enticed the travelers to extend their visit to Petit Trianon, the "little château" that Louis XVI of France gave to his wife Marie Antoinette.

The two friends started out on the path that would take them to the pavilion where Marie Antoinette and her friends had diverted themselves by playing at peasant life, a pastime that was in vogue among the French aristocracy at that time. They made their way down the great steps of the palace and past the fountains. They walked along the central avenue until they reached the fountainhead of the pond, then they turned right, as indicated in their guide book.

The mood of the day seemed to change as they passed the Grand Trianon and turned off the paved walkway onto a broad, grassy drive. In their haste, they missed the path that would have taken them directly to the Petit Trianon. Instead, they crossed it and walked up a lane leading in the other direction. As they proceeded along this route, Moberly saw a woman lean out of the window of a nearby building to shake a dust cloth. Only after they compared notes many days later did Moberly learn that Jourdain had not seen the woman.

The travelers found that their single path suddenly branched out into three. Confused, and believing they had somehow gotten off the main path, they decided they would ask the two men they supposed were gardeners who were walking just ahead of them with a wheelbarrow. The two tourists noticed that the men were wearing very strange three-cornered hats made of black velvet, but they were able to answer Jourdain's question and direct the women to the path that led to the Petit Trianon. But that path ended abruptly when another path intersected it at an angle and led in different direction. The new path seemed like a dividing line between sections of a patchwork quilt; it chopped off the blue-green lawn they had been walking through. The land on the other side of the path resembled wild woodland, with tufts of wild grass and dead leaves scattered all about. The women began to walk down the new path, but the environment they entered looked somewhat unnatural. Though it was still afternoon, the light was suddenly diminished. Although the wind still moved around them, no branches waved, no leaves stirred. The trees almost appeared to be part of a woven tapestry, and they cast no shadows.

Then the women saw a bandstand, and a man who was sitting with his back turned to them. The man was dressed in the same manner as the man that had given them the directions that proved to be incorrect. As the women approached, the man turned toward them and they gasped at the sight of his face. His countenance was dark, his skin was pock-marked, and his mouth drooped like a Greek mask of tragedy, revealing an appearance of decay and evil that could not be concealed by staring, sightless eyes. The two tourists were so stricken by this sight that they did not see the other man until he called to them. The frightened women spun around to face the newcomer and composed themselves enough to ask him for directions. As he pointed the way, he spoke with an accent that neither of the two teachers grasped. They thanked him, nevertheless. At once the man ran off, disappearing into the woods. But still the pair heard the sound of his running footsteps.

Moberly and Jourdain started off in the direction their mysterious guide had indicated. Hurrying along a narrow path nearly roofed by overgrown trees, the women finally found themselves before the Petit Trianon. Rough grass like one might expect to find growing happenstance around the cottage of a French peasant in the days of Louis XVI covered the terrace around the north and west sides of the house. The two tourists noticed a woman who was completely unaware of their presence holding a pad at arm's length and busily sketching the scene. Jourdain could not help remarking that the woman was dressed like a picture she remembered seeing of Marie Antoinette, complete with full skirt and wide white hat. There had to be some kind of historical pageant in progress.

A portrait of Marie Antoinette.

As the two women walked up the steps to the top of the terrace, the strange atmosphere of the place hung over the scene like a musty blanket. When they reached the top, they looked back at the woman with the sketch pad. She glanced up to meet their gaze, and they saw that her face was old and

Real Ghosts, Restless Spirits, and Haunted Places

ugly. A door slammed, and a young man dressed for kitchen work stood before them on the terrace. He carried a broom and seemed to have stepped out to shake the dust form it. He seemed as surprised by their presence as they were with his. He asked if they were lost. The two women politely refused his offer to show them the way and made their way into the Petit Trianon, where they found a wedding in progress. The wedding was not taking place in the time of Marie Antoinette; rather, the event was unmistakably taking place in 1901. As they stood among the cheerful celebrants of a marriage, Jourdain and Moberly felt the cloud of depression that had followed them to the Petit Trianon lift. The women decided to take a carriage back to Versailles.

A week passed and the two women had still not spoken of the strange afternoon they spent walking to the Petit Trianon. After they had discussed what they had seen that day, Jourdain and Moberly concluded that the place was haunted, and they had somehow either walked into scenes from the past or they had encountered a number of ghosts during their afternoon tour of the estate.

Jourdain and Moberly returned to Versailles, separately and together. Jourdain's second visit to the haunted grounds was on January 2, 1902. In contrast to the late summer day on which the two had made their first visit to Versailles, the day of Jourdain's return was cold and rainy. Rather than walking to the Petit Trianon this time, she decided to make the journey in her own carriage. During the drive, she tried to recall the placement of each incident that had occurred when she and Moberly made their memorable trip on foot. Once again she saw the darkness deepen. The same depression she had felt the first time descended upon her with the cold rain. She puzzled over the activity of men who were out in the rain, filling a cart with sticks. She glanced away for an instant, and when she looked back the laborers and their cart were gone and the landscape was barren for as far as she could see. She hastened through the village and found herself lost in a maze of crisscrossing, diagonal paths that all seemed to end in other paths.

Slipping through the dripping woods was a man in the same costume as the one who had given them directions during their first visit. Suddenly, Jourdain felt as if she were being jostled by a passing crowd. She heard voices speaking French, and they seemed very close to her ears, but she saw no one beside her. Music played by unseen musicians drifted in from the distance. Jourdain looked at her map and quickly selected a path, hoping to get out of that other-worldly place as quickly as possible.

She started out, only to find herself drawn to another path by a sense of urgency she could not understand. She bolted onto the path she had first chosen and was immediately lost. The clouds seemed to lower, and the rain became very dense. Grayness was everywhere. Even the raindrops had the look of wet clay. The ground itself appeared to dissolve in grayness and ooze over the edges of the paved walk. Fear all but drew the breath from Jourdain's lungs as she desperately sought her way back to the present. In her haste, she almost ran into a bearded giant of a man who suddenly appeared on the path in front of her. Eleanor was too tired to be frightened. Catching her breath, she simply asked for directions. He told her to follow the path that she was on. The man's directions proved accurate, and soon a badly shaken Jourdain was on her way back to Versailles.

Although Jourdain made several trips to Versailles with classes of her students, it was not until July 1904 that Moberly accompanied her again. As Jourdain had told her incredulous friend, things had changed since their first visit. Gates that were open when the two had first visited the grounds had been closed and locked, and the passing years placed a seal of cobwebs upon them. Only the ghosts that remained at Petit Trianon knew when the doors had last been opened. Marie Antoinette had gone to sketch other scenes, and in her place rose a well-rooted shrub of a size that gave mute testimony to the decades of growth that it had seen come and go.

Had the great wheel of time somehow turned back, bringing the past into the present? Or had the two women somehow managed to summon spirits from an earlier time? Or as some of their critics believe, had they imagined the whole series of remarkable events? When they later published a book describing their strange afternoon at Versailles (*An Adventure*, 1911), both wrote under pseudonyms. The women were not the sort to make brash, emotional statements containing more drama than reason, and they stoutly defended their version of their strange encounter with ghosts of late-eighteenth-century France. They were, after all, academics: Jourdain held the post of Taylorian Lecturer in French at Oxford University, and Moberly was the principal of an Oxford girl's school. Both were daughters of Anglican clergyman. They were both interested in music, not only in the areas of listening or playing but in the theory of harmony itself. Interestingly, both women were psychically sensitive, but they were reluctant to speak of their abilities and instead spoke of their "horror of many forms of occultism."

Opening a Door to the Past

At approximately 8:50 A.M. on October 3, 1963, Colleen Buterbaugh, secretary to Dean Sam Dahl of Wesleyan University, Lincoln, Nebraska, was on her way to deliver a message from the dean's office to a professor when she opened a door and walked into an office that was in the past. As Buterbaugh entered the first room of the professor's suite, she suddenly smelled a musty, intensely disagreeable odor. The room was filled with a deathly silence. Standing before her was a tall, black-haired woman dressed in a floor-length skirt. The woman took no notice of Buterbaugh and raised her right arm toward the top right hand shelves of an old music cabinet. The tall woman was not transparent, but Buterbaugh knew that she wasn't real either. While Buterbaugh looked at the woman, her whole body just faded away, all at once.

Buterbaugh looked out the window. It was then that she received the fright that sent her hurriedly scurrying from the office. There were no modern buildings or streets anywhere in sight. In fact, most of the campus was just an open field. All at once Buterbaugh realized that she was no longer on the college campus in the year 1963. Fearing that she had somehow stepped through a door into another time dimension, she quickly fled the room. Once back in the hallway, she was assured that she had returned to the present.

The startled and confused secretary hurried back to her desk in Dean Dahl's office. She tried to work, but the whole bizarre incident was too much for her to keep to herself. She entered the dean's office, and he got to his feet to help the pale and obviously shaken woman to a chair. He listened courteously and without comment to her story, then he asked her to accompany him to the office of Dr. Glenn Callen, chairman of the division of social sciences, who had been on the Wesleyan faculty since 1900. Once again, the secretary was fortunate to have a listener who heard her out and treated her account with respect.

After a careful quizzing of Buterbaugh and the aid of a number of old college yearbooks, Callen theorized that the secretary had somehow walked into the office as it had been c. 1920. Lengthy research managed to produce a photograph of the campus as Buterbaugh had seen it. The picture had been taken in 1915. More investigation through the college's old yearbooks revealed the picture of a music teacher who fit Buterbaugh's description of the woman she had seen in the office. The teacher's name was Clara Mills, who at some point in the late 1930s had died shortly before 9:00 A.M. in the very office Buterbaugh had seen her in. The filing cabinet that Buterbaugh had seen her opening was found to contain choral arrangements dating back to Mills's tenure at the college (1912–1936).

Psychical researchers Gardner Murphy and H. L. Klemme employed hypnotic time regression as a means of eliciting further details of Buterbaugh's remarkable paranormal experience. After they had placed the secretary in a state of hypnotic trance, they instructed her to relive and describe the events of that most extraordinary morning. Once again, the secretary heard the sound of students practicing music. She dodged the students moving from their first-period classes, and then she entered the first room of the professor's suite. Although she was in a state of hypnotic regression, she was again stopped short by a very musty, disagreeable odor. Buterbaugh told the researchers that when she first walked into the room, everything had seemed quite normal. But after about four steps into the room, the strong odor had hit

The photographer was the only one present when this photo was taken after a 1995 fire at Wem Town Hall in the United Kingdom. In 1677 a fire started by a young girl destroyed the original building.

her. She emphasized the words "strong odor" and said she meant the kind that stopped a person in their tracks and almost choked them. As soon as she was stopped by the odor, she felt as though there was someone in the room with her. It was then that she became aware that there were no noises out in the hall. Everything had become deathly quiet.

She looked up, and something seemed to draw her eyes to the cabinet along the wall in the next room, and there was Mills, standing with her back to Buterbaugh, reaching up into one of the shelves of the cabinet with her right hand, standing perfectly still. Buterbaugh explained that while the woman was not transparent, she knew somehow that "she wasn't real." Then, while the startled secretary was looking at her, she just disappeared.

Until the woman faded away, Buterbaugh said that she was not aware of anyone else being in the office suite. But as the one ghost was fading from sight, the startled secretary suddenly felt as though she was not alone. To her left was a desk, and she had a feeling that there was a man sitting there. She turned around and saw no one, but she still felt his presence at the desk. Then she looked out the window behind that desk, became terribly frightened, and left the room. There wasn't one modern thing out there. The street was not even there. Neither were the new campus buildings. That was when she realized that these people were not in her time, but that she was back in their time.

Researchers Murphy and Klemme received permission to conduct a thorough search of the university files, and they uncovered a photograph dated 1915 that depicted a campus scene similar to the one that Buterbaugh had glimpsed out of the window. The two investigators thought it highly unlikely that the secretary could have ever come across the picture or even one like it prior to the time of her most unusual experience. They also agreed that the picture of Mills found in old yearbooks fit the description of the tall, dark-haired woman whom Buterbaugh had seen in thé office, and they established the fact that Mills had died shortly before 9:00 A.M. in the same building that the secretary had entered at about 8:50 A.M.

In the summer of 1970, I accompanied psychic-sensitive Irene Hughes to the Wesleyan campus and the office in the C. C. White building where Colleen Buterbaugh had stepped into the past. We hoped to test whether a gifted sensitive might elicit a recall of another's psychic experience. Hughes had no idea where we were, other than being on a college campus. "I know that you Don't want to tell me anything about the experiment tonight, Brad," she said, "but I am receiving psychically that it has to do with something that happened in one of these classrooms." Hughes walked directly to the back office of the suite. "I have the feeling that the desk was further over this way," she said, "because I feel like I want my back right to the window. You know," she added, "I am just getting so many different impressions. People ... people

... so many people have been walking through here." Then Hughes began to receive an impression that made us instantly more attentive: "She came as a young lady. I see her in a long skirt that seems to open in the back. Her hair is bouffant ... pompadour ... rolled over. I feel her around in here very much. She seems to be a very pleasant and pretty woman. Involved with teaching."

It seemed as though Hughes was providing us with a description of Mills. "When I look outside this window, it does not look the way it did when I was seeing it through her eyes. Those buildings weren't there. There was only a road or a sidewalk," she added. After a few more minutes, Irene said, "I can see a man in this office. He came in and sat down at the desk. Then I see a secretary walking down the hall and entering the office. She walked in and wanted ... tried to see him at the desk. Then I see the woman in the office—not the secretary, now, but the woman who belongs in there—I can see her hair, and it is very pretty. She is very tall for a woman, and her hair is dark, but not really black. It is worn in a roll and pushed over. I can see her skirt is dark and long. And she has on a white blouse. She has a very pretty smile, and she busies herself around the office."

[In the 1915 yearbook, a picture of Mills bore the caption: "A daughter of the gods thou art, divinely tall and most divinely fair." According to Buterbaugh, the picture and description matched the appearance of the tall, dark-haired woman she had seen in the office. It also seemed to match the description that Hughes had divined through her psychic sensitivity.]

Hughes continued receiving impressions: "I see the secretary walking in and seeing the woman over there (pointing toward the wall where the filing cabinet had been). Then she looked and saw the man sitting at the desk. Then ... then she looked out the window. I think maybe she saw him looking out the window and turned to see what he was looking at. And ... and things weren't the way they are now." I found it very interesting that although Buterbaugh had seen the image of Mills, Hughes seemed to be saying that the man at the desk may have been the stronger entity or vibratory force. We may have had a reverse of what seemed to be obvious to the percipient.

In my opinion, and in the opinions of the researchers who accompanied us to the Wesleyan campus, Hughes accurately described the image of Mills as seen by Buterbaugh in this classic paranormal case. In speaking with knowledgeable faculty members, Mills wore that style of dress all of her life, even after the styles had changed, which made it difficult to determine the date of the paranormal scene that Buterbaugh had witnessed. Mills joined the faculty in 1912, and it would appear that her spirit has not thought of retiring.

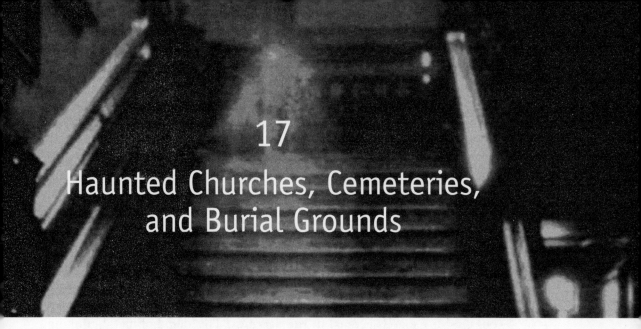

17
Haunted Churches, Cemeteries, and Burial Grounds

An Uninvited Guest Upsets Epworth Rectory

It was on December 1, 1716, that the children and servants brought their complaints to Reverend Samuel Wesley. For several nights they had been heard mysterious groans and sounds in their rooms at Epworth Rectory, Dorcester, South Yorkshire. In addition to those frightening manifestations, they also heard the sound of footsteps ascending and descending the stairs at all hours of the night.

Reverend Wesley was skeptical about the allegations that paranormal manifestations were occurring in his house. After a week of careful nocturnal surveillance throughout the rectory, Wesley had not even uncovered a stirring mouse. He severely lectured the child or servant who brought him any more stories about ghosts prowling the stairs and the bedrooms. One night at dinner, he told his family that he been unable to detect any unusual noises in the rectory.

Wesley decreed that if there were any peculiar sounds in his rectory, they were undoubtedly caused by the silly young men who came around in the evenings to court his daughters. The Wesleys had four grown daughters who had begun to entertain beaus and suitors, and the girls bristled at their father's veiled sarcasm. One of the older daughters wished aloud that the ghost would come knocking at the door to their father's study or bedchamber and give him a fright. The girls were so peeved with their father that they stubbornly vowed to ignore the disturbances until they became so loud that even he would have to acknowledge them. They didn't have long to wait. The very next night, nine loud knocks thudded on the walls of Wesley's bed chamber.

[335]

Wesley could not deny the reality of the harsh intrusions into his time of rest, but he dismissed the notion of a ghost being responsible for the sounds and concluded that some rogue had managed to get into the rectory unnoticed by the servants and was trying to frighten them. Wesley whispered to his wife that in the morning he would buy a large dog "big enough to gobble up any intruder." First thing in the morning, the clergyman obtained a huge mastiff and took it into the rectory. Such a brute would be able to deal with any spook, he decreed.

That night, however, as the knocks began to sound, Wesley was startled to see his canine ghostbuster whimper and cower behind the frightened children. One of the older girls teased that the dog was more frightened than they were. Two nights later, the sounds in the house seemed so aggressively violent that Wesley and his wife were forced out of bed to investigate. As they walked through the rectory, the unseen noisemakers seemed to follow them. Mysterious crashing sounds echoed in the darkness. The sound of metal clinking seemed to surround them. The Wesleys somehow managed to maintain their courage and searched every chamber rectory for the source of the disruptions, but they found nothing.

After he called a family meeting to pool their knowledge concerning the invisible intruder, Wesley learned from one of his older daughters that the disturbing phenomena usually began at about ten o'clock in the evening. The impending commotion was always preceded by a "signal" that sounded something like the winding of a very large clock. The noises also appeared to follow a pattern that seldom altered. They would begin in the kitchen, then suddenly move up to visit one of the children's rooms, where the ghost would knock on the foot and head of the bed. This routine seemed to comprise the ghost's stretching exercises. After it had warmed-up with these preliminaries, it would indulge any spectral whim that appealed to it.

"Why do you disturb innocent children?" Wesley demanded to know one night as the knockings in the nursery became especially explosive. "If you have something to say, come to me in my study." The ghost ignored the clergyman's invitation and continued to bang about on the bedsteads of the children. "You deaf and dumb devil, why do you frighten these children that cannot answer for themselves?" he roared with righteous indignation. "Come to me in my study like a man!" As if in answer to Wesley's challenge, a sharp knock sounded on the door of his study with such force that the cleric thought the boards would splinter. Although there were no more disturbances that evening, Wesley soon found that his invitation not been ignored. While in his study one evening, "an invisible power" heavily pushed him up against his desk. On another occasion he was slammed into the door jamb of his study just as he was entering the room.

When photographer Chris Brackley developed this photograph of the inside of St. Botolph's Church in London, he noticed the strange appearance of a woman in the right upper balcony. Only three people were in the church at the time, none of them upstairs.

Wesley decided to obtain reinforcements for the struggle against the devil that had invaded his rectory. He sent for Mr. Hoole, the Vicar of Hoxley, and told him the whole story. Hoole listened patiently to his fellow cleric's

Close-up of the entity in St. Botolph's Church.

story and told Wesley that he would lead devotions that night. They would see if the thing would dare to manifest in his presence. The ghost was not the least bit awed by the Vicar of Hoxley. That night the ghost put on such a powerful demonstration of paranormal power that the clergyman fled in terror, leaving Wesley to combat the unseen demon as best he could.

The children had overcome their initial fear of the invisible entity in a most remarkable way. They had come to accept its supernatural antics as a welcome relief from the boredom of village life. They had begun to call their unseen guest "Old Jeffery," and the ghost almost achieved the status of a pet. Old Jeffery, it was observed, was a bit testy and temperamental. If any visitor slighted him by claiming that the rappings were due to natural causes, such as rats, birds, or wind, the phenomena would quickly intensify so that the doubter stood instantly corrected.

The preternatural disturbances kept up their scheduled arrival time of ten o'clock in the evening until the day that Mrs. Wesley remembered an ancient remedy for riding a house of evil spirits. Old folklore and texts recommended that those afflicted by bothersome entities should obtain a large trumpet "and blow it mightily throughout every room in the house," she told the family. "The sounds of a loud horn are unpleasing to evil spirits." The eardrum shattering experiment in primeval exorcism was not only a complete failure, but the ghost began to ignore his old schedule of only making appearances at night and started to come around in daylight hours as well. Old Jeffery had either resented being called an evil spirit or simply decided to express its criticism of the terrible trumpeting. Whatever the reason, it retaliating with increased activity.

The children seemed to welcome the fact that Old Jeffery would be available during their playtime hours as well. Several witnesses swore that they saw a bed levitate to a considerable height while a number of the Wesley children squealed merrily from the floating mattress. The only thing that seemed to disturb the children was the sound that Old Jeffery had begun to make. It sounded like a trailing robe was following them wherever they went.

One of the girls declared that she had seen the ghost of a man wearing a long, white robe that dragged on the floor. Other children in the Wesley household claimed to have seen an animal, similar in appearance to a badger, scurrying out from under their beds. A number of the servants testified that they had seen the head of a creature that resembled a rodent peering out at them from a crack near the kitchen fireplace.

Just as the Wesleys were growing accustomed to Old Jeffery's antics, the bizarre phenomena ended as abruptly as they had begun. While the entity never returned to harass Epworth Rectory with its mischief, the memory of its disruptive period of occupancy has remained to challenge both scholars of Christian history and the paranormal for more than two centuries. Among the 19 children of the Reverend Samuel Wesley who witnessed the phenomena were John and Charles, the founders of Methodism and the authors of some of Christendom's best loved hymns.

BORLEY RECTORY: THE MOST HAUNTED HOUSE IN ENGLAND

It was the well-known psychical researcher Dr. Harry Price who applied the title of the "most haunted house in England" to Borley Rectory, located about 60 miles northeast of London on the Essex-Suffolk border. Over the years, the claim of "most haunted" has been contested and the case has become controversial, but the old accounts of the occupants and the teams of researchers still make for chilling reading.

According to one of the legends of Borley, shortly after Reverend Guy E. Smith arrived to take over clerical duties at the rectory in 1928, he opened a cabinet in the library to put away some books and saw a human skull grinning at him from a shelf. Mrs. Smith held her breath as her husband removed the skull from the cabinet and began to examine it. "You don't...you don't suppose," she asked with nervous laughter, "that the rectory really is haunted? You Don't think that could be the skull of the nun that's supposed to walk through these halls, or the skull of one of the poor devils that was buried in the Plague Pit?" Smith cautioned his wife to calm down before she convinced herself that all the weird tales they had heard about Borley Rectory were true. Still, it was difficult to deny the fact that no fewer than a dozen clergymen refused to live there before he accepted the call. Nor could he forget the story about a former rector who had a window in the dining room bricked up because he could not stand to see the ghost of a nun continually peering in at him.

Reverend Smith tried to ignore his wife's suggestion that something evil had made its abode in the rectory. He and the church sexton gave the skull a solemn burial in the churchyard, and he and his wife fought to stave off the

Once known as the "most haunted house in England," Borley Rectory was said to house many different types of phenomena including ghosts and poltergeists. This photograph of the rectory was taken in 1929.

depression that seemed to have enveloped them. However, it was not many nights before they were given awesome evidence of invisible forces at work.

The haunting phenomena usually began shortly after they had retired for the evening. They would be lying in bed, and they would hear the sound of heavy footsteps walking past their door. On several nights Smith crouched in the darkness outside of their room with a hockey stick clasped firmly in his hands, trying to lunge at the invisible *something* that passed their door, but he was never able to strike anything tangible. A female voice began moaning from the center of an archway that led to the chapel. Keys were dislodged from their locks and were found several feet from their doors. Hoarse, inaudible whispers sounded over their heads. Small pebbles appeared out of nowhere and pelted them.

When the Smiths reported their supernatural plight to the London *Daily Mirror*, Dr. Harry Price was notified. In the summer of 1929 Price, his secretary, and C. V. Watts, a reporter for the *Mirror*, set out to visit the rectory and to see for themselves if Reverend Smith and his family were truly beset by authentic haunting phenomena.

Before the trio left London, their research revealed that the rectory, though constructed in modern times, stood on the site of a medieval monastery. There had once been a nunnery close at hand, and its ruins were still visible. There were many legends about the nunnery, but the most famous was about a nun who had been set into one of the convent walls while she was still alive as punishment for eloping with a Benedictine brother, who was later hanged for his indiscretion. Occupants of the rectory and several villagers had reported seeing the ghost of the veiled nun walking through the grounds. About a quarter of a mile away stood a castle where many tragic events had also occurred, ending with a siege by Oliver Cromwell. A headless nobleman and a black coach pursued by armed men had also been listed as frequent phenomena around the rectory.

Borely Rectory was built by the Reverend Henry Dawson Ellis Bull in 1863 (some sources say 1865). The reverend had fathered 14 children and needed a larger home. Bull died in the rectory's blue room in 1892 and was succeeded in occupancy by his son Harry, who died in the rectory in 1927. As a dozen clergymen refused to take up residence at the rectory because of the eerie tales they had heard, the building was vacant for several months, until Reverend Smith and his family accepted the call in 1928.

After Price, his secretary, and C. V. Watts arrived at the rectory, they had lunch with Reverend Smith and his wife and listened to the couple describe the range of psychic phenomena that they had witnessed. While they spoke, a glass candlestick struck an iron stove near Price's head and showered him with splinters. A mothball came rolling down the stairwell, followed by a number of pebbles.

During his stay at the rectory, Price busied himself with research, conducting interviews with the surviving daughters of Reverend Henry Bull, the builder of the rectory, and former servants who had remained in the village. A man who had served as a gardener for Reverend Bull told Price that while he had worked at the rectory, both he and his wife heard footsteps in their rooms over the stables. The sounds were audible every night for the eight months he worked there. Several former maids testified that they had remained in the employ of the Bulls for only one or two days before they were driven away by the strange occurrences.

The eldest of Bull's three surviving daughters said she had seen the nun appear at a lawn party on a sunny July afternoon in 1900. She had attempted to approach the phantom and engage it in conversation, but it disappeared as she had drawn near to it. The sisters all swore that the entire family had often seen the nun and the phantom coach. It was their father who had bricked up the dining room window so that the family might enjoy dinner without the spectral nun peering in at them.

Mrs. Smith said that she had also seen the shadowy figure of a nun walking about the grounds of the rectory. On several occasions, she had attempted to confront the phantom, but it had always disappeared. Before the investigators left the Smiths, Watts wrote an article for the *Daily Mirror* in which he admitted that he had seen the phantom nun and heard the sound of the ghostly carriage and horses' hooves for himself.

The Smiths left the rectory shortly after the investigators concluded their research. Both Mr. and Mrs. Smith had begun to suffer the ill-effects from lack of sleep and the enormous mental strain that had been placed on them.

The supernatural phenomena reached new heights of activity when the Reverend Lionel Algernon Foyster, his wife Marianne, and their four-year-old daughter Adelaide established residence in the rectory on October 16, 1930. Reverend Foyster was a cousin of Caroline Foyster Bull, the wife of Reverend Henry Bull, so he must have had some idea what dreaded things they might face in the rectory after dark. They had lived there only a few days when Mrs. Foyster heard a voice softly calling, "Marianne, dear." Thinking her husband was summoning her, Mrs. Foyster ran upstairs. Foyster told his wife that he had not spoken a word but that he had also heard a voice calling.

On one occasion, Marianne Foyster set her wristwatch by her side as she prepared to wash her hands in the bathroom. When she finished washing, she reached for the watch and discovered that the band had been removed. It disappeared and never again reappeared. When Reverend Foyster realized that the tales that he had heard about Borley Rectory had all been true, he was not frightened, for he believed that he would be protected by his Christian faith. He used a holy relic to quiet the disturbances when they became particularly violent, and he remained calm enough to keep a detailed journal of the phenomena that he and his family witnessed.

For some unknown reason, Marianne Foyster became the brunt of the most cruel and sadistic facets of the haunting. While on the way to their bedroom, she sustained a violent blow to her eye that slashed her skin and left a large black bruise that was visible for several days. On another occasion, she narrowly missed being struck by a flat iron that shattered the chimney of the lamp that she was carrying. Strangely enough, while one facet of the haunting persecuted Mrs. Foyster, another seemed desperate to establish contact with her. Messages were found scrawled on the walls: "Marianne ... please ... get help."

When Reverend Foyster learned that Dr. Harry Price had once shown an interest in the Borley phenomena, he wrote to London to inform the psychical researcher of renewed activity in the rectory. Upon arrival, Price and his two assistants once again set about examining the house from attic to cellar. While Price was in an upstairs room, an empty wine bottle was suddenly thrown through the air by an invisible force and narrowly missed him. Shortly after that welcoming salvo from the haunting, the investigators were startled to hear the screams of their chauffeur, who had remained behind in the kitchen to enjoy a leisurely cigarette. The frightened man insisted that he had seen a large, black hand crawl across the kitchen floor.

Reverend Foyster showed Price the entry he had made in his journal on March 28, when his wife had confronted a grotesque entity while ascending a staircase. She had described it as a black, ape-like monstrosity. It had reached out and touched her on the shoulder with an "iron-like touch." Price soon learned that others had seen the creature on different occasions. The Foysters also told Price and his team that the haunting had begun to materialize items that they knew were not theirs. A small tin trunk had appeared in the kitchen when they were eating supper. A powder box that contained a wedding ring manifested in the bathroom, and after the Foysters had carefully put the ring away in a drawer, it disappeared overnight. In his book *The Most Haunted House in England*, Price documented more than 2,000 incidents of paranormal activi-

Strange messages were written on the walls of Borley Rectory, reportedly by the spirits that inhabited the house. Investigators tried to communicate with the spirits by writing messages back (seen here in large capital letters). Responses would often appear written in pencil, although they were not always legible.

ty that occurred during the Foysters' residency in the rectory. The Foysters endured the supernatural harassment for five years before leaving Borley Rectory in October 1935. After the Foysters left, the bishop wisely decreed that the place should be put up for sale. It should have come as no surprise to the parish to discover that there would be no interested parties waiting in line to bid on it.

In May 1937 Harry Price learned that the rectory was once again vacant and offered to lease the place so that he could create a kind of ghost laboratory. His proposed sum was accepted, and the psychical investigator enlisted a crew of 40 men who would take turns living in the rectory for a period of one year. Price outfitted the place with special ghost-detecting equipment and prepared a booklet of instructions that told his army of researchers how to correctly observe and record any phenomena that might manifest.

Shortly after Price's crew began to arrive, strange messages that seemed to have been written in pencil began to materialize on the walls. Each time a new marking was discovered, it was carefully circled and dated. Two Oxford graduates reported actually seeing the formation of a new message while they were busy cataloging another. It appeared that the entity missed Marianne Foyster. "Marianne … Marianne … M … " it wrote over and over again. "Marianne … light … Mass … prayers … Get lights … Marianne … please … help … get."

Professor C. E. M. Joad, of the Department of Philosophy and Psychology at the University of London, was one of those who witnessed the pencil markings appear on the walls. In the July 1938 issue of *Harpers* magazine, Joad commented on his experience: "Having reflected long and carefully upon that squiggle, I did not and do not see how it could have been made by normal means…. The hypothesis that poltergeists materialize lead pencils and fingers to use them seems to be totally incredible…. And the question of 'why' seems hardly less difficult to answer than the question 'how.' As so frequently occurs when one is investigating so-called abnormal phenomena, one finds it equally impossible to withhold credence from the facts or to credit any possible explanation of the facts. Either the facts did not occur, or if they did, the universe must in some respects be totally other than what one is accustomed to suppose."

The investigators soon discovered a "cold spot" in one of the upstairs passages. Although this is a common aspect of haunting phenomena, it had gone unnoticed in previous explorations by the psychical researchers and the rectors who had lived in Borley. Certain of Price's investigators noted that they shivered and felt faint whenever they passed through it. Another cold spot was discovered on the landing outside of the blue room. Thermometers indicated the temperature of these areas to be fixed at 48°F, regardless of what the temperature may have been in the rest of the house. On the last day of Price's tenancy, the wedding ring that had materialized during the Foysters' occupancy again appeared. To be certain that the ghost would not snatch it away again, the investigator brought it home to London with him.

In late 1938 Borley Rectory was purchased by a Captain W. H. Gregson, who renamed it "The Priory." He was not at all intimidated by stories that the place was haunted, but he was upset when his faithful old dog went wild with terror on the day they moved in and ran away, never to be seen again. He was also somewhat concerned with the strange track of unidentified footprints that circled the house in freshly fallen snow. The captain swore that they were not made by any human or animal. He followed the tracks in an attempt to figure out how they had been made, but they mysteriously disappeared into

The ruins of Borley Rectory, photographed on March 28, 1939. The rectory was derelict until 1944, when the property was razed.

nothingness. On February 27, 1939, Borley Rectory was completely destroyed by flames. Captain Gregson later testified that a number of books had flown from their places on shelves and knocked over a lamp, which led to an immediate explosion of flames.

In December 2000 a book was published with the controversial title *We Faked the Ghosts of Borley Rectory*. In this exposé, Louis Mayerling claimed that Harry Price, a host of other psychical researchers, and the world at large had been taken in by hoaxsters who took special delight in making Borely Rectory appear haunted. Mayerling stated that Borley Rectory had been a second home to him in his younger days. He had been but a lad when he first arrived at Borley Rectory in 1918 and discovered Reverend Harry Bull and his family having great fun perpetuating the local folklore about a phantom nun and other things that went bump in the night. According to the author, the Foysters later got in on the spooky pranks and encouraged Mayerling to don a black cape and stalk the gardens at dusk. Mayerling revealed how those in on the hoax took great delight in ringing bells, tossing pebbles, and making eerie groans and moans. However, he did admit to one incident that he could not explain, which might indicate that there really was something paranormal occurring at Borley Rectory.

On Easter Sunday in 1935, a prestigious group of individuals who believed that paranormal phenomena was occurring at Borely Rectory joined Mayerling and Marianne Foyster for a séance at the rectory. Among those in attendance were the acclaimed playwright George Bernard Shaw; T. E. Lawrence, the heroic "Lawrence of Arabia"; Sir Montagu Norman, governor of the Bank of England; and Bernard Spilsbury, a criminal forensic scientist for the Home Office. According to Mayerling, the kitchen bells all clanged and a brilliant silver-blue light seemed to emanate from the walls and the ceiling, leaving them completely surrounded. From his previous experience as a ghostly imposter, Mayerling knew that it was impossible to cause all the bells to sound at once, and he had absolutely no idea what could have caused the brilliant, lightning-like flash. He admitted that he was, in fact, blinded by the strange phenomenon and eventually recovered sight in only one of his eyes. Shaw and Norman refused to stay the night after such a violent supernatural display, and Mayerling confessed in his book that the memory of that occurrence still unnerved him.

In spite of Mayerling's confession that he participated in "creating" the alleged phenomena at Borley Rectory, the haunting remains controversial and a subject of debate among psychical researchers. Although Mayerling may have joined the Bull family in perpetuating the legends of the rectory and later encouraged the Foysters to play along with the hoax, the admitted pranksters were not present during the years of Reverend G. E. Smith's residency, the year-long observation of extensive phenomena by Price's team of researchers, or the manifestations reported by Gregson after he assumed ownership of Borley Rectory.

THE GENTLE SPIRITS OF MISSION SAN ANTONIO DE PADUA

Monks living at the Mission San Antonio de Padua, one of North America's oldest Roman Catholic spiritual centers, have seen and heard ghosts. The mission is also known for the strange colored clouds that hover above it on hot, otherwise cloudless days. The mission, constructed in 1771, is located in central California's Santa Lucia mountain range, 30 miles north of Paso Robles. A nearby army base is the only other settlement.

Franciscan brother Timothy, a historian at the mission, said that even when the first *padres* settled there in 1770, there were mysteries about the area. Local Indians told them of monks just like them who had come before, but they had come flying through the air. On one occasion in the mid-1980s, Brother Timothy recalled having been in the refectory with some archeologists when they all heard someone moving in the attic above them. Everyone heard the entity take a few paces then step over the crossbeams The consensus among them was that an intruder was on the roof of the refectory. Two of the archeologists went up and searched the roof with flashlights. Nobody was there, and the thick dust was totally undisturbed.

During a visit to the mission, psychical researcher Richard Senate was walking through the mission's courtyard to get a cold drink from the icebox. It was about 12:30 A.M. Through the dense blackness of the night, Senate saw a light on the other side of the courtyard. He finally realized that it was a candle, and he changed his course to see who it was, because the monks were strict about the use of candles, as they can be a fire hazard. He was about 12 feet from the figure when he opened his mouth to speak. Senate could clearly see that the person was wearing a monk's habit and was less than average height. They were both approaching the door to the chapel when the monk vanished right before Senate's eyes. Senate turned on his flashlight, but

In September 1999 a photographer and one other person were taking photographs inside Sefton Church in Merseyside, United Kingdom. Neither individual saw a ghost or a living individual standing in front of the camera before the photograph was taken. The blurred figure of a man remains unexplained.

there was nothing there. The monk couldn't have quietly opened the door, because it was heavy and it squeaked. It was that experience that led the now-famous paranormal researcher to first believe in ghosts. Senate found out later that the timing of the ghost's appearance had been significant. The old *padres* would get up at 12:30 A.M. and pray in the chapel for an hour before they went back to bed. Senate is convinced that he saw a three-dimensional image from the past—the ghost of a long-dead monk going to prayer.

The monks of Mission San Antonio de Padua have often seen a small, colored cloud about three feet square hanging eight feet above the tile roof over the women's guest quarters. The strange cloud changes colors, initially appearing white and then evolving into green, blue, yellow, and red. The monks tell of the day Father John Baptist died and a mysterious cloud appeared, as if it were signaling the priest's passing. Father John had been working in Atascadero, 70 miles away from the mission, when he died, and the monks had not yet gotten the news.

Brother Timothy remembered seeing a wispy white cloud that floated out of the door of the winter chapel. Father Joe saw it as well, and the two of them watched its unbelievable movements. The cloud went along the cloister and then suddenly turned abruptly along the path. As Brother Timothy and Father Joe watched it, it went out to the fountain at the center of the courtyard, hovered there for a minute or two, then turned again and went along the path past the cloister and into the church. The two men ran to follow it, but it had disappeared inside. The clerics noted that the white cloud had taken the exact route Father John had followed each day on his way to say his noon mass. He had always walked the same path, even pausing to feed the goldfish in the fountain. Brother Timothy and Father Joe are convinced that Father John's soul was following his familiar path one last time.

THEY PROVIDED A HOME FOR DISPOSSESSED SPIRITS

In 1971 Donald Page, who had been a medium since the age of 15, revealed that he and an eminent canon of the Church of England, Canon John D. Pearce-Higgins, had been running a home for wayward ghosts for nearly three years. Page said that he kept a spare bedroom in his London apartment expressly for the purpose of offering shelter and spiritual comfort to the ghosts that he had exorcized from their old haunts.

Page said that he and the cleric had been a ghost-hunting team for more then 15 years, and he claimed that they had helped hundreds of ghosts find peace. Canon Pearce-Higgins kept a well-documented account of their activity for the Church of England's Fellowship for Psychical Research. The cleric stated that their primary aim was to help both the haunters and the haunted. When the two men weren't helping restless spirits move along to higher realms, Reverend Pearce-Higgins was minister of London's Southwark Cathedral, and Page headed a Spiritualist church, the Fellowship and Brotherhood of Paul.

When they received a request from someone who was experiencing an unpleasant haunting, they carefully investigated the disturbances to determine if they were truly being caused by a troubled ghost. If they found a restless spirit or an evil earthbound entity to be the culprit, Page would go into a trance and permit the spirit to possess him. Then his spirit guides would take over by removing the spirit from him and escorting it to the small guest room that was decorated with psychical artwork and had become a sanctuary for displaced spirits. The sanctuary allowed the spirit an opportunity to adjust to life in a transitional state before it moved on to a higher, more spiritual plane of existence.

As the Reverend K. F. Lord was photographing the interior of his church, located in Newby, North Yorkshire, United Kingdom, he saw nothing unusual in front of him. When the film was developed, he noticed that a translucent hooded figure seems to be standing next to the altar.

The medium emphasized that one cannot simply remove spirits from the places they haunt and leave them to flounder helplessly in a spiritual twilight zone. Page said that they permitted the ghosts to stay in the sanctuary until they had regained their spiritual equilibrium and were able to move on to the next plane of existence. The spiritual ministers keep their troubled ghosts in the sanctuary for as long as it takes to assist them in their transitional period. During this time of spiritual therapy, Page's spirit guides, the two men and their assistant, Edna Taylor, are able to show the confused ghosts the way to continue their journey on the other side.

Canon Pearce-Higgins, who was also an editor and contributor to *Life, Death, and Psychical Research* (1973), admitted that many people might doubt the efficacy and the validity of their work, but that all he could say for certain was that when they went into a house and performed their procedure and the phenomena stopped, they assumed it was because of what they had done.

Real Ghosts, Restless Spirits, and Haunted Places

THE MALEVOLENT SPIRIT THAT INVADED ST. PAUL'S

In 1972 Peter Chapman of the Saratoga Springs *Saratogian* and Marty Hughes of the *Greenwich Journal and Salem Press* reported that St. Paul's Episcopal Rectory in Greenwich, New York, had received visitations by at least two ghosts. The central figure in the accounts was Reverend William R. Harris of St. Paul's, who gave a detailed account of events in the rectory, including a chilling description of a malevolent entity's attempt to possess him.

Late one night he had awakened with a terrible sensation of pressure being placed at the foot of his bed. The pressure increased, a chill swept over him, and he felt "literally pinioned by an inexpressibly oppressive weight." Suddenly, a scant foot away from his face, he saw a shroud of whitish gray begin to form. In the portion of the shroud that would normally contain a head, he saw fierce, burning, laser-like eyes that were filled with hatred. Reverend Harris sensed a tortured, aggressive, malevolent, and demonic spirit, and he realized intuitively that the spirit might attempt to possess him. As a contemporary man of the cloth, he had previously regarded the notion of possession as a superstitious notion, but now he felt the definite need for counteraction. He thrust his right arm through the ghost and shouted loudly for it to leave in the name of Jesus Christ. And the spirit disappeared.

Reverend Harris described the entity as having a long, sharp, aquiline nose, severe cheekbones, a thin mouth, and angular features that culminated in a pointed chin. He also mentioned seeing wisps of gray beard that hung to the thing's chin like Spanish moss on a tree.

Mrs. Harris reported that one morning in 1968, something invisible attempted to take away a tea tray she was carrying into the kitchen. The Harris daughters, Jan, Julie, and Page, also had encounters with apparitions. Julie and Page once ran to their mother with the startling report that they had seen something white go down the hall "like an old man dressed in clothes from Jesus' time." Julie reported seeing the same apparition perched on the banister in the upstairs hall. As she watched, it went right through the wall.

Reverend Harris's mother encountered a strange visitor in the rectory when she was staying there in the family's absence. She described it as a figure of a woman dressed in the style of clothing that was worn by Puritans. It passed from the living room, across the entry hall, and into the studio. Although Mrs. Harris raced into the studio, nobody was there.

The carefully documented account of the ghosts of St. Paul's Rectory was enhanced even more by an amazing drawing of one of the phantoms done by professional artist Paul Fung. Fung saw a ghost at close range on July 4, 1972, when he returned to the rectory with the Harris family after seeing a circus perform at the Washington County Fairgrounds. Fung, who used to draw the "Blondie" comic strip, felt the coldness that is often associated with ghosts and got a good look at it. He even returned for a second look.

THE GHOSTLY MONK OF BASILDON

A number of cleaning ladies that work overnight shifts at a factory near Holy Cross church in Basildon, England, have seen a phantom monk on several occasions. The women usually finish work at 4:00 A.M., and it is as they are leaving the factory and walking past the old church that they often see the ghost. They agree that the ghost is definitely a monk, and it walks across the church road before it disappears among the graves in churchyard.

One of the women stated that she was once riding her bicycle when she saw the ghost directly in front her. Unable to brake quickly enough, she drove right through the spook. She said that she didn't feel any impact at all, but she described the feeling of traveling through the ghost as cold and clammy.

Witnesses all mention that the monk wears a red cowl and has a chalk-white face that is set in a kind of grim mask. Some have described the ghostly monk as transparent. Others say that the monk's feet don't seem to be touching the ground, as if he were floating. An interesting aside might be interjected at this point regarding reports of ghosts that appear to be "floating" in the air. In one interesting case, a ghost that haunted one particular house was always seen walking or floating about six inches off the ground. Investigation revealed that the floor of the room the ghost appeared in had been lowered six inches after the death of the individual whose image the ghost represented. The same may hold true for the phantom monk of Basildon. The animated ghost of the monk may be several centuries old, and the streets in front of Holy Cross church may have settled over time. If the road had settled quite a bit, it would make the monk that traces the old ground look like he was floating.

THE PLAYFUL SPIRIT IN THE OLD CHURCH

Courtesy of Stephen Wagner at <paranormal.about.com>:
The Personal Experience of Jason M.

"When I was 16 years old, my stepfather helped out at this church built [during] the 1800s in Hartford, Connecticut. It was a hot, late summer day on a Saturday. My friends Ryan, Joey, and I had come along to help my stepfather with some yard work for a few extra bucks. While we were in the janitorial room getting supplies, I told Ryan and Joey about how big [the] place was when no one was [there] and how we could all run around if we could get away from my stepfather.

The "Black Abbot" that is said to haunt the churchyard at Prestbury, near Cheltenham, Gloucestershire, United Kingdom. Photographed in 1990.

"About one hour later, somewhere in the front of the church, Joey and my stepfather were raking and bagging some lawn clippings that [they had] just cut, while Ryan and I were grabbing leaves that had gathered in the lower recesses of where the windows [met the ground]. The heat was intense, and we were soaked with sweat. I had what seemed to be a bright idea: Let's sneak into the nursery daycare to cool off, for that part of the building was always cooler in the summer! [All of the doors to the church were locked,] so the first time we went in the daycare nursery, we had to ask other people working that day to open the door. On our way out, I placed a twig in the lock to the nursery. When [no one was] looking, [Ryan and I crept back to] the nursery. From the windows overlooking the front lawn, we could see the members of the congregation working in the sun. We sat in very small chairs laughing and joking about how we got out of the hot labor. Suddenly, from the hallway by the windows we heard what seemed to be a small kid, like our friend Joey, running down the hallway toward our direction. We thought [he had seen] us disappear and decided to sneak in, too. We were on the other side of the doorway to the hallway, so he couldn't see us. I thought it would make a really funny surprise if we jumped out at him as he came in. The person running down the hallway sounded like he would [walk through the door] in a few seconds. On the count of three, we would jump out and say BOO! When the person got to the very edge of the doorway, we could hear his breath. It sounded just like Joey! So we jumped out to say boo, and when we did … no one was there! Suddenly, a quick gust of wind blew by. It must have been the spirit of a child sensing our playful intent and wanting to join in on our fun."

THE MYSTERIOUS FORCE IN ARENSBURG CEMETERY

In the summer of 1844, the ecclesiastical court that assembled periodically at Arensburg, on the island of Oesel in the Baltic, was stunned by a complaint that had been submitted. A number of people had complained that a mysterious force from one of the private chapels in the cemetery was killing their horses. The first complaint had been registered by a peasant woman on June 22, 1844. The woman had driven to the cemetery for one of her regular visits to her mother's grave. She tethered her horse near the Buxhoewden family chapel, but the animal allowed her only a few moments at her mother's graveside before it began to shriek in terror. By the time she had reached the animal, it had collapsed in a wild-eyed frenzy and was frothing at the mouth. The woman had run for a veterinarian, who managed to save the horse by bleeding it.

On the following Sunday, several people had hitched their horses near Buxhoewden chapel while they attended services in the nearby church. When they had returned to their animals after mass, they were shocked to find their horses trembling in terror. Some people claimed that they could hear weird rumbles and groans coming from within the chapel. On the next Sunday, services were interrupted by the loud stampings and snortings of 11 horses that had been tied near the chapel. As the owners left the church in alarm, they had been startled to find several of the animals struggling on the ground in various stages of nervous collapse. Bleeding was immediately prescribed as treatment, but the veterinarian was too late to save four of the horses. Once again, several people insisted that they had heard strange sounds issuing from within the Buxhoewden chapel.

The consistory chose to ignore the complaints of the people for the time being. Perhaps the horses had eaten some noxious plants. Perhaps there was an outbreak of some new disease. The mysterious death of the horses was obviously a matter for a practitioner of veterinary medicine, not an ecclesiastical court.

However, the strange happenings in and around Buxhoewden chapel became impossible to ignore just a few days after the consistory had dismissed them. During a funeral service in the chapel, the assembled mourners were horrified to hear terrible groans coming from the vault below. After the service had been concluded, those with stouter hearts went down to the vault to prepare for the interment of the latest coffin. They were quite unprepared for the sight that greeted them when they unlocked the heavy vault door and pushed it open. Nearly all of the coffins in the Buxhoewden family vault had been removed from their resting places and had been heaped in a disorderly pile.

It seemed impossible to account for such a disrespectful act. The only man that had a key to open the vault was the same man who stood incredulously before his family's vault, surveying the havoc that had been done to his family's final resting place. A representative of the Buxhoewden family protested to Baron de Guldenstubbe, president of the consistory, that it seemed apparent to them that some enemy of their family had managed to find a way into the vault in order to commit senseless acts of desecration. The baron pointed out that it would be impossible to enter the vault without a key, and the representative of the Buxhoewden family who stood before him had the key that opened the door to the vault. The baron added that there might be more to the matter than met the eye.

Baron de Guldenstubbe convinced two members of the Buxhoewden family to accompany him on an inspection of the vault. All three men gasped in shock when they found the coffins once again strewn about the underground vault. An official investigation committee was formed consisting of eight members, including Baron de Guldenstubbe, the bishop of the province, two other members of the consistory, a physician, the burgomaster, one of the syndics, and a secretary. Their first act was to examine the vault thoroughly. They were hardly surprised when they unlocked the vault to find the coffins again in a state of disarray.

The Baron de Guldenstubbe gave the order to open two or three of the coffins to determine whether or not robbery appeared to be the motive for the desecration. The order was carried out, and all rings, jewelry, and other personal effects buried with the corpses were found to be interred with their earthly possessors. Next the baron speculated that some practitioners of the dark arts of devil worship might have dug a tunnel into the crypt for the sole purpose of terrorizing the village. Workmen took up a section of the floor, the foundations were tested, and the walls sounded, but no evidence of any tunneling was discovered. The committee was temporarily baffled. Perhaps whatever had caused the disturbance had passed over, and the whole thing would simply become a topic for a winter evening's storytelling session around a blazing fireplace.

The baron insisted upon an official test of the phenomenon. After the coffins had been replaced, fine wood ashes were scattered over the floor of the vault. The committee then sealed the door with both consistory and municipal seals and scattered ashes over the stairs leading from the vault to the chapel. As an added precaution against anyone gaining unlawful admittance into the crypt, armed guards would maintain a 24-hour-a-day watch for three days and nights to prevent any person from even approaching the building. The baron proclaimed that it was humanly impossible for anyone to gain entrance into the vault.

At the end of the three-day testing period, the committee returned and ordered the guards to open the vault. The seals remained unbroken until the guards swung the huge door on its hinges. The coating of ashes on the stairs leading down to the vault bore no footprints or markings. The committee could only utter exclamations of frustration and wonder when their sputtering torches revealed the coffins of the Buxhoewdens in a state even worse than before. Many of the coffins bad been set on their ends and one coffin (that of a suicide) had its lid opened. It was as if the strange force responsible for the disturbances had felt compelled to put on an extra exhibition of its abilities for the illustrious gentlemen of the committee. Baron de Guldenstubbe made out an official report, and each of the committee members signed as witnesses. To the committee, the curious occurrences in Buxhoewden chapel were totally inexplicable.

THE HAUNTED GRAVE DIGGER

From the Ghost to Ghost Website <www.ghosttoghost.com>:
The Personal Experience of Ronnie

"I do excavation work and have my own company. I build rural water and sewer systems among other things that come along. One of those other things from time to time is digging graves. I live in a small oil, farming, and ranching town and pretty much know everybody in the surrounding area. Anyway, a lifelong friend's wife had passed away and the family asked that I dig the grave. I told them I would be honored to do so. Now, keep in mind her husband had passed away about four and a half years prior to her death. With

This photograph was taken at Bachelor's Grove Cemetery in Chicago. There was no one seated on the bench when this photograph was taken.

this said, my helper and I dug the grave for my recently deceased friend along-side her husband's.

"Now, like I said, these people were lifelong friends of mine. We were just about done with the grave. All that was left was to get all the measurements right and finish off the bottom of the grave. I stood up and looked down from the back of my backhoe while my helper was bent over measuring the dimensions of the grave.

"As I looked up I saw the deceased woman's husband standing there along with a lifelong working partner of his [who was] also deceased. [I saw them both] in living color. Frank and his friend Mick were standing there with their hands crossed in front of them, looking up at me with smiles on their faces and nodding their heads in approval. I looked back down in the open grave, and then looked back up and they were gone.

"But the kicker of all this was the way Frank was dressed. He was wearing a blue and white bib overall. Whereas Mick was wearing the everyday work clothes that he wore each day, right down to the shiny belt buckle he loved so much. I have asked a few around here if Frank had ever worn bibs in his younger years. But none could remember. You must remember these people were in their eighties when I asked them. That was four years ago and most of them have since passed on. Needless to say, I didn't do any more digging that day."

THE WARRIOR WANTED HIS HEAD REJOINED TO HIS BODY

In 1964 a museum in New Mexico assigned a pair of young archeologists to undertake what had been planned as a very ordinary examination of one of the countless early Pueblo villages that dotted the flatlands of New Mexico. No extraordinary finds were expected, but investigation at the site was overdue. The two young archeologists would be working side by side with Navajo diggers hired to aid in the project.

Work was proceeding as anticipated when a Navajo workman doing rough excavation on a refuse pit at the edge of the village hurriedly approached the team leaders with news of a curious discovery. His shovel had partly uncovered a piece of bone among the rubble that had been deposited there nearly 1,000 years earlier by the inhabitants of the ancient village. Unwilling to touch the bone for fear it might be human and bear a curse, the digger alerted the archeologists to the find and stood back at a respectful distance as they took up the digging. What emerged, to the archeologists' surprise, was the skull of a Native American man whose body had apparently been thrown without ceremony into the garbage pits. It was a strange find, considering the reverence with which the New Mexican tribes were known to bury their dead.

After the two archeologists had searched for hours without finding the rest of the skeletal remains, they returned their attentions to the skull and came up with a gruesome explanation. Death had probably come to the man from a blow to the back of the skull. The shape of the head suggested that it was not a Pueblo tribesman, but probably the skull of one of many Apache invaders who had filtered into the area during a wave of migration in about 900 A.D. A piece of cervical vertebra still clinging to the skull showed marks of having been hacked through by some early weapon similar to an ax.

The aged bones that lay in the refuse heap had belonged to a captive Apache who had been killed and beheaded by the Pueblo, then consigned to the garbage as a further degradation. No further attempts were immediately made to unearth any remaining skeletal bones after the first search of the nearby area had proved fruitless. They were of no great archeological importance, and more urgent work in the heart of the old village required all of the hours that the summer dig would still permit.

In 1946 or 1947 Mrs. Andrews of Queensland, Australia, took a photograph of her daughter Joyce's grave. Joyce had died at the age of 17 in 1945. When developed, the photo of Joyce's grave revealed the appearance of a small child. Mrs. Andrews was sure that there was no child present at the graveyard when she took the picture; she was also sure that the child in the photo was not her daughter. Researcher Tony Healy visited the graveyard in 1995 and found two graves of young infant girls near Joyce's grave.

But then strange events began occurring at the old Pueblo ruin. What appeared to be the work of vandals suddenly began causing havoc at the dig site. When the archeologists and Navajo workmen slept, someone entered the village and smashed unearthed pottery and kicked in carefully excavated trenches. Events took on an even more macabre turn in the week that followed. Frightened workers swore that they saw the glowing head of a man appear before them in their bunkhouse at night. Utter nonsense, the archeologists laughed, until they slept with the workmen one night and saw the faintly phosphorescent glow of what might have been the head of a man. There was no rational explanation for the sight.

Panic at the site reached its peak when the workers became certain they were hearing words in a tribal dialect that they did not understand carried on the winds of the inky desert nights. As a last resort the young archeologists turned to an age-creased shaman at a nearby Navajo reservation to explain what was taking place at the dig and restore progress to the work at the village. The shaman said that the head of the long-dead Apache was seeking his body because he could not enter the spirit world without it. The ghost would haunt the excavation until head and body were joined together in burial. Native superstition, the archeologists agreed, but in order to calm the nerves of the jittery workmen, they would see what could be done about finding the rest of the restless Apache's bones.

Because the Navajo workers reasoned that the vandalism had been a sign to help the diggers, the search for the missing remains centered on the area of the village where the vandalism had occurred. As digging proceeded in the area over several days, the team could not help noticing that the vandalism had stopped. Was it a sign the ghost was pleased? As workmen softly prodded the earth from an old ceremonial circle, a wall of dirt fell away and revealed a set of bones protruding from the soil. When the bones were laid out, they were found to be of a young male missing his head. When the skull that had been discovered earlier was brought out for comparison, the severed vertebrae were an exact match. The bones of the doomed Apache brave reposed together once more.

With the aid of the shaman, the young archeologists gave a reverential burial to the yellowed skeletal remains, and the troubles that had plagued the summer expedition ended at once. When the final report of the diggings at the site was made to the museum, the scientific background of the young archeologists did not permit inclusion of the strange events that had taken place at the site. But they were willing to share those experiences with friends, who puzzled as earnestly as they did over the curious happenings that led them to help a long-dead Apache find peace in the next world. Not a scientific achievement, but a very human one of which they were proud.

18

Haunted Mansions and Plantations

A GHOST VISITS MANNINGTON HALL

Dr. Augustus Jessopp was in high spirits on that chilly autumn night in 1879. Lord Orford had invited him to spend the night at Mannington Hall and had given him permission to examine some very old books in his extensive library. Although Jessopp enjoyed the animated conversation with the other guests, he could hardly wait until the others had gone to bed so that he could begin taking notes from the old books in the library. A dentist by profession, Jessopp was an antiquarian by hobby.

By eleven o'clock, Lord Orford and his other guests had retired for the evening, and Jessopp was alone in the library with the treasured volumes. He immediately set to work, taking notes from six small books. He had four large candles on his desk and a crackling fire in the fireplace. The light was excellent. The evening of stimulating and delightful companionship had left him feeling exhilarated, and he felt as though he could work through the night.

At 1:30 A.M., Jessopp glimpsed something white about a foot from his left elbow. Upon closer examination, the object proved to be a large, extremely pale hand with dark blue veins across its back. Putting his pen aside, Jessopp turned and saw that he shared the desk with a tall, solidly built man, who seemed to be intent upon examining both the dentist and the books he had been studying. The strange visitor had a lean, rugged profile and auburn hair that had been closely cut. He was dressed in the type of black habit worn by clergymen in the early 1800s, and he sat in a posture of complete relaxation with his hands clasped lightly together on his lap. After a few moments, Jessop realized that the man was not staring at him at all; rather, the stranger seemed completely unaware of his presence.

[361]

Jessopp never imagined his visitor to be anything other than a living person, but he did think it most peculiar that he had not met the clergyman earlier in the evening. How had the man entered the room and seated himself so silently at the same desk? It was not until the man vanished before his eyes that Jessopp realized he had been visited by a ghost.

Jessopp was a very stolid sort of individual, not easily frightened or impressed by anything out of the ordinary. After he realized that he had seen a ghost, his most pronounced reaction was one of disappointment, because he had not had the time to make a sketch of the ghostly clergyman. He had returned to his notes, wondering how he could sensibly relate the story of his spectral visitor to Lord Orford. Then the white hands once again appeared beside him. The figure sat in precisely the same position as before, and the expression on his face had not changed in the slightest. The ghostly clergyman still seemed to have an attitude of contemplation or complete relaxation, and he sat with his hands folded on his lap. Jessopp turned to give the ghost his full attention. It had occurred to him that he might speak to the specter, and he tried to form a sentence in his mind. He wanted it to be just the kind of provocative statement that would prompt a ghost to utter a response. Then, before his lips could say a word, the eeriness of the whole situation began to dawn on him. A sense of deep dread and fear began to permeate his entire being. An unconscious reflex knocked a book to the desk, and the ghost vanished instantly at the harsh sound.

The story of Jessopp's encounter with the ghost became so exaggerated as it was retold by others that the dentist allowed the *London Athenaeum* to print an authorized account of the incident about two months after the uncanny experience. In the article, Jessopp emphasized that he was not in the habit of engaging in flights of fancy and did not wish to be regarded as one with mediumistic powers who regularly received supernatural visitations; nor was he suffering from any problems of the nervous system that would make him susceptible to delusions. The dentist stressed the point that he had been in perfect health on the night of the materialization and had not been suffering from weariness or fatigue. He also stated that the discussion that had taken place at Mannington Hall that evening had concerned itself with travel and art and had in no way touched upon the supernatural. The ghost, he added, did not appear wispy or cloaked in a traditional sheet. The figure appeared lifelike, natural, and so solid that it had blocked the light from the fireplace. After the aforementioned experience, there was no question in Jessopp's mind that ghosts do exist.

THE OCTAGON: THE CAPITAL CITY'S FAVORITE HAUNTED HOUSE

In Washington, D.C., there is a brick mansion on the corner of New York Avenue and 18th Street that harbors many legends, and a ghost to go with

Over 200 years old, the Octagon is home to many ghosts.

them. Built in 1800 by Colonel John Taylor, the stately mansion known as the Octagon was temporarily used as an executive residence by President James Madison when the British burned the White House during the War of 1812. Today the mansion is the national headquarters of the American Institute of Architects and a historic shrine.

Caretakers and maintenance men have long told tales of moans, groans, and shifting furniture. The "eye" of the haunting seems to be the main stairwell. A gardener once told a journalist of the "groans of distress" that had followed him up the stairs. A former caretaker told of the unexplained sounds that he had often heard moving up the stairs; several times he had heard someone walking up the stairs, but no one was ever seen. According to legend, one of the young women of the Taylor family either fell or leaped to her death down the elegant stairwell. A maintenance man admitted that upon opening the mansion each morning, he found a corner of the rug at the foot of the stairway turned up. The spot where the rug lays is supposedly the very same area where the young woman died over 190 years ago.

A hostess at the Octagon has said that she has never seen any ghosts, but she has watched the chandelier in the stairwell sway as if a hand moved it. The hostess is at a loss for a rational explanation to explain the swinging chandelier. There is no draft in the house, nor is there any kind of vibration that could cause the ornate fixture to sway.

Another maintenance man recalled that, a few years ago, every bell in the mansion would begin to ring at a certain hour every night. That particular disturbance has ceased, but according to some observers, there remains enough activity in the Octagon to qualify the mansion for the title of the "Capital's favorite haunted house."

GHOSTLY SOUTHERN BELLES AT ROCKY HILL CASTLE

Rocky Hill Castle, an old southern mansion, was built by Reverend Thomas Saunders near Courtland, Alabama, in 1828. Until sometime in the 1950s, the castle still sheltered Reverend Saunders's descendants and the family ghost.

Once, when he was queried by reporters as to why the Saunders family remained on the old estate for so long, Saunders simply replied that they just happened to love the place. During the interview, Saunders admitted that the family had, on occasion, heard the clanking of chains coming from the basement. However, Saunders stated that they had conducted a full investigation into the disturbances and had found nothing that could have produced the mysterious noises. On other occasions, they had heard a persistent tapping coming from the basement. It had long been Saunders family legend that the sounds were made by the two who built the castle and who had died years earlier.

Mrs. Saunders recalled the time she sensed the presence of someone in the room with her. Whenever she turned to look over her shoulder she saw no one, but the strong feeling that she was being watched remained. Finally she dared the *thing* to speak, or go away and leave her alone. According to Mrs. Saunders, a voice replied in a whisper, "Sister, do not be doubting, for I am truly here."

Later that same day, Mrs. Saunders was descending the staircase when she was startled to see a woman she had never seen before standing at the foot of the stairs. The woman was attired in the swirling petticoats of the antebellum era. As a number of nearby towns were celebrating centennial observances at the time, Mrs. Saunders assumed that the woman was a solicitor hoping to secure funds for some historical project in connection with a pageant. Mrs. Saunders recalled that she did not for one moment suppose that the smiling lady at the bottom of the staircase was anything other than a living person. When she reached out her hand to welcome her unannounced visitor, the costumed lady vanished. It was as if the voice had materialized a body to demonstrate that it had been "truly there."

Mr. Saunders had suffered through all the weird noises in his old family mansion very patiently, but he was skeptical about his wife's account of the disappearing lady in swirling petticoats. He had never seen the family ghost, and although he was forced to accept the unaccountable noises in the basement, he did not believe in materializing or dematerializing spooks. A few days after his wife's experience with the family ghost, Saunders was in the basement on an errand and was offered dramatic evidence that changed his mind about the reality of ghosts. Sitting on a trunk right before him was a southern belle from the Alabama of long ago.

A family ghost, built up through generations of psychic reconstruction, can almost become an independent mental mechanism. Whether the ghost actually whispered or Mrs. Saunders's heightened psychic sensitivity allowed her to feel the presence of the ghost prior to its actual materialization makes for interesting speculation.

Sandringham's Christmas Ghost

Servants at Sandringham, one of the country homes of England's royal family, have always found it difficult to sleep. According to those who have inhabited the servants' quarters, the rooms are haunted. A maid who spent several years in service of the royal family said that the disturbances always begin on Christmas Eve. Once the ghost has dumped the Christmas cards on the floor and mussed up the beds, the servants can look forward to enduring the ghost's pranks for a period of six to eight weeks.

For generations, the housemaids have known that the most haunted spot in the house is the sergeant footman's corridor on the second floor. Maids refuse to go there alone and will only clean and dust that corridor in small groups. The ancestral ghost is noted for turning light switches on and off, the sound of footsteps it makes in the corridor, as well as the opening and closing of doors. According to one sergeant, the ghost's most grisly accomplishment is when it makes a wheezing sound that resembles a huge, grotesque lung breathing in and out.

Many of England's ancestral ghosts have been explained by marvelous old legends of unrequited love or grim murder, but researchers have been unable to determine any particular incident that could have put Sandringham's ghost in motion.

SCANDALS AND MURDER SATURATE LONGLEAT MANSION

Longleat, one of England's largest and most elegant Elizabethan mansions, is virtually saturated with history, legend, and tragedy. Of special ghostly prominence is the haunted corridor where, in the 1730s, Viscount Weymouth was said to have strangled his wife's lover. This murderous incident is just one of the tragic events that has occurred in the home since its construction was completed in 1580.

On January 25, 1965, NBC aired a television special entitled *The Stately Ghosts of England*, which explored the shadowy corners of Longleat. In the haunted corridor where Weymouth may have strangled his rival for his wife's affections, the cameras managed to capture a weirdly glowing light that came out of one door, bobbed about, moved about 10 yards down the corridor, then disappeared through another door. A strange light also appeared on film for nearly half an hour, although a light source was never found. Mysteriously, the usable footage had dwindled to 11 minutes by the time technicians began to edit the film for television.

In an article for the June 1966 issue of *Fate*, well-known British psychic-sensitive Tom Corbett provided readers with an account of some behind-the-scenes activity during the filming of the NBC special. According to Corbett, microphones went dead quite inexplicably; a series of annoying minor accidents plagued the crew; light cords were unplugged at crucial moments; and film taken in the mansion "turned out muddy" in spite of the fact that two sets of cameras had been used and they had both been inspected before taping began.

While searching for a prop, the chief cameraman entered the nursery on the third floor and felt something oppressive and cloying envelop him. He left the nursery in extreme shock and later stated that he thought he would have suffocated if he had not been able to wrench himself away. Decorated twice for valorous service during World War II, the chief cameraman was not the sort to be startled by mysterious noises and weird shadows.

On another occasion, two young journalists went to Longleat to have a bit of fun with the "cranks" that were making a film about ghosts. To get them out of the way, Corbett suggested that they go up to the Bishop Ken library where they could see two pictures painted by Adolph Hitler and one by Winston Churchill. Corbett wrote that the young men returned much less full of themselves. After they had seen the beautiful collection of books and paintings in the library, they had locked the door and started down the corridor. They had gone only about 20 feet when they both heard a key turning in the door. Startled, one of the young men shouted that he had the key. Nevertheless, they hurriedly retraced their steps and saw, to their amazement, the handle being turned. They did not investigate this occurrence, knowing that they had just locked an empty room.

GHOSTS OCCUPY THE HOME OF WILLIAM LYON MACKENZIE

When people enter the front door of 82 Bond Street in Toronto, they step into a physically restored scene of the past. Mannequins in period clothing stand about, and in the parlor a nineteenth-century housewife in a red shawl stands delicately poised with a red paper flower in her hand. People in oil portraits with eyes from another time stare down at the visitors, and a family album resting on a tasseled velvet tablecloth offers stiff faces looking up from the heavy pages.

This was the home of William Lyon Mackenzie, first mayor of Toronto and grandfather of William Lyon Mackenzie King, prime minister of Canada (1921–1926, 1926–1930, 1935–1948). Mackenzie immigrated to Canada in the early nineteenth century and became a shopkeeper in York. Having a rebellious and stubborn mind, he founded the newspaper *Colonial Advocate* to provide a means for his scathing attacks on the government. His fiery campaign made him a political hero. Mackenzie was elected to the Legislative Assembly of Upper Canada in 1828 and won reelection five times. He became Toronto's first mayor in 1834.

Mackenzie died in 1861, but the caretakers of his historic home claim that the ghosts of Mackenzie and a lady—either Mackenzie's wife or his daughter, Isabel—still walk the halls of the memory-charged mansion. Some witnesses have said that they have seen a third ghost of a small, bald man in a frock coat.

Mr. and Mrs. Alex Dobban assumed the position of caretakers in April 1960 but resigned after little more than a month because of the effect the place was having on Mrs. Dobban's nerves. They hadn't lived in the mansion long when they heard the footsteps going up and down the stairs. Knowing that they were alone in the house, they were perplexed by the sound. On another night, they were awakened by a rumbling noise in the basement. At first they took it to be the oil burner, but Mr. Dobban checked and found that the furnace was not on. They concluded that the noise was the old printing press that occupied one of the locked rooms in the basement. On some nights, they also heard music coming from the piano in the downstairs front room.

Caretakers Mr. and Mrs. Charles Edmunds were able to withstand the ghostly manifestations for nearly four years before they were forced to leave by the constant, oppressive presence of *something*. Mrs. Edmunds lost 40 pounds from the stress of knowing that an unseen entity was always watching them. On the very day the Edmundses moved into Mackenzie's house, they heard footsteps on the stairs when they were the only people in the house. One night Mrs. Edmunds was awakened by something touching her on the shoulder. She opened her eyes to see a ghostly lady standing over her bed, leaning down "like a shadow." Mrs. Edmunds said that she could see the ghost clearly. The phantom had long dark brown hair that hanged down in front of her shoulders and that framed a long, narrow face. She vanished after a few moments. For two years Mrs. Edmunds was not again awakened by the lady, but when she reappeared the ghost left Mrs. Edmunds with a physical memento of their meeting. According to the Edmundses, the lady reached out and slapped Mrs. Edmunds, leaving her left eye purple and bloodshot and her cheek bearing three red welts. Mrs. Edmunds also reported seeing the ghost of a little, bald man in a frock coat. She would see him for just a few seconds and then he would vanish. She stated that she had seen the bald man or the ghostly lady standing in the third-floor bedroom at least eight or nine times.

Charles Edmunds recalled when their grandchildren, Susan, four, and Ronnie, three, visited them in the home shortly after they had moved in. As the children were getting ready for bed one night, they went from their upstairs bedroom down to a bathroom on the first floor. The Edmunds soon heard their grandchildren screaming. They ran down to the bathroom and found both children huddled in a comer. The children said a lady had walked into the bathroom and then just disappeared. Although Mr. Edmunds never saw either of the two ghosts that seemed to haunt the mansion, he often heard heavy, thumping footsteps on the stairs, as if someone with heavy boots on were treading them.

On July 1, 1960, Archdeacon John Frank performed the rites of exorcism in the house at 82 Bond Street. Toronto *Telegram* staff reporter Aubrey Wice was on hand to observe the ritual means of "laying" an earthbound spirit to rest. The clergyman decided to consecrate all vital spots of the haunting. The bedroom where Mrs. Edmunds claimed to have been struck in the face was the first stop. Wice wrote that after the rites of exorcism had been completed, it felt as though the oppressive air that had saturated the house had been lifted.

Mrs. Winifred McCleary, the caretaker who was employed shortly after the exorcism, maintained that the "oppressive air" had not been lifted high enough to suit her. Mrs. McCleary claimed that the house was still very much haunted when she took over as caretaker. She told of hearing the toilet flush by itself and seeing the tap for the hot water turn on its own. "You thought you were in another world in that house," she told Gary Oakes, a *Telegram* reporter. "You knew you weren't alone." Mrs. McCleary remembered that one of the ghosts was not content to just lurk about in the shadows and engage in phenomena of a mildly annoying nature. It wanted to put its arms around people, the woman said.

A second exorcism was ordered and seems to have put the ghosts to rest. I researched the mansion in the late 1960s, but later curators of the house would not answer my queries concerning any continuing phenomena. It seems that caretakers have not actually lived in the Mackenzie house since July 1967, which is not to imply that curators will not reside in the museum because it is haunted. What it does mean is that no one has been in the position to have experiences similar to those encountered by the Dobbans, Edmundses, and Mrs. McCleary.

York University history professor William Kilborn, who wrote a book about Mackenzie entitled *The Firebrand*, believes the caretakers had valid experiences of some kind or other and expressed the opinion that he wouldn't go out of his way to spend the night there. The *Haunted Ontario* website (<http://www.ghosthuntersinc.com/haunted/ontario.htm>) continues to describe the Mackenzie house as being "full of spirits. People have reported misty figures and orb-like lights. Lights go on and off. Voices are heard, as well as footsteps. One witness saw a woman in one of the bedrooms walk to the window and disappear. There have been many other ghosts and activity reported."

THE WHALEY HOUSE: AMERICA'S MOST HAUNTED MANSION

Old San Diego is the birthplace of California. On July 16, 1769, Father Junipero Serra established the mission of San Diego de Alcala on Presidio Hill. In the early 1820s a small Mexican community was formed that had evolved into El Pueblo San Diego by 1835. Because it was the first permanent Spanish settlement on the California coast, San Diego is as significant to the heritage of the United States as Jamestown, the first English settlement in Virginia. The first United States flag was raised over San Diego in 1846.

Not only have my wife, Sherry Hansen Steiger, and I found San Diego to be one of the most haunted places in North America, but the Whaley

San Diego's Whaley House.

House, constructed in 1857, might just be one of the most haunted mansions. When we were researching the mansion, the director of the Whaley House, June Reading—an amicable and knowledgeable woman who has since passed on—told us that immediately after its completion, the mansion became the center of business, government, and social affairs in San Diego. The oldest brick house in southern California, the Whaley House served as a court-house, theater, and boarding house; it was also the family home of Thomas and Anna Whaley and their children. Located at 2482 San Diego Avenue, in what is now referred to as Old San Diego, the Whaley house has been restored and is now owned and operated by the San Diego Historical Society as a tourist attraction.

Although Whaley House closes its doors to visitors at 4:00 P.M., police officers and passersby say that someone or something walks around the house at night and often turns on all the lights. While conducting tours through the old mansion, members of the society have heard footsteps coming from other parts of the house that were visibly unoccupied.

This photograph was taken by Margaret Jackson during her visit to Whaley House. The photograph has been examined by several paranormal researchers, who have stated that the photograph clearly shows up to 20 different ghosts.

Almost every type of haunting phenomena has been observed or encountered in the mansion. Footsteps have been heard in the master bedroom and on the stairs. Windows, even when fastened down with three or four-inch bolts, have mysteriously opened in the middle of the night, triggering the burglar alarms. As they tour the mansion, people have often noticed the smell of food being prepared in the kitchen, the sweet scent of Anna Whaley's perfume, and the heavy aroma of Thomas Whaley's favorite Cuban cigars. Screams have frequently been heard echoing through upstairs rooms; girlish giggles and rattling of doorknobs are also commonplace. A large, heavy china closet once toppled over by itself. Many people have heard the piano in the mansion's music room being played, although visitors are not allowed near the instrument. The milling and shuffling of ghostly crowds are often heard in the courtroom. Images of Thomas and Anna Whaley have been seen on numerous occasions.

Numerous individuals have sensed or psychically seen the image of a man hanging from a scaffold on the south side of the mansion. According to Reading, 10 years before Thomas Whaley purchased the property and constructed his home, a renegade sailor named Yankee Jim Robinson was hanged on the land. The mansion was built over the site of Robinson's execution. To be more precise, the scaffold Robinson was hanged from was located where there is currently an archway that separates the mansion's music room and living room. Whaley had been an observer when Yankee Jim kept his appointment with the hangman.

In the fall of 1966, a group of reporters volunteered to stay in Whaley House and spend the night with Yankee Jim. Special permission was granted to the journalists by the historical society, and the ghost hunters settled in for their overnight stay. The wife of one of the reporters had to be taken home by 9:30 P.M. She was badly shaken by something she had seen on the upper floor but refused to describe. The entire party of journalists left the house before dawn. They also refused to discuss the reason for their premature departure, but some say they were confronted by the ghost of Yankee Jim, still protesting the horror of his death.

Reading said that other ghosts are also seen at Whaley House, including a young girl named Washburn, who was a playmate of the Whaley children, and the family's dog, "Dolly Varden." Some visitors to the house have reported seeing a gaudily dressed woman with a painted face lean out of a second-story window. In Reading's opinion it could well be the ghost of an actress from one of the theatrical troupes that leased the second floor in November 1868.

The court house wing of the mansion is generally thought to be the most haunted area of Whaley house, due to the violent emotions that were expended there in the early days of San Diego. Many individuals who have visited the old house have heard the sounds of a crowded courtroom in session and the noisy meetings of men in Thomas Whaley's upstairs study. According to many psychical researchers, the fact that this one mansion served as the site

June Reading, former director of the Whaley House Museum, standing by the jury stand, where a ghostly figure is frequently seen sitting.

for so many city functions, in addition to being a family home, almost guarantees several layers of psychic residue permeating the environment. Many sensitive visitors to the Whaley House have also seen the image of Anna Whaley, watching over the mansion that she loved so much. According to a good number of those who have encountered her presence, she seems deeply resentful of the intruding strangers.

June Reading told us that in 1964 the popular television talk show host Regis Philbin saw Anna Whaley as he sat on the Andrew Jackson sofa at 2:30 A.M. The spectral image floated from the study through the music room and into the parlor, where Philbin "dissolved" the apparition with the beam of his flashlight. Since that time, night visits to Whaley House have not been permitted.

Numerous photographs of spirit phenomena have been taken in Whaley House over the years, and many can be seen in a display case in the mansion. As a matter of fact, during a visit to the house, my wife Sherry was able to capture a rather startling image on film. When we returned home and developed the photographs taken during our research trip to Whaley House, to our amazement we discovered a ghostly materialization of the noose that hanged Yankee Jim Robinson. Sherry had photographed the arch between the music room and the living room, the site where the renegade had been executed before that portion of the Whaley House had been constructed. The photo reveals a phantom noose hanging from the ceiling. Sherry also captured several other odd materializations that showed up on the developed film. Sherry took several pictures in areas of the house where many have reported lights being turned on when no one is there. Even though the lights were off during our daytime interview with Reading, the photographs show that the lights were "on."

THE MYRTLES: AMERICA'S MOST HAUNTED PLANTATION

According to the Smithsonian Institution, the Myrtles Plantation located three miles north of St. Francisville, Louisiana, rivals the Whaley House for the title of the most haunted house in the United States. Built in 1794 by General David Bradford, the plantation rests on the site of an ancient Native American burial ground. Since it was constructed, the plantation has been the location for at least 10 violent deaths. Throughout the years, owners and their guests have fled the house in the middle of the night, terrified by the appearance of frightening ghosts. The entities continue to be seen by visitors. With the recent popularity of reality programming and documentaries on the paranormal, the story of Myrtles Plantation has been shown numerous times on television.

The tragic events that set the haunting in motion began when Bradford's daughter Sara Matilda married a young judge named Clark Woodruffe. Although the Woodruffes were happily married and their union had produced two daughters, when Sara Matilda was carrying their third child Clark began an extramarital affair with Chloe, one of the house slaves. Although Judge Woodruffe had a reputation for integrity in matters of the law, those who knew him personally were aware that he was promiscuous. At first, Chloe tried to deny the sexual demands of her master, but she knew that if she fought against Woodruffe's unwanted advances, she could be sent to work in the fields, and she much preferred being assigned to the duties in the mansion. While Sara Matilda suffered through her pregnancy and gave birth to another daughter, Chloe provided the release for her master's sexual needs. Eventually, when the judge grew tired of her and chose another house slave as his new mistress, Chloe feared that she would lose her position as a servant in the plantation house and be ordered to work in the fields doing hard manual labor. She desperately hoped that she might somehow find a way to win back Woodruffe's affections and not be in danger of being sent to do brutal work in the cotton fields.

One evening, as she hovered around the Woodruffes as she worked, she listened for any mention of her name and any clue about her fate. The judge grew irritated by her presence and accused her of eavesdropping on a private, family conversation with his wife. As punishment, the Woodruffe ordered his overseers to cut off one of Chloe's ears. From that time on, Chloe wore a green headscarf with an ear ring pinned to it to hide her missing ear.

Disfigured and dismayed, Chloe felt certain that she would be banished to the cotton fields and life in the crude cabins and barracks of the other slaves. That was when the clever Chloe came up with what she believed might be the perfect plan that would guarantee her status as a house slave and keep her out of the fields. Since she was a very young girl, she had been wise in the ways of herbs and potions. She knew that it was possible to mix up a potion that would make her master love her again, but it would be difficult to find a way to make him drink it. After much thought and deliberation, she devised a much better way to use her expertise with herbs. She would bake a birthday cake for the Woodruffes' oldest daughter and place oleander into the mix. If oleander is used in large doses it is poisonous, but Chloe thought that if she only used a small amount of extract in the mix, the family would only become ill. Then, the loyal maid and servant that she was, she would nobly nurse them back to health.

Tragically, Chloe inadvertently sprinkled too much oleander into the cake mix. Sara Matilda and two of her daughters became extremely ill and died within hours after the birthday party. Because neither the judge nor the baby ate any of the poisoned cake, they survived the mysterious illness that struck down the rest of the family. Stricken with grief and ashamed of what she had done, Chloe confided in another slave that she had only intended to make the family ill, so that she would be the one to take care of them. Chloe made a poor choice for a confidante. Rather than keeping the secret, the woman tattled to her fellow slaves that their mistress's death, and the death of her two daughters, had not been due to some mysterious sudden illness. Chloe had deliberately poisoned them.

An enraged mob made up of both the Woodruffes' slaves and their white neighbors chased Chloe into the surrounding woods, where they caught her and hanged her. Her body later was cut down, weighted with rocks, and thrown into the river. Judge Woodruffe closed off the room where the birthday party had been held and never again allowed it to be used during his lifetime. Judge Woodruffe was unable to enforce his decree for long, for he was murdered a few years later.

The ghost of Chloe has been often sighted both inside and outside of the plantation house. She is most often seen wearing a green headscarf that is wrapped like a turban around her head, with an earring pinned over her missing ear. Her ghost is also held responsible for stealing earrings from many guests over the 200 years since her hanging.

John and Teeta Moss, the current owners of the Myrtles Plantation, have converted the place into a bed and breakfast, and Hester Eby, who manages house tours of the mansion and grounds, states that the haunting phenomena continues unabated. Moss even photographed a shadowy image of Chloe standing near the house. According to Eby and members of the staff, resident ghosts frequently reported include those of the two poisoned Woodruffe girls, who are often heard playing and running in the halls. The spirits of the girls have also been seen playing on the mansion's veranda and seated at the table in the children's dining room. Perhaps they are eternally partaking of that last terrible meal that featured a deadly treat of poisoned cake.

Many guests have heard a baby crying when there are no infants present in the mansion. Some witnesses of this phenomenon have associated the sounds of the crying infant with the ghost of a French woman who wanders from room to room, as if she is looking for someone. Perhaps she is searching for her baby. The ghost of a woman in a black skirt floats a foot off the floor and is seen dancing to music that cannot be heard by the living. Some guests have seen the ghost of a man who was stabbed to death in a hallway over an argument concerning a gambling debt. A more active spirit is said to be that of an overseer who was robbed and killed in 1927; the spirit angrily demands that guests leave the place and return to their own homes. Numerous guests have been awakened by an unseen pianist who plays the grand piano on the first floor but immediately stops if someone enters the room. There is a ghost of a young girl that only seems to appear when a thunderstorm approaches the plantation. She has long curly hair, wears an ankle-length dress, and is seen cupping her hands to peer inside the window of the game room.

Many guests have heard the sounds of footsteps on the stairs and have seen the image of a man struggling to reach the upstairs hallway. Eby said that it is commonly believed to be the ghost of William Winter, an attorney who owned the Myrtles Plantation in the late nineteenth century. On the night of his death, he was reportedly summoned to the porch by a stranger on horseback who claimed to be in desperate need of an attorney. When Winter stepped outside to see how he might be of service, the man shot him and rode away. Fatally wounded, Winter stumbled through the house, painfully climbed the stairs, and died in the arms of his wife.

Throughout the years, many residents and their employees have heard their names called by invisible entities. This particular haunting phenomenon seems to ebb and flow, intensifying and then lessening in its manifestations. Now that the place is also a bed and breakfast hotel, Eby said that the staff knows when they are going to have a bad night by the number of guests who call up by midnight and demand to leave the place at once. Both employees and guests report seeing candles floating up the stairs at night, bobbing up and down as if they are being carried by someone. Many believe that the candle is carried by Sara Matilda as she searches for her errant husband dallying with one of the servant girls. One man who was hired to greet guests upon their arrival at the bed and breakfast became fascinated by a woman who approached his post dressed in a white, old-fashioned dress. Thinking she was merely getting in the mood for her stay in an old southern plantation by dressing like an antebellum belle, he was a bit miffed when she seemed unresponsive to his cherry greeting. In fact, she seemed to take no notice of him at all. He watched the seemingly snobbish woman until she walked up to the main house and vanished through the front door without opening it. He left his job that day and never returned to the Myrtles Plantation.

19
Creepy Castles and Ghostly Royalty

THE INCREDIBLE SUPERNATURAL SIEGE AT CALVADOS CASTLE

A Classic Case from France

All of the inhabitants of Calvados Castle were disturbed by the strange noises that echoed throughout its dark corridors shortly after midnight on October 12, 1875. The next morning, the master of Calvados thought that he knew what had caused the nocturnal knockings and thumpings. Someone was obviously trying to frighten his family away from the castle so that they might purchase the surrounding land at a fraction of its value. The scoundrels who had invaded the castle had no doubt found entrance to the interior by means of some long forgotten passage. The brigands probably thought it a simple matter to drive a man away from an old castle that he had just inherited.

He had no sooner finished discussing his theory with his coachman Emile and gardener Auguste when the three men heard the two formidable watchdogs outside in the garden howling and barking. Rushing to a window, the master of Calvados saw the dogs directing their angry attention toward one of the thickets in the garden. He smiled at the thought that their noisy midnight visitors had tarried too long and found themselves cornered by the dogs. He unlocked his weapons case and thrust rifles into the hands of Emile and Auguste. He selected a double-barreled shotgun for his own use. They would soon have the miscreants at gunpoint.

After the men had posted themselves at the edge of the garden, the dogs were urged to attack. The two brutes rushed into the thicket with vicious growls. There was a moment of silence, and then the hoarse canine rumbles of

[379]

fury turned to plaintive whines and whimpers of terror. The dogs ran out of the thicket with their tails between their legs, and the master could not call them back. Cautiously, the three men entered the thicket, their firearms cocked and ready. They found nothing, not a footprint, not a shred of clothing on a branch, absolutely nothing. "But, what," the master asked of his men after they had searched in all directions, "could have frightened the dogs so?" His question was never answered to his satisfaction.

The mysterious disruptions at Calvados Castle that October night started of one of the most prolonged and terrifying accounts of haunting phenomena. The hauntings that took place in the old Norman castle from October 12, 1875, to January 30, 1876, were written up and published in 1893 as the *Annales des Sciences Psychiques* by M. J. Morice. Although the master of Calvados kept a diary that was later used as a meticulous record of the phenomena, he insisted that his family name not be mentioned in connection with the haunting. He is, therefore, referred to in the narrative only as M. de X. His immediate family consisted of Mme. de X., and their son, Maurice. The remainder of the household consisted of Abbe Y., tutor to Maurice; Emile, the coachman; Auguste, the gardener; Amelina, the housemaid; and Celina, the cook.

On the evening of October 13, Abbe Y. came down to the drawing room and told M. and Mme. de X. that his armchair had just moved without anyone being near it. He insisted that he had seen it move out of the corner of his eye. If the strange incident with the watchdogs had not been so fresh in his mind, M. de X. may have accused his son's tutor of too much after-dinner sherry. He tried to calm Abbe Y. down and returned with him to his room. M. de X. attached gummed paper to the foot of the tutor's armchair and fixed it to the floor. Then he gave Abbe Y. permission to ring for him if anything further should occur.

At ten o'clock that evening, M. de X. was awakened by the ringing of Abbe Y.'s bell. When he entered the tutor's room, he found the man with the covers pulled up to the bridge of his nose, peeking out at his employer like a frightened child. In a trembling voice, Abbe Y. said that the whole room had been moving about, and there had been rappings on the wall. M. de X. saw that the armchair had indeed moved about a yard, and several candlesticks and statuettes had been toppled. He heard a door open behind him and turned to see Amelina peeping out from her room across the hall. Her face was pale. She, too, had heard the rappings. The next evening, the disturbances did not confine themselves to Abbe Y.'s room. Thunderous blows were heard all over the castle. M. de X. armed his servants and conducted a search of the entire building.

They found nothing. The pattern was repeated night after night as the noisy ghost began its siege in earnest. For more than three months, the inhabitants of Calvados Castle would not know a night of unmolested slumber. The curate of the parish and Marcel de X., a relative, arrived to witness the phenomena and to try to determine the origin of the manifestations. That night, the sound of a heavy ball was heard descending the stairs from the second floor to the first, jumping from step to step. After having spent a night in the castle, the parish priest declared that the heavy tread he had heard during the night sounded like the footsteps of a giant, and he proclaimed the activity to be supernatural. Marcel de X. agreed with the priest. He had quickly concluded that this ghost would be a most difficult one to "lay," and declared that he would leave Calvados Castle to the noisy spirit. He wished M. de X. the best of luck and returned to his home.

On Halloween the ghost seemed to outdo itself with a display of paranormal prowess that kept the household from going to bed until three o'clock in the morning. The center of the activity had become the green room. The ghostly machinations seemed to always begin or end with loud rappings in the empty room. The entity's walk had also evolved. By All Hallow's Eve, its tread had begun to sound like wooden stumps repeatedly hitting the floor.

It was during a violent November rainstorm that the spirit acquired a voice. High above the howling wind and rumbling thunder, the household heard a long shriek. Amelina declared that there was a woman outside in the storm calling for help. The cry sounded again and everybody looked curiously at one another. Mme. de X. agreed that the wail certainly sounded like a woman, and she asked Celina to look out a window and see if someone was outside. Celina had just reached the window when a cry sounded from within the castle. The members of the household gathered together in the sitting room as if they hoped to seek strength from their unity. Three sorrowful moans sounded from the staircase. The *thing* was getting closer!

The men of Calvados Castle left the sitting room to inspect the castle. They found nothing. There was no woman in the castle and no sign that anyone or anything had entered the castle from the storm. They heard no further sounds until the following night, when everyone was awakened just before midnight by terrible sobs and cries coming from the green room. They seemed to be the sounds of a woman in horrible suffering. The activity seemed to become intensified as days passed by, and the cries of the sorrowful woman in the green room evolved into shrill, furious, despairing cries, "the cries of demons or the damned."

Shortly after the "weeping woman" had arrived and added to the disturbances at Calvados, a cousin of Mme. de X.'s paid a visit. The gentleman was an army officer, and he scoffed at the wild stories his family told him. Against all their pleas, he insisted upon sleeping in the green room. He told them that he always had a revolver at his side, and that if anything should dare to disturb his sleep it would get a bullet in its hide. The officer strode boldly to the green room, left a candle burning as a nightlight, and went straight to sleep.

He was awakened a short time later by what sounded like the soft rustling of a silken robe. He was immediately aware that the candle had been snuffed out and that something was tugging at the covers on his bed. He gruffly demanded to know who was there. He attempted to relight the candle at his bedside, but as soon as he had a flame something extinguished it. Three times he lighted it, and three times he felt a cold breath of air blow it out. The rustling noise seemed to become louder, and something was definitely determined to rob him of his bedclothes. He cocked his revolver and warned his unwelcome guest that if it did not declare itself, he would shoot. The only answer to his demand was an exceptionally violent tug on the covers.

The officer decided to shoot. It was simple enough for him to determine where his silent adversary stood by the sound of the rustling and the pull on the bedclothes. He fired his revolver three times. The lead slugs struck nothing but the wall, and he dug them out with a knife the next morning. While it appeared that the shots had only hit the wall, the officer's attempt was mildly effective, as the ghost left his covers alone for the rest of the night.

Abbe Y. fared far worse than any member of the household throughout the duration of the haunting. No other room in the castle had to entertain such animated furniture. Whenever the tutor left his room, he always made certain that the windows were bolted and his door was locked. The key to his room hung by a leather strap that he kept belted to his waist. These precautions never accomplished the least bit of good. When he returned to his room, Abbe Y. would invariably find his couch overturned, cushions scattered about, windows opened, and his armchair placed on his desk. On one occasion, all of his books were scattered on the floor. Only the Holy Scriptures remained on the shelves. The tutor once tried nailing his windows closed. He returned to find the windows wide open and the couch cushions balanced precariously on the outside windowsill. The most hurtful attack on the clergyman occurred as he knelt at his fireplace, stirring the coals. Without warning, a huge amount of water rushed down the chimney, extinguishing the fire. The sparks that flew from the chimney blinded Abbe Y., and he was covered in ashes. The cleric somberly concluded that such actions could only be the work of Satan.

One night the ghost roamed the corridors of the castle and sought admittance to the rooms of each member of the household. It knocked once or twice on the doors of several bedrooms, then, true to its aggressive pattern of behavior against the tutor, it paused to deal 40 consecutive blows to Abbe Y.'s door before it returned to the green room.

When a priest from a neighboring parish ventured to stay the night in Calvados Castle, he heard the distinctive sounds of a large animal rubbing itself along the walls. Another visitor took special notice of the sounds the ghost made as it walked through the halls. He said that the steps taken by the ghost were quite unlike human steps and was sure that no animal could have walked in such a manner. He declared it sounded more like a stick jumping on one end.

When the Reverend Father H. L., a Premonstrant Canon, was sent to Calvados by the bishop, there was not the slightest sound from the noisy ghost from the moment the reverend father entered the castle until the moment he left. But as soon as the clergyman had made his departure, there was a loud thud in the first-floor passage that sounded like a body had suddenly fallen to the ground. That disturbance was followed by what sounded like a rolling ball violently striking a door. The ghost had once again begun its torment of the household in earnest.

On January 20, 1876, M. de X. left for a two-day visit to his brother, leaving his wife to keep up the journal of the haunting. Mme. de X. recorded hearing an eerie bellowing that sounded something like a bull and frightened everyone during her husband's absence. A weird drumming sound was also introduced during M. de X.'s absence, as well as a peculiar noise that seemed very much like something striking the stairs with a wand or a stick.

Upon M. de X.'s return to Calvados, the disturbances became more violent than they had ever been. The ghost charged into the rooms of Auguste and Emile and turned their beds over. It invaded the master's study and heaped books, maps, and papers on the floor. The midnight screams increased in shrillness and were joined by the furious cries of animals. Rhythmic tappings moved up and down the corridors as if a small drum and bugle corps were parading in the halls. For the first time the ghost pounded on the door of Maurice, the son of M. and Mme. de X. The force of the successive blows on his door shook every window on the floor.

On the night of January 26, 1876, the parish priest arrived to conduct the rites of exorcism. He had also arranged for a Novena of Masses to be said at Lourdes and coincide with his performance of the ancient ritual. The priest's arrival was greeted by a long, drawn-out cry and what sounded like hoofed creatures running from the first floor passage. The door to Maurice's room began to shake as if something desperately demanded entrance.

The last days of the haunting are significant in that a great deal of the activity began to center around the adolescent son. It was as though the psychic tremors of puberty had somehow set the manifestations in motion or had reactivated unseen forces that had lain dormant in the old castle. The rites of exorcism reached their climax at 11:15 on the night of January 29. From the stairway came a piercing cry, like that of a great beast that had been dealt its deathblow. Rappings began to rain on the door of the green room. At 12:55 A.M., all those present in Calvados Castle heard the voice of a man in the first-floor passage. M. de X. recorded in his journal that the voice seemed to shout twice, "Ha! Ha!" Ten powerful blows to the door of green room shook everything. After one final blow to the door, there was the sound of coughing in the first-floor passage.

The sound of coughing may very well have been the entity's death-rattle. The family rose and cautiously began to move about the castle. The priest slumped in exhaustion from the long ordeal. There were no terrible screams, no moving of furniture, no mysterious knocking. They found a large earthenware plate that had been broken into 10 pieces at the door to Mme. de X.'s room. No one had ever seen the plate before that night.

"Everything has stopped," M. de X. wrote in his journal entry for January 30, 1876. His elation was somewhat premature. Several days after the exorcism had been performed, Mme. de X. was sitting at a writing desk when a packet of holy medals and crosses dropped in front of her. It was as if the ghost had suffered a momentary defeat and was declaring that it must withdraw from the fray for a time to recuperate and lick its wounds. Toward the end of August 1876, soft knockings and rappings began to be heard again. On the third Sunday in September, the ghost arranged the drawing-room furniture in the shape of a horseshoe, with the couch in the middle. When the parish priest heard that the hauntings had returned to Calvados Castle, he was heard to moan that the devil had held council and was about to begin the spiritual warfare again.

The final cycle of the phenomena was very short-lived. The ghost had lost intensity, was less destructive, and appeared content playing the organ and moving an occasional bit of furniture about the room of Maurice's new tutor. The phenomena became progressively weaker, and eventually whatever energy had energized it during the brief cycle dissipated. Finally, the only thing that haunted Calvados Castle was the memory of those terrible months when a ghost with a thundering, hammering fist had run rampant in its corridors and manifested one of the most dramatic hauntings on record.

THE GHOSTLY LADIES AND LORDS OF GREAT BRITAIN

Anne Boleyn

Shortly before World War II, a British music hall comedian sang a song about Anne Boleyn's ghost walking through the Tower of London "with her head tucked underneath her arm," but a phantom such as Anne's is hardly a subject to jest about. Anne *does* haunt a site near Wakefield Tower, in the historic Tower of London. It has been said that her unhappy shade manifests wearing the etheric replica of the fur-trimmed robe of gray damask, crimson petticoat, white collar, and black hood she wore to her execution on May 19, 1536. Anne not only haunts the Tower of London but also Hever Castle, her old home in Kent, and Bollen Hall in Cheshire.

The Tower of London, guarded by its famous Yeoman Warders, also known as "Beefeaters."

Not many years ago, one of the guards at the Tower of London reported to an officer that there was a strange light in the old Chapel of St. Peter ad Vincula, and that it had been seen before. On each occasion the building was known to be locked and empty. The officer obtained a ladder that he propped up near one of the high windows to peer into the chapel, and he was amazed to see a procession of men and women radiating a luminous glow. Among the figures was a woman who resembled the old paintings that he had seen of Anne Boleyn. The officer watched the ghostly scene for several minutes before it suddenly vanished.

Henry VIII

It is a wonder that Henry VIII does not haunt the Tower of London, for the nearby Chapel of St. Peter ad Vincula contains the bones of not only Anne Boleyn but also Katharine Howard and numerous other persons who were victims of Henry's wrath and the headman's axe. For centuries, King Henry's ghost has been seen in Windsor Castle. Witnesses claim that his spirit can often be heard groaning and dragging the ulcerated leg that tormented him in his later years.

Katharine Howard

The ghost of Katharine Howard, another of Henry's unlucky wives, is associated with Hampton Court Palace. While a prisoner in the palace, she managed to escape from her room on November 5, 1541. She ran down a gallery that gave access to the king's private chapel, where her lord and master was at his devotions. She hoped to plead with him to spare her life, but as soon as she had she reached the door of the chapel, she was dragged back by the guards. After her death at the block, her phantom was said to haunt the gallery. Her wraith would appear at the far end, pass as far as the door of the chapel, stop, and then return to utter a piercing shriek, which ended in her vanishing.

Jane Seymour

Jane Seymour, the wife who followed Anne Boleyn, died in childbirth and is also said to haunt Hampton Court Palace. On very rare occasions she has been seen descending one of the staircases, a lighted candle in her hand.

Queen Elizabeth I

King George V saw the ghost of Queen Elizabeth a few years before his death, during one of his periods of illness. He was at Windsor Castle at the time and alone in his bedroom. Suddenly pictures on the wall began to move as if they were being stirred by a draft. At the same time, a woman wearing a black Tudor costume appeared out of one of the walls, crossed the room, and vanished through the opposite wall. The king felt a sensation of coldness that so frequently accompanies psychic manifestations. His nurse told how she, too, had been conscious of an invisible presence in the sick room; she had also seen the pictures stir on the walls.

"View of Hampton Court Palace" by Jan Griffier, c. 1702.

The ghost of Queen Elizabeth I was also seen by a man in the king's service at Windsor Castle. He saw the ghost in broad daylight, and on comparing notes with His Majesty, came to the conclusion that they had both seen the phantom of Elizabeth Tudor.

Real Ghosts, Restless Spirits, and Haunted Places

In 1996 Britain's Queen Elizabeth II met an actress portraying Elizabeth I at the opening of the Royal Armouries Museum.

The Brown Lady of Raynham Hall

Another great lady's ghost that has walked for many generations is that of Dorothy Walpole Townshend, sister of Sir Robert Walpole, the first prime minister of England, and wife of Lord Charles Townshend of Raynham Hall. In 1712 at the age of 26, Dorothy married her childhood sweetheart, Lord Charles, after his first wife died. When Lord Charles learned that Dorothy had been the mistress of Lord Wharton—or so the legend goes—he ordered her imprisoned in her room. Various stories say Dorothy died of a broken heart, a fall down the stairs, or of smallpox.

After Lord Charles's grandson George was made a marquess 1786, he became known for the lavish parties he held for aristocrats at Raynham Hall, located a few miles southwest of Fakenham, in Norfolk. An added attraction for the guests was the opportunity of glimpsing the ghost of Dorothy Townshend carrying a lamp as she walked the darkened corridors of the estate. Her ghost has been seen many times wearing a dress of brown brocade, so her

The famous photograph of the "Brown Lady of Raynham Hall."

specter became popularly known as the "Brown Lady of Raynham Hall." When George IV visited Raynham in the early nineteenth century, he was awakened as he slept in the state bedroom by a pale woman dressed in brown. The ghost so frightened him that he vowed to never again return to Raynham.

In 1835 Colonel Loftus, a gentleman staying at the estate over Christmas, saw the ghost on two occasions in as many days. On the night of his second encounter, she was on the staircase, carrying a lamp. He made a sketch of her, making a particular note of the fact that her eye sockets were hollow and empty. Not many years later, Captain Frederick Marryat, author of numerous popular books for boys, saw the Brown Lady carrying a lamp and followed her. When she turned toward him, she smiled in a manner he deemed diabolical, and he fired his pistol at her. The bullet went right through her and was lodged in a heavy door. After this attempted assault, she vanished for about a hundred years.

When the Brown Lady reappeared again, it was in 1926 to the then Marquess Townshend, who was a boy at the time of the encounter. Ten years later, Lady Townshend hired photographer Indra Shira to take photographs of the interior of Raynham Hall. To the astonishment of the photographer, he saw the ghostly form of a woman descending the stairs. The photographer managed to capture the ghost on film. Shira's photograph appeared in *Country Life* magazine, December 1, 1936, and shows a woman wearing what appears to a wedding gown and a veil, or possibly a shroud.

Some psychical researchers from the United Kingdom claim that Queen Elizabeth II has seen the ghost of Dorothy Walpole on several occasions. According to members of the Queen's staff, the Brown Lady appears with a cold rush of air that makes Her Majesty's dogs start barking like mad.

In the 1950s a famous race car driver sat up all night with two dogs waiting for the phantom. He did not see her, but the dogs sensed a presence that came down a passage in the dead of night, for they suddenly appeared terrified.

The Green Lady of Louth

From the Brown Lady of Raynham, we turn to Green Lady of Louth. Thorp Hall, Louth, was once the seat of Sir John Bolle, an adventurer who set out on an expedition to Cádiz, Spain, in 1596. While there, he fell in love with a beautiful Spanish woman who wanted to be his wife, but this was impossible as he had a wife and family in his native land. Thus, she could not accompany him to England, but as a keepsake she gave him a miniature of herself wearing a green dress. Strange as it may seem, although the woman never visited England during her life, her phantom has occasionally been seen at Thorp Hall. She is usually seen under a tree in the grounds, but she always manifests wearing a green dress.

The Gray Lady of Hackwood

After ladies brown and green comes the Gray Lady of Hackwood. In the 1860s a certain legal gentleman, who was hard-headed and not easily deceived, saw the Gray Lady appear out of a wall in the bedroom he occupied as a guest at Hackwood Hall, near Basingstoke in Hampshire. At first he suspected trickery, but on investigation, a hoax was ruled out after the Gray Lady appeared twice in one night. In the morning he resolved to say nothing to his fellow guests, but on his arrival at the breakfast table they excitedly asked him if he had noticed the shadowy gray form that had followed him up the staircase the previous night.

Amy Robsart

Another famous lady who was reluctant to quit this world was Amy Robsart, wife of Robert Dudley, who was very famous at court in the days of Elizabeth I. Her husband neglected her when royal favor had come his way, and she became despondent. At that time she lived at Cumnor Place in Oxfordshire, and it was there that she met her death on September 8, 1560. The circumstances surrounding her death have always been considered strange. She had given her servants the day off so they could visit a fair at Cumnor Village, and when they returned in the evening they found their mistress dead at the foot of the staircase. Her neck was broken.

Whether she had met with foul play or had an accident will never be known, but her violent passing seemed to result in her becoming an earthbound spirit. Her phantom haunted the staircase from 1560 until the house was demolished in 1810. Twelve clergymen had tried to "lay" her ghost, but their attempts were all in vain.

After the house was pulled down, the ghost of Amy Robsart was occasionally seen in the open parkland. It was said that all who came face to face with her died within a few days of the encounter. Legend says that Amy's ghost appeared to her husband, and during her visit to him she told him that he would shortly die. This proved correct, for 11 days later he was dead.

THE GHOSTLY CASTLES AND MANSIONS OF GREAT BRITAIN

Windsor Castle

Windsor Castle, built in the eleventh century, has been christened by psychical researchers as the "Grand Central Station" for the ghosts of English royalty. Princess Margaret confided in friends that she had encounters with the ghost of Queen Elizabeth I, who died in 1603, and Charles I, who was beheaded in 1649.

Queen Elizabeth II of Britain during 2001's Garter ceremony at Windsor Castle.

King George III, England's monarch at the time of the American Revolution, tragically went mad during his reign and has often been sighted in the castle library. He appears to be studying ancient volumes, perhaps to determine the reason for his spells. He is said to mutter, "what, what," over and over again.

Real Ghosts, Restless Spirits, and Haunted Places

The Monster of Glamis

Princess Margaret was born in a haunted castle that has its own grotesque monster-in-residence. While the British Isles can boast of many spectral visitants, Glamis Castle is the only one that can claim an indestructible, flesh-and-blood monster that resides in a hidden mystery room.

Glamis is one of the most ancient of Scottish castles, and as it is purported to be the scene of Macbeth's foul murder of Duncan, there is little wonder that the old fortress shelters a number of extremely active phantoms. For centuries, inhabitants of the castle have claimed to see numerous ghostly re-enactments of tragedies that have saturated the psychic ether of the environment. Among the phantom recreations are:

1. The erection of the scaffold used for the execution of the widow of the sixth Lord Glamis, who was hanged as a witch.

2. The accidental death of the eighth Lord Glamis.

3. The agonizing natural death of the fifth Earl of Strathmore.

4. The murder of the third Earl of Strathmore during a game of cards at the castle.

One of the more foul deeds committed by one of the lords of Glamis concerns the mass murder of a group of Ogilvies, who arrived at the castle and begged for refuge from a band of pursuing Lindsays. The Lord of Glamis pretended to be sympathetic to the Ogilvie cause and locked them up in a secret dungeon, promising to shelter them from the Lindsays. When the leader of the Lindsays arrived at the castle, Lord Glamis winked, held up the key to the thick stone door, and told the man not to worry about the Ogilvies any longer. Lord Glamis had sealed them away to starve to death.

A later Lord Glamis, who was a bit less awed by manifestations of the supernatural than some of his predecessors, led a number of servants in an investigation of ghostly noises that had been disturbing the household. They managed to trace the spectral sounds to a large room in an unused portion of the castle. Lord Glamis found a key to fit the ancient lock, and as the door swung open, he fainted. The wide-eyed servants, who caught their swooning lord, were horrified to see that the room was filled with skeletons. From the position of the skeletal frames, it was easy to determine that they had died gnawing one another's flesh.

But back to the monster. All chroniclers of Glamis agree that it resides somewhere in a secret room, and generations of servants have sworn that they have heard its shuffling feet and hideous half-human cries as it emerges for its nocturnal prowlings. According to Augustus Hare, who visited the castle in 1877, a ghastly chamber that is deep within a wall hides a secret transmitted

Glamis Castle, Scotland.

from the fourteenth century, which is always known to three persons. When one of the triumvirate dies, the survivors are compelled by a terrible oath to elect a successor. In his famous book *Demonology and Witchcraft*, Sir Walter Scott also wrote about the ritual of the select three that have to hide their terrible secret. Scott wrote that the only people who knew the location of the hidden room were the Earl, his steward, and, upon coming of age, the heir.

According to legend, the monster is a Lord Glamis who received the brunt of a family curse while in his mother's womb. The curse dictated that he be born a half-human monster who should live in misshapen form for all eternity. When the child was delivered, it was found to be a grotesque monstrosity, and the brutish baby was hidden away by his father in a secret room. For centuries, three people have been selected to care and look after for the monster.

A persistent legend tells of one Lady Glamis who was determined to discover the location of the secret room and view the monster for herself. While Lord Glamis was away on a trip, she instructed her guests, who were all quite eager to help her solve the mystery, to hang a towel from every window in the castle. The window without a towel, she reasoned, would be the secret room.

After the party had draped a towel in every visible window, they encircled the castle to see if any opening might be without a tell-tale cloth. One window remained undraped, but the searchers had no luck in locating the hidden room. They could only conclude that the secret chamber lay deep within a wall. Lord Glamis returned home to find the guests and his lady still engaged in their search for the monster. He was enraged, for he had no intention of allowing the terrible family secret to ever become public knowledge. After a violent quarrel with her indignant husband, Lady Glamis left the castle, never to return.

Culzean Castle

Culzean Castle is a picturesque and historic fortress in Turnberry, Ayrshire, Scotland. Today, much of its colorful past has been forgotten, and it is commonly referred to as "Ike's Castle" because former United States President Dwight D. Eisenhower was given a lavishly furnished apartment in the castle as a tribute to his leadership of the Allied armies in World War II.

Visitors and staff often mention ghostly encounters with a beautiful dark-haired girl in an evening dress who approaches them in an empty corridor. Mrs. Harriet Howard, an American tourist, told of a meeting she had with the girl in Culzean Castle. She remembered that the ghost greeted her with the words, "It rains today." Howard nodded in reply, assuming that the beautiful girl must be some kind of hostess-guide for the castle. As the corridor was quite narrow, Howard leaned back against a wall and stated that she would give the young woman some more room to pass. The girl's smile faded. "I do not require any room nowadays," she said wistfully. According to Howard, her entire right side became chilled as the girl brushed past her and continued down the corridor. "And the really strange part of it," the startled woman said later, "was that she didn't really brush up against me, she actually walked through my side."

World's Biggest Ghost Hunt at Tutbury Castle

Walpurgis Night (April 30) has traditionally been regarded as one of the most powerful nights for ghosts, demons, and long-legged beasties. In essence, it is springtime's Halloween, though many practicing witches and occultists believe that Walpurgis Night has an even greater potential for smashing the barriers between the seen and unseen worlds.

On Walpurgis Night, 2003, hundreds gathered at Tutbury Castle outside of Derby to participate in an event publicized as the "World's Biggest Ghost Hunt." According to many of the participants, they received more than

On March 3, 1993, Brenda Ray took a set of photographs in Tutbury, Staffordshire, United Kingdom. Tutbury Castle, quite visible in the background, is home to many ghosts. When Ray had her film developed, one image showed an individual in a flowing cape walking down the middle of the road. Another photograph taken seconds later does not show the hooded figure.

they bargained for. David Clensy, a feature writer for the *Evening Telegraph*, said that he arrived at the castle a cool, calm, and reserved skeptic. When he left, his suit was caked with mud, sweat was streaming from his brow, and he felt "somewhere near a gibbering wreck." Nobody, he said, had anticipated such violent results at the ghost hunt.

Tutbury Castle was originally constructed in 1071 by the Norman Hugh de Avranches. In 1265 Henry III gave the castle to his younger son Edmund, who was granted the title of Earl of Lancaster in 1267, and the estate has remained in the possession of the earls and dukes of Lancaster ever since. Mary Queen of Scots was imprisoned at Tutbury in the late sixteenth century. In 1646 the castle was taken by parliamentary forces during the civil war and ordered to be destroyed, leaving the ruins that exist today.

The King's Chamber, where Charles I took shelter to avoid the roundhead forces, is considered the most haunted area of the castle. Ghosts frequently reported include a monk, a baby, a drummer boy, and

Close up of the mysterious figure walking through Tutbury.

a gray lady. Management of the castle grounds has closed portions of the ruins, including the King's Chamber, because in recent years they have had so many visitors and ghost hunters faint as they enter the room. The spirits within are quite aggressive and have been known to push, slap, and touch people.

Clensy said that although his skeptical mind tried to focus on having only rational thoughts as he entered the King's Chamber, it was hard to do after he saw a husky bouncer from Derby run from the cold, dank place. The man later told Clensy that he had felt a tapping on his shoulder that began to burn. It had left him feeling powerless and terrified. The big man admitted that he had burst into tears he had felt so frightened. And when he had run out into the light and pulled back his collar, there was a long, three-pronged claw mark on his neck that was still bleeding.

The team of four medics stationed at Tutbury Castle said that the bouncer's wounds were the most serious they dealt with that night. Most of the first-aid was directed toward the people who fainted and swooned. The medics observed that fainting was quite common when people felt overcome by strange things going on around them.

On May 3 the sponsors of the World's Biggest Ghost Hunt declared the event an unqualified success. According to Tutbury Castle and Fright Nights (<http://www.frightnights.co.uk/wbgh/>), 750 people attended the event, and nearly 200 reported strange experiences within the castle walls. In addition, dozens of individuals camped all night in the rain and reported further ghostly encounters.

20
Phantoms on Roads and Highways

THE PHANTOM HITCHHIKER

We have all heard at least one variation on the "phantom hitchhiker" story. It may well be the best-known and most universal of all so-called urban legends. Here is a recap of the familiar tale to set the mood for this chapter.

A college student (or a salesman) is driving on a lonely country road late one rainy night when he is startled to see a young woman walking along the shoulder. Immediately, he pulls over, leans across the front seat to open the passenger door, and asks her if she wants a ride. She appears a bit dazed and is soaked to the skin.

With a mumbled word of thanks, she gets inside. The college man reaches behind him, grabs his sweater from the backseat, and offers it to the hitchhiker. In the glow of the dashboard lights, he can see that she is really a very lovely girl.

She smiles her thanks and drapes the sweater over her shoulders, informing him that she has to get home to see her parents. The driver notices for the first time that her face and hands are scratched and bleeding, and he asks what happened to her. She explains that her car slid off the road and into a ditch. She had been standing there for what had seemed like hours, hoping for help, before she decided to walk the rest of the way to her parents' home.

He tells her that there is no problem taking her right to her parents' front door. She thanks him, gestures into the darkness ahead and says that the house is only a few miles ahead.

[399]

As he is summoning the courage to ask her name, she points to the lights of a house down a very short lane. She asks him to stop, and she gets out of the car. He protests that he would be happy to drive her the rest of the way, but she is already running away into the night. As he drives on, he berates himself for not asking her name, but then he remembers that she still wears his sweater. That will be his excuse to drive back to her parents' home and formally make her acquaintance.

Two days later, the student drives back to his mystery girl's home and knocks on the door. He is surprised when a very elderly woman opens the door and invites him to step inside. As he looks about the interior of the front parlor, he notices a framed portrait of the beautiful young girl, and he asks the woman if her granddaughter is home.

Following the student's gaze to the portrait, the woman begins to weep. Her darling daughter, she said, is still trying to come home. The student listens incredulously as the woman tells him that her daughter had been killed in an automobile accident on a dark and rainy night over 40 years before.

He leaves the old woman, concluding that she must be crazy. The hitchhiker he had picked up that night was no more than 19 years old. And she was very much alive.

As he passes a small rural cemetery, something blowing in the wind on one of the grave markers catches his eye. When he enters the graveyard to investigate, he finds his sweater draped over a tombstone that marks the final resting place of a young woman who had died 40 years ago.

Some version of the above account of a phantom hitchhiker has been told and retold with variations since the days of horse and carriage. Each year I receive a number of accounts from individuals who swear that they themselves have stopped to pick up a ghostly hitchhiker—nearly always a lovely young woman.

The stories of phantom hitchhikers translate easily from one culture to another. For many years, taxi drivers in Naha, Okinawa, Japan, have claimed that an attractive woman in her 20s, with short-cropped hair and dressed in black slacks, often hails them for a ride on the road to the U.S. Marine camp. When the cab drivers turn to ask for a specific destination, she disappears. The phantom has been dubbed the "Nightwalker of Nago," because she most often appears on the mountain road leading from the fishing village of Nago to the marine camp.

Resurrection Mary, Archer Avenue, Chicago

Chicago paranormal researcher Richard Crowe has quite a file on "Resurrection Mary," a beautiful phantom hitchhiker who haunts Chicago's South

Side. "She was buried in Resurrection Cemetery on Archer Avenue, which is where she gets her nickname," Crowe explained. "During the 1930s and 1940s, Mary was often picked up at dances by various people. She would ask for a ride toward Resurrection Cemetery, saying that she lived down that way. As people drove her home, she would yell at them to stop in front of the cemetery gates. She would get out of the car, run across the road, and dematerialize at the gate."

Crowe mentioned a report wherein two young men were fascinated by watching this beautiful blonde dance by them, but when she passed near them they got the strangest sensation. That night when they got home, they told their father about this woman. They' d never heard of Resurrection Mary, but their father recognized her by the description they provided.

"I investigated and found out that a week before this sighting, Mary had been seen dancing around the cemetery' s fence," Crowe said.

Crowe told me that he had numerous first-person accounts of people who have had Mary open their car doors and jump in, but he had only one first-person account of someone who met her at a dance and followed up by going to the street address she gave him. According to the man's report, Mary had sat in the front between the driver and him. Their friend sat in the back-seat. When they approached the front gate at Resurrection Cemetery, she asked them to stop and let her out. It was a few minutes before midnight, and the young men had protested, saying she couldn't possibly live there. According to the narrator of the story, Mary said, "I know. But I have to get out."

"So being gentlemen and she being so beautiful, we let her out, and she left without saying another word," he told Crowe. "She crossed the road run-ning, and as she approached the gate, she disappeared."

The young man continued with his account: "She had given me her name and address, so early Monday morning, all three of us guys came to the number and street in the stockyards area. We climbed the front steps to her home. We rang and knocked on the door. The mother opened the door, and lo and behold, the girl's color picture was on the piano, looking right at us. The mother said she was dead. We told her our story and left. My friends and I did not pursue the matter any more, and we haven't seen her again. All three of us went into the service thereafter and lost contact with each other."

THE HAUNTED HIGHWAYS AND ROADS OF GREAT BRITAIN

People have been traveling about at night in carriages and coaches far longer in Great Britain than in the United States, so there seems little question that their shadowy highways should have an inordinate number of ghosts at the side of the road.

The A23

The United Kingdom's most haunted road is said to be A23 between London and Brighton, where numerous motorists have sighted a small girl with no hands or feet, a specter in a white trench coat, and a ghost dressed in cricketer's clothing.

The A465

On a stretch of the A465 near Bromyard in Herefordshire, villagers are concerned that the ghost of an accident from more than 60 years ago could be haunting the country road. A farmer reported as many as 26 drivers crashing into his fence during an 18-month period. Some motorists stated that they mysteriously lost control of their vehicles, that they felt their steering wheels pulled from their hands, as they approached the haunted area.

The A12

On a dark night in the 1970s, a lorry driver was traveling north up the A12 on a narrow stretch of road outside Blythburgh in Suffolk when he was horrified to see in the road ahead of him a man riding in a small cart pulled by a horse and a woman walking beside the cart. He swerved to attempt to avoid hitting them, but the road runs between high banks at that point. Thus unable to leave the road, he slammed into the pair and their horse and cart.

Shaking with dread and remorse, assuming that he must surely have killed the two, the driver stepped down from his cab and began to walk back along the road, fearing at any moment to come upon the grisly remains. He found nothing. He walked back to his truck, looked underneath and around the vehicle. Nothing.

At last he drove on, baffled but relieved that he apparently had not harmed anyone. Later, he learned that the folk of Blythburgh often encounter the cart, the driver, and the woman crossing that piece of road, and the historians among them believe the ghosts date back to the eighteenth century.

Blue Bell Hill

Since 1965 dozens of drivers have slammed on their brakes to avoid hitting a pretty young woman in a flowing white dress standing in the road on Blue Bell Hill in Maidstone, England. The phantom is said to be that of a woman who was to have been a bridesmaid for her best friend when she died in a car crash the night before the wedding. Her spirit appears still dressed in her flowing bridesmaid's gown, still attempting to get to the wedding on time.

The country road by Bosworth Battlefield (near Sutton Cheney, Leicestershire) is said to be haunted by ghostly soldiers and galloping horsemen.

Salisbury

In October 1959 Charles Collins, a salesman for an industrial engineering firm, was returning to London when he decided to spend the night at the

Blue Bell Hill, Maidstone, Kent, United Kingdom, where phantom hitchhikers have been seen.

Spread Eagle, a small eighteenth-century coaching inn on the western edge of Salisbury. Around midnight, Collins suddenly had the urge to get out of bed and look out the window. As he looked over the yard, he saw a man in eighteenth-century costume ride through on a horse. He wore a mask and carried a pistol. Collins was captivated by the sight—until the man suddenly vanished.

In the morning, the landlord unhesitatingly told Collins that he had seen the ghost of a highwayman named Richard Savage, who had been hanged in 1730. Tradition said that he had sought refuge at the Spread Eagle, but the landlord turned him away. Ever since, he had returned to the inn to haunt it.

Historical records of the phantom highwayman go back to 1850, and the ghost has been seen on the average of once every five years. In 1962 Savage's spirit was seen by three American tourists staying at the inn.

THE WEEPING BRIDE OF STOWE, VERMONT

Old-timers in the region state that the ghost that haunts the covered bridge on Hollow Road is that of a young bride who was left waiting at the altar by an irresponsible groom. The jilted woman left the church, heading for her elusive lover's home near the bridge on Hollow Road. As she was crossing the bridge, something startled her horse, causing it to bolt and throw her to her death on the rocks below the bridge.

Traditionally, in the wee hours of morning, the sorrowing bride returns to search for the lover who betrayed her and humiliated her by jilting her on their wedding day. Motorists traveling the road late at night have reported seeing the image of a young woman dressed in a bridal gown driving her carriage resolutely toward the covered bridge. Some have reported making eye contact with the angry ghost and state that the experience chilled them to the bone.

MISTY MISS LATTA ON ARKANSAS 64

Drive the lonely stretch of Arkansas Highway 64, especially on a rainy night, and area residents swear that you will be likely to sight the tormented spirit of Laura Starr Latta, who died a month before her twentieth birthday in 1899. Motorists have claimed to have seen Laura's small, frail frame inside a white nightgown standing on the side of the road across from the cemetery where her body lies. Some old stories say that Laura was accosted by a gang and beaten to death on the way to her wedding. Others say that she was killed by a runaway wagon or murdered by a bizarre cult. The inscription on her tombstone reads, "Gentle Stranger passing by, As you are now, once was I. As I am now, so you must be. Prepare yourself to follow me."

THE SPIRITS OF POCAHONTAS PARKWAY TOLL PLAZA

Over the years I have received numerous reports from truck drivers who make long hauls across the Plains states and who say that they have seen strange things. Most often, in addition to phantom hitchhikers of varying descriptions, they attest to having encountered spirits from the past—ghostly wagon trains, small bands of Native tribespeople, stage coaches, and Pony Express riders.

On July 15, 2002, the driver of a delivery truck reported seeing three Native Americans approaching the recently opened Pocahontas Parkway toll plaza on state Route 895 in eastern Henrico County, Virginia. In a report filed by the toll taker to whom he related the account, the driver remarked that he had seen three breech-clothed warriors carrying torches walking in the middle of the highway. He blasted his horn to warn two more torch-wielding men who were clearly illuminated by his headlights. He wondered if some tribespeople were staging some bizarre kind of protest against the parkway.

The toll taker took the driver's report and added it to the list of stories from motorists who had seen strange and unexplainable phenomena. She

This photograph was taken on a rural road where strange apparitions were often seen.

knew that although she would report the incident to state troopers who would be right on the case, they would find no Native Americans parading with torches in the area.

Troopers who patrol the graveyard shift along the Pocahontas Parkway told Chris Dovi of the Richmond, Virginia, *Times-Dispatch*, that they had responded to dozens of calls similar to the one the delivery truck driver made on July 15. The first was on July 1, then two nights later, when plaza workers reported hearing Indian drums, chants, whoops, and the cries of what seemed to be hundreds of voices. From time to time there would be seen the vague outlines of people running back and forth in the darkness.

Virginia state police spokeswoman Corinne Geller visited the toll plaza late one night in July and said that the high-pitched howls and screams were real. She told Dovi (August 11, 2002) that the sounds were not the kind of screams that a person in trouble would make, "but whooping. There were at least a dozen to 15 [voices]. I would say every hair on my body was standing up when we heard those noises."

An engineer working nights to complete the construction of the bridge in Parkway Plaza said that he and a group of workmen had seen an Indian sitting astride a horse watching them from below on the interstate. They were about to tell him to move on, that he wasn't allowed to ride a horse on the interstate, when both rider and horse disappeared.

Deanna Beacham of the nearby Nansemond tribe confirmed that none of their tribal members were engaged in any kind of protest against the plaza. Although she would not admit to a belief in tribal spirits roaming around near the plaza, she said that there were many rivers, streets, roads, and communities with Native American names in the region, so why shouldn't people see physical manifestations of that impulse.

Dennis Blanton, director of the College of William and Mary's Center for Archeological Research, conducted a dig at the site of the bridge's construction at the plaza. According to his group's findings, there were artifacts scattered all over the site, dating back 5,000 to 6,000 years. Edward Halle, an area historian, agreed that the Pocahontas Parkway location had been home to tribespeople for a long time.

An area resident, who owned a business less than a mile from the toll plaza, said that "hooting and hollering" had been heard near the place for years and that the local Native Americans had long declared that there were many spirits there. In his opinion, the plaza had been built on an Indian burial ground.

THE PHANTOM WARRIOR WHO RACED TRAINS

A traveling salesman was making the night trip from Minneapolis, Minnesota, to Butte, Montana. He had been dozing lightly in a lower berth when he was awakened by what he later described as a "damned uneasy feeling."

He couldn't put a finger on what was troubling him, he told a reporter for a Chicago newspaper in the summer of 1943. There were no strange or unusual noises in the train. He could detect nothing that sounded wrong in the steady clicking of the wheels. For some reason he decided to lift his window shade.

That was when he saw the apparition. Outside of his window, so close that it seemed as if he might be able to touch them if he lowered the glass, was a brightly painted Indian brave on his spirited mount. The warrior bent low over the flying black mane of his horse and looked neither to the right nor to the left. He seemed to be mouthing words of encouragement to the phantom mustang as they rapidly gained on the train.

"I've seen them five or six times after that, in different parts of the Dakotas," the salesman said. "They seem to be solid flesh, but there's a kind of shimmering around them. It's like watching a strip of really old movie film being projected onto the prairie."

Railroad brakemen, engineers, and construction crews in the Dakotas and Wyoming have often spoken of the phantom Sioux and his determined race with their swift, modern iron horses. They couldn't beat the trains when they were alive, one old-timer who knew the legend behind the spectral racers commented, but they seem to have picked up some speed in the afterlife.

According to tradition, Frederic Remington, the famous artist of the Old West, sketched the Sioux brave and his mustang from life as the inexhaustible pair raced the train on which he was riding in about 1888. Remington had heard from several travelers the same tale, of a determined warrior astride a big, bony mustang who tirelessly raced the trains. It was as if the locomotive represented a tangible symbol of the encroaching white man, and the Sioux believed that if he could conquer the iron horses, his people could vanquish the paleface invaders.

With a marrow-chilling war whoop, the warrior would come astride the train engines as they entered a wide-open stretch of the prairie. The mustang would pound the plains until sweat formed on its lean, hard body. Only the greater speed of the locomotives would at last enable them to pull away from the chanting Sioux and his indefatigable mount.

One can easily sense the great admiration Remington had for the spirit of the Sioux and his animal as he painted their images. Remington named his piece "America on the Move."

ROUTE 666: THE SOUTHWEST'S DEVIL'S HIGHWAY

Although U.S. Route 666 is now officially known as U.S. Route 491 or 393, the legend of Camino del Diablo, "the Devil's Road," will be long remembered. The original naming of the highway had nothing to do with the Number of the Beast, or Antichrist—666, as given in Revelation, the last book in the Bible. The highway was so designated because it was the sixth branch of an interstate route then known as U.S. 60. The section linking Chicago to Los Angeles became the legendary Route 66. And the Four Corners detour from Route 66 was renumbered 666 in August 1926. But some say labeling the road with those numerals made it Satan's own road to perdition. The 190 miles of the former U.S. 666 starts at Gallup, New Mexico, wends its way through 70 miles of Colorado, then ends in Monticello, Utah.

According to numerous eyewitness accounts, on nights of the full moon, a black, 1930s-vintage Pierce-Arrow roadster has appeared and run scores of cars, trucks, and motorcycles off the road. The ghostly automobile has been linked to at least five deaths.

Dr. Avery Teicher of Phoenix spent ten years documenting reports of the phantom Pierce-Arrow and the howling hellhounds that materialize to terrorize anyone foolhardy enough to pull off Route 666 and admire the desert landscape. According to Dr. Teicher, two members of a biker gang had both of their arms chewed off by the fiendish ghost dogs, and a third biker had 90 percent of his face eaten away. The least threatening of all reports from the Devil's Highway are those of a phantom female hitchhiker who vanishes whenever someone stops to give her a ride.

On January 21, 2003, New Mexico Governor Bill Richardson stated his support to change the name of U.S. 666. The change became official in May 2003.

A TUNNEL OF GRAYNESS ON I-80

In the late 1950s, I was driving late at night with my family heading west on I-80 near Ames, Iowa. Suddenly we entered a section of road that had the thickest fog I had ever encountered. Intermixed with the incredibly thick fog was a flock of large sheep—or so I believed them to be—who really made the driving hazardous. At last we broke through the patch of fog, to find the highway completely free of the pea soup that had so thoroughly blinded my vision. I had been moving at an extremely slow rate of speed to avoid hitting the animals that had crowded around us, so I accelerated to make up time, cussing out the farmer under my breath for allowing his sheep to run free. Iowa has no open ranges.

I thought back on the strange, unusually thick fog from time to time over the years. Mainly when talk of hazardous driving conditions arose, I could tell of the really thick fog that I had once encountered. I did not really consider the event paranormal until I received the following email from Kent in February 2002:

"I play in a jazz trio around the Cedar Rapids/Iowa City area. Having an interest in the paranormal, I have found that nightclubs are a great place to collect first-hand accounts of strange events. Naturally, after a few drinks people are more willing to talk about subjects they would not normally discuss.

"A second-hand account was recently related to me about a professor from Ames who, with his wife, was driving west on I-80 at about 2:00 A.M. one night. The couple supposedly had to come to a complete stop to allow a herd of 'wild' horses to cross the highway! As the account went, the horses seemed to appear out of a fog and disappear into the mist on the other side of the road.

"My entire family and myself had a very strange incident happen in roughly the same area several years ago, and we still discuss it when we pass that stretch of road. In our case, we seemed to 'jump' about 30 miles up the road in an instant, and arrived at our destination a full half-hour sooner than we should have. Also, there was a strange fog around the highway, which seemed to cover both sides of the road and obscure the scenery totally, but the road itself was clear! That was the really strange part. It was like driving through a tunnel of grayness."

She Hangs by Her Neck During the Full Moon

By now, it is unlikely that anyone really remembers the names of the witnesses who first saw the ghostly image of the young woman hanging from the bridge on the old country road near Mt. Pleasant, Iowa, but nearly everyone agrees that it was two truck drivers who had turned off the main highway at about midnight one night when there was a full moon. As they rounded the bend that approached the old bridge, the driver suddenly slammed on his brakes.

"Look ahead!" he said to his partner. "Look in the full beam of the headlights! There's a woman hanging there on the bridge." As the full impact of the sight penetrated his consciousness, the other man said that they should cut the woman down, as she might still be alive.

There could be few sights creepier than coming upon the swaying body of a hanged woman suspended from the girder of an old country bridge, but the two truckers knew they had to do something—whether it was midnight on a deserted gravel road or not. Their feet had no sooner touched the coarse road when the form of the hanged woman began to fade from their sight.

By the time that they had reached the bridge, the woman, noose and all, had completely vanished. The two men stared at each other with open mouths, mouths no longer capable of articulating the fear and confusion that jammed their brains. Just moments before, they had both clearly seen the wretched figure of a hanged woman swaying above the worn wooden planks of the old bridge.

The second sighting of the ghostly hanging was by a young couple coming home from a Saturday night dance, who saw the same grim apparition on the dark and eerie country road. Then other truckers and townspeople began to see the form of the hanging woman in the light of the full moon.

We decided when our team went to investigate the apparition that we would have to be there on site on a night of a full moon, for the ghost had never been sighted at any other time. So on July 19, 1970, with the moon full above us, we sat in my station wagon with the psychic-sensitive Irene Hughes and a number of others, just a few yards away from that haunted country

This photograph was taken at 14 Mile Creek, Raymond, Mississippi.

bridge. My associate Glenn and I wanted to see if Irene could pick up on the ghost and the events that led to the hanging without having any prior knowledge of what she might see. All Irene knew was that our research team had taken her out in the Iowa countryside and parked at a particular place.

Just a few minutes before midnight, someone whispered that Irene was in a light trance. "There's someone coming down the road," she said. Two or three people agreed with the sensitive. I strained my eyes to perceive a midnight visitor, but I could see nothing more than a traffic sign advising approaching motorists about the narrow bridge and its load limit.

Irene said nothing. She seemed to be tuned into another dimension, which the rest of us could neither see nor hear. The medium sat in silence for a few more moments, then she spoke, slowly, precisely: "I see a woman swinging in a circle. A circle of confusion. She is disturbed, confused. She feels betrayed. She feels like she wants to jump over the side of the bridge." A high, thin wail seemed to come from the direction of the bridge. Was it only the cry of some night-hunting bird, the distorted complaint of some farm animal, or the keen of a tormented soul? The frogs and crickets seemed undisturbed by any of the possibilities.

"I see a circle," Irene said, speaking once more. "I see a woman committing suicide from this bridge." (Again it must be noted that we had not told Irene what she might expect to see at this lonely country bridge.)

"It was suicide," Irene said. "But there was another person involved. This is most unusual. Usually when someone in spirit appears, they are dressed just as they were in life. I have never had any spirit who comes to me wrapped in a sheet like so many people think spirits do. But that is just what I saw on the bridge. I saw what looked like somebody wrapped in a sheet!"

"A shroud?" I asked her.

"A shroud," she agreed. "And she tells me her name is Brown. Or maybe it was O'Brien. She was a brunette. I really don't feel that she was a sick person. I feel that this act was just a sudden thing in her life. I feel that there was a husband, but that he was not close by."

Irene sat quietly for a few moments, apparently sifting through the psychic impressions bombarding her from the bridge. "I'm hearing the name Helen," she said, resuming her reportage. "I feel that this woman was having a love affair with a doctor in the community. And I feel that you will find that there was a doctor who left the town rather quickly after this woman took her life. I don't feel that this woman was mentally ill or anything like that. I feel that her life was okay and then, suddenly, involvement with the doctor began."

A reporter who had accompanied us asked how many years ago this happened. Irene said that she had the feeling that it may not have been more than 16 to 20 years ago, around 1950.

"According to the information that I have," Glenn said "that would seem to be exactly the time that the ghost began to appear."

"Look!" Irene said. "Can you see it? A form was very clear there for an instant."

It may be that our eyes were playing tricks on our group, but on the right-hand side of the bridge, there seemed to be a glowing figure.

"Oh, I see her so clearly," the medium said. "She's wearing a yellow dress." Irene suddenly stopped talking. Then, after several seconds of silence, she said: "She keeps telling me, 'Honey, don't talk. Honey, don't tell them.'"

I asked if there was some reason why she didn't want anyone to know why she killed herself.

"I think it is the doctor," Irene said. "I think she was involved with a doctor who left soon after her death."

By this time the researchers had left the station wagon and were standing in the middle of the bridge. There were holes in the wooden planking, and we had to move our feet cautiously in order that we not twist an ankle.

"I am getting the impression that some member of her family was from Philadelphia, but she came here from Kansas," Irene said. "I'm seeing a huge sunflower, and that is the sunflower state, isn't it?"

As discreetly as possible, we conducted a follow-up investigation after we spent several hours of a full-moon night near the bridge with the legend of the hanging lady. Through one of our sources, we learned that there had been a young woman, originally from Kansas and fond of wearing bright yellow dresses, who had come to the area and become romantically involved with a local doctor. The young woman had committed suicide in despair over their impossible love affair, and public opinion, or conscience, had forced the doctor to leave town. While some informants believed that the ghost of the hanging woman might well be the suicidal Kansan, others said that the young woman in question had not hanged herself and that they were unaware of the legend of the haunted bridge.

It is possible, then, that the spirit of the young woman in the bright yellow dress may have hanged herself at the bridge in an earlier decade than the 1940s or 1950s. Or perhaps the hanging woman is only a mischief-making spirit who takes delight in frightening motorists who travel a dark country road. Or maybe she is only an urban legend, who shall be forgotten—until some night when the moon is full and someone turns the bend toward the old country bridge and sees her ghostly figure hanging there.

21
Haunted Hotels, Motels, and Inns

BENJAMIN "BUGSY" SIEGEL STILL HAUNTS THE FLAMINGO

If you had checked into the Flamingo Hilton prior to 1993 and were feeling flush enough from your Las Vegas winnings to put up $400 a night, you might have asked for the Presidential Suite and spent the evening with the ghost of Benjamin "Bugsy" Siegel.

The stylish mobster lived in the Presidential Suite after its construction in the mid-1940s and before his death in 1947, and countless guests who rented the suite after Siegel's death swore that his ghost still haunted it. The Flamingo was Siegel's desert dream come true, and the casino-resort has anchored the Las Vegas strip since the first slot-machine was pulled and the first dice were thrown in 1946.

While most of the original furniture used by Siegel and his girlfriend Virginia Hill had been replaced after his death, some elements of the suite remained unchanged. The lime-colored bidet and the pistachio-hued toilet and sink were the actual ones that Siegel and Hill used. The green linoleum on the two bathroom floors was also original. In the late 1940s and early 1950s, the ghastly shade of green was considered "class" by the fashionable Siegel.

Although the pool table in the parlor area of the suite was brought in during the early 1970s to replace Siegel's original table, some guests—in addition to getting a glimpse of the ghost of the notorious mobster who created Las Vegas—insisted that they heard the pool balls rolling around in the middle of the night.

Today, a lavish garden grows on the grounds where the original Pink Flamingo building was located. The final wall of Siegel's desert paradise was

[415]

Benjamin "Bugsy" Siegel, 1941.

torn down in 1993, giving way to a luxurious new casino-resort that includes a wildlife habitat and a 15-acre Caribbean-style water playground. In the garden there is a plaque that reads, "On this site, Benjamin 'Bugsy' Siegel's original Flamingo Hotel stood from December 26, 1946 until December 14, 1993."

Some people who have followed the wandering paths of the garden after dark have reported encountering the ghost of a man they believed to be Siegel. Although the gangster was murdered in his house in Beverly Hills, ghostly traditions have long maintained that spirits will return to the place that they held most dear. Others who have stayed in the Presidential Suite of the new hotel state their conviction that they have seen the ghost of Siegel making himself comfortable in the plush accommodations of the new penthouse.

THE HOTEL ROOSEVELT: HOLLYWOOD'S MOST HAUNTED

If gangster ghosts are not your cosmic cup of tingle, how about the spirits of departed movie stars? Travel a bit farther west from Las Vegas and check into the Hollywood Roosevelt Hotel in Hollywood, and you just might encounter the ghosts of Marilyn Monroe, Montgomery Clift, or Carole Lombard.

Lombard shared her fabulous top-floor suite with Clark Gable, and the elegant decor is basically the way the ill-fated actress left it. The essence of romantic Hollywood is nowhere more powerful than at this glamorous star's favorite hideaway. Numerous guests who have shared the romance of this suite have also experienced an encounter with the gorgeous ghost of the actress herself.

Marilyn Monroe posed for her first print advertisement on the diving board of the Roosevelt's pool, and she stayed often at the hotel over the years, preferring a second-floor cabana room overlooking the pool. Her favorite mirror is on display in the lower elevator foyer, and numerous individuals have claimed to have seen Monroe's sensuous image near—or superimposed over—their own when they stop to look in the reflecting glass.

The Flamingo Hilton Hotel in Las Vegas, Nevada, as it looked in 1979.

In December 1990, while my wife, Sherry Hansen Steiger, and I were in the lower elevator foyer taping a "Ghosts of Hollywood" segment for a Japanese television program, a hotel guest, curious as to what we were filming, stopped to watch the proceedings. Suddenly, he stepped briskly aside as if to

Marilyn Monroe in front of her favorite mirror, which is now at the Roosevelt Hotel in Hollywood.

avoid a collision with some unseen person and stifled a cry of surprise, which interrupted the scene that we were filming.

When the director asked the man what was wrong, he replied, somewhat shaken, "Didn't you see that blonde woman who just brushed by me? If I

Real Ghosts, Restless Spirits, and Haunted Places

didn't know Marilyn Monroe was dead, I would have sworn it was her!'

As we quizzed him about his experience, he appeared only mildly interested when we explained that the full-length mirror in the foyer had once been a personal favorite of Marilyn Monroe. "But the woman who brushed by me was solid flesh and blood," he insisted. "She was no ghost!"

The man stalked off a bit indignant, fixing us with an incredulous glare, when we, together with the director and the camera crew, tried to make him understand that there had been no woman visible to the rest of us in the foyer.

Montgomery Clift lived at the hotel for three months during the final stages of filming *From Here to Eternity*. He would often pace the hall outside of his ninth floor apartment, rehearsing his lines, and sometimes practicing bugle calls—much to the consternation of nearby guests who were trying to get some sleep.

Kelly Green, one of the personable staff members of the Roosevelt, told us of the dozens of guests who had heard Clift's

Brad and Sherry Steiger with Kelly Green at the very haunted Roosevelt Hotel in Hollywood.

bugle blowing long after his death in 1966. In November 1990 a witness to the ghostly bugle blasts had been interviewed for inclusion in our segment on Hollywood ghosts for *Entertainment Tonight*. In October 1992 Sherry and I wanted to return to the hotel and try to catch the ghost of Clift in the act for ourselves for the new "Haunted Hollywood" segments that we were filming for the 1992 Halloween edition of HBO's *World Entertainment Report*.

The night before filming, Kelly Green made arrangements to place us in the room next to Clift's haunted room on the ninth floor. It was our intention to film in the room early the next morning, so Sherry and I were disappointed to hear a variety of sounds coming from Clift's room, as if it may have been occupied by a family with children.

We couldn't imagine that the thoughtful Ms. Green would book guests— especially a family—in a room that we wished to utilize the next morning for filming, but we really didn't feel that we could complain. It was quite enough that she was making the room available for us to film the segment the next day.

Sherry and I went to bed sincerely hoping that the next-door guests would check out very early in the morning—a hope that we increasingly felt was in vain, since our neighbors stayed up most of the night, moving noisily about their room. Perhaps it wasn't a family with children next door, for it certainly sounded like a party was in progress with little consideration for the neighbors.

Neither of us seasoned ghost hunters could suppress a small shiver that next morning when we learned that Ms. Green had indeed left orders at the desk for the Clift room to remain unoccupied for the convenience of our filming. The thumps and bumps that we had heard all night had been the ghost of Montgomery Clift and his circle of spooks welcoming us to his portion of Haunted Hollywood.

Later that day, Sherry recalled that she had been awakened sometime during the night by what she had thought at the time was one of the rambunctious kids next door blowing on a horn, but she had been too tired from the seminar that we had just completed at a Los Angeles area college for the eerie significance of the bugle blasts to register fully in her sleep-numbed consciousness.

SLEEPLESS IN BELLINGHAM

The Personal Account of Sherry Hansen Steiger

In the mid-1990s, during one of our frequent speaking tour engagements in which we lecture, conduct seminars, make local radio and television appearances, and do book signings, my husband, Brad, and I had just completed several events on the West Coast and were about to land at the airport in the beautiful state of Washington.

The Washington event was sponsored by our friend Benjamin Smith, who picked us up from the airport, briefed us on the logistics and updates regarding the next few days of our seminars, and then with an extra twinkle in his eye enthusiastically told us of a surprise he'd arranged for our overnight lodging. Ben could hardly contain his excitement, but he made it clear that he didn't want to tell us too much about the castle where we would be guests because he didn't want to influence our opinions or experience of the place.

We had known Ben for quite some time, so during the last segue of the drive from the airport en route to our destination, we chatted, sharing old times and catching up on things before getting back to the business at hand. As we neared Bellingham, it was already far later in the evening than we had hoped to arrive, as inclement weather, plane delays, and the like put us in past dark and served to remind us yet again why we arrive in a city the day before our scheduled appearances.

There was little doubt to us that Ben had worked long and hard to put this seminar together in his usual expert and efficient manner, so Brad and I were certain his surprise had a great deal of thought behind it as well. As we approached the "castle," Ben expressed his regret that we had not been able to view it first during the daylight hours. Any question he might have had regarding our approval of this overnight stay as opposed to our normal hotel accommodations was dashed before he was able to complete the rest of his sentence in declaring, "This is it." I let out a squeal of delight as Brad simultaneously said, "Wow! You weren't kidding."

We could see why Ben referred to the bed and breakfast as a castle. Even through the black hues of a dark and stormy night, the proud, looming structure betrayed its magnificence as it beckoned us into its Victorian elegance and enticed us with her secrets. It almost seemed destined that we should arrive on a stormy night with the stage set for an experience we were never to forget.

We entered through the kitchen, where the owners greeted us warmly, expressed their delight at our being there, and graciously made us feel at home. Promising a more complete tour of the mansion the next day when we wouldn't disturb the other guests (many of whom were most likely already asleep), we were escorted to the room reserved for us—passing the most incredible antiques and luxurious decor at every twist and turn along the way through the halls and up many stairs.

During their many global expeditions, the owners spared no expense in acquiring some of the most elaborate and unusual antiques I had ever seen. And all these treasures had been carefully selected and transported to the Bellingham Bed and Breakfast. Representing what seemed to be every culture from the farthest corners of the earth, there was nary a square inch that didn't have some interesting intrigue or history associated with it and a story to tell.

Differing themes embellished the guest rooms—each one decorated in an elaborate, unusual motif and eclectic style reminiscent of a bygone era, but styled with immense creativity.

After showing us the bathroom we would share with other rooms on our floor, they opened the door to our most amazing room. The wallpaper, drapes, bedspreads, lampshades, overstuffed lounging chairs, as well as a canopy of sorts over the head of the bed were all done in a matching pattern with deep blue hues and an Oriental flair. Although lush, the room was illuminated by low lighting and was somewhat dark, so it was suggested that we leave a light on all night, in case we needed to get up. We said our goodnights as we settled into our room after a very tiring day of traveling. At that time in our lives, we were traveling so much that it wasn't unusual for Brad and I to awaken in the night and forget which city we were in—so we readily agreed to the wisdom of leaving a light on. We chose the floor lamp with a large Victorian shade next to an overstuffed chair on the other side of the room from our bed.

It was late and we were exhausted, so knowing we were going to be up early, we settled into the comfy feather bed and promptly fell into a deep sleep. A few hours later, I was awakened to the pull of the bed covers to Brad's side of the bed. I started to tug some back to cover me, then noticed that Brad seemed restless. Thinking he was just trying to get comfortable in a new bed, I fell back asleep.

Once again I was awakened, only this time when I rolled over and looked at Brad, I saw that he was sitting up on his side of the bed, holding his head in his hands. Thinking he must have a bad headache or not be feeling well, I asked him if he was okay. Getting no immediate response, I asked again, only a bit louder this time. Suddenly I was startled beyond belief when Brad answered me—from a prone position still under the covers and apparently not happily awakened by me!

"Weren't you just sitting up on the side of the bed?" I asked, somewhat confused.

"What are you talking about?" Brad muttered. "I'm trying to sleep!"

Shrugging it off to being overtired, I watched as Brad pulled the covers back over his head and went back to sleep. With his movement of pulling the covers over his head, I could clearly see he definitely was *not* sitting on the bed—now at least—and I drifted back to sleep.

Sometime later, I awakened again and saw that Brad was not in bed. Looking around the room, I saw him sitting in the chair next to the lighted lamp. His demeanor was grim, and it looked as if he was in a great deal of pain with his head down—cradled in his hands—almost like he was crying. Concerned, I cried out to him. "Honey, what's wrong? Do you have a headache? Can I get you some aspirin, water or something?"

There beneath the covers next to me, grumbling with great dissatisfaction that I had disturbed his sleep yet again, Brad uttered loudly, "I am trying to sleep, for heaven's sake!"

With the sound of Brad's voice, the solid image of the man in the chair vanished! I dared not say another word. At this point I was grateful that Brad fell asleep immediately, but I lay there for a few minutes, pondering what in the world was going on.

This strange state of affairs continued on and off on three or four more occasions. Two of the times I distinctly saw Brad—or so I thought—pacing the room, back and forth, back and forth, each time acting extremely upset and disturbed. Another time, he was sitting in the chair again, holding his head and shaking it.

Finally, convinced that Brad was just not wanting to worry me, I blurted out shrilly and loudly enough so that I was worried that I'd awakened whoever was in the rooms next to ours: "Honey, please, please ... tell me what's wrong!"

With that outburst we were both awakened to a shocking realization that the physical being I thought was Brad in distress was not him at all. Aware that Brad was now really awake, I told him what I had been seeing and experiencing. Without too much further discussion, we decided if we were going to be at all coherent for our lectures the next day, we'd better try to get *some* sleep. Suggesting maybe we *both* had better take some aspirin, somehow, we managed to doze off once more.

Mercifully, another few hours passed, allowing us to sleep peacefully, until I was awakened by Brad's hand clasping mine ever so gently under my pillow. Thinking it odd that he would awaken me, yet guessing he was just reassuring me—or *himself*—that we were both really still there in bed, I squeezed his hand.

Dozing off, I felt the squeeze of my hand again. This time, I raised up my head from the pillow, sputtering, "Why are you grabbing my hand?" Then looking over at Brad, I saw that he was facing the *other* direction with his arms and hands on the opposite side. There was no way he could have just squeezed my hand, and furthermore, he was sound asleep.

How I was able to drift off to sleep again, I really don't know, but I did, and thankfully, Brad didn't seem to awaken even with yet another of my outbursts. However, the tranquility was not to last.

A short time later, an electrical sensation pierced my entire body as I was literally shocked into feeling something or someone trying to get my full attention with yet another squeeze of my hand. This time it was with a jolt that startled me to the point of full consciousness. I was wide awake.

With total wakefulness, an awareness hit me and I absolutely *knew* that the hand that had been squeezing mine under my pillow was a *baby's* hand. I could literally feel teeny, tiny fingers wrap around mine and give a gentle squeeze. Seeing that Brad was lying still and facing the other direction, I knew that even if he had been capable of grabbing my hand and rolling over fast in hopes of not being detected as some kind of joke, his hand was ten times larger than the one I felt clasping mine.

Just before the owners of the bed and breakfast had said goodnight to us after showing us to our room, they described a spectacular breakfast feast of homemade goodies that sounded too good to miss. The meal was served in a formal manner in the dining room at an appointed time, and as I glanced at the clock after this final rude awakening, I knew it was time to get ready if we were to be there on schedule. Sitting bolt upright with the many occurrences of the night surging through my mind and body, I didn't quite know what to do next.

Brad rolled over and upon seeing me sitting up said, "I guess it's time to get up if we are to make that early morning breakfast."

"Honey," I said, "I don't know how much you remember of what happened last night, but I have to tell you about it."

Quickly I described the events from beginning of the evening to the present—ending with the squeeze of my hand by what I felt to be a baby's hand. I asked if he would convey my apologies to our hosts for not making the breakfast, as I had looked forward to it, but that I felt a guidance to stay and pray and meditate.

Brad's first concern was for me, that I would need to eat before our lecture and seminar, but he was persuaded that whatever was going on was indeed more important for me to figure out. Acknowledging that he remembered my awakening him with the weird proclamations of his pacing, his sitting holding his head, and his squeezing my hand, he asked what I thought had really taken place since it certainly was not he who had done these things. My answer was that I needed to go into prayer and find out.

Brad dressed and went on down, telling me he'd try to at least bring me coffee or something to nibble on. Telling him not to worry, I went into prayer for guidance. It came to me that there was an infant that truly was clasping onto me for help and that it was somehow "stuck" between worlds not knowing where it was. I filled and surrounded myself with light and a prayer for protection as I was urged to pray the baby into the light. Praying that God's will be done and that I be led to what to do next, I felt a baby's hand grab onto me again and then felt the arms of a blessed angel gently lift the infant with immense love and understanding and carry it off to free it from the earthly realm of confusion.

An hour and a half must have passed before Brad entered the room to find me still in prayer. His presence was exuberant as he could hardly wait to tell me of the discussion that had ensued at the breakfast table. Brad and Ben met before the others joined in, so in addressing Ben's surprise at my not being there, Brad explained a few of my experiences. When the others, including the owners of the bed and breakfast, were all gathered at the table, Brad explained my absence by saying that I had a rather sleepless night. Ben laughed and added that he wasn't surprised at what I had picked up on, said, "Wow, that's why we wanted to put you guys in that room!"

With that, the owners of the mansion were too intrigued to allow the details to wait, so they asked if Brad would mind sharing what I had happen

Brad and Sherry Steiger in their room at the Bellingham, Washington, bed and breakfast where they spent a sleepless night.

throughout the night. As Brad was recounting the rest of the discussion to me, my first impulse was that of dismay that this strange uncanny episode of mine was being made public when I wasn't even certain of what it was. But then, when Brad described what the owners had told him at breakfast what had really happened in that bedroom to the original owners and builders of the mansion, my heart skipped a beat!

The original owner's love and devotion for his wife took form in the physical manifestation of his building the mansion for her, and the two of them had eagerly hoped to fill it with the laughter of children. The expectant joy on the night that his wife was giving birth to their first child was suddenly turned to horror when what seemed at first to be the normal screams of child labor changed to screams from the midwife at something gone very wrong. As the cry of a newborn baby taking its first breath of life was beginning, the wailing and weeping of the midwife revealed the giving up of the last breaths of the beloved mother's life. The husband watched grief-stricken as his dear wife's life was terminated in what seemed a sacrificial act of giving birth. It was as though this terrible scene was etched in the memory banks of the very walls of this bedroom where the tragedy took place. It may have been that I had picked up on the extreme emotions of a sorrow and grief beyond measure.

It was said that the owner was in such despair that he constantly paced his bedroom, back and forth and frequently sat in his chair, holding his head in disbelief and anguish.

The second tragedy that I may have experienced was when the child, while still an infant, succumbed to the dreaded scarlet fever and died in its crib in the middle of the night in that very room. The father's grief was so overwhelming that he was able to do little more than pace and pace and sit on the side of the bed or in his chair, holding his head, and no doubt his heart was broken.

Later, I was asked by the owners of the mansion, who attended our lecture, if I would mind telling my story first before we began our presentation. The owners had found it amazing that without any prior knowledge whatsoever of the history of the house or of the previous owners, I had seemed to pick up on so many details as though I had seen it as it had occurred originally. Whether it was an experience where I traveled back in time or was sensitive enough to perceive an energy that was recorded in the ethers of time and space—like a record or tape—or if ghostly manifestations had called my attention to their unfortunate tragedy, it was without any doubt a sleepless night in Bellingham, and one that neither Brad nor I will ever forget!

HAUNTED HOTELS ACROSS NORTH AMERICA

There are many haunted hotels and motels in North America. Here are just a few of my favorites. Check the directory of haunted places in the back of the book for many more:

St. James Hotel, Cimarron, New Mexico

A glimpse of an old guest register at the St. James Hotel reads like a "Who's Who" of the Wild West: Billy the Kid, Pat Garrett, Bat Masterson, Black Jack Ketchum, Doc Holliday, Buffalo Bill Cody, and the list goes on.

Almost any room in this 120-year-old hotel—a favorite of gunfighters in the 1880s—will produce an active spirit encounter. According to yellowed newspaper accounts, 26 people have died violently at the St. James, and the dining room coiling remains pockmarked with bullet holes. If you should decide to give the St. James a try, it would probably be best to avoid Room 18. Things got a little too wild in that room back in the 1880s, and the spirits there are too hostile and aggressive for most folks.

Bartenders and chefs in the hotel complain that food and crockery disappear from under their noses. Bottles and glasses float in the air and sometimes shatter in loud explosions.

"A lot of gunfighters checked into this old hotel," a bartender exclaimed. "But their spirits have never got around to checking out!"

The Mission of San Antonio de Padua, California

There are guest accommodations in the old Mission of San Antonio de Padua, located in the central California mountains of the Santa Lucia range, 30 miles north of Paso Robles. Constructed in 1771, the mission remains an enchanted, spiritual, haunted place. If you can make arrangements to stay overnight, you might very well catch sight of the ghosts of several monks, the benevolent spirit of Father John Baptist, and the mysterious entity that manifests as a headless woman on horseback.

The monks who reside in the mission speak of having often seen a small colored cloud, about three feet square and about eight feet high above the tile roof over the women's guest quarters. The cloud changes color from white to green to blue, then yellow and red.

On numerous occasions in recent years, the mission has been the scene of remarkable spiritual conversions and hearings. And the monks speak of such miracles as the appearance of white and purple violets on certain graves within the courtyard.

The Dorrington Hotel, Dorrington, California

The ghost of Rebecca Dorrington walks at night in this 120-year-old hotel in the tiny High Sierra hamlet of Dorrington. The town itself was named for Rebecca, the Scottish bride of John Gardener, an 1850s homesteader who also built the old hotel. Rebecca's eerie nocturnal repertoire consists of banging doors open and shut, flashing lights on and off, and shifting furniture about. Some guests have been "treated" to a ghostly re-enactment of Rebecca's fatal tumble down a back stairwell, the accident that cost her her life in 1870.

The Brookdale Lodge in the Santa Cruz Mountains

The sprawling Brookdale Lodge, built in 1924 in the Santa Cruz Mountains near Boulder Creek, California, was a popular hideaway for gangland kingpins in the 1930s. Later, the lodge was a favorite of film legends Marilyn Monroe, Joan Crawford, and Tyrone Power. The colorful inn, which features a brook running through the dining room, has a number of "cold spots," which indicate haunted areas. The most frequently sighted spirit entity is that of a small girl dressed very formally in 1940s-style clothing. The ghost is thought to be that of the five-year-old who drowned in the brook sometime in the late 1940s.

Hotel Monte Vista, Flagstaff, Arizona

The picturesque old Monte Vista Hotel provides a marvelous place for an overnight stay on the way to or from the Grand Canyon. Guests who stay there may encounter the "Phantom bellboy," who knocks on doors and announces, "Room service," in a muffled voice. Others claim to have seen the wispy image of a woman strolling through an upstairs corridor.

San Carlos Hotel, Phoenix, Arizona

Guests have complained about the noisy children in the halls. When they are informed that there are no children running about unattended, some annoyed patrons have set about trying to prove they aren't going crazy by catching the shouting, squealing, laughing kids who are disturbing their relaxation and sleep. Some frustrated guests who have nearly grabbed one of the little rascals have been astonished to see the child disappear before their eyes.

The only explanation that some investigators have offered for this phenomenon is the fact that the old San Carlos Hotel was built sometime in the late 1920s on the site of Phoenix's first adobe elementary school. Perhaps psychically sensitive guests are hearing and seeing the ghosts of schoolchildren from long ago.

The Horton Grand Hotel, San Diego, California

There are so many ghosts at the historic old Horton Grand Hotel in San Diego that the entities often get together and hold dances. Shelly D., who lived at the hotel for two years, claimed to have watched a group of 15 to 20 ghosts dressed in the style of the 1890s, having a dance in the third-floor ballroom.

It was only after she had watched them for a while that Shelly realized that there was something very strange about the costumed dancers. No one paid the slightest attention to her. Everyone appeared to ignore her when she spoke. Then she noticed that there was something very eerie about their eyes, kind of dark and hollow. The ghostly figures didn't seem to mind the intrusion of her physical presence. Shelly wondered if she were observing the recreation of some past scene that had once occurred in the hotel. She remembered that they swung their partners round and round and seemed to be having a great time.

Room 309 receives the most nominations for "most haunted" in the Horton Grand. Research has revealed that a gambler named Roger Whittaker was murdered in that room in the 1880s. Dan Pearson, the owner of the Horton Grand, said that he first became aware that there were strange things happening in Room 309 when he brought workmen in to renovate it in 1986. Later, as Pearson walked by the room with a psychically talented friend, the man stopped suddenly and said, "There's something going on in that room! I feel it strongly!"

Three months later, Pearson said that a guest at the hotel staying in Room 309 found her young daughter carrying on an animated conversation with someone else in the room. "Don't you see him, Mommy?" the girl asked incredulously. "Don't you see the man in our room?"

Our son-in-law, John T., a media specialist, was in San Diego a few years ago filming some of the unique architecture of various structures when one of his technicians shared an experience from his own stay at the Horton Grand.

"He called the front desk to complain that the people above him were making too much noise, as if they were marching up and down the hall," John told us. "The front desk clerk responded, 'sir, there is no floor above you. Perhaps you should have read the diary on the mantle.' The technician checked and found the diary filled with guest experiences with ghosts through the years at the Horton Grand."

Hotel del Coronado, San Diego

In another of San Diego's haunted hotels, the Hotel del Coronado, where our son-in-law and his crew were filming a convention, he said that one of his technicians reluctantly admitted that an invisible someone had brushed against him when no one was around. After they had completed filming the function they were assigned to cover, the entire crew heard strange booming noises coming from a balcony loft area where there was no living, visible person.

Our son-in-law's technician may have brushed up against Kate Morgan, the Hotel del Coronado's principal resident ghost, who died of a gunshot wound to the head; the action was officially ruled a suicide. Kate's body was found in November 1892 on an exterior staircase leading to the beach.

Although most of the sightings of Kate have occurred on the beach and in hotel hallways, Room 3327, where Kate stayed, seems to be the center of most of the paranormal phenomena.

The Old Stagecoach Inn, Waterbury, Vermont

Margaret Spencer, a once wealthy, vivacious beauty who died in 1943 at the age of 98, haunts Room 2 of the Old Stagecoach Inn in Waterbury, Vermont. Margaret is often glimpsed in a wispy, white shawl, and she loves to play tricks on the guests.

The Hotel del Coronado, outside of San Diego, California.

Fifty Ghosts Walk the Streets and Hotel Hallways of Nantucket, Island

Almost any place of lodging near Nantucket's historic section harbors its share of unseen guests. Even the Coast Guard station is haunted.

When author Peter Benchley was on the island writing his bestseller *Jaws*, he encountered the ghost of an old man dressed in eighteenth-century clothing. The entity sat in front of a fireplace in a rocking chair, and Benchley insists that he was not dreaming.

Kennebunk Inn, Kennebunkport, Maine

This 200-year-old inn is haunted by a friendly ghost named Silas, who delights in levitating champagne glasses and tossing beer mugs around the bar. The phantom shade of Silas Perkins has haunted the inn since his demise in the eighteenth century, and weekend vacationers flock there in the hope of getting one of his spiritual uplifts. The Kennebunk Inn is a favorite of former president George H. W. Bush because it is near his seafront estate.

The MisFitz Inn, Southbury, Connecticut

This 165-year-old inn is haunted by a ghost known affectionately as Sadie the Lady, a prostitute who practiced her profession at the inn in the 1890s. Sadie had the misfortune to fall in love with a married patron, who claimed that he returned the heartfelt emotion. However, when Sadie approached her lover when he was dining at the inn with his wife, he denied knowing her. Two days later, Sadie was found dead in her room above the tavern, an apparent suicide. Ever since her tragic end, Sadie has been held responsible for strange noises coming from empty rooms, overturned chairs in the bar, and water being dumped on unsuspecting patrons and employees.

King's Tavern, Natchez, Mississippi

In the late 1700s, Madeline was the mistress of Richard King, the tavern's namesake, until she was murdered by his jealous wife. For over 200 years, Madeline's restless and angry ghost has been held responsible for every squeak, rattle, and rap in the tavern. Patrons regularly report seeing Madeline's large portrait swing back and forth, and some have claimed to have seen the ghost of a slender woman who stands defiantly before them, her hands on her hips. To add to the color and allure of the haunted tavern, in the 1930s a woman's skeleton was found sealed in a brick fireplace with a jeweled dagger in her chest.

The only guest suite remaining in King's Tavern is on the third floor. After the restaurant section closes, the occupants of the room are left alone in the tavern with Madeline's ghost. According to the proprietors, many guests check in, but few remain to check out in the morning.

General Wayne Inn, Merion, Pennsylvania

Located on the old Lancaster roadway between Philadelphia and Radner, the establishment has been in continuous operation since 1704, when

Robert Jones, a Quaker, decided to provide travelers with a restaurant and a place of lodging. During the Revolutionary War, the establishment, originally called the Wayside Inn, played host to General George Washington and the Marquis de la Fayette, as well as a number of their adversaries, the British Red-coats and their Hessian mercenaries. The Wayside was renamed the General Wayne Inn in 1793 in honor of a local hero, General Anthony Wayne.

When Barton Johnson bought the General Wayne Inn in 1970, he was well aware of its reputation for being haunted. Previous guests had claimed encounters with the ghosts of men dressed in Revolutionary Era uniforms. The ghost of Edgar Allen Poe, a frequent guest when he was alive, according to the old register, had been reported in a room known as the Franklin Post Office. Employees working in the bar area, as well as the guests seated there, often saw dozens of wine and other liquor glasses in a wooden rack begin to shake violently for no apparent reason.

In 1972 New Jersey psychics Jean and Bill Quinn conducted a séance in which at least 17 different entities declared their presence and provided a bit of their personal history. When Wilhelm, a Hessian soldier killed in the Revolutionary War, identified himself through the mediums, he explained that most of the time he liked to stay down in the cellar. As far as the restaurant's maitre d' was concerned, Wilhelm could have the cellar to himself. He had seen the ghost so often that he finally told Barton Johnson that he would no longer go down to the cellar.

In addition to Wilhelm, the mediums identified a little boy ghost who cried for his lost mother; two female entities who had worked at the inn and had died young under bizarre circumstances; eight other Hessian soldiers who had once been quartered at the inn and who had died nearby in battle; a Native American who seemed primarily to be watching the other entities; and an African American who chose to remain silent. The spirits of the Hessians had been seen by many customers and employees over the years. Usually they played harmless pranks, such as blowing on the necks of young women, but one of their spectral ranks enjoyed terrifying any employee whose job it was to stay after closing and clean up.

Ludwig, the spirit of a Hessian soldier, materialized for many nights in the bedroom of Mike Benio, a contractor. Ludwig appealed to Benio to unearth his bones, which had been buried in the basement of the inn, and give them a proper burial in a cemetery. When Barton Johnson returned from a vacation, Benio asked permission to excavate a certain area of the cellar that was under the parking lot. Here, Benio found fragments of pottery and some human bones. After giving the remains a proper burial, the ghost of Ludwig was at peace and no longer manifested at the General Wayne Inn.

One night, Johnson placed a tape recorder in the bar. The next morning during playback, he could clearly hear the sounds of bar stools being moved about, the water faucet being turned on and off, and glasses catching the water.

Jim Webb and his partner, Guy Sileo, bought the inn in 1995. Webb was found murdered in his office on December 27, 1996, and Felicia Moyse, a 20-year-old assistant chef, committed suicide on February 22, 1997. Some people felt that the place had added two more ghosts to its roster.

A Phantom Nazi Officer Haunts a Hotel in Ontario

According to reports coming out of Gravenhurst, Ontario, Canada, in September 1968 a deserted hotel was hosting a most unusual kind of ghost for North America. A Nazi officer wearing a German uniform with a swastika cross attached to his jacket was seen on numerous occasions.

One girl told a story of being lifted off the ground and dropped by the ghost, and her account was backed up by the corroborating testimony of several witnesses. A teenager said that he had reached out to touch the phantom and had found the thing to be very cold.

Actually, the appearance of a Nazi ghost in Canada is not as strange as it may seem. The old hotel at which the ghost has been sighted used to house German prisoners during World War II.

Observers have seen the ghost loitering in the dining room and strolling across the grounds. Others have seen the entity as a black cloud drifting across the yard, ranging from six to eight feet in height.

Those who observed the thing in either guise affirm that it was a creature of habit. It always seemed to appear between 11:00 P.M. and 1:00 A.M., and usually followed the same route from the dining room to a certain point on the grounds.

22

Haunted Restaurants, Bars, and Theaters

Two Ghosts Visit a McDonalds in Yuma, Arizona

The Personal Experience of Verne Koenig

"I must relate to you a very strange or weird incident that happened to me during our winter stay in Yuma, Arizona, in 1996. One weekday afternoon I stopped by a McDonald's restaurant for a cup of coffee. On the north side of the restaurant, there are two doors, one going directly up to the counter, the other—further back—that leads to the restrooms and then to a booth area around the corner from the counter. I bought my coffee and sat in the first booth of this area between the two north doors, looking toward the door leading to the restrooms.

"I picked up a newspaper and started looking through it as I was sipping my coffee. There was no one else in this particular booth area, and I noticed just a few customers on the east side area sitting in booths. One waitress was at the counter at that time, and there were a few other employees in the kitchen area.

"Very shortly, I noticed a man and a woman enter the further north door near the restrooms. I did not notice if they came from a car or were walking. They paused, looked around for a moment, and then sat down in the first booth near the door. I couldn't help noticing them because of the way they were dressed and the way they looked. The man was dressed in a nice looking gray suit and wearing a tie, but his complexion was that of a very sick man. He was very pale and seemed to be sweating, although it was not warm outside that day. The woman wore a Hawaiian type dress, flowery and very colorful, and it reached down to her ankles. She was carrying a large cloth type bag.

[435]

They sat for a moment and then the woman reached into her bag and withdrew a large towel of some kind and began wiping the man's face, over and over again. Then she put it back, got up, and went into the ladies restroom.

"I was observing these things, peering over the top of the newspaper I was supposed to be reading. The woman was in the restroom for five or six minutes. When she came out, she took the towel from her bag and again wiped the man's face, neck, and head. They sat there for a few more minutes, apparently conversing, although I couldn't hear what they said. Then the woman went back into the restroom, and the man got up and walked up the aisle towards me. When he reached my booth, he stopped and I could see how pale looking he was, very white. He asked me, 'Do you have some money so I can get something to drink?'

"I guess I was surprised that he would ask me for money. Both of them were so well dressed that I thought surely they would have enough to pay for a drink. I refused him. He looked at me for a moment and then walked back to his booth by the door and sat down. Shortly after, the woman came out of the restroom again. They talked awhile, and then both of them walked up the aisle towards me. Without looking at me, they rounded the corner to the counter area. Out of curiosity, I immediately got up to observe if they were going to buy something, when suddenly, they weren't there! They had completely disappeared.

"I was dumbfounded. I went to the door on the south side of the counter area, looked out, but nobody was there. They could not have reached that door so quickly or gone out without my seeing them.

"And then the weird thing! I stopped at the counter where a single waitress was on duty, and I asked her if some people had just walked by and gone outside. She looked kind of funny at me and said, 'No, there was no one that just walked past here. I assure you I would have seen them.'

"I went outside and looked at the cars that were parked in the lot. All were empty, and there was no sign of the man and the woman I had observed, even driving off in a car.

"Of the few persons in the other part of McDonalds that day, none had seen them, only me. It's truly unexplainable. I often think what if I had given the man some money, what would have happened then? I guess I'll never know."

A HAUNTED GODFATHER'S PIZZA IN OGDEN, UTAH

A Research Project in Progress by Utah Paranormal Exploration and Research (UPER), Contributed by Merrie Barrentine and Michael Zimmer

"Utah Paranormal Exploration and Research (UPER) began its investigation of Godfather's Pizza in the fall of 1999. Traditionally, our group has avoided ghost hunting—jumping around from one site to the next—in order to better focus on a handful of more active sites. At Godfather's Pizza, we've done the standard video filming, digital and 35mm photography, and audio recording for electronic voice phenomena (EVP). We've also recorded many of the restaurant owner/manager's memories of activity over the past 19 years, beginning with his second night there, when the jukebox suddenly began playing even after the power to that end of the building had been shut off. The jukebox remained playing even when the electrical plug was pulled.

"Since that initial encounter, there have been many other events involving the paranormal. A woman, a man, and two different boys have been the most frequent visitors, seen by employees and customers alike. The tile floor in front of the counter bulged up one morning, rising approximately eight to ten inches, before returning to level. When the tile was removed later, the concrete underneath was unbroken.

"Fluorescent lights have shot out of their boxes to arch across the room, as if thrown by unseen hands, until about 40 lights lay shattered on the floor. The owner has heard someone whistling in the kitchen on numerous occasions when no one else was there, and customers have seen figures walk through walls, tables, and railings. The owner said one of the ghost boys walked right through him, an event he described as 'chilling.'

"UPER has done archive research on the restaurant and its riverside location through old books, regional history sources, and microfilm at the local library. There is fairly convincing evidence—as yet unconfirmed—that the site was once a paupers' field. Its location in relationship to the 100-plus-year-old Ogden City Cemetery—just below the hill from it and right on the Ogden River—would seem to support that possibility.

"UPER's best paranormal experience at Godfather's was in 2000. During an after-hours investigation, a vague mist was seen forming in the middle of the room. Although the apparition's physical appearance lasted only seconds, UPER's general manager, Merry Barrentine, was able to snap several photos of the manifestation before it disappeared. It was from one of these that the 'Godfather's boy' appeared.

"The restaurant's owner identified the boy as one he's seen in the restaurant before, but UPER wanted a second opinion and sent the photo to a professional photographer out of state. In response, he noted, 'I opened it (the photograph) in Photoshop 6, cropped the image to the area you now see, increased the resolution to 300ppi, and changed the image size to 7 inches high. Then, I used the unsharp mask filter at 100 percent, with a radius of 3.3, and a threshold of 0. Those were the only settings I used to clean it up. No further enhancement was done on the original image.'

A photograph of the ghost that appeared at Godfather's Pizza in Ogden, Utah, in 2000.

Real Ghosts, Restless Spirits, and Haunted Places

"'My observations with the photo are what you've mentioned.... [One], the very bottom bar is a reflection on the table by the bar above it and the form is behind it and yet there is lens flare above the form [that] suggests the form is in front of the window.'

"'Here is what I see in the image: It appears that the figure is standing *inside* the room, though there doesn't appear to be anyone physically in the room itself. There is some mist-like stuff that seems to be in the area where the person would be standing, if there were someone in the image. By zooming in on the photo, I can sort of see that the person is short, appears to be a boy, though it is impossible to be certain. The person's face is in profile, the nose being obvious as is the ear. The hair seems to be parted on the person's left side, since that is the area of the head that appears in the reflection. A white starch collar is the most prominent feature of the person's clothing, leading us to assume that the figure is a male. Also, it appears that the figure is standing at the front edge of the table (the edge nearest to the camera lens) and is leaning with his/her left hand resting on that flat edge of the table. The shirt is rather blousy and is ill-defined, but is still visible.'"

THE GHOSTS OF SANDY'S RESTAURANT, VENTURA, CALIFORNIA

An Investigation by Renowned Psychic Investigator Richard Senate

"**S**andy's is best known for its steak and seafood, but the regular customers believe this restaurant is haunted by at least two ghosts. The manager states that he has never seen anything, but he does admit that customers tell of odd happenings. Some say that they have seen a dark shadow following them into the place; still others say they hear things in the back room—things like silverware moving about with an odd tinkling sound. Several years ago, a woman witnessed a glass levitate and fly across the room smashing against the wall.

"There is a persistent cold in the back room of the place that is apparent even on a hot day. Could this cold spot be evidence of a ghost? The stories that reached me were so dramatic that I felt I needed to conduct an on-site investigation. I drove out to the very modern looking cinder block restaurant on the corner of Saviers and Bard streets. It was deceptively ordinary looking.

"When I pulled in, I started to get the impression that the stories were just so much folklore or perhaps the product of liquid spirits and nothing supernatural. But when I stepped into the place, the hair on the back of my neck shivered. It was a feeling I had felt many times when I entered a haunted site. As I was drawn into the building, I felt something cold and invisible pass by me. Yes, I was convinced the stories were true—this place was haunted.

"I met with George, the bartender, who confirmed what the patrons had seen. Some said they even saw a dark shadow-like form come through the bar area. The waitress, Lillian, said that a coffee pot had flown across the room and that strange crashing sounds were heard. The bartender confirmed her story and said some time back four people sitting at the bar felt something touch them, turned and looked, but there was nothing there. He went on to say that the odd events seem to take place late at night, after nine.

"The restaurant was built perhaps 40 years ago and was successfully managed by a friendly couple. When ill health forced them to sell, the present owners purchased the establishment. The original owners passed away, and it has been from the time of their deaths that there have been reports of ghosts wandering Sandy's Restaurant. Some speculate that the phantoms are the spirits of the former owners, checking back at the place they worked so hard to establish. Whatever the reason, my visit did confirm that the former owners could find little fault with the steak the present proprietors serve at the place or with the quality of the service. Perhaps that is the cause of the ghostly activity. So many people had so many good times at the restaurant, they return now that they are in spirit.

"The bar area and the front lobby seemed to me to be haunted. There was also a strange feeling in the last booth, as well. If you go there, order the steak, and keep an eye on the bar for moving shadows. And keep a tight grip on the water glass—just be sure it doesn't fly off by itself!"

A VANISHING RESTAURANT OUTSIDE OF AMARILLO

In the early summer of 1987, Sam and Clara were traveling to Amarillo, Texas, on a business trip. Shortly after midnight, they decided to stop to eat at a quaint, rustic-style restaurant that neither of them had ever noticed on previous trips to the region. They remembered that the food was prepared in an excellent down-home country style, and that the waitress, the cook, and even the other customers were so friendly in a sincere manner that Sam and Clara truly meant their promise that they would stop back again.

"And we tried to do exactly that on our return drive," Sam said, "but that great little down-home restaurant was nowhere to be seen. We even looped back a couple of times, thinking we might somehow have driven on by. We even got into an argument, each of us insisting that we remembered exactly where it was. We just couldn't find it, and since the hour was getting very late, we drove on."

Because their business required a number of return visits to Amarillo, Sam and Clara traveled that route on three consecutive weekends, each time keeping a watch for the restaurant with the wonderful cooking, but it seemed as though it had simply vanished.

"Since then, we have driven that route a dozen or more times," Sam said, "but we never again found that friendly little restaurant."

Indeed, Sam and Clara may have been extremely fortunate. What if the "friendly little restaurant" appeared and disappeared every few years? A kind of Texas-style "Brigadoon." They might have been lost in time and space for decades. But at least the food and the company would have been good.

A Protective Ghost at Homestead Restaurant, Jacksonville

Alpha Paynter operated a boarding house in the cabin that later became the Homestead Restaurant in Jacksonville, Florida. Alpha devoted her life to the place, and when she died in 1962, she was buried in the yard behind the building. According to many of those who have patronized the place in recent years, Alpha Paynter has never left the Homestead and remains its protector.

Steve Macri, a former owner of the Homestead, admitted to Michele Newbern Gillis of the *Jacksonville Daily Record* (September 22, 2002) that in the 26 years that he ran the place, there were many things that he could not explain. In October 2001, just before he closed, there were a rash of complaints from women who claimed that an invisible someone was touching them on the shoulders. Macri also mentioned the newly hired dishwasher from out of town who asked who the lady in the long dress was who was watching him from the top of the stairs. A young employee, who was shooting hoops during his break, ran back in the restaurant screaming that he had seen a woman in the backyard half in and half out of the ground.

A new ownership team, which includes Kathy Johansen, whose family owned the Homestead until 1975, reopened the restaurant in September 2002. Although Johansen said that she had never seen the ghost of Alpha, she knew that over the years that her father owned the restaurant, many customers and employees had claimed to have seen her. Contractors working alone in the building after hours complain of being touched from behind. Many have left and never returned to complete their work.

According to tradition, Alpha's spirit appears most often in mirrors in various rooms in the restaurant. Many patrons have reported seeing her leaning over the fireplace in the center room.

Danza's in Brooklyn Is Haunted by Wiseguys

Danza's Restaurant in Bensonhurst was once Tali's Restaurant and Lounge, headquarters of Salvatore "Sammy the Bull" Gravano, where at least two men who co-owned the place with the infamous mob informer were murdered. The present owner, Stephen Carroll, told Al Guart of the *New York Post* (March

10, 2002) that the place was haunted by ghosts that sit down for dinner, disembodied voices, and tablecloths that fluff and drop back down on their own.

Principal among the restless spirits that have never left the restaurant are likely to be that of Michael DeBatt, Gravano's partner, who Sammy the Bull had murdered while he was tending bar, and Joseph D'Angelo, who Sammy claimed was killed by another mobster. Roseanne Massa, DeBatt's sister, believes that her brother Michael may well be haunting Danza's because his spirit is disturbed that Gravano has never really paid or atoned for killing him and 18 others. Sammy spent less than five years in prison for his crimes as the result of a deal that he cut with prosecutors for testifying against Gambino head John "teflon Don" Gotti.

Stephen Carroll said that he had pretty much overlooked the bullet holes that still marked the restaurant's brick walls and the claims of ghosts until his cousin, Angela Perrone, was working alone in the basement. She said that she heard someone speaking to her and thought it was her partner. But then she discovered that he had been outside packing the car the whole time that she was in the basement.

Since that time, Carroll and other members of his staff have seen men sitting down at tables or walking toward the basement, only to vanish. Employees and customers have said that they have heard disembodied voices and had the feeling that they were being watched.

GHOSTS BELLY UP TO BAR WITH PATRONS IN AMERSHAM

At the fifteenth-century bar Boot and Slipper in Rickmansworth Road, Amersham Old Town, England, the staff is too frightened to go down in the cellar alone. They complain that the resident ghost brushes past them, says a few words that cannot really be distinguished, then places its hand on their shoulder.

Patrons say that the Elephant and Castle in Amersham Old Town is just as haunted as the Boot and Slipper. The ghost of a woman in black has been seen gliding to and fro in the kitchen. Barmaids complain that they have their bottoms pinched when there is no one else around who could perpetrate such a personal offense.

The Chequers pub is haunted by a white-hooded figure, and numerous cold spots have been detected in the bar that was built in the 1500s. Some say that people accused of witchcraft and other crimes were imprisoned there while they waited to be burned at the stake.

The Crown Hotel has five ghosts, including a very inhospitable one who shouts at guests to get out. In Room 16, a more maternal spirit exists, that of an old Victorian housekeeper who likes to tuck young men into their beds. Staff members reported some men running down the stairs at three in the morning when the caring housekeeper pays them a visit.

ADMIRAL GROG HEADS THE GHOSTLY CREW AT THE INN

The ghost of Admiral Edward Vernon, remembered as the man who introduced watered-down rum—"grog"—to the British navy, now heads a crew of spirits at the Tuddenham Road Inn in Ipswich, Suffolk, that includes a monk, a drowned seaman, and a publican named George.

Staff members have reported seeing an ash gray figure scamper through one of the upstairs bedrooms. On one occasion, the spirit of a pony-tailed sailor appeared in the back bar and walked right through the landlord. Even witnesses saw this eerie phenomenon, which has made the back bar an extremely unpopular place to have a drink.

The admiral himself, who was Ipswich Member of Parliament from 1741 to 1754, has been seen often, standing fully materialized and in full dress uniform. Those who have seen the ghost say that the admiral appears very authoritative.

WHAT DO YOU GET WHEN A JAIL BECOMES A THEATER?

Employees at the Tolbooth Theatre in Stirling, Scotland, have refused to work in a place that is haunted. In the restaurant portion of the building, a former jail that underwent a multimillion pound renovation in 2002, staff members have witnessed wine glasses become airborne and door handles turn themselves. Because this was the section in the old jail where prisoners awaiting execution were once held, many employees rationalized that there should be little wonder why restless and angry ghosts should inhabit the area.

Operations assistant James Wigglesworth told reporter James Hamilton that although the building had totally changed since it was a jail, there were still things that made the hairs on the back of his neck stand up. Late at night, Wigglesworth said, one could hear things being dragged across the floor of what used to be the cell area upstairs. The bar staff regularly reported wine glasses dashing themselves to the floor, and a ticket seller quit her job when she saw the ghost of man walk across the room.

The owners of the theater hoped they had found the reason for the disturbances when they found the skeleton of a convicted murderer under the concrete floor of the former prison entrance. According to old prison records, the remains were those of Alan Mair, who was hanged outside the Tolbooth in 1843. Mair was given a Christian burial in January 2002. The respect paid to Mair's bones did not alleviate the haunting phenomena. The manifestations continued to plague the staff of the theater and the restaurant of the remodeled Tolbooth. And the hauntings even stretched beyond the confines of the building.

The postman on his regular route stopped by the Tolbooth, and spotting a man he assumed was an actor fully dressed in eighteenth-century costume, he gave a cheery hello. He was terrified when the man returned his salutation with a resounding, "And good morning to you, sir," then disappeared.

In order to placate the nervous staff at the Tolbooth, the owners have promised an exorcism, but parapsychologist Dr. Richard Wiseman of the University of Hertfordshire doubted that the rites would do any good. Theaters attract ghostly experiences, he said, and when they were placed in buildings that were former jails, there would be great "expectations of ghostly events going on."

THE GRAND THEATER INVESTIGATION IN WAUSAU, WISCONSIN

**Research in Progress by the Wausau Paranormal Research Society:
Contribution by Todd Roll**

"Built in 1927 to replace the old Grand Opera House, the Grand Theater has been a Wausau, Wisconsin, landmark for decades. Originally a vaudeville and silent movie house, the Grand has changed functions over the years, showing motion pictures from 1932 to 1985, and, after a renovation project in 1986, the Grand became the feature performing arts theater for north central Wisconsin.

"Over the years the Grand has been host to numerous plays, movies, musical performances, and, if the tales are to be believed, one or more ghosts.

"The earliest reports of ghostly activity at the Grand are from the 1950s, when workers reported movie canisters being moved from the upstairs projection room to the lobby. Over the years other manifestations have been reported, including phantom footsteps, apparitions, electrical malfunctions, cold spots, and areas that are just creepy to be in.

"The Wausau Paranormal Research Society launched an investigation of the Grand Theater in July 2001. At that time the theater was undergoing a major renovation project in which the theater will receive an addition and be linked to two other buildings as part of the 'Arts Block' project, making conditions less than ideal for an investigation, but our hope was that the project might 'stir up' the spirits of the building.

"During our initial research we collected reports of the following paranormal phenomena at the Grand. Many stagehands reported the sound of footsteps walking across the empty stage. When they would investigate, the

This photograph was taken inside the Grand Theater in Wausau, Wisconsin. A number of anomalies were revealed on the negative after development.

source of the footsteps could not be located. A worker closing up the theater for the evening saw an apparition of a man appear along the back wall of the balcony. The apparition was seen in the exact spot where the door to the projection room had been located.

"An apparition, again of a man, was seen in the lighting rack above the stage by a number of people over the years. In one case the apparition walked down the spiral staircase from the lighting rack and crossed the stage directly in front of two witnesses. Lights in the projection area are often turned on when no one is around. Various areas of the theater are reported to be 'cold spots.'

"During the most recent construction project, power would mysteriously shut off in one area of the basement. Electricians would test a wire and find it live, but when they tried to power equipment off of it the same line would be dead, only to become live again moments later.

"A puddle would form in another area of the basement, when no source of water for it could be found. Two staff members reported hearing 'voices' coming out of a room behind the balcony. A search revealed no other people in the building.

"The Wausau Paranormal Research Society decided to concentrate our investigation in two areas, the balcony and third floor offices, and the stage and lighting rack. While taking background photos of the balcony, I snapped a photo of an anomalous blob. I was using standard 35mm 400 speed film and did not see the blob at the time the photo was taken. A photo taken seconds later did not show the blob. When checking the negative, the blob does appear on it. The photo does have some other development flaws on it, but the blob is something different. It should be noted that there was a renovation project going on at the time, and the blob could very well be a dust particle.

"During our third visit we recorded some electronic voice phenomena (EVP) in one of the spotlight rooms in the third floor office area. While setting up equipment in the room, two members reported hearing 'whispering' coming from the far corner of the room. After playing back the tape, a voice can be heard saying, 'Don't come back over here.' The origin of the voice could not be determined at this time.

"The Wausau Paranormal Research Society plans to visit the Grand Theater … to conduct a further investigation of the phenomena reported."

23
Battlefields Where Phantom Armies Eternally Wage War

A Phantom Army in Scotland

In the mid-eighteenth century, Archibald Bell, a farmer of Glenary, Scotland, and his son were walking down a local road. Before long the noise and clatter of many feet alerted the men to the imminent approach of a marching army. As soldiers were not averse to recruiting unwilling victims to serve in their ranks, the two Bells retired hastily to a hiding place some distance above the ground.

They saw pass beneath them a vast army. There was something peculiar about the soldiers, though. They were wearing uniforms unlike any seen in the Highlands. And the cut of their breeches was in the style of another era altogether. Just as the elder Bell was noticing the absence of a ground swell of dust accompanying the soldiers, the army disappeared. The road was empty and untrodden. To their dying days, the elder Bell maintained that the vision had been one of the future, while Bell the younger insisted that they had seen an army of the past.

The Ghostly Army of Kentucky

It was an unusually warm day on the afternoon of October 1, 1863, when a small group of Union soldiers stopped at the Kentucky mountaintop home of Moses Dwyer and asked for a drink of water. Although Dwyer made it clear that his sympathies lay elsewhere, he said that he could not deny the Yankees a drink of water.

The Union sergeant thanked the mountaineer and assured him that his men would be on their best behavior if they might just rest a bit in the shade of his large porch. The members of the Dwyer family offered the troops some freshly baked cookies, and soon the civilians and the soldiers were talking and joking, forgetting about the great schism that was supposed to divide them.

After a few minutes of gentle conversation, one of the Union soldiers noticed a clump of strange clouds and pointed skyward. There, over the ridges of the adjacent hills, were rows and rows of weirdly shaped clouds, about the size and general shape of doors. They seemed to be constructed of smoke or some cottonlike substance rather than water and vapor.

Within moments, the sky had filled with the peculiarly shaped clouds.

The sergeant noted that the clouds seemed to be flying on their own. There was no wind that day, so all the soldiers and the Dwyer family were wondering out loud how the clouds could be moving in such a manner. As neatly regimented as companies of soldiers, the strange clouds sailed swiftly over the heads of the astonished witnesses on the porch of the Kentucky mountain cabin. Their numbers were so great that it required more than an hour for all of the door-sized "rolls of smoke" to pass overhead.

Moses Dwyer had just finished commenting that the sight was the darnedest thing he had ever seen in all his years in the region when suddenly, in the valley below them, thousands upon thousands of what definitely appeared to be human beings materialized, marching at double time in the same direction as the mysterious clouds.

A soldier cocked his musket nervously, muttering that the whole Rebel army was fixing to march on them. The sergeant was as pale as the next man, but he had not yet allowed himself to panic. He quieted his men and spoke to them in a harsh whisper, proclaiming that the strange army approaching them was not made up of living combatants but the ghosts of men who were once soldiers.

The phantoms all wore white shirts and trousers and marched approximately 30 to 40 "soldiers" deep. Oblivious to the attention they were receiving from the startled mountain family and the Union troops, the apparitions strode purposefully across the valley and began to ascend the steep mountain range that surrounded it.

The ghostly marchers could have passed for a mighty earthly army on the move if it had not been for their bizarre appearance. The phantoms were not of uniform size, as their companion clouds had been. Some of the eerie marchers were tall, and others appeared to be quite small. Their legs were seen to move and their arms to swing briskly. While they marched in strict military fashion, they bore no weapons of any kind. As the phantom parade began to ascend the mountain, members of the ghostly march were seen to lean forward, just as men do when negotiating steep terrain.

It took over an hour for the great parade of phantoms to march out of the valley, and the witnesses to the remarkable sight were left speechless and filled with wonder. Some of them, perhaps rightly, interpreted the ghostly marchers to represent the many men who would die in the bloody War Between the States.

Strangely enough, on October 14, 1863, a similar parade of phantoms was observed by ten Confederate soldiers and a number of civilians at Runger's Mill, Kentucky. According to contemporary reports, the phenomenon remained identical in every detail, except that the combined passage of the weird clouds and the eerie marchers took only one hour instead of two.

A Phantom Re-creation of Dieppe

On August 4, 1951, two young Englishwomen vacationing in Dieppe, France, were awakened just before dawn by the violent sounds of guns and shell fire, dive bombing planes, shouts, and the scraping of landing craft hitting the beach. Cautiously peering out of their windows, the two young women saw only the peaceful pre-dawn city. They knew, however, that just nine years previously, nearly 1,000 young Canadians had lost their lives in the ill-fated Dieppe raid.

Being possessed of unusual presence of mind, the young Englishwomen kept a record of the frightening cacophony of sound, noting the exact times of the ebb and flow of the invisible battle. They presented their report to the Society for Psychical Research, whose investigators checked it against detailed accounts of the event in the war office. The times recorded by the women were, in most cases, identical to the minute of the raid that had taken place nine years before.

Spirit Memories of the Battle of Edge Hill

Restored battle scenes offer excellent examples of what seem to be impressions caused by the collective spirit memories of large groups of people under threat of death and the most-severe kinds of physical and emotional stress. Perhaps the best-known, most extensively documented, and most substantially witnessed of such occurrences was the Phantom Battle of Edge Hill, which was "refought" on several consecutive weekends during the Christmas season of 1642. The actual battle was waged near the village of Keinton, England, on October 23 between the Royalist Army of King Charles and the Parliamentary Army under the Earl of Essex.

It was on Christmas Eve that several countryfolk were awakened by the noises of violent battle. Fearing that it could only be another clash between actual living soldiers that had come to desecrate the sanctity of the holy

The village of Radway and the field where the Battle of Edge Hill took place in 1642.

evening and the peace of their countryside, the villagers fled from their homes to confront two armies of phantoms. One side bore the king's colors; the other, Parliament's banners. Until three o'clock in the morning, the phantom soldiers restaged the terrible fighting of two months before.

Real Ghosts, Restless Spirits, and Haunted Places

The battlefield of Edge Hill.

The battle had resulted in defeat for King Charles, and the monarch grew greatly disturbed when he heard that two armies of ghosts were determined to remind the populace that the Parliamentary forces had triumphed at Edge Hill. The king suspected that certain Parliamentary sympathizers had fabricated the tale to cause him embarrassment, so he sent three of his most trusted officers to squelch the matter.

When the emissaries returned to court, they swore oaths that they themselves had witnessed the clash of the phantom armies. On two consecutive nights, they had watched the ghostly reconstruction and had even recognized several of their comrades who had fallen that day.

GHOSTS STILL DEFEND CORREGIDOR

Another area that seems to be drenched with the powerful emotions of fighting and dying men is that of the small island of Corregidor, where in the early days of World War II, a handful of American and Filipino troops tried desperately to halt the Japanese advance against the city of Manila and the whole Philippine Islands. Filipino Defense Secretary Alego S. Santos said after the war was over that the valiant defenders of the Philippines had fought almost beyond human endurance.

According to several witnesses, their ghosts continued to fight. In the 1960s the only living inhabitants of the island were a small detachment of Filipino marines, a few firewood cutters, and a caretaker and his family. And then there were the nonliving inhabitants. Terrified wood cutters returned to the base to tell of encountering bleeding and wounded men who were stumbling about in the jungle. In every instance, they described the men as grim-faced and carrying rifles at the ready.

Marines on jungle maneuvers reported coming face to face with silently stalking phantom scouts of that desperate last-stand conflict of a quarter of a century ago. Many claimed to have seen a beautiful red-headed woman moving silently among rows of ghostly wounded, ministering to their injuries. Most often seen was the ghost of a nurse in a Red Cross uniform. Soldiers on night duty who spotted the phantom have reported that, shortly after she faded into the jungle moonlight, they found themselves surrounded by rows and rows of groaning and dying men in attitudes of extreme suffering.

According to the caretaker and his family, the sounds that came with evening were the most disconcerting part of living on an island full of ghosts. Every night the air was filled with horrible moans of pain and the sounds of invisible soldiers rallying to defend themselves against the phantom invaders.

The supervisor of tourism for Luzon, Florentino R. Das, said that he and his wife had visited the island and heard for themselves the terrible sounds of men in pain. Upon his investigation, he was unable to find any physical cause for the eerie disturbances.

The Shadow Warriors of Crete

How long might the violent emotions of warfare saturate the psychic ether of a terrain? The phantom marchers of Crete have been parading for centuries and seem to be armored men right out of the pages of Homer's *Iliad*.

People come from all over the island to observe the ghostly army, which usually puts in an appearance during the last weeks of May and the first week of June. No trained observer has been able to put the spectral army into any precise historical context. The ghostly ranks are filled with the images of tall, proud men, who wear metal helmets of classic design and carry short, flat swords.

The native islanders call them the "shadow men" or the "dew men," because they always appear just before dawn or just after sunset. They seem to form out of the sea, march directly for the ruins of an old Venetian castle, then disappear with the growing darkness of the night or the light of day. Historians have discarded any theory of a connection between the ghostly army and the medieval castle because of the design of the phantoms' breastplates and weapons.

For almost a century, feature stories on the spectral army have been carried in the major newspapers of Greece. In addition to the local peasants, Greek businessmen, archeologists, and journalists have reported seeing the phenomenon. German and English archeologists and observers have also been on hand for the parade of phantoms. During the Turkish administration of the island in the 1870s, an entire garrison of Turkish soldiers sighted the ghostly marauders and were frightened into readying themselves for combat.

Most theorists have discarded the possibility that the phantom marchers are only a mirage. Mirages have maximum ranges of about 40 miles and only occur in direct sunlight. The army, as has been noted, appears only in the half-light of dawn or dusk. Then, too, a mirage is a reflection of reality. This would mean that within a range of 40 miles, such an army would truly be marching. It would seem beyond all range of imagination to suppose that an entire army of men, who enjoyed conducting annual secret maneuvers in ancient armor, could exist on the island of Crete without being detected by the populace.

THE PHANTOM HUN

My friend John Pendragon of Tunbridge Wells, England, sent me the eerie account of the "Phantom Hun" who was seen in 1916 well behind the British lines between Laventie and Houplines to the northeast of Bethune, France. According to Pendragon, the story was first made public in the 1930s, when Edwn T. Woodhall (late of Scotland Yard and the Secret Service) wrote his reminiscences.

It was the practice during World War I (*c.* 1916) to earmark numerous isolated sites for reserve dumps of explosives that could be drawn upon in an emergency. Such dumps were usually in abandoned villages or farmhouses, well away from the range of enemy guns, and were guarded by one or two soldiers, the guards being changed weekly. From the guard's point of view, such jobs were "cushy," though the loneliness of a deserted ruin could often be rather irksome.

One such dump was located between Laventie and Houplines, and the explosives were hidden in the basement of a ruined farmhouse close to a derelict village. The guards were given rations for a week, plenty of fuel, cooking utensils, books and magazines, and perhaps a dart board. The men used to say that it wasn't so bad during the day, but nights were apt to be eerie—even if one did not believe in ghosts.

From far away there came the rumble of the guns and the frequent ascent of Verey lights. Occasionally an airplane droned over. Although they were in the midst of war, it seemed strangely remote to those in the ruined farmhouse near Laventie.

Then, gradually, stories began to circulate about the site. It seemed, according to reports, that always around the full moon, strange sounds were heard as if the guards were not the only inhabitants of the shambles of the farmhouse. Unaccountable footsteps were heard on the cobbled road that ran past the dump, and one man reported that when the moon was full he had seen a figure some 25 yards from where he stood. He challenged the figure, and receiving no reply, fired his rifle. To his amazement the figure vanished.

Since it was suspected that an enemy agent was at work, the intelligence service was informed, and an officer—Edwin T. Woodhall on the first occasion—was sent with a French policeman to augment the guard. The gendarme was chosen in case the arrest of a civilian was necessary.

The first night passed uneventfully enough. The men had a good fire, plenty of candles and food, and a couple of packs of cards, and after they had amused themselves for a while, they arranged to take turns to keep watch. It was on the second night's vigil that the strange manifestation occurred. Woodhall was taking the first two hours watch while the gendarme and the soldier slept. The latter soon settled themselves and fell asleep, but a little over an hour later they found Woodhall shaking them awake and telling them to listen.

The awakened men listened as they silently reached for their weapons. Above the cellar hideout there came the unmistakable sound of iron-shod boots on the road that ran a few yards away. So heavy and so definite were the footfalls that the vibration caused one or two pieces of plaster and earth to drop from the ceiling of the cellar.

With Woodhall leading, the three men crept to the top of the steps and into the moonlight. Instantly they saw a dark figure move from its place near a wall and vanish into the deep shadow cast by the buildings. For an hour or more, they searched the area but found nobody, not even a stray animal disturbed by the uncanny silence that had fallen upon the moonlit ruins. When daylight came, a more thorough search was made, but again there was no indication of any unauthorized person being on the site or in the derelict village beyond.

The following night brought spectacular events. Again the watch was kept, but the men who were resting did not slumber. They were too expectant and tense. At 2:55 A.M.—a little later than on the previous night—there came once again that characteristic sound of heavy iron-shod boots clumping toward them in the darkness.

Silently the three men crept to the top of the steps and, remaining in the shadows, gazed to the right towards a moonlit wall. A few yards from where they stood, their weapons ready, a German soldier knelt by the wall turning over some fallen bricks. Spellbound, they watched him. There was no doubt in their minds that he was as earthly as themselves. His spiked helmet gleamed in the moonlight. There was, nevertheless, something rather odd about the appearance of his uniform. It was heavily smeared with clay, as if it had been buried.

For more than a minute they gazed at the figure as he turned over the bricks. Then they challenged the German soldier. He responded by half-rising and turning to look at them. Then it was that all three of the men realized that before them was not a German soldier of flesh and blood but a grotesque skeleton. From beneath that spiked helmet a skull nodded while the bony hands dropped the bricks they held.

Shots from three rifles rang out, shattering the stillness of the night. Instantly the phantom vanished. The men kept watch until dawn, but the spectral German soldier did not reappear.

It must be granted that the intelligence staff investigated the case very thoroughly, but not before the explosives were removed from the dump—this being done on the day following the report being made. Acting in collaboration with the French authorities, the British pieced together the history of the village as it existed at the time of the declaration of war in August 1914. Although many of the inhabitants were dead, a number were traced and questioned, and from their various reports the following strange story was patched together.

In the late summer of 1914, the vast army of General Von Kluck swept towards Paris and the Channel ports. German infantry reached the village and overran the place, taking whatever they required but not harming the inhabitants unless they resisted.

The farmhouse was occupied by a sergeant-major and 20 or more men. The farmer had gone, leaving his wife and an infant, together with several villagers who had decided to remain. The cellar that had later been occupied by the British guards was then used as a wine store. The wine was promptly taken by the German soldiery, who settled down to a night's revel—the sergeant-major, in particular, pestering the farmer's young wife with his attentions. The situation became so threatening that the woman left the house and sought the advice and protection of an aged priest, who had remained behind with his parish. He said that he would remain with her until the Germans left, their departure being expected on the following day.

Shortly afterwards the Allies began to shell the village, forcing the Germans to retreat sooner than they had planned. All was confusion. The shouts of the men, the neighing of their horses, and the crash of the exploding shells made the place hell. The sergeant-major, according to the report of witnesses testifying later, was angry that the young mother had sought the old priest, and he denounced her as a spy. Drunkenly he first shot the child, then the mother, and finally the old priest.

The woman and child died instantly, but the cleric lingered for a few minutes, and pointing at the German he said, "Evil man, your spirit will live on, and you will return when your hour comes to haunt this place until God sees fit to absolve your soul!" Then, in the presence of witnesses, the priest died.

Running unsteadily to join his company, the sergeant-major was caught by a splinter from an exploding shell and died on the cobbled road.

The Germans departed, and the few French peasants buried the woman, the child, and the priest in one grave and the soldier in another. All the graves were close to the wall at the spot where the phantom was seen kneeling among the scattered bricks. The bodies were eventually exhumed to testify to the truth of the story.

WITNESSING A GHOSTLY RE-CREATION OF THE "WAR FIGHT"

In his article "Time Marched Backward" (*Fate*, October 1962), William P. Schramm recounts an interesting ghostly reconstruction of the past. The experience occurred to Paul Smiles, a friend of Schramm's, who was on duty with the British Army in Nairobi, East Africa, in 1942. He had taken advantage of a furlough to head for the lion country below Mount Kilimanjaro. Once there, he learned that a pride of lions had put themselves outside the protective laws by hunting native stock. A native guide named Simbia led Smiles to a shooting platform, and the white hunter was directed to await the lions, which would, according to the guide, come down to the pool to drink.

Smiles was about to drift off to sleep when he was brought fully to his senses by the roar of a lion. Just as he was bringing a large male with full, dark mane into his sights, a rifle shot split the night's silence and sent the pride of lions scattering.

The shot had come from the direction of the tree in which Simbia sat perched. The two men had agreed that Bwana Smiles should have the first shot. The Englishman was about to castigate his guide when "a bedlam of rifle fire broke loose, as if hundreds of … troopers had gone into action. Amidst this din, sharp commands rang out in both English and German. The fusillades ensued time after time, interposed with excited commands. Then came silence."

Startled and shaky, Smiles came down from the shooting platform. Simbia stood at the foot of his tree, waiting for him. He had not expected Smiles to be able to shoot a lion on that night, the anniversary of the "War Fight" that had been waged on that ground between the English and the Germans 25 years before. On the first night that Simbia had heard the sounds of phantom warfare, he had thought that he had experienced some kind of nightmare. He had never told anyone what he had witnessed for fear that they would say he was bewitched. That was why he had brought Smiles to that particular shooting platform on that night. He had wanted corroboration of his story.

Simbia led Smiles through the brambles until they came to the open veldt. There under the African moon, Smiles saw rows of crosses marking the graves of both British and German infantry. "Outnumbered ten to one, and maybe taken by surprise, the British regiment had been annihilated. Since then every year on the fight's anniversary night, Simbia explained, the souls of the troopers came back and fought the battle over again."

DO YOU LIVE ON BATTLE-SATURATED SOIL?

In his article "Battles and Ghosts" (*Prediction* magazine, July 1952), John Pendragon sought to establish his theory that in regard to England, the eastern part of the country produces the greatest crop of haunted sites. The late, eminent British psychic-sensitive and researchers stated that such might be due to the fact that the eastern area of the country has been the scene of most of England's battle, especially battles to stave off invasion. Pendragon also made reference to the theory that the districts may, in some unknown way, have become "sensitized" as the result of these emotional conflicts involving bloodshed.

It has for some time been suggested by paranormal investigators that great human emotion can saturate a place or an object with its own particular vibration. On that assumption, is it not possible—or even probable—that the scenes of bloody conflicts have, so to speak, "sensitized" the very soil upon which they took place?

Many readers may be living in a house that is built on the site of an early battle, recorded or unrecorded, or even the scene of a human sacrifice or a terrible murder. Perhaps you smile indulgently, but such a case is by no means impossible. Many a sedate parlor may be standing on a place that has witnessed the most grim and terrifying scenes.

John Pendragon stated that eastern England is an especially haunted area, and its geological composition is composed mainly of soil types of the Tertiary and Quaternary periods, the most recent eras of geological history. The Tertiary era of rock includes marine limestone, clay, shelly sands, and gravels. In the Quaternary era one finds peat, alluvium, silt, mud, loam, and sometimes gravel.

Essex probably contains the greatest number of haunted sites in England, and Essex is 80 percent London clay, with the remainder mostly chalk. This particular county and its clay subsoil may provide a key to the problem of why certain areas are more haunted than others. The question is, are certain subsoils more sensitized than others?

The astrophysicist Robert Millikan discovered that certain soils absorb cosmic waves more readily than others, some soils acting as conductors and others as insulators. The French physicist Georges Lakhovsky noted that the highest incidence of cancer appeared to occur on clay soils and soils rich in ores, and that the lowest incidence was to be found where the soil was sand or gravel. Lakhovsky attributed this fact to the deflection of cosmic waves by the conducting soils, causing an imbalance in body cells, which, he maintained, are miniature oscillating circuits. Therefore, we may deduce that cosmic rays or the deflection of them by a soil consisting predominantly of clay does, in some way yet unknown to us, act as an aid to the production of phenomena that we call haunting by spirits.

It would seem that the clays, chalk, and alluvial soils are more sensitized than the ancient rocks, such as granite, gneiss, coal, old red sandstone, limestone, and so forth. Perhaps clay has the property of storing or deflecting the X energy, while granite and basalt do not. Subterranean water may also play a part. We might also point out that the most haunted places in England are on the "drier side" of the country. Pendragon was convinced that the reason why some areas are more haunted than others lies in a fusion of a number of factors, widely different, but that the geology of the district is one of them.

CHING, THE GHOSTLY VIOLINIST OF KUMSONG

Veterans of the Korean conflict returned with tales of a ghost town that came to life on cold, still nights. By day, Kumsong, Korea, was nothing but piles of battered rubble. The population had long since given over residence of their war-washed village to the rats. The American troops, who looked down on the charred ruins from their positions in the front-line bunkers, called Kumsong the "Capital of No Man's Land."

But, then, on some nights, soldiers would come back from their frozen bunkers with stories of music, singing, and the laughter of women that had drifted up from the ghost town. So many Allied troops heard the ghostly music that "Ching and his violin" became a reality to the front-line soldiers.

One morning the GIs awakened to find that some wit had nailed a poster to the side of a log bunker: "Come to the gala dance this Saturday night—located in lovely, convenient downtown Kumsong. Dancing partners and delicious drinks without cost."

Soldiers who scoffed at the tales of the weird phenomena were invited to put on their long-johns and join the sentries on the hill that overlooked the battered city. A sergeant with a poetic soul wrote the following to celebrate Kumsong's ghostly dance: "There's a place to dance in your combat pants,/And a place to forget the fight;/There's gals galore and no sign of war,/In Kumsong, Saturday night./It's down the line, don't step on a mine,/Far from the battle's din,/Where you can jig to the phantom music/Of Ching and his violin."

GHOSTS ON PORT HUENEME NAVAL BASE

Richard Senate, the experienced paranormal investigator, has found that the Port Hueneme Naval Base in California has many stories of ghosts. "The Officers Club, formerly the Senator Thomas Bard Mansion, has a long history of strange psychic events," Senate said. "Some believe that the ghost of Mrs. Bard walks the halls. Others report the phantom of the old senator himself haunting the second floor. Still others point to sightings of a Chinese servant as the specter that dwells in the three storied house."

Senate has found that new accounts of ghostly behavior point to the new Navy Exchange warehouse as being perhaps more haunted than the mansion. It was built on the site of a clinic, and the sightings of ghosts in that old structure date back to World War II.

"A phantom officer was once encountered late at night," Senate stated. "There were reports of whispering voices that came at a set time each day. When personnel checked, there was no one around or any logical explanation for the sounds. Years ago, two naval personnel witnessed a man run though the building late at night, wearing clothing that resembled the uniform of the Second World War. He ignored them and ran past them. It was a long moment before they the witnesses recalled that all the doors and windows were locked for the night. The man they saw looked as if he was very solid—unlike the commonly held view that ghosts are semitransparent or dressed in white."

Senate remarked that while the old building is history now, the ghosts may not have been evicted with the demolition. A young man was stocking merchandise in the new Naval Exchange warehouse before the store was open when he saw an officer in uniform standing, looking at a rack of uniforms. He got up to inform the office that the store was not yet open but he would be glad to help him. The officer turned to him and abruptly vanished.

Senate told another story about a young man who went to the vending machines in the Naval Exchange late one night for a snack. He walked away and then remembered that he forgot his change. He turned and heard a woman's voice say, "Did you forget something?" There was no one else in the building. He ran away, unwilling to return to vending machine out of fear.

Is the new building haunted? "Perhaps," Senate said. "The files of psychic research are filled with accounts of haunted buildings being torn down, only to have the structures built on the same location haunted with the older spirits."

THE FRENCH CAPTAIN GOES IN SEARCH OF HIS HEAD

In October 1965 the air force airfield of Tan Son Nhut had enough to keep it busy with Viet-cong raids and air strikes without having to worry about restless spirits, but a pesky phantom Frenchman had the nasty habit of setting off flares and keeping the men on edge.

One night staff Sergeant James Hinton of Lexington, Kentucky, an air policeman, was making his customary watch. He was out near the bomb and ammunition dump when someone triggered off one of the flares. The captain in charge of the detail immediately began to fire in the direction of the flare, thinking he saw someone in black pajamas drop into a ditch, but when the men got there, the ditch was empty. The next thing they knew, another flare went off, and there seemed to be someone up in a tree just beyond the old French tower. The captain opened up again and so did the rest of men. No one fell from the tree. The soldiers glanced uneasily at each other on the moonlit-flooded runway. What had caused the flares to go off? The adrenalin was flowing in their veins; their nerves would not be quieted.

Veteran Vietnamese guards explained to the Americans that the ghost was that of a French captain who was on duty in the tower when his outpost was overrun by Vietminh on the last day of the war waged against the French in 1954. The Frenchman put up a fierce, though vain, struggle.

When finally captured, the communists decided to repay him for the trouble he had caused them by beheading him. The French captain pled with his captors to be shot like a soldier instead of beheaded like a criminal, but the communists had made up their minds. He was clad in black pajamas and decapitated.

The Vietnamese soldiers believed that the Frenchman's body was buried in the old Buddhist cemetery out beyond the airport gates, but his head was hidden somewhere near the old watch tower. The Frenchman, now a member of the unquiet dead, must make regular forays to the old tower in search of his head if he was ever to find any rest.

According to Hinton, that was only the first of many spectral visits from the phantom Frenchman. As the soldiers became accustomed to these encounters, they learned to disregard the pajama-clad figure hovering around the old French tower at the edge of the main runway. Flares continued to be set off mysteriously, however.

The Vietnamese soldiers were firm in their beliefs regarding the nocturnal specter. They avoided night watch on the edge of the runway, and they repeatedly refused to allow the old tower to be torn down. When the runways were extended to accommodate fighter jets, all the other towers were removed, but not the one where the disconsolate Frenchman sought his head.

THE STERN GHOST OF THE GURKHA HAVILDAR

No sentry dares to sleep on duty at the Khamba Fort in the mountains of Kashmir. The Indian army men who guard this fort believe that they are watched over by the ghost of the Gurkha Havildar. And he is a harsh taskmaster.

In these mountains, the legend of the Gurkha ghost has become famous. Educated army officers, although disbelieving the legend, are content to let it grow because the Gurkha ghost solves many disciplinary problems in Khamba Fort. Indian troops swear the ghost prowls the fort at night, slapping the faces of sentries who aren't alert and using his best parade ground language to berate slovenly soldiers.

The ghost is said to be that of a Gurkha havildar (sergeant) who performed a heroic one-man assault on Khamba Fort during the bitter 1948 war between India and Pakistan for Kashmir. The fort, held by Pakistani forces, had fought off Indian troops for weeks. Then, the Gurkha havildar found a crack in the fort's steep, thick stone walls, and one night, armed only with grenades and a knife, crept inside. He killed all the defenders but was fatally wounded himself.

On night in June 1965, Lance Naik (Corporal) Ram Prakash said he met the ghost when firing broke out along the cease-fire line. Prakash said that a terrifying voice rose from a turret on the fort's wall: "I have given my life for this post. Why are you so slack?" Then came the sound of a face being slapped. It was learned later, Prakash said, that a sentry in the turret was nodding over his rifle and was punished by the stern ghost.

The men of Khamba Fort know the Gurkha ghost well. Each can describe in detail the clothing worn by the eerie figure that strides the ramparts at night. The troops say that the ghost invariably appears wearing only one shoe. The other apparently was lost in battle more than 50 years ago. The men agree that they are not really afraid of the ghost because they know he is on their side.

The men of Khamba Fort are very careful to put out cups of tea and sweets for the lonely Gurkha ghost who maintains his vigil throughout the night. And, they say, the tea and sweets always are gone by dawn.

24
Ghosts in Civic Buildings and Prisons

ENCOUNTERING A NEBBISHY GHOST IN THE STATE CAPITOL

The Personal Experience of Richard D. Hendricks

Richard D. Hendricks is a researcher with a large Madison, Wisconsin, law firm, the proprietor of Weird Wisconsin (<www.weird-wi.com>), the associate director for the Wisconsin Paranormal Research Center (<www.my.execpc.com/~wisprc/>), and the Newsline editor for The Anomalist *(<www.anomalist.com>).*

"I've heard my share of loud ghost encounters. Fully dressed apparitions, water sluicing off them, materializing in showers, with bloated gray heads, blackened hollows for eyes. Smoky snake entities slithering in through the front door, baleful golden-slitted eyes nailing shock-frozen homeowners to the sofa. Aged frail women wearing yesterday's faded dresses, hair knotted in gray buns, quietly threatening to kill robust young men. Wild and weird encounters; enough to raise goose bumps on even the strongest.

"I hear these stories and rub my hands in anticipation. Maybe this house, this snug secure suburban abode, is finally the place where the screaming bloody revenant all ghost hunters secretly hope for will at last reveal itself in all its gaudy excess.

"Alas. Hours, days spent poking about, with little to show for the effort. No amorphous shape captured on video or film; no eerie voice spitting sibilants on a cassette tape; only ambiguity, and the lingering thought that, if only I had been here sooner. In my lectures, I've worked it into a standard joke: if

[463]

you're afraid of ghosts, the best place to be is with ghost hunters, for only rarely do they ever encounter them.

"Even my own family has had numerous paranormal encounters, not the least of which was the haunted saloon my mother owned in northern Wisconsin. For a decade, well over a dozen members of my extended family saw apparitions, felt cold spots, experienced inexplicable electrical phenomena, heard banging noises, and puzzled over other routine spirited manifestations. But when I visited: nothing. Quiet as the grave. The closest I ever got was years before, when my grandmother phoned my mother to ask how she was doing. From upstairs, I heard my mother answer the phone—and then scream. My grandmother had been dead already for a couple of days. It was my nearest contemporaneous encounter.

"Or so I thought until a few years ago. I work across the street from the state capitol building in Madison, Wisconsin. It's a massive structure, situated on the highest point between two large lakes, built of white Bethel Vermont granite in the form of a Greek cross in the Italian Renaissance style, surmounted by the only granite dome in the United States, and only second in height as a concession to the national capitol in Washington, D.C. It's oriented to the four cardinal directions, with windows throughout, and massive Corinthian columns, carved statuary, and a gilded bronze statue, Miss Forward, symbolizing our state motto, with a stylish badger clinging to her head, atop the dome. Legislative offices, the governor's office, and the Supreme Court share space with the public, who are either visiting, advocating, or simply cutting through to save blocks of walking around its perimeter.

"It's the third building on site; two previous capitol buildings were consumed by fire. Before that, Native Americans camped here for hundreds of years, and the effigy mounds they constructed high above the glittering blue lakes were obliterated without a second thought. In the original badly constructed wooden building, James Morrison boarded pigs in the basement for safe keeping. Bored legislators goaded the hogs into squealing by poking sticks at them through the spaces between shrunken floorboards. In 1882, while two wings were being added, one collapsed, killing eight workers. If, as some people theorize, certain buildings act as enormous energy storage batteries, then this one, with its history of native spiritual practices, horrific fires, sudden deaths, partisan antagonisms, and the concentrated attention of millions of citizens from across the state, must be simmering with potency.

"Are there ghosts? For years, custodians have talked of doors opening and closing, [and of] hearing paper rustling in empty rooms, and a lucky few have encountered a distinguished, bushy-bearded, white haired man striding about. He's Moses Strong, former legislator and lobbyist for the Milwaukee Railroad in the mid-1800s. A portrait of Strong, when straightened, always settled askew, until finally it was considered such a nuisance it was buried away in a dark basement closet. I haven't yet found a reason for Strong's lingering tenancy, but his continued presence amply illustrates the lobbyist's tenacity.

"Until recently, the State Law Library was also in the building. During the hot summer of 1999, I was in the capitol on an errand to the library on the third floor. Finished, I took the elevator to ground level. I poked G, and as the brass door began closing, it abruptly stopped, stuttered, then shrugged open, as if a straggler had stuck an arm in to stop its closure. I've done this often myself; except, no one was there.

"An old building, an old elevator; some glitch, no doubt. Still, I have another old joke, on the off chance there may be someone invisible trying to sneak on. After all, it always pays to be pleasant, particularly in the presence of the unknown. I offered a greeting. 'Hi. How are you?'

"I didn't expect a response, nor did I receive one. The elevator slowly settled to ground level. I continued my gag, 'I hope you don't mind if I get out first; I'm sorta in a hurry.'

"Midway through the opening door, I swear I felt something shoulder past me. I faltered. Lurched to the right. It was weird. Of course, my rational mind immediately discounted the experience. It was the heat; I was woozy; and was still a little unsteady from recent knee surgery. I shrugged, and thought no more of it. And it would have ended there had I not been back in the building within the hour on a new errand. I was on a different elevator to the third floor. My ride was uneventful.

"I'm always in a hurry, even with a gimpy knee. A wide marble staircase was in front of me as the door opened. I ducked to the right, to take a hallway past legislative offices to reach my destination on the other side. Just as I rounded the corner, I nearly collided with a small nondescript man, a bit smaller than me, about five-foot-four, short brown hair, glasses, wearing a mustardy colored polo shirt, and also seemingly in a hurry.

"'Excuse me,' I blurted out, neatly sidestepping this nebbishy little man and allowing my momentum to carry me along the hallway.

"At the end of the corridor, I turned left. On my left was the gallery from which I had just come, across the wide expanse of the marble staircase. There, some 50 feet away, was the same nebbishy man I had nearly collided with, already in the act of waving at me.

"He was moving slowly, partly in profile, looking back at me, waving his right arm in an exaggerated languorous sweeping gesture, a goofy grin spread across his narrow face. Strange. At the rate he had been traveling, and from his position where we had nearly collided, he should have been well past this point, perhaps vanished. It was as if he had waited just around the bend of the hallway, and had started waving before I turned my corner, knowing that I would look back across to where I had been. As if to say, See me now?

"I immediately flashed back to my elevator ride an hour earlier. It was just flat-out weird. Was it coincidence? Did I weave a connecting narrative on the fly from two discontinuous and utterly mundane events? Or was it something more?

"I've long suspected that every individual clothes a discarnate entity in his or her own individual design. If ghosts are some form of free-floating energy, then each person particularizes it. The same energy—but one person may see a bent old man painfully hobbling down a hallway, another a girlish figure skipping merrily. And in a psychic locus, where millions of citizens project their thoughts, their desires, their dreams, their fears, their concern over faceless bureaucrats and archetypal state workers, surely something could poke up that did not have an onsite historical antecedent. Something like a scurrying nebbishy little man in a polo shirt.

"For years I've thought of this figure. Was it a ghost? It would be nice to have a loud, excessive ghost encounter—scary, then over with, and done. Paranormal? Who knows. Its ambiguity resonates through the years, making it seem more spooky. Unknown, and ultimately unknowable."

GHOSTS IN THE OLD STATE CAPITOL IN RALEIGH

For many years there has been talk of slamming doors, muffled voices and ghosts walking the corridors of the 164-year-old capitol building in Raleigh, North Carolina. A number of persons hired as night watchmen have quit after only one night on duty, complaining of doors opening and closing and invisible footsteps following them on their rounds. In July 2002 a staff member working late thought she heard the sounds of a reception in progress on the first floor, but when she reached the foot of the stairs, she found the rotunda empty, and all noises suddenly ceased.

Sam P. Townsend, a retired capitol administrator, recalled the state library room on the third floor as being particularly creepy. Late one night as he approached the library door, he remembered a cold, dank air falling on his head and neck, and he decided his work could wait until the next day.

Although the capitol had gone through a considerable number of watchmen who declined the privilege of working in the building after one night on the job, Owen J. Jackson, 84, stuck with the task for 12 years before he retired in 1990. He simply shrugged off the angry slamming of doors that sounded behind him and the thumping noises that followed him on his rounds.

Capitol historian Raymond Beck admitted that he didn't like to work in the capitol after dark. He always made it a point to be out of the building by

The old State Capitol Building, Raleigh, North Carolina.

quitting time, because when darkness fell, he could sense the whole atmosphere changing.

In February 2003 psychic investigator Patty Ann Wilson of the Ghost Research Foundation released the findings of her group's research into the capitol conducted in November 2002. Their biggest coup, she told Lorenzo Perez, staff writer for the Raleigh *News and Observer,* was to record a spectral whisper and to photograph a ghost in Reconstruction-era clothing as it sat in the third chair in the third row of the old House chambers.

THE PHANTOM OF HARRINGTON'S CITY HALL

Jan Almquist, city manager of Harrington, Delaware, said that she had actually bumped into the ghost that walks the hallways of the city hall after dark. She remarked that it felt something like a "soft pillow," but she was able to walk right through it. At that very moment, she caught the image of a man, about five-foot six and solidly built, reflected in the window glass.

Real Ghosts, Restless Spirits, and Haunted Places

Other city employees have reported locked doors opening themselves, then slamming shut again. Some have heard unseen footsteps creaking down the hallways and treading up and down the stairs. Police officers working late on night duty frequently hear footsteps clearly sounding in another part of the building. When they investigate, they hear the noises in the area that they just left. City Clerk Norma Short said that she had seen the ghost on three different occasions. She also reported the manifestation of a gray form standing in the library that disappeared when she approached it.

Although no one can identify the ghost for certain, some residents of Harrington have nominated Millard Cooper as the mysterious specter. Before the building, which was constructed in the early 1900s, housed the city government, library, and police headquarters, it was Cooper's Funeral Home. On February 25, 1971, mortician Cooper committed suicide, and longtime residents of Harrington comment that the description of the ghost could well fit the undertaker as he appeared in life.

Are There Ghosts in the Federal Building in Jonesboro?

For some years now, employees have claimed that there are a number of ghosts in the E. C. "Took" Gathings Federal Building and U.S. Courthouse in Jonesboro, Arkansas. While Bill Collier, who retired after 15 years as the General Services Administration building superintendent, said that he had never spotted a ghost during his period of service, he acknowledged that there were plenty of complaints of strange night noises and of objects being mysteriously moved. Collier also admitted that nearly every employee and security guard in the building had complained of unusual activities at one time or another.

Ernest Mungle, who had worked in the building as a custodian, told Larry Fugate, a reporter for the *Jonesboro Sun* (October 13, 2002), that he had once heard voices from an empty and locked jury room and even had met a ghost on the third floor many years ago. He didn't worry about its presence and had given it the nickname of Charlie.

One of the offices in the building hired a carpet installation crew to work in the evenings when the rooms were vacant. After only two shifts, the crew refused to work in the place after dark.

Two employees of the Internal Revenue Service complained of hearing rickety-ticky piano music, such as the kind that was heard in the old saloons. When a longtime resident of Jonesboro heard the stories, he explained to the employees that a saloon had once stood near the front entrance of the downtown office building.

A TALL, MUSTACHED GHOST IN HATBORO'S BOROUGH HALL

On a Friday morning in December 2000, Viki Connolly, the administrative assistant at the Loller Building, the borough hall in Hatboro, Pennsylvania, had come to work early. Because she knew she was the only one in the building, she was surprised when she saw the tall, sad-eyed mustached man standing in the tax collector's office. There was something about him that immediately transmitted to Connolly that he was not human. As she watched from her desk, about 15 feet away, the stranger crossed the office in five quick steps and vanished.

Later, recreating the scene for John Anastasi, a staff writer for *The Intelligencer* on October 2, 2002, Connolly said that the ghost simply walked from one corner of the room to the opposite corner and disappeared when it got to the wall. She stated that she was not frightened by the entity, for his facial expression was "sad or sick or tired," and she felt sorry for him. She described the ghost as tall with a mustache, salt and pepper hair, wearing his long hair pulled back in a ponytail. He was dressed in a gray military uniform.

The building that currently houses Hatboro's administrative offices, council chambers, and district court was constructed originally in 1811 as a school. While no one stepped forward to admit seeing paranormal visitors in the building, District Justice Paul Leo stated that he considered Ms. Connolly to be a very credible person. Justice Leo, whose courtroom is on the second floor of the Loller Building, said that there had been evenings when he had come in the courtroom for arraignments that he had suddenly felt as if he wasn't alone, that someone stood behind him.

A JUSTICE OF THE PEACE BROUGHT A HAUNTING ON HIS FAMILY

The Classic Case of the Drummer of Tedworth

In March 1661 John Mompesson, a justice of the peace of Tedworth, England, had an ex-drummer in Oliver Cromwell's army brought before him. The former soldier, whose name was Drury, had been demanding money of the bailiff by virtue of a suspicious pass. The bailiff had believed the pass to be counterfeit, and Mompesson, who was well acquainted with the handwriting of the official who had allegedly signed the note, judged the paper to be a forgery.

Drury beseeched Mompesson to verify his story with Colonel Ayliff of Gretenham, who, the drummer insisted, would vouch for his integrity. Mompesson responded to the drummer's pleas that he not be put into jail, but he told Drury that he would confiscate his drum until he had checked out his

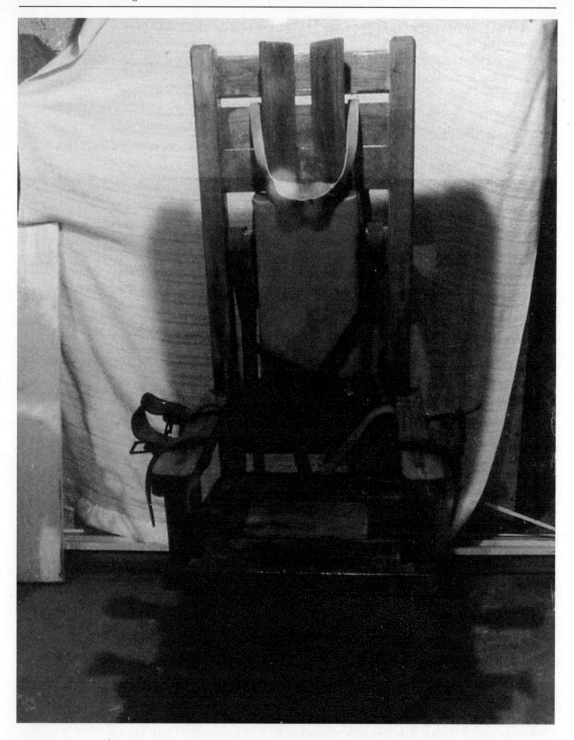

Five different entities have been seen in this photo of Tennessee's retired electric chair.

story. Drury begged that he be allowed to take his drum with him, but Mompesson told the man to be on his way and to be thankful that he did not sentence him to wait out the time until Colonel Ayliff could be contacted residing in a cell in Tedworth Goal (jail).

Mompesson had the drum sent to his house for safekeeping, then left on a business trip to London. When he returned, his wife informed him that the household had been frightened by noises in the night that she attributed to burglars trying to break into the house. On the third night of his return, Mompesson was awakened by a loud knocking that seemed to be coming from a side door. With one pistol cocked and ready and another tucked in his belt, he opened the door. There was no one there. But knocking sounded at another door. When he opened that door and found no one there, he walked around the outside of the house in search of the prankster. He found no one, nor could he account for the hollow drumming sound that came from the roof.

From that night on, the sound of drumming came always just after the Mompessons had gone to bed. After a month, the disturbances moved from the roof down into the room where Mompesson had placed Drury's drum. Once there, the ghostly drummer favored the family with two hours of martial rolls, tattoos, and points of war each evening.

The ghost began beating on the children's bedsteads at night, sometimes raising and lowering their beds in time with its drumming. When it would at last cease pounding the invisible drum and hoisting their beds in the air, it would lie under the beds, scratching at the floor. The Mompessons tried moving their children to another bedroom, but the drummer moved along with them. The knocking became so loud that it awakened neighbors several houses away. The Mompessons' servants also received nocturnal visits from the ghost. It would wait until they drifted off to sleep, then it would lift their beds. On occasion, it would curl up around their feet.

The unseen drummer soon had achieved such strength that it could hand boards to a servant who was doing some repair work in the house. This remarkable display of spirit energy was observed by numerous witnesses, but Mompesson stepped in and forbade the servant to encourage such familiar interaction with the demon. Perhaps Mompesson should have been more judicious in his designation of the unseen spirit's character, for the entity emitted offensive, sulfurous fumes. The stench convinced the justice of the peace that their unwelcome visit had come directly from the pit of Hell.

A Reverend Cragg was summoned to conduct prayers and a kind of exorcism in the house. The drummer kept quiet until the minister's closing "amen," then it began to move chairs about the room, throw the children's shoes into the air, and toss objects about the room.

The drummer particularly enjoyed wrestling with a muscular servant named John. It delighted in wrapping itself around the big man and holding him fast, as if he were bound hand and foot. Only by exerting the full extent of his brute strength could John free himself from the hold of his invisible opponent.

On the night in which Mrs. Mompesson gave birth to another child, the drummer kept respectfully silent. For three weeks, there were no sounds of drumming in the Mompesson home. The family had begun to think that the mysterious and annoying sounds had ended. But then one night the drummer began the rolls again. It was as if it had maintained a period of quiet to allow the mother to recover some strength before it began its mischief in earnest.

By January 10, 1662, nearly a year after the disturbances began, the ghost had acquired a voice and the ability to simulate the sound of rustling silk and the panting of animals. It had begun by singing in the chimney, then moved into the children's bedroom, where it frightened them with its chanting that it was a nasty witch. On a particularly cold and bitter winter's night, the ghost came to Mompesson's bedside, panting like a large dog. Even though the bedroom did not have a fireplace, it soon became very hot and filled with a stifling, disagreeable odor. The next morning, Mompesson scattered fine ashes over the bedroom floor to see what sort of footprints might be made by the obnoxious entity. The ghost entered the bedroom again that night, and on the following morning, Mompesson was baffled by the discovery of the markings of a great claw, some letters, circles, and other strange imprints.

Reverend Joseph Glanvil was attracted to the case by the reports that had reached him, and he arrived to conduct his investigation. The phenomena provided the clergyman with ample evidence of their existence from the very first moment of his arrival. It was eight o'clock in the evening and the children were in bed, suffering their nightly ritual of scratching, bed-liftings, and pantings. Reverend Glanvil tried desperately to trace the source of the disturbances but could find nothing. Later that night, when Reverend Glanvil and a friend retired for the evening, they were awakened by a loud knocking. "What would you have to do with us?" the clergyman asked the entity. "Nothing with you," a disembodied voice answered him.

The next morning, Reverend Glanvil's horse was found in a state of nervous exhaustion. A puzzled servant pronounced his opinion that it appeared as though the animal had been ridden all night. Glanvil mounted the horse for his return trip, and it collapsed. Although the horse was well attended and cared for, it died within two days.

On one occasion, Mompesson fired his pistol at a stick of firewood that had suddenly become animated, and he was astonished to see several drops of blood appear on the hearth. The firewood fell to the floor, and a trail of blood began to drip on the stairway as the wounded ghost retreated. One wishes that a modern pathologist's laboratory could have had an opportunity to analyze the drops for blood-type.

When the thing returned three nights later, it seemed to take out its anger for Mompesson's attack on the children. Even the baby was tossed about and not allowed to sleep. In desperation, Mompesson arranged to have the children taken to the house of friends. Later that night when the ghost pounded on the door to Mompesson's bedroom, it showed itself to a startled servant. "I could not determine the exact proportion," the terrified man told his master, "but I saw a great body with two red and glaring eyes, which for some time were fixed steadily upon me."

A friend of Mompesson's, hoping to be of some assistance to the justice of the peace, had all of his coins turn black during the course of his overnight stay. His horse was discovered in the stables with one of its hind legs firmly fastened in its mouth. It took several men working with a lever to dislodge the hoof from the unfortunate beast's jaws.

About this time, Drury, the man whose drum Mompesson had confiscated, was located in Gloucester Gaol, where he had been sentenced for thievery. Upon questioning, he freely admitted putting a spell on Tedworth's justice of the peace and "witching" him. "I have plagued him," the man boasted, "and he shall never be quiet 'till he hath made me satisfaction for taking away my drum."

It is likely that the haunting at Tedworth began quite independently of the bitter ex-soldier who claimed to have put a curse on John Mompesson. It would not seem at all inconsistent with Drury's character to conjecture that after he learned of the disturbances at Tedworth, he might have taken the credit for originating the manifestations. On the other hand, one should recognize the terribly potency that some people accredit to "curses," the direction of negative suggestion.

Justice of the Peace Mompesson had Drury tried for witchcraft at Sarum, and the drummer was condemned to be transported to one of the English colonies. Certain accounts have it that the man so terrified the ship's captain and crew by raising storms that they took him back to port and left him on the dock before sailing away again.

With the drummer either on his way to the colonies or set free from jail to do as he would, the manifestations in the Mompesson house ceased. By the time a king's commission had arrived to investigate the alleged haunting, the phenomena had been quiet for several weeks. The cavaliers spent the night with the family, then left the next morning, pronouncing their consensual verdict that the entire two-year haunting had been either a hoax or the misinterpretation of natural phenomena by credulous and superstitious individuals.

Whatever the truth of the manifestations in the Mompesson home, the demon of Tedworth is so much a part of the legend and folklore of England that ballads and poems have been written in celebration of the incredible series of events.

Later, Reverend Joseph Glanvil wrote *Saducismus Triumphatus,* his account of witnessing the phenomena at Tedworth while it was in progress. Expressing his frustration with the king's investigators and their final verdict regarding the phenomena, Glanvil wrote: "It was bad logic to conclude a matter of fact from a single negative against numerous affirmatives, and so affirm that a thing was never done.... By the same way of reasoning ... the Spaniard inferred well that said 'There is no sun in England, because I was there for six weeks and never saw it.' This is the common argument of those that deny the being of apparitions. They have traveled all hours of the night and have never seen any thing worse than themselves (which may well be) and thence they conclude that all ... apparitions are fancies or impostures."

THE WHITE LADY OF SHEPTON MALLET

On Tuesday, January 17, 1967, the British press carried the story of six prison warders who complained of frightening experiences while on night duty at Shepton Mallet, Somerset.

The guards told of a "chilling atmosphere" and a "weird presence" that seemed to permeate the tiny, blue-tiled duty room. Each of the men testified that he had heard unaccountable bangings and the sound of heavy breathing, and had had the feeling that something or somebody was in the room with him. One of the guards told a reporter that he personally would not do another night in the duty room for a thousand pounds.

The warden of the prison, Barry Wigginton, sent a full report to the home secretary, Roy Jenkins, stating that he had been unable to find any satisfactory explanation for the happenings. Wigginton said that he had spent a night in the guard room and had found nothing unusual. He had also called in two chaplains to calm his frightened staff. By the time the story had appeared in the British press, the incidents had ceased, but some prison officers were still reluctant to spend the night alone in the duty room.

One senior warder told a journalist that they had all been scared stiff and nobody had yet come up with an explanation. Someone brought up the legend of a "white lady"—a woman who was beheaded in 1680—that had been known to haunt the 360-year-old prison in autumn and winter.

"If this has been the white lady doing this," a prison officer commented, "and she comes back again, the night duty staff is going to wear thin."

In 1988 Lars Thomas was on a guided tour of the Viaduct Inn's cellar, which used to be cells of London's notorious Newgate Prison. He took a photograph inside one of the empty cells, but when he developed the film, this figure appeared on the photograph.

AN EERIE VISITATION AT PENTRIDGE PRISON

**From the Ghost to Ghost Website <www.ghosttoghost.com>:
The Personal Experience of Karen Linstrom, Governor (Retired),
HM Prison Service, Victoria, Australia**

"I worked in the Victorian Prison Service, Australia, for 16 years. I began my career at HM Pentridge Prison, Coburg Victoria. The site, now partially torn down, was home to 1,200 male and female prisoners at any one time. The ghostly encounter that I am going to describe took place in 'D' Division, originally constructed for female prisoners in 1880 but currently the remand facility for 320 maximum security male prisoners.

"One night, a young male prisoner had slashed his wrists and arms in a suicide attempt. He had lost a life threatening amount of blood, and six of us were desperately trying to stem the flow while waiting for the intensive care ambulance to arrive. At one point, the Senior Prison Officer requested that I run out of the infirmary, up a shot landing to call [your equivalent of 911] to get an ETA on the ambulance.

"As I ran up the stairs I hit what felt like an ice wall and was momentarily stopped in my tracks. The air around me became instantly chilled, and although this was in the middle of summer, I was cold and could see my breath. I was then able to get up the last six steps, but when I turned around, I saw an opalescent fog crystallize into the form of a woman. She wore long skirts, a cap on her head, and when she turned her face towards me, I got the impression of a woman old before her time, with uncountable horrors and sorrows written in the depth of her startling blue eyes. She then vanished, and the air around me returned to its warm and humid state.

"I have never forgotten her face, and that five to ten second interlude. I went in search of files and possible photographs to try and find this restless soul. I now have it narrowed down to three possible women, all transported from England, all of Irish extraction, all for seven to 14 years hard labor for crimes such as stealing one shilling's worth of bread.

"She saved me from annoying an already busy emergency service, and made me acutely aware of how much of us we leave behind for other people to learn from."

THE RESTLESS SPIRIT OF A MONK WHO VISITED A PRISON CELL

A Classic Case from Germany

On a September night in 1835, Dr. Henry Kerner was confronted by a problem that had never been outlined in textbooks or explained by men under whom he had studied. That night he left his room near the Weinsberg prison grounds and walked to a cell where he intended to shut himself in with a 38-year-old female inmate who appeared to be suffering from strange delusions. The prison guards let him pass with a nod, and the turnkey opened the cell of Mrs. Elizabeth Eslinger.

Dr. Kerner asked the woman how she felt before he removed his cloak and sat in the cell's single chair. She replied that she was fine, and Kerner knew her answer to be the truth, for he had examined her himself that afternoon. The minutes passed slowly until an hour had elapsed, then another. Finally, at 11:30 Kerner heard a sound as though some hard object had been thrown down on the side of the cell opposite where the woman sat.

Mrs. Eslinger immediately began to breathe more rapidly and informed the doctor that the ghost she had seen for so many nights had appeared in the cell again. Dr. Kerner put his hand on the woman's forehead and told the evil spirit to depart. Immediately, there sounded a strange rattling, cracking noise all around the walls of the cell, which finally seemed to go out through the window. The woman said the spirit had departed.

Thus, for Dr. Kerner, the reality of the woman's story was established beyond a doubt. He had been decidedly skeptical when he had first heard of the prison ghost, but after examining the woman and hearing the testimony of her fellow prisoners, Dr. Kerner decided that he must investigate the phenomena personally before he could write his report.

According to Mrs. Eslinger, the ghost was the shade of a Roman Catholic priest of Wimmenthal, Germany, who had lived in 1414 and had committed many crimes. In particular, he and his father had worked a fraud upon his own brothers. Since his death, the monk had existed as a spirit in despair. His presence was often accompanied by groans and moans and sometimes by an earthy smell. Although he could not be touched when Mrs. Eslinger reached for him, she claimed that she could feel his hand, which became warmer as time passed and his visits increased.

Prison officials considered the particular cell block to which Mrs. Eslinger had been confined to be nearly impenetrable. With no windows and thick walls on the first floor and only closely barred, narrow windows on the second, they felt that no person could enter the block without passing the guards who were on duty 24 hours a day. Yet the apparition visited the cell nightly, and its presence had been attested to by Mrs. Eslinger's fellow prisoners.

Mrs. Eslinger told Dr. Kerner that the spirit had been sorely troubled when the doctor had called it an evil spirit, protesting that it deserved pity. It had entreated Mrs. Eslinger to pray for it nightly.

For more corroboration (and perhaps to protect his reputation), Dr. Kerner brought his wife to Mrs. Eslinger's cell on October 18. Once again, the woman's breathing quickened, and this time, the doctor asked quite gently that the spirit trouble the woman no longer. The same noises rattled around the cell, then down the passageway.

On October 20 Dr. Kerner again stayed in the cell, this time with Justice Heyd. At midnight Dr. Kerner saw a yellowish light come through the window that had been shut tight against the weather. Simultaneously, he felt a cold breeze and smelled a strong odor. The same sensations awoke Justice Heyd, who had been dozing, and Dr. Kerner described his face feeling as if ants were running over it. Mrs. Eslinger had fallen to her knees next to her cot and had begun to pray fervently. While she prayed, the men saw the light move up and down the cell, then heard a moaning, hollow, resonant voice that Dr. Kerner could not ascribe to any human.

On December 9 the doctor and the wife of the prison deputy warden, Madam Mayer, were again in the cell. Suddenly a small cloud of light about the size of a small animal, like a cat, came into the cell and moved across it. At the same time there came such a noise at the window that Dr. Kerner thought the panes of glass inside the bars would surely be broken. Mrs. Eslinger told her guests that the ghost had seated itself on a stool in the cell. After the ghost had arrived they heard footsteps, as if someone paced up and down on the floor. Although they saw nothing, Dr. Kerner again felt a cold wind, and a little later he and Madam Mayer heard the same hollow voice say, "In the name of Jesus, look on me!"

Both Dr. Kerner and Madam Mayer could then see a light surrounding them. Once again they heard footsteps and the voice asking, "Do you see me now?"

Dr. Kerner for the first time perceived the form of the being. The ghost was dressed in the loose robe of a medieval clergyman. Dr. Kerner saw it several times again that night, often standing near Mrs. Eslinger as she prayed. Once it approached Madam Mayer, and she commanded it, "Go to my husband in his chamber and in his chamber leave a sign you have been there."

The voice replied that it would accept the challenge. The door to the cell, still locked and bolted, swung open easily, then fell shut again, and a shadow seemed to float down the hall while the sound of footsteps filled the quiet block of cells. Fifteen minutes later, it had returned near the window, and when asked if it had completed its task, a hollow laugh filled the cell. Later in the morning, without prompting, Deputy Warden Mayer remarked that the door to his bed chamber, which he was certain not only had been locked but also bolted, had been standing open when he arose.

In concluding his report, Dr. Kerner did not attempt to explain away what he had observed, but he re-emphasized the fact that he and other witnesses had indeed seen *something* in Mrs. Eslinger's cell, and whatever it was, he knew of no natural explanation for it.

The published report, with its admirably objective viewpoint, created a great stir throughout Germany. The report had influence not only among the general public but among scientists as well, and many learned men sought entrance to the Weinsberg prison to investigate the phenomena. In all, over 50 men of science visited Mrs. Eslinger, and nearly all of them observed some unexplainable phenomena. Although many of them tried to duplicate the manifestations, none were successful. The bars that rattled so easily at the passing of the ghost could not be shaken by the effort of many men, nor could the awesome voice be duplicated. Two German surgeons claimed that they had heard a sound as if gravel were falling to the ground while they awaited admittance, and that upon entering the cell, the sound was repeated for them by the ghost at their request.

Another time two physicists, Dr. Sicherer and Dr. Fraas, visited Mrs. Eslinger and described a thick cloud that hung near her head. They also heard a loud pounding noise and observed the phenomenon of the locked cell door swinging open, then clanging shut with great violence. These strange occurrences repeated themselves eight times during the night in which they stayed in the cell.

All during the remainder of Mrs. Eslinger's prison term, the ghost continued to haunt the cell block. On Mrs. Eslinger's release, the ghost promised to return to the cell and did so two nights later, whereupon it manifested new sounds at the request of Mrs. Mayer.

The ghost did not bother Mrs. Eslinger after her release from prison, but during the months it had been with her in the cell, it had asked her many times to journey to Wimmenthal to pray for its soul. After much deliberation, Mrs. Eslinger went to Wimmenthal, and witnesses said that when she prayed, the form of a man appeared, accompanied by two small specters. When Mrs. Eslinger ended her prayer, she fell into a faint. After she had been revived, Mrs. Eslinger said that the ghost had asked for her hand. She extended it after taking the precaution of wrapping it in her handkerchief. When the ghost had touched her hand, a flame shot from the cloth. Finger-like marks were scorched into the handkerchief, providing physical proof of the ghost's presence.

The Weinsberg Prison ghost was front-page news in Germany for six months and is certainly one of the best-documented manifestations in the annals of psychic research. It is interesting to note that the prison files on Mrs. Eslinger made mention of the fact that she claimed always to have been a "ghost-seer," although her first actual communication with a ghost did not occur until the specter of the Catholic priest began to appear to her during her internment in Weinsberg Prison.

The administration building of the former Ohio State Reformatory, photographed in 2002. The prison was closed in 1990 and reopened for tours in 1996.

It would seem that Mrs. Eslinger had long had mediumistic abilities and would, therefore, be of the proper mental makeup to serve as an energy center for a restless spirit. How and why the ghost of the priest became attracted to the imprisoned widow is beyond speculation at this point.

SPIRITS SEEK REDEMPTION AT SHAWSHANK PRISON

The old Ohio State Reformatory at Mansfield, Ohio, made famous by the motion picture based on Stephen King's novella, *Rita Hayworth and the Shawshank Redemption,* is said to be haunted by the ghosts of inmates and guards alike, all of whom seem to be seeking some kind of spiritual redemption and peace.

When the reformatory was constructed in 1886, the architect Levi T. Scofield intended his Romanesque-Gothic design to be one that would uplift, inspire, and overpower people. It was Scofield's intent to build a prison that would fulfill the ideals of the mid-nineteenth century—to teach the incarcerated individuals a skill, instill within them a fear of God, and return them to society as contributing citizens. The prison has the largest freestanding steel cellblock in the United States, with cells stacked six tiers high, 593 cells designed for 1,200 inmates. The idealistic precepts held by the architect and the wardens were realized in the early days of the reformatory's existence. Historical records indicate that more than 65 percent of the inmates did not return to its cells. But as the early ideals of reformation faded, recidivism rose, and eventually prisoners were crammed four to a cell that had been designed for two.

The state of Ohio abandoned the old reformatory in 1990. In 1995 the Mansfield Reformatory Preservation Society convinced the state to rehabilitate the sprawling, castle-like prison. In 1999 the society was permitted to purchase the reformatory and 17 acres for one dollar.

After the motion picture *The Shawshank Redemption* was released in 1994, the reformatory became popular both with

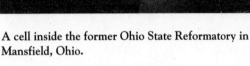

A cell inside the former Ohio State Reformatory in Mansfield, Ohio.

movie fans and with ghost hunters. Among just a few of the restless spirits reported in the Ohio State Reformatory are the following:

1. The inmate in Cell 17, who killed himself by dousing himself with lighter fluid then lighting up his own body.

2. The inmate in Cell 35, who had his head crushed when someone slammed a steel door shut on him.

3. The inmate who had his throat cut with a straight edge razor in the barbershop.

4. The wife of warden Arthur Glattke, who died under suspicious circumstances in 1950.

5. Arthur Glattke himself, whose spirit has been seen in numerous spots in the reformatory.

6. Urban Wilford, a guard who was killed during a prison break attempt in 1926.

Writing in the October 13, 2002, issue of the *Detroit Free Press*, travel writer Gerry Volgenau described the spirit manifestations of the reformatory: "Ghostly images appear. Faces emerge in the shadows.... Visitors hear voices, sometimes singing.... Most unnerving of all, people say they've been touched: a flick to the ear, a finger poke in the shoulder, a push from behind, an ankle grabbed on the stairwell. And ... they were utterly alone. Or were they?"

25

Phantoms Seen
on Seas and Lakes

THE GHOST OF THE HMS *EURYDICE*

March 24, 1878, was a clear spring day, and inhabitants along the west coast of England were basking in the good feeling of another winter gone. Suddenly a large cloud, coming from the northwest and heading southeast toward the Isle of Wight and the English Channel, appeared on the horizon. The cloud was estimated to have been 24 miles in length and a half a mile in depth. And though there was no wind that day, the cloud passed overhead with unusual speed.

The sky through which the incredible mass passed was clear and calm, but watchers below heard a steady roaring from within it, not unlike the sound of tornado winds, and they felt a numbing cold. Snow flurries could be seen occasionally within the cloud. When the cloud had passed, though, no trace of the wind or cold remained, and the springtime weather returned.

Cruising the English Channel at the time of the appearance of the strange cloud were two sailing vessels, the HMS *Eurydice*, a 921-ton naval training ship with 360 men aboard her, and, about a mile behind her, the merchant schooner *Emma*.

Five-hundred-foot-high cliffs along the coast of the Isle of Wight hid the approaching cloud mass until it was almost upon the *Eurydice*. Her captain had no time for emergency preparation. Just as the order to take in the sails was given, the tornado winds of the weird mass hit the defenseless vessel. A howling darkness descended upon the *Eurydice*, and she was lashed by heavy snow and icy spray.

[483]

For a full half hour the hapless ship wrestled beneath the mysterious energy mass, until finally the badly battered vessel ceased to struggle, capsized, and sank beneath the channel. Only two of the 360 men aboard her survived. Meanwhile, only a mile behind the *Eurydice,* the *Emma* breezed by, completely untouched by the violent sudden storm that had sunk her sister ship beneath the waves.

For more than 200 years, seamen have claimed to have seen the ghost of the HMS *Eurydice* on rainy nights at sea, and the mystery of the sudden storm that swept out of nowhere and destroyed the vessel has haunted many a sailor on night watch. Then, on October 17, 1998, the London *Mirror* reported that Prince Edward and a motion picture crew saw the ghost ship while filming the second installment of his *Crown and Country* television series on the Isle of Wight. According to Edward, he had been telling the story of the HMS *Eurydice,* the 26-gun frigate that had capsized and sank in Sandown Bay during a sudden and mysterious blizzard in 1878. The crew had been discussing how they might illustrate the incident when a three-masted schooner suddenly appeared.

Excited to be able to film a vessel similar in appearance to the HMS *Eurydice,* the cameramen began to focus on the schooner. And then it disappeared. Robin Bextor, the program's producer, told reporter Gerry Lovell that they had filmed the vessel for a while, then decided to wait so they could catch it sailing off into the horizon. "We were pleased at our stroke of luck at seeing it because it would save us time and money getting footage of a similar vessel. We took our eyes off it for a few minutes, but when we went to film it again, it had gone."

Officials of the Sail Training Association added to the mystery by saying that they knew of no vessel in the area at the time Edward and his television crew saw the ghost ship. The officials stated that they did have two three-masted training ships, but on that particular week they were both away.

Prince Edward said that he was convinced that as far as ghosts were concerned, "there are too many stories, coincidences, occurrences, and strange happenings. There is definitely something out there.... I cannot believe it is just people's imagination. There is more in it than that."

And in this particular sighting of a phantom ship, the television crew had the good fortune to have captured it on film.

VANISHING GHOST SHIPS

The ghost image of a British gunboat that was sent to harass the French forts along the eastern seaboard of Canada puts in sporadic appearances at Cape d'Espoir in Gaspe Bay. Observers of the phenomenon down through the

The ghost ship commonly referred to as "The Flying Dutchman" is one of the best-known in the world.

Real Ghosts, Restless Spirits, and Haunted Places

decades have stated that ghostly crewmen line its decks, and at the wheel stands a man with a woman at his side. As the vessel approaches the shore, its lights gradually go out, and it appears to sink at exactly the same spot where the British gunboat sank 200 years ago.

In 1647 a ship was seen to vanish in full view of a crowd of people who had been awaiting its arrival at New Haven, Connecticut. Five months earlier, the ship had put out from New Haven and had been feared lost. When her sails and rigging were spotted coming into the harbor, the word quickly spread, and a crowd of eager friends and relatives gathered to welcome the ship home. Then, before their startled eyes, the vessel became transparent and began to slowly fade from view. Within a few moments, the astonished crowd was left staring at the empty harbor.

THE LEGEND OF THE *PALATINE*

Dozens of reputable witnesses claimed to have heard the terrible screams that issued forth from the ghost ship *Palatine* just five miles off the coast of Rhode Island. John Greenleaf Whittier committed the legend to poetry, and the story of the ghostly ship has found its way into several formal histories of New England. Although the ghostly recreation of the disaster was last officially reported in the 1820s, there are several old-timers in the Block Island area who can relate the details of the phantom ship.

The story of the tragic ship *Palatine* and her final voyage goes back to November 1752. With a full passenger list of immigrants, all bound for the prospering districts around Philadelphia, the vessel set sail from a Dutch port. The immigrants carried everything they possessed with them, for none planned to return to the Old World.

The voyage was uneventful until the *Palatine* reached the vicinity of the Gulf Stream, at which point it seemed as if all the fury of the North Atlantic was hurled upon them. Storm after storm smashed the ill-fated ship, driving her far off course into uncharted seas.

The captain had become ill shortly after the *Palatine* had set out, and the turbulence of the storm soon drove him to his bed. With their captain in quarters, the ship's crew began to slack off. For weeks the little vessel was mauled by the vicious sea while the crew did little to get her on course. Without their captain to drive them, the seamen stayed below and let the sea rule the *Palatine*.

When the captain died, all hope was lost for the ship's passengers. Ambitious young officers, backed by the crew, seized control of the provisions. To those passengers who could pay their exorbitant prices, the greedy officers doled out meager rations of food and water. Those without money starved to death and were cast overboard.

The supplies gave out around Christmas time. The crew took to the lifeboats and abandoned the *Palatine* and its surviving passengers to the whims of the sea. The vessel drifted for several more days, until it finally ran aground on the sandy shoals of Block Island. Most of the surviving passengers left on board had suffered mental breakdowns.

Residents of Block Island removed the survivors to the safety of village homes. One woman had become so crazed by her suffering and by the death of her loved ones that she refused to leave the ship. She maintained that she had to stay aboard to await the return of her family so they could all disembark together.

The islanders decided to allow the woman to remain on board and selected a committee that would be responsible for providing her with food and water. The *Palatine* was towed into a cove, and the villagers planned to salvage any usable cargo and to dismantle the ship at their convenience. Perhaps by that time, they reasoned, the poor woman might have regained her senses.

One day while the islanders were working on the *Palatine*, the ship was blown adrift by a sudden storm. In his haste to leave the ship, one of the workmen accidentally tipped a brazier of coals. Flames began leaping upward from the dry timbers, and the work crew scrambled for their boats. As they rowed toward the shore, the islanders looked back at the *Palatine*, its deck enveloped in flames. Then the men heard the agonizing screams lifting from the flaming vessel. The "daft woman" had been left behind.

The workmen were filled with shock and pity. They knew the flames were too intense to risk going back to the *Palatine*. There was nothing they could do for the trapped victim except to offer a prayer for her soul. They watched, horrified, as the rising wind slowly pushed the blazing vessel out to sea.

In flames, the *Palatine* sailed into legend. There are some people in the area who claim that the ship returns every year on the anniversary of her destruction. Others contend that the *Palatine* came back only as long as any member of her original crew remained alive. Historians found dozens of witnesses who claimed to have seen the image of the burning ship and to have heard the terrible screams of the dying woman.

Dr. Aaron Willey reported having viewed the lights of the *Palatine* on several occasions. His story exactly paralleled other reports: a blazing fire the size of a ship appears near shore, then slowly recedes until it is only a tiny light on the horizon.

PHANTOMS OF THE *QUEEN MARY*

During the years that the 1,019-foot luxury liner the *Queen Mary* was in service (1936–1967), there were 41 passengers and at least 16 crew members who died on the high seas of various illnesses and accidents. In addition to the deaths that occurred directly in her cabins or on her decks, the *Queen Mary* was responsible for the deaths of 300 seamen during World War II. This latter tragedy occurred when the liner was painted gray and was pressed into military service as a transport to carry American troops to and from Europe. Nicknamed the "Gray Ghost," the ship's great speed helped it to elude Nazi U-boats, but it was also that speed and power that accidentally sliced her escort ship HMS *Curacao* in two and drowned most of its crew.

Since the *Queen Mary* was permanently docked in Long Beach in 1967, hundreds of visitors have claimed to have seen materialized ghosts, moving objects, and eerie lights floating through its hallways. Disembodied voices are frequently reported, and many individuals say that they have heard screams and the harsh sound of ripping metal in the bow area, terrible echoes of the night the Gray Ghost tore the *Curacao* in half.

While there have been reported sightings of ghostly officers, crew members, and soldiers, perhaps the most often seen apparition is that of an 18-year-old crewman who was crushed to death deep among the pipes and girders of the engine room by hydraulic door no. 13 during one of the luxury liner's final voyages. Many witnesses claim to have seen a young man in coveralls on the catwalks of the engine room who vanishes before their eyes. Others have met him in narrow walkways and have even stepped aside to let him pass, only to see the young man disappear after a few steps.

THE USS *HORNET*: THE SHIP OF SOULS

The USS *Hornet* has a distinguished record of service for her country. The massive aircraft carrier has a flight deck that is 894 feet long. It weighs 41,000 tons and is outfitted with a full hospital, three barbershops, a tailor shop, a cobbler shop, and seven galleys. During World War II as many as 3,500 sailors served aboard her at one time, and the aircraft carrier won nine battle stars during naval action. Because of the many battles that she endured during her years of service (1943–1970), there may have been as many as 300 military personnel who died during combat or shipboard accidents.

In 1969 the *Hornet* retrieved the Apollo 11 astronauts from the sea after their return from the Moon. In 1995 she was docked at Alameda Point, outside of Oakland, California, named a National Historic Landmark, and opened to the public as a museum.

Among the ghosts most commonly sighted on the *Hornet* is that of a khaki-clad officer who is often seen descending the ladder to the lower deck. Some witnesses claim to have followed him, fully believing him to be a member of the museum staff or a visiting naval officer, only to have him disappear before their astonished eyes. Understandably, most of the ghosts that have been seen are male because of the World War II term of service of the aircraft carrier. Some witnesses have sworn that they have recognized the ghost of Admiral Joseph James ("Jocko") Clark, who commanded the ship during the years of heavy fighting during World War II.

Well-known psychical researcher Lloyd Auerbach has conducted a number of investigations on the *Hornet* with the psychic Stache Margaret Murray, and researchers David Richardson, Fred Speer, and Dinny Anderson. Of the many decks, compartments, nooks, and crannies on the huge aircraft carrier (Auerbach says it's like investigating a small city), the team of researchers located 27 different areas that they assessed as "hot" and a number of others that were "lukewarm" on the ghost scale. Because of the great range of spirit activity on the *Hornet,* Auerbach has christened it the "Ship of Souls."

Psychical researcher Loyd Auerbach.

The researchers deemed two locations as psychically interesting: the medical bay and hangar bay no. 3 in the stern of the ship. One can imagine, Auerbach suggests, the emotions that would be absorbed in a place where medical personnel treated those individuals suffering from war-time wounds. The feelings felt by the psychically sensitive could be "downright oppressive." Interestingly, Auerbach writes in the October 2000 issue of *Fate* magazine that the two psychics on their team "picked up ... a feeling that there were spots we needed to stay away from, at least until we were fully accepted by the ghosts."

In the area of the hangar bay, Auerbach felt as though he was walking through a heavy curtain of thicker air, and he immediately felt nauseated. When he backed out of the area, he felt fine. The psychics and other members of the team sensed negative energy in the "nausea zone."

"Just outside, in hangar bay no. 3, is an area where several apparitions have been seen," Auerbach says, "and an area where I felt 'something' very strong on one of my first visits. Also, at the end of the hangar bay is the fantail section.... It too is a spot where people have reported activity."

Real Ghosts, Restless Spirits, and Haunted Places

ADRIFT AT SEA BUT KEPT ALIVE BY A LOVING, LOYAL GHOST

In the summer of 1991, three fishermen—Tabwai Mikaie, Nweiti Tekaman-gu, and Arenta Tebeitabu—set out on a fishing trip from their South Pacific island of Kiribati, in the Republic of Kiribati. Not far from land, off a coral atoll called Nikunau, they were suddenly pummeled by a powerful, unexpected cyclone that capsized their 12-foot boat and tossed them into the sea. Although the men lost their outboard motor, they managed to climb safely back into the boat. However, since they were no longer able to power the tiny vessel, they began to drift farther and farther out into deeper waters, thus commencing a voyage that at times must have seemed endless.

Incredibly, the three men remained adrift for 175 days and nearly a thousand miles. By using a spear and a fishing line, they were able to survive on fish. From time to time they achieved some variety in their diet when they were able to snare a coconut floating by. To supplement their meager water supply, they collected rainwater. On numerous occasions, razor-jawed sharks circled their boat, but the fishermen turned the tables on the monsters and caught and ate no fewer than 10 of the voracious predators during their six months adrift. Tabwai Mikaie, 24, said that they prayed to God four times a day, asking for his tender mercies to save them.

Tragically, after a seeming eternity of helpless drifting, Nweiti Teka-mangu, 47, died when they were at last in sight of land. Although his friends wept and pleaded with him to hold on for just a few days longer, Tekamangu's heart simply gave out after such a strenuous ordeal, and his sorrowful companions had no choice other than to cast his body overboard.

The survivors, Mikaie and Tebeitabu, were now terrified by the thought of the formidable ordeal that lay before them. Since they were now only a few days from the mountainous island of Upolu in Western Samoa, they would soon have to maneuver their little 12-foot boat through some of the most treacherous reefs in the South Pacific. In their weakened condition, the task seemed impossible.

Tekamangu, the oldest of the tiny crew, had also been the most experienced and by far the most accomplished navigator. If he were still alive, he would have been able to guide them to a safe harbor. Mikaie and Tebeitabu began to resign themselves to what appeared to be their certain destiny: They, too, would perish before they reached land.

Just as it seemed certain that the boat would be shattered into a thousand pieces of driftwood, the two men were astonished to see the spirit of their dead friend rise from the depths of the turbulent sea. The ghost of Tekamangu told them to listen to him and they would be safe. Although there were sharp and treacherous reefs on each side of their weather-beaten and sea-battered

In 1924, while the oil tanker SS *Watertown* traveled down the West Coast of the United States on its way to the Panama Canal, two men died in an accident on board and were buried at sea. For several days following their burial, two faces were seen following the ship.

boat, Mikaie and Tebeitabu placed their complete confidence in the commands of their ghostly comrade, who masterfully guided them through the murderous offshore rocks to the safety of the beach on Upolu. Soon the two half-dead fishermen were being lifted from their little boat and taken to a hospital.

Later, while authorities and journalists decreed the feat of their having survived six months adrift at sea as a miracle, Tebeitabu and Mikaie testified that it was only the supernatural presence of their friend that had enabled them to live. In their statements to the authorities, they declared that if Tekamangu's love and loyalty had not sent his spirit back to help them, they would surely have been dashed to splinters on the reefs of Upolu.

LEGEND OF YAQUINA BAY LIGHTHOUSE

The Yaquina Bay Lighthouse in Newport, Oregon, was built in 1871 and used for only three years until the Yaquina Head Lighthouse was constructed. According to legend, one dark and stormy night a hundred years ago, a group of teenagers crept into the abandoned lighthouse to explore its empty hallways, but one of them never came out. All that was left of the young lady was her bloody handkerchief at the bottom of the third-floor staircase. Ever since that girl met her mysterious fate in the lighthouse, people have seen an eerie light in the upstairs window and heard cries and moans issuing from the darkened interior.

In November 1998 Cathy Kessinger, writing in *MidValley Sunday*, quoted Walt Muse, who oversees the lighthouse for the state parks department, as stating that there wasn't a "shred of evidence to support the spooky tale of the young woman who disappeared, leaving only a bloody handkerchief and a few drops of blood behind." Muse said that he had heard all the stories about people seeing lights on in the lighthouse and hearing and seeing strange things to support the legend. He himself was surprised one night to see a single light in the third-floor window. After a careful examination, he concluded that the source of illumination must have been light escaping from the beacon above.

Muse said that he is continually surprised by tourists who want to visit the haunted lighthouse. He often hears people saying that they "feel something" within its walls. Some people have sent Muse pictures they took while touring the lighthouse that purport to show something passing in front of the camera, like an apparition.

Perhaps the expectations of hundreds of people over the years have created a spirit and a mysterious light at the Yaquina Bay Lighthouse, and these same expectations have kept the "ghost" alive for more than 100 years by feeding it with their collective psychic energy.

"WILLIE" HAUNTS BIG BAY POINT LIGHTHOUSE

As far as Norman and Marilyn Gotschall were concerned, one need not bother with theories of collective psychic energy and expectations when it came to "Willie," the ghost that haunted the 18 rooms of the historic lighthouse at Big Bay Point, Michigan. When they moved into the place in December 1986, Norman said that he did not believe in ghosts. After a few nights in the lighthouse, he changed his mind.

On the very first evening of the Gotschalls' arrival, the wind suddenly began to howl and shutters started banging. From the sounds of things, there was a terrible storm brewing on Lake Superior. But when Norman and Marilyn looked outside, it soon became apparent that the only storm was inside the lighthouse. Later, they figured that weird phenomena was just Willie's way of welcoming them.

"Willie" was William Pryor, a former military man who manned the lighthouse in 1896. A perfectionist who took his position very seriously, Pryor was thrown completely off balance when, after a few years on the job, his 20-year-old son committed suicide. A week later, in his grief and shame, Pryor hanged himself.

Marilyn Gotschall said that on one occasion shortly after they took up residence in the lighthouse, she heard someone calling her name from one of the upstairs rooms. Believing it to be Norman, she walked upstairs to find the area completely empty. "Willie" called her name two more times, then, seemingly satisfied with her friendly nature, he was quiet.

In 1990, when the Gotschalls were in the process of converting the lighthouse into a motel, one of their early guests claimed to have seen a man in a military uniform with bright gold buttons standing at the foot of her bed. The man told the guest that he was upset by all the commotion at the lighthouse and said that he wouldn't be content until all the restoration work was completed. Then he vanished, leaving the guest more confused than frightened.

The Gotschalls explained to their guest that Willie was their resident ghost and that he was a bit particular about the condition in which they managed the lighthouse.

THE GIRL GHOST OF WHITE ROCK LAKE

Texans who live near White Rock Lake in Dallas have reported the nocturnal visits of a girl ghost in a dripping wet evening gown who appears on the lakeshore. Young couples, who have parked beside the lake to take full advantage of the bright moon reflecting on the placid waters, have told some hair-raising tales about the phantom. One young man said that he would

White Rock Lake in Dallas, Texas.

never forget the sight of the shimmering ghost looking in the car window at him and his frightened date.

Frank X. Tolbert, a columnist for the *Dallas Morning News*, dealt with the legend of the alleged girl ghost and received hundreds of letters and phone

Real Ghosts, Restless Spirits, and Haunted Places

calls in response to his article. Apparently the apparition had been seen and firmly attested to by a good number of people.

Mr. Dale Berry told Tolbert that he and his family had purchased a home near White Rock Lake in September 1962. On their first night in their new home, Berry hurried to the door to answer the ringing of the bell. There was no one there. The bell rang a second time. In spite of Berry's rapid dash to the door, whoever had rung the bell had vanished by the time he opened the door.

The third time the bell rang, Berry's daughter answered the door. Soon the entire family was clustered around the front door in response to the girl's screams. There, on the porch, were large puddles of water, as if someone dripping wet had stood there. There were large droplets of water on the steps and the walk leading up to the front door, yet the sprinkler system had not been turned on, the rest of the yard was dry, and the night was clear and cloudless. Moreover, the neighbors were not the sort to indulge in practical jokes.

It appeared that the girl ghost of White Rock Lake had been trying to pay the newcomers a visit to welcome them.

DID THEY DISCOVER A LAKE RESORT FOR GHOSTS?

The Personal Experience of Roy

"We drove into the bush one day and paddled up a river for 45 minutes or so to a small lake, totally inaccessible, except by a canoe. There are no roads or trails to it, and the canoe route was only accessible by small boat because of the shallowness of the river and many beaver dams.

"It was my first visit to the lake. My cousin had urged me to go with him as he had been shown the lake by his father but had never fished it, although it was rumored (correctly) to have very large northern pike. When we finally arrived at the lake, my cousin was totally surprised that a very large and beautiful log home, complete with large dock, had been built on the north shoreline. The building was not a small log cabin but a large and well-crafted log home. And as the lake is only a pothole of a lake and only a few hundred feet across at its largest point, the building stood out clearly and magnificently in the natural setting.

"My cousin marveled at how someone had somehow built such a large structure in such a short time, and we wondered how all the building materials could have been brought in. I suggested that the lake couldn't have much fish if there was a large building on it with people coming and going. It was early in the evening when we arrived there, and there seemed to be a strange kind of static in the air. We soon left, convinced that the lake couldn't hold big fish if people were visiting regularly and living on it.

"Eventually, we decided to give the lake another chance, and packed up our gear and returned. Incredibly, on the *exact* spot where we had seen the building, there was nothing except unspoiled nature. There were not the slightest indications that anything had ever been there except for a beaten down lean-to a few feet in size that had obviously been there for years and years and [that was] probably the remnant of a trapper's shack! There were no trees cut down, no old stumps, no rubble or garbage. In fact, there were old trees on the spot! The lake was exactly as it had been when my cousin had gone there originally ... without any sign of human habitation or activity! We have wondered about this for about 30 years now. My cousin muses that maybe one day we will go there and such a building will have materialized and that somehow we were looking at the future."

A Most Unusual Fishing Companion

On April 26, 2000, during the *Jeff Rense Program*, a woman named Jenny called in to tell Jeff and me that she had had a most perplexing experience occur to her some years before when she lived in Arizona c. 1986. But what began as a colorful anecdote told by an articulate and charming woman suddenly took a sharp detour into a rather chilling ghost story.

Because her husband was out of town a great deal of the time on business, Jenny was attempting to be both mother and father to their young son. Although she had never really been fishing before, she bought rods and reels and all the other necessary equipment and took her son to a lake outside of Tucson, because that was the kind of thing that a father and son would do.

No one else was near their spot on shore that afternoon, and Jenny was having difficulty putting the worms on the hook for her son and casting the line far enough from shore to attract the fish. As she grew increasingly frustrated with the whole idea of fishing in order to please her son, a man in his mid-twenties came up behind her and offered to help her bait the hook. He told her that she had to make a knot in the worm so it would not come off the hook, and he demonstrated the art of baiting the hook and casting the line.

The man stayed with them through the entire afternoon, and the three of them had a great deal of fun fishing together, and they even managed to catch some fish. At the end of the day, Jenny invited him to come back with them to the picnic area where she planned to have a barbeque. He accepted the invitation, and they all ate heartily of the burgers and other food that she prepared. It was the perfect ending to a wonderful day, and Jenny took a picture of the man and her son as they posed for the camera.

The next day, Jenny took the film to a one-hour photo shop to be developed, and when she saw the man's beautiful smile, she was touched with the manner in which he had unselfishly shared his day with them. He had no doubt come there to do some serious fishing, and he had diverted his own precious free time away from the office to help make the afternoon more meaningful for Jenny's son. She decided that she would send him a copy of the photograph as a thank-you for the fishing lessons.

Several times during the previous afternoon he had told them his full name and the place where he worked, so Jenny got the telephone number from information and called the store. When she asked for him, the receptionist connected her to a man who rather brusquely asked why she wished to speak with him and what her business was. Rather impatiently, Jenny explained the circumstances and her wish to send a photograph in an effort to repay the man for his kindness.

The man on the telephone asked her to describe their fishing companion. When Jenny did, the man gasped and said that she had described perfectly his younger brother who had drowned at that lake five years before.

Stunned, Jenny at first thought the man was playing a cruel joke on her, but she verified his account by checking newspaper records at the public library. Thinking the man would want to see her proof of his brother's spirit on the photograph, she sent him a copy. But the letter was returned to her, unopened. She put the picture away in a drawer, but it appeared again on the top of her desk. She grew increasingly uncomfortable with the picture in her possession. No matter what she did with it, it would return to a place where she could not ignore it. She even tried ripping it up and burning it, but it kept materializing and returning to her.

At last Jenny drove out to the lake where she had met the man and spoke into the lake, as if she were addressing him face-to-face. In a solemn manner, she said that she felt that it was time that he went into the Light, that it was not right for him to remain around the lakeshore any longer. She would pray for his soul to be at peace.

Jenny drove back home and went to bed. At three o'clock in the morning, the telephone rang at her bedside. With her husband traveling away from home, she feared an emergency call. When she picked up the receiver, she heard a great deal of static, as if the call were coming from a great distance away, then a male voice said, "Thank you," and hung up.

Jenny told Jeff Rense and me that the next day, she could not find the photograph of the man. It was gone at last, and it has never reappeared.

26
Ghosts on Trains, Planes, and Automobiles

GHOST TRAINS THAT COME AND GO

The Phantom Train of Pittsfield, Massachusetts

Several Pittsfield, Massachusetts, residents are convinced of the existence of a phantom train and swear that they have seen the specter on a stretch of track between the North Street bridge and the junction, and passing the Union Depot. One of the most impressive sightings occurred one afternoon in February 1958, when John Quirk and several of his customers in the Bridge Lunch saw the phantom train of Pittsfield go by.

Regardless of what anyone else would try to tell them, Quirk told reporters, the phantom train consisted of a baggage car and five or six coaches. Quirk and his customers could describe that locomotive down to the last bolt. It was so clear and plain that they were even able to see the coal in the tender.

Railroad officials replied that they had operated no steam engine on that line for years. There has definitely not been a train that has passed Union Depot or the junction at the times when certain witnesses claim to have seen a locomotive in the area.

At 6:30 A.M. one frosty March morning, Bridge Lunch employees and customers caught another glimpse of the ghost train. The place was full of customers and every one of them saw the ghost train, according to waiter Steve Strauss. "Just like every time before, the steam engine pulled a baggage car, five or six coaches, and was high barreling east toward Boston."

[499]

A Phantom Train in Texas

Thomas Phillips of Pasadena, Texas, told of the time when, on a business trip in the 1960s, he stopped for a train between Belleville and Sealy, Texas. He first saw the train coming off to his right, about 300 feet ahead. Strangely enough, the train, pulled by an old style locomotive, had seemed to move out of a cloud of fog.

As he drummed his fingers impatiently on the steering wheel waiting for the train to pass, Phillips suddenly realized that there were no crossing lights, signs, or signals. As the freight cars passed slowly in front of him, he also noticed that the train seemed to be lighted by a source entirely apart from the lights of his car. When the last boxcar passed before him, Phillips saw to his surprise that there was no sign of a railroad bed, not even a break in the pavement where one ever had been.

A Ghostly Engineer Looks for His Head on the Tracks

For more than 80 years, the people in the town of St. Louis, Saskatchewan, have been seeing the light from a phantom train and the subsequent light from a lantern, as the ghost of a Canadian National Railway engineer seeks his lost head. According to the story, a CNR engineer was checking the tracks near St. Louis when he was struck by a train and decapitated.

Mayor Emile Lussier told CBC News on November 1, 2001, that he was present when a scientist came to the site to investigate the mysterious appearance of the ghost light. According to Lussier, the scientist left baffled by the maneuvers of the engineer's lantern. The light would appear behind them, but when they turned around, the ghostly illumination appeared right at their heels.

Haunted Railway Sites in Newfoundland and Labrador

Dale Jarvis, a columnist for the St. John's, Newfoundland, *Telegram*, often features paranormal subjects. In his column for December 4, 2002, he discussed a number of railway ghost stories across Newfoundland and Labrador. Among the haunted trains or railway sites he listed were the following:

1. A ghostly conductor who manifests on the Port Union and Bonavista branch line.

2. The spirit of a young girl who haunts the railway trestle in Clarke's Beach.

3. The phantom train that materializes on the company rail line built by the American Smelting and Refining Company.

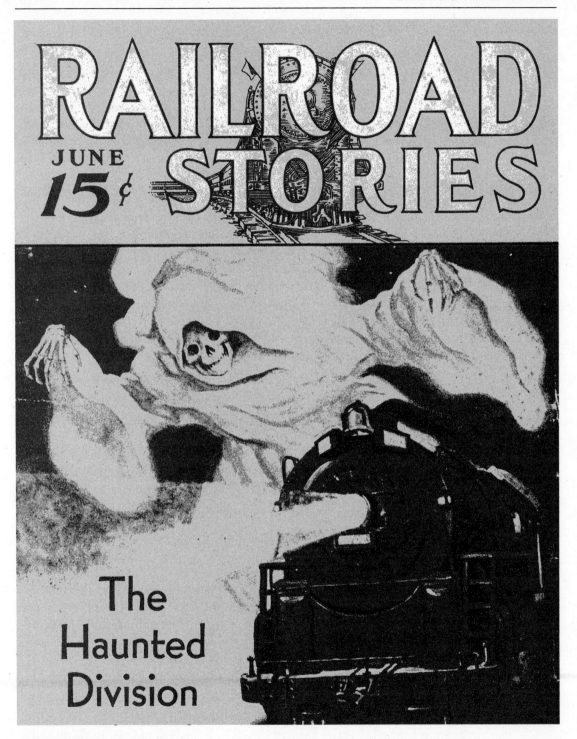

Cover of *Railroad Stories*, June 1933.

Real Ghosts, Restless Spirits, and Haunted Places

Strange Disturbances at the Tamaqua, Pennsylvania, Train Station

They say that light bulbs won't stay lit in the 1874 Tamaqua, Pennsylvania, train station. Many people attribute this phenomena—and several others, including sudden icy drafts and the sighting of ghosts—to the spirits of five members of the Molly Maguires, a group accused of taking violent action on behalf of mine workers' rights. On June 21, 1877, known as "Black Thursday" and the "Day of the Rope," 10 alleged members of the Molly Maguires were hanged. Five of those bodies were kept packed in ice overnight inside the Tamaqua train station, then only three years old.

THE PILOT CAME BACK TO CLEAR HIS REPUTATION

In May 1913 a small group of pilots and mechanics near a workshop hanger at Britain's Montrose Air Training Station were inspecting a newly arrived airplane on the grounds. The man most interested in the craft was the pilot who would fly it for the first time, Lt. Desmond Arthur, a black-haired young Irishman who was enthusiastic about what he considered the advanced lines of the airplane. The senior mechanic agreed that the craft was nice to look at, but he was skeptical about its ability to bear any extra strain.

"We'll find out now," Arthur said confidently, stepping into the cockpit. A mechanic spun the prop, then jumped away as the motor caught. Without hesitation, the young pilot taxied the plane into the wind, then picked up speed. The plane lifted from the ground.

The spectators watched carefully as the accomplished pilot took the plane to nearly 4,000 feet before he leveled off and began to test the new model's maneuverability with a series of stunts.

In the middle of a twisting roll, the plane heeled over on its back, then shed a wing. The machine and the pilot dropped to the ground like a falling stone. By the time the men of the Montrose Station arrived at the scene of the crash, Desmond Arthur was dead.

The tragedy did not receive official comment until 1916, when authorities blamed the accident on misjudgment by the pilot. The official report based its findings on the immediate investigation by military authorities after the accident and their evaluation of the testimonies of witnesses to the crash. There were those, including the senior mechanic, who protested that the crash was due to faulty construction of the aircraft, but the investigators' assessment discounted such testimony.

A few weeks after the report was published, a mechanic at Montrose Station learned that the Desmond Arthur tragedy could not be dismissed so easily. While working on the inside bracing of an airplane, he noticed an officer in flight clothes approaching the craft. The mechanic continued work until the officer came very close and stood directly over him.

Becoming a bit uneasy at the man's silence, the mechanic finally asked, without looking up, if the officer wished to fly the craft. When the officer did not reply, the mechanic slid out from under the brace, and looked up at the silent man.

The officer's face was contorted with rage; his lips moved furiously and he gestured as if he were shouting, but he made no sound. The mechanic fell away from the strange flier; the wrench he had been holding clattered to the floor. Before the mechanic could turn and flee, the officer disappeared. Terrified, the mechanic ran until he came to Flight Sergeant Wilkens.

"I've seen him," the man gasped, out of breath. "The ghost of Desmond Arthur! The officers were right. He's come back."

The Montrose ghost first appeared in August 1916, to Second Lieutenant Ralph Peterson. Peterson had entered his room and found a fellow airman leaning against the wall. Surprised by the officer's presence, Peterson had just begun to question the man when the visitor melted into the wall. When Peterson reported the incident, Colonel James Rutherford dismissed it as imagination and warned the junior officer of the hazards of alcohol.

A few days later, two officers, whose testimony the station commander could not question, saw the same strange flier. Major Jenkins and Captain Edward Milner, two senior officers who shared a room, had just retired. The bed lamp had not been off more than a few minutes when the sound of footsteps caused both officers to sit up in their beds. Before either of them could move, their door swung open and a young man in flying kit entered. He gestured wildly and seemed to be shouting at the two officers, neither of whom could testify that any sound issued from the angry visitor.

When one of the officers switched on the light, the figure faded before the astonished eyes of the two officers. They quickly had the building secured and ordered all exits guarded. Guards reported that no person had attempted to leave the building. After the officers had conducted a bed check, they were convinced that their visitor had not been a living man.

The next officer to see the restless ghost recognized its form. Lieutenant Edwards, the station adjutant and an officer in the regular army, swore that he had seen Desmond Arthur come into his room. Edwards had known Arthur well, and he, too, described a man who seemed to be shouting at the top of his lungs, yet made no sound.

The Montrose ghost added a bizarre note to the aviation news, but in 1916, aviators did not receive much good press. The high cost of World War I was bearing hard on the British, and it had become fashionable to take pot shots at the fledgling air corps and its personnel. It was in this spirit that the report on the Desmond Arthur crash had been compiled, and even though a few devoted airmen had fought to remove the blight from Arthur's otherwise clean record, their efforts had been overpowered by a rising tide of criticism against the corps. In addition to the great cost of the war, British air losses reached their peak in 1916, and Parliament appointed a committee to investigate the matter. The air corps cringed under the double obligation to reduce costs and increase efficiency at the same time.

But the ghost of Desmond Arthur seemed determined to bring about a change in the record the report had left of him. The story gained momentum, and soon the tale of the ghost of the airbase spread to the Continent and even to the enemy. In one instance, a German soldier, shot down behind Allied lines, asked almost immediately for news of the Montrose ghost.

Meanwhile, the parliamentary committee had found that to increase Britain's aviation efficiency would entail increased, not lowered, costs. Machines arriving at French bases were ill-equipped, seldom outfitted with essential parts, and the personnel arriving in the war zone often came prepared with only a few days' training.

It was at this point that C. G. Gray, the editor of the British aviation magazine the *Aeroplane*, took up the reinvestigation of the Desmond Arthur case. "With training and machines in such bad shape now," Gray wrote, "imagine what [conditions] would have been in 1913."

With the aid of a friend, Commander Perrin, one of Britain's earliest fliers, Gray prodded the authorities into a reinvestigation. In a few weeks, the Royal Air Club's Safety and Accident Investigation Committee announced that Desmond Arthur had not, after all, been guilty of an error in judgment. With the help of influential men in Parliament, these findings were finally incorporated into the parliamentary record on November 12, 1916.

About two months later, the Montrose ghost appeared for the last time. The phantom materialized first to Lieutenant Edwards, then to Major Jenkins and Captain Edward Milner. All three claim that the ghost smiled broadly at them. The Montrose ghost had vindicated his memory, and he has not been seen since that day in January 1917.

THE LEGEND OF BRICK BARTON

Here is one of my favorite ghost stories from World War II. It may be a legend from the war, but as a child of those years of conflict who had a cousin flying P-51s out of England, and two uncles in B-24s—one out of England, the other out of Italy—it has always spoken to me of the heroism and sacrifice of the aviators of that period in our nation's history.

Captain Brick Barton of Auburn, New York, was a pilot of a B-24 bomber out of an English base during World War II. One day Barton and his crew had just completed their mission over Frankfurt, Germany. The copilot confirmed that all targets had been approached and all bombs dropped. Now they could go home.

Barton nodded. They had completed their mission successfully. It would be good to get back to the base. As Barton was in the process of turning the bomber back toward England, a German fighter made a strafing pass at the B-24. The pilot's compartment was riddled, and several bullets struck Barton.

The copilot, seeing that his captain had been hit, took immediate control of the plane. He heard the harsh chatter of the bomber's machine gunners, and he knew that he would not have to worry about the German fighter any longer. But how, he asked himself, was he going to get this giant airplane back to England all by himself.

"Don't worry, kid," Barton told him, managing a weak grin. "You just take control, and I'll give you instructions on how to get us home. I'll be with you all the way."

As the B-24 neared the base in England, the copilot radioed the tower and told them to prepare an ambulance for Barton. When the relieved young officer stepped out of the plane, the flight surgeon complimented him on a safe landing.

"Thank you, sir," said the copilot, "but I couldn't have done it without the help and advice of Captain Barton. He kept talking to me and giving me pointers from the moment he was hit over Frankfurt. You had better see to him right away."

The flight surgeon hurried into the pilot's compartment. A few minutes later, visibly shaken, he left the bomber and approached the copilot.

"You say Captain Barton spoke to you, that he helped you land the airplane?"

"That's correct," the copilot acknowledged, frowning his bewilderment at the surgeon's strange barrage of questions.

"Well, that's impossible," the surgeon said. "Captain Barton died instantly, and he's been dead for almost an hour."

REPORTS OF A CAR ACCIDENT THAT WASN'T REVEALED A FATAL CRASH THAT WAS

It is doubtful that the dispatcher at the police station who took the call from motorists reporting a crash off the A3 in Surrey at 7:20 P.M. on Wednesday,

This photograph was taken at the Henry Ford estate. Although no one was sitting in this classic car when the photograph was taken, the image of a man is clearly visible in the driver's seat.

December 11, 2002, realized that he was actually taking down a report of a chilling ghost story. The witnesses all told the same story: a car had swerved off the road at Burpham, near Guildford, its headlights blazing, and crashed in

Real Ghosts, Restless Spirits, and Haunted Places

the undergrowth off A3. When officers investigated, they found no sign of the alleged accident. It was apparent because of the thick undergrowth off A3 that no vehicle had crashed through it.

But witnesses persisted that they had seen a car that had veered off the A3, headlights brightly burning, crashing into the undergrowth. Police officers returned in the daylight and began foraging in the thick and twisted undergrowth. They were amazed to discover a wrecked Vauxhall Astra automobile, nose-down in a ditch, invisible from the road. However, it could not have crashed with headlights blazing on the night before. The car had been hidden there for a good while. So long, in fact, that it contained a decomposed body. Puzzled, the officers kept searching, but they could find no signs of a recent crash, only one that had obviously taken place some months ago.

On December 13, 2002, the authorities revealed that the corpse was that of Christopher Chandler, who was being hunted for an alleged robbery. He was reported missing by his brother on July 16. Surrey

A close-up of the ghost in the classic car.

police stated that it was obvious from the physical evidence that the accident that had claimed Chandler's life had occurred in July, not December, and that the body and the Vauxhall Astra had remained undiscovered for five months, just yards from the dual carriageway that was used daily by thousands of motorists.

The question that will never be answered to everyone's satisfaction is whether the motorists who witnessed the crash in December saw a ghostly replay of the accident that had actually taken place unnoticed in July.

GHOST AUTOMOBILES ON THE HIGHWAY

Mary Passed a Car That Disappeared

Mary of Portland, Oregon, writes to say that she was driving east out of Bend on the Bend–Burns Highway early one morning. "The road is raised up somewhat banked from the desert, and it is a long, easy slope down from Horse Ridge. I wasn't going very fast, just enjoying the drive, when I came upon a black sedan moving slowly. I hit my passing gear and zoomed past. As I passed, I looked in to see if there was anyone I knew in the sedan. There was just an older man and woman who looked back at me."

But when Mary glanced in her rearview mirror, just as soon as she had passed the black sedan, there was no car behind her. "The highway behind me was empty."

Mary had a frightening thought that the older couple had somehow gone over the bank, which, at that point, was several feet high. "I came to a quick stop at the edge of the road and got out. I went to the back of my car and looked and looked, but I couldn't see the black sedan anywhere. There were no access roads around or any other cars around. Besides, the car was only out of my sight for a couple of seconds."

As Mary stood there looking around for some sign of the mysterious black sedan with the older couple inside, "a light breeze sprang up and blew across me, and I can tell you that the hairs on the back of my neck and my arms stood up. I jumped in my little car, locked all four doors, and got out of there. I was both frightened and puzzled. I guess I still am. I still get that creepy hair-rising-on-back-of-neck-and-arms feeling whenever I recall the car that disappeared and the breeze that sprang up out of nowhere."

Max Encountered the Ghost of a 1941 Chevrolet

Early on a Sunday evening in 1991, Max was driving with his family outside of Albany, New York, when he became impatient with the way an old car, which he guessed to be a 1941 Chevrolet sedan, was slowing traffic. Max figured that the car was going to or coming from some antique auto show or rally and he wanted to be tolerant, but they were returning from a family outing at Lake George and he wanted to get home to do some paperwork.

"I had to be at work early the next morning with my presentation ready to go, and I had some factors that I needed to sharpen," Max said. "As I approached nearer to the Chevy, I was surprised that it didn't have those special license plates that owners of those old cars are supposed to display. I hated to be a jerk, but I really leaned on my horn, something I usually don't do when following a slow-moving vehicle."

Max recalled that he could see the driver of the Chevy turn around and look at him with what appeared to be shock. "I expected an angry, hostile look, and maybe an obscene gesture or two, but this guy looked as if I had genuinely startled him. As if he had somehow imagined himself to be driving all alone on the highway."

Then, before the startled, incredulous eyes of Max, his wife, and their three children, the old Chevrolet sedan in front of them began to fade away. "It was as if it were some old photograph dissolving bit by bit before us, just fading away until there was nothing left to prove that it had ever been there. The antique Chevy and its driver had completely disappeared in about 30 seconds."

A Wagonload of Hay from Another Dimension

Inez M. of Ely, Minnesota, reported her experience during the winter of 1924, when she and four others found themselves stalled in the snow near an old country school house near Embarrass, Minnesota. As they were shoveling their way free, they looked up to see a wagonload of hay pulled by a team of horses fast approaching them on the narrow road. Two men sat on top of the hay, seemingly unconcerned with the plight of those in the stalled automobile.

As the wagonload of hay came abreast, Inez said, she jumped aside on her side of the road. Her friend Martha jumped to the other side. Then, just as the team drove between them, it disappeared. Where moments before Martha and she had been unable to see each other from the sides of the road because the hayrack was in the way, they now stood facing each other in amazement. When they recovered somewhat from the shock, they looked for a trail to show them where the wagon had been, but they found none.

A Phantom Car Approaches Their Front Porch

Deborah from Montana wrote to say that her friends in Montana have a ghost car that goes by their front porch. "Their driveway (which ends on their property) used to be the county road," she said. "The county road used to pass by their front porch (about 30 feet from their front porch) and continue up through their pastures and on into the rolling hills. I have sat on their front porch and heard cars come down their driveway, past their front porch and into the pastures. I can never see the cars, but I can certainly hear them crunch on the gravel.

"I have heard the car(s) on just about every trip I have made to their ranch. My friend, who does not believe in ghosts, says it is only the wind, but I have never heard the wind crunch gravel as does a car."

THE PHANTOM CAR THAT COMES TO A MIDWEST FARM AGAIN AND AGAIN

The Personal Encounters of Mark

"**I** was listening to a past Halloween show with you and Jeff Rense, and you told a story about a phantom car that hit home. I live with my family in the rural central Midwest. I grew up here until I graduated high school in

1974, then I moved to Illinois to farm. With lowering prices and more government involvement in the farming industry, I quit farming five years ago and went to write and design for a magazine. I was the production supervisor there until I left a couple of years ago.

"My father retired from farming, and he and my mom moved into my grandmother's house, across our pasture, and my wife and I moved back to my childhood home. The old two-story farmhouse we live in is over 100 years old, and my mother and uncle also grew up here.

"As far back as I can remember, we have been visited by a phantom car. It comes a few times a year but is most noticeable in the summer. (With the windows open you can hear the engine and the tires crunching the gravel.) The phantom car can be seen just after dusk as it turns off the highway and into our long gravel lane. You can see and hear the car coming up the lane clearly and solidly. It appears to be a car from a different era, as it has large round headlights on either side of the car's hood like they are sitting on fenders. The car drives all the way up the lane and stops in front of our house on the circle drive. Then the engine shuts off, the lights turn off, and two car doors open and close.

"As the 'occupants' come crunching across the gravel, their footfalls stop. Nothing is ever out there! This phenomenon has been seen by everyone in my family, and a couple of times by a whole house full of people celebrating birthdays.

"My wife had a visit by it one night while on the phone with my dad. She told him that I had just driven up. She went outside with the remote phone and told my dad that nothing [was] here, but she [knew] she had just been watching me drive up and thought I had someone with me because she heard two car doors open. I had never told her about the car.

"I found the attached picture over at my mom's. It is a picture of our house from April 1937. It was taken from the sky, as you can see. The original photo was brown with age and faded. I scanned the photo into Photoshop and turned it back into a grayscale picture and adjusted the levels so it is clearer.

"What struck me in the photo is the car sitting on the circle drive. It is in the exact position that the phantom car is in when it stops, the engine shuts off, the lights turn off, and two doors can be heard opening and closing. The sounds of walking also match the spot it is sitting in! I know very little of the cars from that period. But if it had large headlights on either side and an engine that had the underlying sewing machine sound, it could be the phantom car.

"I found out from my mom that my grandparents were married in 1916 and moved into this house in 1918. The house was originally one story. My grandfather built the second story in 1929. (Yes, during the depression.) I had

Real Ghosts, Restless Spirits, and Haunted Places

Mark's photograph of the car that he believes still visits his family's farm.

told you in an earlier e-mail that I thought my grandparents were also visited by the phantom car. I was wrong. The earliest my mom remembers [seeing it] is in the 1960s. My grandfather died in the late '50s when I was three or four years old.

"This doesn't solve the mystery, however, because two doors open and shut and two people are heard walking. (My grandmother lived to be 100 years old.) It makes me wonder if the car in the drive is actually my grandparents' car or someone who came to visit (and continues to come to visit).

"The latest on the phantom car (April 2, 2003) is that its visits are becoming more infrequent, but it does still make the journey. Now perhaps only once every three or four months at least that we see it. (As you can imagine, that makes it even harder to out-guess it and get any photos, etc. It tricks us into thinking we are getting company every time it appears, and it is gone about the same time we realize what it is.)

"The last sighting of it was at a time when I was waiting for someone to come to our house. So I did watch its whole 'performance.' I realized what it was just when it stopped on the circle drive. No interior lights come on as the doors open. In fact, you can't tell by watching that they do open, but you hear them shut distinctly. It does appear to be the car in the old photo, or one very similar.

27
When Ghosts Visit Stores and Office Buildings

THE GHOST OF LADY MARTHA

A business acquaintance of mine in a nearby city called to inform me that he had found what seemed to be a classic haunting. According to the information he had gathered, the ghost of a strong-willed woman was haunting an entire office complex. The woman, whom everyone respectfully had called "Lady Martha" in life, was, according to certain startled witnesses, even more imposing in death.

Before she had passed on, Lady Martha had strongly opposed smoking, and she was bold enough to walk up to a total stranger on the street, slap a cigarette out of his mouth, and deliver a blistering lecture on the evils of nicotine. If cigarettes aroused her ire, beer and liquor drove her into an absolute frenzy. Those who had known Lady Martha and her opinions said that her oratory on temperance and prohibition were well known in the community.

Some time after Lady Martha's death, so went the story that was told to my friend, an executive in the office building that she had owned and in which she had maintained a top floor apartment, shook a cigarette out of a pack on his desk. He hung the cigarette on his lower lip and reached for a match, but before he could light the tobacco, the cigarette and the pack on his desk had vanished. A thorough search of the office could not turn up even one crumb of the man's tobacco. Word began to spread that Lady Martha's no-smoking rule still held firm in her office building, and what is more, the lady herself was somehow still around to enforce it.

A clothing store located in the same building had been undergoing a series of peculiar happenings that seemed to reach a bizarre climax one night

[513]

after work, when certain of the sales personnel decided to have a few relaxing beers in a basement storeroom. Since the salesmen were married and the saleswomen were young coeds from the local college, a decision was made to bolt the fire door behind them so that someone would not happen upon their after-work libation and misinterpret the scene to the men's wives.

As the beer was being distributed, one of the men jokingly commented that it was a good thing that Lady Martha was in her grave or she would be able to smell the booze in her basement. According to all those in attendance on that occasion, the words had scarcely been uttered when the bolted door swung open with a violence that slammed it against the wall. Then, to their immediate astonishment and their subsequent fear, a shimmering replica of Lady Martha drifted into the storeroom and shook a scolding finger at each participant in the after-hours gathering.

When my friend began to hear repeated accounts of such ghostly confrontations in Lady Martha's office building, he called me and asked if he might arrange for me to visit the scene of the manifestations. I agreed with his assessment that he had uncovered a haunting with an interesting investigative potential, and I asked him if he would tape record an interview with some of the witnesses of the phenomena so that I might better evaluate the material before I made arrangements to travel to his city.

My friend earnestly complied with my request, but it was that simple act of tape recording that led to the witnesses' fearful squelching of my visit to the haunted office building of Lady Martha. At first the businessmen had no objections to granting interviews to my friend regarding the phenomena that they had witnessed, and they had no objections to me conducting an investigation in the basement storeroom where Lady Martha's ghost had so dramatically and forcefully appeared. But then, as a courtesy to them, my friend offered to play back the tape so that they would be able to hear their comments before he mailed the cassette to me.

Unexplainably, anytime one of them mentioned Lady Martha's name, the tape went blank, so that it was full of such lines as, "Yes, I remember the time that_____ stopped me in my office to lecture me about smoking. Boy, could_____ ever preach against man's enslavement to tobacco."

And that was that. Before my friend left them that evening, the businessmen were no longer eager to have an investigator of the strange and unknown visit their building. They had had enough of the strange and unknown happening about them every day, and that little demonstration that evening had convinced them that Lady Martha did not wish to have any spook hunters prowling around her building. More than one of the men expressed his concern that if things had been weird up to then, think what it would be like if Lady Martha really got angry with them for bringing in an outsider.

"Brad, we have a situation in which a group of normally hard-nosed, tough-minded businessmen are actually afraid of a ghost," my friend summed it up over the telephone. "I'm sorry I blew it," he apologized. "I never should have played back the tape for them."

I told my friend that he could hardly be held responsible for the strange malfunctioning of his tape recorder, which may have presented us with a most peculiar audio proof of life beyond the grave. As difficult to believe as it may be for the skeptical reader in our twenty-first century world of science and technology, scores of sensible, well-educated, practical men and women still fear the supernatural. Moviegoers may enjoy being cinematically frightened and titillated by horror films and afterward engage in bold laughter and self-conscious analysis of the manner in which they were able to temporarily suspend reality and enter into the frightening illusion created by the motion picture. But take these same individuals, place them in an environment of moss-covered crypts, moldering mansions, and mournful midnight sighs floating up circular stairwells, and some peculiar atavistic mechanism transforms them into shuddering, haunted men and women.

And when ghosts come to the office or store, they seem to be playing out of bounds. Ghosts should be hanging out in spooky houses and cemeteries, not bothering anyone at work.

THE NOISY GHOST IN THE ARMY SURPLUS STORE

When Mr. A. M. Sharp took over the Lancashire, England, army surplus store on that Monday morning in the spring of 1952, he was still puzzled by the former owner's odd behavior and the weird story that he had told as he handed over the keys on the previous Friday. The man had actually seemed reluctant to allow Sharp to take ownership of the store, not because of any regrets about selling the place, but because he seemed to fear for Sharp's well-being.

His story had been strange. He told Sharp that as he readied the store for new ownership, he had heard peculiar noises coming from the upper floor. It had seemed as though someone were walking around up there, and the longer the fellow walked, the bigger and heavier he became. By late afternoon, the footsteps sounded as if they were those of a giant. The man was certain that there was no one upstairs and that there had been no one up there all day. When it came time for him to catch the evening train, he realized that he had left his coat on the upper floor. He started for the stairway, then as a particularly violent bump sounded from above, he bolted and left the store on the run.

Sharp was bewildered by the man's story. He had known him for several years and was aware that he was an ex-commando who had taken part in some of the bloodiest campaigns of World War II. It was indeed difficult to imagine the man running from some silly bumps on the floor. Obviously the poor fellow was breaking up. It was a good thing he had decided to retire.

Sharp was soon to learn, however, that whatever his friend had heard clomping around in the upper room, it could hardly be written off so lightly as a case of nerves. He later told journalists that it was shortly after he had taken over the store and was working late one evening that he heard distinctly the steady tread of footsteps on the floor above. He knew that there was no one but himself in the shop. He ran out of the store to see if there was anybody about next door. The place was deserted.

Sharp was determined to find out what was going on, and he started to run up the stairs. As he reached the third step, his legs seemed suddenly to freeze. He looked up and sensed, more than saw, a figure walking along the small passageway at the top of the stairs. At this point, Sharp admitted that he was really frightened.

The next morning when Sharp opened up the surplus store, he was dismayed to find that several shelves of army ankle-boots, which had been carefully stacked the previous afternoon, had been scattered about the shop. His first thought was that a burglar had broken into the shop and, finding only a few coins in the cash register, had decided to express his disappointment with an act of vandalism. Sharp checked the back door and all the windows, but he could discover no way by which an intruder might have gained entrance to the store.

It wasn't until he discovered the boots dumped about the floor on the next morning that Sharp began to connect the mysterious noises on the upper floor with the senseless violation of the shelves. The pattern was repeated on several mornings, until Sharp could plan on his picking up the scattered boots as a matter of course.

One night, when he stayed after the closing hour to catch up on some book work, Sharp was startled to feel the pressure of a hand on his shoulder. He spun around on his chair, but there was no one there, only the sound of retreating footsteps.

Eventually, rumors of strange goings-on in the army surplus store began to reach the ears of inquisitive journalists. With the permission of Sharp, some reporters from the Lancashire *Evening Post* decided to conduct an evening's vigil in the shop. One reporter assured Sharp that there was a perfectly normal explanation for the seemingly odd occurrences and that they would have the cause of his "walking boots" ready for simple explanation on the following morning.

One of the journalists carefully inspected the upper rooms and found them to be completely empty. Because of his reluctance to enter the area after dark, Sharp had long since ceased using the area for storage. The reporters were also careful to test the rooms for loose boards, noisy shutters, or gnawing rats.

This bureau was photographed for a trade furniture dealer. Photographer Montague Cooper could not explain the hand that mysteriously appears in the photograph.

Throughout the evening, the journalists heard a great variety of sounds, especially heavy bumping and thumping sounds. At other times, there were noises like metal scraping the floor. It was just after midnight when they seemed to hear the sound of a chain being rattled across the floor. By this time, the journalists were all quite nervous. They had become convinced that they were not hearing rats and mice, nor the antics of some jokester.

Shortly after midnight, most of the journalists left the noisy upper floor for the comparative quiet of the shop area. With the coming of dawn and the cessation of the activity, the reporters made another inspection of the storage rooms. They were amazed to discover a long chain lying in one corner of a room. They all agreed that there had been no chain in any of the storage rooms when they made their first inspection. Upon opening a closet door, a reporter called the attention of his fellow journalists to a broken, three-legged chair that they had previously noted as hanging from one of a series of wall pegs. It now dangled from one of the other pegs on the closet wall.

Each of the journalists accused the other of having crept upstairs and moved it. While they were arguing over which one had played ghost, Sharp arrived and put the clincher on their debate. He swore that when he had left that previous evening, there had been no chair at all in the upper floor. Nor, he insisted, had he ever seen that particular chair before in his life. When the journalists left the army surplus store that morning, they had to confess that rather than solving any mystery, they had merely complicated it.

Although the ghost that inhabited the upper floor had contented itself with producing mild amusements for the journalists during their overnight stay, by the next morning it had reverted to raising havoc with Sharp's merchandise. The harried shopkeeper opened his door that next day to find boxes emptied of their contents, army boots strewn about the shop, shirts unpinned and draped across shelves, and trouser legs tied together in knots.

Frank Spencer, a British clairvoyant, paid a visit to the haunted army store and later told reporters that he had seen a number of entities inhabiting the building. Each of these entities had wailed of an injustice or a great sorrow that kept it earthbound. Investigation later revealed that the surplus store had been built on the site of an ancient jail. An unused section of the basement was found to be paved with flagstones and contained an old room that may very well have been an old cell.

When last interviewed in the spring of 1952, Sharp was less concerned about who or what was causing the disturbance in his store than he was with why they insisted upon making such a terrible mess of his surplus store. Eventually, after a few more months of havoc, the disturbances ceased.

THE POLTERGEIST THAT TRASHED A COURT REPORTER'S OFFICE

When Jim Hazelwood, editorial writer for the *Oakland Tribune*, arrived at the office of court reporter George W. on Franklin Street on June 15,

1964, the ghost had already been active for two weeks. The first manifestations, according to Helen R., concerned themselves with the telephones in the office. The row of lights on each telephone base would light up in rapid succession, but there would be no one on the line. The telephone company insisted that there was nothing wrong with the instruments.

The disturbances centered next on the electric typewriters. The coil springs beneath the keys began to go limp, twisted together, and balled up. When the repairmen came to take them away, they left replacement machines in order that work in the office might go on without interruption. The springs on the loan machines, however, began to suffer from the same mysterious mechanical affliction. When the original typewriters were returned to George W.'s office, their springs once again began to twist and bend.

Bob G., a sales representative for the typewriter company, told Hazelwood that the typewriter springs in question normally lasted for the life of the machine. They hadn't replaced more than three of the springs in the last 10 years. But during the past few days, they had replaced about 100 in George W.'s machines. They had practically exhausted the stock of springs in the Bay area.

Hazelwood arrived at the office about 15 minutes after Officer Charles N. had completed an inspection tour of the suite. The inhabitants of the besieged office had decided to suffer in silence no longer. The staff members of George's office included, in addition to himself, his wife, Z., court reporters Robert C. and Calvert B., and two transcribers, Helen R. and John O. Hazelwood quickly surveyed the office and saw that it was in a shambles. A cracked ashtray littered the floor along with a pile of smashed crockery. A puddle of water had seeped out of a broken flower vase that rested against a corner of George's desk.

Officer N. told Hazelwood that when he had first arrived, the broken vase had been on a shelf 18 inches deep. It flew across the room and made a right turn to smash itself on the floor. While the policeman spoke, he was interrupted by a banging sound from the room on the left. One of the telephones had fallen to the floor. Hazelwood later wrote that they had quickly become tired of picking up telephones. While he was in George W.'s office on June 15th, all eight of the phones kept sliding off the desks and falling to the floor with monotonous regularity.

Jim E., a staff photographer for the *Tribune*, arrived and asked John O. to pose beside a pile of debris. Jim snapped the picture, and the two men turned to leave. Their attention was brought sharply back to the room when they heard a loud crash behind them. The floor was now covered with white powder from a large jar of cream substitute that had jumped out of the coffee cupboard and smashed on the floor.

The phenomena called a halt to its unwelcome activities that afternoon at precisely 4:00 P.M. George W. announced that he was going to move some of his equipment into an empty office downstairs in an attempt to escape the wild thing that had mysteriously beset them. It was imperative that the staff get caught up on work that had been accumulating because of the ghost's rampages.

The next day, George's frustrations were multiplied when he learned that the ghost had followed them into the new suite. In addition, other offices on the second floor had been afflicted by the phenomena. Ralph and Jeanetta R., who ran an engineering insurance service, had their typewriter fly off a desk and several coffee cups explode. Their telephone fell to the floor and was broken. In another office on the second floor, dental technician Frank B. was mixing some paste when an asbestos board suddenly tore loose from the nails holding it to the wall.

Reporter Hazelwood arrived shortly after 10:00 A.M. and went up to the third floor office where some of the staff were still trying valiantly to conduct business. The journalist resolved to keep a logbook of the occurrences for one hour. During those 60 incredible minutes, a metal dictaphone foot pedal with cord wrapped around it flew out of the cabinet, struck a wooden counter and fell to the floor; light bulbs broke in the stairwell between the third and fourth floor; paper cups were strewn around the water cooler; a metal card index file fell the floor; a typewriter top flew out an open window to the street below; and a two-pound can of coffee left the cabinet and landed 10 feet away.

Later that day, a 30-pound typewriter leaped off a table in an empty room and fell to the floor. A large electric coffee percolator slid off a table, and several coffee cups exploded. Bob G., the harassed typewriter repairman, saw a heavy wooden filing cabinet turn sideways and fall over.

Dr. Arthur Hastings, who at that time was a professor at Stanford and who had gained an excellent reputation as an investigator of the unusual and unexplained—one that he still maintains—offered his opinion that the office was the scene of a genuine poltergeist phenomenon. Hastings told Hazelwood that this was the first time that he had ever heard of a poltergeist case taking place in an office. But the phenomenon was real enough to convince even the most hard-nosed skeptic that this particular poltergeist preferred the typewriters and filing cabinets of an office to the domestic surroundings of a home.

On Wednesday morning, June 17, the phenomena reached a climax shortly after Cal B. and John O. opened the office. In rapid succession, the water cooler tipped over, soaking the left office and covering the floor with broken glass, a large wooden cabinet of office supplies came thudding down, and a movable counter flipped over onto its back.

Hastings predicted that the phenomena would not return. "This is usually the pattern with the poltergeist phenomena," he told Hazelwood. "They start slowly, build up to a climax, and then stop altogether. I don't think we'll see any more of these occurrences. Of course," he added, "I could be wrong."

It appeared at first as though Hastings' prediction had been accurate. The poltergeist was quiet for nine days. Then, on June 26, it once again caused havoc at George W.'s office. Z., his wife, said that she tried to prepare for it as soon as the first tell-tale signs showed up. When springs started breaking in all three typewriters, she knew that it had come back.

Z. started placing breakable objects on the floor. She had no sooner set a cup down and turned her back when the cup leaped eight feet across the room and shattered against a filing cabinet. Almost simultaneously, two glass ashtrays smashed to the floor and a stapler bounded from a desktop. Z. said that they didn't know what was systematically attacking their office, but whatever it was, they were sick and tired of it.

Hastings said that he still believed that the "eye of the storm" had passed on and that only the weaker manifestations remained. It appeared that this time Hastings was correct. After that last dramatic manifestation, things at the office seemed to quiet down for good. But both Hazelwood and Hastings were shocked when John O. confessed to the police that he had caused all the objects to fall by "flipping them behind his back."

Hazelwood had been away on an assignment in San Francisco on June 29, the day that the police had called the press conference to air O.'s confession. John had asked to speak first with Hazelwood, but the police convinced him that he should make his confession public before reporters from all the media. At the press conference, the police had outlined the 20-year-old court transcriber's confession, and John O. soberly nodded his head and agreed to the charges that the police read. The story of the young man's admission of guilt and trickery went out over all the wire services and was broadcast live on television. Another poltergeist case was "exposed" as the work of a hoaxster.

Immediately upon his return from San Francisco, Hazelwood started for John O.'s apartment, taking Leo C., a staff photographer, along as a witness. Hazelwood said that he knew and John knew that he couldn't have thrown all those things around the office. Almost in tears, John said that of course he wasn't responsible, but it was easier to admit to the disturbances and get the police off his back. The police interrogators kept suggesting ways that he could have caused things to fly and typewriters to break down. At the same time, they assured him that he would probably not be prosecuted. At last, to end the incessant interrogation as quickly as possible, John had simply agreed with them.

The two journalists informed the police of John O.'s repudiation of his confession, but the police had solved the case to their satisfaction and great relief. Hastings said that John O. could conceivably have caused some of the accidents by trickery, but that there were too many aspects of the case that could not be explained by sleight of hand or by any natural causes.

Although the classic poltergeist formula usually has a young person present who is in the throes of puberty, it was pointed out by reporter Hazelwood that John O. was emotionally high-strung and sensitive. He was upset to the point of illness that the police should even consider him guilty of the disturbances. It should also be noted that John had been recently married. Poltergeists have been known to plague those making marital adjustments as well as those entering puberty.

Hazelwood remained convinced of John O.'s innocence. In a letter dated July 30, 1965, Hazelwood told me: "I suspected him (John O.) almost from the first and would have loved to have been able to expose him as the trickster. It was just not possible to do so. At the same time, all activity ceased the moment John O. left the building. This happened on several occasions.... In fact, he was out of the room, but not the building, more often than not when the events occurred. I went into this as a hard-nosed reporter with almost 20 years in the business. I was prepared to scoff, expose, disbelieve. I came out of it absolutely convinced that the poltergeist phenomenon is a real one which cannot be explained by our present knowledge of natural laws."

THE HAUNTED ARTS AND CRAFTS STORE IN SCAPPOOSE, OREGON

An Investigation by Dr. Sharon A. Gill and Dr. Dave R. Oester

Dr. Sharon A. Gill is a licensed and ordained minister and holds a doctorate in metaphysical counseling from the University of Metaphysics. Her thesis was on grief counseling. Dr. Dave R. Oester is a licensed and ordained minister who holds a Doctor of Divinity and a Doctor of Philosophy in Religion through his religious affiliation. Gill and Oester's ministry focuses on teaching people how to confirm there is life after death, and they believe the spirits of the dead are the evidence that life exists beyond the grave. They have appeared on many prime time television shows on the History Channel, the Discovery Channel, the Learning Channel, Arts and Entertainment, Fox, and ABC. Their website, <www.ghostweb.com>, is one of the most popular and largest ghost hunting websites on the Internet. They have over 9,000 ghost photos and 300 Electronic Voice Phenomena ghost voices posted on the site.

Dr. David Oester begins the narrative:

"In 1994 Sharon and I had moved from the quiet little coastal town of Seaside to Warren, Oregon, along the Columbia River. We moved into an old house built in 1928 that had many of the original features, including the lead pipe plumbing. It was a wonderful old place with lots of character. It also

Dr. Sharon Gill and Dr. Dave Oester.

seemed as though the original tenant had remained there to share our home. Her name was Amelia, and she let us know when she was around in terms that were unquestionable. We coexisted there with her for over three years.

"Before we moved to the area, we had been driving over to Scappoose for two years to visit my mom. When visiting the town, we would frequent the local arts and crafts store. It was the only one around without having to go clear into Portland, and it usually carried the supplies we were looking for. I had been there many times prior to our move and knew the store well. Once we moved to the area, I got to know the owner and his family. Something very strange was taking place in the store, yet the owner, a young man, was not talking about it.

"Ghosts were the furthest thing from the young man's mind. Yet after he closed the store and retired to his apartment on the second floor, things would happen. Often he would catch sight of a shadow moving and turn quickly to see if it was one of his cats. Nothing was there. His cats would react to things that he could not see, and it unnerved him, not knowing what was taking place. The activity picked up when he started to redecorate the apartment, and things were happening down in the store, too. Finally he consulted us about the strange occurrences.

"We were able to meet Chris, the mother of the young man who owned the store, who often worked in the store. She was very talkative and shared stories of many of the ghostly hauntings that were taking place in the store. Each time we came into the store, she would relate another experience about their ghost.

"Our interest was piqued, so we decided to investigate the history of the building and determine if any other stories about a ghost surfaced. Sharon and I visited the local library and searched for historical records relating to the building. The crafts store was next door to a tavern, and behind the tavern in the same building was an abandoned doctor's office.

"After some research, we found some local residents who recalled going to this doctor, over 50 years ago. They remembered that a ghost had haunted Doc's office. That portion of the building had documented history of a haunting. Now we had established evidence of a historical haunting that had spanned some 50 years. The crafts store and the abandoned doctor's office are in the same building.

"The top floor of the crafts store was adjacent to the old ball room above the tavern. This ball room was a favorite of the locals on Saturday night. According to newspaper accounts, a fire destroyed the ball room and also resulted in people burning to death.

"During one conversation with Chris, she had mentioned that she had heard people upstairs laughing and thumping around, almost like they were dancing country-western style. When she investigated, she would find nothing out of place and no living person upstairs. The newspaper accounts of the fire and the deaths may provide clues that account for the sounds that Chris was hearing upstairs. Some of the people killed in the fire were still dancing away in the ball room.

"Since Sharon and I had established that the building had been haunted some 50 years ago by a ghost, we arranged a time after the store closed for us to go down to the store to investigate. Some of the ghostly occurrences the owner experienced while upstairs in his apartment were crashing sounds down in the store, yet he would find nothing disturbed. He would go downstairs in the morning to open the store and find that cans of paint that had been neatly arranged on a top shelf were now sitting on the floor, yet no one had been in the store since he had closed it the night before. One morning he found an entire display sitting at the foot of the stairs. Everything had been moved during the night while he slept. His first thought was that someone had broken into the place, but there were no signs of an intruder.

Real Ghosts, Restless Spirits, and Haunted Places

"A family member who worked in the store agreed that something very strange was going on, and we were looking forward to being able to investigate and maybe learn more about the spirit who remained there. We took our cassette recorders and cameras one evening at 7:00 P.M. and met Chris and her grandson in the old building. We spent the first hour talking with them, learning about what had been taking place for quite some time."

Dr. Sharon Gill picks up the storyline:

"It was during the interview that I heard music playing. It sounded like a music box playing softly in the background. Since the music had caught my attention, I had to find out where it was coming from. The grandson, about 10 years old, heard it, too, so we went deeper into the store to find the source.

"We found nothing in the store itself, though we searched thoroughly. I decided to go upstairs to the apartment to find the music. I followed David up the dark stairs, slowly, as they were steep. When I was almost to the top, I turned and snapped a picture down the stairway. I can only explain that the reason I took the picture at that moment stemmed from a feeling I had. After we had investigated the apartment, David said he had felt a cold draft come by him, as though it was rushing past us down the stairs. I had not felt the cold, but I had felt the need to take a picture.

"The resulting picture was the first vortex captured by us and is the photograph on the cover of our second book, *Haunted Reality*. When taking the picture, the camera strap on the Pentax UC-1 was around my wrist. It has always been my policy to use the camera strap to prevent dropping the camera and to keep the strap away from the lens.

"At the end of the evening, we suggested to Chris that she give the ghost a name. When things started to happen again, she could talk to it and tell it to stop the pranks and scaring the animals. Chris named the ghost 'Billie.' We asked her why the name Billie, but she didn't know why. It was a name that had come to her mind.

"While working in the store during the day, the bell on the front door would ring, alerting the clerks to customers coming in. The bell rang regularly, but the clerks found that no one had entered. It was something that started to get on their nerves, because they would drop everything to see who had entered.

"The problem was complicated after the story of Billie had come out in our second book. The media had filmed the story for television, and folks were coming to the store to see the ghost. The owner feared that they would start to go upstairs to his apartment without his knowledge. He decided to install a security system at the bottom of the stairs to alert him to anyone going up to his living quarters.

"The security system included a motion sensor that would ding like a doorbell if someone walked in front of it. The only trouble with the security system was that they had not accounted for such a playful ghost. Billie enjoyed setting off the motion sensor almost immediately, and some days it would ding almost constantly. The constant dinging occurred, but no living person would trigger the sensor. Finally, giving up on the whole idea, the owner decided to have the system removed, as it was driving the clerks crazy while they tried to work in the store. We all enjoyed a good laugh when hearing how the ghost had outsmarted modern technology.

"Late one afternoon, one of the clerks was upstairs in the warehouse putting stock away. She had a bag filled with Pogs in her hand, and though she was aware of Billie and the antics, her mind was on getting her work done. She knew the warehouse well, as she had been up there a hundred times. On this particular day, however, something happened that she never expected. As she looked up from where she was putting the Pogs on the shelf, she saw a mist at the end of the aisle. It moved around the shelves to the other side of where she was standing. At that moment, she screamed, Pogs flew everywhere, and she took off running back out through the apartment, down the stairs, and into the store below.

"As she described to Chris what was happening, she calmed herself. It was not so much that the ghost scared her, but it was more the element of surprise to which she had reacted when she saw the mist. She and the other clerks had felt cold spots down in the store, saw items moved from one location to yet another location, and heard things banging upstairs on many occasions. On this day, Chris and the clerk went back up the stairs to the warehouse. They had to see if Billie would show herself again.

"As they entered the warehouse, they saw the Pogs all over the floor. They walked the aisles, but found no mist or sign that Billie had been messing around. Chris told the clerk to pick up the Pogs, and she went back downstairs to tend to customers. The clerk finished her job upstairs and the rest of the day was uneventful.

"One evening remains clearly fixed in my mind. As we were at the store purchasing a few items, another customer was in the store holding yarn in her hands to purchase. As Chris was adding up our bill, we spoke about Billie and recent events. The woman standing in line behind us was listening to the conversation. Suddenly she threw down the yarn and said the store had demons, and she was not going to buy anything there.

"I looked at Chris, who had experienced a lot in the store and had come to understand Billie and had actually become very fond of her. The tear in her eye said it all. Billie was no more a demon than any one of us standing there, but the woman had no understanding of the spirits that remain on this physical

A photograph of the "vortex" inside the crafts store in Scappoose, Oregon.

plane. Many people judge ghosts as something demonic, which cannot be farther from the truth in most cases. There are ghosts with attitudes and ghosts who are negative, but not demons as this woman was speaking of them.

"We have worked with hundreds of people and helped them to understand the nature of ghosts. They remain here for a purpose, which we may or may not understand. They are people without physical bodies who have unresolved issues or things left unsaid or undone at the time of their deaths.

"Billie continued to make herself known to the owner and his employees. She became an accepted part of the old building. By understanding Billie, the owner coexisted with her and set limits to her antics. The cats would still react at times, but mostly they calmed down and just watched as Billie moved about the room.

"The owner sold the building a few years later, and we learned that it is now a restaurant. The new owners do not believe in ghosts, so whether they have experienced Billie or not, we will never know. They refuse to discuss the subject.

"The events that took place at the arts and craft store were real to those who experienced them. The photograph validated to us that there was at least one spirit at the store. We learned a lot from investigating and sharing that story. The reversed J-shaped anomaly captured on film was coined a 'vortex' by us. The vortex captured on film cast a shadow on the wall, meaning that it was dense in nature and the flash did not penetrate through it. We did not see anything on the stairs that night, yet the camera recorded the energy moving behind me. David had felt its chill as it moved by him. The interesting aspect of the photo was that the vortex's shadow was at a 45-degree angle from the vortex, instead of directly behind the vortex.

"In July 1996 we posted this vortex photo on our website. The response to the photo was remarkable, and by November 1996 we had established the International Ghost Hunters Society on the Internet."

28

Mysterious Entities and Dark, Hooded Bedroom Invaders

In recent years, dozens of men and women have sent me accounts of their mysterious encounter with a dark-robed hooded entity. Some believe that this increased interaction between spirits and humans is due to the barriers between the two worlds becoming thinner, as our physical world approaches nearer to a great time of transition. Others theorize that these hooded beings come from some dimension that occasionally rubs up against ours and believe that these entities are curious about our species. Still others speculate that the mysterious nocturnal visitors are aliens from an extraterrestrial world who invade human bedrooms in order to conduct certain physical and mental tests to learn more about what it is to be an earth-dweller.

My own experience seemed more in the nature of a spiritual teaching mechanism in which the hooded entity imparted certain information to me and subsequently assumed the role of a kind of spirit guide.

THE AUTHOR'S ENCOUNTER WITH A HOODED ENTITY

I was awakened one night in 1972 by an unusual kind of buzzing sound, and I sat up to encounter a dark, hooded figure standing at my bedside. In the dim light issuing through the shades and curtains from an outside streetlight, I could see that the unexpected bedroom intruder, who looked very much like a cowled monk, was waving his arms over me in a peculiar manner.

Interpreting his movements as threatening, I was instantly wide-awake. I rolled out of bed, stood up, and prepared to deliver as solid a punch as I could

[529]

Real Ghosts, Restless Spirits, and Haunted Places

manage right into the face of the person who had invaded our home and posed a threat to my sleeping wife and four children.

My blow never landed. I felt all the strength drain from my body. My arms dropped limply to my sides—and this was back in my iron-pumping, jogging days. But at that moment, I had never felt so weak, so helpless. I collapsed in a heap back on the bed. I remember that I actually began to weep in fear and confusion. I was completely at the mercy of whoever or whatever had come into our bedroom.

It was then that the hooded being spoke. "Don't be afraid," it said in a quiet whisper. "We won't hurt you."

And the next thing I knew, the morning sunlight was making me squint into wakefulness. There was no physical trace that a hooded entity or anyone else had been in our bedroom during the night, but strangely, within my mind there had been planted the seed of an idea for a book about the contemporary revelatory experience. I had dreamed concepts for books before, but I had a peculiar kind of feeling that the cowled monk was not simply a character in a bizarre nighttime vision meant to inspire me. As I reflected on the incident throughout the day, I became more and more convinced that an actual visitation had occurred and that some kind of entity had come to our bedroom in the night.

The next evening, I was just falling asleep when I became aware of a peculiar buzzing that sounded like the noise a metallic bumblebee might make. I realized at once that it was just such a sound that had awakened me the night before when the hooded being invaded our bedroom.

I was instantly wide-awake. When I focused my attention on the open door to the bedroom, I perceived a greenish-colored light emanating from somewhere in the stairway. My pulse quickened as I saw a green globe of softly glowing light moving down the hallway toward our bedroom.

On one level of consciousness, I knew that somehow the glowing orb was associated with the hooded entity. The being was returning for some purpose I had not yet ascertained. But I resolved that on this, his second visit, I would not under any circumstances allow him to "knock me out" the way he had done on the preceding visitation. I would stay alert and mentally analyze every moment of the experience.

The greenish globe entered the bedroom and hovered near the bedside, and I heard a deep, but very pleasant, male voice command me: "You will listen!"

I perceived only a glimpse of the hooded figure as he somehow extricated himself from the glowing orb—then, at once, my physical self and my questioning brain were silenced.

Once again, my next conscious memory was that of the morning sunlight streaming through the bedroom windows. But I now had bursting within the creative corridors of my psyche the passionate conviction that my next book was to be about the experiences of men and women who had entered into spiritual contact and communication with a higher intelligence. And I knew that I would entitle the book *Revelation: The Divine Fire*. I also realized that my cowled after-midnight visitor had not come to frighten me but to inspire me.

Revelation: The Divine Fire was published in 1973 by Prentice-Hall. Wherever I have lectured or presented seminars in the past 30 years, there have always been a number of individuals who will tell me that that particular book was the one that turned their lives around or that gave them the spiritual tools they required at a particular time in their lives. I tell them that I can only take credit for having been a competent stenographer for the book.

It was nearly eight years later before the hooded figure appeared to me again. This time I was permitted to remain conscious as my spirit teacher presented me with the exact information for which I had been seeking to complete a very important project. He also told me that his name was Elijah, and he allowed me to see his face—a countenance that shone with a spiritual light, framed with long gray hair and a full beard.

About a year later, Elijah, my cowled spirit mentor, came to me when I was suffering with painful boils and skin eruptions that covered a good portion of my body. I lay miserable on my bed, unable to bear even the touch of a sheet on my skin. Elijah took pity on my suffering and gave me certain specific instructions of a seemingly bizarre combination of ordinary food to ingest. Within two or three hours, all traces of the horrible boils had vanished from my body, never to return.

In 1987 a most important visitation from my hooded advisor occurred in my apartment in Scottsdale, Arizona, when he confirmed that Sherry Hansen was to be the one with whom I was to walk together on a mutually rewarding spiritual and physical life-path. He has not appeared to me since that time.

THE ANGEL OF LIFE

As the following account demonstrates, one aspect of the mission of the hooded bedroom invaders may be to tell the recipient of their visits some things about their lives that they need to know in order to better carry out their own mission on Earth.

An Observation from Mark

"I saw something on our local television news program on Halloween (2000) morning that made me consider the actuality of those hooded figures that you've been reporting that appear to people in their bedrooms or other places.

"A reporter was interviewing children and adults who were dressed in Halloween costumes. She stopped to speak with a little fellow who was no more than four to six years old. He was dressed in black hood and long black robe and it looked like he didn't have a face, as he had a black, opaque nylon covering the opening in the hood.

"The reporter asked him who he was supposed to be, and the little boy said, 'I'm the Angel of Life.' Now remember, he was dressed all in black, the universal color for death.

"The reporter then asked him who the Angel of Life is. The boy replied, 'The Angel of Life is someone who comes to talk to you. He tells you things about your life.'

"The boy's mother had a helpless, embarrassed look on her face as she explained that she had no idea where her son ever came up with such thoughts. The conviction in the little boy's face and the non-hesitant way in which he explained who he was has me thinking that, at some time, he actually had talked to the Angel of Life."

HOODED ENTITIES PROLONGED HIS MOTHER'S LIFE AND GAVE HIM A HEALING

The Personal Encounter of Douglas Stingley

"I was for 17-plus years the medical caregiver for my mother. During the early summer of 1991, a short time after my mom's first major stroke, she got better for no apparent reason. [Previously] she had a profound speech impediment and a total lack of ability to reason or to focus on mental tasks. It was that way until a single day when her problems stopped all at once with a near total return to normalcy. Around three years after that period of time, I had a dream recall of what really happened to make my mother's quality of life so much better before her death. I was sitting in the family room, watching the last part of *Late Night with David Letterman* on television, when I saw the hall light go on. My mom had already gone to bed around an hour before. I got up and went to the west end of the dining room and looked down the hall. Her door was closed, and everything was quiet.

"Something made me sit down at the dining table and look down the hallway. Out of the third bedroom, a couple of creatures of humanoid form came out and moved through the wooden door of mom's bedroom without opening it. They came in and out of her bedroom for what seemed to be a period of two and a half to three hours. They always returned to the third bedroom as their staging area. They wore light hooded robes [that were] dark brown, with tan accents. They were too thin of body compared to their height. But what was shocking was their faces—solid black without eyes, nose, mouth, or ears, and no indication of such. Their head was like an egg colored with a black felt marker. They did not walk as much as they glided across the floor.

"Whatever they did in that room restored my mother to a near-normal state. They carried whatever they needed inside small gray-colored boxes no larger than large rectangular tissue boxes. One odd note about this is that they paid no attention to me to the point that one could wonder if I was even on their plane of existence. Also during this period, our pet cat Mitzi could not be seen. (Mitzi was lined up at her feed dish the very next morning, like nothing had happened.)

"A next follow-up is on Mom. She suffered a massive stroke that totally destroyed all memories of me or anyone in 1997. However, due to those creatures, she had an additional six years of peaceful retirement.

"I myself had a healing by the hooded ones some years ago. This was when I was a 13-year-old boy in 1971. During that summer, the Willamette Valley of Oregon was struck by a strep epidemic that had hospitals filled to the brim. It was a very hard-to-treat strain. I got this infection and was hospitalized for a life-threatening kidney infection that despite all the drugs used seemed to get worse instead of better. I think I was close to death. None of the antibiotics seemed to work.

"A 'nurse' wearing a grayish white hooded robe came to my bedside at Salem Memorial Hospital. Somehow I could sense that inside the robe was the body of a chubby, round of body, older-type person. I looked at her face in the dim room light, and it was covered by plastic-like skin. Her nose was only a V-shaped ridge. She implanted thoughts into my head instead of talking to me, and she gave me the information that she had a solution to my problem. She said not to look at what she was doing. She then moved her arm down as if to give me an injection, but I felt no needle, only a cold pressure like an ice cube pressed against my body.

"I began to get better within 24 hours. I asked a day-shift nurse about this 'nurse,' but was told there was no one like her working there. I think now her face must have been some sort of mask."

"INSIDE THE HOOD WAS ONLY BLACKNESS"

The Personal Encounter of Judith

"**B**ack in 1973 in Fountain Valley, California, I had become extremely psychic, and at the same time had developed a habit whereby it always took me a long time to fall asleep. Restless and unusually agitated, with my eyes closed I visualized that I was looking out the bedroom window at the neighborhood.

"The night was quiet, due to the late hour, and I 'saw' no activity in the neighborhood with my mind's eye until my attention was directed to a corner of the street where I saw two men dressed in monk habits with hoods over their heads wearing odd looking pointed-toe slippers. Their unusual footwear attracted my attention, and only then did I realize that they were not walking, but floating, a few inches above the sidewalk. My view of them was long-ranged, yet detailed.

"I watched one lone monk figure reach our house, float up the walkway, pass through our closed and locked door, move up the entry hall, make the sharp left through the open bedroom door, and stop at the foot of the bed. Throughout the entire perception my eyes had been closed, and I had become increasingly stressed and frightened. Now I had to open my eyes to prove that the astounding horror in the cold, dark room really was not there. When I opened my eyes, I was wrong. It was!

"The monk-like figure had moved around the room to stand beside my bed. He towered over me. I thought I would die from heart failure when he bent over me to stare into my face. But inside the hood, instead of a face, I saw only empty blackness. And then, the next thing I knew, it was morning."

THREE STRANGE ENCOUNTERS WITH HOODED BEINGS

The Personal Encounters of Michael G.

"I do not recall the month, but I will never forget that Sunday afternoon in 1999. I had been to church, and I was full of energy on this beautiful, sunny afternoon. About a half an hour after getting home, I still felt energized but I began to feel a sensation around my forehead as I have many times since. I suddenly felt weak. I went in and sat at the foot of my bed. I remember feeling light-headed, then I fell back slowly on the bed and passed out. I have never been given to fainting or passing-out spells, but I didn't fall asleep—I passed out cold.

"When I woke, I had no concept of time. My first reaction was that I had fallen asleep and woke up later that night, as it was pitch dark. But things were different. I was now wide awake, and I was aware that I was naked and lying on my back on what felt like a metal table. As I looked upward, I noticed two very tall dark figures standing in front of me in black-hooded robes.

"At this point my normal first reaction would have been to shake myself into consciousness, as I would have thought it to be some kind of nightmare. But then I felt intense pain, and I realized that it was the pain that woke me in the first place. I struggled to get up, but could not move an inch. The two creatures just stood and watched as if they were observing my response to the pain. However, I could tell that they were responsible for the pain.

"I lost track of time. Soon my eyes started to adjust to the dark, and I could start to make out small images around the room. I couldn't tell if they were machines or people—it was still too dark. I was very scared, but I gathered the courage to stretch forward what little I could. I looked closely into the face hole of the hoods. I just started to get focused on some sort of facial features when the creature to my left waved his hand (which seemed to have longer fingers than should be normal) in front of my face—and I passed out cold again.

"I woke later in my apartment on my bed, but not quite in the same position. If I had to take a guess, I believe I was gone/out/whatever for about an hour, maybe a little more. When I was back I saw the sun was still out, and I got up and felt fine—but I was somewhat sore. I don't know where those creatures took me or what they did—or for what reason—but I do know I was nowhere near my home. This was the first time in my life I 'remember' encountering these strange creatures.

"Regarding my second encounter, I had not seen or heard anything from the beings since that initial experience, and I had no desire to meet them again. It was late one night in February 2003. I recall being startled suddenly awake. As I woke, I remember feeling as though all my senses were heightened. When I looked over at my sleeping wife, I saw a tall, dark hooded figure standing right beside her.

"I couldn't see much detail because it was dark and we sleep with the blinds shut, but I could make out the round hood facing me. It stood very tall. Maybe seven or eight feet. The hooded entity looked as startled—momentarily at least— to see me as I was to see it. When it saw that I saw it, it turned to the side quickly. I sat still, not really knowing what to do, but ready to react if it tried to harm either my wife or myself. As it turned to the side it moved very fast two steps forward toward the wall at the foot of the bed and then vanished.

"I did make out its form before it disappeared. It was tall, dark and wearing a hooded shroud of some sort. It had small arms that protruded out of its sleeves, and I could only make out four fingers. The thing I noticed most was its shape. The entity's form seemed to be that of a large snake dressed in a dark hood and gown. I was wide awake when I saw the physical shape of it, and it had blocked my view of the mirror behind it—so I know that at least for a few moments it was a solid figure.

"The third time (so far) that I have experienced these beings was just as unexpected as the first two. The Saturday after the second encounter, I was working at my job in an office supply store. It was late and not terribly busy when I was walking about five aisles down in the middle row. I looked over in aisle two—and there was one of those creatures. It saw me look at it and jumped behind a shelf and disappeared into thin air. This one was a little short-er than the previous creatures that I had encountered—maybe only seven feet this time. I asked the guy in the back if he had seen anyone, but he hadn't.

"I am truly at a loss to explain who these beings are and what they want, but I know for a fact they are real."

SOME GHOSTLY MANIFESTATIONS MAY BE ANGELS— OR EVIL SPIRITS

The Personal Experience of Journalist Michael Shinabery

"Ghostly manifestations, be they God's angelic messengers or evil spirits, are not uncommon throughout history. Jesus walked on the water and calmed the storm, and so afraid were his disciples huddled in the boat that—at first—they called Jesus a ghost. In the Bible, Satan perverts everything that is of God. Therefore, it is no stretch to believe in ghostly, even malevolent, manifestations—because if there is a Holy Spirit, there must be evil spirits.

"On June 30, 1995, a long-time friend in Colorado awoke one morning, padded from her bed to the living room, and went down, dead, on the floor. [She was] only 43; a heart attack ended her life on Earth. Ironically, the house's previous owner, an older woman, fell dead of a heart attack in the exact same spot.

"Not long after the funeral (which I attended), her daughter called me late one night, waking me from sleep. Terror was unmistakable in her voice. Her husband, brother, and my friend's six-year-old son had gone to the house to gather up my friend's belongings. Pulling dinnerware from kitchen cabinets, they were unnerved when they heard heavy pounding from the basement. It was an area of the house my friend had said made her feel uneasy.

"The brother, husband, and her son fled the house when blood bubbled up from the cabinet's wood shelves. The daughter had one frantic request: pray. Please. Prayers can be easily spouted. Persuasive prayers in the face of such oppression are another challenge. My prayer was in the Spirit, or praying in tongues.

"I do not know how long I prayed, lying in bed, but—as is not always the case—I did pray with what the Bible terms 'understanding.' The Holy Spirit was clear in what happened to my friend. In recent months, she had been sliding from her faith, delving into areas and things that made me uncomfortable, and I had told her so as delicately as possible. From the 'understanding,' my friend, an influential Christian, was demonically oppressed to lead others astray. Delving into occult areas had opened the door to that influence. Others with less or no faith would see her as a devout woman involved in this and that occult practice, and because they knew she was Christian, it must be OK.

"Ergo, the spirit that persecuted her—including tempting her over time with substances (drugs and alcohol) and foods that weakened her heart—was there to use her further, but not cause her death so soon. Yet in its fervor the effect was final. Its subsequent rage at having failed, thus worsening its own eternal state, was taken out on the three who entered the house that night.

"I have no idea how far I was into my prayer, lying in bed, when the attack turned to me. The demonic laughter was undeniable, and suddenly I could not breathe because my chest was being so tightly squeezed. So tight that I could not utter a word.

"Just before I thought I was going to lose consciousness, however, I squeezed out the name 'Jesus,' then struggled to repeat it slowly, like a mantra, until the attack diminished and finally subsided.

"Talking to my friend's family soon after, we realized that about the same moment I conquered the demonic attack, the manifestations that night in Colorado stopped. The family reentered the house over several days, boxed up her belongings, and never went back.

"Over the next several months, though, I struggled with late night manifestations. I would be awakened from sleep, unable to breathe, hearing demonic laughter. Only speaking 'Jesus' with great effort would stop the nocturnal attacks."

THE HAUNTED GUITAR

Today, Patrick Cross is a recognized paranormal researcher who travels throughout Canada and the United States, investigating ghosts and hauntings. Cross grew up in a house in Rexdale, Toronto, built on a murder-suicide site, and he recalls mysterious blood spots appearing and reappearing on the basement floor. There was an organ upstairs that would play eerie music—even when unplugged.

"When I was only five or six years old, ghosts scared me all the time," Cross recalled, "then I just tried to live with them. I wanted to find out what was happening and why. I began researching the paranormal."

In 1995 Cross, who is also an accomplished musician, bought a white electric guitar in the shape of a "V," a copy of the more famous guitar made by Gibson, called a Gibson "Flying V." The guitar purchased by Cross was made of heavy maple wood and looked like it had been passed down by various musicians.

"It was made in 1989, and it was in very good shape considering it was used," Cross said. "Other than a slight crack on the top of the neck of the guitar, as if it had been dropped, it played well—or so I thought. The guitar had come from a fire in a Michigan bar, where a band was playing and a fire broke out. Everything in the bar was burned to a crisp—all except the guitar, which survived without any burn marks and fully intact. Apparently, someone in the band had died in the fire, and the guitar was sold, ending up in Oakville, Ontario."

Cross recalled that he was strangely drawn to the guitar. "It was as if it called to me saying, 'play me.' As soon as I picked it up to play, I felt a tingling electric sensation, like it knew I wanted it and it was right for me. I didn't even check out the other guitars, since I couldn't put this one down. It was an odd feeling, but most musicians will understand.

"The guitar played fine in the store, jamming to some bluesy rock riffs and some classic chords, but when I got it home, it seemed to go out of tune when I picked it up to play it. I thought this was odd, since it played fine before—and now it started de-tuning itself. When I started playing something like 'Smoke On the Water,' by Deep Purple, and 'Purple Haze,' by Jimi Hendrix, the guitar played back in tune. It felt like it really liked a dark, heavy sound, and it played better than ever. I put the guitar away and went about my business."

After two days, Cross began to hear weird sounds in the apartment. "The noises seemed to be coming from the closet in the second bedroom where the guitar was stored. I opened the closet door, heard nothing, looked at the guitar, looked around, didn't see anything—but I heard what sounded like men's voices arguing with each other. It was as if an argument was going on in the closet between two men. One sounded Spanish, the other Mexican, and they were talking about money. I heard this from the front room, then went into the bedroom to the closet to look. Again, everything stopped."

As the days passed, weird things started happening around the inside of Cross's apartment: "My car keys would disappear, then re-appear sometime later. I saw shadows move on the wall, heard footsteps and bangs or knocks. Cupboard doors opened and closed on their own. Lights turned back on after I shut them off. The television set was on when I would come home, even though I remembered turning it off before I went out. My cat would look in the air, as if she saw something move in the air, and then look in the other bedroom as if she could see someone walking around. If the guitar was left out, I could feel a chill around it—like cold air or cold wind."

As Cross began to use the guitar in his rock band, "SCI-FI Prodigy," strange things would also happen at music rehearsals and band performances.

"We experienced power failures on our equipment and heard weird voices coming through the music amplifiers. Lights would go off and on and blow out and on several occasions, actual fires started from the floodlights in the room for no reason. The drummer experienced his cymbals falling off and his drums go out of tune every time he started to play. The band members also heard other people talking in the room around the guitar when we were out of the room.

"As we started playing our songs, the haunted guitar would go out of tune on the fifth and sixth strings, repeatedly. I had to put it down and play my other guitar, because the Flying V could not be played. If we started playing songs with negative lyrics or heavy metal, the guitar would play perfectly fine. The guitar particularly liked one song I wrote and played called, 'Something Is Out There,' which is all about ghosts and evil entities with emphasis on something coming to get you. It's an X-Files type of feeling. This was one of the very few songs during which the guitar would stay in tune.

"The guitar had a presence of evil—a bad aura around it. It seemed to be three feet of cold presence. Other people, including Rob McConnell from the *X-Zone Radio Show* and Janet Russell from *Beyond the Unexplained*, also felt this."

More things of a paranormal nature occurred to Cross as time went on. "I had a series of bad luck, which I believe was related to the guitar being in my apartment. I lost my job; my health started to suffer; rashes and sores appeared on my legs for no apparent reason. My car would shoot out flames from the top of the engine every time I started it, even though there was no mechanical reason to account for this.

"At times, there was a stench that seemed to come from the guitar—like a burnt dead smell. Then the terrible odor would go away as quickly as it appeared. I could hear heavy breathing around my amp and guitar when it was out in the bedroom. Yet when I walked back into the room, the sounds faded away."

Cross began to take pictures of the guitar and investigate why all these bizarre happenings and bad luck occurrences should be taking place. He captured some "ghost orbs" around the guitar many times, and on occasion he could see a misty presence.

"It always felt cold when I would pick up the guitar, and I would get small electrical shocks even when it wasn't plugged in," Cross said. "Everywhere I went with the guitar, it seemed to cause things to happen. On one occasion in London, Ontario, where our band was performing, a fire broke out in the bar area. Glasses filled with water would shatter as they passed near the table where the guitar lay."

On May 16, 1999, Cross was a guest speaker at a UFO-ghost conference, the X Zone Symposium, in St. Catharines, Ontario. He brought his haunted guitar along to see if he could find some individuals who could psychically channel anything that might explain the phenomena surrounding it.

"Psychics said that they felt weird around the guitar and expressed their opinion that it contained an evil presence," Cross recalled. "Two people who said they could help were psychic-sensitives Janet Russell and Eugenia Macer-Story. Eugenia proceeded to channel the guitar and found out it had a living entity attached to it. The entity was inside the wood of the guitar. She found it had a controlling effect on me and anyone who touched or felt it. It seemed to have intelligence and was clearly talking to Eugenia, saying it did not wish to be put on display, but wanted to cause evil and destruction. It wanted to fly like a condor with large wings, and it called itself, 'Eye of the Condor.' We later found out this was a popular song in Mexico and South America, where condors do live. The guitar wanted to start fires. It wanted me to kill with it. Actually use it to kill, swinging it like an axe. This was its way of having me worship and glorify it."

Cross felt sickened when he heard these words being channeled by Eugenia, for many times, he had had frightening images enter his mind of wanting to kill when he was around the guitar. He had also experienced very vivid dreams of going out to commit murder, using the instrument as if it were an axe.

The entity that possessed the guitar went on, saying that it had started many fires and survived while all else burned. It said it had been spawned by the Devil, and it was here to rise up to do its father's bidding in the world. It wanted to fly free, like a condor, spreading evil throughout the world.

"Eugenia found the guitar had the most powerful of Voodoo hexes, EXU (pronounced 'Echu'), placed on it by previous musicians who had owned it," Cross said. "The hex was supposed to bring wealth to anyone who owned it and did its bidding. The EXU hex back-fired on the owners who were involved with drug money and they were killed."

The spirit inside the guitar wanted to be released into human form in order to kill and destroy. It liked Cross to play only dark, evil music and said it de-tuned itself if the music was good, happy, or up-tempo. The entity said that it never wished to become good. It only wanted to commit evil acts.

"It used profanity, swearing, and vulgar language as it spoke to Eugenia, trying to latch onto her," Cross said. "The spirit said that it wanted to come into her body and kick out her soul. Eugenia felt the presence coming into her, and she let go and moved away from the guitar as it tried to possess her."

Eugenia confirmed that many of Cross's personal problems were from the "Devil-guitar." She said the only way to fix the problem was to bless it or to destroy it completely. When she asked the guitar if it wanted to be blessed, the entity responded by saying no, and speaking in Spanish, began blaspheming Christ and God.

Patrick Cross (right) and his "Flying V" electic guitar.

On the advice of Eugenia, Cross put the guitar in its case and covered it with salt to contain the energy. Then he wrapped the outside of the case with a light blue cloth in an effort to keep the negative spirit energy from leaving the case.

"On Sunday night after the conference, I took the guitar to destroy it," Cross said. "I didn't want any more bad things to happen, and I wanted to get rid of the guitar for good. I took the guitar to a remote park just after 9:00 P.M. I found an area that was secluded with a steel garbage can. I took the guitar out of its case, doused it with lighter fluid and gasoline, and put it in the garbage container. Before lighting the guitar aflame, I poured salt all around the garbage can to stop the entity from escaping or attempting to attach itself to me. I recited the Lord's Prayer three times and told the entity to go back where it came from. I demanded it to leave in God's name.

"After I said these things, I saw a misty cloud of air rise up inside the garbage can. There was wind all around me. Minutes before, it had been calm. I attempted to light the guitar, but the fire kept going out. I poured more gasoline all over it. I found some wood to put around it. Finally, after 25 minutes, it was on fire. It started to burn at last.

"As the flames went higher, I heard a high-pitched shriek coming from the burning guitar. It sounded like a sick, wounded animal. I was standing there, watching it burn, adding more gasoline to the fire, when some of the flames jumped on my arm. Now I was on fire, and as I tried to put it out, I dropped the full can of gasoline. I was horrified—because now the whole can of gas could explode and engulf me in flames.

"I panicked, but somehow I managed to put out the flames that had begun to burn my clothes. I breathed a sigh of relief as I watched the guitar burn away, into a charred chunk of wood.

"After an hour, I made sure the flames had burned out. I poured more salt over the burned up guitar, just to make sure it would contain whatever spirit energy was still left. I left the guitar in the garbage can and took the case, closed it up with salt inside it, and wrapped the blue cloth back around the case. I was shaking, but I felt good that I had destroyed the evil entity. Hoping that it wouldn't haunt or possess anything else again, I left the park around 10:30 P.M."

Immediately after returning home, Cross felt a sense of relief. He didn't hear any voices or see or feel any more ghostly activity around him. The next day, Monday, everything immediately changed for the better. "I had a phone call for a new job, my health was coming back, my sores and rashes had all disappeared, and my plants came back to life," he said. "I won $150 on a Bingo scratch ticket, there were no more power failures on my TV, and my car started normally. Miraculously, everything that had been going bad changed over night since getting rid of the haunted guitar."

Since 1999 Cross has investigated all sorts of hauntings and ghost activity, but he has never had anything happen as bad or bizarre as when he owned the haunted guitar.

TOUCHED BY AN APPARITION

In October 2001 Barry Conrad, a psychic investigator and documentary filmmaker (*California's Most Haunted*), went to a woman's home in San Diego to film and interview her. She had reported being touched and held down in her bed and said that her small son had been seeing an apparition of a soldier that would appear in his room.

"While we were there, my girlfriend, Lisa McIntosh, was standing off by herself, snapping pictures, when she later told me she felt a hand go across her back. She turned and finding no one there, took pictures of the area she was standing in." Attached is a picture of McIntosh and one of the pictures she snapped of the area behind her; this latter photo is similar to the photos taken during the Entity case (a famous case investigated by Conrad and a team of investigators, including the well-known parapsychologist Barry Taff and documented in the film *Unknown Encounter*).

For her part, McIntosh noted that "When we first arrived at this woman's home, the first thing that gave me a very strange feeling was that there were no sounds at all outside. No birds, crickets or anything. It was as if the ground her house stood on was 'dead.' It was also an area that was in complete darkness around her home. There were no street lights or anything like that because she was very far from a main road.

"After entering her home all of a sudden I had mixed emotions about being there. I felt like something was with us in every room we went in. Going in to her home the first time, I did not know how vicious the attacks on her had been. While Barry started to film her, she began telling about the events that had been taking place in her home. I was listening, but was off by

Lisa McIntosh.

myself and was standing near some sort of vent on the floor taking pictures of her and just snapping random shots when all of a sudden, I felt a hand go across the lower part of my back. At first I thought someone had walked up behind me, so I turned around only to discover there was no one there or anywhere around me. I felt stunned, frozen and although instinct dictated to run, being a ghost researcher, I decided to take more pictures where the incident happened. Never in my wildest dreams did I think I would capture what developed.

"I was not touched again the remainder of the time we were there but before I ever took the first picture in this house, I felt an uneasiness that is hard to put into words. I think for some reason I dreaded to have to be there but I didn't know why.

"The woman eventually had to move from this home and has reported to me that her tenants renting the home are beginning to have trouble there as she did."

This photograph was taken by Lisa McIntosh after she felt something touch her back and realized that no one was standing behind her.

29
Strange Beings
That Masquerade as Humans

There is a category of ghosts that I consider among the very strangest of all, because they seem to function as some sort of independent entities who masquerade as human beings for some unknown reason. These mysterious spirit beings literally walk among us, sometimes pretending to be us to achieve some goal that is at present beyond our ability to ascertain.

If, when we encountered these entities, we might come away from the experience concluding that we had met angels unaware, higher beings who were trying to teach us something or who were cleverly guiding our footsteps along the path to higher spiritual awareness, we could justify their incomprehensible actions by rationalizing that they were working to fulfill a greater plan than we are capable of comprehending as material beings. But their agenda not only lies beyond our knowing, it in fact seems designed to confuse us rather than enlighten us.

FIVE STRANGE CUSTOMERS IN A TOBACCO SHOP

The Personal Encounter of Rick Aiello

"**I** had finished shopping for groceries with my wife and stopped next door at the tobacco store to buy her some cigarettes. I walked in as usual, but I stepped into a scenario for which I was not prepared. Standing in front of the counter were five people, all about in their mid-twenties. They all had their backs to me but one. The one facing me was standing at the end of the counter right in front of me.

"What struck me as odd right away was the way he was dressed. First let me say that he was tall and very thin and wore strange, small black frame glasses. He was very white and pale complexioned. He had on a black suit with a black tie and the brightest, whitest shirt that I have ever seen. As I was standing there waiting for my turn, I noticed him fidgeting with something in his hand. He had a gold, 1940-ish type, thin cigarette case open in his hand. He was putting white candy cigarettes in the gold case and talking about how important it was that he had them.

"Strange ... but the whole impact had not hit me yet. I was still waiting for my turn, and at that moment of impatience tried to see why I was having to wait. The four others still facing the woman behind the counter had been talking to her. She had just finished seeing all their IDs, and I caught her asking, 'Where are you people from?' They all had identification from different states, and at one point the clerk said, 'Come on!' like they had fake IDs or something. Then she asked, 'What are you people up to? Who are you?'

"I've been going to this store for five years, and I have come to know this woman. I had never heard her ask such questions or act that way. I do know that she knows her stuff when it comes to IDs. Here in New York, accepting a false ID is no excuse for selling tobacco products to minors, and the state takes it very seriously.

"Anyway, now I'm tuned in and really watching these five strangers and taking a real interest in what the hell is going on. Now I really look the people over. They all [wore] odd clothing, some articles that were stylish in the 1940s. One of the group, the only female, wore a very large ribbed corduroy jumper-type dress and a pair of real leather, white 1960s go-go boots. She wore a cotton/wool '40s type coat the like you have not seen since watching the movie *It's a Wonderful Life*. Now I'm tingling from the energy in the room. The three others also wore very old-style clothing. No Nikes ... nothing from the present ... nothing!

"After taking all this in so far, I start to look at their faces and listen to them talk. They all had very pale faces, and in retrospect, they all acted peculiarly. I think the more I felt they were not 'right,' the more they tried to act more casual. They all acted very friendly in a kind of superficial way.

"None of the five answered any more of the clerk's questions after she appeared to sense something odd about them. They paid for a couple of cigars and seemed overly cheerful to avert our attention from their strange appearance and off-kilter behavior. After the clerk took their money, they turned toward me and started toward the door. For the first time I noticed that at the door are five suitcases that belong to them. They assembled at the door, grabbed their individual suitcase, and walked out the door.

"Each suitcase was individually just as strange as the people were. Remember the old-fashioned type that looked as if they were made of fabric, with a kind of basketweave design? Okay, that was one suitcase. The rest were equally dated, as if they were from the 1930s or '40s. Not one of the suitcases was even modern enough to be made of plastic, like a seamless Samsonite type. All of them were very, very old styles, but they looked like they were only about a year old—leather straps and all.

"When they were out the door, I felt my body buzz and tingle, as if it had been touched with electricity. I turned to the woman behind the counter, and she [was] as white as a sheet. I asked her what was the matter, but she didn't answer. I asked what they had said to her, and she replied that she didn't know what they were talking about. She said she remembered them standing there at the counter, but she could not remember what had been said.

"Puzzled, I reminded her that I had been standing in line and could see that they had engaged her in conversation. I said that she had certainly appeared to be intent on what they were talking about. The clerk said that she didn't even notice me come in until they left.

"I told the clerk that I had heard her ask the five weird strangers what they were up to and where they were from and that they had answered that they 'came from afar' and they needed the cigars for a play. None of the five had made eye contact with me all the while they were in the tobacco store. Nor did they turn and look at me when I came in as most people would. Even after I stood right behind them up in line, they acted as if I was not there.

"After the five bizarre people walked out of the tobacco shop, they began to cross the parking lot, which [was] empty except for my car and some others way down the plaza. The smoke shop is at the end of the plaza, and unless someone is getting cigarettes or cigars, that end is empty. I had a clear view of them, and as they [were] walking away I asked the clerk again what it was they talked to her about. She was still confused and scattered, but finally she said, 'I don't know what those people are up to but they are not who they look like.' That was all she could say.

"As I was talking to her, we both watched this strange group cross this wide open lot, and I wondered where their car was. At that point, they disappeared! POOF! At two o'clock in the afternoon in broad daylight, they vanished.

"I blurted out to the clerk that the five strangers who were in her tobacco shop just disappeared into thin air, but she did not appreciate the statement. She was still freaked from whatever happened in there.

"I left the store, wondering if my senses had somehow deceived me, and rejoined my wife, who had been sitting right out front waiting for me. She was annoyed, because she thought I was in the smoke shop shooting the breeze with the clerk and not concerned about how warm it was for her in that parked car. (Remember, I told you those people had 1940s-style winter coats on? And it was a hot afternoon.) She angrily wondered why it had taken me so long in the tobacco store.

"When I told her that the store was busy with five customers who were there before me, she really got steamed. 'Are you telling me that you had to wait for five people?' she demanded. 'Well, I've been sitting here waiting for you to come out and *nobody* has come out since you went in.'

"Incredulously, I asked her if she hadn't seen those five strangely dressed people with suitcases walking across the parking lot. 'They had to walk right in front of you,' I said. My wife, who really is not normally pushy, said, 'I've been here for ten minutes and was about to come in to see what the holdup was. No one has come out of that store.'

"Then I told her the whole story. She swore that she was glaring at the door, waiting for me—and nobody came through the door. The funny part emotionally for me was a sense of well-being after leaving the store. I was kind of tickled to think that I was part of something special of sorts. Maybe for just a moment I had rubbed elbows with higher energy beings. Why do I say that? They left me with a very good feeling. I was elated and smiling, because the more I reflected on the incident, the more I picked up on details of the exchange.

"The five out-of-place strangers seemed benevolent in a funny way, and the manner in which they were dressed seemed to indicate that they didn't appear on this plane often. They all looked very young, but no one in their early twenties would wear those 'uncool' clothes, especially the shoes, which were definitely off style and appearance. And winter coats? It was 78 degrees outside. The suitcases were the icing on the cake. Right out of Hollywood props. That's the story, and the experience will be with me a long time."

Perhaps some readers who have considered Rick Aiello's encounter with the spirit masqueraders might suggest that we are dealing with entities from another dimension of time and space—perhaps even time travelers from a distant future who wanted to explore life in the twenty-first century but who didn't read the guide book closely enough when it described the items of apparel that would be in vogue in our time.

Or maybe the five strange entities, who bought candy cigarettes to place in a gold case and who bought cigars as part of a role in a play, really were angels, higher spirit beings, just playing at life as a material being for a few hours before they vanished back to their dimension of spirit. Perhaps that was why Rick felt such a strange sense of well-being and elation after his encounter with the fantastic five.

The experience of Jerry and his girlfriend Kelly indicate that these bizarre beings might be from some other dimension of reality, but their motives are suspect and less than angelic.

A Spirit Imposter Tried to Woo His Girlfriend

Jerry told me that during a two-week period in 1997, his girlfriend, Kelly, received a number of telephone calls from someone or something pretending to be him. The first time that Kelly received a call from the entity posing as Jerry, he asked her to meet him at a park on the edge of town as quickly as possible. She was getting ready and would soon have left her apartment when Jerry knocked on her door. She was puzzled when she opened the door to admit him.

Jerry had come directly from his job at the dry cleaners, and he had stopped by to see if Kelly wanted to take in an early movie. Kelly wanted to know why he suddenly changed his plans. He had just called 20 minutes ago and asked her to meet him at the park on the edge of town. When Jerry adamantly denied making such a call, they assumed it was some friend trying to pull a prank on them. So they laughed it off and went to the movies.

The next evening, however, when Kelly knew Jerry would be working very late, she answered the telephone and heard her boyfriend's familiar voice. But she was baffled when he asked where she was the night before and why she hadn't met him at the park.

Kelly grew impatient and told Jerry that he wasn't funny. Whereupon Jerry, who never raised his voice in anger, snapped at her and warned her not to get "sassy" with him. In addition, he called her a "little twit."

When Jerry continued to rage, Kelly hung up the telephone. It was only after she had calmed down that she began to play back the rude conversation in her mind. "Twit"? Where had Jerry come up with that one? And "sassy"? The more she analyzed the whole weird telephone call, the less it really sounded like Jerry's voice.

Kelly picked up the phone and called Jerry at work. She knew his boss didn't like Jerry to receive personal calls at work, especially when the employees were putting in overtime, but she considered this an emergency. Jerry nervously came to the phone, gently remonstrating with her for calling him at the dry cleaners when he was on overtime. He laughed ironically when she asked if he had called her apartment earlier that night. In fact, if he didn't get off the phone immediately, he said, his boss would have a seizure.

Kelly was satisfied that it hadn't been Jerry on the telephone calling her a twit. But two hours later when the telephone rang again, she wasn't quite so certain. It was Jerry again, asking her to drive her car to meet him out by Miller's Pond, near the old mill.

Kelly protested that it was late and that he must be tired from working such long hours overtime. Jerry responded that seeing her, his little pigeon, would wake him up. Kelly heard the warning buzzer go off in her mind. Jerry had never called her a "little pigeon" before. This could not be the real Jerry.

"Whoever you are," she said calmly, keeping her voice even and under control, "leave me alone."

The voice at the other end pleaded with her. If she would not meet him at Miller's Pond, wouldn't she at least come down to the corner and speak with him.

She knew that she may have been acting foolishly, but Kelly gave the voice a "maybe." She kept watching the corner for any sign of a man she might suppose was the person pretending to be Jerry on the telephone. She wanted to get all the weirdness resolved. If it was a friend of theirs playing a joke, she would give him a piece of her mind. Amazingly, around midnight, she saw Jerry walk slowly up to the street corner in front of her apartment building and look up at her window. He waved and smiled, and she waved and got her sweater.

When she got about six feet away from him, she stopped and looked very carefully. He did look an awful lot like Jerry, but he was wearing some kind of heavy work boots, a baseball cap, and a brown leather jacket, kind of like the type she had seen in old movies that pilots wore in World War II.

He reached out his hand and asked her to come with him. The light from the streetlamp was fairly bright, and she could clearly see that, except for the way he was dressed, he certainly did look like Jerry.

But then she said, "Jerry, you always told me you hated to wear baseball caps." When he took off the cap, the imposter had a crewcut, a hairstyle that Jerry would not have in a million years.

Kelly started to run back into the apartment building. At that same moment, the real Jerry pulled up in his car next to the imposter. The phony Jerry let out a high-pitched scream and literally disappeared.

"Whatever this thing really was," Jerry said, "it tried to contact Kelly just once more, about five days later. Kelly thought for sure she was talking to me until 'he' asked her to drive out to the park and meet me for a picnic after work. The park is four miles out of town, and Kelly knew that I knew that her car was in the garage for a few days. She screamed at the false Jerry to leave her alone and never to call again. And, thank the Lord, he never has."

Neither Jerry nor Kelly have any theory to offer as to why this spirit masquerader wished to appear as him or why it was so persistent in attempting to pursue her. They soon became engaged and were married four months after their bizarre experience. Could the interloper from another dimension have been sent to play a weird version of Cupid in order to insure and hasten the union between Jerry and Kelly to fulfill some larger purpose?

HARASSED BY SPIRIT MASQUERADERS FOR 20 YEARS

Some years ago I received a fascinating account from a young professor in the graduate department of a major university. There seemed no purpose in the nightmarish experience that Jim had with spirit masqueraders other than sadistic harassment. His adventure across the murky borders of the supernatural began when he was 17.

Jim's father had been a senior sales representative for an import company based in the South Pacific, and from March 1964 to May 1968, they had lived in New Zealand. In March 1967, shortly after he had turned 17, Jim had gone on holiday at the beach near the little New Zealand ocean town of Kawhia and had been swimming around a section of shoreline that was not usually penetrated by tourists. It was here that he found a flat, smooth metallic object under a tidal rock.

The object was oval-shaped, rounded at the edges, and engraved with peculiar symbols. It weighed about one pound, and when Jim found it, it had been tightly wedged between two tide-level boulders that were only exposed at low tide. The object looked very old. Algae and other sea deposits encrusted it.

When such objects are found in New Zealand, they are most often taken for Maori relics, which are in high demand. Jim's father immediately advised him to take the oval-shaped object to a knowledgeable Maori to have it examined. Two weeks went by, during which time the object passed from hand to hand among Maoris who were experienced in appraising the relics of their people. At last the consensus was delivered to Jim: the object did not come from any time in their culture and they did not recognize what it could be.

Jim could not later recall if a metallurgical analysis of the object had ever been made, but he did remember that the curio ended up in a dresser drawer in their home in Te Awamutu, where it was to remain until his father received orders to move to New York in May 1968. As Jim recalled, that was when he first discovered that the object was missing. When he came to pack it for moving, it was not there. It had disappeared.

As they waited for the flight from Auckland International Airport in May, Jim's parents were saying good-bye to some friends at some distance from him when he was approached by two young Polynesian men, who claimed to be from New Zealand Inland Revenue. They asked him if he were taking anything illegal out of the country, and they were especially interested in learning if he had any relics, art objects, or the like.

The two men intimidated Jim, and he did his very best to explain that he had no relics in his possession—but then they insisted that he go with them to a hotel to undergo a private baggage check. It was at that point that he called for his father, who demanded to see their identification and asked why they couldn't examine his son's baggage right there in the airport. When their answers didn't make sense, Jim's father summoned a patrolling constable to intervene. His mere arrival seemed to frighten the two men away.

That fall, back in the United States, Jim enrolled at Columbia University for his freshman year. Shortly after the term began, he was approached by an art dealer who said that he had heard that Jim had spent some time in New Zealand and indicated that he was interested in purchasing any relics or curios that Jim might have brought with him. Although the alleged art dealer was polite and businesslike, he was annoyingly persistent. In spite of Jim's repeated denials that he had any such relics to sell him, the man approached him three times before the winter holidays.

Through correspondence, Jim learned that three of his closest friends in New Zealand had been questioned by men who seemed to fit the description of the two strange men who had attempted to search his luggage at the airport. In one instance, the New Zealand police had to be called in to block continued harassment. In another case, a girl's life had been threatened. According to their letters to Jim, each of his friends had been questioned about whether or not he had given them anything to keep before he left New Zealand. They all used words like "spooky," "weird," and "creepy" to describe the men who had persistently troubled them.

In 1970 Jim transferred to Stanford University. He had no sooner moved into his apartment and had the telephone installed when he received a call warning him never to return to New Zealand. During a later call, a woman with a high-pitched voice informed Jim that he was being kept under surveillance by a group who felt that he had acted unjustly in the past by not returning things to their proper owners.

In 1972 Jim decided to teach high school for a time before he continued with his graduate work. That summer, a few weeks before he was to begin his first job in the Sacramento school system, he was vacationing in San Francisco. Late one night, the telephone rang in his hotel room, and Jim answered it to hear a voice tell him that he had acted wisely by not returning to New Zealand.

Jim emphasized to me that he had led a very quiet life as an undergraduate. Yet at both Columbia and Stanford he probably received 30 or more

Real Ghosts, Restless Spirits, and Haunted Places

telephone calls from anonymous voices advising him not to return to New Zealand. In other instances, the voices reprimanded him for having taken something that did not belong to him. Jim said that he didn't carry a sign with him declaring that he had lived in New Zealand, and he seldom discussed his life there with any but a few of his closest acquaintances. Who could possibly have cared about his finding that metallic slab? And who could possibly have taken such a long-term interest in him because of a casual act committed a few days after his seventeenth birthday?

About the third day after classes had begun in the suburban community of Sacramento where Jim had accepted a high school teaching position, a student unknown to him stopped by his classroom to say hello. Jim knew that such an act was hardly unusual, since students will often do this to look over a new teacher, but from the first moment he stepped in the room, the boy acted strangely inquisitive.

Jim was astonished when the teenager stepped to the blackboard and drew the same design that he had first seen on the mysterious metallic object that he had found in New Zealand. He smiled at Jim, then asked if he knew what the symbols meant. When Jim pressed the boy, in turn, for some answers, the student erased the design, laughed, and said that he was just fooling around, that he didn't mean anything by it.

Jim never saw the alleged student again. He described him to a couple of the teachers and to a bunch of students, but no one was able to identify him. Jim doubted very much if he actually went to the school at all.

After four years of high school teaching, Jim was awarded a teaching assistantship at a major university and arrived in the fall of 1976 to begin his doctorate program. He hadn't been at the university more than four days when someone rang his room and scolded him for taking things that didn't belong to him. The voice told Jim that he should always leave things where they were.

At the time that Jim contacted me in the mid-1980s, he was receiving only an occasional mysterious telephone call in which the voice at the other end chastised him for taking that strange metallic object from where he found it. If the 17-year-old Jim had discovered a strange key to other dimensions, the entities had long since reclaimed it. But apparently, some spirit masqueraders were determined that he should never forget the day he disturbed an artifact from another level of being.

"WE ARE ALL RELATED"

When Kent was a student at a midwestern university, he may have received some kind of clue to the identity of at least some of the spirit masqueraders. One day he was out driving in the countryside, trying his best to clear his brain and prepare for an important test in economics the next afternoon. As he drove farther away from the city, he became aware that he was passing through a tiny village that presently supported a general store, a gas station, a couple other buildings of indeterminate use, and lots of apparently deserted business locations. However, on the outskirts of the village, there appeared to be some kind of celebration in progress on the grounds of an old country church. Kent heard polka music and saw a small crowd of people playing games and lining up beside what appeared to be a generous smorgasbord table.

The college student couldn't resist pulling his car over to the side of the road, getting out, and walking over to the cheery partygoers. Suddenly his way was blocked by a big man who glared at him with ice-cold eyes. And then a tall, smiling man stepped between the brute and the student. He introduced himself as Erik and inquired of Kent his full name. When the student answered, Erik's face lit up, and he asked if Kent were related to the G. family of Boscobel, Wisconsin. When Kent said that he was, Erik loudly called to everyone at the picnic that he was distantly related to them and to make a place for him. With his arm around Kent's shoulder, Erik took him around to various people and introduced him. What Kent had so fortuitously stumbled into, Erik explained, was a gathering of the descendants of the early immigrants who had settled the little dying village that he had just found that afternoon.

Kent admitted that for him the high point of the afternoon was meeting Kari, a beautiful, blue-eyed blonde who appeared to be about his own age. After only a few moments at her side, he found her completely enchanting. While other members of the gathering came from all over the United States for the annual reunion of settlers' families, he was delighted when Kari said that she was a local resident.

After many hours of dancing to polka music with Kari, Kent asked to see her again. Although she had seemed so warm and friendly during the afternoon and had seen to it that he had received generous portions of the lavish smorgasbord, she now appeared cool and indifferent. Whenever he pressured her for her telephone number or address, she turned away and told him that it would not be wise to pursue a relationship.

Kent knew that it was time for him to get back to his studies. And all around him the families were packing up their things. Looking around in puzzlement, he asked where they had parked their cars. Erik explained that they had all left their vehicles in the village and had walked out to the picnic grounds. That was part of the annual ritual they observed.

Kent got back in his car and waved good-bye to Kari, who returned his wave with an expression of sorrow, which he took to be a sign of encouragement that she already missed him and wanted to see him again. Later that night, Kent found that study was impossible. He spent half the night disturbing his roommate, as he tried to write a paper for an English literature class, regaling him with his descriptions of the wondrous Kari.

In the local telephone book, Kent found many listings under the last name that Kari had given him, but when he rang the numbers, none of the families said that they had a daughter named Kari. Determined to find her, he drove back to the small village and inquired of all the present residents about Kari. But none of them gave him the slightest satisfaction as to her whereabouts.

Perhaps as disconcerting as his inability to find Kari was his discovery of the charred remains of a church—exactly where he thought that he had danced polka after polka with the girl of his dreams. When he asked when the church had burned, a farmer looked at him suspiciously and refused to answer. Kent concluded that he had been mistaken about the location of the celebration. It had to have been at another country church.

Persistent to the bitter end, on his next excursion to the locale, Kent drove down the long lanes of every farm within a radius of 15 or 20 miles, seeking somehow to find the beautiful Kari.

One night, several weeks later, Kent was seated at the counter in an all-night diner when he looked up to make sudden eye contact in the large counter mirror with Erik, who was sitting in a booth directly behind him. Kent was startled to see him there, for he was certain there had been no one else in the diner but one other man seated at the far end of the counter. Erik beckoned for Kent to join him.

Erik told Kent that he and his friends had really liked him, but he should stop trying to find Kari. A relationship with her was out of the question. When Kent asked about Erik's statement at the picnic that he was related to him, Erik smiled and said that was true.

"We are related, but not in the way that you probably understand it," Erik tried to explain. "We are related to you as companions, as friends. There are those among us some who have some resentment toward your kind because truly, we were here first, and sometimes we feel supplanted by you and your kind. But hear me now, young man, because we feel a true affection for you, we are telling you to give up your search for Kari. What you hope for, can never be."

The waitress yelled that Kent's hamburger was ready, and when he turned away from the counter, Erik had vanished. Kent ran out in the street because he had so many questions that he wanted answered, but Erik was nowhere to be seen.

Three years later, when Kent was visiting a friend in New York, he was certain that he saw Kari and Erik walking amidst the crowd in Times Square as he rode in a cab.

"Like an idiot," Kent said, "I rolled down the window and shouted their names. I know they saw me and heard me, for they looked directly at me, then turned quickly away and stepped into the lobby of a movie theater. I cannot help wondering how many 'Eriks,' 'Karis,' and all of our other 'relatives' walk among us, skillfully blending in with the crowd, carefully shielding their true identities and their true purpose from us."

Many years ago, in his book *Adventures with Phantoms*, British author Thurston Hopkins wondered similarly about the mysterious entities that he had encountered while walking the streets of London. Hopkins thought these beings were "not fully quick, nor fully dead." In his opinion, these entities mimic us and pretend to be as we are, but they are not truly of our kind.

"They are creatures who have strayed away from some unknown region of haunted woods and perilous wilds," Hopkins wrote. "They dress like us; pretend that they belong to mankind and profess to keep our laws and code of morals. But in their presence we are always aware that they are phantoms and that all their ideas and actions are out of key with the general pitch and tone of normal life."

30
Ghosts from Outer Space

FLYING SAUCERS AND UFO CONTACTEES

One night I stood with several other witnesses observing what we all thought was a brightly lighted unknown object—a UFO—moving across the sky. When a skeptic in the group guffawed that it was only the running lights of a 747, the mysterious glowing object—seemingly on cue—split itself in half. As if that were not startling enough, the two illuminated halves of the object then made a complete arc high above us before they came back together as one light moving purposefully against a backdrop of stars.

I know that we had not witnessed a conventional aircraft. Nor can I conjecture an extraterrestrial spacecraft that would bother to respond to the oral challenge of some totally insignificant human many thousand feet below. Even if it could, why would it? Enough people report UFOs without the obliging ETs staging special showings. And no secret Air Force project could accomplish those kinds of weird maneuvers and handle the speeds at which the self-dissecting object appeared to travel.

However, perhaps by some fortuitous circumstances we had witnessed the playful maneuvers of another form of intelligence that shares our planet, most often unseen. Maybe what we have thus far been labeling "spaceships" are actually some kind of multidimensional mechanism or psychic construct by which our paraphysical companions transport themselves. As we have seen a number of times in this text, many psychical researchers suggest that the "orbs," those darting globs of light seen at the scene of so many hauntings, are the paraphysical vehicles by which spirits move about between their dimension of being and ours. To go one step farther, perhaps the glowing lights in the sky and

[557]

the orbs on the ground are the higher intelligences themselves, rather than the vehicles that transport them. Perhaps that is how spirits really appear to one another in their nonmaterial world, and they do not assume a humanlike appearance until they manifest in our material, three-dimensional world.

I began researching "flying saucers" in the mid-1950s. In those days, there was a general consensus among UFO investigators that the lights in our skies were nuts and bolts extraterrestrial spacecraft and that their alien crews had come to invade our planet or to keep it under surveillance until they decided what to do with us. The mystery was considered a physical one that was being controlled by material entities in material craft.

At the same time that flying saucer researchers were combing fields and forests for tangible evidence that material spacecraft had been touching down on Earth to take soil samples and specimens of vegetation, a number of men and women became convinced that they had encountered alien "space intelligences" and that they remained in direct communication with them through telepathic thought transference. These individuals, who were called "UFO contactees," also claimed a heightening of extrasensory perception after the contact experience. Along with increased psychic abilities, the contactee was given a timetable of certain predictions of future events and an almost religious fervor to spread the message that had been given to them by the space beings.

The Contactee Gospel contained such percepts as: (1) Brothers and sisters from outer space have come to Earth to help those humans who will accept the concept of a larger universe. (2) The space beings want humankind to become eligible to join an intergalactic spiritual federation. (3) The space beings have come to assist the people of Earth to lift their spiritual vibratory rate so they may enter new dimensions. (According to the contactees, Jesus, Krishna, Confucius, and many of the other leaders of the great religions came to Earth to teach humanity these very same abilities.) (4) The citizens of Earth stand now in the transitional period before the dawn of a New Age of peace, love, and understanding. (5) Earthlings must raise their vibratory rate within a set period of time or severe Earth changes and major cataclysms will take place.

According to the UFO contactees in those years, the space beings' most prominent characteristic was wisdom. However, practical-minded Earth scientists remained singularly unimpressed with the lack of any specific technical information that was relayed by the contactees. Messages advising humans to "raise their vibratory rate" and issuing cautions about a coming period of transition simply sounded hollow to the scientists, who were hoping that beings from a more greatly advanced technological society would bring information to share on how to advance Earth's own technology.

I began to take a special interest in the UFO contactees, and as I studied the phenomena closely I began to see numerous correlations between those who claim to be in telepathic communication with a Space Being and those mediums or psychic-sensitives who claim to be in communication with spirits. The medium or channel enters a trance state and works with a guide or a control from the other side who relays information from spirits of deceased human personalities. Likewise, the UFO contactee goes into some state of trance and channels information from Space Beings. The similarities between spirit mediums and UFO contactees—as well as their spiritual messages—become all the more striking when it is discovered that so many of the early well-known contactees, such as George King, George Van Tassel, Gloria Lee, and George Hunt Williamson, had been members of psychic development groups.

After almost 50 years of investigating the mysteries of the paranormal and the UFO, I have become convinced that in so many areas of human experience the two phenomena are one. And yet so many of my fellow researchers maintain that the accounts of hooded beings and greenish balls of light in peoples' homes are not evidence of ghostly phenomena but are really reports of extraterrestrial aliens who have crossed millions of light years to come to Earth to frighten people. The poltergeistic energy that tosses books from shelves and upsets furniture is the work of ETs, not the explosion of psychokinesis from someone entering puberty or undergoing emotional stress. The nightmarish horror of aliens who invade people's bedrooms and abduct them by going right through walls is not an experience of the astral body or a projection of the psyche, but an actual physical happening by extraterrestrials who can never get enough of examining human sexuality. And all those ghosts that materialize before humans in dark and lonely places or in creepy castles and moldering mansions are merely extraterrestrials who have explored the universe to find victims for their pranks.

Let me state clearly that I do not exclude the extraterrestrial hypothesis to explain some sightings of UFOs. There may, indeed, be other intelligent life-forms elsewhere in the universe. What I am saying is that I believe so much of the UFO mystery to be the activity of ghosts, spirits, multidimensional beings—call them what you like—rather than the machinations of aliens from other planets. And I also believe that many of these spirit entities have the ability to influence the human mind telepathically in order to project what may appear to be three-dimensional images.

In our era of space-age science and popular movies and television series dealing with extraterrestrials and UFO invaders, it seems that some multidimensional entities, who may exist right around the corner in another space-time continuum, may use the device of flying saucers and aliens to divert humans from their true motives.

The UFO entities always seem to have an inordinate interest in our measurement of time, an aspect of the mystery that has led a number of

Real Ghosts, Restless Spirits, and Haunted Places

researchers to theorize that the supposed alien beings might really be time travelers, perhaps even our descendants from the future.

In his paper "Toward an Extraterrestrial Anthropology," Dr. Roger W. Wescott states that "time as Western Man conceived it at least since the Renaissance Period, is single in dimension, uniform in pace, and irreversible in direction. If time should turn out to have more than one dimension, discontinuity of pace, or reversibility of direction—or if space should turn out to have more than three dimensions—then it would be quite possible for solidly and prosaically material beings from the 'real' world to pass through our illusively constricted space-time continuum as a needle passes through a piece of cloth."

If such interdimensional traffic should exist, Wescott suggests, we might consider such beings to be supernatural because from our perspective they would seem to materialize and vanish inexplicably. We might, in fact, dismiss them from our reality as hallucinations or hoaxes.

"Rather than existing in space and/or time in the conventional sense of these terms," Wescott offers, "our planet may exist in hyperspace and/or hypertime, where hyperspace is understood to mean space with four or more dimensions and hypertime to mean time which permits events and processes to occur in other than an irreversible linear and unidirectional manner."

On such a "hyperhistorical" sphere—or, alternatively, such a historical "hypersphere"—Wescott says, "All the supernatural beings and all the miraculous occurrences known to us from religion and folklore would become explicable as intrusions from the larger earth of reality into the smaller earth of our self-habituation."

THE BIZARRE ORDEAL OF AN IOWA FARM FAMILY

An Iowa farmer named Gary C. saw a UFO one night as he was working late in the field during spring plowing. The next morning over breakfast, he learned that his wife, Melanie, 14-year-old son Jake, and 12-year-old daughter Lisa had also seen the bright object as the kids were getting ready for bed.

That day at school, a man who claimed to be from the state board of education asked to interview Jake. He told the principal of the junior high school that the boy had attracted attention because of his high scores in the state tests and that Jake had been selected to participate in a special educational project.

The principal allowed the man to speak to Jake in a private room, but he had become suspicious of the man's motives. The principal was aware that Jake was an above-average student, but he knew that the boy's test scores were hardly exceptional enough to warrant a special visit from a representative of the state board. A call to the state office revealed that they had no one on their staff by the man's name, and they had no special project for junior high students in progress.

When the principal entered the private room to confront the imposter, he found a puzzled Jake sitting alone. The teenager could only shrug that the special state project must be about space travel, for all the man asked him were questions about UFOS, aliens, and life on other planets. Jake had glanced away from his interrogator for just a moment, and when he looked back at him, he seemed to have vanished.

[*Author's note: Interestingly, I have spoken to a number of individuals— most of whom are now adults—who recalled a similar experience when they were called into a room at school and a man, allegedly from a state educational office, asked them questions about UFOs, aliens, and outer space. In most cases, the individuals had sighted strange lights in the sky that they had thought were UFOs.*]

About the time that Jake was being interviewed by the mysterious stranger at school, out on the farm Gary and Melanie received a visit from two men dressed in black while they were eating lunch. The men identified themselves as agents of a special government task force investigating UFOS and said they had learned that the family had sighted a bright object in the sky on the previous evening.

Melanie and Gary were puzzled, since they had not told anyone of their sighting. The alleged government agents suddenly adopted a threatening manner and demanded that Melanie and Gary turn over any photographs they may have taken of the UFO. The farm couple said that they had taken no photographs, but the two agents refused to accept their denials and threatened that they had better cooperate if they knew what was good for them.

"You must cooperate," the taller of the two men said, "for your own good, the good of your country, the good of your world."

At that point, one of the agents began to choke and seemed to have difficulty breathing. Without another word, the two men quickly left the farmhouse and drove off in their car, which Gary said later looked like a bizarre blending of three or four different makes of automobile.

Later that afternoon, Gary was certain that he saw the two men watching him from the shadows of his machine shed while he fed the cattle on the feedlot. In the farmhouse, Melanie answered the telephone on four occasions to hear nothing but a peculiar static. Finally, on the fifth ring, a voice in a strange accent told her to forget all she knew about UFOs or terrible things would happen to her entire family.

That night, shortly after the children went to bed, Lisa began screaming that some animal had crawled under her covers. When Gary and Melanie investigated, they found nothing, but then Jake yelled that his bed was jumping up and down. As they ran to his room, they could hear the thumping sounds of his bed lifting and slamming to the floor.

Such poltergeistic disturbances continued on a nightly basis for nearly a week before dissipating. And during the day, all four members of the family felt that mysterious, shadowy figures were keeping a close watch on them—at school, out in the fields, and in their home. The eerie harassment of the family continued intermittently for about a month, then abruptly ended. However, there was one final display of supernatural prowess.

About 10 days after the strange disturbances in his family's home had ceased, Gary had to fly to North Dakota to attend an uncle's funeral. As he was about to board the plane in his town's small local airport, Gary saw the two "government agents" behind him going through security. It was obvious that they were tailing him and that they were still keeping him under surveillance. He felt especially uneasy when the two men dressed in black took seats directly behind him. Although Gary wanted to turn and confront them, he decided that it was best to sit still and ignore them.

About halfway through the flight, one of the men leaned forward and whispered in Gary's ear, "Remember, in one way or another, we'll always be around to keep an eye on you."

Angrily, Gary turned around—to face empty seats. The two men had disappeared. Gary felt dizzy, disoriented, and nauseated. He heard several of the passengers near him complaining loudly to the night attendants about a terrible smell. Some began to cough; others reached for vomit bags. All around them was the foul, suffocating odor of rotten eggs or burning sulfur.

Several minutes later, after the terrible odor had dissipated, Gary asked one of the flight attendants what had happened to the two passengers who had been sitting behind him. Neither she nor any of the other passengers remembered seeing anyone in the seats directly behind him. Gary felt as if he were going insane. He got up to walk the aisle of the small plane and to check the restrooms to see if the two men had hidden themselves somewhere on board the airplane. Somehow Gary managed to control his frayed nerves until the plane landed.

He waited in the airport for over an hour, watching the grounded aircraft, monitoring the hallways of the terminal, knowing without question that he really had seen the two strange men enter the aircraft and take the seats directly behind him. Finally, satisfied that the men in black had not hidden somewhere on the airplane and were not going to exit surreptitiously, Gary left the airport, sensing that his family's ordeal had finally ended.

STRANGE SHAPE-SHIFTING ENTITIES
TORMENTED A MINISTER FOR OVER 25 YEARS

Gary and his family got off easy in their interaction with the bizarre entities compared to Reverend Martin J., who underwent one of the most harrowing accounts with these mysterious multidimension, shape-shifting intelligences that I have ever encountered. For Gary, Melanie, and their kids, the ordeal lasted about a month from the initial incident until the incredible disappearing act aboard the passenger plane. For Reverend Martin, the nightmare continued for more than 25 years—and may not be over still.

On Halloween 1968, Martin J., a Protestant minister, was trick-or-treating with his four-year-old daughter when he happened to glance up and see a bright light moving in a zigzagging motion across the sky. Since the night was cloudy with a light rain falling, he knew that he had not seen a star, and because of the erratic motion of the object, he knew that he had not seen any kind of conventional aircraft.

He mentioned the sighting to his wife and his nine-year-old son that night around the dinner table, but the matter was soon dropped. Later that evening, however, Martin had a vivid dream of a strange entity who came to stand beside his bed and warn him not to tell anyone else about the sighting.

The next day, as he was going about his normal ministerial duties, Martin became aware of someone—or something—following him. Once when he turned around quickly at the sound of footsteps, he caught a glimpse of what appeared to be a tall thin man dressed completely in black ducking behind a parked truck. Another time, he blinked his eyes at what appeared to be some kind of large, reptilianlike creature sitting on a high tree branch staring at him.

That next Sunday in church, as Martin was in the midst of his sermon, the entire building seemed to be filled with the nauseating odor of rotting flesh. Several members of the congregation became ill and had to leave. Martin himself became so nauseated that he could barely continue.

Word soon spread that the building had been overrun by rats, and church attendance dropped so severely that the denomination's board of supervisors considered closing its doors. When exterminators were summoned, they stated that they could find no evidence of rats or any reason why the terrible stench remained in the church. The next day, the church was officially closed.

As for Martin, it seemed as though a bizarre series of happenings afflicted him wherever he went. When he and his wife went to a movie theater to attempt to get their minds off their troubles, they were accused of releasing a noxious odor and were asked to leave. A drive in the country resulted in a minor accident and a traffic ticket when the automobile that the pastor had left in park with the emergency brake applied jumped the curb and smashed into five other parked cars before it came to a halt. And on every night since Halloween, the entire family was haunted by dark, shadowy figures that lurked about the home and frightened the children in their beds.

By the autumn of 1970, two years after he had seen the strange light in the sky on Halloween, Martin found himself without a church position. He also found himself without a wife. Connie, his wife of 14 years, was on the brink of a nervous breakdown. She said that she was truly sorry, but she felt that a divorce and her restored mental equilibrium would make her a better mother than institutionalization for insanity. In utter confusion, Martin signed the divorce papers and left for another city in another state. For 10 years thereafter, he worked as a counselor in a halfway house. He found it impossible to accept another parish ministry because of the ongoing series of weird events that continued to haunt his existence.

On Halloween night in 1978, the tenth anniversary of his sighting of the strange bright light, he received three most unusual visitors to his apart-ment. Three nondescript, smallish entities manifested before his astonished eyes. They looked almost completely human—and yet, upon close scrutiny, there was some vague, undefinable difference that set them apart. They said that they hoped there were no hard feelings for the harassment he had endured over the past 10 years. However, he had set some things in motion that could not be stopped once they had begun. To demonstrate their good-will, they would now permit him to do what no human had ever been allowed to do: he could take their pictures as they demonstrated just a small portion of their repertoire of guises.

Within the next several hours, the frightened and astonished minister saw the three entities change shape, glow in the dark, and materialize and dematerialize right in front of him. While he snapped away with his Polaroid, it became apparent that the beings could assume whatever physical form they chose. As he watched, they shifted forms from grotesque gargoyles to winged angelic beings, from hollow-eyed ghosts to woodland elves.

The next day, feeling secure with his photographic evidence, Martin believed that he held some kind of cosmic trump card that would somehow keep the things away from him. Suffused also with feelings of vindication, he called his parents; his ex-wife, Connie, who had since remarried; his son, now a sophomore at a church college; and a half dozen of his friends in the ministry and told them that he now had proof that he was not crazy and had not been making up weird stories for the past 10 years.

Two days later, three police officers appeared at Martin's apartment. With broad smiles they explained that when they weren't on duty they were serious UFO buffs and had heard about his remarkable photographs of alien beings. Although the minister was surprised that the few people in whom he had confided had broadcast his coup of having obtained snapshots of other-worldly beings, these men, after all, were the police. And they weren't laughing at him. The three men were very serious when they examined the dozens of photographs, and they were firm in their arguments that such solid proof of alien beings among human society should be widely published in the media.

Martin was very reluctant. He had endured enough ridicule since his initial sighting a decade before. The police officers were extremely sympathetic when Martin told them a little about the ordeal that he had endured. They spoke in disgusted tones about the fickle nature of the average human in today's society. They shook their heads in disbelief that Martin's church had turned him out rather than sticking by him. They were openly contemptuous of a wife who would leave a man when he most needed her support and love. Martin was long overdue for his day in court. It was time that he was vindicated.

The officers told him that they were extremely well informed about constructive public relations campaigns. They assured him that they would use their credentials to get the pictures published and to restore his credibility as a clergyman. Together, the four of them would prove to the world at large that such creatures were walking among humankind and that the UFO and paranormal phenomena were very real.

That night, for the first time in a decade, Martin slept peacefully. At last he had the support of three fine men who would help him clear his name and restore his reputation as a minister.

However, when the officers arrived unannounced the following night, they threatened Martin, confiscated his photographs, taped his hands behind his back, pulled a stocking cap over his face, and tossed him roughly into the back of a van. After the policemen drove him around for a while, loudly debating whether or not they should kill him, they finally released him in a remote wooded area.

Although Martin felt fortunate that he was still alive, he realized that his proof of the alien entities had been taken by the phony police officers—who, he now understood, were actually the paraphysical beings assuming yet another disguise. A few days later, he began to notice strange physical effects on his body. The upper portion of his torso became scaly. His vision became blurred, and from time to time he was temporarily blind for several days.

I learned of Martin's plight when he was interviewed by an incredulous journalist, who was convinced by the minister's apparent sincerity but completely unnerved by his incredible story. At that time, after 25 years of torment by alien beings, the beleaguered clergyman was receiving emotional support from other ministers—and praying without ceasing that the ghosts, shape-shifters, angels, or demons had finally decided to leave him alone.

I have learned through firsthand investigations and some personal experiences of my own that such ordeals as those of the Iowa farm family and the clergyman are very real and that the victims are not simply suffering from particularly eerie delusions.

The important thing to remember if you should be confronted by such entities is not to play their game—and especially not to cast them in the role of villain. If you permit hostility, then that is what you are likely to receive. In my opinion, the phenomenon is the manifestation of a single source and is, of itself, neither good nor evil. How these ostensibly menacing figures conduct themselves depends in large part upon the behavior of the human percipient with whom they are interacting.

In metaphysical works, these entities are sometimes referred to as the "Brothers of the Shadow." In UFO lore, they are the infamous "Men in Black." Whoever or whatever they may really be, there is an aspect of their appearance that is suggestive of the "trickster" figure that is common to all cultures and well-known to ethnologists and anthropologists. The trickster plays pranks on hapless humans, but often at the same time he is instructing people or transforming aspects of the environment for the good of his human charges.

Most cultures view the trickster as a supernatural being with the ability to change his shape at will. Although basically clever and wily, he can at times behave in a stupid, childish manner, and may often appear to end up as the one who is tricked. The trickster does not hesitate to lie, cheat, and steal. Often he seems to be the very essence of amoral animalism.

The trickster figure frequently manifests in the guise of a cultural hero. To the Native Americans of the Southwest, he appeared as the wily coyote. To the Norse and the Greeks, the trickster manifested often in the role of a mischievous, but not really demonic, god.

Perhaps to communicate to our contemporary culture, the trickster, who is ageless and as old as time, must draw upon the ancient myths and combine them with our emerging fascination with other worlds in order to fashion the figures of wily and amoral extraterrestrial aliens. We have the ability, however, to exorcise the negative aspects of the trickster by refusing to play its silly games, thereby allowing us to concentrate on the positive aspects that he can bring to us.

TOUCHED BY FALLEN ANGELS

Some researchers have theorized that such spirit entities as the Brothers of the Shadow, and the Men in Black might be angels—with the emphasis on *fallen* angels, the nonmaterial beings who serve evil, rather than good, and who try their best to ensnare humans in their nasty plans to supplant our species. An angel (*angelos* in Greek; *malach* in Hebrew) is a messenger, one who is sent to accomplish whatever mission has been assigned to him or her. In relation to God, the Supreme Being, the obedient angels of righteousness stand as courtiers to a king. They themselves are not gods but are created beings, as subject to God's will as are humans. In spite of an age-old misconception, humans do not become angels when they die. The angelic ranks were formed long before humankind was scooped from the dust of Earth.

Although angels are frequently called spirits, it is often implied in the Bible that they can possess corporeal bodies when seen on Earth. Even though angels throughout history have often been mistaken for ordinary humans when judged by their appearance alone, those individuals who have confronted them have often felt the physical effects of the beings' other-worldly powers.

In the teachings of Islam, there are three distinct species of intelligent beings in the universe. There are first the angels (*malak* in Arabic), a high order of beings created of Light; second are ethereal, perhaps even multidimensional, entities known as al-jinn; and third are human beings, fashioned of the stuff of Earth and born into physical bodies.

The Ahrimanes, Fallen Angels Who Seek to Enslave Humankind

According to Persian and Chaldean tradition, the *Ahrimanes* are fallen angels who, out of revenge for being expelled from heaven, continually torment the apex of God's creation, the human inhabitants of Earth. The old legends have it that the Ahrimanes decided to inhabit the *Ahrimane-Abad*, the space between the Earth and the fixed stars.

Military and aviation historian Trevor James Constable has come to the conclusion that it is the Ahrimanic powers that are trying to seize control of our planet. He believes that Inner Space, not Outer Space, is the invasion route chosen by the Ahrimanic powers. The choices we make, Constable says, and the extent to which we utilize balancing forces to neutralize the Ahrimanic attacks, will bring us victory or defeat.

Because from time to time the Arhimanic entities have revealed themselves riding in etherically propelled vehicles that appear to represent a material technology far in advance of that possessed by humans, people have assumed that such UFOs are spacecraft from a scientifically superior extraterrestrial world. In addition, the Arhimanic beings have devised contact encounters with ingenuous human beings who can be used to serve certain ends in promulgating the thought that the Space Brothers come from outer space, rather than being deceivers from a nonmaterial dimension near at hand.

Constable decrees that the overall consequence of such deceptive contact encounters, wherein humans are set upon by the Ahrimanic humanoids, is that the world is led to believe that material craft and physical alien beings are involved. And if people are not convinced by the contactee, then he or she is labeled just another "flying saucer nut." Either way, the world gets a lie overlaid with confusion and ridicule while the Ahrimanic humanoids depart from view.

The Ahrimanic deceivers are everywhere, Constable warns, "unrecognized and often aided by humans who don't know that the Devil is indeed alive and well—and coming to Earth within the lifetime of millions now living."

One is always wise to "test the spirits" and attempt to determine if the counseling entity serves the dark side or the light side of the force. And such caution should be doubled in reports of UFO encounters, for in Constable's opinion, the Ahrimanic messengers inject themselves into such events in order to sow confusion, disorientation, and distrust among UFO investigators. Humans are constantly being seduced into doing the work of the nether forces because they simply do not acknowledge that such forces exist, let alone recognize how they work *into* and *upon* Earth life.

"Incomprehension of spiritual forces and the institutionalized denigration of the spirit in formal education make humanity pitifully vulnerable to dehumanizing, life-negative, and destructive trends," Constable says. "The Arhimanic intelligences confront humankind with a bewildering armory of advanced technical devices, transcendental abilities, and mind-bending powers. Armed only with mechanistic thought and an unbalanced technology ... the human posture for meeting this stupendous and unavoidable event is both unstable and inadequate."

Constable maintains that the hope of humankind lies in the expansion of human awareness. "If man can be shown where the battlefield is, the nature of the terrain, and the ways in which he is already being assaulted in this inner war, then the right tactics and strategy can be brought to bear against the inimical forces."

For centuries, the Ahrimanic entities have held as their goal the total enslavement of humankind. If they are unopposed, they will overwhelm humanity and take evolution wholly under their control. We must realize that in the struggle for mastery of Earth, we human beings and our souls are at once the goal of the battle and the battleground itself.

Cities, Towns, and Villages in North America Heavily Populated by Ghosts

There is not a single city, town, village, or hamlet in the world that does not have its own stories of ghosts, apparitions, phantoms, and haunted houses. For this directory, I have only selected a handful of places that best illustrate the commonality of human interaction with the world of spirits.

Anchorage, Alaska

Room 201 of the Courtyard by Marriot is haunted by a man who was found dead in that room. Another ghost, named Ken, roams the parking lot and the courtyard. A phantom cat is often reported in rooms 103 and 107.

The Dimond Center mall was built over a sacred tribal burial ground, which obviously disturbed many spirits because ghosts are frequently seen in the restrooms and corridors.

The ghost of a young girl is seen by custodians and students in the hallways of Hanshew Middle School.

The Historic Anchorage Hotel, the city's oldest hotel, is plagued by hauntings. Water faucets turn themselves off and on in rooms 215 and 217; a young girl is often seen in the second floor hall; and footsteps are often heard on the stairs although no one is on them.

Weird humanoid monsters are seen in the basement and auditorium of West High School; the beings may be the spirits of forest creatures that once roamed the land where the school was built.

Asheville, North Carolina

The ghost of a man who was murdered in the pantry of the Old Battery Park Hotel, now an apartment building, is still seen by residents.

When Clyde Erwin High School was built just outside Asheville in the 1970s, the Old County Home Graveyard was disturbed, thereby causing many restless spirits to haunt the school.

[569]

The Lady in Pink takes spectral delight in tickling the toes of guests who stay at the Grove Park Inn.

Visitors to the sprawling Biltmore Estate commonly report sightings of ghosts, as well as the sounds of voices, screaming, and maniacal laughter.

Albuquerque, New Mexico

Back in the 1800s, the building that currently houses the Job Corps Center was a convent where nuns looked after small children. One day, a sister went insane and began to kill her young charges, throwing many down a well. Awful, terror-filled cries of children are frequently reported, and some witnesses have seen the ghost of a woman dressed in black.

The Kimo Theater had its opening night in the autumn of 1927, and many spirits from that era were so impressed that they return again and again.

Guests at the Desert Sands Motel on W140 report cold spots, ghostly voices, and doors that unlock and open of their own volition.

Glowing lights, mysterious black-robed figures, and the sounds of crying voices manifest in the Carrie Tingly Children's Hospital.

The lobby and certain rooms on the bottom floor of the Ramada Hotel are haunted by a woman who was murdered by a lover who had grown tired of her.

At the Radisson Hotel, screaming can be heard issuing from vacant rooms. Female guests complain of being shaken awake by the hands of ghost children.

Bakersfield, California

A lady with a long, flowing robe is seen walking along the canal in Central Park just before dawn.

The ghosts of a girl in a prom dress and a boy wearing a letterman's sweater are seen in the top row of the bleachers at Bakersfield High School.

Witnesses have seen the ghost of a workman who fell from the rafters during the construction of Harvey Auditorium at Bakersfield High.

Spirits have pushed, groped, and grabbed customers at the bar in Club Paradise.

Melodrama Musical Theatre is haunted by the ghost of the former owner of the building.

Visitors to Pioneer Village frequently report seeing ghost children in front of the old school building.

Baltimore, Maryland

Fort McHenry shelters a host of ghosts who still guard Baltimore vigilantly. Lights, shadowy figures, and voices have been reported for many decades.

A floating lady and a man who walks out of his grave are regularly seen by visitors to the Gardens of Faith Cemetery.

Todd's Farm is home to numerous ghosts, including a lady who sits by a candle in the attic window, awaiting the return of her soldier lover.

North Oakes Retirement Community was formerly Mt. Wilson State Hospital, a sanitarium for tuberculosis patients, whose moans and cries for medical help can still be heard.

The house of Edgar Allan Poe is said to be haunted by the spirit of a rather rotund female dressed in gray. Those wishing a glimpse of the master of the macabre's ghost are said to have a better chance at Westminster Church graveyard, where Poe is buried beside his wife Virginia.

The ghosts of three sailors who were killed in action aboard the USS *Constitution* remain on duty.

Boston, Massachusetts

The ghost of one of the city's former mayors has been seen many times in the seat where he died at the Emerson Majestic Theatre (built in 1903).

Numerous ghosts have been reported by employees and guests at the Parker House Hotel. Most of the apparitions sighted have been of people from the early 1800s.

Boston Common is the home for many ghosts, including two aristocratic women in nineteenth-century attire who vanish when witnesses approach them.

The Pilot House was built in 1839 and originally served as a dormitory for visiting pilots and captains. For many years, witnesses have heard the sounds of men laughing and talking and doors opening and closing.

A lady in black haunts Fort Warren, which served as a prison during the Civil War.

Burlington, Vermont

Among the numerous restless spirits that seem to have enrolled for eternity at the University of Vermont are: A female ghost in 1890s-era clothing appears in the agriculture department; poltergeists disturb the Center for Counseling and Testing; Converse Hall is haunted by the spirit of a student who committed suicide; Redstone Hall has a ghost that runs through walls and frightens female students; Coolidge Hall harbors a number of ghosts, including one who awakens sleeping residents by standing over their beds and staring at them.

An employee who committed suicide haunts the basement and kitchen area at Carbur's Restaurant.

An abandoned building on the outskirts of the Castleton State College campus houses antiques and museum pieces that continually get rearranged and tossed about—although no one ever enters the place.

Calgary, Alberta, Canada

Grace Hospital is haunted by a woman who died in one of the delivery rooms during childbirth.

The ghostly form of a woman is seen walking in the shallow area of Bow River, where she is said to have drowned in 1910.

Visitors to Heritage Park have seen the spirit of a beautiful, smiling woman holding her baby.

Witnesses claim the woods next to St. Mary's College are haunted by weird entities.

The ghosts of murder victims and individuals who committed suicide are seen in the upstairs bedrooms of Deane House.

Chicago, Illinois

For years witnesses have heard the cries and seen the ethereal form of the Sobbing Woman of Archer Woods Cemetery.

Over the decades more than 100 glowing ghosts have been sighted in Bachelor's Grove Cemetery. See the photograph of the young woman taken by the Ghost Research Society elsewhere in this book.

In 1929 Al Capone held a gory Valentine's Day party at S-M-C Cartage Company for seven of Bugs Moran's men, who were lined up against a brick wall and killed. Over the years, many witnesses claim to have seen seven shadowy spirits and heard screams and machine-gun fire. Although the building where the massacre took place has been torn down, people still believe the site to be haunted.

Patrons of the Dome Room nightclub claim that haunting phenomena occurs nightly in the building, which once housed a morgue.

Guests and employees have reported a large number of paranormal occurrences at the Congress Hotel.

Cincinnati, Ohio

Security guards report that an extremely tall entity frequents one of the sarcophagi at the Cincinnati Museum of Art.

Employees and guests at the Country Hearth Hotel have noted mysterious phenomena occurring in room 331, as well as in room 431, which is directly above it.

The ghost of a little, blond, blue-eyed girl in a blue dress haunts King's Island theme park. She is said to be joined by spirits that haunt the observation deck of the Eiffel Tower, the roller coaster, and the Octopus ride.

Sister Mary Carlos haunts the auditorium at Mother of Mercy High School.

Cincinnati Zoo remains the stalking ground of the spirit of a lioness, whose glowing eyes have stared unblinkingly at many patrons from shadowed areas.

Colorado Springs, Colorado

Employees and guests at the Broadmoor Hotel claim to have heard the screams and cries of the desperate victims of a fire that occurred there many years ago.

The spirits of laborers who died building Gold Camp Road, originally a railroad line from Colorado Springs to Cripple Creek, are often sighted by those who travel the road.

Years ago a school bus filled with elementary school children was in a terrible traffic accident in the Camp Road tunnels. The ghosts of the bus driver and the children who were killed are seen in and around the tunnels.

Pioneer's Museum is haunted by the spirit of a manager who was murdered in the late 1950s by an employee over a salary dispute.

Dearborn, Michigan

Many witnesses have reported seeing a ghost in an old-fashioned uniform at the Henry Ford estate; some believe it to be Ford's butler. See the photograph elsewhere in this book taken by the Michigan Ghost Watchers of the ghostly image of a man in one of Ford's automobiles.

When a new gym was being added to Divine Child High School, a construction worker fell from the scaffolding, and witnesses say the building is haunted by his spirit.

Firefighters at Fire Station No. 2 claim that the tall, shadowy figure they see in the station after dark is a fireman who won't allow death to force him into retirement.

Crestwood High in Dearborn Heights has experienced a wide range of haunting phenomena, including sightings of ghosts, objects being moved, and the sounds of voices echoing through empty hallways.

El Paso, Texas

Shortly after midnight, an area of Concordia Cemetery that contains the graves of dozens of children—all victims of an early smallpox epidemic—reverberates with the sounds of children laughing and playing.

The ghosts of cavalry troopers have been seen in Fort Bliss, including that of a soldier who hangs from the rafters in Building 13.

On the outskirts of the city, many witnesses claimed to have seen "El Muerto," the "dead one," with his head hanging by a rawhide throng attached to the saddle as he rides his ghostly steed through the desert.

The J.C. Machuca Apartments were built over a tribal burial ground, and residents complain of shadowy figures in their rooms.

Ysleta High School is haunted by the ghost of a cheerleader who committed suicide in a restroom, and by a small boy who died when he fell off the stage in the auditorium.

Gainesville, Florida

The "Blue House" of the Sweet Water Bed and Breakfast Inn has a ghost that may hearken back to the days when the place was a plantation. The maids complain of furniture moving around, and some guests feel the spirit pressing down on their chests at night.

The ghost of a female patron who was killed in the upstairs restroom of the Purple Porpoise is often seen and felt. On occasion, the hostile spirit of her murderer also manifests and molests female guests.

A female student at the University of Florida who jumped to her death from Beatty Towers haunts the halls and some of the rooms in the towers.

Gettysburg, Pennsylvania

Many visitors have reported witnessing spirit re-enactments of segments of the great battle that took place near here on July 1–3, 1863. Frequently cited are areas near Devil's Den, Cemetery Hill, and Gettysburg National Military Park.

Farnsworth House Inn is considered by many to be one of the most haunted houses in the United States. Among the numerous ghosts seen are a midwife attending to a young woman in labor and three Confederate soldiers at their post in the garret of the house. The voice of a soldier singing to comfort his dying friend is also heard.

Houston, Texas

Motorists on Christman Road look out for a phantom female hitchhiker in a purple dress.

Jefferson Davis Hospital was built upon the final earthly resting place of 3,000 Civil War veterans and victims of yellow fever epidemics. Certain hallways and rooms are teeming with the spirits of nurses, doctors, and patients.

Beer mugs and plates loaded with food fly across the room at the Ale House Pub and Eatery.

Although Klein Collins High School is new, it was built over an old burial ground, thereby provoking many mysterious sounds and paranormal experiences in its rooms and hallways.

Indianapolis, Indiana

Nighttime security officers at the Old Central State Hospital and Asylum claim a nightmarish cacophony of screams, groans, and cries for help, as well as sightings of people who vanish.

The House of Blue Lights on Meridian Street is haunted by the spirit of a woman whose sorrowful husband could not part with his beautiful young wife after her death. He kept her body in a special glass coffin in their home, as he couldn't bear to bury her.

The ghost of a young firefighter, who died in the early 1990s as he valiantly tried to extinguish the flames at the Indianapolis Athletic Club, often awakens guests in the middle of the night.

There are those who claim to have seen a spirit re-enactment of the 1960s' murder of a witness in an elevator at the Indianapolis City-County Building.

Kansas City, Missouri

According to witnesses, there are eight ghosts in the Donaldson House/Kansas City Art Institute, but only one is a friendly spirit.

The ghosts of young girls in long white dresses have been sighted as they merrily play together in Elmwood Cemetery.

Many individuals claim that the entire shoreline around Houston Lake—with emphasis on the beach area—is haunted by some very bizarre entities.

Several guests of the Hotel Savoy who have stayed in room 505 have had the ghost of Betsy Ward manifest in the tub as they take a bath.

Strawberry Hill has evolved from a mansion to an orphanage and is currently a museum. The ghosts of the couple that built the mansion have been sighted, as well as two nuns, who attended to the children when the place was an orphanage.

Laredo, Texas

The building that currently houses La Posada Hotel was formerly a convent, which explains the spectral nun that guests often see in the halls; but nothing can truly explain the actions of a ghost that assumes the exact image of employees for the purpose of tricking the staff and management.

The Civic Center is said to be haunted by the spirit of a custodian who was killed when curtain weights fell on the stage.

When Martin High School was built, no attention was given to the task of moving the bodies from the old cemetery on which the building would rest. Consequently, strange sounds are heard throughout the school, and shadowy figures haunt the gym.

The ghost of a mud-caked woman in a white dress is said to walk in the water near the banks of Zacate creek.

Los Angeles, California

Belmont High School is haunted by the spirit of a young girl who died in a fire during the early 1900s, when Belmont was a private school for girls.

Strange phenomena in the building of Southwest Law School, built in 1929 and formerly home to an I. Magnum/Bullocks department store, are attributed to the spirit of a little girl who was said to have been pushed into an elevator shaft sometime in the 1930s.

Apparitions of weird entities haunt the 18th floor and the parking garage at the Los Angeles Airport Marriott. Guests have reported strange odors, sounds, and being engulfed by feelings of absolute terror.

Employees and security officers report three ghosts at the Neutrogena Corporation factory. The wife and son of Neutrogena's founder were murdered execution style in the building, and individuals working late in the factory have seen a woman dressed in white and a child. The third entity has not been seen, but a menacing growl signals its arrival.

Westchester High School is haunted by a student who died when he fell while playing basketball, crushing his skull and breaking his neck. Two other spirits, a boy and a girl, have been sighted in various places in the school.

The performances never end at the Palace Theatre. Over the years, employees and psychical researchers have determined that as many as 24 ghosts of actors, stage hands, and audience members haunt the building.

Louisville, Kentucky

The ghost of a girl in a prom dress is seen at the top of the hill on Mitchell Hill Road, near the spot where she and her date are said to have been killed on prom night.

The Deaf Community Center was once a private mansion inhabited by the Hampton family. The sounds of the lavish parties and balls that the Hamptons hosted can still be heard, and Mrs. Hampton has been seen walking the hallways.

The ghost of a male student who was shot and killed in the lobby of Meyzek Middle School has haunted the school since the 1930s.

Milwaukee, Wisconsin

Perhaps because the Stritch dormitory at Cardinal Stritch University was a former convent, today's students often encounter the ghosts of nuns in their rooms and in the halls.

Students residing in Humphrey Hall at Marquette University must learn to live with the ghosts of children who died in the building when it served as the Milwaukee Children's Hospital. Even the security monitors have picked up images of singing, laughing, screaming children.

The bar area in the Walker House is haunted by the ghost of a horse thief who was hanged on a tree outside the establishment.

Customers and security guards at the Grand Avenue Mall are perplexed by the figure of a dancing ghost on the second floor.

New Orleans, Louisiana

Some guests craving a ghostly encounter choose rooms on the third floor of the Castle Inn. The bed and breakfast is haunted by the playful spirit of a little girl and by a black man who burned to death in one of the wood sheds.

Numerous ghosts appear at various places in the French Quarter, but locals warn against the handsome specter of a man who was allegedly a real-life vampire and reportedly still takes delight in assaulting women.

Le Petit Théâtre du Vieux Carré is said to be haunted by the ghost of a young bride who fell to her death in the courtyard below, the specter of an old man seated in one of the theater rows, and spirits who touch actors with cold but invisible hands when they are backstage.

According to tradition, at least four spirits haunt O'Flaherty's Irish Channel Pub—two victims of a murder-suicide and two former owners.

The Morgue Bar and Lounge is well named, for the building in which it is housed served as the city's first integrated mortuary during the yellow fever epidemic of 1853. Paranormal activity has been reported throughout the place, but the ladies' restroom is particularly active.

During the Civil War, the Hotel Provincial was converted into a hospital. Numerous guests and employees have reported viewing spirit re-enactments of the terrible days when wounded troops lay screaming in pain and frantic doctors and nurses worked desperately to save lives.

Portland, Oregon

There is something so frightening in the basement of the Lotus nightclub that most employees refuse to venture down there alone.

The ghost of a hanged horse thief and his dog haunt the camp ground at Scapponia Park.

The Fairmount Apartments once housed a grand hotel that was built in 1905 to celebrate the centennial of the Lewis and Clark expedition. Residents on the lower floors report a sinister presence.

The ghost of a young woman dressed in Victorian-era clothing haunts the theater at the University of Portland.

The Villa St. Rose School for Girls is haunted by the spirits of small children who died there when the place was an orphanage maintained by nuns.

Salt Lake City, Utah

The City-County Building harbors ghosts on all five floors. According to employees and visitors, ghosts include two children who were killed in an accident during construction; a woman who seems to be searching for lost children; a former judge; and a former mayor of Salt Lake City.

Even nonbelievers in the spirit world are creeped out when they read that Lilly's tombstone in the Salt Lake City Cemetery decrees that she was a "victim of the Beast 666."

Several murders in bygone days have led to poltergeist phenomena appearing in many buildings in the West Temple and 2nd South area.

A lady in a purple dress seems to head a veritable community of spirits at the Utah State Historical Society building.

San Antonio, Texas

The atmosphere is extremely melancholy at the Alamo. Some sensitive people have viewed spirit re-enactments of the fierce struggle that took place there in 1836.

Shadowy figures have been sighted in the halls and rooms of Brackenridge Villa Mansion. The building was constructed in the 1840s, over a site held sacred by Native American tribespeople.

The spirits of soldiers and tribespeople have often been seen walking at the side of Old Nacogdoches Road.

Our Lady of the Lake University is haunted by the ghost of a former janitor who dwells in the basement of the library, and by the spirits of nuns who walk the halls.

Through the years employees, staff members, and guests claim to have encountered as many as 38 ghosts at the Menger Hotel, including Teddy Roosevelt and a number of his Rough Riders.

San Diego, California

A woman in white appears at a table in a shadowy corner of El Fandango Restaurant.

The sounds of marching ghosts and other phenomena have kept many a guest awake throughout the night at the Horton Grand Hotel.

The ghost of Kate Morgan haunts room 3312 and the beach area in front of the Hotel Del Coronado.

Yankee Jim, Thomas Whaley, and an entourage of spirits both welcome and unnerve visitors to the Whaley House.

Your prayers for the peace of her soul will please the ghost of "Amanda," a tall, former model who committed suicide in room 325 of the Vagabond Motel when she was depressed over her addiction to drugs.

San Francisco, California

A headless man, thought to be the ghost of a victim of the 1989 earthquake, knocks on the windows of cars driving toward Oakland on the Bay Bridge.

Before the Queen Anne Hotel offered the elegant, Victorian style accommodations that it provides today, it served as a school for girls. Guests and employees frequently encounter the spirit of the headmistress, who died heartbroken when the school was closed.

In the 1920s a young woman committed suicide by by leaping into Stowe Lake because she sought to hide her unwelcome pregnancy from her parents. The woman's ghost can still be seen walking in despair around Strawberry Hill in Stowe Lake Golden Gate Park.

The San Francisco Arts Institute attributes its various restless spirits to the possibility that it was built over the graves of earthquake victims from the early 1900s.

Savannah, Georgia

Before guests may stay in room 204 at the 1790 Inn, they must sign a waiver at the front desk stating that the management is not responsible for any items of clothing stolen by "Anne," the ghost who haunts the inn.

Hanging Square derived its name quite logically, as it was the place where the city's criminals were executed. Spanish moss will not grow on the bough where Anna Reilly, a teenaged murderess who was the first woman hanged in Georgia, was executed, and a stiff, cold breeze is always felt around the tree.

The Hamilton-Turner Inn was built in 1837 by Samuel Hamilton, a wealthy jeweler and former mayor of Savannah. Many guests at the inn have learned that the "ghost bird" carvings on the roof will not keep away spirits who open and close doors and windows, directing cold drafts toward them.

The Forsyth Park Inn, built in 1896 as a private residence, is haunted by the ghost of Lottie, a young girl who murdered a woman she suspected of being her uncle's mistress by poisoning her tea, only to learn that she had killed the wrong woman. Lottie's mother is also said to haunt the stairway and hallways of the inn.

Savannah was settled in 1733, and as Georgia's oldest city it has seen fierce Revolutionary War battles, three deadly yellow fever epidemics, and a harsh period of occupation during the Civil War. Because of the city's tumultuous past, many researchers claim that hundreds of hotels, inns, and private homes harbor ghosts.

Seattle, Washington

Both employees and guests complain of the loud party taking place on the ninth floor of the Claremont Hotel—which stops abruptly whenever anyone investigates. Witnesses say that judging from the music that blares forth from the unseen merrymakers, it sounds like a party from the Roaring Twenties.

The spirit of a Native American woman haunts the Pike Place Public Market, walking the area that was once sacred ground to her tribe.

When the University YMCA is devoid of human occupants, footsteps and voices still issue from the upper floors of the building. An eerie presence is often felt in the basement.

The Hunt Club Bar in the Sorrento Hotel plays host to the antics of entities that enjoy moving objects, especially glasses, across the room.

St. Louis, Missouri

A noisy ghost named George, who is often seen in a white suit and white hat, haunts Powell Symphony Hall.

The Lemp Mansion has numerous cold spots, and visitors often have the feeling that they are being watched and have reported being touched by invisible beings.

Although the Old City Hospital has not been used since the 1960s, witnesses have reported seeing shadowy figures moving behind windows that are not boarded, and hearing screams issuing from the vacant building.

Six Flags Theme Park is home to the ghost of a little girl, a spirit named Stella, and a bizarre entity that makes an eerie squealing noise that sounds like a pig.

People claim to have heard babies crying in Coopers Cemetery. Others report the ghost of an old man carrying a lantern.

Toronto, Ontario, Canada

Custodians and security guards on night duty at the Goodwill executive offices at 108 George Street have reported that electrical appliances turn themselves off and on, and voices are often heard coming from empty offices.

The spirits of a number of soldiers who capsized their boat and drowned in Grenadier Pond in the 1800s are sighted on nights with stormy weather.

The Mackenzie House has a wide variety of poltergeist and spirit activity, including misty, glowing figures.

A ghost with a nasty disposition that inhabits the Mynah Bird Coffee House likes to make chairs, dishes, and other objects become airborne.

The Lady in Red mysteriously appears, sings a bit of a tune, and disappears near the Old Bay Street Subway Station.

Tucson, Arizona

The ghost of a woman in a long white dress often pushes employees at Centennial Hall off balance. The more benevolent spirit of man seems to be on duty to assist anyone who might be harmed by the nasty entity.

The Fred G. Acosta Job Corps Center is haunted by the ghost of a young girl who committed suicide in the restroom on the second floor.

The rebuilt Pioneer Hotel is said to be haunted by the spirits of those who died in a fire that wrecked the original building.

Ghostly miners with their glowing headlamps have been seen in the San Miguel Magma cooper mine.

The victim of a jealous boyfriend haunts the room at the Radisson Hotel where she was discovered with another man. Another female spirit is heard weeping in the ballroom area.

Winnipeg, Manitoba, Canada

The Fort Garry Hotel is haunted by a ghost that takes delight in crawling in bed with the guests. Maids have claimed to have seen blood on the walls of room 202, where a despondent female guest hanged herself.

The spirits of three hanged men haunt the parking lot of Little Mountain Park.

Watchful presences are sensed and clearly audible voices are heard among the ruins of the old St. Norbert Monastery.

Some researchers feel that the spirits of actors Laurence Irving and Mabel Hackney may be responsible for much of the ghostly phenomena at the Walker Theatre. The couple died in 1914, after less than a week of their run at the theatre. They may have felt cheated by fate and continue to perform in spirit.

The old St. Vital Hotel appears to be haunted by the ghost of a man who was murdered outside the back door in the 1970s.

Resources

Haunted Cemeteries: <www.zerotime.com/ghosts/cemet/.htm>.

Hauk, Dennis William. *Haunted Places*. New York: Penguin USA, reprint edition, 1996.

———. *International Directory of Haunted Places*. New York: Penguin, 2000.

Kerman, Frances. *Ghostly Encounters: True Stories of America's Haunted Inns and Hotels*. New York: Warner Books, 2002.

Mead, Robin. *Haunted Hotels: A Guide to American and Canadian Inns and Their Ghosts.* Nashville, TN: Rutledge Hill Press, 1995.

Norman, Michael, and Beth Scott. *Historic Haunted America.* New York: Tor Books, 1996.

————. *Haunted Heritage.* New York: Forge, 2002.

Obiwan's Ghosts, Hauntings, and Other Strange Phenomena <www.ghosts.org>.

Shadowlands: <www.shadowlands.net>.

Smith, Susy. *Haunted Houses for the Millions.* Los Angeles: Sherbourne Press, Inc., 1967.

————. *Prominent American Ghosts.* New York: Dell, 1969.

Taylor, Troy. *Beyond the Grave.* Alton, IL: Whitechapel Productions Press, 2001.

Wlodarski, Anne Powell, and Robert James Wlodarski. *Dinner and Spirits: A Guide to America's Most Haunted Restaurants, Taverns, and Inns.* iUniverse.com (print on demand), 2001.

GHOST HUNTERS, RESEARCHERS, AND RESOURCES

Adventures Beyond
<www.adventuresbeyond.com>
Documentary filmmaker Bob Schott and his crew have produced excellent films (Witches, Ghosts, and Phantoms and America's Most Haunted) dealing with the Bell Witch, ghosts, and mysterious phenomena.

Rick Aiello
E-mail: rickdxer@aol.com
Rick Aiello's many personal experiences with the paranormal have led him to become a collector of accounts that deal with the unexplained, and a researcher of the unknown and unusual.

American Association of Electronic Voice Phenomena
<www.aaevp.com>
E-mail: aaevp@annap.annap.infi.net

American Ghost Society
<www.prairieghosts.com>
The American Ghost Society was founded in 1996 by Troy and Amy Taylor. The goals of the group are to seek out and authenticate evidence of ghosts and conduct research into paranormal activity.

American Society for Paranormal Research and Investigation
Brian A. Schill, Founder
4661 Donovan Street
Orlando, FL 32808
E-mail: aspiusa@aol.com

American Society for Psychical Research Newsletter
Fax: (212) 496-2497

Atlantic Paranormal Society
<www.the-atlantic-paranormal-society.com>
The Atlantic Paranormal Society provides a list of 50 "carefully chosen groups across the country" that have shown excellence and discretion in handling paranormal investigations.

Avalon Foundation
<www.theavalonfoundation.org>
Nicholas Reiter and his partner Lori Schillig have conducted research into ghostly and paranormal phenomena since 1996. They have a large amount of quality material on their website and in their files, including some excellent photographic evidence. For a scholarly look at a particular ghost photograph: <www.alliancelink.com/users/avalon/m1photo .htm>; for information on ghost photography

[581]

in general:
<www.alliancelink.com/sers/avalon/photos.ht
m>. Go to <www.alliancelink.
com/users/avalon/fieldstudies.htm> for investigative case reports.

Barcon Video Productions
<www.barcon.com>
3653 Mesa Lila Lane
Glendale, CA 91208
*Director of photography Barry Conrad heads a
group of researchers and documentary film-
makers who have produced high-quality films
such as* Unknown Encounter *and* California's Most Haunted.

Paul Bartholomew, Author, Lecturer, Investigator of the Unexplained
56 Mt St.
Whitehall, NY 12887
E-mail: yetimanape@yahoo

Clarisa Bernhardt, Intuitive
P.O. Box 1922 Stn. Main
Winnipeg, Manitoba
R3C 3R2 Canada
E-mail: clarisabernhardt@hotmail.com
*Highly respected intuitive-medium Clarisa
Bernhardt provides interdimensional and paranormal explorations. She is a popular conference speaker and has conducted several
workshops regarding the development of intuitive abilities. Bernhardt serves as an intuitive
consultant and advisor to presidents of several
international companies.*

Carissa of the Spirits
<www.carissas.homestead.com>
*Carissa's interaction with paranormal phe-
nomena have been documented by her grandmother Norma and mother Terri for many
years. They were featured on a segment of
ABC's* World's Scariest Ghosts Caught on
Tape *(October 2000).*

Celestial Visions School of Metaphysical Arts
<www.cvsop.com>

*Director Clark Schmidt, PhD, has studied the
fields of metaphysics and parapsychology for
42 years. The website <www.paravision.
homestead.com> contains information about
the school's para-plasma and orb research.*

Patrick Cross, Ghost Researcher
<www.globalserve.net/~scifi/enter.htm>
*Patrick Cross has investigated and researched
ghosts and paranormal phenomena for over 15
years and is considered one of Canada's top
authorities in the field. Cross also conducts
walks and tours on the ghostly folklore of
Burlington, Ontario, Canada.*

Richard T. Crowe, Researcher, Folklorist, Ghost Tour Director
<www.ghosttours.com>
*Richard T. Crowe conducted his first Chicago
Ghost Tour while he was completing his stud-
ies at DePaul University in 1973. Intent on
pursuing ghostlore wherever the quest may lead
him, Crowe has visited Ireland, England,
Scotland, Yugoslavia, Jamaica, Hong Kong,
Mexico, and many cities in the United States.
He appears often on radio and television, and
his lectures and tours fill up fast.*

Daytona Beach Paranormal Research Group
<www.dbprginc.org>
<www.hauntsofdaytona.com>
E-mail: hauntsofdaytona@aol.com
*It took 18 months to do all the background
research and documentation necessary for the
the initial Haunts of the World's Most Famous
Beach Ghost Tours. The Daytona Beach
Paranormal Research Group is now a nonprofit corporation, and a large percentage of
income garnered from the popular tours goes to
cemetery preservation and restoration. The
tours blend local history, folklore, and scientific data. The Riverfront Park Ghost Walk is a
two-hour-long walking tour of the downtown
business district. The Deland Ghost Walk is
90-minute-long walking tour through the business district.*

Delaware Paranormal Investigations
<pages.zdnet.com/dprs/ghosts/>

Henry Dorst, Researcher, Vancouver, British Columbia
<www.vitalenergy.biz/vital_means.html>
In 1984 Henry Dorst began to inspect homes for stressful levels of EMF's and Geopathic Earth Radiation, as well as to provide remedial methods for those afflicted by haunting phenomena. Dorst states: "In one case [ghosts] stayed at the skeleton of a house destroyed in a fire, making the property [unsellable] for several years. In this case, within a week of their 'release' this property sold."

Ghost Hunter
<www.rb59.com/ghosth>
Robert Benjamin has created some very user-friendly software for the ghost hunter.

Ghost Research Society
<www.ghostresearch.org>
The Ghost Research Society was formed in 1977 as a clearing house for reports of ghosts, hauntings, poltergeist, and life-after-death encounters. Society members actively research and investigate private homes and businesses. They also analyze alleged spirit photographs, video, and audio tapes. The GRS is currently helmed by the well-known and highly respected ghost researcher Dale Kaczmarek, who also produces the Ghost Trackers Newsletter. Kaczmarek often appears on television and radio programs, and he has contributed to numerous books and periodicals. He has amassed one of the world's largest collections of authentic spirit photographs and tape-recorded spirit voices. His personal goal is to prove the existence of ghosts and life after death through his continuing research, study, and investigations.

Ghosts and Haunts in Missouri
<www.missourighosts.net>
<www.stlghosts.net>
Terry, Joe, Cathe, Doug, Adam, Luke, and Milos actively conduct free investigations of private residences in the St. Louis area. The research group has about 100 online members. Check their websites for information about their two ghost videos, filmed during actual investigations of St. Louis mansions, cemeteries, and downright spooky places.

Ghost Stalkers of West Tennessee
<www.ghoststalker.topcities.com>
Ghost Stalkers does not claim to exorcise spirits or to know all the answers about ghost phenomena. The group's main goal is to "help people, conduct extensive investigations, provide documentation, and ultimately prove that there is life after death."

Ghost Trackers Newsletter
<www.ghostresearch.org>

Irene F. Hughes, Intuitive, Medium, Seer
<www.irene-psychic.com>
E-mail: espirene@aol.com
Irene F. Hughes is one of the most accurate psychic-sensitives and mediums in the United States. Her talents have been employed by numerous police departments, and she is responsible for locating many missing people. Her abilities as a medium are featured several times in this book.

International Ghost Hunters Society
<www.ghostweb.com>
Dr. Sharon A. Gill and Dr. Dave R. Oester believe the spirits of the dead provide evidence that life exists beyond the grave, and their ministry focuses on teaching people how to confirm that there is life after death. It was Dave and Sharon who coined the term "orb" to describe the mysterious balls of light often seen in places with haunting phenomena. Today, the ghost-hunting community universally accepts "orb" as a name to describe spirit entities. Their website is one of the largest and most popular ghost-hunting websites on the Internet, with over 9,000 ghost photos and 300 EVP ghost voices posted on the site. In 1998 they offered the first home study course for certification as a ghost hunter. In 2000 they added a certification

course for paranormal investigators. Currently, their membership rolls exceed 14,000 members from 87 countries worldwide, and they still offer free membership to their Internet-based ghost-hunting organization. Dave and Sharon have coauthored the following books: Twilight Visitors, Haunted Reality, and America's Haunted Highways Revealed. The couple appears on prime time television programs on The History Channel, Discovery, TLC, Arts & Entertainment, Fox, and ABC; they also appear on the popular radio show The Jeff Rense Program on a monthly basis.

Lafayette Ghost Trackers

<www.indianaghosts.org>
Linda Schumm is the director of the Lafayette chapter of Indiana Ghost Trackers, which was started by herself and Dave Edwards. They have 100 members with chapters in Merriville, South Bend, Indianapolis, Lafayette, and Evansville.

Maryland Ghost and Spirit Association

<www.marylandghosts.com>
This group was founded a few years ago by Beverly Listsinger with her husband and daughter. It is dedicated to investigating ghost and paranormal phenomena at Civil War and other sites throughout Maryland. The group currently has over 800 members.

Michigan Ghost Watchers

www.ghostwatchers.org>
E-mail: ghostwatcher@comcast.net
Michigan Ghost Watchers is composed of a group of serious paranormal investigators. According to their president, Cindy Blake, "It is our goal to acquire proof that the spirit world exists. We use scientific techniques to collect our data, including cameras, temperature sensors, electromagnetic field detectors, and the like. We feel our research is vital to gain an understanding of ourselves and the world around us."

Lee Moorhead, Medium and Psychic-Sensitive

<www.stargaze.com>
Lee Moorhead has been known for many years as the "Psychic of the Hamptons," and she is highly regarded for her intuitive abilities.

MVD Ghostchasers

<members.tripod.com/azspiritchaser/home.htm>
Founded in 1995 by Debe Branning, MVD Ghostchasers conducts investigations throughout the state of Arizona.

New England Society for Psychical Research

<www.Warrens.net>
<www.NESPR.com>
NESPR Journal
Cheryl Wicks, editor
P.O. Box 41
Monroe, CT 06468
Ed and Lorraine Warren, the internationally famous ghost investigators and demonologists, can be reached at their personal website or at their New England Society for Psychical Research website.

Frank "Nick" Nocerino

<www.crystalskullsociety.org/meetnick.htm>
Many consider Frank Nocerino to be the dean of American ghost researchers and an expert on the paranormal.

Office of Paranormal Investigations (OPI)

<www.mindreader.com>
P.O. Box 875
Orinda, CA 94563-0875
E-mail: esper@california.com
Established in 1989 by its director, internationally known author-lecturer-teacher-researcher Loyd Auerbach, the Office of Paranormal Investigations provides a number of services to the general public, the media, as well as the scientific, business, and legal communities. Investigations of apparitions, poltergeists, and hauntings are conducted, as are explorations of

other psychic and anomalous experiences. Reasonable fees are charged for investigations and consulting services. OPI conducts seminars, offers seminars and lectures on videotape, and provides a number of audiotapes to the general public. Also visit the site of the new international group, the Paranormal Research Organization (PRO) at <www.paranormal-research.org>. Founded by both professional and amateur paranormal investigators in 2002, PRO includes a variety of experienced and knowledgeable parapsychologists, paranormal investigators, counselors, and experts in other fields. PRO's goals include creating a network of knowledgeable and ethical field researchers and investigators; providing a central web-based repository for researchers to share data; offering a website with information pages specifically designed for the general public and the media; publishing materials for the interested public; and providing educational materials and opportunities for those who are interested in increasing their knowledge and skills in paranormal investigations.

Paranormal Investigations

P.O. Box 77
Barnegat, NJ 08005-0077
E-mail: PsiQuest@aol.com
Director T. Clarke Lynes received his formal training in paranormal investigations from famed researcher Loyd Auerbach, but his interest in the paranormal and haunting phenomena began in 1948. Lynes states: "I enter into an investigation with the serious intent of gathering as much information as is possible from the witnesses and from anyone else who has knowledge of the events. The goal is to be able to make an informed determination of the possible cause of the events—whether they may have natural explanations or possibly be paranormal in nature." On occasions, Lynes enlists the services of medium Linda Marrero of Edison, New Jersey, to accompany him.

Pennsylvania Ghost Hunters Society

<home.supernet.com/~rfisher/pghs.html>

Rick Fisher founded the Pennsylvania Ghost Hunters Society in 1997, and he has taught thousands through the Haunted Workshops and the Pennsylvania Paranormal Conference that he hosts each year. Fisher is currently a part time instructor at a local community college, where he gives classes on investigating the paranormal. The Pennsylvania Ghost Hunters Society conducts numerous active investigations and has obtained both photographic and EVP evidence that proves the existence of ghosts.

Janet Russell

<www.janetrussellpresents.com>
Janet Russell is a popular psychic-sensitive who also hosts her own television program, Beyond the Unexplained, and sponsors numerous psychic fairs in New York.

Richard Senate

<www.ghost-stalker.com>
E-mail: Ghostlamp@ojai.net
Since 1972 Richard Leonard Senate has investigated more than 200 haunted houses. He has visited Hawaii and the United Kingdom and was pleased to find both places haunted. Senate believes that the main focus of any psychic investigator is to collect and save data on paranormal events and then attempt to use the information to formulate a theory that explains why a place is haunted (if it really is) and name the identity of the ghost. He tries to examine each site as scientifically as possible. In 1995 he was the first ghost hunter on the internet with a website. Senate often appears on television and radio, and he conducts classes and special ghost tours for the public. He is the author of eight published books on the paranormal, including The Ghost Stalker's Guide to Haunted California, The Ghosts of the Ojai Valley, The Haunted Southland, and Ghosts of the Haunted Coast. For a reasonable fee and transportation, Senate is willing to travel anywhere to give lectures or to act as a consultant in psychic investiga-

tions. *Speaking engagements fill early, and he has lectures booked up to a year in advance.*

Michael Shinabery, Author and Researcher

P.O. Box 169
Cloudcroft, NM 88317

South Jersey Ghost Research

<www.southjerseyghostresearch.org>
South Jersey Ghost Research is a professional group of investigators that can trace its roots back to 1955. SJGR will assist people troubled by ghost phenomena in New Jersey, eastern Pennsylvania, Delaware, and New York City without charge. Investigations are discreet.

Spring Spirit Seekers

<www.springspiritseekers.com>
Founded in 2001 by Chris and Ginger Pennell in Spring, Texas, the group terms themselves "semi-scientists" and utilize instruments such as electromagnetic field readers and laser thermometers in their investigations.

Toronto Ghosts and Hauntings

<www.torontoghosts.org>
Toronto's oldest and best-known established society dedicated to the collection of data pertaining to ghosts and hauntings.

Utah Paranormal Exploration and Research

<www.uper.freewebspace.com>

Members of Utah Paranormal Exploration and Research make up a responsible team of investigators who do not trespass or go on to property uninvited. UPER is a nonprofit organization composed of professionals who share an interest in the unknown.

Washington State Ghost Society

<www.washingtonstateghostsociety.org>
Henry Bailey states that the Washington State Ghost Society is a nonprofit organization assisting individuals who believe or know they are experiencing paranormal activity: "We provide a free service to examine such activity, provide support, make recommendations, assist [in determining] whether the phenomena is, indeed, paranormal in origin or possibly could be attributed to the paranormal. The service is free and completely confidential. The society also endeavors to provide education and information regarding the field of paranormal investigations, primarily involved with the field of the paranormal relating to ghosts and survival after death."

Wausau Paranormal Research Society

<www.pat-wausau.org>
303 Sturgeon Eddy Road
Wausau, WI 54403
Todd Roll is the lead investigator of the Wausau Paranormal Research Society of Wausau, Wisconsin, a group that actively pursues reports of ghost phenomena in that region.

Appendix C

SELECTED FILMOGRAPHY

Ghost Stories with the Most Authentic Shudders

The Uninvited (1943)

I first saw this movie when I was seven years old, and some of the scenes left an indelible impression upon me. I have seen the film many times since that initial viewing, and on each occasion I've savored the intelligent and superbly paced script by Frank Partos and Dodie Smith that is eerie, compelling, and chilling. *The Uninvited* remains, in my opinion, one of the most authentic depictions of haunting phenomena ever placed on film. The principals, Ray Milland and Ruth Hussy, do a splendid job of portraying two intelligent, rational people who must deal with a house that is occupied by an evil entity. Roderick Fitzgerald (Milland) and his sister Pamela (Hussey) purchase a home in Cornwall that has been abandoned for many years. When Roderick goes off to London on business, Pamela soon discovers that the house is haunted. Gail Russell (a lovely, tragic actress who later committed suicide) plays Stella Meredith, a young woman with mediumistic abilities whose mysterious past is inextricably linked with the old house and the restless spirits within its dark corridors. Directed by Lewis Allen, the film was adapted from the novel by Dorothy Macardle and has a strong supporting cast, including Donald Crisp, Cornelia Otis Skinner, and Alan Napier. Special effects are virtually nonexistent. The film is extremely subtle in presenting the spirits, and therein lies much of its ability to seize the imagination and to provoke genuine chills. Wisely, director Allen never overplays his hand, but instead concentrates on allowing the audience to feel the mysterious threat from the spirit world along with the actors.

The Haunting (1963)

This film's portrayal of a serious investigation into haunting phenomena has made it one of my favorites. I especially appreciate director Robert Wise's use of subtlety in his presentation of the ghosts. Richard Johnson portrays Dr. Markway, a professor of anthropology who is interested in psychical research. He arrives at Hill House with the intention of conducting a number of experiments to see whether local stories of the mansion being cursed and haunted by evil spirits are true. To assist him in his research, he brings Eleanor (Julie Harris) and Theodora (Claire Bloom), two women who have had psychic experiences. Luke (Russ Tamblyn), the heir to Hill House, joins them, hoping that Dr. Markway will somehow exorcise the demons that have plagued his home so that he can sell the property. The presentation of the haunting phenomena in this film is extremely effective; Wise uses camera angles and lighting techniques that emphasize a sense of a terrible reality within the surrealistic world of the supernatural. Although the motion picture contains a number of chilling scenes, the spirits are ambiguous and at the same time very frightening. As the movie unfolds, perceptive viewers question how much of the paranormal phenomena is occuring in the minds and imaginations of the investigators. After viewers have pondered those questions, they will begin to wonder how much is going on in their own imaginations. While Wise's version of *The Haunting* (an adaptation of Shirley Jackson's novel, *The Haunting of Hill House*) remains one of the best haunted-house movies of all-time, the 1999 version by Jan De Bont, starring Liam Neeson, Lili Taylor, and Catherine Zeta-Jones includes over-emphasized, massive sets and extraordinary special effects that effectively eliminate any possibility of an eerie, scary atmosphere and remove nearly all traces of authentic psychical research.

The Changeling (1980)

Some consider this film the best haunted-house movie since *The Haunting*. A newly widowed man (George C. Scott) moves into an old mansion and discovers that the creepy place is haunted by the spirit of a murdered child. Scriptwriters William Gray and Diana Maddox provide a truly eerie ghost story that director Peter Medak builds skillfully into a superior supernatural tale. Other cast members include Trish Van Devere, Melvyn Douglas, and Barry Morse.

The Entity (1983)

Although many consider the story of a malicious entity that viciously molests a widowed mother (Barbara Hershey) too far-out to be believable, the fact that I know the investigators involved in the case this film is based on makes it all the more frightening to me. Frank de Felitta respectfully adapts the events of the Los Angeles haunting/possession, and director Sidney J. Furie maintains a suspenseful atmosphere in telling the story of a real-life incubus.

Ghost Story (1981)

Four successful, elderly men, members of the Chowder Society, have shared a terrible secret and suppressed their guilt for 50 years. Although the Peter Straub novel upon which this film is based presented many more levels of ghostly phenomena in a believable manner, director John Irvin does a good job of translating a multigenerational ghost story from the printed page to the motion-picture medium. The advertising tagline for the film was "The time has come to tell the tale," and a superb cast is used to great advantage in revealing the gruesome secret that has haunted the memories and dreams of the four men (Fred Astaire, Melvyn Douglas, Douglas Fairbanks, Jr., and John Houseman) and certain unfortunate members of their families. The fascinating and seductive ghost in the story is presented as a multidimensional presence that is at times very physical and at others only ethereal, yet it is always something different than it appears.

The Exorcist (1973, 2000)

William Peter Blatty, the author of both the book and the Academy Award–winning screenplay for *The Exorcist*, once said that he had experienced paranormal phenomena since his earliest childhood. When he worked on the film version of his novel, which was based on an actual case of spirit and/or demonic possession, Blatty's principal objectives were to convey the types of supernatural experiences that he had so often encountered in his own life, and to instill a feeling of absolute terror in the audience. Critics and audiences agree that Blatty and director William Friedkin succeeded in creating what may be the most frightening film ever made. In June 2001 the American Film Institute released its list of the top "100 Most Thrilling American Films," naming *The Exorcist* number three, below number two, *Jaws,* and number one, *Psycho.* While her movie-star mother, Chris MacNeil (Ellen Burstyn), is shooting a film on location, innocent and cherubic 12-year-old Regan MacNeil (Linda Blair) begins playing with an ouija board to pass her lonely days. It's not long before eerie thumps and bumps sound throughout the house, and Regan's bed becomes airborne. When medical science and psychiatry cannot determine the cause of the manifestations, and it appears that her daughter may somehow have been responsible for the death of her director (Jack MacGowan)—whose body was found at the bottom of a steep flight of stone stairs outside Regan's bedroom window—a desperate Chris turns to Father Karras (Jason Miller), who is both priest and psychiatrist. After he becomes convinced the phenomenon afflicting the child is genuine, Father Karras enters a request for an exorcism with church authorities, who, in turn, summon the experienced exorcist Father Merrin (Max von Sydow). The scenes leading up to the exorcism and the rites themselves are punctuated by numerous effects that are not for those with queasy stomachs. There are levitations, blasphemies, an abundance of foul language straight from the demon's mouth, and the much-referenced green "pea soup" projectile vomiting.

The Sixth Sense (1999)
Cole Sear's (Haley Joel Osment) tearful complaint to child psychologist Malcolm Crowe (Bruce Willis) that he can see dead people became one of the most familiar quotes of 1999. M. Night Shyamalan won the Academy Award for best original screenplay and was nominated as best director for this film. Because the audience is able to see the spirits of the dead along with Cole, the ghosts are presented as solid, physical beings, rather than wispy, ethereal images. Many psychically sensitive individuals said that they could very much identify with the character of Cole, who realizes his paranormal abilities as a child. The film has a surprise ending that brought many audiences back for a second viewing.

The Innocents (1961)
Henry James's *The Turn of the Screw* has been adapted many times for both the small and big screen. This cinematic interpretation is particularly effective due to director Jack Clayton's decision to allow the audience to only see the ghosts through the eyes of the central character, governess Miss Gliddens (Deborah Kerr), which allows both a paranormal and psychological interpretation of the events. As Miss Gliddens catches a fleeting glimpse of someone in the shadows of the manor, both the audience and Gliddens come to accept that two former members of the household staff who have died have become spirits and are negatively affecting the children, Flora (Pamela Franklin) and Miles (Martin Stephens). Gliddens resolves to save the children from the two evil spirits that she fears are slowly possessing them. The film is a psychological masterpiece.

Lady in White (1988)
Writer/director Frank La Loggia fashioned a classic ghost story that takes place in Willowpoint Falls, New York, on Halloween 1962. Ten-year-old Frankie (Lukas Haas) falls victim

to a schoolboy prank and is locked in the school cloak room on the scariest night of the year. While imprisoned in the cloak room, he views the ghostly re-enactment of a murder. Melissa (Joelle Jacobi), was the victim of a mysterious serial killer who has struck ten times in over a decade. In addition to the spirit of Melissa, Frankie encounters the "Lady in White" who haunts the small town. To his horror, Frankie finds that he must evade the murderer, who would like to make him the 11th victim. Other cast members include Len Cariou, Alex Rocco, and Katherine Helmond.

The Others (2001)

Alejandro Amenábar, who both wrote and directed the film, crafted a haunted-house story with nicely sustained suspense. The Stewart children (James Bentley, Alakina Mann) suffer from a disease that does not allow them to be exposed to direct sunlight. Understandably, such a rare condition puts an additional stress on their mother, Grace Stewart (Nicole Kidman), as she awaits the return of her husband in the final days of World War II. The Stewarts live in an old mansion on the island of Jersey, and Grace sternly orders all the domestic help to keep window shades lowered and never to open a door until they have closed the previous one. The home must be kept in complete darkness at all times. The children begin to complain that the large, old house is haunted, and insist that they have actually seen ghosts materialize in certain rooms. Grace dismisses such talk, and she sternly informs her principal domestic Bertha Mills (Fionnula Flanagan) that no member of the household staff should encourage such childish fantasies. But such orders become increasingly difficult to fulfill as the children and servants become more and more aware of *the others* invading the mansion. Eventually, in a shocking turn of events, Grace Stewart must also face the reality that has overtaken them all.

Poltergeist (1982)

I was disappointed with this film upon my initial viewing, because in interviews prior to its release screenwriter Steven Spielberg stated that he and director Tobe Hooper sought to walk the thin line between the scientific and the spiritual. Based on my interpretation of those remarks, I went to the film expecting a storyline based on the generally accepted parapsychological theory of a poltergeists as an explosion of psychokinetic energy. However, in the course of viewing the motion picture it became clear that Spielberg and Hooper had based the film on the premise that poltergeists are disembodied spirits who don't know they are dead and need a guide to take them into the next plane of existence. Upon a second viewing of the film, I set aside my prior expectations and was able to appreciate the movie on its own terms. The film focuses on Steve and Diane Freeling (Craig T. Nelson and JoBeth Williams), who are completely unaware that their new home has been built over a graveyard. The tension in the film centers on the couple's daughter Carol Anne (Heather O'Rourke), who announces that "they're here," shortly before the entities pull her into a spiritual vortex. The challenges faced by the Freeling family as they struggle to reclaim Carol Ann from the spirit world make for a presentation of unrelenting suspense. While purists may carp that the special effects were overdone and far too elaborate for anything other than a Hollywood-type haunting, scenes such as when their son Robbie (Oliver Robbins) must face a sinister and animated clown doll, or when Diane must enter the vortex to bring Carol Ann back to the world of the living, are very effective. Zelda Rubenstein, as the diminutive medium Tangina Barrons, is a believable guide into the unknown, a role that she reprised in *Poltergeist II: The Other Side* (1986) and *Poltergeist III*. Neither of the sequels was able to maintain the edge-of-the-seat tensions of the original film.

The Shining (1980)

An isolated mountain hotel has been vacated by its staff for the winter months and is inhabited by caretakers Jack Torrance (Jack Nicholson), his wife Wendy (Shelley Duval), and their young son Danny (Danny Lloyd). Danny has what the hotel handyman Dick Hallorann (Scatman Crothers) calls "the shining," a mediumistic and telepathic ability to perceive spirit entities and "hear" others' thoughts. At first he is the only one able to see the ghostly inhabitants of the sprawling mountain resort. The entities—all murderers or murder victims—become increasingly menacing as Jack Torrance sinks deeper into depression over his inability to write productively. Later, as Jack's nerves grow frayed by his lack of productivity and the monotony of the family's forced snowbound isolation, the ghosts appear to work on the writer's weaknesses and bring him into their evil mindset. Little Danny is tormented by the phrase "red rum," which comes to be clearly understood as "murder" when Torrance hunts his wife and son with an axe. In this adaptation of the Stephen King novel, director Stanley Kubrick crafted a film that interacts with the viewer's own imagination on many levels, thereby making the appearance of the ghosts and Torrance's descent into violence and insanity even more credible.

Ghost Stories for the Chills

The Amityville Horror (1979)

Although the initial motion picture has spawned a cinematic cottage industry that has produced at least six sequels of varying quality, the original movie, based on the bestseller by Jay Anson, is certainly the best and contains a number of scenes that will forever remain in the viewer's memory banks. This story of a husband and wife (James Brolin, Margot Kidder) who move into a haunted house has left horror and paranormal buffs arguing over which elements in the film are fact or fiction, but the general audience is content to be swept away by the suspense of the nightmarish sequence of events so powerfully captured by director Stuart Rosenburg. The cast also includes Rod Steiger, Murray Hamilton, Don Stroud, and John Larch.

The Legend of Hell House (1973)

The great fantasy writer Richard Matheson adapted his own novel for this chilling cinematic recounting of an attempt to exorcise an accursed mansion. Roddy McDowell is excellent as the sole survivor of an earlier attempt to rid the Hell House of evil who is persuaded to join a medium (Pamela Franklin) and a physicist (Clive Revill) in having another go at the place. The film was directed by John Hough, who skillfully keeps the tension of the storyline taut at all-times.

The Fog (1980)

The restless spirits of pirates come in with the fog and exact terrible revenge on the contemporary residents of a coastal California town. Director John Carpenter, who cowrote the script with producer Debra Hill, is a bit heavy on the gore and violence, but the film proceeds with the eerie atmosphere of a spooky campfire tale. The film costars Jamie Lee Curtis, Adrienne Barbeau, and Hal Holbrook.

The Girl in a Swing (1989)

This adaptation of the Richard Adams novel delivers an effective supernatural film that tells the story of the ghostly visitations endured by a recently married woman (Meg Tilly) who is suppressing a terrible secret from her past. The film was directed by Gordon Hessler and also stars Rupert Frazier and Elspet Gray.

The Green Man (1990)

Director Elijah Moshinsky fashions a subtle, yet scary ghost story in this movie based on the novel by Kingsley Amis. Albert Finney plays the proprietor of a country inn called The Green Man that is haunted by the spirit of a seventeenth-century master occultist. The sinister ghost appears to have the ability to manipulate the boundaries of time and space and is able to lure the unsuspecting into the dark corners of the psyche. The film also stars Linda Marlowe, Sarah Berger, and Nicky Hensen.

Haunted (1996)

James Herbert's novel was adapted for the screen by Tim Prager and directed by Lewis Gilbert. *Haunted* is an intriguing ghost story that will greatly benefit from a second viewing. Aidan Quinn is excellent as the skeptical debunker of the supernatural who finds himself seduced into a bizarre alternate reality by a family of eccentrics who occupy a lovely mansion in the English countryside. The old nanny Tess (Ann Massey) insists that there are ghosts in the mansion, but the family members (Kate Beckinsale, Anthony Andrews, and Alex Lowe) humor her and dismiss her tales of things that go bump in the night.

Nomads (1985)

Written and directed by John McTiernan, this film is unique in its treatment of the nomadic shadow people, evil spirits that masquerade as humans and wander the fringes of society. Actor Pierce Brosnan plays an anthropologist who is persecuted by demons after he runs afoul of them; he involves a nurse played by Lesley Anne Down in his fantastic story when he is placed in a mental institution. This is a genuinely eerie and haunting film.

Ghost Ship (2002)

Although the plot has a few scenes that have been seen before in other films, the movie contains enough fright scenes and suspense to keep you watching. A salvage crew finds a a passenger ship in a remote region of the Bering Sea that has been missing since 1962, which they decide to board to investigate. There is a bit more gore than is necessary, especially in the opening flashback scene. The movie was directed by Steve Beck and stars Julianna Margulies, Gabriel Byrne, Ron Eldard, and Desmond Harrington.

Ghost Stories for Laughs

Topper (1937)

Directed by Norman Z. McLeod, the film was adapted from the Thorne Smith novel about Cosmo Topper, a meek and mild banking executive who is the only one able to see George and Marian Kerby, a ghostly couple that harasses him and attempts to persuade him to enjoy a more relaxed lifestyle. The fact that the ghostly couple is played with charm, wit, and stylish sex appeal by Cary Grant and Constance Bennett boosted the popularity of the film. Roland Young played Topper, and Billie Burke was his loving, but always confused, wife. The motion picture made ghostly phenomena appear to be so much fun that the Hal Roach studios released the sequels *Topper Returns* in 1939 and *Topper Takes a Trip* in 1941. Cosmo and George and Marian Kerby were played by Leo G. Carroll, Robert Sterling, and Anne Jeffreys in a television series (1953–1955) based on the successful Topper films.

Ghostbusters (1984)

With their specially designed laser devices and a unique ghost trap, three parapsychology professors (Bill Murray, Dan Aykroyd, and Harold Ramis) who lost their university funding set about ridding Manhattan of obnoxious ghosts. Things go so well for the ghostbusters that they add another man (Ernie Hudson) to their crew. Supernatural storm clouds gather when Dana Barrett (Sigourney Weaver) discovers an ancient god in her refrigerator, becomes possessed by the gate keeper Zuul, and is united with the key master, Vinz Clortho (Rick Moranis). The Ghostbusters save the world in a hilarious conclusion. Written by Dan Aykroyd and Harold Ramis and directed by Ivan Reitman, *Ghostbusters* offers an original premise for a comedy, and has excellent special effects. The sequel, *Ghostbusters II* (1989), lacked the energy and excitement of the original.

Ghost Breakers (1940)

The comic genius of Bob Hope demonstrates how a movie can be funny and scary at the same time when he visits a haunted house in Cuba owned by a character played by the beautiful Paulette Goddard. The movie was directed by George Marshall and featured Anthony Quinn, Richard Carlson, Paul Fix, and Willie Best.

Beetlejuice (1988)

Director Tim Burton appears to have told screenwriters Michael McDowell and Warren Skaaren to observe no boundaries for this supernatural comedy, in which the ghosts played by Alec Baldwin and Geena Davis try to frighten the new occupants out of their former home. Michael Keaton has the title role of Betelguese, their bizarre advisor, who exorcises humans. Catherine O'Hara, Jeffrey Jones, and Winona Ryder are in the roles of the family plagued by the spirits that refuse to leave their home.

Heart and Souls (1993)

This film is based on the old adage that every time someone leaves for the other side, there is a soul born on the earthplane to take its place. However, this film takes that theory to the extreme by having four people who died in a San Francisco bus accident act as spirit guides to a baby born at the moment of their death. This supernatural fantasy has a kind of contagious charm skillfully wrought by Robert Downey, Jr., as the not-always-grateful recipient of advice from the spirit world. Directed by Ron Underwood with a cast that includes Charles Grodin, Alfre Woodard, Kyra Sidgwick, Tom Sizemore, and Elisabeth Shue.

Love Beyond the Grave

Ghost (1990)

Directed by Jerry Zucker and written by Bruce Joel Rubin, this film demonstrates how a man's (Patrick Swayze) love for his partner (Demi Moore) holds him to earth until he is certain that she will be safe from the man who murdered him and will be able to make the transition from grief to wholeness. Whoopi Goldberg received the Oscar for best supporting actress for her role as spiritualist Oda Mae Brown, and the film was nominated for best picture.

The Ghost and Mrs. Muir (1947)

The emphasis is on unrequited love in *The Ghost and Mrs. Muir*, which stars Rex Harrison as the restless spirit of a handsome sea captain and Gene Tierney as the beautiful widow who has moved into a picturesque New England seaside cottage. The popular film was transformed into the television series *Ghost and Mrs. Muir* (1968–1970) with Edward Mulhare and Hope Lange.

Dragonfly (2002)

This film effectively combines accounts of near-death experiences with spirit manifestations in a story about a grieving doctor (Kevin Costner) struggling with the death of his wife (Susanna Thompson). There are a number of authentic shudders and some emotionally moving scenes that should satisfy the person seeking both a ghost story and a demonstration of love beyond the grave. The movie was directed by Tom Shadyac and features accomplished performances by Kathy Bates, Ron Rifkin, and Joe Morton.

Truly, Madly, Deeply (1990)

The novelty of seeing Alan Rickman, who has been the consummate villain in so many films, portraying the spirit of a loving man who has returned to help his grieving companion (Juliet Stevenson) adjust to his death is but one of the treasures in this unique ghost story. In the guise of an off-beat story of love beyond the grave, this film deals passionately with the grief that accompanies the death of a loved one. The film was written and directed by Anthony Minghella.

What Dreams May Come (1998)

This film literally takes place in the afterlife. Chris Nielson (Robin Williams) is killed in a car accident, and his spirit ascends to his soul's concept of heaven, which is beautifully wrought by computer magic. After a time, he learns that his sorrowful wife (Annabella Sciorra) has committed suicide in her loneliness and despair, and he is compelled to search for her soul. The film also stars Cuba Gooding, Jr., Max von Sydow, and Rosalind Chao. Ronald Bass adapted Richard Matheson's novel for the screen, and the movie was directed by Vincent Ward

References

Clarens, Carlos. *An Illustrated History of the Horror Film*. New York: Capricorn Books, 1968.

Hardy, Phil. *The Encyclopedia of Horror Movies*. New York: Harper and Row, 1986.

Internet Movie Database Inc. <us.imdb.com>.

Katz, Ephraim. *The Film Encyclopedia*. New York: Perigee Books, 1982.

Maltin, Leonard. *Leonard Maltin's 1999 Movie and Video Guide*. New York: Dutton Signet, 1998.

Stanley, John. *Creature Features: The Science Fiction, Fantasy, and Horror Movie Guide*. New York: Boulevard, 1997.

Appendix D

BIBLIOGRAPHY

Angoff, Allan. *Eileen Garrett and the World Beyond the Senses.* New York: William Morrow, 1974.

Asala, Joanne, ed. *Scandinavian Ghost Stories.* Iowa City, IA: Penfield Press, 1995.

Atwater, P. M. H. *Beyond the Light.* New York: Avon, 1997.

Baird, A. T., ed. *One Hundred Cases for Survival After Death.* New York: Bernard Ackerman, 1944.

Barbanell, Maurice. *Spiritualism Today.* London: Herbert Jenkins, 1969.

Bardens, Dennis. *Ghosts and Hauntings.* New York: Ace Books, 1965.

Bayless, Raymond. *The Other Side of Death.* New Hyde Park, NY: University Books, 1971.

Begbie, Harold. *More Twice-Born Men.* New York and London: G.P. Putnam's Sons, 1923.

Bell, Charles, and Harriet P. Miller. *Mysterious Spirit: The Bell Witch of Tennessee.* Forest Knolls, CA: Elders Publishing, 1985.

Bodin, Ed. *Scare Me!* New York: Orlin Tremaine Company, 1940.

Boone, J. Allen. *Kinship with All Life.* New York: Harper and Row, 1954.

Brown, Slater. *The Heyday of Spiritualism.* New York: Hawthorn Books, 1970.

Bryd, Elizabeth. *The Ghosts in My Life.* New York: Ballantine Books, 1968.

Caidin, Martin. *Ghosts of the Air: True Stories of Aerial Hauntings.* Introduction by John Keel. St. Paul, MN: Galde Press, 1995.

Carrington, Hereward. *The Case for Psychic Survival.* New York: The Citadel Press, 1957.

———. *Essays in the Occult: Experiences Out of a Lifetime of Psychical Research.* New York: Thomas Yoseloff, 1958.

Carrington, Hereward, and Nandor Fodor. *Haunted People.* New York: New American Library, 1968.

Clark, Jerome. *Unexplained!* Detroit and London: Visible Ink Press, 1999.

Clarke, Ida Clyde. *Men Who Wouldn't Stay Dead*. New York: Bernard Ackerman, Inc., 1945.

Copper, Arnold, and Coralee Leon. *Psychic Summer*. New York: The Dial Press, 1976.

Crawford, W. J. *The Psychic Structures of the Goligher Circle*. New York: E.P. Dutton and Company, 1921.

Crookall, Robert. *Intimations of Immortality*. London: James Clarke Company, Ltd., 1968.

———. *More Astral Projections*. London: Aquarian Press, 1964.

Denning, Hazel M. *True Hauntings*. St. Paul, MN: Llewellyn Publications, 1996.

Dingwall, Eric J., and John Langdon-Davies. *The Unknown—Is It Nearer?* New York: New American Library, 1968.

Ebon, Martin, ed. *True Experiences in Communicating with the Dead*. New York: Garrett Publications, 1959; College of Psychic Science, 1962; New American Library, 1968.

Edsall, F. S. *The World of Psychic Phenomena*. New York: David McKay Company, 1958.

Estep, Sarah Wilson. *Voices of Eternity*. New York: Ballantine Books, 1988.

Farris, David A. *Mysterious Oklahoma: Eerie True Tales from the Sooner State*. Edmond, OK: Little Bruce, 1995.

Fiore, Edith. *The Unquiet Dead*. New York: Doubleday, 1987.

Flammarion, Camille. *Death and Its Mystery After Death: Manifestations and Apparitions of the Dead; The Soul After Death*. Translation by Latrobe Carroll. New York and London: The Century Co., 1923.

———. *Haunted Houses*. London: T. Fisher Unwin, 1924.

Floyd, Randall. *Ghost Lights and Other Encounters*. Little Rock, AR: August House, 1993.

Fodor, Nador. *These Mysterious People*. London: Rider and Co., 1935.

———. *An Encyclopedia of Psychic Science*. Seacaucus, NJ: The Citadel Press, 1935.

———. *Mind over Space and Time*. New York: The Citadel Press, 1962.

Ford, Arthur, and Jerome Ellison. *The Life Beyond Death*. New York: G. P. Putnam's Sons, 1971.

Gaddis, Vincent H. *Mysterious Fires and Lights*. New York: Dell Books, 1968.

Garrett, Eileen. *Many Voices: The Autobiography of a Medium*. New York: G. P. Putnam's Sons, 1968.

Gauld, Alan. *Mediumship and Survival*. London: William Heinemann, Ltd., 1982.

Hall, Trevor. *The Spiritualists*. London: Duckworth, 1962.

Hauk, Dennis William. *Haunted Places*. New York: Penguin USA, reprint edition, 1996.

———. *International Directory of Haunted Places*. New York: Penguin, 2000.

Hein, Ruth. *Ghostly Tales of Minnesota*. Cambridge, MN: Adventure Publications, 1992.

Holmes, M. Jean. *Do Dogs Go to Heaven?* Tulsa, OK: JoiPax Publishing, 1999.

Holzer, Hans. *Yankee Ghosts*. New York: Ace Books, 1966.

Hudson, Thomson Jay. *The Law of Psychic Phenomena: A Working Hypothesis*. Chicago: A.C. McClurg and Co., 1917.

Hyslop, James H. *Borderland of Psychical Research*. Boston: Small, Maynard and Co., 1906.

Jacobson, Laurie, and Mark Wanamaker. *Hollywood Haunted*. Los Angeles: Angel City Press, 1999.

Johnson, George Lindsay. *Does Man Survive?* New York and London: Harper and Brothers, 1936.

Kerman, Frances. *Ghostly Encounters: True Stories of America's Haunted Inns and Hotels*. New York: Warner Books, 2002.

Kleiner, Dick. *The Ghost Who Danced with Kim Novak and Other True Tales of the Supernatural*. New York: Ace Books, 1969.

Kolb, Janice Gray. *Compassion for All Creatures*. Nevada City, CA: Blue Dolphin Publishing, 1997.

L'Aloge, Bob. *Ghosts and Mysteries of the Old West: True Accounts of New Mexico and the Old West*. Las Cruces, NM: Yucca Tree Press, 1994.

Lamb, John. *San Diego Specters*. San Diego, CA: Sunbelt Productions, 1999.

Le Braz, A. *Dealings with the Dead: Narratives from La Legende De La Mort En Basse Bretagne*. Authorized translation by Mrs. A. E. Whitehead. Chicago: De Laurence Scott and Co., [n.d.].

LeShan, Lawrence. *The Medium, the Mystic, and the Physicist*. New York: Viking Press, 1974.

Martin, MaryJoy. *Twilight Dwellers of Colorado*. Boulder, CO: Pruett Publishing, 1985.

May, Antoinette. *Haunted Houses and Wandering Ghosts of California*. San Francisco: San Francisco Examiner Division, 1977.

McComas, Henry C. *Ghosts I Have Talked With*. Baltimore, MD: The Williams and Wilkins Company, 1937.

Mead, Robin. *Haunted Hotels: A Guide to American and Canadian Inns and Their Ghosts*. Nashville, TN: Rutledge Hill Press, 1995.

Murphy, Gardner. *The Challenge of Psychical Research*. New York: Harper and Row, 1970.

Norman, Michael, and Beth Scott. *Historic Haunted America*. New York: Tor Books, 1996.

———. *Haunted Heritage*. New York: Forge, 2002.

Oppenheim, Janet. *The Other World: Spiritualism and Psychical Research in England*. Cambridge: Cambridge University Press, 1985.

Post, Eric G. *Communicating with the Beyond*. New York: Atlantic Publishing, 1946.

Price, Harry. *The Most Haunted House in England*. London: Longmans, Green & Co., 1940.

———. *Poltergeist over England*. London: Country Life, Ltd, 1945.

Ramsland, Katherine. *Ghost: A Firsthand Account into the World of Paranormal Activity*. New York: St. Martin's Press, 2001.

Rider, Fremont. *Are the Dead Alive?* New York: B.W. Dodge and Company, 1909.

Rider, Geri. *Ghosts of Door County Wisconsin*. Sioux City, IA: Quixote Press, 1992.

Ring, Kenneth. *Life at Death*. New York: Coward, McCann and Geoghegan, 1980.

Roberts, Nancy. *Civil War Ghost Stories and Legends*. Columbia, SC: University of South Carolina, 1992.

Saltzman, Pauline. *Strange Spirits*. New York: Paperback Library, 1967.

Scott, Beth, and Michael Norman. *Haunted Wisconsin*. Minocqua, WI: Heartland Press, 1988.

Sculthorp, Frederick C. *Excursions to the Spirit World*. London: Almorris Press, Ltd., 1961.

Sitwell, Sacheverell. *Poltergeists*. New York: University Books, 1959.

Smith, Alson J. *Immortality: The Scientific Evidence*. New York: Prentice Hall, 1954.

Smith, Scott S. *Pet Souls: Evidence that Animals Survive Death*. Thousand Oaks, CA: Light Source Research, 1994.

Smith, Susy. *Haunted Houses for the Millions*. Los Angeles: Sherbourne Press, Inc., 1967.

———. *Prominent American Ghosts*. New York: Dell, 1969.

Spaeth, Frank, ed. *Mysteries of the Deep*. St. Paul, MN: Llewellyn Publications, 1998.

Sparrowdancer, Mary. *The Love Song of the Universe*. Charlottesville, VA: Hampton Roads Publishing Company, Inc., 2001.

Spence, Lewis. *An Encyclopedia of Occultism*. New Hyde Park, NY: University Books, 1960.

Stallings, Nancy L. *Show Me One Soul: A True Haunting*. Baltimore, MD: Noble House, 1996.

Steinour, Harold. *Exploring the Unseen World*. New York: The Citadel Press, 1959.

Stevens, William Oliver. *Unbidden Guests*. New York: Dodd, Mead and Company, 1957.

Stirling, A. M. W. *Ghosts Vivisected*. New York: The Citadel Press, 1958.

Stonehouse, Frederick. *Haunted Lakes: Great Lakes Ghost Stories, Superstitions, and Sea Serpents*. Duluth, MN: Lake Superior Port Cities, Inc., 1997.

Sullivan, Lawrence E., ed. *Death, Afterlife, and the Soul*. New York: Macmillan Publishing Company, 1989.

Tabori, Paul. *Companions of the Unseen*. New Hyde Park, NY: University Books, 1968.

———. *Pioneers of the Unseen*. New York: Taplinger, 1973.

Tanner, Amy E. *Studies in Spiritism*. New York and London: D. Appleton and Company, 1910.

Tucker, George Holbert. *Virginia Supernatural Tales*. Norfolk, VA: Donning Company, 1977.

Tyrrell, G. N. M. *Apparitions*. New York: Collier Books, 1963.

Uphoff, Walter, and Mary Jo Uphoff. *New Psychic Frontiers*. Gerrards Cross, Bucks, Great Britain: Colin Smythe, Ltd., 1975.

Van Dusen, Wilson. *The Presence of Other Worlds: The Findings of Emanuel Swedenborg.* New York: Harper and Row, 1974.

Walker, Danton. *I Believe in Ghosts.* New York: Pyramid Books, 1970.

Watson, Lyall. *The Romeo Error.* New York: Dell Books, 1976.

White, Steward Edward. *The Betty Book: Excursions into the World of Other-Consciousness.* New York: E. P. Dutton and Company, 1937.

———. *The Road I Know.* New York: E.P. Dutton and Company, Inc., 1942.

Willis-Brandon, Carla. *One Last Hug Before I Go: The Mystery and Meaning of Deathbed Visions.* Deerfield Beach, FL: Health Communications, 2000.

Winer, Richard. *Ghost Ships: True Stories of Nautical Nightmares, Hauntings and Disasters.* New York: Berkley Publishing Group, 2000.

INDEX

Note: (ill.) indicates photos and illustrations.